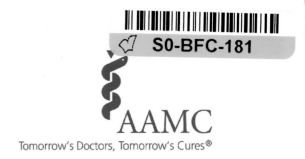

AAMC

Tomorrow's Doctors, Tomorrow's Cures®

Minority Student Opportunities

In United States Medical Schools

2009

19th Edition

Edited by Lily May I. Johnson
Diversity Policy and Programs

Learn
Serve
Lead

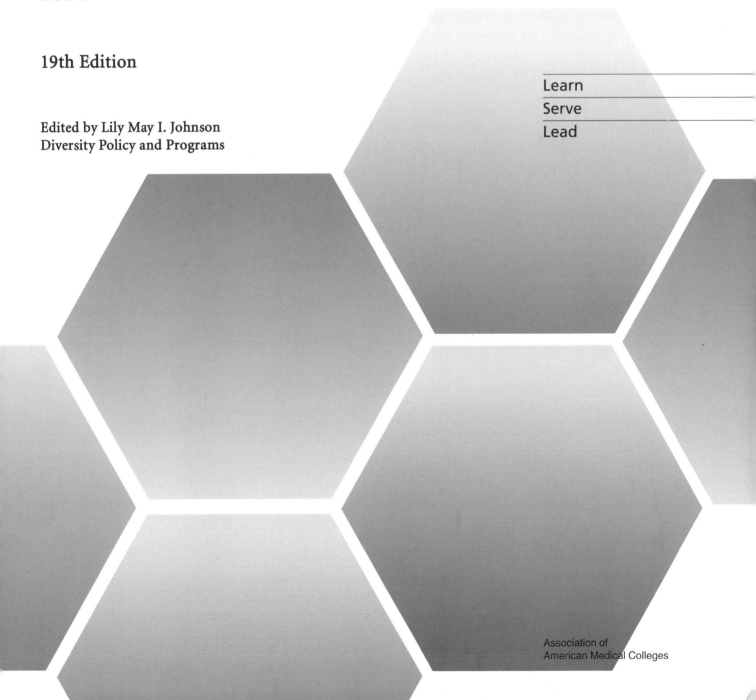

Association of
American Medical Colleges

To order additional copies of this publication, please contact:

Association of American Medical Colleges

Customer Service and Order Fulllfillment

2450 N Street, NW

Washington, DC 20037

Phone: 202-828-0416

Fax: 202-828-1123

www.aamc.org/publications

Price: $15, plus shipping

(Item code: MSOUSMS09)

Remittance or institutional purchase order must accompany order.

ISBN 978-1-57754-086-1

Acknowledgments

The editor thanks Darrell G. Kirch, M.D., President and CEO of the Association of American Medical Colleges (AAMC), and Charles Terrell, Ed.D., Chief Diversity Officer, Diversity Policy and Programs at the AAMC, for their support. She also thanks the medical school officials who provided the information for this book. Thanks also go to AAMC staff, especially Kehua Zhang, Ph.D., Angela Moses, Ann Steinecke, Ph.D., and Hugo Dubon for providing invaluable advice and support throughout the process of revising and laying out the book.

Preface

Medical schools supply the information in this book in response to a questionnaire from the AAMC's Diversity Policy and Programs. The questionnaire asks schools to update the information published in the previous edition of MSOUSMS (2007). Unless otherwise noted by an asterisk, all schools submitted updated information on their programs and policies related to minority student opportunities in medical schools.

In the Table of Contents, medical schools are listed both alphabetically and by geographical location to help readers locate information about specific medical schools. Most entries cover seven topics: (1) recruitment, (2) admissions, (3) academic support programs, (4) enrichment programs, (5) student financial assistance, (6) educational partnerships, and (7) other pertinent information. Each school's entry also contains a table showing the most recent data on applicants and matriculants by gender and race, ethnicity.

In addition to the schools' entries, two appendices present (1) selected AAMC data of interest and (2) a table consolidating enrichment activities at medical schools. For more detailed information regarding any program, policy, or procedure please contact the school in which you are interested. Contact information is provided for each medical school.

We have also included information about AspiringDocs.org throughout the book. AspiringDocs.org was launched in 2006 by the AAMC to provide students with the information, encouragement, and support they need to choose careers in medicine. Although targeted to minority students, the interactive Web site contains features and information that will be valuable to any student considering a career in medicine.

Our hope is that prospective applicants will find this book useful, along with other resources such as AspiringDocs.org, in determining where to apply to medical school. Among the items to examine when making a decision are a medical school's program and philosophy, geographic location, state residency requirements, and the cost of attending. Be sure to discuss this and other information with a premedical advisor at your undergraduate institution, as well as with the minority affairs representatives at the medical schools to which you are applying. This book should be used in conjunction with the Medical School Admission Requirements (MSAR™), which is also published by the AAMC and is available for purchase at (http://www.aamc.org/students/amcas/start.htm).

Policies and procedures regarding recruitment and admissions programs described in this book are those of each medical school, not those of the AAMC.

Group on Student Affairs-Committee on Diversity Affairs (GSA-CODA) July 2009

Chair
Karen A. Lewis, M.S.
Assistant Vice President for
Student Services,
Enrollment Management and Registrar
Meharry Medical College

Central
Gloria V. Hawkins, Ph.D.
Assistant Dean for Multicultural Affairs
University of Wisconsin School of
Medicine and Public Health

Northeast
Carlyle H. Miller, M.D.
Associate Dean for Student Affairs
and Equal Opportunity Programs
Cornell University
Weill Medical College

Southern
Brenda A. Latham-Sadler, M.D.
Associate Professor of Family &
Community Medicine
Assistant Dean for Student Services
Director of Diversity and Development
Initiatives
Wake Forest University Health Sciences

Western
Linda K. Don, M.Ed.
Assistant Dean
Office of Outreach and Multicultural
Affairs
University of Arizona College
of Medicine

AAIP Liaison
Joycelyn Dorscher, M.D.
Director, Center of American Indian
and Minority Health
University of Minnesota
Medical School

Liaison to COA
Ronald D. Garcia, Ph.D.
Assistant Dean for Minority Affairs
Stanford University School of Medicine

Liaison to COSFA
Martha C. Trujillo
Director for Student Financial Services
Stanford University School of Medicine

Liaison to COSA
Virginia D. Hardy, Ph.D.
Senior Associate Dean,
Academic Affairs
The Brody School of Medicine at
East Carolina University

Liaison to COSR
Sonia Beasley
Office Manager
Office of Student Affairs
University of Maryland
School of Medicine

GSA
Dwight Davis, M.D.
Associate Dean for Admissions &
Student Affairs
Pennsylvania State University
College of Medicine

OSR
Phillip Murray
(4th year student)
Medical College of Georgia

NAAHP Liaison
Michael Ellison, Ed.D.
Assistant Dean & Pre-Health Advisor
Chicago State University

AAMC Staff
Lily May Johnson, M.S.
Manager
Diversity Policy and Programs
Association of American
Medical Colleges

Henry Sondheimer, M.D.
Senior Director
Student Affairs and Programs
Association of American
Medical Colleges

Table of Contents

Appendices

Alphabetical Listing of Medical Schools

Geographical Listing of Medical Schools

Foreword

It is with great pleasure we present the 2009 edition of *Minority Student Opportunities in United States Medical Schools (MSOUSMS)*, the one-of-a-kind resource for minority students and others traditionally underrepresented in medicine. I recently had the opportunity to review a copy of the very first *MSOUSMS*, published by the AAMC in 1969. Bound with staples and a faded blue cover, the contents are simply the Xerox copies of each school's typed descriptions of their efforts to increase minority representation. As a piece of history, it is fascinating to read. In comparison to the *MSOUSMS* you now hold in your hand, it is remarkable to see how far we have moved efforts to deliver information about careers in medicine to students who have traditionally faced significant barriers.

Three years ago, the AAMC called for a 30 percent increase in medical school enrollments by 2015. As new schools open and current schools examine ways to expand access for all qualified students interested in careers in medicine, opportunities for enhancing diversity in medical education abound. Diversity Policy and Programs at the Association of American Medical Colleges (AAMC) continues to support our constituents and pursue innovations that are changing the face of medicine as a means of achieving quality health care for all. When the last edition of *MSOUSMS* was released, we had only just launched AspiringDocs.org. This comprehensive, Web-based marketing campaign has directed information and resources to nearly 6,500 registered site users almost a half a million site visits. AspiringDocs information site is continually refreshed and updated, making it a resource interested students can return to again and again.

The AAMC has also begun to use new social media to improve our outreach and alumni activities. For example, Summer Medical and Dental Education Program (SMDEP)—funded by the Robert Wood Johnson Foundation and jointly directed by the AAMC and the American Dental Education Association—now hosts an alumni Facebook Fan Page, where over 18,000 SMDEP alumni can join, remain connected to the program, and share their stories of success.

Since it was first published, *MSOUSMS*, has remained a unique source of essential information for increasing minority student representation in medicine. *MSOUSMS* contains information on each medical school, including school-specific data on minority student applicants, acceptances, enrollments, and graduates. This information is crucial for assisting students, their families, and their advisors with decision-making about the possibilities for careers in medicine.

We wish you luck in your pursuit, and we welcome any suggestions or ideas that will make this publication more useful to you in the future.

Charles Terrell, Ed.D.
Chief Diversity Officer
AAMC

Information
About Medical
School Programs

Association of
American Medical Colleges

University of Alabama School of Medicine

Dr. Anjanetta Foster-Alexander
Assistant Dean for Diversity and
Multicultural Affairs,
University of Alabama
School of Medicine
Medical Student Services
1530 3rd Avenue S, VH 102F
Birmingham, AL 35294-0019
205-934-7975, 800-707-3579;
205-996-2575 fax
afoster@uasom.uab.edu
http://medicine.uab.edu

Recruitment

The University of Alabama School of Medicine (UASOM) has a fundamental commitment to the identification, recruitment, retention, and career advisement of minorities and students from disadvantaged populations. Staff of the Office of Medical Student Services and the Office of Diversity and Multicultural Affairs, a division of the Office of Medical Student Services, participate in high school and college recruitment activities throughout Alabama. Other recruitment activities include participation in local and national conferences such as the Minority Access to Research Careers/ Minority Biomedical Research Support annual conference. Minority and disadvantaged students interested in the study of medicine are identified, provided literature, and offered counsel. A relationship with the identified students is maintained through their academic advisors. Visits to appropriate college campuses are made at least once each year by recruitment officers and, when possible, by minority medical students. Through these visits, information on the admissions process, curriculum, financial aid, and personal development programs is given to interested students. Individual conferences are arranged, especially with junior-level college students.

Admissions

Applications submitted by minorities and students from disadvantaged backgrounds are reviewed by members of the Admissions Committee. Particular emphasis is placed on students who are residents of Alabama, and all students so designated are offered on-campus interviews. Area interviews are offered, when possible, and are frequently coordinated with the college visitation program. Considerable effort is expended to make the interview process convenient for the student.

Academic Support Programs

Enrichment and academic aid programs designed to assist minorities and disadvantaged groups are offered on an as-needed basis. The School of Medicine maintains a sophisticated and extensive educational development office that prepares, evaluates, and administers self-development instructional materials. Other study aids and tutorial assistance are also available to students. The tutorial sessions are available to all students upon request and as the need is identified by the faculty. Considerable effort is made to identify minority tutors.

University of Alabama School of Medicine
Applicants, First-Time Applicants, Matriculants by Gender, Race and Ethnicity, 2007-2008

| | 2007 | | | | | | | | | 2008 | | | | | | | | |
| | APP | | | F-time APP | | | MAT | | | APP | | | F-time APP | | | MAT | | |
	Women	Men	Total	Women	Men	Total	Women	Men	Total	Women	Men	Total	Women	Men	Total	Women	Men	Total
Hispanic/Latino																		
Cuban	5	8	13	4	7	11	0	0	0	6	6	12	5	5	10	0	0	0
Mexican American	11	12	23	8	11	19	1	1	2	12	11	23	9	9	18	0	1	1
Puerto Rican	4	4	8	2	4	6	0	0	0	2	4	6	2	2	4	0	0	0
Other Hispanic	17	16	33	11	13	24	0	0	0	14	23	37	7	20	27	0	0	0
Multiple Hispanic/Latino*	1	2	3	1	1	2	0	0	0	5	2	7	5	2	7	0	0	0
Subtotal	38	42	80	26	36	62	1	1	2	39	46	85	28	38	66	0	1	1
Non-Hispanic/Latino**																		
Black	163	64	227	121	50	171	9	2	11	158	54	212	112	42	154	11	2	13
Native American/AK	7	4	11	5	4	9	1	1	2	3	3	6	3	3	6	0	1	1
Native Hawaiian/OPI	1	4	5	1	3	4	0	0	0	4	1	5	3	1	4	1	0	1
White	531	717	1,248	443	535	978	47	87	134	551	758	1,309	436	578	1,014	52	81	133
Asian	138	193	331	108	135	243	13	12	25	148	180	328	98	125	223	9	11	20
Other Race		0	0	0	0	0	0	0	0	1	1	2	1	1	2	0	0	0
Multiple Race*	23	20	43	17	14	31	1	0	1	23	14	37	18	12	30	3	2	5
Unknown	4	11	15	4	9	13	0	1	1	14	14	28	13	13	26	0	2	2
Subtotal	867	1,013	1,880	699	750	1,449	71	103	174	902	1,025	1,927	684	775	1,459	76	99	175
Foreign	15	15	30	11	13	24	0	0	0	7	15	22	4	10	14	0	0	0
Total	920	1,070	1,990	736	799	1,535	72	104	176	948	1,086	2,034	716	823	1,539	76	100	176

*Since 2002, students can select more than one race and / or ethnicity. **Those who did not choose 'Hispanic/Latino' or 'Non-Hispanic/Latino' are listed under 'Non-Hispanic/Latino'. Data Source: AAMC Data Warehouse: Applicant-Matriculant File, as of 1/16/2009.

Student Financial Assistance

The university waives application fees for disadvantaged students upon verification of need. The Mineral District Medical Society (MDMS), a community-based association of practicing minority physicians, awards scholarships annually to minority medical students. In support of UASOM's goals to increase the number of minorities that enter and graduate, the university has developed merit and need based scholarships for incoming students.

Educational Partnerships

In an effort to facilitate minority access, a positive mentoring relationship has been developed between the UASOM and the MDMS. These mentors serve as role models and student advisors to UASOM minority medical students.

Other Pertinent Information

In support of the institution's goals of increased minority participation at the UASOM, an Office of Minority Enhancement was developed to assist minority students in preparing to enter and graduate from the University of Alabama School of Medicine. As a component of the Office of Medical Student Services, the Office of Minority Enhancement can assist students in utilizing the full range of services available to medical students. Programs and activities include:

- counseling and support for academic and personal concerns;
- tutorial programs as needed;
- financial assistance;
- assistance with finding and securing research opportunities; and
- liaison activities among the UASOM, minority students, and medical organizations.

University of South Alabama College of Medicine

Dr. Hattie M. Myles,
Assistant Dean—Student Affairs and Educational Enrichment
University of South Alabama
College of Medicine
307 University Blvd.,1005 MSB
Mobile, AL 36688-0002
251-460-7313; 251-460-6761 fax
hmyles@usouthal.edu
http://www.southalabama.edu/com/dream.shtml

Recruitment

Representatives from the Admissions Office and the Office of Student Affairs visit colleges in Alabama, and adjoining service areas in Mississippi and Florida, to provide pre-professional students with information on preparing for medical school. When possible, medical students participate in these recruitment visits. Disadvantaged underrepresented medical students are especially encouraged to visit historically black colleges and universities to share their experiences in the College of Medicine with prospective minority applicants. Interested pre-medical students are interviewed, and their academic record, background, and financial resources are reviewed for further consideration for special programs and medical school preparation activities.

Admissions

All applicants are evaluated by the Admissions Committee of the College of Medicine. This committee is composed of faculty, members of the local community (medical and non-medical), and medical students. There are no special admissions procedures for any applicants. Selection is made on a competitive basis using academic qualifications; Medical College Admission Test (MCAT) scores; and personal qualities and abilities such as maturity, leadership, determination, and motivation for a career in medicine.

Academic Support Programs

Because of the relatively small size of the College of Medicine's classes, academic assistance is readily available to all students. This assistance is provided both by other medical students and by faculty. Tutorials, academic and personal counseling, and other support can be obtained by the individual or coordinated through the Office of Student Affairs. Study skills information, including specialized preparation for board exams, is also available through this office.

Enrichment Programs

Diversity Recruitment and Education for Admission into Medicine (DREAM) Program
The University of South Alabama College of Medicine offers this special summer program designed for disadvantaged underrepresented undergraduates who are first-time sophomores. It offers a direct process for conditional acceptance into the University of South Alabama College of Medicine. Summer students participate in MCAT preparation sessions and are introduced to the first year of medical school through a series of medical courses, lectures, seminars, and clinical experiences by medical school faculty and staff. They also receive information for applying to medical school and for financial aid.

The Office of the Dean Summer Research Program
A limited number of research positions are available for incoming first-year students and rising second-year students. The program provides students with the opportunity to work with clinical

University of South Alabama College of Medicine
Applicants, First-Time Applicants, Matriculants by Gender, Race and Ethnicity, 2007-2008

	2007									2008								
	APP			F-time APP			MAT			APP			F-time APP			MAT		
	Wo-men	Men	Total	Wo-men	Men	Total	Wo-men	Men	Total	Wo-men	Men	Total	Wo-men	Men	Total	Wo-men	Men	Total
Hispanic/Latino																		
Cuban	3	5	8	2	4	6	0	0	0	9	4	13	7	4	11	0	0	0
Mexican American	5	9	14	2	6	8	0	0	0	7	4	11	7	3	10	0	0	0
Puerto Rican	2	2	4	2	2	4	0	0	0	3	3	6	3	0	3	0	0	0
Other Hispanic	5	9	14	4	5	9	0	0	0	16	14	30	10	9	19	0	0	0
Multiple Hispanic/Latino*	1	1	2	1	1	2	0	0	0	1	2	3	1	1	2	0	0	0
Subtotal	16	26	42	11	18	29	0	0	0	36	27	63	28	17	45	0	0	0
Non-Hispanic/Latino**																		
Black	67	34	101	46	30	76	2	2	4	85	34	119	62	27	89	3	2	5
Native American/AK	5	4	9	4	4	8	0	0	0	1	3	4	1	3	4	0	1	1
Native Hawaiian/OPI	1	1	2	1	1	2	0	0	0	3	2	5	2	1	3	0	0	0
White	278	383	661	222	258	480	25	33	58	283	454	737	221	307	528	27	32	59
Asian	62	94	156	44	62	106	5	4	9	85	101	186	64	63	127	4	1	5
Multiple Race*	9	9	18	6	6	12	0	1	1	12	5	17	7	5	12	2	1	3
Unknown	3	5	8	3	4	7	0	1	1	5	8	13	4	5	9	1	0	1
Subtotal	425	530	955	326	365	691	32	41	73	474	607	1,081	361	411	772	37	37	74
Foreign	26	31	57	21	22	43	0	1	1	25	40	65	16	34	50	0	0	0
Total	467	587	1,054	358	405	763	32	42	74	535	674	1,209	405	462	867	37	37	74

*Since 2002, students can select more than one race and / or ethnicity. **Those who did not choose 'Hispanic/Latino' or 'Non-Hispanic/Latino' are listed under 'Non-Hispanic/Latino'. Data Source: AAMC Data Warehouse: Applicant-Matriculant File, as of 1/16/2009.

and basic science faculty on a variety of research projects. These projects are presented in August at Student Research Day, and abstracts from these presentations are published in the Alabama Journal of Medical Sciences.

Student Financial Assistance

State scholarships and a variety of federal loan programs are available to qualified applicants. These programs are handled through the Office of Financial Aid of the College of Medicine. Each year, a limited number of tuition waiver scholarships are available to qualified disadvantaged underrepresented medical school matriculants.

Educational Partnerships

The relationship between the University of South Alabama College of Medicine and the historically black colleges of Alabama allows priority consideration to their students for participation in the summer programs and regards these schools as primary feeders for disadvantaged underrepresented students.

University of Arizona College of Medicine

Dr. Ana María López, MPH, FACP
Associate Dean, Outreach and
Multicultural Affairs
University of Arizona
College of Medicine
www.diversity.medicine.arizona.edu

Tucson Campus

Linda K. Don, Assistant Dean,
Outreach and Multicultural
Affairs – Tucson

Dr. Oscar Beita, Associate Director,
Office of Outreach and Multicultural
Affairs – Tucson
P.O. Box 245140
1501 North Campbell Avenue,
Room 1119B
Tucson, AZ 85724-5140
520-621-5531; 800-841-5948;
520-626-2895 fax

Phoenix Campus – *in partnership with Arizona State University*

Dr. Douglas Campos-Outcalt,
Assistant Dean, Outreach and
Multicultural Affairs – Phoenix

Patricia Rodriguez, Associate Director,
Office of Outreach and Multicultural
Affairs – Phoenix
550 East Van Buren Street
Phoenix, AZ 85004-2230
602-827-2027; 602-827-2127 fax

Recruitment

The University of Arizona College of Medicine (UA COM) is strongly committed to efforts to achieve the educational benefits associated with a diverse student body. Additionally, the college strives to educate physician leaders that will provide culturally and linguistically sensitive health care for Arizona communities and who will dedicate their efforts to eradicating health disparities in our state and nation. A combined M.D./M.P.H. program, with opportunities to concentrate on health disparities issues, is offered through collaboration with the Mel and Enid Zuckerman College of Public Health. Interested applicants should ask the College of Medicine Admissions Office for contact information for this program.

Outreach and Multicultural Affairs (OMA) works closely with the Office of Admissions at both of our College of Medicine campuses. OMA recruitment and pre-admissions activities include mock interviews, mock MCATs, informational workshops, and the Arizona Applicant Academy. The OMA sponsors a statewide pre-health professions student organization, Fostering and Achieving Cultural Equity and Sensitivity (F.A.C.E.S.) in the health professions. F.A.C.E.S. encourages any student who is interested in diversity issues in health care and health professions education to participate in its activities. There are F.A.C.E.S. chapters on various campuses in the state, offering opportunities to develop leadership skills, volunteer with health care projects that target underserved populations, and shadow community physicians and other health professionals.

Admissions

The University of Arizona College of Medicine is committed to the concept of individualized, holistic review of applicants. In evaluating applicants, the Admissions Committee considers many factors including the applicant's entire academic record, performance on the

University of Arizona College of Medicine
Applicants, First-Time Applicants, Matriculants by Gender, Race and Ethnicity, 2007-2008

	2007 APP Women	Men	Total	F-time APP Women	Men	Total	MAT Women	Men	Total	2008 APP Women	Men	Total	F-time APP Women	Men	Total	MAT Women	Men	Total
Hispanic/Latino																		
Cuban	1	0	1	0	0	0	0	0	0	0	2	2	0	2	2	0	0	0
Mexican American	25	32	57	20	27	47	9	1	10	22	18	40	17	12	29	6	3	9
Puerto Rican	1	2	3	1	2	3	0	0	0	1	2	3	1	2	3	1	1	2
Other Hispanic	9	4	13	4	2	6	0	1	1	10	11	21	7	10	17	2	2	4
Multiple Hispanic/Latino*	3	2	5	3	1	4	1	1	2	3	2	5	2	2	4	1	0	1
Subtotal	39	40	79	28	32	60	10	3	13	36	35	71	27	28	55	10	6	16
Non-Hispanic/Latino**																		
Black	12	12	24	10	8	18	2	3	5	16	13	29	11	11	22	1	1	2
Native American/AK	10	3	13	6	1	7	1	0	1	8	5	13	4	3	7	0	0	0
Native Hawaiian/OPI	2	1	3	1	1	2	1	0	1	1	0	1	0	0	0	1	0	1
White	263	293	556	197	217	414	56	31	87	261	289	550	176	193	369	56	45	101
Asian	56	48	104	41	32	73	10	11	21	78	65	143	59	49	108	20	13	33
Multiple Race*	10	12	22	8	9	17	1	2	3	13	13	26	9	12	21	3	1	4
Unknown	3	6	9	3	6	9	2	1	3	4	10	14	4	8	12	0	0	0
Subtotal	356	375	731	266	274	540	73	48	121	381	395	776	263	276	539	81	60	141
Foreign	2	2	4	2	2	4	0	0	0	3	5	8	3	4	7	1	0	1
Total	397	417	814	296	308	604	83	51	134	420	435	855	293	308	601	92	66	158

*Since 2002, students can select more than one race and / or ethnicity. **Those who did not choose 'Hispanic/Latino' or 'Non-Hispanic/Latino' are
listed under 'Non-Hispanic/Latino'. Data Source: AAMC Data Warehouse: Applicant-Matriculant File, as of 1/16/2009.

MCAT, personal statement, interviews, and letters of recommendation. Applicants are chosen on the basis of their career goals, motivation, academic ability, integrity, maturity, altruism, communication skills, and leadership abilities. Clinical, research, or community service experience is viewed favorably. The Admissions Committee strives to accept a student body with diverse backgrounds in order to best meet the medical needs of the people of Arizona. Priority consideration is given to applicants who demonstrate a willingness to practice in medically underserved areas of Arizona. No preference is given to any particular type of undergraduate major. Since many of the patients who receive care at the College of Medicine's affiliated clinics and hospitals speak Spanish as their primary language, it would be useful for University of Arizona medical students to be conversant in Spanish.

Academic Support Programs
The staff of the Office of Student Development offers extensive individual and small-group sessions that help students adjust their study skills for successful completion of the curriculum. Special attention is given to the transition into medical school in a week-long Medical Student Bridge Program for non-traditional students. Additionally, the Student Development staff provide support for preparation for all steps of the United States Medical Licensing Exam (USMLE), including a six-week, structured review for those students needing to repeat the USMLE Step 1.

Student clubs and organizations provide valuable peer networks for study and social support. They also afford opportunities to improve clinical exam, communication, and other professional skills, as well as exposure to the concerns of diverse communities. The University of Arizona College of Medicine has active chapters of the Association of Native American Medical Students (ANAMS), Asian Pacific American Medical Student Association (APAMSA), Latino Medical Student Association (LMSA), and Student National Medical

Association (LMSA), to name but a few of the organizations.

Enrichment Programs
OMA operates summer programs and other activities for high school and college students. These provide some employment and numerous volunteer opportunities for medical students to engage with members of Arizona's diverse communities. Med-Start, a program established in 1969, offers five weeks of educational enrichment activities for Arizona high school students to explore health professions career opportunities and experience the academic demands of college life. Additional information can be found at (www.medstart.arizona.edu).

Arizona Maximizing Medical Education Potential (AZMMEP)
AZMMEP is a highly structured college co-curricular program that provides a pathway for preparing for medical school application and the demands of medical education, while introducing the concepts of health disparities and cultural competence. AZMMEP is particularly beneficial for students who are from ethnic groups that are underrepresented in medicine, first in their families to graduate from college, economically/educationally disadvantaged, and/or from rural or reservation communities. Web-based activities and options are currently under development to enable students to participate regardless of where they are located.

Student Financial Assistance
The University of Arizona College of Medicine provides three financial aid staff members, located at the College of Medicine Financial Aid Office at the Tucson Campus, to work exclusively with the medical students. The Phoenix Campus has a Coordinator of Financial Aid Services as well. This permits a high degree of personalized service for students as they seek financial assistance for their medical education. Students who are willing to repay their loan debt by practicing in a medically underserved area in Arizona upon completion of residency may be eligible for

the Arizona Medical Student Loan Program. The College of Medicine is able to provide some funding through institutional scholarships and grants.

Educational Partnerships
OMA and other programs work together to provide a comprehensive academic and social support network for Arizona pre-medical and medical students. The College of Medicine is a charter member of Hispanic-Serving Health Professions Schools (HSHPS) and has been recognized nationally for its enrollment and support of Hispanic and American Indian medical students. For example, *Hispanic Business Magazine* has recognized the College of Medicine as one of the top ten medical schools for Hispanics. The Arizona Hispanic Center of Excellence provides a resource network to support Hispanic pre-medical and medical students, as well as Hispanic faculty. The University of Arizona and Inter Tribal Council of Arizona Indians into Medicine (INMED) Program offers students academic advising and tutoring, health career forums, and talking circles, as well as funding to attend Association of American Indian Physicians (AAIP) conferences and workshops.

University of Arkansas for Medical Sciences College of Medicine

Dr. Billy R. Thomas, Associate Dean
Bill E. Bauknight, Director
Center for Diversity Affairs
University of Arkansas
College of Medicine
4301 West Markham,
Slot 625
Little Rock, AR 72205-7199
501-686-7299; 501-686-7439 fax
www.uams.edu/com/eda

Recruitment

The Center for Diversity Affairs (CDA) assists in the early identification, recruitment, and retention of minority students for the University of Arkansas for Medical Sciences (UAMS) College of Medicine. The CDA conducts programs designed to identify, inform, motivate, and assist prospective candidates for medical school admission. These programs pay special attention to minority and disadvantaged students in the state.

Over the years, high school counselors and pre-medical advisory personnel at undergraduate institutions have worked with the CDA staff to inform academically gifted and academically disadvantaged students of opportunities offered at UAMS. This network of dedicated and committed individuals provides the College of Medicine with young and enthusiastic minority students from which to increase the applicant pool.

The Associate Dean, Directors, and Project Coordinator in the Center for Diversity Affairs are responsible for recruitment. In previous years, the CDA staff focused primarily on college and university students; however, over the last few years, the staff have developed a recruitment module for K-sixth grades along with junior and senior high school students. The CDA staff members visit junior high schools, high schools, and colleges, throughout the state that have high concentrations of African-American and other underrepresented minority students. Resources for reaching these students include counselor recommendations, Health

Career Occupation classes, science classes, National Merit semifinalists and finalists, school visitations, College Day Programs, Governor's School attendees, and tours of the University of Arkansas campus. These sources have provided an extensive and ever-expanding list of students for follow-up counseling. Lastly, in an effort to increase our applicant pool the recruitment efforts of the CDA have been expanded through the addition of a Director of Diversity and Recruitment for all five UAMS colleges. Over the past three years the COM has increased its freshman class size to 175. This has resulted in increased recruitment efforts both in and outside of the state.

Retention

The Minority Recruitment and Retention Committee (MRRC), appointed by the Dean of the College of Medicine, consist of faculty members, students, and Center for Diversity Affairs staff. This committee reviews the recruitment and retention strategies of the Center for Diversity Affairs and the College of Medicine and offers recommendations

University of Arkansas for Medical Sciences College of Medicine
Applicants, First-Time Applicants, Matriculants by Gender, Race and Ethnicity, 2007-2008

	2007									2008								
	APP			F-time APP			MAT			APP			F-time APP			MAT		
	Women	Men	Total	Women	Men	Total	Women	Men	Total	Women	Men	Total	Women	Men	Total	Women	Men	Total
Hispanic/Latino																		
Cuban	1	6	7	1	5	6	0	0	0	5	9	14	4	7	11	0	0	0
Mexican American	12	18	30	9	12	21	0	1	1	13	16	29	12	13	25	0	2	2
Puerto Rican	2	3	5	2	3	5	0	0	0	3	4	7	3	3	6	1	0	1
Other Hispanic	9	15	24	5	11	16	0	1	1	17	24	41	13	16	29	0	2	2
Multiple Hispanic/Latino*	1	2	3	1	1	2	0	0	0	1	2	3	1	1	2	0	0	0
Subtotal	25	44	69	18	32	50	0	2	2	39	55	94	33	40	73	1	4	5
Non-Hispanic/Latino**																		
Black	63	29	92	39	20	59	3	2	5	59	29	88	37	17	54	12	2	14
Native American/AK	3	6	9	2	6	8	0	0	0	5	8	13	4	5	9	0	0	0
Native Hawaiian/OPI	3	5	8	3	3	6	0	1	1	3	2	5	2	1	3	0	0	0
White	291	453	744	229	332	561	45	79	124	336	550	886	250	382	632	39	80	119
Asian	109	144	253	77	100	177	5	14	19	154	209	363	119	147	266	7	6	13
Other Race	2	0	2	2	0	2	0	0	0	0	1	1	0	1	1	0	0	0
Multiple Race*	8	20	28	6	14	20	1	1	2	12	25	37	7	18	25	1	0	1
Unknown	1	5	6	1	4	5	1	1	2	8	11	19	8	11	19	0	2	2
Subtotal	480	662	1,142	359	479	838	55	98	153	577	835	1,412	427	582	1,009	59	90	149
Foreign	7	12	19	6	11	17	0	0	0	9	7	16	7	5	12	0	0	0
Total	512	718	1,230	383	522	905	55	100	155	625	897	1,522	467	627	1,094	60	94	154

*Since 2002, students can select more than one race and / or ethnicity. **Those who did not choose 'Hispanic/Latino' or 'Non-Hispanic/Latino' are listed under 'Non-Hispanic/Latino'. Data Source: AAMC Data Warehouse: Applicant-Matriculant File, as of 1/16/2009.

to ensure diversity and fairness of treatment for minority applicants and students. Once a student has applied to the College of Medicine, every assistance is given to her/him in the processing of the necessary forms to complete the admissions process. Information concerning financial aid availability and procedures is covered in detail later. Members of this committee also serve as advisors to, and advocates for, minority students.

The Dean's Minority Advisory Committee (DMAC) is another committee appointed by the Dean of the College of Medicine, with the advice of the staff of the CDA and members of the Arkansas Medical, Dental, and Pharmaceutical Association (AMDPA)—an association composed of minority health care professionals in Arkansas. This committee meets four times each year and has the responsibility of advising the dean on recruitment, retention, and problems that may be encountered by minority students. Members of this committee, and of AMDPA, serve as mentors for medical students and often provide them with counsel and financial assistance.

Admissions

The Admissions Committee is composed of 15 members appointed by the Board of Trustees of the University of Arkansas and selected from a list submitted by the Dean of the College of Medicine. The committee is subject to the approval of the Vice President of Health Sciences, the President of the University System, and the Board of Trustees. Six of the committee members are on the faculty of the College of Medicine; two members are appointed from each of the four Congressional Districts, as established by ACT 337 of 1971, and are apportioned on the basis of members from each district; and one member is appointed from the state-at-large. All members of the committee serve one-year terms and may be reappointed for not more than three consecutive terms. All medical school applicants are reviewed by this committee.

Academic Support Programs

The progress of each student is carefully monitored and, when additional help is needed, it is made available on an individual basis. Each department has review and tutorial sessions available for any student.

Counseling is available for all students by the Office of the Dean, Center for Diversity Affairs, the Office of the Associate Dean for Academic Affairs, and the Office of Educational Development. The latter is an instructional support agency at UAMS that works directly with students to help them to be successful in their educational experiences. The staff works with the students in areas such as enhancing learning strategies, improving test-taking skills, managing time effectively, improving interpersonal skills, note-taking, and establishing efficient study habits.

Four different retention activities are offered to medical students:

- A four-week summer pre-matriculation program for incoming minority/disadvantaged students: Students are selected based on Medical College Admission Test (MCAT) scores, grade-point average (GPA), and other criteria for disadvantaged (rural background and socioeconomic conditions) status. Lectures in microanatomy, gross anatomy, biochemical and physiological aspects of cellular function, learning and testtaking skills, and other seminars are given.
- A five-week preparation/review program for at-risk sophomore students who are required to pass United States Medical Licensing Examination (USMLE) Step 1 before entering into the junior year of medical school: At-risk students are those whose basic science course grades are marginal and those who have relatively low MCAT scores and undergraduate GPA. This course is taught by faculty of the College of Medicine and basic science courses are reviewed;
- A five-week intense science review program for students who failed, for the first time, the USMLE Step 1 ex-

amination: Key features of this program are lectures and frequent testing of students.

A four-week clinical science review program for students who fail to pass the USMLE Step 2 examination: This program is taught by College of Medicine faculty and reviews all clerkships taken in the clinical years.

Enrichment Programs

Due to cuts in Title VII funding (e.g. Health Careers Opportunity Program) the number and length of academic enrichment programs supported by the CDA have been reduced.

Undergraduate Summer Science Enrichment Program (USSEP)

This program, funded by the Health Careers Opportunity Program (HCOP) in the College of Medicine, is designed to acquaint college students with the rigors of the first-year medical school curriculum. The five-week program provides students with an opportunity to work with basic science and clinical faculty in encapsulated versions of the courses taken by freshman. Mock exams, labs, study skills, test-taking skills, and reading skills are integral parts of this program. Sophomore students focus mainly on academics; whereas with junior and senior students the major emphasis is on test-taking skills and MCAT review. Students are also given the opportunity to shadow minority practitioners and UAMS faculty at least five mornings each year during the program to gain firsthand knowledge of the medical practice. This year a total of 15-20 students will participate in the program.

Arkansas Commitment

This program targets junior and senior high school students. Students are identified in high school and placed in research laboratories on the UAMS campus. In addition students are given the opportunity to shadow local minority physicians and UAMS faculty. Students are paired with local physicians and UAMS faculty who act as mentors. Once students are identified and participate in the program, they remain in the program until graduating from college. This program began in 2000, and to date there have been 43 students who have participated in the program.

Summer Science Discovery Program (SSDP)

In addition to programs targeting undergraduate schools, the CDA has been able to develop a program targeting K-sixth grade students, the Summer Science Discovery Program (SSDP). The program is concentrated during the summer and has a primary objective of exposing students to science and the possibility of a career in health care. A total of 200 students participate in the program each summer.

Student Financial Assistance

The medical school participates in the American Medical College Application Service and, under its fee waiver program, will waive the $10 UAMS application fee. Financial assistance is available to all students and is based on individual need. Need is determined in consideration of previous educational debts, parental resources, dependent siblings, and retirement status. In addition to the standard sources, there are other institutional funds administered on either an academic or need-based measurement.

Educational Partnerships

The College of Medicine has an educational partnership with three schools from the public school system in Little Rock, the Museum of Discovery, Greater Friendship Incorporated (a community-based organization), two local historically black colleges, a local community college, and a majority undergraduate institution that is strategically located in the Northeast corner of the state. In addition, the College of Medicine, the AMDPA, and the Arkansas Mentoring and Networking Association (AMNA) have an educational partnership. The AMDPA is an association whose membership includes minority physicians and pharmacists. Members of the association serve as advisors to the Dean of the College of Medicine and as mentors and external support persons for medical students.

The AMNA is an association whose membership includes local community leaders, faculty members from local universities, and individuals from multiple health care specialties.

David Geffen School of Medicine at UCLA

Patricia Pratt, Director, Academic Enrichment and Outreach
David Geffen School of Medicine at UCLA
10833 LeConte Ave,
Suite 13-154CHS
Los Angeles, CA 90095-6990
310-825-3575; 310-206-7180 fax
ppratt@mednet.ucla.edu
www.medstudent.ucla.edu/prospective

Recruitment

The David Geffen School of Medicine at UCLA is firmly committed to attracting and educating qualified disadvantaged students. The school's interest in promoting quality and equity in medical education has led to the development of a continuum of support extending from early pre-medical contact with disadvantaged students, to medical school admissions, through graduation, postgraduate medical education, minority faculty development, and alumni networking. Recruitment, support services, and retention are the primary elements that structure the scope of work of the Office of Academic Enrichment and Outreach (OAE&O).

In addition, UCLA offers a six-week summer enrichment program, UCLA PREP, a nationally recognized program that was established in 1982, and the UCLA ReApplicant Program, established in 2000 (see Enrichment Programs). In 2006, UCLA became part of The Robert Wood Johnson Summer Medical and Dental Education Program (SMDEP), which offers a six-week summer enrichment program which targets disadvantaged community college students.

Faculty, administrators, and medical students are actively engaged in various aspects of the recruitment process. They participate in national, regional, and local conferences and programs for students in the medical education pipeline. David Geffen School of Medicine at UCLA encourages campus visits and can often arrange visits to acquaint prospective students and groups with current medical students and the School of Medicine's facilities. In compliance with the current California legislation prohibiting the consideration of race, ethnicity, or gender in the admissions of students, the David Geffen School of Medicine at UCLA has increased its efforts to maintain the excellent diversity within its student body. The OAE&O also provides technical support, conferences, and workshops designed to increase the number of underrepresented minorities in the national physician work force.

Admissions

The David Geffen School of Medicine at UCLA's Admissions Committee is devoted to the consideration of applicants with disadvantaged backgrounds and/or who are from historically underserved communities. The committee includes faculty and medical students who have themselves overcome socioeconomic and/or educational disadvantages and who have experience in evaluating the non-cognitive aspects of these applications.

The committee evaluates all applications on the basis of academic performance, Medical College Admission Test (MCAT) scores, letters of recommendation, and personal comments—as does the full Admissions Committee. Careful consideration is given to those factors

University of California, Los Angeles David Geffen School of Medicine
Applicants, First-Time Applicants, Matriculants by Gender, Race and Ethnicity, 2007-2008

	2007 APP Women	Men	Total	2007 F-time APP Women	Men	Total	2007 MAT Women	Men	Total	2008 APP Women	Men	Total	2008 F-time APP Women	Men	Total	2008 MAT Women	Men	Total
Hispanic/Latino																		
Cuban	6	13	19	5	9	14	0	0	0	15	12	27	14	11	25	0	0	0
Mexican American	133	122	255	107	93	200	2	4	6	121	111	232	96	85	181	2	4	6
Puerto Rican	13	13	26	10	11	21	0	0	0	15	9	24	10	6	16	0	0	0
Other Hispanic	86	77	163	65	57	122	1	3	4	78	85	163	62	66	128	0	1	1
Multiple Hispanic/Latino*	11	13	24	7	11	18	0	0	0	20	11	31	16	8	24	0	1	1
Subtotal	249	238	487	194	181	375	3	7	10	249	228	477	198	176	374	2	6	8
Non-Hispanic/Latino**																		
Black	120	89	209	93	68	161	2	0	2	149	81	230	116	65	181	3	5	8
Native American/AK	5	5	10	4	5	9	0	0	0	3	6	9	3	5	8	1	1	2
Native Hawaiian/OPI	18	11	29	17	9	26	0	0	0	19	12	31	15	10	25	1	0	1
White	1,154	1,354	2,508	957	1,075	2,032	24	30	54	1,104	1,379	2,483	870	1,093	1,963	25	28	53
Asian	1,015	1,066	2,081	833	841	1,674	26	24	50	980	1,065	2,045	765	798	1,563	20	19	39
Other Race	2	4	6	2	3	5	0	1	1	3	6	9	2	5	7	0	0	0
Multiple Race*	110	103	213	100	78	178	2	1	3	114	104	218	89	76	165	2	2	4
Unknown	29	42	71	27	36	63	0	1	1	73	91	164	68	83	151	2	4	6
Subtotal	2,453	2,674	5,127	2,033	2,115	4,148	54	57	111	2,445	2,744	5,189	1,928	2,135	4,063	54	59	113
Foreign	99	110	209	80	84	164	0	0	0	83	104	187	69	74	143	0	0	0
Total	2,801	3,022	5,823	2,307	2,380	4,687	57	64	121	2,777	3,076	5,853	2,195	2,385	4,580	56	65	121

Note: In 2008, one applicant, who declined to report gender, was not included here.

*Since 2002, students can select more than one race and / or ethnicity. **Those who did not choose 'Hispanic/Latino' or 'Non-Hispanic/Latino' are listed under 'Non-Hispanic/Latino'. Data Source: AAMC Data Warehouse: Applicant-Matriculant File, as of 1/16/2009.

that might have affected the applicant's past academic record or future achievement. Course requirements are the same for all applicants. Special consideration is given to each applicant's potential contribution to the university's goals and society's needs.

Academic Support Programs

The Office of Academic Enrichment & Outreach monitors individual student performance in the medical curriculum in order to identify and address problems as early as possible. Services offered include confidential counseling; learning skills diagnosis; study skills consultation; a United States Medical Licensing Examination (USMLE) review course; tutoring, stress, and anxiety reduction strategies; and a summer pre-entry course.

Enrichment Programs

UCLA Prep

An intensive six-week summer program provides pre-medical and pre-dental students from disadvantaged backgrounds with a means of strengthening their ability and readiness to study medicine and dentistry. Program participants are exposed to the rigors of academic medicine, with hands-on clinical preceptorships in clinical and research settings and are mentored by accomplished medical students.

UCLA ReApplicant Program (RAP)

UCLA RAP is a comprehensive program designed to assist promising students from disadvantaged backgrounds who have been unsuccessful in gaining admission to any U.S. medical school. The 11-month program is conducted in two sessions that begin with an intensive six-week summer session focused on MCAT preparation. Distinguished guest lecturers provide workshops discussing academic skills, extensive science reviews, self development, time management, financial planning, medical school re-application, and interviewing skills. Each participant is given a study-skills diagnostic assessment to aid in developing a successful plan for academic achievement. An individualized academic-year program of a sci-

ence coursework follows, and participants work in close consultation with program advisors to select courses through UCLA Extensions or a local California Sate University.

Prologue to Medicine

The optional summer pre-entry course, Prologue to Medicine, is conducted for a one-week period immediately preceding the first year of medical school. Prologue has been designed to help students from non-traditional backgrounds and with a wide variety of learning styles to navigate UCLA's problem-based learning curriculum. The interdisciplinary approach and small-group study sessions lend themselves well to the introduction of the major basic sciences. The faculty consists of members of the basic science and clinical departments, enabling students not only to sample various styles, but more importantly, to know some of their professors before fall semester. Subject matter, per se, is secondary to the development of learning behavior that will enable students to cope with the new rigors of medical education. The pace, although slower at first, builds up to that which will be encountered when medical school actually begins in the fall. The aim is to make the experience as realistic as possible, permitting the students and faculty to anticipate possible trouble spots and work toward early solutions. Participation is open to accepted students from non-traditional and disadvantaged backgrounds.

Celebrations in Diversity

From the first day of class and throughout the four years of medical training, students participate in activities to promote appreciation and effective communication with many diverse cultures. Each year a multimedia theatrical presentation, "A Slice of Rice, Frijoles and Greens," serves as the foundation for the cultural competency components of the medical curriculum. "Standing on the Shoulders of Giants: A Survey of 5,000 years of Contributions by Blacks to Health, Healing and Medicine" is a permanent exhibit, which is displayed annually. Hispanic Heritage Month activities include a variety of events in-

cluding a film festival, food sharing, and community health fairs. Similar activities are sponsored by student organizations including the annual city-wide "Minority Health Conference," sponsored by the Asian Pacific American Medical Student Association, the Latino Medical Student Association, and the Student National Medical Association.

UCLA PRIME

UCLA PRIME is a five-year dual-degree program designed to develop the leadership skills of a select group of UCLA students who have experience with and a commitment to serving the medically underserved and disadvantaged. Applicants considering UCLA PRIME file a separate AMCAS application to the program and are considered through a distinct rigorous process. UCLA PRIME students have opportunities to participate in seminars and electives focusing on health care for the underserved and are expected to complete a research/leadership project focusing on improving an aspect of health care for the disadvantaged.

Student Financial Assistance

The Admissions Committee makes an effort to seek out qualified applicants. If a supplemental application is requested, a processing fee of $40 is required, but may be waived, on the basis of economic need.

The School of Medicine provides assistance towards meeting the financial needs of admitted economically disadvantaged students from university funds, as well as private scholarship and loan money from a variety of sources. The financial needs for living and medical school expenses, as evaluated from the scholarship-loan application forms, can be met in several ways. Students eligible for campus-based aid are generally offered a combination or package of various types of aid (loans, grants, and scholarships).

Educational Partnerships

Through the outreach programs conducted by the Office of Academic Enrichment and Outreach and in individual departments of the School of Medicine, UCLA has established educational partnerships that are designed to facilitate access to medical careers for students from disadvantaged backgrounds:

- "The Magic of Medicine" Undergraduate UCLA Course;
- UCLA PREP, Summer Pre-medical Enrichment Program;
- UCLA SMDEP
- UCLA Re-Application Program (RAP);
- Affiliation with local colleges, community colleges, high schools, and middle schools;
- Affiliation with Charles R. Drew University of Medicine and Science;
- Combined-degree programs with other UCLA professional schools; and
- Academic Advancement Program on the UCLA undergraduate campus.

UCLA RAP is a member of the California Postbaccalaureate Consortium that includes the postbaccalaureate programs at all five of the University of California medical schools.

Keck School of Medicine of the University of Southern California

Althea Alexander, Assistant Dean
Office of Diversity
Keck School of Medicine of the
University of Southern California
1333 San Pablo Street, MCH51C
Los Angeles, CA 90033-9152
323-442-1050; 323-442-3575 fax
aalexand@usc.edu
http://www.usc.edu/schools/medicine

Recruitment

Consistent with the premise that the choice of a career in the health professions requires early academic preparation and planning, the Keck School of Medicine of the University of Southern California's Office of Diversity recruitment effort is multifaceted and multileveled. At the undergraduate level, an active recruitment program is conducted through regular visits to local colleges and universities, as well as liaison with pre-medical advisors and student organizations. The Student National Medical Association and the Latino Medical Student Association are very active in recruiting efforts at the local high schools, middle schools and undergraduate campuses.

Admissions

The Committee on Admissions considers all qualified applicants. Each applicant is assessed on the basis of his/her potential as a physician. The Assistant Dean of the Office of Diversity is a member of the Admission and Screening Committee. All qualifying minority students are interviewed at the Keck School of Medicine of the University of Southern California. Great care is taken to ensure that qualified students from disadvantaged backgrounds are accepted. There are 18 members of the admissions committee and student representatives from second, third, and fourth year also sit on the committee. The Assistant Dean of the Office of Diversity is a permanent member of the Admissions Committee.

Academic Support Programs

Throughout the academic year, tutoring services are provided for all students. Complete advisement and retention activities are offered to all medical school matriculants.

Enrichment Programs

In the summer, the Keck School of Medicine offers a three-week Bridge Program for incoming freshman students that will give them an overview of the curriculum and introduce them to gross anatomy.

Student Financial Assistance

The dean has provided 11 four-year scholarships and limited monies are available for tuition through privately endowed scholarships. Students have access to several low-interest loan funds. The dean has also committed a significant amount of money to be set aside for minority students' scholarships.

Educational Partnerships

The School of Medicine has partnerships with many universities, colleges,

Keck School of Medicine of the University of Southern California
Applicants, First-Time Applicants, Matriculants by Gender, Race and Ethnicity, 2007-2008

	2007									2008								
	APP			F-time APP			MAT			APP			F-time APP			MAT		
	Wo-men	Men	Total	Wo-men	Men	Total	Wo-men	Men	Total	Wo-men	Men	Total	Wo-men	Men	Total	Wo-men	Men	Total
Hispanic/Latino																		
Cuban	11	10	21	6	7	13	1	0	1	14	14	28	12	13	25	0	1	1
Mexican American	128	127	255	105	99	204	4	5	9	113	110	223	91	79	170	8	10	18
Puerto Rican	10	10	20	9	7	16	0	0	0	8	10	18	7	6	13	0	1	1
Other Hispanic	93	82	175	68	58	126	4	2	6	90	82	172	69	61	130	3	1	4
Multiple Hispanic/Latino*	11	13	24	6	9	15	0	0	0	21	8	29	15	6	21	1	1	2
Subtotal	253	242	495	194	180	374	9	7	16	246	224	470	194	165	359	12	14	26
Non-Hispanic/Latino**																		
Black	112	80	192	85	62	147	2	1	3	133	83	216	98	60	158	4	4	8
Native American/AK	6	3	9	5	3	8	0	0	0	2	4	6	2	4	6	0	0	0
Native Hawaiian/OPI	20	11	31	17	9	26	1	0	1	22	15	37	17	10	27	0	0	0
White	1,316	1,477	2,793	1,060	1,099	2,159	38	61	99	1,219	1,622	2,841	940	1,217	2,157	29	39	68
Asian	1,116	1,173	2,289	885	879	1,764	15	18	33	1,122	1,192	2,314	836	852	1,688	20	19	39
Other Race	2	3	5	2	2	4	0	0	0	1	8	9	0	6	6	0	0	0
Multiple Race*	117	125	242	99	92	191	4	4	8	124	123	247	103	86	189	6	4	10
Unknown	28	42	70	25	36	61	0	0	0	73	99	172	67	87	154	0	2	2
Subtotal	2,717	2,914	5,631	2,178	2,182	4,360	60	84	144	2,696	3,146	5,842	2,063	2,322	4,385	59	68	127
Foreign	141	163	304	111	122	233	4	0	4	143	163	306	114	124	238	2	4	6
Total	3,111	3,319	6,430	2,483	2,484	4,967	73	91	164	3,085	3,533	6,618	2,371	2,611	4,982	73	86	159

*Since 2002, students can select more than one race and / or ethnicity. **Those who did not choose 'Hispanic/Latino' or 'Non-Hispanic/Latino' are listed under 'Non-Hispanic/Latino'. Data Source: AAMC Data Warehouse: Applicant-Matriculant File, as of 1/16/2009.

and high schools throughout Southern California to encourage and support interest in the health professions. They include tutorial programs with local high schools (Bravo Medical Magnet, Stevenson, and Bell Gardens) and campus tours coordinated with pre-medical organizations: Minority Association of Pre-Health Students (MAPS) at nearby undergraduate institutions (California State University at Long Beach and San Bernadino, Fresno, and University of Nevada at Las Vegas). Two student organizations, Latino Medical Student Association and Student National Medical Association, conduct health fairs at the local high schools; hold monthly meetings at two elementary schools, one in the black community and one in the Latino community; and sponsor annual pre-medical conferences. The medical school visits with the following high schools to promote interest in health professions: Manual Arts, Loyola, Sacred Heart, and Dorsey.

Loma Linda University School of Medicine

Dr. Daisy D. DeLeón,
Assistant to the Dean for Diversity
Loma Linda University
School of Medicine
Dean's Office, Coleman Pavilion
Loma Linda, CA 92350
909-558-4630; 909-558-0475 fax
ddeleon@llu.edu

Recruitment

Loma Linda University School of Medicine (LLUSM) recognizes diversity as an integral component in its commitment to achieve excellence in education. Central to LLUSM statement of purpose is to "assist in the fulfillment of our mission by preparing students with skills necessary to deliver culturally competent health care to a diverse community. Efforts to identify recruit and retain students from groups underrepresented in medicine and disadvantaged backgrounds" are coordinated between the Associate Dean for Admissions, the Assistant to the Dean for Diversity, and the Director of the Office for Maximizing Student Diversity (OMSD). The Associate Dean for Admissions and the Assistant to the Dean for Diversity jointly participate in recruitment visits to Seventh-Day Adventist colleges with a significant enrollment of underrepresented students. During these visits students are interviewed and informed of LLUSM programs designed to assist them in preparing for and gaining entrance into medical school.

Admissions

Assessment of all applicants is based on the overall academic record, pattern of academic performance, motivation, extracurricular activities, ability to relate to people, emotional stability, and life styles that are in accordance with the standards and policies of the school. The admissions committee includes student representation and diverse faculty, as well as the School of Medicine's Assistant to the Dean for Diversity and the Loma Linda University President's Assistant for Diversity.

Academic Support Programs

All students matriculating at the Loma Linda University School of Medicine have access to tutoring, study-skills help, and other academic-aid services. Students can also participate in the Faculty Mentoring program available during the academic years at LLUSM. These services are provided by a qualified professional counseling center, selected faculty, and graduate students. Medical students are also supported to attend the Teaching Learning Center (TLC) that assists students to improve their reading, study, and learning skills. Students can attend the TLC after admission but prior to starting classes or they can choose to attend once enrolled at the school. In addition, the School of Medicine holds a study-skills workshop, SILVER, that teaches advanced, graduate-level study skills. These resources provide support to the student who is identified as needing such assistance at the time of admission to the medical school, those students interested in improving their performance, and those students who may experience academic difficulty.

Enrichment Programs

LLUSM has developed programs to target students at all educational levels ranging from middle school to college. The diverse initiatives are designed to widen the pipeline for disadvantaged and underrepresented students in medicine. For a detailed description of the

Loma Linda University School of Medicine
Applicants, First-Time Applicants, Matriculants by Gender, Race and Ethnicity, 2007-2008

	2007									2008								
	APP			F-time APP			MAT			APP			F-time APP			MAT		
	Women	Men	Total	Women	Men	Total	Women	Men	Total	Women	Men	Total	Women	Men	Total	Women	Men	Total
Hispanic/Latino																		
Cuban	8	11	19	8	8	16	0	0	0	11	11	22	10	9	19	0	1	1
Mexican American	79	83	162	60	63	123	0	3	3	70	87	157	56	65	121	0	2	2
Puerto Rican	10	10	20	7	7	14	2	1	3	20	6	26	19	5	24	1	0	1
Other Hispanic	68	53	121	44	38	82	4	7	11	72	63	135	53	41	94	4	8	12
Multiple Hispanic/Latino*	7	10	17	5	6	11	0	1	1	13	7	20	11	4	15	0	1	1
Subtotal	172	167	339	124	122	246	6	12	18	186	174	360	149	124	273	5	12	17
Non-Hispanic/Latino**																		
Black	126	79	205	88	57	145	7	2	9	134	77	211	98	58	156	4	4	8
Native American/AK	4	5	9	1	3	4	0	0	0	4	5	9	3	4	7	0	0	0
Native Hawaiian/OPI	16	9	25	13	7	20	0	0	0	22	16	38	16	10	26	0	1	1
White	845	1,066	1,911	636	770	1,406	33	49	82	777	1,173	1,950	557	825	1,382	21	62	83
Asian	659	719	1,378	499	513	1,012	22	25	47	691	732	1,423	492	486	978	15	24	39
Other Race	1	2	3	1	1	2	0	0	0	2	4	6	2	4	6	0	0	0
Multiple Race*	68	72	140	51	40	91	1	0	1	51	67	118	37	47	84	4	3	7
Unknown	18	29	47	16	26	42	0	0	0	37	57	94	31	52	83	1	0	1
Subtotal	1,737	1,981	3,718	1,305	1,417	2,722	63	76	139	1,718	2,131	3,849	1,236	1,486	2,722	45	94	139
Foreign	128	142	270	101	104	205	6	9	15	127	137	264	90	101	191	5	4	9
Total	2,037	2,290	4,327	1,530	1,643	3,173	75	97	172	2,031	2,442	4,473	1,475	1,711	3,186	55	110	165

*Since 2002, students can select more than one race and / or ethnicity. **Those who did not choose 'Hispanic/Latino' or 'Non-Hispanic/Latino' are listed under 'Non-Hispanic/Latino'. Data Source: AAMC Data Warehouse: Applicant-Matriculant File, as of 1/16/2009.

enrichment programs to increase diversity at LLUSM please visit *(http://www.llu.edu/llu/medicine/ chdmm/index.html)*

Loma Linda University School of Medicine Pipeline programs:

Initiative for Maximizing Student Diversity (IMSD)
IMSD is founded by an NIH-NIGMS grant and targets underrepresented groups in the health sciences (10-15 students). The program features tuition and stipends for Ph.D. and M.D./Ph.D. students and travel and research supplies support.

Minorities in the Health Sciences (MITHS)
MITHS is funded by LLUSM and targets African American SDA high school juniors (10-15 students). The program features a three-week, on-campus, intensive academic program in basic science, reading, writing and math skills.

Apprenticeship Bridge to College (ABC)
ABC is founded by an NIH-NCMHD grant and targets high school students in the local community who are underrepresented in the biomedical sciences (15-20 students). The program features an eight-week summer research program with academic skills development.

Medical Scholars Program (MSP)
MSP is funded by LLUSM and targets underrepresented students interested in academic medicine (2-4 students). The program features two full-tuition scholarships per year for students with potential to become school of medicine faculty.

Advanced Post-Baccalaureate Learning Experience (ABLE)
ABLE is paid by students' tuition and targets disadvantaged medical school applicants who have been denied admissions, with potential to succeed (3-6 students). The program features one-year program with guaranteed admission to SOM if student's performance is equal or above freshman class average.

Si Se Puede (Yes You Can)
Yes You Can is funded by LLUSOM and targets community Hispanic high school students (45-50 students). The

program features a one-week introductory program to health careers.

Undergraduate Training Program (UTP)
UTP is funded by an NIH-NCMHD grant and targets college students underrepresented in the biomedical sciences (15-20 students). The program features a ten-week undergraduate research program with academic skills development in basic science, reading, writing and math skills.

Medical Students Summer Research Program (MTP)
MTP is funded by an NIH-NCMHD grant and targets medical students underrepresented in the biomedical sciences from LLU or LCME accredited schools (10 students). The program features an eight-week program in health disparities research with weekly seminars and professional development workshops.

Student Financial Assistance
Application fees are waived for disadvantaged students when requested in writing. Financial support is available to underrepresented students on the basis of scholarship (academic performance) and demonstrated financial need. The scholarships for disadvantaged students can provide a four-year, tuition scholarship. In addition, for students who qualify for the Medical Scientist Training Program (M.D.–Ph.D.), a full scholarship with stipend is available for the duration of the student's graduate and medical education at Loma Linda University School of Medicine.

Educational Partnerships
The Hippocrates Program
This program is a collaborative effort with Kaiser Permanente that targets eighth graders from underrepresented groups who are interested in medicine and have excelled in science at local public schools from San Bernardino and Riverside counties. Approximately 175 (four groups of 40-45 students) each year participate in activities scheduled throughout a six-month period, which include conferences, physician shadowing, hospital tours, and visits to LLU School of Medicine. This experience exposes young students to a

unique close-up look at medicine and the opportunities available to them in high school and college. Hippocrates circle represents the earliest pipeline program in our local community and is primarily funded by Kaiser Permanente.

The Inland Empire Scholarship Fund (IESF)
The IESF provides 60-80 scholarships to promising financially disadvantaged Hispanic students in the Inland Empire. The IESF is a leading foundation in the region and has established a partnership with the LLU Center For Health Disparities and Molecular Medicine to assist in identifying high school and undergraduate candidates from the immediate community that show promise and interest in medicine and biomedical research.

The Medical Scholars Program
This program has a unique partnership with colleges in Alabama, California, Massachusetts, Michigan, and Puerto Rico to develop faculty from underrepresented and disadvantaged backgrounds. The program identifies sophomore students at partnership colleges who have an interest in academic medicine and have exhibited academic and teaching excellence. Once selected into the program, students participate in a summer research experience at LLU before their matriculation in medical school. Students who meet pre-determined performance criteria can qualify for early decision acceptance to the Loma Linda University School of Medicine. Students accepted through this program receive the benefits of the enrichment components of the program, as well as a financial package commensurate with their scholarship and financial need. The School of Medicine also benefits as these students can function as tutors and Problem-Based Learning Course Facilitators for all School of Medicine students.

Other
Each year, medical and scientific advances offer new opportunities for the improvement of health for all Americans. Yet, a disproportionate burden of diseases such as diabetes, stroke, cancer,

and HIV/AIDS affects minority and medically underserved populations. The Center for Health Disparities and Molecular Medicine (CHDMM) at Loma Linda University School of Medicine is proud to be recognized as a Research Center of Excellence by the National Center on Minority Health and Health Disparities. The CHDMM houses research projects and student training programs funded primarily by the National Center on Minority Health and Health Disparities (NCMHD) and the National Institute of General Medical Sciences (NIGMS). These two NIH initiatives provide synergy to implement a robust research and educational plan to eliminate health disparities through research, education, and community engagement. The CHDMM integrates a diverse team of research scientists and clinicians engaged in training a diverse and new generation of health disparities scholars and physicians. The Medical Training Program (MTP) provides basic research and scientific experience to medical students interested in integrating biomedical research in health disparities in the practice of medicine. MTP students also attend a weekly lecture series addressing issues in health disparities. This program is available to medical students at LCME accredited schools.

Stanford University
School of Medicine

Dr. Ronald Garcia, Assistant Dean for
Minority Affairs
Stanford University
School of Medicine
Center of Excellence
251 Campus Drive, MSOB x361
Stanford, CA 94305-5404
650-725-0354; 650-725-7855 fax
Ron.garcia@stanford.edu
http://coe.stanford.edu

Recruitment

The Stanford University School of
Medicine sends recruiters—faculty and
students—to visit a number of summer
programs in which minority pre-medical students are enrolled. In addition,
the medical school participates in career day programs throughout the country. The Center of Excellence, the Office
of Admissions, and Stanford University
Minority Medical Student Alliance cosponsor a pre-medical student conference, "SUMMA," in early February.

Yearly, specially prepared brochures de-
scribing the medical school program
are sent to a large number of minority
students on the Medical Minority Applicant Registry list. The medical school
students are encouraged to inform minority students at their own undergraduate colleges about the program.

Admissions

Stanford is committed to being a premier research-intensive medical school
that improves health through leadership, collaborative discoveries, and in-
novation in patient care, education, and
research. Stanford will identify, accept,
and recruit the future leaders of medicine. In particular, it seeks individuals
whose leadership will result in significant advances in the ability to care for
patients. Whether through careers in
basic biomedical research, in clinical research, in health policy research, or in
community and/or international service based on original scholarship, Stanford's medical students will contribute
uniquely and importantly.

Stanford is committed to ensuring that
each graduate has fully explored his/her
potential as a student and as a scholar.
Key goals of the curriculum are the
melding of 21st century laboratory and
medical sciences, and helping each student build in-depth expertise in an area
of personal, scholarly interest. While
traditional courses and clerkships are
required for graduation, the duration of
study leading to the M.D. degree may
vary from four to six years. All M.D.
candidates must satisfactorily complete
at least 13 quarters of in residence course
work. Fees for additional quarters are
nominal. Courses are graded pass/fail.

Scholarly concentrations provide medical students with independent, creative
scholarly experiences in areas of personal interest. This required component
of the curriculum develops critical
thinking, skills in evaluation of new
data, and hands-on experiences with
the methods by which new scholarly information is generated.

Stanford does not discriminate on the
basis of race, religion, national origin,
sex, marital status, age, or disability.

Stanford University School of Medicine
Applicants, First-Time Applicants, Matriculants by Gender, Race and Ethnicity, 2007-2008

	2007 APP Women	Men	Total	F-time APP Women	Men	Total	MAT Women	Men	Total	2008 APP Women	Men	Total	F-time APP Women	Men	Total	MAT Women	Men	Total
Hispanic/Latino																		
Cuban	7	13	20	6	10	16	0	1	1	14	12	26	12	12	24	3	0	3
Mexican American	111	116	227	95	93	188	2	4	6	98	111	209	83	87	170	2	3	5
Puerto Rican	16	16	32	11	12	23	0	0	0	13	17	30	13	15	28	0	0	0
Other Hispanic	80	80	160	69	63	132	0	2	2	80	103	183	70	85	155	3	1	4
Multiple Hispanic/Latino*	14	9	23	10	7	17	0	0	0	19	14	33	13	12	25	1	0	1
Subtotal	228	234	462	191	185	376	2	7	9	224	257	481	191	211	402	9	4	13
Non-Hispanic/Latino*																		
Black	126	112	238	108	90	198	0	2	2	140	101	241	109	83	192	2	0	2
Native American/AK	7	11	18	5	10	15	0	0	0	4	11	15	3	11	14	0	0	0
Native Hawaiian/OPI	16	5	21	13	3	16	0	1	1	13	12	25	12	9	21	0	0	0
White	1,343	1,725	3,068	1,188	1,457	2,645	10	22	32	1,236	1,847	3,083	1,056	1,561	2,617	19	18	37
Asian	947	1,045	1,992	821	854	1,675	12	21	33	888	1,046	1,934	729	844	1,573	12	15	27
Other Race	2	5	7	2	4	6	0	0	0	1	4	5	0	2	2	0	0	0
Multiple Race*	112	113	225	104	98	202	3	0	3	118	118	236	97	92	189	3	0	3
Unknown	34	56	90	33	48	81	1	1	2	94	106	200	90	95	185	0	0	0
Subtotal	2,587	3,072	5,659	2,274	2,564	4,838	26	47	73	2,494	3,245	5,739	2,096	2,697	4,793	36	33	69
Foreign	142	194	336	117	159	276	3	1	4	170	177	347	150	141	291	1	3	4
Total	2957	3500	6457	2582	2908	5490	31	55	86	2888	3679	6567	2437	3049	5486	46	40	86

*Since 2002, students can select more than one race and / or ethnicity. **Those who did not choose 'Hispanic/Latino' or 'Non-Hispanic/Latino' are
listed under 'Non-Hispanic/Latino'. Data Source: AAMC Data Warehouse: Applicant-Matriculant File, as of 1/16/2009.

The applicant's state of residence is irrelevant in the selection process. Applicants whose Medical College Admission Test (MCAT) scores are below the national mean are highly unlikely to be admitted to the medical school.

For more details, please see Medical School Admissions Requirements (MSAR), published by the AAMC.

Academic Support Programs

Stanford has a formal, required curriculum that includes two years of basic pre-clinical training followed by two years of clinical experience. However, the curricular plan gives students the option of extending their period of study to five or more years. This arrangement allows students to enrich their training with research or other types of experience and, in addition, offers them the possibility of adjusting their academic load according to their individual needs and capacities.

If academic difficulties arise, tutorial assistance is available to help students improve their performance. Instruction is also available on the general problems of time management and study skills. Peer study groups are also an important source of help to minority students. In addition, a learning strategist is available to assist students.

Center of Excellence in Cultural Diversity
The Center of Excellence (COE) seeks to prepare the next generation of medical leaders to address the issues of health disparities. The COE sponsors initiatives to expand the diversity of the health professions; to promote cultural competence in medical education; to support scholarly interests and projects to eliminate health disparities. See the COE Web site: (http://coe.stanford.edu).

In addition, the COE facilitates student and faculty research on topics related to minority health issues and health care disparities. The COE sponsors curriculum offerings in the area of cultural competence. The COE staff provide advising to medical students regarding career and guidance

Community College Outreach
This program is designed to reach out to students attending community colleges. It provides an opportunity for students at community colleges to learn about how to prepare for medical school and other health professions. Staff visit community colleges, conduct admission workshops, and provide individual and group advising sessions. In addition, guidance is offered in developing leadership activities and establishing premedical student health profession clubs.

Cultural Competence

Stanford adopted cultural competence as an educational objective in 2001: "To promote cultural competency in the science and practice of medicine." This has resulted in a variety of activities related to cultural competence in the curriculum beginning with a presentation during orientation, "Faces of the Community," which introduces students to the diversity of the student community. Throughout the curriculum, presentations, workshops, and courses are offered that examine the role of culture in the context of medical care. Cultural competence is an area that continues to expand each year.

Enrichment Programs

Leadership in Health Disparities Early Matriculation Program
The Center of Excellence sponsors this program for entering Stanford medical students interested in learning about health disparities. This eight-week summer precedes the start of the first year of medical school and includes: introduction to faculty leaders, research opportunities, introduction to health disparities and cultural medicine, early clinical experiences, leadership skills, presentations on the integration of concepts of basic science with clinical science, and an introduction to histology.

Leadership in Health Disparities Program
This program is a continuation of the Early Matriculation Program and is offered throughout the year. This year-long seminar series explores leadership as it pertains to topics dealing with the

nation's health disparities. Students learn skills to be competent, confident, and effective leaders. In addition, students meet distinguished minority leaders in health.

Student Financial Assistance

Available grant and loan funds are awarded to students on the basis of demonstrated need. For federal aid, students are considered independent. For university-based aid, students are considered dependent up until the age of 30, and the school will consider the student's parents' ability to contribute to the cost of financing the student's education in determining eligibility for loans and grants. Foreign students must complete a certification of finances reflecting an escrow account of funds to cover the cost of education for the M.D. degree.

Other Pertinent Information

The Stanford University School of Medicine provides an environment where the individual is judged on intellectual and academic merits. Training is rigorous and every student is expected to develop a sound basis of professional competence. However, Stanford does not wish to mold its students into a specific kind of professional person; instead the aim is to help students achieve and sharpen their own unique professional capabilities and to develop an inquiring and critical approach to medicine in tune with their individual interests. Because of the school's commitment to seeing increased representation of minorities on medical school faculties in the future, special efforts are made to increase students' awareness of the opportunities open to them in careers in academic medicine.

The Admissions Committee recruits outstanding minority applicants with a potential for leadership in medicine and makes every effort to identify those with promise for an eventual academic career. The admission process includes a review of the applicant's entire application with consideration for the context of the candidate's achievements.

Stanford University School of Medicine is situated on the campus of the university, and it is possible for medical students to take academic work in other schools on campus concurrently with their medical studies.

It is hoped that students will make use of this opportunity, together with the flexibility of the medical school curricular schedule, to develop other academic interests relevant to their long-term goals in medicine.

Stanford is world-renowned for the quality of its clinical care. It receives referral cases on a worldwide basis. It offers medical students excellent opportunities for clinical training through clerkships, not only at the Stanford University Hospital but also at the Santa Clara Valley Medical Center, a county hospital; the Palo Alto Veterans Administration Medical Center; the Packard Childrens' Hospital; and the Kaiser Permanente Hospital, an HMO hospital. Overall, these facilities provide nearly 2,100 teaching hospital beds. Students also have the opportunity to take clerkships in other approved institutions either in the United States or abroad. They may also gain experience of primary care at community clinics, including two local student-run free clinics, Arbor Clinic and Pacific Clinic, which mainly serve low-income, immigrant, and diverse patient populations. These clinical experiences have allowed Stanford minority students to enter some of the most prestigious residency training programs in the United States.

UCLA/Drew Medical Education Program

Dr. Daphne Calmes, Dean for Student Affairs
Charles R. Drew University of Medicine and Science
173 East 120th Street
Los Angeles, CA 90059
323-563-4957 fax
www.cdrewu.edu

Recruitment

The UCLA/Drew Medical Education Program is committed to its founding mission of training medical students who intend to practice in medically underserved communities. The program is strongly interested in identifying students who have demonstrated the potential and interest to serve as leaders and innovators dedicated to ameliorating disparities in health care access and delivery. Recruitment for the UCLA/Drew Medical Education Program is accomplished through a wide variety of national and local efforts, which include but are not limited to:

- Information Days for prospective applicants and pre-medical advisors.

- Mentoring and application assistance for disadvantaged pre-medical students.
- Faculty, student, and alumni attendance at national and local meetings for (pre)medical students (e.g., the Latino Medical Student Association, Student National Medical Association, and AAMC).

Admissions

Selection criteria consist of successful completion of all pre-requisite courses, Medical College Admission Test (MCAT) scores, a personal statement, letters of recommendation, interviews, and demonstration of commitment to working with underserved populations. The highly competitive process results in the selection of 24 students from a large and exceptionally competent applicant pool annually.

Application Process

Applicants who seek admission to the UCLA/Drew Medical Education Program are required to apply through the American Medical College Application Service (AMCAS). The Admission Committee members review all AMCAS applications to determine the students' academic competitiveness and potential for serving medically

underserved populations. The Admission Committee strives to ensure that UCLA/Drew medical students receive the optimal training for the challenges of delivering culturally competent health care to the underserved. To that end, a careful consideration of the secondary application and the interview process will determine the applicant's suitability for the program and the program's ability to provide the training, which matches the applicant's goals and interests. Application fees for economically disadvantaged applicants are commonly waived upon verification of need.

Academic Support Programs

The UCLA/Drew Medical Education Program is committed to ensuring that all students have the necessary tools to successfully navigate their medical school experience. To achieve that goal, the program begins with a week-long summer pre-matriculation program designed to facilitate the students' transition into medical school. The program provides hands-on exposure to study and test-taking skills, time and stress management, and a comprehensive overview of the first-year curriculum. Throughout the academic year, the

UCLA/Drew Medical Education Program
Applicants, First-Time Applicants, Matriculants by Gender, Race and Ethnicity, 2007-2008

	2007 APP Women	Men	Total	F-time APP Women	Men	Total	MAT Women	Men	Total	2008 APP Women	Men	Total	F-time APP Women	Men	Total	MAT Women	Men	Total
Hispanic/Latino																		
Cuban	5	5	10	4	3	7	0	0	0	4	2	6	3	1	4	0	0	0
Mexican American	80	69	149	62	49	111	3	2	5	66	57	123	51	37	88	3	5	8
Puerto Rican	6	3	9	4	2	6	0	0	0	5	1	6	4	1	5	1	0	1
Other Hispanic	48	31	79	31	22	53	2	0	2	45	34	79	30	24	54	1	1	2
Multiple Hispanic/Latino*	3	5	8	1	4	5	0	0	0	12	4	16	10	2	12	1	0	1
Subtotal	142	113	255	102	80	182	5	2	7	132	98	230	98	65	163	6	6	12
Non-Hispanic/Latino**																		
Black	131	60	191	91	41	132	7	2	9	113	68	181	82	48	130	5	2	7
Native American/AK	4	1	5	2	1	3	0	0	0	0	1	1	0	1	1	0	0	0
Native Hawaiian/OPI	8	7	15	6	6	12	0	0	0	12	5	17	9	3	12	0	0	0
White	267	287	554	219	211	430	0	0	0	252	230	482	171	169	340	1	1	2
Asian	321	302	623	244	222	466	0	6	6	310	281	591	219	190	409	0	3	3
Other Race	0	1	1	0	0	0	0	0	0	1	4	5	1	4	5	0	0	0
Multiple Race*	43	35	78	39	24	63	2	0	2	30	25	55	21	16	37	0	0	0
Unknown	10	10	20	9	7	16	0	0	0	16	24	40	13	22	35	0	0	0
Subtotal	784	703	1,487	610	512	1,122	9	8	17	734	638	1,372	516	453	969	6	6	12
Foreign	24	29	53	18	21	39	0	0	0	28	26	54	18	23	41	0	0	0
Total	950	845	1,795	730	613	1,343	14	10	24	894	762	1,656	632	541	1,173	12	12	24

*Since 2002, students can select more than one race and / or ethnicity. **Those who did not choose 'Hispanic/Latino' or 'Non-Hispanic/Latino' are listed under 'Non-Hispanic/Latino'. Data Source: AAMC Data Warehouse: Applicant-Matriculant File, as of 1/16/2009.

students meet with learning-skills advisors to develop study plans and strategies, necessary to improve performance. The Office of Academic Enrichment and Outreach at the David Geffen School of Medicine at UCLA provides the students with additional academic support including tutoring by upper classmen medical students. UCLA/Drew students have access to a comprehensive library of online and print study guides and reference materials regarding United States licensing and clinical shelf examinations.

Enrichment Programs

Charles Drew University hosts various pipeline programs that begin as early as elementary school. A nationally recognized Saturday Science Academy provides k-12 students with after-school academic resources and exposure to biomedical sciences. Partnership for Progress provides high school juniors and seniors from the CDU service area with a medical student mentor and various academic enrichment and college preparation activities. The NIH-Step Up provides underrepresented high school students with the opportunity to participate in biomedical science research projects sponsored by the National Institutes of Health. The CDU College of Science and Health offers a post-baccalaureate program for students who have decided on medicine as a second career path.

Student Financial Assistance

Financial aid for the UCLA/Drew Medical Education Program is coordinated through the David Geffen School of Medicine at UCLA. Need-based financial assistance in the form of scholarships and federal loan programs is available to all qualified students. Students are encouraged to apply for competitive private merit-based scholarships and research grants.

University of California, Davis, School of Medicine

Dr. Darin Latimore, Director,
Medical Student Diversity
Office of Diversity
University of California,
Davis-School of Medicine
4610 X Street, Suite 4101
Sacramento, CA 95817
916-703-5567; 916-703-5568 fax
darin.latimore@ucdmc.ucdavis.edu
http://www.ucdmc.ucdavis.edu/
diversity

Recruitment

The School of Medicine at the University of California (UC), Davis remains committed to providing opportunities in medical education for students from educationally and socioeconomically disadvantaged backgrounds.

Recruitment and undergraduate student development efforts include high school outreach activities, recruitment at targeted community colleges and universities, a Medical College Admission Test (MCAT) preparation program, and various pre-medical applicant training through conferences and workshops. A year-long post-bac-calaureate program is also offered for applicants to medical school.

Faculty, staff, community-based physicians, medical school students, and residents are all involved in the school's recruitment efforts. This involvement ranges from visiting undergraduate campuses for pre-medical advising to offering mentor relationships, academic support, and clinical exposure.

Admissions

The School of Medicine selects students for admission with a view to meeting the needs of the medical profession, the school, and society at large. Because we live in a pluralistic society, it is felt that medical training and practice is enhanced by the interaction of students from various backgrounds. The school has become a leader in attracting and maintaining such diversity in its student body. This is reflected in the school's continuing commitment to expanding opportunities in medical education for individuals from groups traditionally underserved in medicine and to increasing the number of physicians practicing in medically underserved areas.

With a founding mission that emphasizes community service, UC Davis School of Medicine recently launched a new program to help increase health care access for underserved populations living in rural areas.

Called "Rural-PRIME," this unique program is designed to train the best and the brightest students for a fulfilling career in rural primary care medicine. It is an opportunity that offers a range of experiences, from public health and community service to the use of leading-edge medical technologies like telemedicine.

Rural-PRIME is a combined, five-year M.D. and master's degree program. It focuses on developing physicians who can become leaders and advocates for improving health care delivery throughout the state's smaller, more isolated communities.

The Admissions Committee is composed of individuals from a variety of backgrounds and abilities, and represents a broad spectrum of medical disciplines. The committee evaluates applicants on the basis of the following factors: academic accomplishment; experience in the health care field; research

University of California, Davis, School of Medicine
Applicants, First-Time Applicants, Matriculants by Gender, Race and Ethnicity, 2007-2008

	2007									2008								
	APP			F-time APP			MAT			APP			F-time APP			MAT		
	Women	Men	Total	Women	Men	Total	Women	Men	Total	Women	Men	Total	Women	Men	Total	Women	Men	Total
Hispanic/Latino																		
Cuban	4	11	15	3	7	10	0	1	1	9	8	17	8	7	15	0	0	0
Mexican American	120	120	240	99	92	191	4	4	8	112	98	210	88	73	161	3	5	8
Puerto Rican	11	5	16	8	3	11	0	0	0	10	9	19	9	7	16	0	1	1
Other Hispanic	72	59	131	50	40	90	5	1	6	75	71	146	56	52	108	1	0	1
Multiple Hispanic/Latino*	12	5	17	7	5	12	1	0	1	19	9	28	15	6	21	0	0	0
Subtotal	219	200	419	167	147	314	10	6	16	225	195	420	176	145	321	4	6	10
Non-Hispanic/Latino**																		
Black	86	66	152	65	49	114	1	1	2	107	67	174	81	53	134	2	2	4
Native American/AK	5	5	10	5	5	10	0	0	0	3	5	8	3	5	8	0	0	0
Native Hawaiian/OPI	15	10	25	14	8	22	0	0	0	22	14	36	17	9	26	0	1	1
White	996	1,048	2,044	819	777	1,596	27	18	45	998	1,139	2,137	777	844	1,621	28	17	45
Asian	902	899	1,801	718	679	1,397	22	16	38	921	939	1,860	687	670	1,357	20	15	35
Other Race	2	4	6	2	3	5	0	0	0	2	3	5	1	3	4	0	0	0
Multiple Race*	98	79	177	88	60	148	2	1	3	104	86	190	81	60	141	4	3	7
Unknown	29	40	69	27	34	61	0	1	1	64	75	139	60	67	127	1	0	1
Subtotal	2,133	2,151	4,284	1,738	1,615	3,353	52	37	89	2,221	2,328	4,549	1,707	1,711	3,418	55	38	93
Foreign	72	86	158	59	67	126	0	0	0	72	72	144	61	56	117	0	0	0
Total	2,424	2,437	4,861	1,964	1,829	3,793	62	43	105	2,518	2,595	5,113	1,944	1,912	3,856	59	44	103

*Since 2002, students can select more than one race and / or ethnicity. **Those who did not choose 'Hispanic/Latino' or 'Non-Hispanic/Latino' are listed under 'Non-Hispanic/Latino'. Data Source: AAMC Data Warehouse: Applicant-Matriculant File, as of 1/16/2009.

experience; and such personal traits as character, motivation, capacity for work, career objectives, and the motivation of the individual to make a positive contribution to society, the profession, the discipline, and the school.

The faculty has set specific academic requirements and policies to govern the evaluation of candidates for admission. The Admissions Committee seeks those applicants who have demonstrated academic potential for a lifetime of self-directed study. It also seeks those individuals who are cognizant of the physician's role and its demands, have demonstrated ability in effective interpersonal relations, have leadership potential, and who show promise of serving the needs of our evolving society. As our society increases in diversity, it is felt that physicians should reflect a similarly diverse spectrum. The school, through its Admissions Committee, actively seeks out individuals from a wide variety of backgrounds and interests who can share experiences and knowledge of representative population groups.

The University of California, in compliance with Titles VI and VII of the Civil Rights Act of 1964, Title IX of the Education Amendments of 1972 (45 CFR 86), and Sections 503 and 504 of the Rehabilitation Act of 1973, does not discriminate on the basis of race, color, national origin, religion, sex, or handicap in any of its policies, procedures, or practices; nor does the university, in compliance with the Age Discrimination in Employment Act of 1967 and Section 402 of the Vietnam Era Veterans Readjustment Act of 1974, discriminate against any employees or applicants for employment on the basis of their age or because they are disabled veterans or veterans of the Vietnam era. This nondiscrimination policy covers admission, access, treatment in university programs and activities, and application for university employment.

Academic Support Programs

UC, Davis offers a wide variety of support services to all of its students. Because of the relatively small class size of

approximately 105 students, close and frequently collegial relationships between faculty and students are possible. In addition, each student has a faculty advisor who serves as a source of guidance and support. Students at UC Davis also have the option to extend the first two years of the curriculum to three years, in order to make use of the additional time to individualize their educational program.

In addition to these offerings, the Office of Medical Education provides an array of supplemental academic support services to its medical students.

Academic tutoring is available to all students upon request. Tutoring is offered by peers who excel in the subject, particularly in the first two years of the curriculum. Faculty members also provide tutorial assistance.

Academic assistance is offered to aid in such areas as test taking, time management, and study skills for those students wishing such instruction. A preclinical retention program is also available for medical students to assist them in making the transition from the preclinical to clinical years. This is an academic, year-round program for students who are in their first two years of medical school, and is conducted at one of five student-run, community-based clinics in Sacramento. These clinics, Clinica Tepati, Paul Hom Asian Clinic, Shifa Clinic, Joan Viteri Memorial Clinic, and the Imani Clinic, operate under the auspices of the UC, Davis Department of Family Practice and Division of Medicine.

To prepare second-year students for the United States Medical Licensing Examination (USMLE) Step 1, various review activities are offered including small-group tutorials, intensive test-taking skills sessions, content review sessions, and self-study guidance. In addition, the Office of Medical Education Opportunity Programs offers supplemental support for students experiencing difficulty with academic coursework and USMLE.

Enrichment Programs

Summer Pre-Entry Program (SPEP)
The school offers a special pre-matriculation program for all interested incoming disadvantaged students. Anatomy, Physiology, Biochemistry, and Introduction to the Physical Examination are taught by UC, Davis faculty. Financial assistance may be available to cover students' living expenses over the duration of the program. The SPEP Program is voluntary; however, students are strongly urged to attend.

Post-Baccalaureate Program
Beginning in the summer and extending through the spring quarter, this program is designed to assist educationally and socioeconomically disadvantaged applicants gain admission to medical school through a variety of structured offerings ranging from an intensive summer MCAT prep program to upper division science course work during the school year.

Student Financial Assistance

The School of Medicine will waive the application fee for disadvantaged students who qualify under the American Medical College Application Service (AMCAS) fee waiver guidelines. If a waiver is not granted by AMCAS, a waiver request may be completed for this institution separately along with a letter from the Financial Aid Office of the undergraduate college and/or graduate school confirming the student's financial situation. Upon receipt of the application and letter, the fee waiver is generally granted.

Although no financial help is available to offset the cost of interview trips, an attempt is made to arrange for overnight accommodations with current medical students, as needed.

Financial aid programs are administered through the School of Medicine's Financial Aid Office and are primarily provided on the basis of need. In addition to a variety of federal, state, and private programs, the School of Medicine offers two types of grants/scholarships. Regents Scholars are selected on the basis of academic excellence and involve a stipend of $7,500 renewable for all four years. Chancellor Grants are awarded to academically promising students from disadvantaged backgrounds and include a scholarship of up to $7,500 per year, renewable for four years. In addition, Smith Scholars are awarded to students with proven academic excellence and have proven achievement in the areas of research, leadership, community service, athletics, and the arts of public service. These scholarships are awarded up to $7,500 for four years.

University of California, Irvine, School of Medicine

Dr. Ellena Peterson, Associate Dean of Admissions and Outreach
Dr. Alberto Manetta,
Associate Dean of Diversity
University of California Irvine
School of Medicine
Berk Hall
P.O. Box 4089
Irvine, CA 92697-4089
949-24-388, 800-824-5388;
949-824-2485 fax

Recruitment

The University of California, Irvine School of Medicine is dedicated to a strong commitment to identify and recruit applicants from socioeconomic disadvantaged backgrounds. Outreach efforts are focused on a variety of educational institutions, including high schools, community colleges, and universities within California. Presentations and information are provided at career fairs, pre-medical club meetings, health professions conferences, and other appropriate recruitment venues.

The Office of Admissions and Outreach participates in local, state, and national conferences to discuss the school's efforts to attract and retain our diverse student population. Also, each fall in partnership with the UC Irvine School of Medicine student organizations, a pre-medical conference is held that includes seminars, panel discussions, and interactive workshops aimed at informing potential applicants on the admissions process. Topics include the American Medical College Application Service (AMCAS) application, Medical College Admission Test (MCAT) preparedness, interview skills, post-baccalaureate programs, and personal essays. In addition upon request, admission counselors visit campuses that otherwise may not have access to pre-medical conferences and resources.

Admissions

The Admissions Committee is composed of faculty, medical students, and community representatives. This committee reviews all applications for admission. Approximately one third of the applicant pool is invited to submit a secondary application. Applicants granted interviews are chosen by the Admissions Committee from those submitting a secondary application. The factors emphasized in the selection of applicants for admissions from those interviewed are academic strength, clinical and/or research experiences, community commitment, motivation, interpersonal skills, and leadership.

Program in Medical Education for the Latino Community (PRIME-LC)
PRIME-LC is a five-year M.D./M.P.H. or M.D./M.B.A. program in which 12 students per class are invited to participate. The primary goal of the program is to develop leaders that will serve the underserved Latino community in California. Students receive immersion courses in Spanish, Latin-American culture, geography, and history. Throughout their medical training they work with Spanish- speaking patients and in areas with a predominance of underserved Latino patients. PRIME-LC students host a number of community service events as part of their training.

Academic Support Programs
Academic Monitoring Program
This ongoing program, beginning with enrollment, is coordinated by the Office of Educational Affairs to assist students in achieving academic success in their course work. Basic Science Course

University of California, Irvine, School of Medicine
Applicants, First-Time Applicants, Matriculants by Gender, Race and Ethnicity, 2007-2008

	2007									2008								
	APP			F-time APP			MAT			APP			F-time APP			MAT		
	Wo-men	Men	Total	Wo-men	Men	Total	Wo-men	Men	Total	Wo-men	Men	Total	Wo-men	Men	Total	Wo-men	Men	Total
Hispanic/Latino																		
Cuban	2	11	13	1	6	7	0	0	0	10	7	17	8	6	14	0	0	0
Mexican American	121	117	238	97	88	185	1	3	4	108	111	219	84	81	165	6	0	6
Puerto Rican	10	5	15	7	3	10	0	0	0	11	8	19	9	7	16	1	0	1
Other Hispanic	76	60	136	53	40	93	3	2	5	73	68	141	55	46	101	1	5	6
Multiple Hispanic/Latino*	9	11	20	6	8	14	0	1	1	15	9	24	13	7	20	0	0	0
Subtotal	218	204	422	164	145	309	4	6	10	217	203	420	169	147	316	8	5	13
Non-Hispanic/Latino**																		
Black	76	57	133	54	41	95	1	1	2	102	62	164	76	47	123	1	2	3
Native American/AK	8	3	11	8	3	11	0	0	0	2	0	2	2	0	2	0	0	0
Native Hawaiian/OPI	16	9	25	14	7	21	0	0	0	20	15	35	16	11	27	1	0	1
White	870	956	1,826	706	713	1,419	23	23	46	866	1,022	1,888	657	745	1,402	19	28	47
Asian	909	900	1,809	725	678	1,403	18	17	35	897	929	1,826	666	659	1,325	12	23	35
Other Race	2	3	5	2	2	4	1	0	1	1	6	7	0	5	5	0	0	0
Multiple Race*	101	84	185	89	64	153	3	3	6	87	77	164	69	49	118	2	2	4
Unknown	24	35	59	22	29	51	1	3	4	63	68	131	59	60	119	1	0	1
Subtotal	2006	2,047	4,053	1,620	1,537	3,157	47	47	94	2,038	2,179	4,217	1,545	1,576	3,121	36	55	91
Foreign	22	39	61	18	30	48	0	0	0	28	30	58	27	19	46	0	0	0
Total	2246	2,290	4,536	1,802	1,712	3,514	51	53	104	2,283	2,412	4,695	1,741	1,742	3,483	44	60	104

*Since 2002, students can select more than one race and / or ethnicity. **Those who did not choose 'Hispanic/Latino' or 'Non-Hispanic/Latino' are listed under 'Non-Hispanic/Latino'. Data Source: AAMC Data Warehouse: Applicant-Matriculant File, as of 1/16/2009.

Directors and Associate Deans meet monthly to discuss the academic progress of all first and second year medical students. Third and fourth year student's progress is monitored in a similar fashion by the Clinical Course Directors. Students experiencing academic or professional difficulty are identified and an action plan is developed to encourage them to utilize the tutoring and other services available in order to assist them in their academic endeavors. A Peer Tutoring Program is available to all medical students to provide tutorial assistance in the basic and clinical sciences. A Learning Skills Specialist, who aids with study skills training, as well as a Clinical Psychologist is available to provide additional support services to students. A United States Medical Licensing Examination Review Course is also offered on campus.

Enrichment Programs

Post-baccalaureate Program
The UC Irvine School of Medicine Post-baccalaureate Program is composed of students that have not yet applied to medical school, reapplicants, and those chosen by the Admissions Committee to be granted a conditional acceptance. The purpose of this program is to give individuals from underserved communities and/or disadvantaged backgrounds the opportunity to become a successful medical school applicant. It is also a goal of these programs to eventually increase the number of underrepresented and disadvantaged students who, upon completion of their M.D. degree, will practice in medically underserved areas of California.

The post-baccalaureate program is composed of two phases. In Phase I, students are given a battery of diagnostic tests and participate in an intense six-week summer MCAT Review Course. In Phase II, students are placed in upper division courses chosen after taking into consideration the individual's academic need. Since the programs are tailored to strengthen the student's deficiencies, the curricula vary. The UC Irvine School of Medicine has had over 20 years of experience with this and other educational initiatives that are exemplary models of outreach and enrichment programs. In particular, the UC Irvine School of Medicine Post-baccalaureate Program has an 85 percent success rate in the placement of participants who complete the program and are accepted into medical and/or osteopathic schools.

Student Financial Assistance

Financial assistance is available to all students based primarily on financial need. The School of Medicine participates in all publicly recognized financial aid programs. The aid programs consist of scholarships, grants, and loans. Currently, 80 percent of the students receive aid of some type. In addition, the School of Medicine has a limited amount of scholarships from private and discretionary funds for disadvantaged students and funds that may be used for emergency situations.

Other Pertinent Information

The Office of Educational Affairs provides proactive programmatic experiences for medical students at different points during the process of medical education in order to enrich students' personal and professional development. Examples of programs include workshops on stress management, interpersonal relations, and career development; professional and peer counseling; and student/faculty colloquia. A variety of speaker series and support for students through professional organizations have been benchmarks for a positive medical school educational experience.

University of California, San Diego, School of Medicine

Dr. Christine Moutier, Interim Assistant Dean of Diversity & Community Partnerships
University of California San Diego School of Medicine
9500 Gilman Drive, MC 0092
La Jolla, CA 92093-0092
858-534-7696; 858-534-5293 fax
somdiversity@ucsd.edu
http://meded.ucsd.edu/diversity/index.html
http://meded.ucsd.edu/HCOE
http://som.ucsd.edu

Recruitment

Recruitment is conducted by University of California, San Diego, (UCSD) School of Medicine's medical students, faculty, and administrators who are representatives themselves of disadvantaged backgrounds. Conferences, seminars, and workshops are held on campus to inform and encourage students, counselors, and pre-medical advisors of current opportunities in medicine and health-related fields. Speakers visit schools with high disadvantaged student populations and high interest in health-related careers. On campus, the Office of Community Outreach of the medical school serves as a focal point for information pertinent to the health sciences, in general, and the UCSD School of Medicine, in particular.

Admissions

The Recruitment and Admissions Committee (RAC) screens applications, selects applicants to invite for an interview, and interviews selected applicants. Within the RAC, there is an Executive Committee whose membership consists of faculty from disadvantaged and other backgrounds and medical students with voting privileges. The Executive Committee has the consideration of applicants with disadvantaged and/or special backgrounds as one of its functions. This committee makes recommendations on students to the Admissions Committee which, in turn, makes admissions decisions on all students.

Academic Support Programs

After matriculation to UCSD School of Medicine, ongoing tutorial services are available, and the use of these services is encouraged. Tutorial services, in various basic science areas, are performed by professionals who are intimately familiar with the lecture material. Special student guides and study programs have been developed by the tutorial services. Similar programs, services, and assistance are available in preparation for the United States Medical Licensing Examination Step 1. These services are individualized to meet specific needs. The students also have access to learning skills experts who can analyze and treat learning problems.

Enrichment Programs

The primary goal of the UCSD School of Medicine's academic enrichment programs is to train a new generation of health care providers who are prepared to address issues confronting populations at risk for health disparities. These programs include:

The Community Outreach Partnership Center (Grades seven-12)
This program sparks an interest in scientific research in young students from disadvantaged backgrounds through advanced instruction and involvement in scientific research. COPC students have a 100 percent high school graduation rate.

University of California, San Diego School of Medicine
Applicants, First-Time Applicants, Matriculants by Gender, Race and Ethnicity, 2007-2008

	2007 APP Women	2007 APP Men	2007 APP Total	2007 F-time APP Women	2007 F-time APP Men	2007 F-time APP Total	2007 MAT Women	2007 MAT Men	2007 MAT Total	2008 APP Women	2008 APP Men	2008 APP Total	2008 F-time APP Women	2008 F-time APP Men	2008 F-time APP Total	2008 MAT Women	2008 MAT Men	2008 MAT Total
Hispanic/Latino																		
Cuban	8	11	19	6	8	14	0	0	0	13	10	23	11	10	21	0	1	1
Mexican American	135	131	266	113	97	210	3	6	9	124	126	250	103	97	200	4	5	9
Puerto Rican	12	11	23	9	9	18	0	0	0	14	11	25	12	11	23	1	1	2
Other Hispanic	84	77	161	61	54	115	1	0	1	86	96	182	68	75	143	0	2	2
Multiple Hispanic/Latino*	13	8	21	9	5	14	0	0	0	21	12	33	15	9	24	0	0	0
Subtotal	252	238	490	198	173	371	4	6	10	258	255	513	209	202	411	5	9	14
Non-Hispanic/Latino**																		
Black	86	76	162	67	64	131	1	0	1	111	81	192	82	64	146	1	0	1
Native American/AK	7	3	10	7	3	10	1	0	1	4	7	11	3	6	9	1	0	1
Native Hawaiian/OPI	18	12	30	15	10	25	0	0	0	18	13	31	13	8	21	0	0	0
White	1,146	1,362	2,508	960	1,061	2,021	32	34	66	1,101	1,389	2,490	884	1,093	1,977	29	29	58
Asian	940	984	1,924	771	779	1,550	24	25	49	899	985	1,884	708	737	1,445	22	29	51
Other Race	3	4	7	3	3	6	0	0	0	2	6	8	1	5	6	0	0	0
Multiple Race*	120	99	219	107	79	186	4	1	5	121	101	222	93	72	165	2	3	5
Unknown	35	47	82	34	40	74	2	0	2	81	85	166	77	78	155	2	2	4
Subtotal	2,355	2,587	4,942	1,964	2,039	4,003	64	60	124	2,337	2,667	5,004	1,861	2,063	3,924	57	63	120
Foreign	32	36	68	26	29	55	0	0	0	19	30	49	17	23	40	0	0	0
Total	2,639	2,861	5,500	2,188	2,241	4,429	68	66	134	2,614	2,952	5,566	2,087	2,288	4,375	62	72	134

*Since 2002, students can select more than one race and / or ethnicity. **Those who did not choose 'Hispanic/Latino' or 'Non-Hispanic/Latino' are listed under 'Non-Hispanic/Latino'. Data Source: AAMC Data Warehouse: Applicant-Matriculant File, as of 1/16/2009.

UniversityLink Medical Sciences Program (Community College Grades 13-14)
This program improves community college transfer, retention, and graduation rates for students from disadvantaged backgrounds who are interested in health sciences through a summer residential and year-long academic skill building and mentoring program. Ninety three percent of program participants transfer to university compared with the 66 percent national transfer rate.

The Research Training Lab (Grades 11-16)
This lab trains students from disadvantaged backgrounds in basic and advanced biological laboratory techniques and places them with mentors in research environments.

The First-Time Applicant and Re-applicant Post-Baccalaureate Program
This program assists highly motivated students to acquire the academic skills needed to succeed in medical school, prepare for the MCAT, complete a competitive application to a health professions school, and prepare for the admission interview. Students in the post-baccalaureate program are two times more likely to gain admission to a medical school than are students who did not participate in the program.

The Conditional Acceptance Program
Students must be selected by the Admissions Committee of the UCSD School of Medicine to participate in this program. They are enrolled in a one-year post-baccalaureate program and are guaranteed admission into the School of Medicine if they maintain a GPA of 3.5 in designated courses. All the students (24) who have participated in this program have entered medical school.

The Pre-matriculation, Cognitive Strategies, and United States Medical Licensing Examination (USMLE) Review Programs
Review programs provide quality instruction in study skills, time management, standardized test-taking, reading speed, and comprehension for students in medical, pharmacy, and graduate schools as well as students in undergraduate academic enrichment and

post-baccalaureate programs.

Student Financial Assistance
Financial aid is awarded to students on the basis of demonstrated need. Intensive efforts are made to provide ample support for individuals from groups traditionally underrepresented in medicine. A Support Scholarship has been instituted, with the support of the financial aid officer, as an incentive to recruit students from disadvantaged backgrounds who show great promise. This is being provided as a stimulus in securing an early decision from applicants to matriculate into UCSD School of Medicine and not to hold multiple acceptances. These students will have the highest priority for funding throughout their stay at UCSD School of Medicine.

Educational Partnerships
The goal of UCSD's educational partnerships is to significantly increase the number of qualified educationally, socially, and/or economically disadvantaged students from urban and rural areas that enter the region's health care work force. The objectives include developing a competitive applicant pool, recruiting talented students for participation in academic enrichment and research training programs, and providing career awareness and exposure to community-based primary health care services. UCSD School of Medicine has established partnerships with:

- The San Diego State University Pre-College Institute (PCI) and School of Public Health
- The San Diego Border Area Health Education Center (SD/AHEC)
- Nine Community Colleges in San Diego and Los Angeles County
- The Health Careers Opportunity Program, San Diego Regional Consortium
- 14 "feeder" middle and high schools
- UCSD Moores Cancer Center
- San Diego County Health and Human Services Department of Public Health
- San Diego Police Department Multi-cultural Relations Office

University of California, San Francisco, School of Medicine

Dr. Alma Martinez, Director of Outreach and Academic Advancement
University of California,
San Francisco, School of Medicine
Office of Admissions
521 Parnassus, Room C-200
San Francisco, CA 94143-0408
415-476-4044
admissions@medsch.ucsf.edu
www.medschool.ucsf.edu/admissions
http://www.medschool.ucsf.edu/outreach

Recruitment

UCSF is proud to announce our new Program in Medical Education for the Urban Underserved (PRIME-US). This program is a special five-year track for medical students interested in working with urban underserved populations. PRIME-US will accept 11 new students from the entering class at UCSF and four new students from the entering class at the Joint Medical Program (JMP) at UC Berkeley. The goals of the PRIME-US program are to attract medical students from diverse backgrounds who have a strong interest in caring for the urban underserved in the United States and

- Provide a medical education experience for these students to equip and support them to become leaders in the care of urban underserved communities.
- Enable these students to serve as a catalyst for others at UCSF and the JMP to appreciate the rewards and challenges of caring for the urban underserved.
- Increase the number of UCSF medical school graduates who choose to pursue careers devoted to improving the health care and health of the urban underserved through leadership roles as community-engaged clinicians, educators, researchers, and social policy advocates.

Admissions

Commitment to Diversity

The School of Medicine welcomes applicants from all ethnic, economic, and cultural backgrounds without discrimination. The School of Medicine has a long-standing commitment to increasing the number of physicians who are members of minority groups that are underrepresented in the medical profession. As a result, over the last 35 years, UCSF has had one of the highest minority enrollment and graduation rates of U.S. medical schools. In addition, the medical school welcomes applications from socioeconomically disadvantaged persons.

Undergraduate Majors

We welcome applicants who have pursued a wide range of undergraduate disciplines. Students who elected to major in the humanities and social sciences are also expected to complete the required science courses. This does not mean that we encourage students to pursue a smattering of knowledge in a great many subjects. Rather, we believe that you gain the richest, most

University of California, San Francisco, School of Medicine
Applicants, First-Time Applicants, Matriculants by Gender, Race and Ethnicity, 2007-2008

	2007 APP Women	Men	Total	2007 F-time APP Women	Men	Total	2007 MAT Women	Men	Total	2008 APP Women	Men	Total	2008 F-time APP Women	Men	Total	2008 MAT Women	Men	Total
Hispanic/Latino																		
Cuban	11	9	20	8	7	15	0	0	0	12	10	22	11	10	21	0	0	0
Mexican American	116	116	232	99	94	193	10	7	17	99	107	206	84	77	161	7	9	16
Puerto Rican	16	11	27	13	9	22	3	0	3	15	10	25	14	9	23	0	0	0
Other Hispanic	96	66	162	72	51	123	2	5	7	81	89	170	67	75	142	4	6	10
Multiple Hispanic/Latino*	14	10	24	9	10	19	0	1	1	20	11	31	15	10	25	0	0	0
Subtotal	253	212	465	201	171	372	15	13	28	227	227	454	191	181	372	11	15	26
Non-Hispanic/Latino**																		
Black	109	87	196	93	71	164	8	5	13	132	81	213	102	65	167	7	3	10
Native American/AK	9	5	14	8	4	12	1	0	1	5	8	13	5	8	13	0	0	0
Native Hawaiian/OPI	14	10	24	12	9	21	1	0	1	13	9	22	10	6	16	0	0	0
White	1,437	1,577	3,014	1,243	1,308	2,551	33	19	52	1,304	1,539	2,843	1,100	1,274	2,374	39	24	63
Asian	1,014	1,008	2,022	852	809	1,661	20	18	38	914	983	1,897	735	770	1,505	19	19	38
Other Race	2	4	6	2	3	5	0	0	0	2	5	7	1	3	4	0	0	0
Multiple Race*	128	111	239	116	91	207	8	4	12	122	98	220	92	79	171	3	6	9
Unknown	43	51	94	41	46	87	1	1	2	96	98	194	92	88	180	6	0	6
Subtotal	2,756	2,853	5,609	2,367	2,341	4,708	72	47	119	2,588	2,821	5,409	2,137	2,293	4,430	74	52	126
Foreign	75	84	159	65	67	132	0	0	0	74	93	167	66	78	144	0	0	0
Total	3,084	3,149	6,233	2,633	2,579	5,212	87	60	147	2,889	3,141	6,030	2,394	2,552	4,946	85	67	152

*Since 2002, students can select more than one race and / or ethnicity. **Those who did not choose 'Hispanic/Latino' or 'Non-Hispanic/Latino' are listed under 'Non-Hispanic/Latino'. Data Source: AAMC Data Warehouse: Applicant-Matriculant File, as of 1/16/2009.

satisfying intellectual experience from the in-depth study of a subject that captures your passion.

Academic Performance
Academic excellence is one of several ways students may demonstrate a high degree of motivation and capability for the medical profession. At UCSF, academic performance is evaluated in the context of other factors, such as the difficulty of the course of study selected, the number of units attempted, and an individual's background. Although applicants who have a grade-point average (GPA) below 3.20 generally are not considered favorably for admission, applicants who have nontraditional backgrounds should not be discouraged. In addition, students should not select courses only for the purpose of raising their GPA.

Selection Factors
Selection is based on an appraisal of those intellectual and personal characteristics that the admissions committee regards as desirable for prospective medical students and physicians. Both cognitive (primarily academics) and non-cognitive factors, such as the applicant's statement and extracurricular activities play an important part in the selection process. Based on the evaluation of these factors, a limited number of applicants (500) are selected for interview.

Academic Support Programs
The Student Affairs Office coordinates programs and support services fro students such as the Student Well Being Program and the Advisory College Program for academic advising.

The Office of Outreach and Academic Advancement works to help maintain a welcoming and supportive environment for an increasingly diverse group of students. This office coordinates pipeline activities for undergraduate students, directs the UCSF Post Baccalaureate Program, and coordinates a Mentoring Program for underrepresented medical students.

Enrichment Programs
Summer research opportunities are not intended for pre-medical students, but rather for students interested in careers in bioresearch. These are listed below. Find further info at the web site: *(http://graduate.ucsf.edu/ summerprograms/applicants/summer-research-opportunities).*

UCSF Summer Research Programs
Students selected for summer research at UCSF will participate in seminars, presentations, and social events throughout the summer, creating a cohesive community of student researchers. The organization and funding for the UCSF summer research programs comes from:

Summer Research Training Program (SRTP)
The SRTP provides undergraduate and master's students with the opportunity to conduct research in the biological and biomedical sciences and make them more competitive candidates for Ph.D. programs. Students are supported in this program by funds from the Howard Hughes Medical Institute, National Science Foundation's Alliances for Graduate Education and the Professoriate, Genentech, the University of California Office of the President, and the UCSF Graduate Division.

Amgen Scholars Program
Supported by a grant from the Amgen Foundation, the Amgen Scholars Program provides summer research opportunities at UCSF for 25 undergraduate students in science and biotechnology. In addition to the summer research experience, participants in the Amgen Scholars Program will join other Amgen Scholars from across the country at a Symposium, at which they will share their summer research findings.

Molecular Biosciences Research Experience for Undergraduate (REU)
The Molecular Biosciences REU program at UCSF combines an outstanding laboratory research experience with activities designed to foster scientific communication and facilitate a transition to graduate school. Funded by a grant from the National Science Foundation, this program provides 12 students with research opportunities.

Biophysics Program Internship
The Graduate Group in Biophysics offers students the opportunity to sharpen their research skills and enhance their graduate applications. College sophomores and juniors who are considering a career in academic research are invited to apply, particularly students from groups underrepresented in the sciences. In addition to laboratory research, our interns will participate fully with the Summer Research Training Program (SRTP) for a comprehensive summer experience.

Student Financial Assistance
The mission of the financial aid program is to help students marshal the resources they will need to attend the UCSF School of Medicine. In other words, we are here to help. In 2004-2005, 89 percent of students received some form of financial aid, while 87 percent received either grants or scholarships. *(http://saawww.ucsf.edu/ financial/general/welcome.htm)*

Educational Partnerships
The Science & Health Education Partnership (SEP) is a collaboration between the University of California, San Francisco and the San Francisco Unified School District. Scientists and educators from both organizations work in partnership to support quality science education for K-12 students.

SEP, founded in 1987 and currently housed in the Department of Biochemistry & Biophysics, is nationally recognized as a model partnership between a university and a local public school system. Since 1989, SEP has been awarded nearly $9 million in competitive federal, private, and state awards. SEP is currently funded by the Howard Hughes Medical Institute, by an NIH-Science Education Partnership Award (SEPA) from the National Center for Research Resources (NCRR), the Bechtel Foundation, the UCSF Chancellor's Office, the UCSF School of Medicine, and the California Science Project.

University of Colorado, Denver, School of Medicine

Dr. Maureen J. Garrity,
Associate Dean Student Affairs
Dr. Steven Lowenstein, MPH,
Associate Dean Faculty Affairs
University of Colorado
School of Medicine
13120 East 19th Avenue
Aurora, CO 880045
303-724-6407

Recruitment

The School of Medicine at the University of Colorado at Denver and Health Sciences Center has a standing committee on Diversity. There is also an Office of Diversity serving the School of Medicine, School of Dentistry, School of Nursing, and School of Pharmacy as well as other programs at the Health Sciences Center. The School of Medicine's standing committee consists of faculty and students committed to recruitment, retention, and support of a diverse faculty and student body. The Office of Diversity has three basic objectives: to discover, motivate, develop, and sustain the interest of postsecondary minority and disadvantaged students in a health sciences career track; to increase the numbers of qualified minority students admitted to the health sciences programs; and to support the schools in providing optimal conditions for these students to successfully complete their training.

Admissions

The Admissions Committee for the School of Medicine is composed of approximately 80 basic science and clinical faculty members and community practitioners. The faculty members have a variety of educational, cultural, and professional backgrounds. The committee is chaired by the Associate Dean of Admissions, School of Medicine. One hundred fifty six students are admitted to the School of Medicine each year. There is a strong commitment to admit and graduate ethnic minority and disadvantaged students.

Both cognitive and non-cognitive factors are considered in the admissions process. Specifically, criteria such as overall grade-point average (GPA), science GPA, senior year GPA, Medical College Admission Test (MCAT) scores, ethnicity, medically related work experience, and two personal interviews are quantified and integrated into an overall evaluation of each applicant. There is flexibility in the process in that the students with the highest scores, both minority and non-minority alike, are not necessarily the individuals who ultimately matriculate into the School of Medicine.

Student Support Programs

The Office of Student Affairs assists students with personal, academic, and financial concerns and makes referrals to appropriate campus and community services. This Office has access to many resources for assisting students who have academic difficulties, including tutoring. The services provided are available to all medical students; however special focus is given to minority and disadvantaged students and the office works closely with the staff in the Office of Diversity in helping students.

Student Financial Assistance

Financial aid generally consists of a combination of long-term, low-interest loans, grants and, in some cases, part-time employment. All financial aid is awarded on the basis of financial need.

University of Colorado School of Medicine
Applicants, First-Time Applicants, Matriculants by Gender, Race and Ethnicity, 2007-2008

	2007									2008								
	APP			F-time APP			MAT			APP			F-time APP			MAT		
	Women	Men	Total	Women	Men	Total	Women	Men	Total	Women	Men	Total	Women	Men	Total	Women	Men	Total
Hispanic/Latino																		
Cuban	8	8	16	8	7	15	0	0	0	5	5	10	4	5	9	1	0	1
Mexican American	49	46	95	39	31	70	4	0	4	42	62	104	36	45	81	2	3	5
Puerto Rican	6	9	15	4	7	11	0	1	1	5	8	13	5	6	11	0	0	0
Other Hispanic	40	27	67	35	20	55	2	1	3	34	41	75	24	30	54	2	0	2
Multiple Hispanic/Latino*	5	2	7	4	2	6	0	0	0	11	4	15	8	3	11	1	0	1
Subtotal	108	92	200	90	67	157	6	2	8	97	120	217	77	89	166	6	3	9
Non-Hispanic/Latino**																		
Black	40	23	63	30	14	44	2	1	3	49	31	80	31	22	53	1	2	3
Native American/AK	5	3	8	5	2	7	0	0	0	8	14	22	8	11	19	0	0	0
Native Hawaiian/OPI	7	3	10	5	3	8	0	0	0	9	3	12	6	2	8	0	0	0
White	959	1,142	2,101	754	836	1,590	58	68	126	1,062	1,373	2,435	832	1,009	1,841	58	60	118
Asian	209	189	398	154	135	289	2	6	8	216	258	474	145	180	325	7	8	15
Other Race	2	2	4	2	1	3	1	0	1	0	1	1	0	1	1	0	0	0
Multiple Race*	40	38	78	34	30	64	4	2	6	53	57	110	41	36	77	1	3	4
Unknown	19	17	36	18	17	35	1	4	5	48	55	103	47	49	96	3	3	6
Subtotal	1,281	1,417	2,698	1,002	1,038	2,040	68	81	149	1,445	1,792	3,237	1,110	1,310	2,420	70	76	146
Foreign	26	29	55	19	17	36	0	0	0	25	39	64	19	33	52	1	0	1
Total	1,415	1,538	2,953	1,111	1,122	2,233	74	83	157	1,567	1,951	3,518	1,206	1,432	2,638	77	79	156

*Since 2002, students can select more than one race and / or ethnicity. **Those who did not choose 'Hispanic/Latino' or 'Non-Hispanic/Latino' are listed under 'Non-Hispanic/Latino'. Data Source: AAMC Data Warehouse: Applicant-Matriculant File, as of 1/16/2009.

Financial need is defined as the difference between the cost of attendance as defined by the institution (tuition and fees, books and supplies, room and board, transportation, and essential incidental expenses) and total resources available to the student. All applicants for aid must be admitted to a professional program or be degree candidates and registered as full-time students to be eligible for financial aid.

Financial aid applications can be obtained in the Office of Financial Aid. Applications are not available to students who have not been officially accepted to a program at the Health Sciences Center. The deadline for submitting applications for financial aid is April 1 preceding the academic year for which assistance is desired or 30 days after the date of the letter of acceptance for entering students. Late applications will be accepted and considered after those received by the deadlines. For inquiries and requests contact: Office of Financial Aid, University of Colorado Health Sciences Center, 4200 East 9th Avenue, Box A-088, Denver, CO 80262 or call 303-315-8364.

Educational Partnerships

The Office of Diversity works to develop K-12 linkages to the Health Sciences Center programs. The School of Medicine has several major scholarships designed to recruit students. The Florence Sabin Scholarship for Commitment to Community Health honors the famous Colorado public health pioneer Florence Sabin and is a four-year award for a student who has shown a commitment to community health and who has plans related to community health as a physician. The Justina Ford Scholarship for Commitment to the Underserved honors the first African-American woman physician in Colorado. This four-year award is given to a student who has demonstrated commitment to the underserved and who has future plans relating to care of the underserved.

Aurora LIGHTS (LeadInG the way in HealTh Sciences careers) Program is a

new comprehensive partnership among the University of Colorado Denver, Aurora Public School District, Community College of Aurora, Metropolitan Community Provider Network, and Central Colorado Area Health Education Center. This consortium's ultimate goal is to create a more competitive pool of individuals from disadvantaged backgrounds who enter and graduate from health or allied health professions programs for Aurora, the Denver metro region, and Colorado. This project has funds to support the school's post-baccalaureate, pre-medical program and to improve the retention rates of disadvantaged health sciences professional students by improving academic and financial support, counseling and mentoring.

University of Connecticut School of Medicine

Dr. Marja M. Hurley,
Associate Dean and Director
Department of Health Career
Opportunity Programs
University of Connecticut
School of Medicine
Farmington, CT 06030-3920
860-679-3483;860-679-1875 fax
http://medicine.uchc.edu/
prospective/enrichment/
hcop/index.html

Recruitment

The University of Connecticut School of Medicine recruits a diverse group of applicants nationally through the Department of Health Career Opportunity Programs (HCOP). Visits to area colleges and to Historically Black Colleges and Universities, attendance at recruitment programs, use of community resources, and summer enrichment programs are some of the methods used to interest qualified applicants to the School of Medicine's programs. The Student National Medical Association and other students enrolled at the School of Medicine are actively encouraged to participate in the recruitment process.

Admissions

Applications from candidates for admissions receive a thorough and sensitive review and are selected on a competitive basis. Minority candidates invited for an interview meet with the staff of the Department of Health Career Opportunity Programs and with minority medical students who answer questions in an informal setting. The Department of Health Career Opportunity Programs is represented on the Admissions Committee.

Academic Support Programs

Academic support is available on an individual basis through the Associate Dean and Director of the Department of Health Career Opportunity Programs. Academic advising and counseling is provided. The "HCOP Newsline," a monthly publication of the department, publishes intramural and extramural academic opportunities available to medical students. A time management, test-taking skills course is provided on an individual basis and is available for all incoming freshman students.

Student Financial Assistance

The application fee may be waived. The financial aid program available to all students has in the past been able to meet approximately 85-90 percent of estimated financial needs. Financial aid packages typically consist of scholarships, tuition remissions, and loans.

Educational Partnerships

The University of Connecticut Health Center, in collaboration with the Hartford School District, Central Connecticut State University, University of Connecticut at Storrs, and Wesleyan University, has designed a comprehensive program of educational enrichment and support activities for disadvantaged students from Connecticut. Its goal is to increase the number of these students applying to professional and graduate programs in medicine, dental medicine, biomedical research, allied health, nursing, and pharmacy. Implementation of the program is through the formal educational consortium consisting of the University of Connecticut Health Center and the universities and school district.

University of Connecticut School of Medicine
Applicants, First-Time Applicants, Matriculants by Gender, Race and Ethnicity, 2007-2008

	2007									2008								
	APP			F-time APP			MAT			APP			F-time APP			MAT		
	Women	Men	Total	Women	Men	Total	Women	Men	Total	Women	Men	Total	Women	Men	Total	Women	Men	Total
Hispanic/Latino																		
Cuban	7	10	17	6	9	15	0	0	0	8	6	14	7	4	11	0	0	0
Mexican American	31	18	49	22	13	35	1	1	2	11	15	26	8	9	17	0	0	0
Puerto Rican	19	16	35	15	13	28	0	0	0	18	4	22	13	3	16	0	1	1
Other Hispanic	44	32	76	36	24	60	2	2	4	42	44	86	32	30	62	1	1	2
Multiple Hispanic/Latino*	8	1	9	5	1	6	0	0	0	5	7	12	4	5	9	0	0	0
Subtotal	109	77	186	84	60	144	3	3	6	84	76	160	64	51	115	1	2	3
Non-Hispanic/Latino**																		
Black	139	82	221	102	69	171	4	3	7	153	80	233	112	58	170	6	1	7
Native American/AK	2	0	2	1	0	1	0	0	0	3	3	6	3	2	5	0	0	0
Native Hawaiian/OPI	4	7	11	3	6	9	0	0	0	7	1	8	5	1	6	0	0	0
White	731	796	1,527	585	634	1,219	30	20	50	711	777	1,488	551	570	1,121	30	29	59
Asian	297	348	645	232	256	488	7	6	13	254	320	574	197	215	412	3	6	9
Other Race	0	2	2	0	1	1	0	0	0	0	2	2	0	2	2	0	0	0
Multiple Race*	37	24	61	30	14	44	2	0	2	31	24	55	24	20	44	2	0	2
Unknown	20	23	43	20	20	40	0	1	1	43	37	80	41	31	72	2	1	3
Subtotal	1,230	1,282	2,512	973	1,000	1,973	43	30	73	1,202	1,244	2,446	933	899	1,832	43	37	80
Foreign	142	136	278	109	106	215	2	0	2	132	121	253	100	95	195	1	1	2
Total	1,481	1,495	2,976	1,166	1,166	2,332	48	33	81	1,418	1,441	2,859	1,097	1,045	2,142	45	40	85

*Since 2002, students can select more than one race and / or ethnicity. **Those who did not choose 'Hispanic/Latino' or 'Non-Hispanic/Latino' are listed under 'Non-Hispanic/Latino'. Data Source: AAMC Data Warehouse: Applicant-Matriculant File, as of 1/16/2009.

High School Student Initiatives

Jumpstart Program

The Jumpstart Program is an enrichment program for ninth- and tenth-grade students attending Hartford public and/or magnet schools. This program is comprised of an academic-year session and a six-week summer session. The program consists of:

- Enrichment experiences both in and outside of the classroom.
- Daily classes in language arts, math, science, career and college awareness preparation, integrating CAPT strategies and support across the curriculum.
- Assessments and evaluations throughout a student's affiliation with Jumpstart, including pre, mid, and post testing; student and parent surveys, mid and final progress reports, etc.
- 20 Saturday Academies during the academic year, where students continue to strengthen their academic skills and college preparation, and are exposed to careers in the health professions.

Juniors Doctors Academy

The Juniors Doctors Academy is an enrichment program for rising 11th - grade students attending Hartford public and/or magnet schools. This program is comprised of a six-week summer session and a 20-week Saturday academic-year program. The academic components focus on math, language arts, and proven test-taking strategies to increase SAT scores. Student participants are registered to take the SAT, with clear emphasis on career and college preparation. Criteria for admission include:

- Minimum of B- average in science, math and language arts,
- Interest in health careers,
- Entering 11th grade,
- Submission of a 150-word essay explaining interest in joining the program, and
- Two letters of recommendation from science or English teachers or guidance counselors.

Seniors Doctors Academy

The Seniors Doctors Academy is an enrichment program for rising 12th-grade students attending Hartford public and/or magnet school. This program is comprised of a six-week summer session and a 20-week Saturday academic-year program. The academic year components focus on pre-calculus and inorganic chemistry with clear emphasis on pre-medical/pre-dental college preparation.

- Minimum of B- average in science, math, and language arts;
- Interest in health careers;
- Entering 12th grade;
- Submission of a 150-word essay explaining interest in joining the program, and
- Two letters of recommendation from science or English teachers or guidance counselors.

High School Student Research Apprentice Program

The High School Student Research Apprentice Program (HSSRAP) is a six-week summer program for Connecticut high school students who have completed their junior or senior year and have indicated an interest in medicine, dental medicine, or biomedical research. This program provides the students with a research experience in one of the basic science or clinical laboratories at the University of Connecticut Health Center or Central Connecticut State University. Students report the results of their research in a presentation before faculty, preceptors, other program participants, and invited guests during the final week of the program. Selected participants must be able to commute daily to the University of Connecticut Health Center or Central Connecticut State University. Students who are selected to participate in the summer research program also have the opportunity to participate in the High School Mini Medical/Dental School Program during the following academic year.

Pre College and College Student Initiatives

The Pre College Enrichment Program

The Pre College Enrichment Program is comprised of two components:

Pre College Academic Enrichment Program

The Pre College Academic Enrichment Program is a six-week summer program held on the campus of the University of Connecticut Storrs for college pre-freshmen who will be matriculating at the University of Connecticut. The program is focused on enhancing the preparation of high school seniors for college and is designed to provide solid development of scientific (biology and chemistry), mathematical (pre-calculus), communications, problem solving, and test taking skills.

Pre College Research Program

The Pre College Research Program is a six-week summer program held on the campus of the University of Connecticut Storrs for college pre-freshmen who will be matriculating at the University of Connecticut. The program is focused on enhancing the preparation of high school seniors for college by providing them with a research experience in a basic science laboratory.

College Enrichment Program

The College Enrichment Program is a six-week summer program held on the campus of the University of Connecticut Storrs for enrolled UConn freshmen and sophomores designed to provide sound development of scientific and mathematical skills. Courses in individual programs of study include: organic chemistry, biochemistry, calculus, or physics.

Medical/Dental Preparatory Program

The Medical/Dental Preparatory Program (MDPP) is a six-week summer program designed to provide a reinforcement and enrichment experience for students from disadvantaged backgrounds who expect to apply to professional schools of medicine and dental medicine. The purposes of the program are to (a) facilitate the entry of these students into professional school by improving their performance on admissions tests and through professional development activities and, (b) to increase the retention of successful matriculants to professional school through early exposure to professional education. Two tracks are available:

Track One-MCAT/DAT Preparation Course
This course is for students who will be taking the Medical College Admission Test (MCAT) or Dental Admissions Test (DAT) in the fall. The program will focus on MCAT/DAT test preparation, clinical interaction with preceptors, and introduction to problem based learning through case studies.

Track Two-Basic Medical Science Course
This course is for all other students not on Track One. This track consists of basic medical science courses emphasizing essential principles of cell and molecular biology correlated to problem-based learning case studies. Clinical experiences and professional development exercises are also presented.

The program provides room and board and a stipend. Priority consideration is given to former program participants.

Summer Research Fellowship Programs
The Summer Research Fellowship is a ten-week summer program for college sophomores, juniors, seniors, or recent graduates interested in a career in medicine, dental medicine, or biomedical research and for applicants who have completed some college coursework in biology and chemistry (preferably through organic chemistry). The program is designed to provide a research enrichment experience and some exposure to clinical or dental medicine.

The Clinical Summer Research Fellowship Program is a six-week summer program for rising college sophomores through recent graduates interested in medicine, dental medicine, and Ph.D. programs in biomedical or behavioral health research. Students perform clinical research and shadow in community health centers and clinics. Both pro-

grams provide room and board and a stipend. Priority consideration is given to former program participants.

Post-Baccalaureate Program
The School of Medicine, in cooperation with the College of Arts and Sciences at the University of Connecticut, offers two non-degree study programs for capable college graduates wishing to prepare for application to medical schools. One program serves the non-traditional students who have little or no science preparation. It is intended to provide an opportunity for these students to complete medical school science prerequisites. The second program is intended to provide these students an opportunity to demonstrate academic excellence in upper division science coursework. To apply, a student must have completed a baccalaureate degree program from an accredited college or university. Admitted students normally present at least a B-/B+ average each semester. Courses available to students participating in these programs are normal course offerings of the University of Connecticut. Counseling for the program course selection is available on an individual basis from the Pre-Professional Evaluation Committee and representatives of the School of Medicine.

Other Pertinent Information
The University of Connecticut School of Medicine is a small institution, 80 per class, where the student does not get lost in the institutional shuffle. A counseling and adult development program is available to all students. A student-based tutorial program is also available.

Yale University School of Medicine

Dr. Forrester A. Lee, Professor of Medicine, Assistant Dean of Multicultural Affairs
Yale University School of Medicine
P.O. Box 208036
367 Cedar Street, ESH 320
New Haven, CT 06520-8036
203-785-7545; 203-737-5507 fax
omca@yale.edu/
http://www.med.yale.edu/omca

Recruitment

Yale University School of Medicine seeks to achieve diversity among students and actively recruits qualified students from groups underrepresented in medicine. Programs to increase student diversity are centered in the Yale Office of Multicultural Affairs (OMCA).

Yale University School of Medicine employs a variety of activities to assist in carrying out its recruitment efforts. Direct mailings are sent to students identified from the AAMC Medical Minority Applicant Registry. Campus visits are made, with special attention given to those colleges/universities with large enrollments of underrepresented stu-

dent groups. These visits are made by the director and staff of the Office of Multicultural Affairs and by Yale medical students to inform prospective applicants and advisors about Yale University School of Medicine and its programs. Students and premed advisors may visit the Yale University School of Medicine to meet with medical students, admissions office staff, members of the Admissions Committee, faculty, and financial aid representatives.

Admissions

Minority applications are considered by the same general procedures as all applications. The Admissions Committee composition at Yale University School of Medicine has good representation from minority faculty members, students, and women. At least one of a minority applicant's interviews is with a minority member of the Committee. When interviewing, minority applicants are invited to meet and have lunch with members of the minority student body and to meet with the Dean and staff of the Office of Multicultural Affairs. All minority applicants are contacted prior to their interview dates by the OMCA and offered overnight hosting with an

on-board minority student if they wish to do so.

Academic Support Programs

Any student who has difficulty or wishes assistance during his/her time at the medical school can receive tutorial assistance from students or faculty member. The Yale Programs of Medical Education offers the student considerable flexibility for individual curriculum planning. Grades are not given and rank order is not established during the first two years. Exams are offered but taken anonymously. Written evaluation of performance in the first two years is provided by the faculty based primarily based on faculty–student interactions and engagement in small-group sessions. More traditional evaluation and grading systems are in place for the final two years. All Yale students are required to submit a research thesis as a requirement for graduation. Students work directly with faculty mentors who supervise research activities which may include any health-related area of inquiry.

Yale University School of Medicine
Applicants, First-Time Applicants, Matriculants by Gender, Race and Ethnicity, 2007-2008

| | 2007 | | | | | | | | | 2008 | | | | | | | | |
| | APP | | | F-time APP | | | MAT | | | APP | | | F-time APP | | | MAT | | |
	Wo-men	Men	Total	Wo-men	Men	Total	Wo-men	Men	Total	Wo-men	Men	Total	Wo-men	Men	Total	Wo-men	Men	Total
Hispanic/Latino																		
Cuban	9	14	23	6	12	18	1	1	2	11	12	23	10	10	20	0	0	0
Mexican American	45	49	94	36	44	80	1	1	2	44	48	92	40	35	75	2	1	3
Puerto Rican	21	23	44	21	19	40	1	0	1	10	19	29	8	16	24	0	0	0
Other Hispanic	64	65	129	60	47	107	0	2	2	55	74	129	49	64	113	3	1	4
Multiple Hispanic/Latino*	6	7	13	5	6	11	0	0	0	6	12	18	6	11	17	0	1	1
Subtotal	145	158	303	128	128	256	3	4	7	126	165	291	113	136	249	5	3	8
Non-Hispanic/Latino**																		
Black	129	120	249	105	102	207	4	7	11	152	111	263	125	89	214	4	3	7
Native American/AK	1	2	3	1	1	2	0	0	0	9	5	14	7	5	12	0	0	0
Native Hawaiian/OPI	7	6	13	6	6	12	0	0	0	8	5	13	7	5	12	0	0	0
White	1,096	1,369	2,465	998	1,205	2,203	15	26	41	1,055	1,447	2,502	940	1,244	2,184	21	23	44
Asian	630	751	1,381	565	631	1,196	13	10	23	572	770	1,342	492	617	1,109	11	16	27
Other Race	1	3	4	1	3	4	0	0	0	3	4	7	2	2	4	0	0	0
Multiple Race*	78	72	150	75	62	137	2	0	2	75	61	136	66	51	117	3	1	4
Unknown	30	41	71	29	37	66	0	1	1	74	98	172	71	84	155	1	1	2
Subtotal	1,972	2,364	4,336	1,780	2,047	3,827	34	44	78	1,948	2,501	4,449	1,710	2,097	3,807	40	44	84
Foreign	177	205	382	147	166	313	10	4	14	204	228	432	166	186	352	6	2	8
Total	2,294	2,727	5,021	2,055	2,341	4,396	47	52	99	2,278	2,894	5,172	1,989	2,419	4,408	51	49	100

*Since 2002, students can select more than one race and / or ethnicity. **Those who did not choose 'Hispanic/Latino' or 'Non-Hispanic/Latino' are listed under 'Non-Hispanic/Latino'. Data Source: AAMC Data Warehouse: Applicant-Matriculant File, as of 1/16/2009.

Enrichment Programs

The Office of Multicultural Affairs conducts three summer academic enrichment programs for college and high school students interested in careers in medicine and science. These programs are designed to increase the numbers of students from groups underrepresented in biomedical science careers.

BioSTEP (Biomedical Science Training and Enrichment Program)

Introduced in 1992, this program is designed to provide intensive, short-term training in research for college students underrepresented in biomedical science. The program has been supported continuously by grants from the National Heart, Lung, and Blood Institute. Over 300 trainees have participated in the program with 95 percent of participants progressing into graduate or professional biomedical science training and education programs after completing college. Many BioSTEP students have entered Yale as M.D. and M.D./Ph.D. students.

Trainee selection is competitive. Program participants carry out research projects in the laboratories and training sites of Yale University School of Medicine. Each trainee works in the laboratory of a Yale faculty member who serves as the trainee's mentor. Investigative opportunities ranging from fundamental molecular biology to applied clinical research.

The ten-week program conducted from early-June to mid-August is open to students who have completed at least one year of undergraduate work at an accredited college or university. Each student participant receives a stipend, travel allowance, and lodging.

SMDEP (Summer Medical and Dental Education Program)

Yale University School of Medicine is one of the 12 sites of SMDEP, a national program of The Robert Wood Johnson Foundation. Approximately 80 students attend Yale each summer. The program provides an intensive six-week exposure to college biology, chemistry, organic chemistry, and physics and limited involvement in clinical shadowing. The academic program also provides instruction in writing and communications along with career planning and counseling pertinent to applying to medical and dental school. Yale SMDEP exposes students to an academic environment that emphasizes collaborative, group-facilitated learning. In classroom and seminar settings, teachers cover topics in basic and clinical sciences and provide highly individualized instruction in writing and verbal communication skills. Students develop a foundation of knowledge and skills needed to become successful medical and dental school applicants and future physicians.

Yale S.C.H.O.L.A.R (Science Collaborative Hands-on Learning and Research)

This is a tuition-free, summer science academic enrichment program for students enrolled at New Haven's magnet science high school —the Hill Regional Career High School. The goals of the program are 1) to reinforce and sustain students' interest in the sciences by providing a fun, intensive educational experience that will academically prepare students for higher level science courses and 2) to increase the success of Career High School students in pursuing health and science-related careers. Approximately 60 students participate each summer. Yale students and faculty serve as instructors and advisors in the program.

Student Financial Assistance

The application fee is generally waived upon request. All applicants, including international students, are eligible for need-based financial assistance. Ample scholarship support is available to cover need not met by personal or family resources. To assure equitable distribution of aid, all applicants are required to provide parental financial information and all recipients are required to borrow an annually determined minimum amount (or base loan) before becoming eligible for institutional scholarship funds. The financial aid office collects and evaluates financial information from FAFSA, the Need Access Application, and a Yale financial aid application.

The George Washington University School of Medicine and Health Sciences

Dr. Yolanda C. Haywood,
Assistant Dean for Student Affairs
The George Washington University
School of Medicine and
Health Sciences
2300 I Street, NW
Washington, DC 20037
202-994-4242; 202-994-1753 fax
emdych@gwumc.edu

Recruitment

The committee has targeted the traditionally Black colleges and universities, Hispanic and Native-American communities, and several MED-PREP programs around the country for visits by members of the committee, to discuss the School of Medicine and Health Sciences' program with minority students.

Admissions

The Committee on Admissions seeks a balanced but heterogeneous student body of gifted, sensitive, mature individuals who will excel in the art, as well as the science, of medicine. In order to identify a diverse group of individuals best suited to the school's program of medical education, admissions decisions are based on a multiplicity of factors. There is no discrimination in the selection process because of race, sex, color, religion, or national or regional origin. The School of Medicine and its Committee on Admissions is committed to increasing numbers and proportions of students from ethnic, racial, and socioeconomic groups currently underrepresented in the field of medicine, and to continuing to seek out qualified applicants from the District of Columbia.

The admissions brochure explicitly describes the selection process. A copy of this brochure is sent to all applicants. Applicants may write to the Office of Admissions for a copy of this brochure prior to application or review our Web site.

Applicants should submit applications and all requested materials as early as possible. In this way, the committee has ample time to review their biographical data and personal comments, and evaluate non-cognitive factors such as motivation, interest in medicine, and dedication. Personal comments are an important element in the evaluation of the applicant's personal characteristics.

Academic Support Programs

The Committee on Admissions attempts to select those applicants, minority or otherwise, who demonstrate the academic promise and commitment to successfully complete the course of study. This policy, as well as active participation of students and faculty, has kept low the number of students who experience academic difficulties. Second-year students mentor first-year students. Students with difficulties are evaluated by the Assistant Dean for Student Affairs, who can then guide the student to the appropriate support services (e.g., tutoring, or counseling center). In order to offer students with great personal promise but less well proven academic ability an opportunity to study medicine, the School of Medicine has a five-year decelerated program. Students are registered in the School of Medicine Special Program Division and take the first year of medical school course work over two years.

George Washington University School of Medicine and Health Sciences
Applicants, First-Time Applicants, Matriculants by Gender, Race and Ethnicity, 2007-2008

	2007									2008								
	APP			F-time APP			MAT			APP			F-time APP			MAT		
	Women	Men	Total	Women	Men	Total	Women	Men	Total	Women	Men	Total	Women	Men	Total	Women	Men	Total
Hispanic/Latino																		
Cuban	46	41	87	34	32	66	1	0	1	43	40	83	36	37	73	0	0	0
Mexican American	126	105	231	100	80	180	0	0	0	104	112	216	81	81	162	0	0	0
Puerto Rican	51	42	93	40	39	79	0	1	1	37	38	75	31	26	57	0	0	0
Other Hispanic	169	158	327	129	112	241	1	1	2	178	139	317	131	101	232	3	0	3
Multiple Hispanic/Latino*	20	12	32	13	10	23	0	0	0	26	11	37	18	6	24	1	0	1
Subtotal	412	358	770	316	273	589	2	2	4	388	340	728	297	251	548	4	0	4
Non-Hispanic/Latino**																		
Black	564	275	839	421	225	646	14	6	20	557	225	782	403	175	578	22	2	24
Native American/AK	9	7	16	8	6	14	0	0	0	6	4	10	6	3	9	0	0	0
Native Hawaiian/OPI	26	16	42	20	13	33	1	1	2	19	16	35	12	13	25	0	0	0
White	3,431	3,504	6,935	2,750	2,613	5,363	59	33	92	3,216	3,840	7,056	2,470	2,800	5,270	38	42	80
Asian	1,740	1,765	3,505	1,310	1,269	2,579	26	17	43	1,748	1,727	3,475	1,274	1,159	2,433	32	14	46
Other Race	3	8	11	2	3	5	0	0	0	6	10	16	4	9	13	0	0	0
Multiple Race*	207	159	366	157	112	269	1	5	6	182	162	344	144	118	262	3	3	6
Unknown	66	79	145	63	71	134	4	3	7	160	175	335	149	153	302	6	3	9
Subtotal	6,046	5,813	11,859	4,731	4,312	9,043	105	65	170	5,894	6,159	12,053	4,462	4,430	8,892	101	64	165
Foreign	228	225	453	181	172	353	0	3	3	260	252	512	209	186	395	5	3	8
Total	6,686	6,396	13,082	5,228	4,757	9,985	107	70	177	6,542	6,751	13,293	4,968	4,867	9,835	110	67	177

Note: In 2008, one applicant, who declined to report gender, was not included here.
*Since 2002, students can select more than one race and / or ethnicity. **Those who did not choose 'Hispanic/Latino' or 'Non-Hispanic/Latino' are listed under 'Non-Hispanic/Latino'. Data Source: AAMC Data Warehouse: Applicant-Matriculant File, as of 1/16/2009.

Students who perform satisfactorily in the decelerated program are promoted into the second year of the M.D. program. There is no separate application process for this program. Students admitted to this program are chosen from a group of applicants who have demonstrated a commitment to service, a high level of self awareness, and the commitment to successfully complete the rigorous medical school curriculum.

University Counseling Center services help students resolve personal social, career, and study problems that can interfere with their academic progress and success. Services include workshops and groups on topics such as time management, study skills, procrastination prevention, family and relationship issues, stress management, conflict management, and self-esteem. Clinical services including crisis intervention and brief personal counseling for issues related to university life are also available.

Enrichment Programs

Students can mentor minority high school students through programs such as the American Medical Student Association's Students Teaching Aids to Students, Science in Our Lives, SHAPED (Study Health and Promote an Education Degree), a Latin American youth health care program, and Upward Bound. The Interdisciplinary Student Community Oriented Patient Education Service (ISCOPES) is currently an elective program designed to provide hands-on experience and training in population-based community-oriented health promotion activities. Over a year and a half period an interdisciplinary team of medical, physician assistant, nurse practitioner, health administration, and public health students works closely with their community site to develop a health promotion project that will be of benefit to the population or community served by the site. Both university and community faculty serve as team supervisors. The team presents its work at an ISCOPES Poster Session twice each year.

Through the Interdisciplinary Student Community Oriented Patient Educa-

tion Service (ISCOPES), students enhance their understanding of community-oriented primary care and cultural competency. Needs of the community are addressed. A combined M.D./M.P.H. program is offered.

Student Financial Assistance

Financial aid is awarded to students on the basis of need. The school's financial aid funds are limited, but the services of the Financial Aid Office are available to assist accepted students to develop plans to meet their financial obligations. There are a limited number of merit-based scholarships available. The application fee is waived for disadvantaged students. The Admissions Committee will utilize regional interviews to avoid having disadvantaged applicants travel to the medical center from substantial distances.

All students are required to attend financial planning workshops.

Educational Partnerships

The Upward Bound Program is a partnership with the DC public school system designed to encourage students to pursue careers in the sciences.

DC Health & Academic Prep Program (DC HAPP)
The DC Health and Academic Prep Program is a four-week program for Washington, DC graduating high school seniors, who are going to a college or university in Fall 2009, to engage in and explore various medical and public health careers. Working directly with graduate students, doctors, and other medical professionals, DC HAPP scholars learn about various medical professions as possible career paths for their future, as well as prepare for their upcoming college experience. Scholars who satisfactorily complete the four-week program will earn a $1,000 stipend, as well as be eligible to earn an $8,750 college scholarship. The program is hosted by and housed at George Washington University. *(http://www.gwumc.edu/dchapp/dchapp.html).*

Georgetown University School of Medicine

Joy Phinizy Williams,
Associate Dean for Students
Georgetown University
School of Medicine
14 Butler Annex,
3900 Reservoir Rd., NW
Washington, DC 20057-1423
202-687-1645; 202-687-7660 fax
williamj@georgetown.edu
http://GEMS.georgetown.edu

Admissions

The Committee on Admissions reviews all applications to the School of Medicine and evaluates them based on established academic parameters and fair and equitable guidelines. Each application is considered individually to enable the committee to have an opportunity to select persons who will add diversity and strength to the class.

The Committee on Admissions is made up of Georgetown University faculty and student representatives. Invited applicants are interviewed individually by a member of the faculty, alumni, or a fourth-year medical student. The School of Medicine and the committee are committed to maintaining a diverse student body and to increasing the numbers of physicians from groups currently underrepresented in the field of medicine.

Academic Support Programs

The Georgetown University Experimental Medical Studies Program (GEMS) GEMS is a one-year post-baccalaureate course of study. Its primary purpose is to offer highly motivated, underrepresented minority students, with modest pre-medical academic records, an opportunity to demonstrate their academic capabilities by passing selected courses taught to first-year students at Georgetown University School of Medicine.

In concert with this primary objective:

• GEMS students must be U.S. citizens who are either from minority groups that have been traditionally underrepresented in medicine (African Americans, mainland Puerto Ricans, Mexican Americans, and Native Americans) or others who meet all other criteria and show evidence of their ability to satisfy the social and educational goals of this program.

• Special consideration is given to residents of the District of Columbia.

• Applicants to the GEMS Program must have successfully completed one year each of general chemistry, organic chemistry, biology, physics, and college mathematics. Appropriate preparation in the laboratory will be required in biology, chemistry, and physics.

• All applicants must show evidence of having earned a baccalaureate degree from an accredited college or university.

• Participants take courses selected from the first-year medical school curriculum and are graded on the same basis as other students enrolled in these courses. The GEMS course requirements are equivalent to half the full-time, first-year course requirements. GEMS students who successfully complete the program are encouraged to apply to the School of Medicine. If accepted, these students will take the remaining first year courses the following academic year.

For additional information about the GEMS Program, send an e-mail to gemsprogram@georgetown.edu or telephone 202-687-1406 or write GEMS

Georgetown University School of Medicine
Applicants, First-Time Applicants, Matriculants by Gender, Race and Ethnicity, 2007-2008

| | 2007 | | | | | | | | | 2008 | | | | | | | | |
| | APP | | | F-time APP | | | MAT | | | APP | | | F-time APP | | | MAT | | |
	Women	Men	Total	Women	Men	Total	Women	Men	Total	Women	Men	Total	Women	Men	Total	Women	Men	Total
Hispanic/Latino																		
Cuban	27	36	63	20	29	49	0	0	0	41	39	80	36	36	72	0	2	2
Mexican American	89	79	168	71	63	134	0	1	1	70	101	171	52	78	130	2	0	2
Puerto Rican	29	38	67	22	35	57	1	0	1	29	35	64	26	27	53	1	1	2
Other Hispanic	135	121	256	109	90	199	3	1	4	131	128	259	102	103	205	2	3	5
Multiple Hispanic/Latino*	18	12	30	15	10	25	0	0	0	18	16	34	15	12	27	0	0	0
Subtotal	298	286	584	237	227	464	4	2	6	289	319	608	231	256	487	5	6	11
Non-Hispanic/Latino**																		
Black	346	185	531	267	149	416	10	5	15	389	207	596	290	165	455	10	1	11
Native American/AK	9	7	16	8	7	15	0	0	0	6	6	12	5	5	10	0	0	0
Native Hawaiian/OPI	24	16	40	20	13	33	0	0	0	22	8	30	13	6	19	0	0	0
White	2,716	3,031	5,747	2,282	2,392	4,674	58	70	128	2,593	3,452	6,045	2,116	2,676	4,792	51	66	117
Asian	1,379	1,464	2,843	1,106	1,113	2,219	17	13	30	1,381	1,499	2,880	1,060	1,074	2,134	23	24	47
Other Race	2	3	5	1	1	2	0	0	0	3	9	12	2	8	10	0	0	0
Multiple Race*	161	145	306	134	117	251	1	2	3	172	127	299	139	89	228	1	1	2
Unknown	52	62	114	51	56	107	2	0	2	133	158	291	126	140	266	3	1	4
Subtotal	4,689	4,913	9,602	3,869	3,848	7,717	88	90	178	4,699	5,466	10,165	3,751	4,163	7,914	88	93	181
Foreign	249	208	457	193	157	350	0	6	6	249	215	464	196	163	359	0	2	2
Total	5,236	5,407	10,643	4,299	4,232	8,531	92	98	190	5,237	6,000	11,237	4,178	4,582	8,760	93	101	194

*Since 2002, students can select more than one race and / or ethnicity. **Those who did not choose 'Hispanic/Latino' or 'Non-Hispanic/Latino' are listed under 'Non-Hispanic/Latino'. Data Source: AAMC Data Warehouse: Applicant-Matriculant File, as of 1/16/2009.

Program, Georgetown University School of Medicine, 3900 Reservoir Rd., NW Washington, DC 20057-1423. Contacts for the GEMS Program are Joy P. Williams, Associate Dean for Student Affairs and Special Programs, 202-687-1645 or David Taylor, Senior Facilitator, 202-687-5411 or Ben Walker, Ph.D., Facilitator, 202-687-1491.

The faculty of the School of Medicine is strongly committed to the academic development of all students, and individual faculty members are generally available to conduct group and individual tutorials.

Student Financial Assistance

Application fees may be waived upon request and justification of need for financially disadvantaged applicants.

Education Partnerships

Georgetown University School of Medicine has a partnership agreement with Eastern Senior High School, Health and Medical Sciences Academy, a magnet program in the District of Columbia public schools for students who aspire to careers in health and or human services.

Howard University College of Medicine

Dr. Dawn L. Cannon, Associate Dean for Student Affairs & Admissions
Judith Walk, Admissions Director
Ann Finney, Admissions Officer
Howard University College
of Medicine
Washington, DC 20059
202-806-6279; 202-806-7934 fax
jwalk@howard.edu

Recruitment

Recruitment activities are coordinated by the Associate Dean for Student Affairs and the staff of the Admissions Office. Efforts are made to achieve more effective communication between the college, pre-medical students, and their advisors. The college conducts year-round undergraduate pre-medical student recruitment efforts, including travel to colleges and universities in various geographic locations across the nation. These efforts are aimed at identifying potential student applicants at an early stage in their college careers and at working to increase the representation of minority students underrepresented in the medical profession.

Another important facet of recruitment is the highlighting of Howard's special programs (e.g., the B.S./M.D. Program, academic reinforcement programs for admitted and enrolled students, M.D./Ph.D programs, the Human Genome Center, the Center for Sickle Cell Disease, the Howard University Cancer Center), and other related programs that may be of particular interest to applicants. The university's Center for Pre-professional Education sponsors two workshops for pre-medical students that serve as an orientation to the medical school application process and allow participants to interact with medical school representatives from across the nation. Although recruitment activities have operated primarily at the undergraduate college level, some efforts are aimed at the secondary school student.

Since Howard University is the oldest and largest predominantly minority medical school in the country, it is concerned with the preparation of pre-medical students in underrepresented minority group communities. The College of Medicine has a sincere commitment to identify, at the earliest stage of undergraduate training, the highly motivated and academically qualified minority student who has expressed an interest in pursuing a medical career.

Admissions

The primary mission of the College of Medicine is to train physicians to practice in medically underserved communities and facilities. The college's admissions policies and procedures are in accord with this mission. The college is an historically Black institution, yet has one of the most diverse student bodies in the country. Candidates for admission and alternates are selected from those applicants who have competitive academic credentials and desirable personal and social traits, and who are most likely to practice in communities or facilities needing physician services.

The college participates in the American Medical College Application Service (AMCAS). The deadline for filing the completed AMCAS application is December 15 of the year immediately preceding the year the applicant expects to enter. All applicants to the college must also take the Medical College Admission Test (MCAT) no earlier than three

Howard University College of Medicine
Applicants, First-Time Applicants, Matriculants by Gender, Race and Ethnicity, 2007-2008

	2007									2008								
	APP			F-time APP			MAT			APP			F-time APP			MAT		
	Women	Men	Total	Women	Men	Total	Women	Men	Total	Women	Men	Total	Women	Men	Total	Women	Men	Total
Hispanic/Latino																		
Cuban	10	20	30	7	17	24	0	0	0	20	17	37	17	12	29	1	0	1
Mexican American	55	47	102	42	29	71	0	1	1	53	47	100	42	33	75	3	0	3
Puerto Rican	26	18	44	19	14	33	1	1	2	22	24	46	17	15	32	0	3	3
Other Hispanic	84	71	155	58	41	99	5	2	7	96	93	189	67	58	125	2	2	4
Multiple Hispanic/Latino*	10	7	17	6	5	11	0	0	0	8	7	15	5	3	8	0	0	0
Subtotal	185	163	348	132	106	238	6	4	10	199	188	387	148	121	269	6	5	11
Non-Hispanic/Latino**																		
Black	1,217	549	1,766	873	408	1,281	47	42	89	1,235	541	1,776	865	396	1,261	39	33	72
Native American/AK	6	3	9	5	1	6	0	0	0	6	3	9	4	3	7	1	0	1
Native Hawaiian/OPI	13	9	22	8	7	15	0	0	0	13	15	28	8	10	18	0	0	0
White	531	582	1,113	391	404	795	2	3	5	567	613	1,180	399	432	831	1	0	1
Asian	716	788	1,504	523	534	1,057	3	7	10	769	752	1,521	532	484	1,016	9	7	16
Other Race	4	4	8	3	1	4	0	0	0	2	8	10	2	5	7	0	0	0
Multiple Race*	93	62	155	66	43	109	1	3	4	75	60	135	56	38	94	3	0	3
Unknown	22	19	41	21	15	36	0	0	0	27	38	65	21	32	53	0	0	0
Subtotal	2,602	2,016	4,618	1,890	1,413	3,303	53	55	108	2,694	2,030	4,724	1,887	1,400	3,287	53	40	93
Foreign	300	244	544	245	191	436	5	7	12	281	242	523	217	186	403	6	4	10
Total	3,087	2,423	5,510	2,267	1,710	3,977	64	66	130	3,174	2,460	5,634	2,252	1,707	3,959	65	49	114

Note: In 2008, one applicant, who declined to report gender, was not included here.

*Since 2002, students can select more than one race and / or ethnicity. **Those who did not choose 'Hispanic/Latino' or 'Non-Hispanic/Latino' are listed under 'Non-Hispanic/Latino'. Data Source: AAMC Data Warehouse: Applicant-Matriculant File, as of 1/16/2009.

years prior to the year of expected matriculation. Letters of recommendation from a health professions committee, or from two science faculty, a secondary application form, and an application fee of $75 are required, as is a personal interview. The application fee cannot be waived.

Academic Support Programs

An academic support program for basic science courses has existed at the Howard University College of Medicine since 1963. Sessions are sponsored and coordinated by the Office of Medical Education.

Each freshman student is assigned two advisors: a faculty advisor and a student advisor. The faculty advisor is a member of the college's faculty who will serve as a counselor throughout the years of medical study. The student advisor is a second-year student who provides support and important study materials and helps guide the entering student through the transition to undergraduate medical education. Additionally, students are assigned a Senior Faculty Advisor, who will assist them in their transition to postgraduate medical education.

During freshman orientation week, and periodically throughout the year, workshops are offered presenting techniques for understanding and memorizing information, taking lecture notes, taking multiple-choice examinations, and managing time in the medical curriculum. Counseling is offered to all students in academic difficulty. These students may receive tutorial support, assistance with learning skills, or referral to other university services. Aid in preparing for the United States Medical Licensing Examination (USMLE) Step 1 is provided through a commercial review course.

Freshman and sophomores may remove one or two course deficiencies through reexamination or by attending the Summer Directed Study Program and then passing an examination administered at the end of the program.

Enrichment Programs

Preliminary Academic Reinforcement Program (PARP)
PARP was organized during 1971 for a small group of incoming medical freshmen and has continued each successive summer. PARP is a six-week summer program that introduces selected entering freshmen to the basic medical sciences, strengthens their learning skills, and provides some measure of their ability to handle the freshman medical curriculum. The subjects taught mirror the blocks of the new integrated curriculum: structure and function, molecules and cells, and medicine and society. Satisfactory completion of the program, a requirement for students selected, is determined on the basis of examinations, attendance, and professionalism. No credit is offered for PARP courses, and the program neither satisfies course prerequisites for medical school nor replaces any courses in the freshman medical curriculum. Participating students may be given some assistance with expenses for room and board. No tuition is charged.

Students for this program are selected by the Admissions Committee from the pool of AMCAS applicants. No direct application to the PARP program is possible.

Summer Medical and Dental Education Program
SMDEP is a free (full tuition, housing, and meals) six-week summer medical and dental school preparatory program that offers eligible undergraduate students intensive and personalized medical and dental school preparation.

The mission of the Howard University Summer Medical Dental Education Program is to provide an educational experience of exceptional quality that will strengthen the overall academic preparation of underrepresented minority, disadvantaged, and low-income students who express interest in admission to medical or dental school.

SMDEP strives to enhance the university's ability to contribute well-qualified, socially conscious medical and

dental school candidates committed to improving the health and quality of life for all communities throughout this nation and the world, especially those communities underserved by the health professions.

Student Financial Assistance

About 85 percent of the students enrolled in the College of Medicine receive some sort of financial assistance. Financial aid awards are based on an analysis of the student's need and academic scholarship. Financial aid applicants are required to file the Free Application for Federal Student Aid.

Several kinds of financial aid are available to the student in need. Scholarships are awarded by the college and are applied to the cost of tuition. Guaranteed and non-guaranteed student loans are available from a number of sources, including the university. While the college attempts to ensure that all its students have financial resources to meet the cost of attendance, we cannot provide financial assistance for application or interview travel.

Educational Partnerships

The College of Medicine is a partner with the Center for Pre-professional Education of the Howard University College of Arts and Sciences in preparing underrepresented minority and disadvantaged students for medical school. In addition to providing counseling and support for pre-medical students, the Center for Pre-professional Education sponsors several special programs. Among these are the B.S./M.D. Program; a Post-Baccalaureate Pre-medical Program; a summer program for undergraduate pre-medical students; and the MED-DENT START Program.

B.S./M.D. Program
This program enables highly qualified students to complete requirements for the B.S. degree and for the M.D. degree within six years after graduation from high school. Students in this program can complete all requirements for admission to the College of Medicine by the end of their sophomore under-

graduate year and may at that point be admitted to the College of Medicine.

The B.S. degree is awarded to these students upon the successful completion of the sophomore year in medical school, and the M.D. degree is awarded upon successful completion of the final two years of the medical curriculum.

Pre-professional Advanced Enrichment Program
The Center for Pre-professional Education offers this six-week summer program to prepare undergraduate college students for the MCAT; to introduce them to basic medical science courses as taught by medical school faculty; to provide clinical hospital experience; and to improve communication, reading, analytical, and exam-taking skills.

MED-DENT START Program
This program provides pre-medical and pre-dental students with supervised and planned clinical experiences in the Howard University Hospital. Staffed largely by minority physicians, the Howard University Hospital is the largest minority-owned and run health care facility in the country and serves a large minority population.

For further information regarding any of the above programs offered by the Center for Pre-professional Education, in cooperation with the College of Medicine, please contact:

Julie C. Andrist, M.Ed., Assistant Coordinator/ Pre-professional Advisor, Center for Pre-professional Education, College of Arts and Sciences, 2225 Georgia Avenue, NW, Room 518 Howard University, Washington, DC 20059, 202-238-2363.

Florida International University, Herbert Wertheim College of Medicine*

Dr. Luther Brewster, Assistant Professor, Medicine & Society
Florida International University
Herbert Wertheim College
of Medicine
11200 SW 8th Street – HLSII 364B
Miami, Florida 33199
305.348.1455; 305.348.0650 fax
brewster@fiu.edu

General Information

In August 2009, the College of Medicine welcomed the inaugural class. The four year program, leading to the M.D. degree, involves in-depth exposure and training in all areas of medical education with specific focus on family and community medicine. Key in the medical training is the focus on the importance of the doctor-patient relationship in diverse patient populations.

For more information about this institution, visit *(http://medicine.fiu.edu)*

*No data available; new medical school.

Florida State University College of Medicine

Dr. Eugene A. Trowers, Jr., Assistant Dean for Diversity and Outreach
Florida State University
College of Medicine
1115 West Call Street
Tallahassee, FL 32306-4300
850-645-2826; 850-645-2846 fax
Eugene.trowers@med.fsu.edu
http://med.fsu.edu

Recruitment

The Florida State University (FSU) College of Medicine was created to train physicians to serve the health care needs of underserved populations in Florida. Because of this unique mission, the FSU College of Medicine (FSUCOM) actively recruits individuals from rural, inner city, and other underrepresented population groups throughout the state. In 1993, prior to the establishment of the FSUCOM, the FSU Program in Medical Sciences implemented the outreach program, Science Students Together Reaching Instructional Diversity and Excellence (SSTRIDE). SSTRIDE was developed to increase the interest and achievement in science and mathematics of a diverse group of middle and high school students. Because of this very successful recruitment program, SSTRIDE has expanded its outreach to include college and post-baccalaureate programs at FSU and programs for middle and high school students in surrounding rural counties. In cooperation with educational, professional, and physician partnerships, outreach/recruitment activities include in-school coursework in anatomy and physiology, after-school mentoring and tutoring, standardized test preparation, career-shadowing experiences, and pre-medical advising.

SSTRIDE programs run continuously throughout the academic year and an on-campus residential summer program is available to upcoming 11th- and 12th-grade students from nearby rural areas. Students are encouraged to remain in the SSTRIDE program until graduation from college, thereby creating a recruiting pipeline to FSU's medical school and other higher education programs. SSTRIDE outreach/recruitment programs are sponsored and implemented by administrators and pre-health professions advisors within the Division of Student Affairs, Admissions, and Outreach at the FSUCOM and the Big Bend Area Health Education Center (AHEC). Representatives from FSU College of Medicine, Division of Student Affairs regularly attend pre-medical and pre-health forums throughout the state of Florida, particularly those targeting underrepresented groups, to recruit students to health care professions. Students enrolled in the College of Medicine also aid in recruitment efforts through active participation with SSTRIDE, and inner city and rural schools, giving guest lectures to address health issues, career in health professions, and biomedical research.

Admissions

Consistent with its mission, the FSU College of Medicine Admissions Committee is especially interested in students who have demonstrated consistent motivation for service to others. Students from underrepresented minority groups, rural and inner city, and non-traditional backgrounds are of particular interest to the committee.

Academic Support Programs

During orientation and throughout the year, FSUCOM students are provided

Florida State University College of Medicine
Applicants, First-Time Applicants, Matriculants by Gender, Race and Ethnicity, 2007-2008

	2007 APP Women	Men	Total	F-time APP Women	Men	Total	MAT Women	Men	Total	2008 APP Women	Men	Total	F-time APP Women	Men	Total	MAT Women	Men	Total
Hispanic/Latino																		
Cuban	49	62	111	31	48	79	1	2	3	68	63	131	56	47	103	2	6	8
Mexican American	12	4	16	5	3	8	0	0	0	9	18	27	7	11	18	1	0	1
Puerto Rican	12	16	28	8	11	19	0	0	0	31	27	58	24	19	43	0	0	0
Other Hispanic	65	62	127	48	38	86	2	2	4	89	93	182	68	69	137	3	5	8
Multiple Hispanic/Latino*	13	5	18	11	4	15	0	0	0	20	10	30	17	9	26	2	0	2
Subtotal	151	149	300	103	104	207	3	4	7	217	211	428	172	155	327	8	11	19
Non-Hispanic/Latino**																		
Black	135	52	187	94	36	130	10	1	11	206	88	294	144	59	203	8	1	9
Native American/AK	1	0	1	1	0	1	0	0	0	5	6	11	3	4	7	0	0	0
Native Hawaiian/OPI	1	3	4	0	2	2	0	0	0	6	2	8	5	2	7	0	0	0
White	341	394	735	266	299	565	44	41	85	490	570	1,060	389	420	809	33	31	64
Asian	104	130	234	74	97	171	8	5	13	216	239	455	176	181	357	10	13	23
Other Race	0	1	1	0	0	0	0	0	0	0	1	1	0	1	1	0	0	0
Multiple Race*	17	15	32	12	9	21	2	1	3	23	24	47	13	17	30	1	0	1
Unknown	3	5	8	3	4	7	0	0	0	16	26	42	15	25	40	1	1	2
Subtotal	602	600	1,202	450	447	897	64	48	112	962	956	1,918	745	709	1,454	53	46	99
Foreign	1	2	3	1	2	3	0	0	0	11	12	23	10	11	21	0	0	0
Total	754	751	1,505	554	553	1,107	67	52	119	1,190	1,179	2,369	927	875	1,802	61	57	118

*Since 2002, students can select more than one race and / or ethnicity. **Those who did not choose 'Hispanic/Latino' or 'Non-Hispanic/Latino' are listed under 'Non-Hispanic/Latino'. Data Source: AAMC Data Warehouse: Applicant-Matriculant File, as of 1/16/2009.

information regarding study skills, coping skills, and instructional support materials. Students are assigned a specific faculty advisor upon matriculation and another is assigned when students relocate to a regional campus. With the help of faculty, student performance is monitored. If a student is identified as not performing at the appropriate level in course work, counseling and tutoring are provided. Study groups are formed early in the first semester but are very fluid as students' academic needs change or emerge. Full-time student support staff is available throughout the four years of medical school. All intervention services and counseling are coordinated by the Director of Student Development and Program Initiatives who works in conjunction with the Student Support Coordinators assigned to each medical class. To facilitate the success of the medical students and to support the unique mission of the College of Medicine, small-group, problem-based instruction with early and extensive clinical experiences are part of the curriculum delivery throughout the four-year program of study. Students are also part of learning communities (consisting of 25-30 students) that have designated facilities conducive to the dialogue of learning and information assimilation.

The Post-Baccalaureate Bridge Program is designed to provide assistance for a small number of identified students who apply to medical school but whose backgrounds may place them at an academic disadvantage for immediate entry into medical school. These students are enrolled in a year-long program, which allows them to take selected medical school courses; enroll in upper level science, bioethics, and psychosocial courses; take personal skills development workshops; and develop and participate in a community service activity to prepare for entry into medical school. Successful completion of this structured program will ensure entry into the next College of Medicine class.

Individualized intervention activities are possible and utilized by all students regardless of background or ethnicity.

The student learning communities provide social and educational opportunities for students. Each community is served by a student support coordinator, who can, along with the help of the Director of Student Development and Program Initiatives and peer counselors from the senior-class identify any psychological issues that may emerge and can direct students to help from university and private resources.

Enrichment Programs

Through SSTRIDE, middle and high school students are exposed to enrichment activities that include an elective anatomy and physiology course offered during the school day, science and mathematics tutorials, hands-on laboratory activities, career shadowing, science and math competitions, and test preparation activities. During the summer months 11th- and 12th-grade students from the Rural SSTRIDE program are provided an intensive three-week residential experience called RIPE (Rural Introduction to Pre-medical Education). RIPE is designed to motivate students to excel academically, expose students to a variety of clinical sites and training opportunities, teach students about scholarships and university based mentoring programs, expose them to college campuses, and inspire students to consider careers in health care professions in medically underserved communities.

Undergraduate students from FSU and Florida A&M University (FAMU), minority students, non-traditional students, and students from rural/inner city backgrounds participate in the Multicultural Association of Pre-health Students (MAPS) and in the College of Medicine's pre-health advising program. These students are offered academic advisement, test preparation activities, mathematics and science tutorial services, study group activities, interview workshops, career workshops, review of personal statements, and participation in local and national pre-health conferences. They can also apply to participate in the Physician Partnership Program and a medical assistant

training program sponsored by the College of Medicine and Big Bend Area Health Education Center (AHEC) with Lively Vocational Technical College. After medical assistant training, these students, many of whom must work to support themselves, are able to find employment in a health care setting, obtain valuable medical experiences, and confirm their commitment to medicine. Web site: (http://www.med.fsu.edu/Student Affairs/default.asp).

Student Financial Assistance

A number of need-based and minority scholarships are available to students. In addition, emergency loans are extended to students who are having difficulty meeting living expenses and tuition fees. During orientation and throughout the year, a financial aid liaison in the College of Medicine provides individual budget counseling to help students develop personal budgets and access to available resources.

Educational Partnerships

Educational partnerships exist between FSUCOM and school districts in Leon, Gadsden, Okaloosa, and Madison County schools. In addition, we have partnerships with the Big Bend AHEC, Lively Vocational Technical Center, Kaplan Educational Testing Center, Princeton Review, Putzer's Review Incorporated, Project Motivational Math, Tallahassee Orthopedic Surgical Center, The Children's Clinic, Wakulla County Health Department, Neighborhood Health Services, Shand's Hospital, and numerous community physicians. Partnerships for third- and fourth-year clinical training exist with physicians, health plans, and hospitals and physician offices in Pensacola, Sarasota, Orlando, and Tallahassee.

University of Central Florida College of Medicine

(Robert) REL Larkin,
Director of Admissions
University of Central Florida
College of Medicine /Admissions
12201 Research Parkway
Orlando, FL 32826-0116
407-823-4244; 407-823-4048 fax
mdadmissions@mail.ucf.edu
http://www.med.ucf.edu/admissions

Recruitment

The University of Central Florida College of Medicine (UCF COM) actively recruits undergraduate students from underrepresented groups for its medical program. Visits are made by the Director of Admissions to undergraduate colleges, including several located in the southeastern United States.

Admissions

The UCF COM recognizes that enhancing diversity requires leadership and commitment. Activities that will foster diversity in the medical school class are coordinated between the COM Admissions Office and the Office for Diversity and Inclusiveness. Both offices will work closely on recruitment practices and will participate at student recruitment events at college campuses around Florida. The offices will review current admissions data to ensure a thorough review of those students who are identified as under-represented in medicine. The Admissions Office will review all completed files to determine that all minimum requirements have been met. Completed applications that meet the minimum requirements will be evaluated to determine competitiveness for an interview invitation. The Medical School Admission Committee (MSAC) chair provides guidance to the director of admissions regarding the qualities and attributes that the MSAC is seeking in applicants who will be selected for interview.

The evaluation rubric for selecting applicants for an interview by the director of admissions will consider the following:

- Possesses the academic skills to succeed in the curriculum – indicators include prior academic program and major, academic rigor by semester, required coursework, and a minimum 3.0 in biology, physics, chemistry, and mathematics and overall GPA, as well as a minimum 24 score on the MCAT. The MSAC will consider applicants with GPA/MCAT scores below the minimum requirements on a case-by-case basis, if the applicant offers unique characteristics which add to the diversity of the class.
- Demonstrates a motivation toward medicine – indicators include a consistent history of medical-related volunteerism, physician shadowing, biomedical research, and other activities that expose the applicant to medicine.
- Demonstrates good communication skills and interpersonal relations – indicators include community service-related volunteerism, teamwork, leadership, and written materials.
- Contributes toward the diversity of the physician workforce – diversity in factors include ethnic/racial, rural/urban, academic degree/major/institution, underserved and socioeconomic factors, as well as other unique experiences. The College of Medicine does not discriminate on the basis of age, color, disability status, national origin, race, religion, or sex and is committed to the principle of a diverse classroom.
- Demonstrates leadership such as having been elected to a position by their peers, participating in extracurricular activities that require leadership skills, founding an organization, or creatively initiating something new to benefit others.
- Demonstrates the ability to persevere or persist and follow through with an activity at the highest level such as research, sports, etc.

Academic Support Programs
Advisor/Mentor Programs
As a new medical program our charter class and following incoming medical students are paired with a clinical faculty member who shares the student's areas of clinical and research specialty interest. For support and guidance, every student will have a faculty advisor throughout the medical curriculum. They will have the opportunities to shadow and participate in research.

Office for Diversity and Inclusiveness
This office works with the Dean of Student Affairs for all students in the medical program. The office can assist with confidential counseling and personal issues regarding the stress and anxiety of participating in the rigors of the medical school curriculum. This office will also provide support and direction to the various student support groups for all medical students.

Enrichment Programs
The Director for the Office of Diversity and Inclusiveness will serve as the advisor to the Student National Medical Association (SNMA) and Minority Association of Pre-medical Students (MAPS). The MAPS is organized under the umbrella of the SNMA.

Student Financial Assistance
For our Charter Class, full-tuition and living expenses scholarship is available for all entering medical students. For each class every effort will be made to meet each student's total financial need through additional scholarships or loans when necessary.

*No data available; new medical school.

University of Florida College of Medicine

Dr. Donna M. Parker
Dr. Michelle E. Jacobs
Dr. Kendall M. Campbell,
Assistant Deans for Minority Affairs
University of Florida
College of Medicine
P.O. Box 100202
Gainesville, FL 32610-0202
352-273-6656; 352-392-5647 fax
parkerd@ufl.edu
mejacobs@ufl.edu
kmarvinc@ufl.edu
http://www.med.ufl.edu/oma

Recruitment

The College of Medicine actively recruits undergraduate students from underrepresented groups for its medical, physician assistant, and interdisciplinary biomedical science research programs. Visits are made by the Assistant Deans for Minority Affairs and students to undergraduate colleges, including several located in the southeast with predominant underrepresented student populations.

Admissions

The Medical Selection Committee reviews applications and compares the applicant's Medical College Admission Test scores and grade-point average with those of other medical students who attend their undergraduate college or are currently enrolled in the College of Medicine. In addition, the applicant's record of clinical experience, research, and volunteerism is taken into consideration. The College does not have a separate minority admissions committee. The College of Medicine is aware of underrepresentation of many groups in the health care workforce, and it is committed to helping to alleviate this problem. Hence, the committee looks critically at applicants' experiences in serving the underserved.

Academic Support Programs

Advisor/Mentor Programs
All incoming medical students are paired with a clinical faculty member who shares the student's area of specialty interest. Students have the opportunity to shadow their advisor and/or participate in their research. Mostly, the advisor/mentor introduces students to a career in medicine and

provides them with individual support and guidance. During the third year, students may select a new advisor/mentor upon determining the specialty area they wish to pursue for residency training.

Office of Student Counseling and Development
Confidential counseling and workshops are offered to help students with personal issues (e.g., stress, anxiety, depression), academic issues (e.g., study skills, test taking), and career issues (e.g., medical specialty decision making, residency application, and interviewing). In addition, support groups for spouses and significant others meet weekly when there is sufficient interest.

Tutoring
The Offices of Medical Education and Student Counseling and Development coordinate tutorial services for students who are referred for this assistance.

The services listed above are conducted by Dr. Beverly Vidaurreta.

Enrichment Programs

Health Care Summer Institute
The Office of Minority Affairs and the Area Health Education Centers co-

University of Florida College of Medicine
Applicants, First-Time Applicants, Matriculants by Gender, Race and Ethnicity, 2007-2008

	2007									2008								
	APP			F-time APP			MAT			APP			F-time APP			MAT		
	Wo-men	Men	Total	Wo-men	Men	Total	Wo-men	Men	Total	Wo-men	Men	Total	Wo-men	Men	Total	Wo-men	Men	Total
Hispanic/Latino																		
Cuban	47	60	107	32	48	80	3	3	6	60	58	118	52	49	101	1	5	6
Mexican American	17	16	33	12	13	25	0	0	0	15	22	37	11	14	25	0	0	0
Puerto Rican	28	26	54	21	23	44	0	0	0	24	26	50	20	17	37	0	0	0
Other Hispanic	75	74	149	60	54	114	2	3	5	92	96	188	71	76	147	5	2	7
Multiple Hispanic/Latino*	12	9	21	9	6	15	1	0	1	17	12	29	14	8	22	0	1	1
Subtotal	179	185	364	134	144	278	6	6	12	208	214	422	168	164	332	6	8	14
Non-Hispanic/Latino**																		
Black	180	85	265	150	65	215	5	2	7	168	85	253	131	66	197	5	2	7
Native American/AK	3	1	4	3	0	3	0	0	0	4	1	5	4	1	5	0	0	0
Native Hawaiian/OPI	7	6	13	7	6	13	0	0	0	5	3	8	5	2	7	0	0	0
White	561	719	1,280	475	567	1,042	32	45	77	597	803	1,400	488	632	1,120	41	44	85
Asian	222	273	495	176	221	397	17	18	35	238	295	533	196	214	410	6	12	18
Other Race	1	4	5	1	0	1	0	0	0	1	2	3	1	2	3	0	0	0
Multiple Race*	37	26	63	24	21	45	0	1	1	31	25	56	24	17	41	3	1	4
Unknown	12	7	19	11	6	17	0	0	0	22	38	60	22	35	57	3	1	4
Subtotal	1,023	1,121	2,144	847	886	1,733	54	66	120	1,066	1,252	2,318	871	969	1,840	58	60	118
Foreign	16	26	42	10	21	31	0	0	0	23	21	44	20	15	35	0	0	0
Total	1,218	1,332	2,550	991	1,051	2,042	60	72	132	1,297	1,487	2,784	1,059	1,148	2,207	64	68	132

*Since 2002, students can select more than one race and / or ethnicity. **Those who did not choose 'Hispanic/Latino' or 'Non-Hispanic/Latino' are listed under 'Non-Hispanic/Latino'. Data Source: AAMC Data Warehouse: Applicant-Matriculant File, as of 1/16/2009.

sponsor a four-week summer camp for rising high school seniors interested in health care careers. Participants attend workshops in study skills, take an SAT prep course and shadow several health care professionals. Health professions students who serve as the camp counselors also provide mentoring.

Summer Research Program
The Short-Term Summer Research Training for Minority Students Program is funded by the National Institutes of Health to increase the number of ethnic minority students entering research and academic careers. Preference is given to undergraduates; however, the program is also open to the professional students and others wishing to pursue graduate education. Students are compensated with a stipend, housing, and travel allowance.

Advisement
The Assistant Deans for Minority Affairs serve as the faculty advisors to the Student National Medical Association (SNMA) and Minority Association of Pre-medical Students (MAPS). The MAPS is organized under the umbrella of the SNMA. Our local SNMA chapter is very active and also provides advisement and mentoring to the members of MAPS.

Student Financial Assistance
A partial- or full-tuition scholarship is available to all qualified underrepresented students. Every effort is made to meet each student's total financial need through additional scholarships and loans.

University of Miami Miller School of Medicine

Dr. Robert Hernandez, Senior Associate Dean for Medical Student Administration
University of Miami Miller School of Medicine
PO Box 016960 (R-128)
Miami, FL 33101
305-243-2003, 305-243-8389 fax
Rhernan2@med.miami.edu
www.mededu.miami.edu/minorityaffairs

Recruitment

Students, faculty, and members of the administration visit various college campuses in the southeast to recruit students. In addition to this, the Associate Dean for Minority Affairs tries to visit the predominantly Black colleges and universities in the state of Florida, as well as some of the institutions in the southeast, to recruit minority and disadvantaged students. These visits may occur on career days, depending upon the convenience of the schools and the schedule of the Associate Dean for Minority Affairs. At these visits an attempt is made to have pre-medical and science major students present, along with faculty advisors, science teachers, etc., to discuss with the group the requirements for admission to medical schools, the planning of necessary courses prior to taking the Medical College Admission Test (MCAT), etc.

Admissions

Applicants for admission must complete an American Medical College Application Service (AMCAS) application. The AMCAS application is used to identify applicants about whom the Admissions Committee would like more information. These applicants will be invited to complete a supplemental application, which includes letters of recommendation, a photograph, and a residency statement and validation form, among other information. An evaluation interview, conducted by a member of the Committee on Admissions, is an integral part of the selection process. Interviews are conducted only by an invitation extended by the Committee on Admissions. The Committee on Admissions gives careful consideration to many factors when evaluating a candidate for admission. Some of these factors are scholastic aptitude, interpersonal skills, intellectual curiosity, maturity, motivation, and compassion. Applications from women and socioeconomically disadvantaged candidates are especially encouraged, as are those from older applicants who have had several years of work experience or graduate study. It has long been a policy of the school to admit students with widely differing backgrounds in order to meet the many needs of medicine.

Special efforts and programs are in place to achieve our goal of increasing the enrollment, retention, and graduation of underrepresented minority students.

Academic Support Programs

A system of volunteer tutors, from the faculty and student body, has been established for one-to-one tutorial sessions with all currently enrolled students.

Enrichment Programs

Minority Students Health Careers Motivation Program
In 1976, the school established a summer enrichment program for minority students interested in health careers. This program, referred to as the Minor-

University of Miami Leonard M. Miller School of Medicine
Applicants, First-Time Applicants, Matriculants by Gender, Race and Ethnicity, 2007-2008

	2007									2008								
	APP			F-time APP			MAT			APP			F-time APP			MAT		
	Wo-men	Men	Total	Wo-men	Men	Total	Wo-men	Men	Total	Wo-men	Men	Total	Wo-men	Men	Total	Wo-men	Men	Total
Hispanic/Latino																		
Cuban	57	75	132	40	57	97	4	6	10	72	74	146	58	56	114	15	7	22
Mexican American	38	37	75	28	29	57	1	0	1	28	37	65	22	24	46	0	0	0
Puerto Rican	35	29	64	27	24	51	2	0	2	37	35	72	31	24	55	0	1	1
Other Hispanic	107	123	230	83	94	177	3	7	10	131	139	270	108	108	216	0	3	3
Multiple Hispanic/Latino*	17	11	28	13	8	21	0	0	0	25	13	38	22	11	33	1	1	2
Subtotal	254	275	529	191	212	403	10	13	23	293	298	591	241	223	464	16	12	28
Non-Hispanic/Latino**																		
Black	224	106	330	174	77	251	7	4	11	211	121	332	159	94	253	6	6	12
Native American/AK	4	4	8	3	3	6	0	0	0	5	4	9	3	3	6	0	0	0
Native Hawaiian/OPI	6	11	17	4	8	12	0	0	0	8	6	14	5	5	10	1	0	1
White	1,003	1,373	2,376	803	1,085	1,888	47	55	102	972	1,428	2,400	770	1,091	1,861	47	65	112
Asian	416	539	955	325	409	734	10	22	32	450	559	1,009	355	392	747	15	15	30
Other Race	2	6	8	2	2	4	0	0	0	1	6	7	1	5	6	0	0	0
Multiple Race*	54	59	113	35	42	77	1	6	7	54	58	112	44	45	89	3	2	5
Unknown	14	23	37	13	19	32	0	1	1	52	69	121	49	60	109	3	3	6
Subtotal	1,723	2,121	3,844	1,359	1,645	3,004	65	88	153	1,753	2,251	4,004	1,386	1,695	3,081	75	91	166
Foreign	20	33	53	12	31	43	0	0	0	21	22	43	18	15	33	0	0	0
Total	1,997	2,429	4,426	1,562	1,888	3,450	75	101	176	2,067	2,571	4,638	1,645	1,933	3,578	91	103	194

*Since 2002, students can select more than one race and / or ethnicity. **Those who did not choose 'Hispanic/Latino' or 'Non-Hispanic/Latino' are listed under 'Non-Hispanic/Latino'. Data Source: AAMC Data Warehouse: Applicant-Matriculant File, as of 1/16/2009.

ity Students Health Careers Motivation Program ("Motivation Program") is the university's priority program for facilitation of entry of minority students to medical school.

The Motivation Program is a seven-week, full-time program for college students, particularly juniors and seniors, who are interested in health careers, primarily medicine. Occasionally, a few college graduates are accepted to the program. Generally, the students selected are majors in one of the biological or physical sciences. Priority is given to Florida residents. The main goal of the Motivation Program is to facilitate the entry of minority/disadvantaged students, particularly Blacks, into health professions schools. This goal is met in part by providing the participants with a challenging curriculum composed of several pre-clinical medical school courses (biochemistry, histology, gross anatomy, and microbiology). An intensive reading and study-skills course accompanies the science curriculum. Clinical correlation conferences and visits to designated clinical areas give students opportunities to learn and also expose them to a wide variety of clinical activities. Seminars and workshops are presented to participants desiring to attend Preparing for Medical School (which includes the planning of credentials, application process, interviewing, the personal statement, reapplying, and alternative careers). Each of the participating students receives a stipend. The Associate Dean for Minority Affairs is the Project Director.

A seven-week, full-time nonresidential Medical College Admission Test (MCAT) preparation program is offered to underrepresented minority students who plan to take the MCAT the following August. The goal of the program is to have 70 percent of each group of participants score no less than eight on the verbal reasoning, and physical and biological sciences sections of the test and a score no less than N on the writing sections. The form of the comprehensive review program consists of several components designed to keep participants alert and involved. They

include small classes, trained instructors, comprehensive science sessions, unparalleled verbal reasoning and writing programs, five full-length tests and detailed diagnostic score reports, and a comprehensive set of course review and practice materials. The course is offered at no cost to Florida residents living within commuter distance to the University of Miami/Jackson Memorial Medical Center.

Student Financial Assistance
Considerable financial aid is provided to students who demonstrate financial need through the Office of Financial Assistance Services. (www.mededu.miami.edu/osfa)

Educational Partnerships
The Office of Minority Affairs at the University of Miami Miller School of Medicine has entered into formal, written partnership agreements with Miami-Dade County Area Health Education Center (M-DCAHEC), University of Miami Schools of Arts and Sciences and Medicine, Miami-Dade County Public Schools Division of Schools of Choice: 100 Black Men of South Florida, Inc. and Miami-Dade Chapter, and the National Medical Association. Each agreement specifies the resources and support the entity will contribute to our comprehensive programs. Our programs provide assistance to is advantaged/minority students aspiring to careers in medicine and other health professions. These programs create an array of activities commencing early in the educational pipeline, supporting the career aspirations of disadvantaged/minority students, and allowing for a greater likelihood of successful entry into health professions careers.

University of South Florida College of Medicine

Suzanne Jackson, Director, Office of
Student Diversity & Enrichment
Nazach Rodriguez-Snapp,
Coordinator, Office of Student
Diversity & Enrichment
University of South Florida
College of Medicine
12901 Bruce B. Downs,
Blvd. MDC 24
Tampa, FL 33612
813-974-2562; 813-396-9463 fax
sjackson@health.usf.edu
813-974-7592; 813-396-9463 fax
nazrodri@hsc.usf.edu
www.hsc.usf.edu/medicine/osde

Recruitment

The Office of Student Diversity and Enrichment (OSDE) encourages and promotes an environment at the University of South Florida (USF) College of Medicine that welcomes and embraces diversity in the student body. We strive to ensure that all students feel supported and accepted in order to optimize their educational experience. The Office of Student Diversity and Enrichment participates in all major recruitment activities in the state of Florida and at selected schools through out the United States. Recruitment activities are held during the summer and academic years. Minority pre-medical student organizations are encouraged to invite the OSDE director and coordinator to present at meetings and conferences.

Admissions

Applicants are encouraged to apply early and complete applications as soon as possible. Since we operate on a weekly "rolling admissions" environment, our Admissions Committee may vote to admit highly qualified applicants in such a way that the class could be filled earlier than the final application deadline. Once the class is filled, interviewed applicants will be able to enter the class via the wait-list process.

Students applying for admission to the USF College of Medicine M.D. Program must complete the requirements for a bachelor's degree at an accredited university or college by the time of matriculation. Applicants will be evaluated on the basis of personal attributes and achievements, academic record, performance on the MCAT, personal references, interviews, and their demonstrated motivation for medicine and helping others. These motivations are mainly demonstrated by a consistent history of medical and community service, volunteering, some physician shadowing, teamwork, leadership, and basic science-related research. Applicants who are currently pursuing graduate-level work toward a Ph.D. degree or other professional degree are obligated to complete all degree requirements prior to matriculation into the MD Program.

To be considered for an interview applicants should have both a science (biology, chemistry, physics, math) GPA and overall GPA of at least 3.0 on a 4.0 scale and a minimum MCAT score of 24. Over the last three years, the matriculating class has averaged GPAs and MCATs at about 3.65 (biology, chemistry, physics, math), 3.70 (overall), and 30, respectively.

You must be a U.S. citizen or Permanent Resident Alien (PRA) with a Green Card in your possession before we will consider your application for a possible interview.

University of South Florida College of Medicine
Applicants, First-Time Applicants, Matriculants by Gender, Race and Ethnicity, 2007-2008

| | 2007 | | | | | | | | | 2008 | | | | | | | | |
| | APP | | | F-time APP | | | MAT | | | APP | | | F-time APP | | | MAT | | |
	Women	Men	Total	Women	Men	Total	Women	Men	Total	Women	Men	Total	Women	Men	Total	Women	Men	Total
Hispanic/Latino																		
Cuban	52	70	122	35	54	89	2	3	5	66	63	129	51	48	99	0	1	1
Mexican American	22	15	37	15	9	24	2	1	3	15	29	44	11	17	28	0	1	1
Puerto Rican	29	23	52	21	19	40	0	2	2	31	26	57	25	19	44	2	1	3
Other Hispanic	93	85	178	71	60	131	0	4	4	102	95	197	78	66	144	1	0	1
Multiple Hispanic/Latino*	18	6	24	14	4	18	1	0	1	22	12	34	19	10	29	1	0	1
Subtotal	214	199	413	156	146	302	5	10	15	236	225	461	184	160	344	4	3	7
Non-Hispanic/Latino**																		
Black	198	94	292	150	61	211	3	3	6	183	99	282	136	74	210	5	4	9
Native American/AK	2	0	2	2	0	2	0	0	0	6	5	11	4	4	8	0	0	0
Native Hawaiian/OPI	3	7	10	2	6	8	0	0	0	5	1	6	4	1	5	0	0	0
White	616	700	1,316	491	530	1,021	32	34	66	628	794	1,422	502	610	1,112	39	34	73
Asian	213	261	474	159	191	350	15	15	30	272	272	544	215	188	403	11	11	22
Other Race	2	5	7	1	1	2	0	0	0	0	1	1	0	1	1	0	0	0
Multiple Race*	31	28	59	20	21	41	1	1	2	37	29	66	26	20	46	4	2	6
Unknown	9	10	19	8	9	17	1	0	1	24	30	54	24	27	51	0	3	3
Subtotal	1,074	1,105	2,179	833	819	1,652	52	53	105	1,155	1,231	2,386	911	925	1,836	59	54	113
Foreign	14	16	30	12	12	24	0	0	0	17	16	33	14	13	27	0	0	0
Total	1,302	1,320	2,622	1,001	977	1,978	57	63	120	1,408	1,472	2,880	1,109	1,098	2,207	63	57	120

*Since 2002, students can select more than one race and / or ethnicity. **Those who did not choose 'Hispanic/Latino' or 'Non-Hispanic/Latino' are listed under 'Non-Hispanic/Latino'. Data Source: AAMC Data Warehouse: Applicant-Matriculant File, as of 1/16/2009.

The College of Medicine is committed to the principle of a diverse classroom. According to the AAMC, our program is in the top 25 percent of medical schools in the nation for ethnic and racial diversity. But diversity means much more and includes factors such as gender, various educational degrees from varied institutions, life experiences, rural, city, and disadvantaged backgrounds, and many more.

Applicants should clearly indicate their state of residency. The M.D. Program is state-supported and a vast majority of our matriculating class will be Florida residents. But, since the entering class of 2004, a growing number of non-Florida residents have matriculated into this program.

A Florida resident, for purposes of admission, lower tuition, and other university classification needs, is one whose parents or guardian (if the applicant is dependent) or the applicant (if independent) is a citizen of the U.S. or a PRA and has established legal residence and resided permanently in Florida for at least 12 months preceding registration at the university. The owning of property in Florida, while being physically located in another state does not qualify a person to claim Florida residence. In those instances where residency is in question, an applicant is requested to submit a Declaration of Domicile one year in advance of matriculation for tuition purposes. Please visit (http://www.registrar.usf.edu/Residency/Definitions.php) for additional residency requirement information.

Interview invitations for all applicants are at the discretion of the Admissions Committee. An invitation to interview means only that the initial evaluation is sufficient to warrant further consideration by the committee. An accepted applicant is given two weeks to reply to an admissions offer to the M.D. Program. That response must be a written statement of intent to attend with an original signature. If an accepted applicant is later offered a position by another medical program, the applicant is obligated to notify each program of their intent

to attend/withdraw as rapidly as possible. Any offer of acceptance is provisional pending the satisfactory completion of all requirements and conditions of admission. An acceptance offer may be canceled failing to meet requirements or failure to maintain high scholastic standards.

Enrichment Programs

Pre-medical Summer Enrichment Program (PSEP)

The PSEP is an intensive six-week full-time summer program for highly motivated students who are preparing for medical school. The program will help participants to enhance the science and communication skills needed for quality performance on the MCAT; explore test-taking strategies to enhance learning skills; provide exposure to medicine through clinical experiences; and offer medical school admissions information through interaction with medical school faculty, staff and students. The program is designed for undergraduates interested in medical school. To be eligible, students must have completed a minimum of 60 hours with an overall GPA no less than 3.0 prior to start of the program. Applicants whose overall GPA is less than 3.0 will not be considered. Students receive a $1,500 stipend for participation in the PSEP program. Stipends are paid out in two installments. Students participate in the following five areas:

1. *Academic Enhancement:* Biology, Chemistry and Physics: Participants will be provided the opportunity to review and enhance their comprehension of concepts in biology, general and organic chemistry, and physics.

Verbal Reasoning and Writing Skills: Participants will be provided the opportunity to enhance their reading and reading-inference skills as well as gain writing experience through personal essays and other assignments.

Test Preparation: Participants will take science-based pre- and post-half tests and simulated MCAT exams during the program.

2. *Test-Taking Strategies:* Participants will work closely with L.E.A.R.N. Program faculty in the areas of reading skills, test-taking skills, etc. Utilizing a proven model of metacognition and intentional learning, students utilize the results of such assessments to develop individualized plans to improve or enhance essential learning skills.

3. *Clinical Experience:* Participates will be paired with physicians in the local community and you will have the opportunity to develop an appreciation of the "real world of medicine" through weekly clinical experiences.

4. *Clinical Seminars:* Participants will take part in one hour per week of exposure to the "real world of medicine" through clinical topics such as health disparities, obesity, diabetes, heart disease and more.

5. *Workshop Series:* Participants will participate in one hour per week of workshops on admissions procedures, financial planning, study skills, test taking, time management, stress management and interviewing techniques. (http://health.usf.edu/medicine/osde/psep.html)

Pre-matriculation Program

Pre-matriculation is a four week program for entering first year medical students who may benefit from an early exposure to the rigorous medical curriculum.

The goals of the program are:

- Facilitate the adjustment of the medical student to the academic environment of medical school
- Facilitate academic success in the medical curriculum via assessment and application of the following skills:
    - Time management
    - Reading comprehension
    - Test taking strategies
    - Communication
    - Identifying learning issues
    - Identifying and formulating knowledge objectives
    - Researching new information

- Provide a "jump start" for students to the curriculum and educational process of the medical school
- Researching new information
- Identify potential at-risk students and provide a remedial educational program along with an introduction to basic medical services
- The pre-matriculation program has two essential components that are integrated and applied in a case-based, small group learning curriculum.
- Case-Based Learning – Each week a patient oriented case will be presented to the student small groups. Students will be required to identify research and share learning issues necessary to solve the case. The cases are designed to encompass information from all the basic science disciplines involved in the first two years of the medical school curriculum. At the conclusion of each case an exam will be given that reflects the style, format, and level of difficulty that can be anticipated in the first two academic years.
- Skill Assessment and Development – Each student will be evaluated for learning style, reading skills, test taking skills, etc. Based on this assessment, an individualized plan will be developed to improve and enhance these essential learning skills. The application and practice of these skills will be integrated with the Case-Based Learning Component. Additional practice and improvement will be provided through laboratory exercises.

This program may benefit students who identify themselves as first generation college student, English as a second language, economically disadvantaged, or as non-traditional students (second career, returned to school after an absence, non science major).

Interdisciplinary Medical Science Degree (IMS)
The Interdisciplinary Medical Science degree (IMS) is designed to provide qualified students with advanced training in the science basic to the practice of medicine. Students successfully completing the program will have a foundation that fosters opportunities in the private sector, teaching, or the pursuit of further advance degrees. A primary goal of this concentration is to provide promising medical school applicants an opportunity to develop the knowledge, skills, and attitudes that would enable them to have a career in the medical sciences. This concentration creates a unique opportunity for students interested in graduate work with a broad medical base. Students will take courses that, while not identical to the first year of medical school, will provide the same level of depth, breadth and intensity, allowing successful participants to demonstrate their readiness for the rigors of a medical school curriculum. Alternatively, appropriate selection of elective courses will allow any student who completes the program to tailor their educational experience to best suit their future plans and aspirations.

Eligibility Requirements
Candidates for the IMS degree are students who do not meet the University of South Florida, College of Medicine admissions requirements. Ideally, candidates will meet the following requirements: GPA: 3.0, MCAT: 22, completed one year of the following undergraduate coursework in general chemistry, organic chemistry, general biology, and general physics. Please note that GRE scores will not be accepted. You must take the MCAT

Student Financial Assistance
In addition to federal loan programs and National Medical Fellowships, the university has two special grant funds that are designated for minority students. These are the Delores A. Auzenne Fellowship and the University of South Florida College of Medicine Minority Tuition Scholarship.

Emory University School of Medicine

Dr. Robert Lee, Associate Dean and Director Multicultural Medical Student Affairs
Emory University School of Medicine
1648 Pierce Drive, Ste – P-396
Atlanta, GA 30322
404-727 0016; 404-727 0045 fax
robert.lee@emory.edu

Recruitment

College Students

The Associate Dean for Multicultural Medical Student Affairs visits eight to ten college campuses per year to meet with students and faculty to discuss careers in medicine, answer their questions, and encourage them to apply to Emory University School of Medicine.

We make use of the Medical Minority Applicant Registry (Med-MAR) to provide information to candidates who have taken the April Medical College Admission Test (MCAT). By writing to selected candidates, we encourage them to apply for the next entering class. Generally, 1,000 potential candidates are encouraged to apply, resulting in an applicant pool of students-of-color and from disadvantaged backgrounds totaling almost 750 per year. The Committee on Admissions is very supportive and active in the efforts to recruit these men and women.

High School Students

The Summer Science Academy has two levels. Students who will enroll in the ninth and tenth grades during their next academic year will be enrolled in The Lower Academy. Students who will enroll in the 11th and 12th grades during their next academic year will be enrolled in The Upper Academy. Our Mission Statement: To provide high school students from traditionally underrepresented minority backgrounds the opportunity to develop a better understanding and appreciation of science by exposing them to an educational environment that is conducive to learning, motivating, and challenging.

Our core beliefs are:

• Science is all around us and is a vital part of our lives.
• All students are able to learn sophisticated principles of science and should be encouraged to enroll in science courses in high school.
• Science knowledge is achievable for students from underrepresented minority backgrounds (African Americans, Hispanic, Native Americans, and Pacific Islanders).
• Students who are female are capable of and should be encouraged to enroll in science courses and pursue careers requiring a background in science and technology.
• With many other career options available, the number of African-American and Hispanic-American males in science related fields is dwindling. Male students from these backgrounds should be encouraged to pursue careers in science and technology.
• It is OK to be smart and be a high achiever, especially in the science, math, and technology areas.

The Summer Science Academy is a six-week program, comprised of sessions lasting two weeks each session, which introduces students to the areas of biology, anatomy, chemistry, diseases common to humans, and neural science. Courses are taught by medical students, residents and medical school faculty. Guest lecturers also teach periodically during the summer programs.

Emory University School of Medicine
Applicants, First-Time Applicants, Matriculants by Gender, Race and Ethnicity, 2007-2008

	2007 APP Women	2007 APP Men	2007 APP Total	2007 F-time APP Women	2007 F-time APP Men	2007 F-time APP Total	2007 MAT Women	2007 MAT Men	2007 MAT Total	2008 APP Women	2008 APP Men	2008 APP Total	2008 F-time APP Women	2008 F-time APP Men	2008 F-time APP Total	2008 MAT Women	2008 MAT Men	2008 MAT Total
Hispanic/Latino																		
Cuban	18	21	39	15	17	32	0	0	0	21	22	43	17	20	37	0	0	0
Mexican American	34	33	67	27	25	52	0	0	0	31	26	57	24	21	45	1	0	1
Puerto Rican	17	15	32	15	11	26	0	1	1	12	11	23	8	7	15	0	0	0
Other Hispanic	70	63	133	54	48	102	1	4	5	65	74	139	52	56	108	1	0	1
Multiple Hispanic/Latino*	8	3	11	7	1	8	0	1	1	13	5	18	11	4	15	0	0	0
Subtotal	147	135	282	118	102	220	1	6	7	142	138	280	112	108	220	2	0	2
Non-Hispanic/Latino**																		
Black	426	189	615	342	154	496	2	3	5	453	181	634	359	153	512	6	6	12
Native American/AK	4	2	6	3	1	4	0	0	0	2	3	5	2	3	5	0	0	0
Native Hawaiian/OPI	3	5	8	3	5	8	0	0	0	6	4	10	6	4	10	0	0	0
White	1,418	1,660	3,078	1,224	1,325	2,549	46	35	81	1,446	1,761	3,207	1,235	1,381	2,616	42	47	89
Asian	615	642	1,257	504	500	1,004	15	16	31	601	704	1,305	475	534	1,009	9	7	16
Other Race	1	4	5	1	1	2	0	0	0	1	3	4	1	2	3	0	0	0
Multiple Race*	90	61	151	77	46	123	1	1	2	83	63	146	63	50	113	0	1	1
Unknown	23	27	50	22	23	45	0	1	1	59	87	146	57	77	134	3	0	3
Subtotal	2,580	2,590	5,170	2,176	2,055	4,231	64	56	120	2,651	2,806	5,457	2,198	2,204	4,402	60	61	121
Foreign	139	145	284	112	103	215	1	2	3	171	147	318	144	107	251	4	1	5
Total	2,866	2,870	5,736	2,406	2,260	4,666	66	64	130	2,964	3,091	6,055	2,454	2,419	4,873	66	62	128

*Since 2002, students can select more than one race and / or ethnicity. **Those who did not choose 'Hispanic/Latino' or 'Non-Hispanic/Latino' are listed under 'Non-Hispanic/Latino'. Data Source: AAMC Data Warehouse: Applicant-Matriculant File, as of 1/16/2009.

Increased numbers of visitation to high school career days by the Associate Dean for Multicultural Medical Student Affairs, the Associate Director of the Multicultural Medical Student Affairs and members of the Student National Medical Association (SNMA) provide information about the programs and careers in the health sciences and increase the programs' visibility for these students.

Medical School Application Process

All candidates to Emory University School of Medicine must apply to through the American Medical College Application Service (AMCAS) and authorize this school to receive their application. Our AMCAS school code is #121. October 15th of each year is our AMCAS deadline, and December 1 of each year is the official deadline for the completion of our Supplemental Application. Candidates are encouraged to complete and submit the AMCAS and Emory Supplemental Applications well in advance of the announced deadline dates. The later one completes their application, the less likely they are to receive an interview, regardless of strength of their academic records.

The following factors are significant in the review of applications:

• Science and non-science grades and grade trends
• Scores on the Medical College Admission Test
• Extracurricular and leadership activities of the candidate
• Letters of recommendation by faculty, administrators, and mentors who have known the candidate; and
• Personal interview, if authorized, by the Committee on Admissions.

Our interview season begins in early October and concludes in the last week of February. The Committee makes no decision regarding interviews until ALL application documents have been submitted. If candidates take or re-take the August MCAT, a decision will be rendered when the scores arrive and all other supporting documentation is re-ceived. Applicants are reminded that the submission of an application, receipt of an invitation to apply, and/or an invitation to interview are not guarantees of being accepted at Emory University School of Medicine. We practice "rolling admissions" and announce decisions each month following the meeting of the Committee on Admissions.

The Office of Multicultural Medical Student Affairs sponsors the *Emory Revisited* Program beginning the third Wednesday of March each year. Successful candidates from underrepresented groups who are admitted by that time are invited to return for a "second look" at Emory. Hosted by members of the Emory SNMA Chapter, faculty, and administrators, this program allows face-to-face, one-on-one opportunities to meet members of the Emory family and other candidates who have been accepted and learn more about the school, the university, and the City of Atlanta. Some out-of-pocket expenses will be reimbursed to the participants.

Academic and Personal Support

We believe that all candidates admitted to Emory University School of Medicine are prepared and able to succeed, based on the review of academic credentials and personal interview. On the occasion where a student may encounter academic difficulty, faculty are available for one-on-one tutoring, extra personal and/or small-group "help sessions," and personal counseling. Personal counseling is available through the Office of Multicultural Medical Student Affairs, the Executive Associate Dean for Medical Education and Students Affairs, the students' Medical Society Mentors, as well as University Student Counseling and Health Services. As warranted, students can be seen in the Student Counseling Center of Emory University. It has been our experience that difficult personal situations may be manifested in academic performance. In the event a student becomes medically ill, the mandatory health insurance covers the medical needs, including hospitalization and/or Emory physicians and other professional faculty in the appropriate discipline.

Student Financial Assistance

Need-based financial aid is available to students to help pay for their medical education and related expenses. Grants and loans are available to help meet need. Accepted students must file the Free Application for Federal Student Financial Aid (FAFSA) (beginning January 1st) and the CSS Financial Aid Profile® (beginning October 1st). Early submission is encouraged!

There are two scholarships of note:

The Woodruff Scholarship—Five scholarships are awarded in the School of Medicine for students in the regular M.D. degree program.

The Dean's Scholarship—The number varies from year to year. Scholarships are awarded to students from diverse backgrounds (e.g., educational, financial, and geographical areas of the country).

We encourage students to borrow only the amount of money they need to avoid excessive debt. Students find that having a roommate helps to keep their debt as low as possible. Financial aid is administered centrally at Emory and financial aid advisers are available to assist students.

Medical College of Georgia School of Medicine

Wilma A. Sykes-Brown, Assistant Dean
Office of Educational Outreach and Partnerships
Medical College of Georgia School of Medicine
CB 1801, Research & Education Building
Augusta, GA 30912-1900
706-721-2522; 706-721-8203 fax
wsykes@mail.mcg.edu
http://www.mcg.edu/careers/specop/pipeline.htm

Recruitment

The Medical College of Georgia conducts an extensive recruitment program utilizing the team approach to assure that students benefit from a targeted recruitment strategy as well as multiple contact persons who may be able to assist them as they prepare for medical school. Faculty and staff in the Office of Educational Outreach and Partnerships, in the Office of Admissions in the School of Medicine, enrolled medical students, and Clinical Faculty, visit colleges throughout Georgia, especially colleges with a preponderance of un-

derrepresented students. Additionally, visits are made to out-of-state colleges that have large enrollments of Georgia residents who are underrepresented in the health professions.

Admissions

Applications to the first-year class of the Medical College of Georgia (MCG) are considered on the basis of the assessment of potential for meeting the health care needs of Georgia, the applicants' motivation and potential for serving as a physician, personal interviews, and academic ability and achievement as measured through college grades and scores on the Medical College Admissions Test (MCAT).

The Admissions Committee is composed of 25 voting members including 18 faculty, three medical students, one community member, one physician from the community, and the Associate Dean for Admissions. There is no application fee to apply for admission to the Medical College of Georgia. Application through the Early Decision Program is encouraged for Georgia residents. The MCG School of Medicine encourages qualified students

from groups underrepresented in medicine to apply.

Academic Support Programs

The Office of Educational Outreach and Partnerships sponsors academic enrichment programs designed to meet the special needs of underrepresented, non-traditional, and disadvantaged students at the pre-admission, pre-matriculation, and matriculation stages of the educational pipeline. Additionally, academic support services are available to all students enrolled in each of MCG's five colleges to enhance student retention and graduation from their specific programs of study.

The Office of Educational Outreach and Partnerships administers the following programs:

• *The Student Educational Enrichment Programs (SEEP)*, a seven-week summer program for high achieving pre-college and college students, designed to enrich their academic backgrounds and strengthen test-taking abilities in preparation for careers in the health professions.

Medical College of Georgia School of Medicine
Applicants, First-Time Applicants, Matriculants by Gender, Race and Ethnicity, 2007-2008

		2007								2008							
		APP			F-time APP			MAT		APP			F-time APP			MAT	
		Wo-men	Men	Total	Wo-men	Men	Total	Wo-men	Men	Total	Wo-men	Men	Total	Wo-men	Men	Total	Wo-men	Men	Total
Hispanic/Latino																		
Cuban		5	10	15	5	9	14	0	0	0	12	7	19	12	7	19	1	1	2
Mexican American		7	10	17	5	8	13	1	0	1	15	11	26	12	10	22	0	1	1
Puerto Rican		9	6	15	7	6	13	0	1	1	5	1	6	3	0	3	0	0	0
Other Hispanic		21	25	46	17	18	35	1	3	4	22	22	44	15	16	31	0	1	1
Multiple Hispanic/Latino*		4	2	6	2	1	3	0	1	1	2	3	5	1	2	3	0	0	0
Subtotal		46	53	99	36	42	78	2	5	7	56	44	100	43	35	78	1	3	4
Non-Hispanic/Latino**																		
Black		264	88	352	192	65	257	9	2	11	222	94	316	151	70	221	9	5	14
Native American/AK		2	1	3	1	1	2	0	0	0	1	2	3	0	1	1	0	0	0
Native Hawaiian/OPI		4	3	7	4	2	6	0	0	0	4	0	4	4	0	4	0	0	0
White		458	548	1,006	360	382	742	49	85	134	474	647	1,121	362	492	854	45	78	123
Asian		166	185	351	115	141	256	18	17	35	205	211	416	146	154	300	25	17	42
Other Race		1	1	2	1	0	1	0	0	0	0	1	1	0	0	0	0	0	0
Multiple Race*		27	16	43	19	9	28	0	1	1	24	21	45	17	18	35	1	2	3
Unknown		7	8	15	5	6	11	1	0	1	17	15	32	16	13	29	2	2	4
Subtotal		929	850	1,779	697	606	1,303	77	105	182	947	991	1,938	696	748	1,444	82	104	186
Foreign		35	37	72	29	27	56	1	0	1	28	36	64	19	24	43	0	0	0
Total		1,010	940	1,950	762	675	1,437	80	110	190	1,031	1,071	2,102	758	807	1,565	83	107	190

*Since 2002, students can select more than one race and / or ethnicity. **Those who did not choose 'Hispanic/Latino' or 'Non-Hispanic/Latino' are listed under 'Non-Hispanic/Latino'. Data Source: AAMC Data Warehouse: Applicant-Matriculant File, as of 1/16/2009.

- *The Supplemental Instruction Program (SIP),* a retention program for matriculating underrepresented, non-traditional, disadvantaged, and other students in need of academic assistance.
- *The Pre-matriculation Program,* a six-week summer program for students who have been accepted into our Schools of Medicine, Dentistry and Graduate Studies. The program is designed to facilitate the academic adjustment of underrepresented, non-traditional, and disadvantaged students and to increase retention of students in the targeted groups. The program is held the summer immediately prior to the beginning of students' first fall semester.

Student Financial Assistance

The Medical College of Georgia's Office of Student Financial Aid assists students in financial planning for meeting educational expenses. Approximately 80 percent of all medical students receive some form of financial aid. Financial assistance includes loans, scholarships, and part-time employment. Non-federal scholarships administered by the Medical College of Georgia are awarded by the School of Medicine Scholarship Committee. Of note, applicants are encouraged to apply for the Stoney Diversity Scholarship which can be accessed at the following Web site addresses: *(http://www.mcg.edu/careers/specop/Sch olarshipEligibilityCriteria.pdf).* Financial aid application materials are distributed electronically via the internet at (www.mcg.edu/students/finaid). Students are encouraged to apply for financial aid as soon as possible after January 1 and to complete the process by March 31. For more information, contact the Office of Student Financial Aid, Medical College of Georgia, AA-2013, Augusta, GA 30912-7320; 706-721-4901.

Educational Partnerships

The Medical College of Georgia partners with local high schools and colleges throughout Georgia, with the statewide Area Health Education Centers (AHECs), and with non-Georgia colleges with large numbers of Georgia residents, to assure that underrepresented, non-traditional, and disadvantaged students have access to health career opportunities. The Office of Educational Outreach and Partnerships maintains long-standing collaborations with the following colleges: Albany State University, Augusta State University, Clark Atlanta University, Fort Valley State University, Georgia College and State University, Georgia Southern University, Hampton University, Kennesaw State University, Morehouse College, Paine College, Savannah State University, State University of West Georgia, University of Georgia, and Xavier University. The Assistant Dean, Office of Educational Outreach and Partnerships, serves as Faculty Advisor for MCG student organizations that include the Student National Medical Association and the Junior Medical League.

(http://www.mcg.edu/students/finaid/ documents/MCGStoneyDiversity ScholarshipEligibilityCriteria.pdf)

Other Pertinent Information

The Medical College of Georgia is the health science university of the state of Georgia. It is strategically located in Augusta, the second largest city in the state, and is 2.5 hours from Atlanta, 2 hours from Savannah, 2.5 hours from Charleston, and 55 minutes from Columbia, South Carolina.

Mercer University School of Medicine

Dr. Maurice Clifton, MSEd, Associate Dean for Admissions and Student Affairs
Mercer University School of Medicine
1550 College Street
Macon, GA 31207
478-301-2542; 478-301-2547 fax
admission@mercer.med.edu
http://medicine.mercer.edu

Recruitment

The mission of the Mercer University School of Medicine (MUSM) is to educate physicians and health professionals to meet the primary care and health care needs of rural and medically underserved areas of Georgia. Although we are a private institution, we only accept residents of the state of Georgia. We have a unique problem-based medical education program that provides early patient care experiences. Such an academic environment fosters the early development of clinical problem-solving skills and instills in each student an awareness of the place of the basic medical sciences in medical practice. The basic science learning is achieved in a small-group setting of approximately

eight students. The small class size also makes possible a close and collegial student/faculty relationship, individualized attention, and supportive atmosphere that enables every student to realize their potential for learning.

The Admissions Counselor, Dean for Admission and Student Affairs, and current students visit Georgia universities and colleges, including historically black universities such as, Spelman College, Clark Atlanta University, Fort Valley State University and Savannah State University. These visits are designed to be a resource for pre-medical advisors, potential applicants, and pre-medical minority organization group members to identify the needs of the students interested in a career in medicine. Recruiting efforts also consist of participation in conferences and graduate fairs. In addition, applicants are encouraged to schedule an appointment with the Admission Counselor for advisement and tours. MUSM provides "a day in the life of a MUSM medical student" experiences for groups of potential applicants. These programs include work with standardized patients, a mock admissions committee meeting, practice interviewing, and a sample of problem-based learning.

Admissions

The Admissions Committee is committed to admitting qualified individuals from groups underrepresented in medicine. The committee defines a diverse student body as an inclusive collection of individuals and groups who bring varied human characteristics, backgrounds, interests and points of view to enrich the medical school community and the practice of medicine. These characteristics are not limited to, but include rural background, socioeconomic status, culture, race, ethnicity, sexual orientation, and life or work experiences. MUSM uses a holistic method of admissions, taking numerous components of an applicant's record into account including racial, ethnic, socioeconomic backgrounds and demographic factors such as being from a rural area.

- The Admissions Committee seeks candidates with experience relative to health care for Georgia's medically underserved, community service and who demonstrate leadership skills.
- The requirements, which include (please see our Web site for full details):

  The pre-medical requirements are one-year laboratory courses in gen-

Mercer University School of Medicine
Applicants, First-Time Applicants, Matriculants by Gender, Race and Ethnicity, 2007-2008

	2007									2008								
	APP			F-time APP			MAT			APP			F-time APP			MAT		
	Wo-men	Men	Total	Wo-men	Men	Total	Wo-men	Men	Total	Wo-men	Men	Total	Wo-men	Men	Total	Wo-men	Men	Total
Hispanic/Latino																		
Cuban	1	1	2	0	1	1	0	0	0	0	2	2	0	2	2	0	0	0
Mexican American	3	2	5	2	2	4	0	0	0	8	4	12	6	3	9	0	0	0
Puerto Rican	5	1	6	4	1	5	0	0	0	2	0	2	2	0	2	0	0	0
Other Hispanic	5	10	15	4	6	10	1	0	1	7	7	14	4	4	8	0	1	1
Multiple Hispanic/Latino*	1	0	1	0	0	0	0	0	0	0	0	0	0	0	0	0	0	0
Subtotal	15	14	29	10	10	20	1	0	1	17	13	30	12	9	21	0	1	1
Non-Hispanic/Latino**																		
Black	105	42	147	76	27	103	1	0	1	95	45	140	60	39	99	1	0	1
White	151	220	371	112	144	256	20	32	52	187	246	433	135	173	308	37	40	77
Asian	71	71	142	47	52	99	3	4	7	74	71	145	49	47	96	5	4	9
Other Race	0	1	1	0	0	0	0	0	0	0	1	1	0	0	0	0	0	0
Multiple Race*	9	5	14	6	1	7	0	1	1	6	8	14	4	7	11	1	0	1
Unknown	1	4	5	1	3	4	0	0	0	5	3	8	4	3	7	0	1	1
Subtotal	337	343	680	242	227	469	24	37	61	367	374	741	252	269	521	44	45	89
Foreign	4	0	4	3	0	3	1	0	1	0	2	2	0	1	1	0	0	0
Total	356	357	713	255	237	492	26	37	63	384	389	773	264	279	543	44	46	90

*Since 2002, students can select more than one race and / or ethnicity. **Those who did not choose 'Hispanic/Latino' or 'Non-Hispanic/Latino' are listed under 'Non-Hispanic/Latino'. Data Source: AAMC Data Warehouse: Applicant-Matriculant File, as of 1/16/2009.

eral biology, general or inorganic chemistry, organic or an organic/biochemistry sequence, and general physics
Residency in the state of Georgia
The MCAT
- Application process:
MUSM participates in the American Medical College Application Service (AMCAS) and reviews only those applications initiated through that service. Applications to MUSM should be sent directly to AMCAS, Section for Student Services. The AMCAS-E application may be obtained at the AMCAS Web site on the internet at *(http://www.aamc.org)*. Mercer's AMCAS application deadlines are August 1st for early decision application and November 1st for regular pool application. The Mercer Medical School Code Number is GA-832.

Academic Support Programs

The Dean of Student Affairs routinely meets with individuals who are concerned with their academic progress. The rigorous medical curriculum is often more than a student expects, and the problem-based format is new to all. Often, students need new test-taking strategies, study strategies, and better time management than they used in college. For many students it may be the first time they experience an academic failure. Each student is assigned to an academic advisor who helps them navigate the curriculum. Students who fall into academic difficulty have a series of steps that include individual planning in order to achieve success. There are both counseling and referral services available.

Enrichment Programs

There is a wide variety of ongoing community service programs managed by the students at MUSM. In addition, MUSM's students run the Macon Volunteer Clinic on Saturdays. The Macon Volunteer Clinic is run completely by donations and physicians who volunteer their time to serve the working uninsured. Every summer MUSM's

first-year students have the opportunity to participate in a summer mission trip. Over the past three years MUSM's students have traveled to Honduras and Mexico to provide medical care to the needy in addition to gaining clinical experience. For more information on MUSM's enrichment programs please see our Web site or email *admissions@med.mercer.edu.*

Educational Partnerships

Mercer University School of Medicine has multiple programs in collaboration with community service organizations, high schools, colleges, and the Area Health Education Centers (AHECs). MUSM is devoted to enabling applicants from diverse backgrounds and the opportunity to enter the health sciences. For more information on specific programs please see our website or email *admissions@med.mercer.edu.*

Student Financial Assistance

- 93 percent of MUSM's students receive some form of financial aid.
- A non-refundable processing fee of $50 is required with submission of the Online Supplemental Application. If a student has received a waiver of the AMCAS application fee, the student is eligible for a waiver of the $50 fee.
- Funds available for medical students:
    Loans
    Scholarships
- A wide variety of outside sources of funding is available to medical students. We encourage students to take some time to research opportunities for alternate funding.
- Financial application material:
    It is the responsibility of the Office of Student Financial Planning to assure that all students have easy access to information concerning every aspect of financial aid programs available, including updates in federal regulations that relate to these programs and financial planning and debt management techniques. The staff fulfills this responsibility using a variety of publications and workshops.

- For more information: *(http://medicine.mercer.edu/Admissions/admissions_financial)*

Other Pertinent Information

Mercer University School of Medicine has two campuses. The original location is on the main campus of Mercer University in Macon, Georgia and is affiliated with the Medical Center of Central Georgia. The site in Savannah, Georgia was expanded to a four-year campus at Memorial University Medical Center in Savannah. There is a centralized application process, curriculum, and evaluation process used across the two campuses. For the 2009 year, MUSM is accepting 90 students into the entering class, 60 of those students in Macon and the other 30 in Savannah.

Morehouse School of Medicine

Dr. Ngozi Anachebe, Assistant Dean for Admissions and Student Affairs
Morehouse School of Medicine
720 Westview Drive, S.W.
Atlanta, GA 30310-1495
404-752-1651; 404-752-1824 fax
nanachebe@msm.edu
http://www.msm.edu/Admissions

Recruitment

Recruitment is conducted by the Office of Admissions and Student Affairs. The admissions officer and other student affairs staff members, administrators, faculty, and students participate in the recruitment process.

The recruitment efforts—to identify, inform, and encourage prospective minority and disadvantaged candidates—are multifaceted. Approaches designed to accomplish this include: recruitment visits at state and private colleges and universities; seminars and conferences within the Atlanta University Center; contacts made with pre-medical advisors and counselors; and participation in many local, state, and national conferences and career fairs. Arrangements

can be made to tour Morehouse School of Medicine on an individual or group basis through the Office of Admissions.

Admission

The primary mission of Morehouse School of Medicine is to admit and educate students who will become primary care physicians for medically underserved rural areas and inner cities, including low-income and minority communities. The Admissions Committee seeks candidates who possess the academic qualifications judged necessary for the successful study and practice of medicine. Equally important, but less tangible, are personal factors such as character, maturity, integrity, perseverance, and motivation.

Because of the urgent need for physicians in the state of Georgia, preferential consideration will be given to qualified residents of Georgia. However, Morehouse School of Medicine welcomes applications from well qualified out-of-state students.

Applicants must apply through the American Medical College Application Service (AMCAS) and request that their application, along with Medical College

Admission Test scores, be forwarded to Morehouse School of Medicine. The school's code number is GA825. Each application received from AMCAS is reviewed individually. Following the initial screening, applicants granted further considerations are requested to submit supplementary materials. Only completed applications are then evaluated for interview. A completed application consists of an AMCAS application form, all supplementary materials, and the $50 application fee. Applications not completed by given deadlines are withdrawn from consideration.

Academic Support Programs

Complete advisement and retention activities are offered to all medical school matriculants. Upon matriculation, each student is assigned to a faculty advisor. Available to all students are a wide range of academic support services such as student tutors, study-skills and test-taking strategies, the Kaplan Board preparation program, and personal counseling from Counseling Services. Retention activities are designed to meet the needs of the individual student and may include a flexible curriculum schedule.

Morehouse School of Medicine
Applicants, First-Time Applicants, Matriculants by Gender, Race and Ethnicity, 2007-2008

	2007									2008								
	APP			F-time APP			MAT			APP			F-time APP			MAT		
	Wo-men	Men	Total	Wo-men	Men	Total	Wo-men	Men	Total	Wo-men	Men	Total	Wo-men	Men	Total	Wo-men	Men	Total
Hispanic/Latino																		
Cuban	7	18	25	5	13	18	0	0	0	15	12	27	14	9	23	0	0	0
Mexican American	36	31	67	28	20	48	0	0	0	36	25	61	30	20	50	0	0	0
Puerto Rican	17	10	27	13	7	20	1	0	1	11	14	25	8	7	15	0	0	0
Other Hispanic	56	46	102	37	28	65	0	0	0	72	58	130	51	38	89	0	0	0
Multiple Hispanic/Latino*	6	8	14	3	4	7	0	0	0	7	7	14	5	3	8	0	0	0
Subtotal	122	113	235	86	72	158	1	0	1	141	116	257	108	77	185	0	0	0
Non-Hispanic/Latino**																		
Black	959	425	1,384	655	305	960	26	13	39	964	438	1,402	648	322	970	25	17	42
Native American/AK	1	4	5	1	3	4	0	0	0	6	1	7	5	1	6	0	0	0
Native Hawaiian/OPI	8	3	11	6	2	8	0	0	0	5	5	10	2	3	5	0	0	0
White	349	429	778	258	294	552	1	2	3	386	462	848	267	310	577	1	2	3
Asian	456	526	982	329	364	693	3	5	8	510	481	991	364	311	675	8	3	11
Other Race	4	3	7	2	0	2	0	0	0	0	6	6	0	3	3	0	0	0
Multiple Race*	50	41	91	34	28	62	0	1	1	46	40	86	35	26	61	0	0	0
Unknown	8	13	21	7	9	16	0	0	0	20	23	43	16	19	35	0	0	0
Subtotal	1,835	1,444	3,279	1,292	1,005	2,297	30	21	51	1,937	1,456	3,393	1,337	995	2,332	34	22	56
Foreign	58	51	109	51	40	91	0	0	0	52	50	102	43	36	79	0	0	0
Total	2,015	1,608	3,623	1,429	1,117	2,546	31	21	52	2,130	1,622	3,752	1,488	1,108	2,596	34	22	56

Note: In 2008, one applicant, who declined to report gender, was not included here.

*Since 2002, students can select more than one race and / or ethnicity. **Those who did not choose 'Hispanic/Latino' or 'Non-Hispanic/Latino' are listed under 'Non-Hispanic/Latino'. Data Source: AAMC Data Warehouse: Applicant-Matriculant File, as of 1/16/2009.

Enrichment Programs

Summer Pre-matriculation Program: The Morehouse School of Medicine offers a five-week summer pre-matriculation program for rising college seniors and post-baccalaureate students. This program includes courses in human morphology, biochemistry, epidemiology/ bio-statistics, test taking and study skills, and time management. This program is identical to the curriculum of the first-year students and begins approximately the first week of July. The 11-month curriculum for first-year students also begins at this time.

Student Financial Assistance

A non-refundable processing fee of $50 is required with submission of the On-line Supplemental Application. If an applicant has received a waiver of the AMCAS application fee, that applicant is eligible for a waiver of the $50 fee. The school does not have funds available to help with interview trips. Morehouse uses a needs-analysis system to determine students' eligibility for financial aid. The demonstration of need is the key factor in all financial aid awards. The School of Medicine's scholarships are awarded to qualified applicants on the basis of established criteria and in accordance with the stipulation of the donors.

Educational Partnerships

Below are existing programs for elementary, middle, and high school students:

Benjamin Carson Science Academy Partnerships: Morehouse School of Medicine and Metro Atlanta schools.

The Benjamin Carson Science Academy consists of a summer science camp and a Saturday science component. It provides an enrichment program for elementary and middle school students to enhance their knowledge of science, mathematics, and health careers. The students are involved in hands-on interactive activities that are designed to challenge them while making the learning of science fun. The students also have an opportunity to explore health careers, participate in educational field trips, and participate in

recreational activities. These recreational activities include chess, martial arts, and dance. Students are recruited for the program after completion of the third grade and continue until they complete the eighth grade.

Medical Post Explorers Program Partnerships: Morehouse School of Medicine, Boy Scouts of America, and Metro Atlanta Public School districts.

The Medical Post Explorers *(MedPost)* Program was established at Morehouse School of Medicine in conjunction with the Boy Scouts of America in 1991. The program was designed to introduce and encourage high school students to pursue a college education in the sciences that will ultimately lead to a career in the medical, biomedical science, allied health, or technologies fields. Current Morehouse School of Medicine medical students and *MedPost* alumni volunteer their time to assist MedPost students during the 'hands-on science' laboratory experiments; they also serve as tutors, mentors, and positive role models for the participants.

Vivien Thomas High School Research Program Partnerships: Morehouse School of Medicine and Metro Atlanta Public School districts.

This program is for high school students and was established in 2001 to provide experiences in the research laboratories at the Morehouse School of Medicine. The students conduct research under the direction of a medical school faculty member and learn the content, process, and methodology involved in inquiry science. They serve as apprentices in biomedical research laboratories and conduct scientific research in conjunction with real research being investigated by Morehouse School of Medicine faculty, research professors, and laboratory technicians. At the end of this summer experience the students present their research findings to the faculty and staff at Morehouse School of Medicine Priority is given to rising ninth and tenth grade students who have participated in the Benjamin Carson Science

Academy or the *MedPost* Program.

Existing Programs for College Undergraduates
SNMA/MAPS Mentoring Program Partners: Morehouse School of Medicine, Atlanta University Center Schools, Georgia State, and University of Georgia.
Location: Morehouse School of Medicine.
Participants: Undergraduate students of Atlanta University Center Schools, Georgia State, and University of Georgia.

The SNMA/MAPS Mentoring Program is conducted by Morehouse School of Medicine medical students who are members of the Student National Medical Association (SNMA) and the Minority Association of Pre-Medical Students (MAPS). They serve as mentors for undergraduate students. Students in the Morehouse School of Medicine college cohort are enrolled in this program.

Public Health Fellowship Program for Minority Students
The Public Health Fellowship Program for Minority Students is a summer program that provides rising college seniors or recent graduates a hands-on experience in public health. The program includes opportunities in epidemiological or community intervention research under the supervision of a mentor. One example of research is surveying mothers of pre-school children in public health clinics regarding risk factors for lead poisoning.

Other Pertinent Information

Morehouse School of Medicine, as a two-year basic medical science institution, admitted its charter class in 1978. In 1985 the school received full accreditation by the Liaison Committee on Medical Education (LCME) and awarded its first M.D. degrees on May 17, 1985.

Students are required to pass the United States Medical Licensing Examination (USMLE) Step 1 for promotion into the clinical phase of the curriculum. Passage of the USMLE Step 2 Clinical Knowledge and Clinical Skills examinations is required to receive the M.D. degree.

Morehouse School of Medicine also offers academic programs leading to the Ph.D. in the Biomedical Sciences, Master of Science in the Biomedical Sciences, Master of Science in Clinical Research, and the Master of Public Health Degrees. For more information, contact the admissions office at 404-752-1650.

University of Hawai'i at Mānoa, John A. Burns School of Medicine

Dr. Mary Ann Antonelli, Director, Office of Student Affairs, Minority Affair Officer
University of Hawai'i at Mānoa
John A. Burns School of Medicine
651 Ilalo Street
Honolulu, HI 96813
808-692-1000; 808-692-1251 fax
mantonel@hawaii.edu

Recruitment

Significant recruitment efforts at the University of Hawai'i at Mānoa John A. Burns School of Medicine are directed towards increasing the number of individuals from educationally, socially, or economically disadvantaged backgrounds who have demonstrated a commitment to serve areas of need in Hawaii and the Pacific. Priority for admission is given to applicants with strong ties to the State of Hawaii and the Pacific.

An extensive network has been established with key officials and advisors in local public and private schools, scholarship officers, local legislators, mass media, and college students studying in the United States. Recruitment is conducted by the faculty and staff alumni and students who serve as role models and help to encourage and motivate the men and women of Hawaii to pursue health careers. Students have run a "Medical Student Mentoring Program" to help students in local colleges learn about application and preparation for medical school. Many students return informally to their intermediate and high schools to encourage health careers for current students. Mechanisms are in place to encourage health careers on all Hawaiian Islands.

Admissions

Applicants are screened by an Admissions Committee composed of faculty and medical practitioners. All applicants are considered without discrimination on the basis of age, sex, race, creed, national origin, or handicap. Standards are high, and the criteria are both objective and subjective. Judgments are made on an individual basis, the intent being to select the candidates deemed most likely to become humanistic physicians. Important in the selection process is an evaluation of what the potential student might contribute to the welfare of the people of Hawaii and the Pacific. Preference is given to the residents of Hawaii. For further information see our Web site: *(http://jabsom.hawaii.edu)*.

Academic Support Programs

In medical school, all first-year students are assigned faculty advisors. All students are offered assistance in study skills, test-taking skills, speaking and writing skills. Imi Hoola, the post-baccalaureate program, continues to offer enrichment to students who have entered the medical curriculum from that program. All sudents are screened for learning differences and are assessed for learning styles in order to offer opportunities for enhanced enrichment services when requested or suggested. The progress of all students is reviewed regularly and help is offered as needed, either informally or formally as requested by the Evaluation, Remediation and Review Committee. Enrichment sessions are included as part of the curriculum in transitioning students problem-based learning paradigm. Curriculum may be decelerated for individuals with academic or personal need, but there is no formal decelerated curricular track.

University of Hawaii, John A. Burns School of Medicine
Applicants, First-Time Applicants, Matriculants by Gender, Race and Ethnicity, 2007-2008

	2007 APP Women	Men	Total	F-time APP Women	Men	Total	MAT Women	Men	Total	2008 APP Women	Men	Total	F-time APP Women	Men	Total	MAT Women	Men	Total
Hispanic/Latino																		
Cuban	2	5	7	2	5	7	0	0	0	4	3	7	3	2	5	0	0	0
Mexican American	22	19	41	19	17	36	0	0	0	28	18	46	24	13	37	0	0	0
Puerto Rican	5	4	9	3	2	5	0	0	0	4	4	8	4	1	5	0	0	0
Other Hispanic	26	26	52	19	18	37	0	0	0	23	30	53	18	17	35	0	0	0
Multiple Hispanic/Latino*	5	3	8	3	1	4	0	0	0	6	3	9	6	2	8	0	0	0
Subtotal	60	57	117	46	43	89	0	0	0	65	58	123	55	35	90	0	0	0
Non-Hispanic/Latino*																		
Black	16	15	31	12	12	24	0	0	0	33	18	51	30	12	42	0	0	0
Native American/AK	5	0	5	4	0	4	0	0	0	2	2	4	2	2	4	0	0	0
Native Hawaiian/OPI	15	12	27	12	9	21	2	2	4	26	12	38	15	11	26	3	0	3
White	338	526	864	267	392	659	5	3	8	333	487	820	249	361	610	4	5	9
Asian	287	327	614	220	235	455	19	12	31	298	295	593	228	198	426	19	16	35
Other Race	0	3	3	0	2	2	0	0	0	1	3	4	1	3	4	0	0	0
Multiple Race*	58	45	103	43	27	70	10	7	17	56	44	100	44	30	74	6	4	10
Unknown	10	14	24	10	11	21	0	0	0	12	38	50	10	34	44	1	2	3
Subtotal	729	942	1,671	568	688	1,256	36	24	60	761	899	1,660	579	651	1,230	33	27	60
Foreign	46	67	113	38	51	89	1	1	2	45	67	112	31	51	82	1	1	2
Total	835	1,066	1,901	652	782	1,434	37	25	62	871	1,024	1,895	665	737	1,402	34	28	62

*Since 2002, students can select more than one race and / or ethnicity. **Those who did not choose 'Hispanic/Latino' or 'Non-Hispanic/Latino' are listed under 'Non-Hispanic/Latino'. Data Source: AAMC Data Warehouse: Applicant-Matriculant File, as of 1/16/2009.

Enrichment Programs

The Imi Hoʻola Post-Baccalaureate Program

The University of Hawaiʻi at Mānoa John A. Burns School of Medicine conducts a post-baccalaureate program designed to provide medical educational opportunities for individuals from disadvantaged backgrounds who are deemed capable of succeeding in medical school. This program prepares students for the academic rigors of medical school and provides individual counseling, tutoring, and support. Each year, up to ten students are selected to participate in the 12-month program. Upon successful completion, they will matriculate into the first-year class at the John A. Burns School of Medicine.

The Native Hawaiian Center of Excellence (NHCOE)

NHCOE is one of 37 Centers of Excellence in the U.S. funded by the Division of Health Professions Diversity, Bureau of Health Professionals, Health Resources Services Administration, Department of Health and Human Services. The mission of the center is to improve the health and wellness of Native Hawaiians through research, leadership training, faculty and curriculum development, cultural competency, information resources, and networking. Programs and activities include:

- Continuing education focusing on Native Hawaiian health and cultural competency
- Fellowship and Faculty Training Program
- Oral History Project
- Secondary School Recruitment Program
- Rural Placement Services
- Student Retention Program
- Native Hawaiian Research Elective
- Historic Medical Documents Reprint Series

- Native Hawaiian Health Database Resource

Administratively, the Imi Hoʻola Program and Center are under the Department of Native Hawaiian Health, interim chair Dr. Kalani Brady.

Student Financial Assistance

Financial status is not a factor in considering applicants for acceptance. AMCAS application fees are waived for those qualifying for fee waiver. Efforts are made to assist students in obtaining loans and scholarships whenever possible. Students are encouraged to speak with a financial aid counselor during the application process, and throughout their time at JASOM. Students in financial need are eligible for assistance from funds administered by the University of Hawaiʻi's Financial Aid Office and scholarships, grants, and awards available through the University of Hawaii Foundation. Organizations and governments outside the university and the state also offer assistance, especially to students of Hawaiian, Samoan, Micronesian, and Filipino ancestry, and students are alerted to apply for any and all opportunities. There are both need-based and merit-based grants and scholarships from various sources. Additionally, long-term and emergency short term loans with no interest are available.

Other Pertinent Information

- The John A. Burns School of Medicine (JABSOM) is one of the most ethnically diverse medical schools in the United States, reflecting the multiethnic population of the State of Hawaii and the Pacific Rim.
- The principal mode of instruction at JABSOM is problem-based learning (PBL). This innovative method of instruction is well suited to the learning styles of many students from underrepresented groups.
- Students have formed Special Interest Groups for Indigenous Medical Students, Philippino Students, LGBT students, and Women in Medicine, among many others.
- All first-year students spend one half

day per week in a variety of community health settings or projects, ranging from health care of the homeless to research in health care delivery to Native Hawaiians, to creating and executing health curricula in local public high schools.

- Students may be selected for our Longitudinal Clerkship Program, matching students to rural and/or underserved communities on Oahu and other Hawaiian Islands

Chicago Medical School at Rosalind Franklin University of Medicine and Science

Dr. Timothy R. Hansen, Vice President for Academic Affairs
Rosalind Franklin University of Medicine and Science
3333 Green Bay Road,
North Chicago, IL 60064
847-578-8734; 847-775-6537 fax
tim.hansen@rosalindfranklin.edu
www.rosalindfranklin.edu

Recruitment

Recruitment is conducted primarily through field visitations and visits to local universities with large minority enrollments. Groups of students from these universities are invited to visit the medical school campus for group discussions and individual conferences with the Admissions Office staff and the Minority Affairs Officer. Minority students enrolled at the medical school are very much involved in this process. Administrative persons taking part in these programs are the Assistant Dean of Educational Affairs and the Director of Admissions. Considerable contact is maintained between these officials and many of the special minority programs offered both within the university and by other schools.

Admissions

A separate committee for minority applicants is not utilized. All applicants are processed in the same manner. The Admissions Office and the Office of Educational Affairs both respond to admission information requests from minority applicants. Additionally, efforts are made to facilitate contact between minority applicants and interviewees with minority students of the medical school by direct introduction during visits to the university, exchange of phone numbers, or letters.

Academic Support Programs

Academic skills programs are available (optional) to all students early in their first term. Academic-skills counseling, tutoring, personal counseling, and time management information are available to all students. These services are presented through academic departments and several Chicago Medical School offices, including Educational Affairs and Student Affairs, and the University Division of Student Development. Students who encounter academic problems are counseled by the Senior Associate Dean for Student Affairs and referred to the appropriate university office for assistance. Modifications to the medical school program, which may or may not require an extended period of medical study, can be designed.

Enrichment Programs

Pre-matriculation Program
Rosalind Franklin University, in collaboration with the Chicago Area Health and Medical Careers Program (CAHMCP), offers a Pre-matriculation Program for minority students working in the CAHMCP program. Students recommended by CAHMCP and selected by Rosalind Franklin University of Medicine and Science for this program are enrolled in selected courses with first-year medical students and are given access to all the support services of the university. Demonstration of academic excellence in this curriculum is seen as a strong indicator of success by the Chicago Medical School (CMS) Admissions Committee.

Student Financial Assistance

Low interest living expense loans are available to students who have minimal personal and family resources and/or,

Chicago Medical School at Rosalind Franklin University of Medicine & Science
Applicants, First-Time Applicants, Matriculants by Gender, Race and Ethnicity, 2007-2008

	2007									2008								
	APP			F-time APP			MAT			APP			F-time APP			MAT		
	Women	Men	Total	Women	Men	Total	Women	Men	Total	Women	Men	Total	Women	Men	Total	Women	Men	Total
Hispanic/Latino																		
Cuban	27	22	49	20	15	35	0	0	0	21	26	47	16	24	40	0	0	0
Mexican American	96	86	182	76	67	143	0	0	0	90	101	191	74	77	151	1	0	1
Puerto Rican	22	9	31	15	6	21	0	0	0	23	17	40	20	13	33	0	0	0
Other Hispanic	96	90	186	68	60	128	1	0	1	118	98	216	91	63	154	0	1	1
Multiple Hispanic/Latino*	13	11	24	6	6	12	0	1	1	19	11	30	14	3	17	1	0	1
Subtotal	254	218	472	185	154	339	1	1	2	271	253	524	215	180	395	2	1	3
Non-Hispanic/Latino**																		
Black	243	137	380	163	105	268	6	4	10	257	128	385	157	99	256	10	1	11
Native American/AK	5	10	15	4	9	13	0	0	0	5	8	13	4	5	9	0	0	0
Native Hawaiian/OPI	26	15	41	17	10	27	0	0	0	23	17	40	14	10	24	0	0	0
White	2,379	2,511	4,890	1,780	1,748	3,528	49	49	98	2,347	2,831	5,178	1,661	1,887	3,548	44	53	97
Asian	1,439	1,583	3,022	1,023	1,079	2,102	24	38	62	1,507	1,532	3,039	1,039	965	2,004	25	32	57
Other Race	4	5	9	1	1	2	0	0	0	4	11	15	4	8	12	0	0	0
Multiple Race*	126	120	246	85	87	172	1	0	1	120	139	259	82	91	173	3	2	5
Unknown	31	38	69	26	31	57	0	0	0	88	126	214	79	108	187	3	2	5
Subtotal	4,253	4,419	8,672	3,099	3,070	6,169	80	91	171	4,351	4,792	9,143	3,040	3,173	6,213	85	90	175
Foreign	356	335	691	288	244	532	9	8	17	356	365	721	270	269	539	5	4	9
Total	4,863	4,972	9,835	3,572	3,468	7,040	90	100	190	4,978	5,410	10,388	3,525	3,622	7,147	92	95	187

*Since 2002, students can select more than one race and / or ethnicity. **Those who did not choose 'Hispanic/Latino' or 'Non-Hispanic/Latino' are listed under 'Non-Hispanic/Latino'. Data Source: AAMC Data Warehouse: Applicant-Matriculant File, as of 1/16/2009.

because of academic status, do not have access to state and federal financial aid programs. In addition, disadvantaged students are given consideration for deferral of tuition payments for a limited period. All students are encouraged to discuss their needs with the Financial Aid Office, in advance of matriculation, to obtain a realistic view of their needs and the availability of funds.

Educational Partnerships

Chicago Area Health and Medical Careers Program (CAHMCP). Rosalind Franklin University is an active participant in the CMS and CAHMCP partnership, which presents the Pre-matriculation Program noted above.

Loyola University of Chicago Stritch School of Medicine

Mr. Adrian Jones, Assistant Dean for Admissions and Recruitment
Loyola University of Chicago Stritch School of Medicine
Office of Admissions
Bldg. 120, Room 200
2160 South First Avenue
Maywood, IL 60153
708-216-3229; 708-216-9160 fax
Ssom-admissions@lumc.edu
www.meddean.luc.edu/admissions

Recruitment

Loyola University of Chicago Stritch School of Medicine welcomes applications from students with diverse backgrounds, including those who are economically disadvantaged or belong to a group that is underrepresented in medicine. Loyola's efforts to recruit and encourage minority and disadvantaged students to pursue scientific and health-related careers include participation in community outreach programs and promotion of reciprocal campus visitation programs. Faculty, medical students, and administration all contribute to the success of Loyola's recruitment efforts.

Admissions

Applicants to the Stritch School of Medicine demonstrate academic competence and the potential to satisfactorily complete Stritch's four-year interdisciplinary curriculum. Loyola's Committee on Admissions, composed of basic and clinical science faculty, administrators, and students, reviews all applications. In the evaluation process, committee members look not only at an applicant's academic ability, but also at his/her ability to solve problems, handle responsibility, and work effectively with others. Ideal candidates for admission to the Stritch School of Medicine demonstrate leadership, involvement in community service, and the ability to work with a diverse patient population.

Academic Support Programs

The Stritch School of Medicine's Office of Student Affairs supports students in their studies through academic counseling and referral to a network of faculty and other resources. To help students adjust to the rigor of the curriculum, the Stritch Teaching and Learning Center sponsors workshops and offers materials on topics such as effective study strategies, problem-solving techniques,

memorization, time management, test taking, and the use of computer applications for learning and testing. Students are encouraged to meet with the program's director to talk about particular concerns, either in a small-group setting or one on one. Through all four years, students are paired with mentors and role models within the curriculum or in tandem with it. During the first year, students are assigned to a clinical faculty advisor who helps guide their academic pursuits and progress. Loyola's faculty is noted for its accessibility to students, and their interest in fostering formal and informal learning and professional growth.

Enrichment Programs

The Summer Enrichment Program (SEP) at Loyola University of Chicago Stritch School of Medicine is a six-week experience for pre-medical students. The program offers students a variety of educational experiences designed to enhance their preparation for a career in medicine, including academic lectures by Stritch faculty, shadowing experiences at Loyola physicians, mock admissions interviews, mentoring by current Stritch medical students, and

Loyola University Chicago Stritch School of Medicine
Applicants, First-Time Applicants, Matriculants by Gender, Race and Ethnicity, 2007-2008

	2007									2008								
	APP			F-time APP			MAT			APP			F-time APP			MAT		
	Wo-men	Men	Total	Wo-men	Men	Total	Wo-men	Men	Total	Wo-men	Men	Total	Wo-men	Men	Total	Wo-men	Men	Total
Hispanic/Latino																		
Cuban	18	28	46	13	24	37	0	0	0	22	32	54	18	25	43	0	0	0
Mexican American	97	84	181	85	70	155	3	3	6	80	108	188	61	86	147	1	2	3
Puerto Rican	20	16	36	14	12	26	2	1	3	19	23	42	18	16	34	0	1	1
Other Hispanic	91	76	167	70	60	130	0	0	0	114	111	225	84	72	156	1	0	1
Multiple Hispanic/Latino*	17	7	24	12	4	16	1	0	1	15	17	32	10	10	20	0	1	1
Subtotal	243	211	454	194	170	364	6	4	10	250	291	541	191	209	400	2	4	6
Non-Hispanic/Latino**																		
Black	198	118	316	157	92	249	4	1	5	236	105	341	183	79	262	8	1	9
Native American/AK	5	8	13	4	8	12	0	0	0	5	7	12	5	6	11	0	0	0
Native Hawaiian/OPI	23	13	36	20	10	30	0	0	0	18	17	35	9	9	18	1	1	2
White	2,759	3,016	5,775	2,187	2,222	4,409	60	52	112	2,743	3,361	6,104	2,053	2,373	4,426	48	53	101
Asian	1,199	1,339	2,538	885	963	1,848	5	13	18	1,245	1,339	2,584	871	884	1,755	6	8	14
Other Race	3	4	7	2	1	3	0	0	0	4	11	15	4	9	13	0	0	0
Multiple Race*	127	115	242	96	76	172	0	0	0	124	134	258	96	87	183	5	1	6
Unknown	29	52	81	27	44	71	1	0	1	101	132	233	94	115	209	2	5	7
Subtotal	4,343	4,665	9,008	3,378	3,416	6,794	70	66	136	4,476	5,106	9,582	3,315	3,562	6,877	70	69	139
Foreign	11	14	25	9	12	21	0	0	0	4	15	19	4	14	18	0	0	0
Total	4,597	4,890	9,487	3,581	3,598	7,179	76	70	146	4,730	5,412	10,142	3,510	3,785	7,295	72	73	145

*Since 2002, students can select more than one race and / or ethnicity. **Those who did not choose 'Hispanic/Latino' or 'Non-Hispanic/Latino' are listed under 'Non-Hispanic/Latino'. Data Source: AAMC Data Warehouse: Applicant-Matriculant File, as of 1/16/2009.

field trips and social activities in and around the Chicagoland area. The program targets students who will enrich the diversity of our medical student community, have the potential to become successful practitioners and leaders in the health care profession, and demonstrate a commitment to service in communities experiencing health care disparities. SEP participants will develop an understanding and appreciation of the skills and attributes needed to deliver compassionate health care and work collaboratively to promote equity in healthcare for underserved communities. Please visit the Web site for more information: *(http://www.stritch.luc.edu/node/120)*

Student Financial Assistance
A fee waiver is granted to applicants who have received a fee waiver from the American Medical College Application Service, or who submit a letter explaining their situation from a college financial aid officer. The Stritch Financial Aid Office works closely with the Stritch Admissions Office on minority recruitment and has been successful in funding minority and disadvantaged students through need-based financial aid programs, including Loyola Stritch grant and loan funds. Debt-planning management sessions are held with each student prior to graduation. Stritch has maintained a zero percent default rate and all past graduates have repaid loans within an average of seven years.

Northwestern University The Feinberg School of Medicine

Sunny Gibson, M.S.W., Director
Office of Minority and Cultural Affairs
Northwestern University
The Feinberg School of Medicine
Morton 1-658
303 East Chicago Avenue,
Chicago, IL 60611
312-503-0461; 312-503-4474 fax
s-gibson@nothernwestern.edu
www.medschool.northwestern.edu

Recruitment

Student recruitment is conducted at the college level, primarily, with emphasis placed on candidates who have distinguished themselves academically, personally and professionally, and come from a multiplicity of backgrounds and interests. The medical school facilitates recruitment through visits to the institution, pre-arranged group tours of the medical school, premedical enrichment programs and advising, and extensive communication by mail, email and telephone. Feinberg is committed to diversity and excellence, which go hand in hand in enrolling the best and brightest students.

Admissions

Applications to the medical school are reviewed and evaluated by a diverse group of faculty and students, who compose the Committee on Admissions. The admission of minority student applicants is determined on a competitive basis with the same process used to evaluate all applicants. Inclusive in the evaluation process is attention to trends in performance, employment history, extracurricular involvement, scholarly activities, the personal comments of the applicant, and the evaluations included from letters of recommendation. Please see the admissions Web site for specifics:
*(http://www.medschool.northwestern.edu /admissions/md/index.html) or contact admissions at:
(med-admissions@northwestern.edu).*

Academic Support Programs

All students at Feinberg have the full support of the Feinberg community: course directors, assigned mentors, associate deans, fellow students, and staff. In addition, the Director of Academic and Career Counseling in the Office of Student Programs provides workshops and one-on-one assistance to students seeking additional academic guidance. Every effort is made to ensure that students have the tools to successfully meet their academic and career goals. Third- and fourth-year students also offer formal and informal advice and support to first- and second-year students as they progress.

Enrichment Programs
Pre-Matriculation Program
Beginning in the summer of 2007, the Office of Minority and Cultural Affairs will sponsor selected underrepresented matriculating students to participate in an individualized pre-matriculation program in bench research, clinical research, or community/educational partnership. Students will receive a stipend, and have the opportunity to acclimate to the medical school environment and meet fellow students and faculty early on, as well as acclimate to the City of Chicago community.

Ongoing Activities

The Feinberg School of Medicine is regularly involved in providing information, resources, and guidance to college, post-baccalaureate students, and occasionally high school students interested in pursuing medical school. The med-

Northwestern University The Feinberg School of Medicine
Applicants, First-Time Applicants, Matriculants by Gender, Race and Ethnicity, 2007-2008

	2007 APP Women	Men	Total	F-time APP Women	Men	Total	MAT Women	Men	Total	2008 APP Women	Men	Total	F-time APP Women	Men	Total	MAT Women	Men	Total
Hispanic/Latino																		
Cuban	13	14	27	12	12	24	0	0	0	17	15	32	15	14	29	1	0	1
Mexican American	62	53	115	50	42	92	3	1	4	48	52	100	40	38	78	1	0	1
Puerto Rican	17	14	31	16	11	27	0	0	0	14	14	28	12	10	22	0	0	0
Other Hispanic	60	69	129	53	53	106	3	2	5	71	69	140	62	54	116	1	5	6
Multiple Hispanic/Latino*	5	10	15	1	9	10	0	1	1	9	14	23	8	11	19	0	2	2
Subtotal	157	160	317	132	127	259	6	4	10	159	164	323	137	127	264	3	7	10
Non-Hispanic/Latino**																		
Black	174	119	293	143	100	243	3	4	7	189	104	293	151	84	235	1	0	1
Native American/AK	4	4	8	4	4	8	0	0	0	4	4	8	4	4	8	0	0	0
Native Hawaiian/OPI	15	7	22	14	7	21	1	0	1	13	5	18	6	4	10	1	0	1
White	1,885	2,184	4,069	1,654	1,806	3,460	39	42	81	1,671	2,231	3,902	1,407	1,823	3,230	35	39	74
Asian	985	1,105	2,090	836	908	1,744	26	24	50	925	1,062	1,987	734	844	1,578	26	39	65
Other Race	4	2	6	3	2	5	0	0	0	3	5	8	2	5	7	0	0	0
Multiple Race*	118	105	223	105	84	189	3	2	5	108	98	206	90	76	166	1	2	3
Unknown	28	53	81	25	51	76	1	4	5	97	129	226	91	116	207	5	3	8
Subtotal	3,213	3,579	6,792	2,784	2,962	5,746	73	76	149	3,010	3,638	6,648	2,485	2,956	5,441	69	83	152
Foreign	213	205	418	172	152	324	5	5	10	213	228	441	182	174	356	2	5	7
Total	3,583	3,944	7,527	3,088	3,241	6,329	84	85	169	3,382	4,030	7,412	2,804	3,257	6,061	74	95	169

*Since 2002, students can select more than one race and / or ethnicity. **Those who did not choose 'Hispanic/Latino' or 'Non-Hispanic/Latino' are listed under 'Non-Hispanic/Latino'. Data Source: AAMC Data Warehouse: Applicant-Matriculant File, as of 1/16/2009.

ical school also nurtures a community partnership infrastructure that allows us to invest more heavily in the surrounding Chicago neighborhoods and still maintain continuity as our students progress from year to year. Please see our Web site: *(http://www.medschool.northwestern. edu)* for updates on our program development.

Student Financial Assistance

Supplemental application fees are waived upon receipt of a fee waiver from the American Medical College Application Service, or upon written request from the applicant's undergraduate college financial aid officer. Any applicant experiencing financial hardship and needing assistance in the admissions process should call or email the Office of Minority and Cultural Affairs to explore possible solutions.

Cultural Competency and Diversity

Cultural Dynamics in Medicine (CDM) CDM was added as a part of the Patient, Physician, and Society curriculum in 2004. This six-week course is mandatory for first-year students and focuses on fundamental cultural competency skills. Throughout the curriculum, issues of cultural competency are addressed including communication and language barriers, health care disparities, and how personal biases can impact patient care.

Diversity
The medical school has active chapters of the Student National Medical Association (SNMA), Latino Cultural Medical Association (LCMA), Asian Pacific American Medical Student Association (APAMSA), South Asian Medical Student Association (SAMSA), Queers and Allies (Q&A), and American Medical Women's Association (AMWA). Our student groups are involved in outreach in the surrounding community, both educational and clinical.

For a full list of student groups, please visit: *(http://www.medschool.northwestern.edu/student-programs/orgs/studorgs.html)*.

Rush Medical College of Rush University Medical Center

Sharon D. Gates, Director of Multicultural Affairs
Rush Medical College
600 South Paulina Street,
Suite 1080K
Chicago, IL 60612
312-942-3670; 312-942-3127 fax
sharon_gates@rush.edu
http://www.rushu.rush.edu/medcol

Recruitment

Rush Medical College seeks to attract candidates who can help make the student body more representative of our national population and more realistically informed about social problems affecting the delivery of health care in this country. Rush welcomes applications without regard to race, creed, national origin, or sex.

Minority pre-medical groups are encouraged to visit the Rush University Medical Center to meet with students and faculty to see the facilities. Such visits can be arranged through the Office of Admissions.

Academic Support Programs

Each student is assigned a carefully selected and trained academic advisor who will provide counseling and guidance throughout all four years of medical school. Students experiencing academic difficulty are provided a range of assistance including: individual and group instruction in time management, study skills, and test-taking strategies; peer tutors; and individualized instruction. Students have the option of modifying and extending their schedules so as to proceed at a slower pace during the pre-clinical years.

Student Financial Assistance

Financial aid, in the form of loans and non-refundable aid, is available to all students based primarily on need and accrued educational debt. The application fee is waived for applicants meeting the requirements for fee waivers by American Medical College Application Service. Financial assistance for interview trips is not available.

Rush Medical College of Rush University Medical Center
Applicants, First-Time Applicants, Matriculants by Gender, Race and Ethnicity, 2007-2008

	2007									2008								
	APP			F-time APP			MAT			APP			F-time APP			MAT		
	Women	Men	Total	Women	Men	Total	Women	Men	Total	Women	Men	Total	Women	Men	Total	Women	Men	Total
Hispanic/Latino																		
Cuban	13	13	26	12	10	22	0	0	0	16	16	32	11	15	26	0	0	0
Mexican American	54	51	105	47	35	82	3	3	6	51	64	115	38	51	89	2	1	3
Puerto Rican	11	8	19	8	5	13	0	1	1	15	12	27	14	9	23	0	0	0
Other Hispanic	55	56	111	39	46	85	0	2	2	81	72	153	65	49	114	4	3	7
Multiple Hispanic/Latino*	8	6	14	5	4	9	1	0	1	14	12	26	11	6	17	0	0	0
Subtotal	141	134	275	111	100	211	4	6	10	177	176	353	139	130	269	6	4	10
Non-Hispanic/Latino**																		
Black	154	75	229	111	57	168	0	1	1	192	96	288	134	74	208	1	1	2
Native American/AK	7	5	12	5	5	10	0	0	0	4	6	10	3	4	7	0	0	0
Native Hawaiian/OPI	11	6	17	10	4	14	0	0	0	17	8	25	11	6	17	0	1	1
White	1,552	1,606	3,158	1,222	1,158	2,380	33	43	76	1,644	1,905	3,549	1,211	1,326	2,537	34	45	79
Asian	748	797	1,545	542	566	1,108	17	20	37	930	964	1,894	653	629	1,282	23	8	31
Other Race	2	2	4	1	0	1	0	0	0	2	9	11	2	8	10	0	0	0
Multiple Race*	73	62	135	57	41	98	2	1	3	86	83	169	64	52	116	5	0	5
Unknown	17	25	42	15	19	34	1	0	1	49	83	132	44	74	118	1	1	2
Subtotal	2,564	2,578	5,142	1,963	1,850	3,813	53	65	118	2,924	3,154	6,078	2,122	2,173	4,295	64	56	120
Foreign	20	20	40	16	14	30	0	0	0	20	25	45	16	22	38	0	0	0
Total	2,725	2,732	5,457	2,090	1,964	4,054	57	71	128	3,121	3,355	6,476	2,277	2,325	4,602	70	60	130

*Since 2002, students can select more than one race and / or ethnicity. **Those who did not choose 'Hispanic/Latino' or 'Non-Hispanic/Latino' are listed under 'Non-Hispanic/Latino'. Data Source: AAMC Data Warehouse: Applicant-Matriculant File, as of 1/16/2009.

Southern Illinois University School of Medicine

Dr. Wesley G. Robinson-McNeese,
Executive Assistant to the
Dean for Diversity and
Minority Affairs
Southern Illinois University
School of Medicine
P.O. Box 19620
Springfield, IL 62794-9620
217-545-6012; 217-545-0786 fax
wmcneese@siumed.edu
http://www.siumed.edu

Recruitment

Members of the Southern Illinois University (SIU) School of Medicine's Office of Student Affairs routinely visit regional college campuses and minority student groups to discuss the programs and curricula offered at SIU. We also participate in statewide and regional recruitment fairs, taking medical students with us whenever possible. In addition, elementary, high school, and college students are invited to orientation visits and Career Days at the school's Carbondale and Springfield campuses. SIU medical students also participate in various educational events at local and area schools.

Admissions

Academically qualified U.S. citizens and foreign citizens with permanent resident visas who are residents of the State of Illinois are encouraged to apply to the SIU School of Medicine. A limited number of out-of-state residents are considered for the M.D./J.D. program.

All applicants must present scores from the Medical College Admission Test (MCAT). Applicants are expected to have a good foundation in the natural sciences, social sciences, and humanities and demonstrate facility in writing and speaking the English language.

A minimum of 90 semester hours of undergraduate work in an accredited, degree-granting college or university is required. At least 60 semester hours must be completed at a U.S. or Canadian college or university. Preference is given to those applicants who will have earned a baccalaureate degree by the time of matriculation to medical school and who have had sufficient and recent academic activity to demonstrate a potential for successful completion of the rigorous medical school curriculum.

Before issuing an acceptance to an applicant, the Admission Committee looks beyond proven scholastic ability for evidence of responsibility, maturity, integrity, compassion, proper motivation, identification with the goals of the school, exploration of medicine as a career, service orientation, and good interpersonal skills. Meeting the admission requirements does not insure admission, as the school is limited to a freshmen class of 72 students. Although the Admissions Committee uses no quotas, active efforts are made to recruit qualified applicants from groups traditionally underrepresented in the medical profession.

The Southern Illinois University School of Medicine Admissions Committee, separate and apart from the MEDPREP Admissions Committee, is composed of basic science and clinical faculty from the Carbondale and Springfield campuses. Medical students are also voting members on this committee. The Office of Student Affairs and Admissions encourages minority applicants to make

Southern Illinois University School of Medicine
Applicants, First-Time Applicants, Matriculants by Gender, Race and Ethnicity, 2007-2008

	2007									2008								
	APP			F-time APP			MAT			APP			F-time APP			MAT		
	Wo-men	Men	Total	Wo-men	Men	Total	Wo-men	Men	Total	Wo-men	Men	Total	Wo-men	Men	Total	Wo-men	Men	Total
Hispanic/Latino																		
Cuban	0	3	3	0	2	2	0	0	0	0	3	3	0	1	1	0	0	0
Mexican American	16	13	29	15	9	24	2	0	2	10	6	16	9	5	14	0	0	0
Puerto Rican	4	2	6	4	1	5	1	0	1	3	8	11	2	5	7	0	0	0
Other Hispanic	13	9	22	9	7	16	1	0	1	16	10	26	13	7	20	1	0	1
Multiple Hispanic/Latino*	1	2	3	0	1	1	0	0	0	1	4	5	0	1	1	0	1	1
Subtotal	34	29	63	28	20	48	4	0	4	30	31	61	24	19	43	1	1	2
Non-Hispanic/Latino**																		
Black	70	33	103	40	22	62	2	5	7	65	26	91	45	18	63	6	3	9
Native American/AK	1	0	1	0	0	0	1	0	1	0	0	0	0	0	0	0	0	0
Native Hawaiian/OPI	5	2	7	4	2	6	0	0	0	2	3	5	1	2	3	0	0	0
White	348	426	774	273	316	589	24	26	50	305	378	683	225	282	507	19	32	51
Asian	167	217	384	118	170	288	3	3	6	137	141	278	100	101	201	4	2	6
Other Race	1	0	1	0	0	0	0	0	0	0	1	1	0	1	1	0	0	0
Multiple Race*	15	18	33	9	11	20	3	1	4	9	19	28	7	9	16	2	2	4
Unknown	4	2	6	4	2	6	0	0	0	11	12	23	9	12	21	0	0	0
Subtotal	611	698	1,309	448	523	971	33	35	68	529	580	1,109	387	425	812	31	39	70
Foreign	4	4	8	3	2	5	0	0	0	1	3	4	1	3	4	0	0	0
Total	649	731	1,380	479	545	1,024	37	35	72	560	614	1,174	412	447	859	32	40	72

*Since 2002, students can select more than one race and / or ethnicity. **Those who did not choose 'Hispanic/Latino' or 'Non-Hispanic/Latino' are listed under 'Non-Hispanic/Latino'. Data Source: AAMC Data Warehouse: Applicant-Matriculant File, as of 1/16/2009.

application to the Southern Illinois University School of Medicine, and a particular effort is made to interview those minority students who apply.

Academic Support Programs

The curriculum is designed to prepare students for careers as health care professionals in a rapidly changing field, while providing a means for developing the knowledge and skills necessary for licensure, residency, and future accreditation examinations. The emphasis of the curriculum is on developing self-directed and lifelong learning skills that will help students maintain their knowledge and experience throughout their careers.

Students are assigned to mentors who work with them as they develop and build their clinical skills. In year four, students mentor second-year students as part of a Doctoring Curriculum that runs throughout the entire four years. Year-four students also choose an Electives Advisor to work with them as they choose and participate in electives that will most appropriately prepare them for their chosen specialties.

Every student must attain the predefined levels of competence established by the faculty. Evaluations are designed to measure levels of competence in knowledge, skills, and attitudes, not to compare students. Decisions regarding student progress are made on the basis of whether students demonstrate the prescribed levels of competency. Determining whether students demonstrate appropriate attitudes, concepts, and skills is accomplished through oral and computer-based examinations, faculty evaluation of cognitive and non-cognitive attributes, and performance based examinations.

The school's *Student Progress System (SPS)* prescribes the standards of academic conduct that must be met by students in order to graduate. The SPS also describes how student academic performance and professional conduct are evaluated. A Student Progress Committee, composed of students, faculty and administrators, monitors the process.

Counseling services are available for all medical students, with an emphasis on academic and personal guidance as needed.

Southern Illinois University School of Medicine sponsors a non-degree, post-baccalaureate Medical/Dental Education Preparatory Program (MEDPREP) on the Carbondale campus. MEDPREP is designed to assist students from groups currently identified by the AAMC as underrepresented in their preparation for medical school. Illinois rural white applicants from disadvantaged educational or economic backgrounds, as well as other minority group members, are considered for the program on a space-available basis.

MEDPREP students are recruited nationwide. That recruitment process includes visits to campuses by MEDPREP personnel. It also includes attending national meetings such as National Association of Minority Medical Educators and AAMC. Also, the admissions officers at many other health professional schools help identify likely candidates for MEDPREP.

Students interested in MEDPREP may obtain application forms and information from that program's Admission Coordinator. There is no application fee to MEDPREP. Invited MEDPREP applicants come to the Carbondale campus for an Admissions Day, which includes a series of tests, interviews with the faculty, and meetings with MEDPREP students in order to learn more about the program.

All students enrolled in MEDPREP must have completed at least two years of college coursework and maintained an overall grade-point average (GPA) of 2.0 and a math/science GPA of 2.0; a majority of MEDPREP participants are post-baccalaureate students. Each year, approximately 60 minority and disadvantaged students participate in MEDPREP. Most students participate in the program for two academic years.

MEDPREP offers a series of tutorials, courses, and seminars covering many phases of pre-professional preparation

for medical education. The curriculum is tailored for students as determined by analytic tests, a review of previous academic history, student preferences, and the admissions requirements of the medical schools to which the student plans to apply. MEDPREP and other university courses are available for developmental and advanced work in both basic sciences and learning skills. Students have an opportunity to prepare for the MCAT, the Dental Admissions Test (DAT), and are exposed to the medical school faculty and curriculum. MEDPREP emphasizes small classes and close faculty interaction and supervision.

Acceptance to, or success in, MEDPREP does not guarantee admission to Southern Illinois University School of Medicine or any other medical school. MEDPREP does, however, use the MEDPREP Alliance Program as a portal to the SIU School of Medicine. MEDPREP students who are Illinois residents and meet the Alliance criteria are guaranteed admission to Southern Illinois University School of Medicine, and other health professional schools.

Enrichment Programs

Southern Illinois University School of Medicine invites high school students to its campuses on a regular basis throughout the school year, setting up Career Day-type experiences. Similar tours and workshops are arranged for college students, especially pre-medical students.

The School of Medicine also participates in a High School Research Apprenticeship Program that brings students to Carbondale and Springfield to participate in a paid, six-week research experience. The students make a formal presentation of their research project at summer's end.

The Office of Student Affairs supports and coordinates cultural and ethnic observances throughout the school year. These functions are spearheaded by student organizations in cooperation with local community groups.

MEDPREP (Post-baccalaureate Program)

This two-year program, as noted above, is an enrichment program, which begins in June and runs through the entire year. Every attempt is made to make the student aware of areas of strength and weakness. A major purpose is to promote student self-learning. During the second year of the MEDPREP experience, enrichment courses in areas such as cardiovascular physiology, hormonal regulation, and medical immunology are taught. The enrichment courses offer the student advanced medical school level work. Contact: Layla Murphy, 618-453-1554.

Student Financial Assistance

Approximately 85 percent of the students at Southern Illinois University School of Medicine rely upon financial assistance to meet their educational costs.

Southern Illinois University School of Medicine participates in all major Federal Student Aid programs. All applications for financial assistance must include a summary of the family's financial situation. This summary is analyzed by an approved need analysis service to determine the expected family contribution. SIU School of Medicine utilizes the Free Application for Federal Student Aid (FAFSA) for this purpose.

The School of Medicine assists students in developing their financial aid package and works to provide the difference between the student's total educational expenses and the existing resources. Most financial need is met by combining various loan programs. Scholarship and grant aid is generally limited to students who demonstrate exceptional need. A limited number of institutional and outside scholarships are available and offer students a means of minimizing their educational debt.

Educational Partnerships

The MEDPREP Alliance Program is a partnership with the SIU School of Medicine. MEDPREP students who meet predetermined criteria are admitted to the SIU School of Medicine. Additionally, more than a dozen admissions officers from various medical schools across the country visit MEDPREP each year. Students from MEDPREP are often admitted to those medical schools. In a typical year, about 30 MEDPREP students matriculate to health professional school; those 30 students are accepted to 20-25 different schools around the country.

Other Pertinent Information

Questions about medical school minority student affairs should be directed to: Dr. Wesley G. Robinson-McNeese, Executive Assistant to the Dean for Diversity, Southern Illinois University School of Medicine, P.O. Box 19620, Springfield, IL 62794-9620, 217-545-7334, (wmcneese@siumed.edu). Questions about MEDPREP should be directed to Layla Murphy, Admissions Coordinator, MEDPREP, Southern Illinois University, School of Medicine, 210 Wheeler Hall, Mail Code 4323, Carbondale, IL 62901-4323, 618-453-1554, *(medprepadmissions@siumed.edu).*

University of Chicago Division of the Biological Sciences Pritzker School of Medicine

Dr. William A. McDade, Associate Dean for Multicultural Affairs
Rosita Ragin, Assistant Dean for Multicultural and Student Affairs
University of Chicago Pritzker School of Medicine
924 East 57th Street, BSLC 104
Chicago, IL 60637-5416
773-702-1617; 773-702-2598 fax
sickledoc@aol.com
rragin@uchicago.edu

Recruitment

The University of Chicago, located on the south side of Chicago, is an integral part of an ethnically diverse neighborhood. It has a long-standing tradition of academic excellence and places particular emphasis on recruiting students who seek to be leaders in research and clinical care. Both the university and the Pritzker School of Medicine are involved in a studious effort to increase minority representation at all levels. Significant strides have been made in attracting underrepresented minority students into the medical school, residency programs, and into faculty positions. High levels of effort continue in all three areas and are showing tangible results. The percentage of minority students entering medical school at Pritzker has more than doubled in the last five years and currently ranges between 18-23 percent of the entering class.

The Pritzker School of Medicine is particularly interested in seeking diversity among its students and is sensitive to society's need for an increasing number of minority men and women as physicians. It sends representatives, including enrolled minority students, to regional and national events to recruit underrepresented minority students and offers numerous campus tours and discussions. Students are encouraged to come to the campus for a variety of programs offered during the summer and throughout the academic year. Increased effort has been directed toward community outreach with medical students.

The Pritzker School of Medicine has had a longstanding presence at national meetings of minority pre-medical Society for Advancement of Chicanos and Native Americans in Science and Annual Biomedical Research Conference for Minority Students and medical school meetings of the Student National Medical Association (SNMA). Multiple recruitment trips are made annually to college campuses to connect with minority pre-medical students.

Admissions

The University of Chicago utilizes the AAMC's Medical Minority Applicant Registry (Med-MAR) to contact prospective students. The Admissions Committee is composed of a diverse group of faculty, students, and administrators who value diversity within the medical school class. Students who are invited for interviews will, under most circumstances, be given the opportunity to meet with the Associate or Assistant Dean for Multicultural Affairs and a minority faculty member or student as part of the admissions interview day. Housing is typically available with student hosts from SNMA.

Academic Support Programs

All students are assigned to a Career Advisor through their membership in one of the four Pritzker Societies. The Pritzker Societies provide a context and

University of Chicago Division of the Biological Sciences The Pritzker School of Medicine Applicants, First-Time Applicants, Matriculants by Gender, Race and Ethnicity, 2007-2008

	2007									2008								
	APP			F-time APP			MAT			APP			F-time APP			MAT		
	Women	Men	Total	Women	Men	Total	Women	Men	Total	Women	Men	Total	Women	Men	Total	Women	Men	Total
Hispanic/Latino																		
Cuban	16	20	36	14	15	29	0	0	0	12	19	31	11	17	28	0	0	0
Mexican American	72	72	144	58	60	118	3	2	5	59	61	120	48	47	95	2	3	5
Puerto Rican	16	20	36	15	16	31	4	0	4	19	18	37	17	13	30	0	0	0
Other Hispanic	78	70	148	67	61	128	0	2	2	67	72	139	59	57	116	0	0	0
Multiple Hispanic/Latino*	12	10	22	7	8	15	0	0	0	14	14	28	8	11	19	0	0	0
Subtotal	194	192	386	161	160	321	7	4	11	171	184	355	143	145	288	2	3	5
Non-Hispanic/Latino**																		
Black	206	119	325	171	100	271	10	2	12	201	106	307	169	81	250	5	5	10
Native American/AK	5	5	10	4	5	9	1	0	1	2	4	6	2	4	6	0	0	0
Native Hawaiian/OPI	16	5	21	15	5	20	1	0	1	13	10	23	6	8	14	0	0	0
White	1,881	2,229	4,110	1,620	1,793	3,413	23	30	53	1,573	2,228	3,801	1,307	1,781	3,088	24	28	52
Asian	1,024	1,169	2,193	842	948	1,790	15	11	26	865	1,075	1,940	687	839	1,526	13	12	25
Other Race	1	4	5	1	2	3	0	0	0	1	7	8	0	7	7	0	0	0
Multiple Race*	103	111	214	89	87	176	0	4	4	111	99	210	86	80	166	2	1	3
Unknown	26	50	76	25	44	69	0	0	0	77	122	199	74	110	184	0	1	1
Subtotal	3,262	3,692	6,954	2,767	2,984	5,751	50	47	97	2,843	3,651	6,494	2,331	2,910	5,241	44	47	91
Foreign	224	223	447	175	171	346	2	2	4	225	240	465	183	184	367	3	1	4
Total	3,680	4,107	7,787	3,103	3,315	6,418	59	53	112	3,239	4,075	7,314	2,657	3,239	5,896	49	51	100

*Since 2002, students can select more than one race and / or ethnicity. **Those who did not choose 'Hispanic/Latino' or 'Non-Hispanic/Latino' are listed under 'Non-Hispanic/Latino'. Data Source: AAMC Data Warehouse: Applicant-Matriculant File, as of 1/16/2009.

opportunity for gaining advice over time from a broad array of individuals such as peer students, students who are farther along in their training, and faculty. In addition to the academic advising societies, the students are offered scheduled quarterly meetings with the deans to discuss well-being issues and academic plans. Additional opportunities are provided by the Bowman Society and its bimonthly lecture series that covers career development and the development of a biomedical scientific community interested in health care disparities. This positive networking provides both basic information and a valuable framework for assisting students in understanding the best ways to negotiate the four years at Pritzker. It also reduces the isolation students may initially feel, while additionally identifying any individuals who might benefit from personal counseling or other types of assistance. Faculty are strongly committed to each student's success.

Enrichment Programs

Young Scientist Training Program (YSTP)
YSTP is a high school/college program sponsored by the National Institute of Diabetes, Digestive Diseases and Kidney Disease designed to help develop minority students' interest in biomedical research. Ten students are recruited locally and commute to the university to work with distinguished minority faculty mentors for ten weeks during the summer. Students are selected from the most outstanding cohort of science-oriented high school freshmen through college seniors. Stipends are paid to participants. An annual symposium participation experience is required.
(http://pritzker.bsd.uchicago.edu/about /diversity/ pipeline/ysp.shtml)

Summer Research Program (SRP)
SRP is sponsored by the National Heart, Lung and Blood Institute. This program provides an 11-week research experience for 15 entering underrepresented minority medical students and those students who have completed their first year at Pritzker. Participation in weekly

research-cluster interest groups and an end of summer symposium is required. Participants engage in basic science and clinical research projects. Stipend is paid to participants.

Pritzker School of Medicine Experience in Research (PSOMER)
PSOMER is a residential program for minority junior and senior college students. Students are recruited from around the United States, and for eight weeks in the summer they are mentored by University of Chicago faculty, work on research projects that range from bench to clinical projects, and attend various seminars relevant to medical education. Participants augment their research work with weekly colloquiums. All participants are required to present their work at a poster session at the end of the program. Stipends are paid to the participants.
(http://pritzker.bsd.uchicago.edu/about/ diversity/pipeline/psomer.shtml)

The Chicago Academic Medicine Program (CAMP)
CAMP is a non-residential six-week summer program for minority freshman or sophomore pre-medical students or graduating high school seniors. The goal of the program is to build the academic success skills of the students by providing group-learning and team-building projects using a curriculum that covers three organ systems in a mini-medical school style format. The curriculum is enhanced by daily medical education and learning skills seminars, weekly book club sessions, and clinical experiences held one morning each week. Participants are provided with various opportunities to meet the faculty by attending group meetings with professors and mentors and individual meetings with the deans. Students are selected locally or must have a local residence to reside at during the program. This tuition free program also provides a stipend and funding for local transportation.
(http://pritzker.bsd.uchicago.edu/about /diversity/pipeline/camp.shtml)

Academic Support Programs

Minority students are welcomed to the Pritzker School of Medicine at a reception where students, house staff, and faculty are invited, thus building an informal network of academic support. Mentorship of regular academic advisement is provided by the Office of Multicultural Affairs. The Pritzker Societies provides an opportunity for students to obtain advice over time from peer students, students who are farther along in their training, and faculty. All current students are equally divided into four societies, each with a head and five adjunct faculty advisors. Each class at Pritzker has an annual symposium/retreat that has a diversity component.

Student Financial Assistance

The University of Chicago has a variety of resources (both scholarships and low interest loans) to help students meet their educational expenses. Pritzker's support of students is need-based, and the new Dean's Promise Scholarships is offered to outstanding candidates. As a private institution, our student indebtedness is below the median for all graduating seniors with debt. Applicants who receive fee waivers from the American Medical College Application Service (AMCAS) will automatically receive a fee waiver for the Pritzker Supplemental Application. Students without an AMCAS fee waiver may petition to waive Pritzker's fee with appropriate documentation from their college's financial aid office.

Other Pertinent Information

Students obtain early exposure to clinical medicine as they begin patient contact the first week of medical school. During the first two years, students develop important clinical skills that give them confidence in placing their focus on the patient while a full-time clinical student in the third year. The six junior-year clerkships, as well as the largely elective fourth year, give students an excellent background with which to enter residency and ultimately the practice of medicine.

The Summer Research Program, student/faculty dinners, and a number of organizations give students opportunity to work closely with faculty mentors. Students interested in obtaining the Masters in Business Administration, Masters in Public Policy, Masters in Health Studies, or Masters in Public Realm are encouraged to do so. Currently six students are enrolled in combined degree programs pursuing Ph.D. degrees in science. Six students are in the Medical Scientist Training Program, one is on an NIH Pediatrics Growth and Development Training Grant, and one is on an NIH Minority Predoctoral Fellowship.

The Office of Multicultural Affairs created the Bowman Society Lecture Series, which is named in honor of one of Pritzker's outstanding minority emeritus professors, Dr. James E. Bowman. Dr. Bowman's legacy is one of excellence and distinguished service, and he has been a role model to many Pritzker students. The Bowman Society features nationally renowned faculty presenters in a bimonthly lecture series followed by a meeting of the Society whose membership includes faculty, graduate and medical students, fellows, and house staff where the principal topics of discussion are career development and forging a strong biomedical scientific community interested in health care disparities.

Students are active in community health centers and neighborhood schools to disseminate health information or provide care directly. Underrepresented minority students who attend Pritzker traditionally assume leadership roles during and after their medical school experience. The University of Chicago Hospital is a major health care provider to residents of the south side of Chicago, and as such, the diversity in patient population is large. There is a significant outreach program in geriatrics care, where students are involved in a senior companion program. Students also volunteer in two community health centers. Some student-led outreach groups include Remedy

Cuba/Peru, Maria Shelter, Washington Park Clinic, Community Health Clinics, Adolescence Substance Abuse Program, Prostate Cancer Awareness Program, HIPCORPS, Doctors Back to School Program, and Project Brotherhood. In addition, many of our enrichment activities involve mentorship of younger students by older medical students and provide excellent leadership and teaching experience for our minority medical student population. Numerous opportunities exist for students to initiate other outreach programs where they may perceive a need to exist.

A wide variety of student organizations sponsor programs and activities on numerous topics, including cultural sensitivity and diversity. Organizations such as the SNMA are dedicated to increasing the awareness of serving the unique health care needs of minority communities and working toward the abolition of the barriers that obstruct the fulfillment of those needs. The last two national presidents of SNMA (past and current) are from the University of Chicago. Pritzker students have won one of the ten national AMA Minority Scholar Awards in both the past and current academic year. They specifically focus on educating students and physicians about problems facing minority communities, recruiting and supporting minority medical students, and improving the health status of these communities. Students are also encouraged to attend a variety of annual festivals and events highlighting the arts, publications, and politics of a wide variety of communities.

University of Illinois at Chicago College of Medicine

Dr. Javette C. Orgain, MPH,
Assistant Dean Urban Health
Program
University of Illinois at Chicago
College of Medicine
1819 West Polk St., Rm 145 CMW
Chicago, IL 60612-7333
312-996-6491; 312-996-3548 fax

Recruitment

Primarily, staff of the Urban Health Program conduct recruitment activities targeted at underrepresented minority and/or disadvantaged students. Recruitment activities are carried out in the community, at the high school, and undergraduate levels. Recruitment efforts consist of providing workshops and seminars to a wide range of audiences, as well as participation in local and national conferences aimed at targeting pre-medical students. Minority medical students and faculty in the college also actively participate in the recruitment efforts. The Urban Health Program administers an intensive local outreach program, as well as visits other states to encourage out-of-state underrepresented minority and/or disadvantaged students to apply.

Admissions

In order to be considered for admissions, students must apply to the University of Illinois College of Medicine (UIC-COM) through the American Medical College Application Service (AMCAS). When the college receives the application from AMCAS, a determination is made of whether the applicant is to receive the college's supplemental application. All applicants must meet minimum academic criteria to be offered a supplemental application. Upon the college's receipt of the supplemental application and three letters of recommendation (or school's composite letter), the application is initially screened by a panel composed of members of the full Admissions Committee. Following the review of the application, a recommendation is made to the full Admissions Committee. All candidates being considered for admission must participate in an interview. Minority candidates are encouraged to contact staff members of the Urban Health Program for assistance before and during the process.

Academic Support Programs

The Urban Health Program developed the Academic Assistance Program to identify and aid students with the challenges of the medical curriculum. Academic Skills Specialists (one at each of the four campuses) work with faculty and administrators to identify appropriate interventions (i.e., test-taking skills, group and/or individualized tutoring, crisis management, etc.).

Retention programming activities include a comprehensive orientation to introduce the rigors of medical education and to provide information regarding resources and multiple approaches to overcoming academically related obstacles. The Learning and Study Skills Inventory (LASSI) is used to assist in identifying factors that are predictive of success in medical school.

The two minority medical student organizations at the College of Medicine campus, National Network of Latin American Medical Students-La Raza Medical Student Association (NNLAMS-LaRAMA) and the Student

University of Illinois College of Medicine
Applicants, First-Time Applicants, Matriculants by Gender, Race and Ethnicity, 2007-2008

	2007									2008								
	APP			F-time APP			MAT			APP			F-time APP			MAT		
	Women	Men	Total	Women	Men	Total	Women	Men	Total	Women	Men	Total	Women	Men	Total	Women	Men	Total
Hispanic/Latino																		
Cuban	18	32	50	13	27	40	2	0	2	22	26	48	18	20	38	3	0	3
Mexican American	102	105	207	79	74	153	10	12	22	92	88	180	65	63	128	18	3	21
Puerto Rican	24	11	35	20	8	28	1	2	3	22	17	39	18	13	31	3	1	4
Other Hispanic	77	93	170	56	66	122	8	6	14	102	93	195	76	60	136	12	9	21
Multiple Hispanic/Latino*	10	14	24	6	9	15	0	0	0	14	15	29	9	8	17	0	2	2
Subtotal	231	255	486	174	184	358	21	20	41	252	239	491	186	164	350	36	15	51
Non-Hispanic/Latino**																		
Black	314	177	491	205	128	333	14	9	23	296	138	434	196	107	303	19	6	25
Native American/AK	7	7	14	5	6	11	0	0	0	7	5	12	5	4	9	0	0	0
Native Hawaiian/OPI	13	10	23	10	7	17	0	0	0	12	11	23	6	7	13	1	0	1
White	1,722	1,941	3,663	1,368	1,408	2,776	56	85	141	1,461	1,914	3,375	1,090	1,362	2,452	59	75	134
Asian	987	1,172	2,159	724	880	1,604	42	52	94	936	1,028	1,964	656	705	1,361	45	38	83
Other Race	1	3	4	1	2	3	0	0	0	1	7	8	1	7	8	0	1	1
Multiple Race*	102	83	185	79	64	143	3	2	5	91	96	187	66	66	132	2	6	8
Unknown	27	31	58	26	26	52	1	2	3	73	78	151	67	73	140	2	3	5
Subtotal	3,173	3,424	6,597	2,418	2,521	4,939	116	150	266	2,877	3,277	6,154	2,087	2,331	4,418	128	129	257
Foreign	5	5	10	4	4	8	0	0	0	28	37	65	24	29	53	0	0	0
Total	3,409	3,684	7,093	2,596	2,709	5,305	137	170	307	3,157	3,553	6,710	2,297	2,524	4,821	164	144	308

*Since 2002, students can select more than one race and / or ethnicity. **Those who did not choose 'Hispanic/Latino' or 'Non-Hispanic/Latino' are listed under 'Non-Hispanic/Latino'. Data Source: AAMC Data Warehouse: Applicant-Matriculant File, as of 1/16/2009.

National Medical Association (SNMA), also provide academic assistance to first- and second-year students through reviews and mock practicals.

Enrichment Programs

Underrepresented minority and/or disadvantaged students can take advantage of the following summer and enrichment programs.

The Summer Pre-matriculation Program (SPP)

SPP is a six-week program offered to students who have been admitted to the College of Medicine, either traditionally or conditionally. The purpose of the program is to introduce students to the first-year curriculum. Preview courses in biochemistry, gross anatomy, tissue biology, and physiology are offered. Faculty and upperclass medical students organize lectures and laboratory sessions for the participants.

In addition, the Urban Health Program offers summer programs for college and high school students. The Medical College Admission Test (MCAT) Review Program is a seven-week summer program designed to provide participants with an intensive review of the basic sciences in preparation for the MCAT examination. The Verbal Reasoning Workshop is a supplement to the MCAT Review Program. The workshop is an eight-session academic-year program, which offers participants an opportunity to focus on enhancing reading, comprehension, and writing skills in preparation for the MCAT.

The Post-baccalaureate Admission Program (PAP)

PAP is an invitation-only program. To be considered, one must apply for traditional admission through the AMCAS. The PAP is a 14-month, guaranteed admission program designed to provide an opportunity for selected students to demonstrate their academic abilities in preparation to matriculate to medical school.

Student Financial Assistance

All students are awarded financial assistance based on need as the sole criterion. Personal need of each accepted applicant is reflected in the award. To make it financially feasible for out-of-state underrepresented minority applicants to attend the University of Illinois, students may apply to have the non-resident portion of their tuition waived through tuition differential coverage. It is important to apply for financial aid early in the process, even if an acceptance offer has not been made.

Educational Partnerships

The Urban Health Program maintains a formal partnership with several high schools in the Chicago Public School system; a Chicago Community College; two community-based organizations; two Illinois state four-year colleges; and our own undergraduate institution on two campuses. The partnerships foster collaborative efforts to facilitate summer and academic-year program activities designed to facilitate access to medical school for students from underrepresented minority and disadvantaged backgrounds.

Indiana University School of Medicine

Krystal Ardayfio, Director of
Multicultural Affairs
Indiana University School of Medicine
635 Barnhill Drive, MS 166
Indianapolis, IN 46202-5120
317-274-1939; 317-274-4309 fax
kardayfi@iupui.edu

Recruitment

The Indiana University School of Medicine (IUSM) is committed to expanding its efforts to identify, advice, and recruit underrepresented minority individuals who have potential and promise for education and training in medicine. The school's efforts include contact with appropriate administrators, teachers, and advisors in Indiana high schools, and colleges, and universities across the nation. Recruitment activities are developed and implemented primarily through the admissions office and in collaboration with the Office of Multicultural Affairs. Such activities consist of on-campus visitations to conduct pre-medical seminars and converse with students on a one-to-one basis or in small groups. IUSM participates in high school career opportunity programs and also reaches out to the community formally with the Howard Hughes Medical Institute-funded Crispus Attucks Medical Magnet High School Outreach Program, the Area Health Education Center-funded Dr. Camp, and Camp Medical Detectives. IUSM also connects with the community through information sheets or brochures, visual aids, and tours of the medical center. The tours are available to students and small groups by appointment. Additionally, minority medical students share their experiences with local high school students through a "Doctor Back to School" program and through a partnership with a local "Center for Leadership Development Program" for high school students.

Admissions

The School of Medicine's Admissions Committee evaluates all applicants, minority and non-minority, on the basis of scholarship, character, personality, references, performance on the Medical College Admission Test (MCAT), and a personal interview. Indiana University School of Medicine participates in the American Medical College Application Service (AMCAS). The AMCAS application, and transcripts, must be submitted to AMCAS no later than December 15th. It is essential that all applicants follow appropriate admissions procedures and promptly return necessary materials. Although applications are reviewed at various times throughout the year, the Admissions Committee will take action on an application only if all required materials have been received.

Academic Support Programs

The Indiana University School of Medicine currently makes use of several academic reinforcement programs for disadvantaged students. Matriculants are mentored by upperclassmen through the Student National Medical Association (SNMA). The Office of Multicultural Affairs (OMCA) conducts Lunch and Learns geared toward minority students at which a faculty mentor is made available to foster a strong support system. The OMCA also makes available writing seminars and covers the fees for contracted private writing coaching as well as individual personal

Indiana University School of Medicine
Applicants, First-Time Applicants, Matriculants by Gender, Race and Ethnicity, 2007-2008

| | 2007 | | | | | | | | | 2008 | | | | | | | | |
| | APP | | | F-time APP | | | MAT | | | APP | | | F-time APP | | | MAT | | |
	Wo-men	Men	Total	Wo-men	Men	Total	Wo-men	Men	Total	Wo-men	Men	Total	Wo-men	Men	Total	Wo-men	Men	Total
Hispanic/Latino																		
Cuban	7	12	19	6	9	15	0	1	1	6	6	12	4	4	8	0	0	0
Mexican American	23	35	58	17	21	38	3	7	10	21	30	51	17	19	36	1	2	3
Puerto Rican	5	7	12	4	6	10	0	0	0	4	9	13	4	8	12	0	0	0
Other Hispanic	30	27	57	22	18	40	1	3	4	35	44	79	26	28	54	2	5	7
Multiple Hispanic/Latino*	2	6	8	2	4	6	0	0	0	7	7	14	6	4	10	0	0	0
Subtotal	67	87	154	51	58	109	4	11	15	73	96	169	57	63	120	3	7	10
Non-Hispanic/Latino**																		
Black	158	80	238	96	55	151	9	3	12	161	90	251	113	61	174	15	1	16
Native American/AK	5	3	8	3	2	5	0	1	1	5	4	9	2	2	4	1	0	1
Native Hawaiian/OPI	7	2	9	6	0	6	0	0	0	9	7	16	7	5	12	0	0	0
White	910	1,115	2,025	733	842	1,575	95	111	206	818	1,186	2,004	621	873	1,494	91	132	223
Asian	288	404	692	213	300	513	19	25	44	299	395	694	223	260	483	14	26	40
Other Race	1	4	5	1	1	2	0	0	0	1	2	3	1	1	2	0	0	0
Multiple Race*	36	54	90	29	42	71	5	5	10	31	41	72	22	29	51	5	1	6
Unknown	5	14	19	4	11	15	0	2	2	28	50	78	27	44	71	2	4	6
Subtotal	1,410	1,676	3,086	1,085	1,253	2,338	128	147	275	1,352	1,775	3,127	1,016	1,275	2,291	128	164	292
Foreign	110	140	250	88	110	198	1	3	4	123	150	273	99	118	217	4	2	6
Total	1,587	1,903	3,490	1,224	1,421	2,645	133	161	294	1,548	2,021	3,569	1,172	1,456	2,628	135	173	308

*Since 2002, students can select more than one race and / or ethnicity. **Those who did not choose 'Hispanic/Latino' or 'Non-Hispanic/Latino' are listed under 'Non-Hispanic/Latino'. Data Source: AAMC Data Warehouse: Applicant-Matriculant File, as of 1/16/2009.

statement writing sessions offered directly from the OMCA.

Special tutorial programs are offered on a regularly scheduled basis by the faculty of each of the basic science courses for all students whose academic performance is below par.

Academic Counseling

The Office for Mentoring and Student Development offers both group and individual services designed to identify academic problems early. Academic counseling services include:

- Learning-style assessment
- Time management
- Test-taking skills
- Peer tutoring
- Liaison with faculty for students having difficulty
- Resources for course and board preparation
- Learning disability evaluation referrals and advocacy

Career Advising

The Office for Mentoring and Student Development offers the following resources designed to assist students in specialty selection and getting into a residency:

- AAMC Careers in Medicine
- Career values and interests workshops and individual consultations
- CV and personal statement workshops and individual consultations
- Mock residency interviews
- Annual residency survey

Enrichment Programs

Master of Science in Medical Science Program.
The Master of Science in Medical Science (MSMS) Program was established in 1995 at Indiana University School of Medicine to expand the pool of successful medical school applicants from underrepresented minority and disadvantaged backgrounds. The program enhances the preparation and confidence of its students to be successful in a medical curriculum. The Admissions Committee at IUSM identifies and selects MSMS students from its pool of medical school applicants.

The MSMS Program's two-year curriculum includes graduate medical science courses taught by IUSM faculty, collaborative problem-based learning courses, and a research experience. Students must maintain a B (3.0) average in the program and complete 35 credits to obtain the MSMS degree. The curriculum of the MSMS Program was designed to allow first- and second-year students to apply for medical school admission. Students who are admitted to medical school after one year in the program may apply 11 credits of basic medical science course work with grades of at least "B" toward completion of the requirements for the MSMS degree. The university underwrites a major portion of the cost, but tuition is charged. Financial aid is available.

Medical College Application Test Preparation Program
The MCAT Preparation Program begins in June as an intensive ten-week academic experience. The goal of the program is to enhance and reinforce academic skills that are essential for both improved MCAT performance and success in rigorous graduate course work. Approximately 30 hours per week are spent in class, with an emphasis on cooperative learning in small groups. Subject matter includes biology, chemistry, organic chemistry, physics, verbal reasoning, and writing. Critical thinking skills are stressed. Physical conditioning is encouraged. At least three hours per week of regularly scheduled physical exercise is strongly recommended. Enrollment in the MCAT Preparation Program is limited to students admitted to the MSMS Program. For more information visit: (www.msms.iu.edu).

Student Financial Assistance

Indiana University School of Medicine has one endowment scholarship from American States Insurance Company. The amount available annually is $10,000 committed to one student over four years.

The Eli Lilly Company Scholarships support several tuition scholarships annually. Endowed in 1993 by the Eli Lilly Company, the dean appropriates $150,000 annually to support renewals as well as select new recipients. In 1998, Lilly agreed to fund two additional scholarships to cover tuition, fees, books, and a stipend. A distribution is made by the Eli Lilly Company each year to cover these commitments. This is in addition to what is awarded through the endowed funds.

The Wishard Memorial Foundation provides tuition scholarships to one or two underrepresented minority students from Indiana each year in the form of four-year renewable scholarships. The George H. Rawls Scholarship began in 1998 in an effort to increase the number of minority physicians in the Indianapolis area. The scholarship commits the recipient to practicing within the area of Indianapolis. There is no specialty restriction.

The George and Lula Rawls Academic Excellence Award totals approximately $1,400 and is divided into three awards. The first award is given to a student with the highest academic performance in the MSMS Program; the second one is awarded to a second-year medical student with the highest academic performance after the first year; and a final award is given to a student in the upper second-to-fourth years with the highest academic performance.

The Indiana University School of Medicine's Dean's General Funds, used to recruit Indiana's best and brightest students, and provides 20 percent-100 percent tuition scholarships. Among those students being recruited are URM's that fall in the top 30-40 entering students.

The Aesculapian Medical Society awards three external scholarships annually ($2,000 each) in the spring semester. The scholarships target students with the highest academic performance in the first and second year as well as a student in the final two years. This is not a school scholarship, although Indiana University School of Medicine assists the Aesculapian Society in identifying the recipients. The Aesculapian Society annually solicits its membership to fund the scholarships.

Educational Partnerships

IUSM has a partnership with the Center for Leadership Development *(www.cldinc.org)*.

Indiana University School of Medicine's educational outreach programs are implemented at the Crispus Attucks Medical Magnet High School (CAMMHS), a grade six-12 Indianapolis Public Schools district (IPS) magnet program. Indianapolis Public Schools is the largest school district in Indianapolis as well as in the state of Indiana with approximately 34,000 students. IPS has a 2008-09 student ethnic breakdown of 57% Black; 23% White; 15% Hispanic; and 5% Multiracial. The percent age of students on free and reduced lunch is 75 and 7, respectively. The students attending CAMMHS are recruited from across the IPS school district.

Our educational partnership aims to attract Indianapolis Public Schools Crispus Attucks Medical Magnet High School students to life science and medical professions. The programmatic components of the partnership include: 1) Howard Hughes Medical Institute Precollege Program, 2) field trip to the medical school for sixth grade students, and 3) Crispus Attucks Students Interest Group for sixth and seventh graders. For more information visit *(http://www.msms.iu.edu/body.cfm?id=6 994)*

The Bridges to the Doctorate initiative, funded by the National Institutes of Health, represents a formal partnership between Jackson State University (JSU), a historically black institution, and Indiana University-Purdue University at Indianapolis (IUPUI). The purpose of the partnership is to enhance the quality and quantity of underrepresented minority students who are being trained as the next generation of scientists by providing a structured "bridge" between the JSU Master's program and the IUPUI doctoral program. This program guarantees a 12-month stipend

and fee remission for all Bridges students *(http://www.iupui.edu)*.

University of Iowa Roy J. and Lucille A. Carver College of Medicine

Barbara Barlow, Program Associate for Student Affairs
University of Iowa Roy J. and Lucille A. Carver College of Medicine
1213A MERF
Iowa City, IA 52242-1101
319-335-8057; 319-335-8049 fax
barbara-barlow@uiowa.edu

Recruitment

The University of Iowa Roy J. and Lucille A. Carver College of Medicine maintains a long tradition of identifying, admitting, and graduating qualified applicants from ethnic groups underrepresented in U.S. medicine. This commitment has been demonstrated by the number of underrepresented minority students who have successfully entered and graduated from the college. Since 1970, more than 300 students have earned their M.D. degree and entered their chosen medical specialty.

The College of Medicine actively encourages minority students to seek information regarding its programs and welcomes applications to the college of medicine. Efforts to promote minority applications include:

- Faculty and administrative staff visits to undergraduate campuses and minority summer programs to present information and speak informally with individual students;
- Visits by students who hold membership in the Student National Medical Association to high schools and colleges for the purpose of presenting and sharing information related to medical education;
- Information packets mailed to selected registrants of the Medical Minority Applicant Registry; and
- Diversity weekend held the first weekend in December for students interviewing who would like to learn more about programs promoting diversity at Iowa.

Admissions

The College of Medicine participates in the American Medical College Application Service (AMCAS). Personal interviews are conducted and generally begin in early fall. There is no geographical restriction placed upon the selection of candidates.

The Admissions Office staff screens all applications forwarded to the College of Medicine by AMCAS. Students are asked to complete a University of Iowa College of Medicine application, arrange for the submission of three evaluation forms, and respond to several short essay topics. AMCAS applications should be submitted as early as possible to allow time for the return of supplementary materials and subsequent committee evaluation. Supplemental application materials must be on file in the College of Medicine by December 15.

All applicants must meet the high standards of the Admissions Committee to be offered admission to the College of Medicine. Selection for admission is based upon a careful review of each applicant's academic performance and potential, as well as a number of non-cognitive characteristics considered to be important in future physicians.

University of Iowa Roy J. and Lucille A. Carver College of Medicine
Applicants, First-Time Applicants, Matriculants by Gender, Race and Ethnicity, 2007-2008

| | 2007 | | | | | | | | | 2008 | | | | | | | | |
| | APP | | | F-time APP | | | MAT | | | APP | | | F-time APP | | | MAT | | |
	Women	Men	Total	Women	Men	Total	Women	Men	Total	Women	Men	Total	Women	Men	Total	Women	Men	Total
Hispanic/Latino																		
Cuban	3	6	9	3	3	6	0	0	0	6	5	11	3	4	7	0	0	0
Mexican American	48	52	100	34	37	71	4	2	6	52	51	103	42	31	73	4	5	9
Puerto Rican	4	4	8	3	4	7	0	0	0	9	9	18	8	6	14	0	0	0
Other Hispanic	23	29	52	14	18	32	0	0	0	29	34	63	16	18	34	1	0	1
Multiple Hispanic/Latino*	4	3	7	3	1	4	0	0	0	6	5	11	5	3	8	0	0	0
Subtotal	82	94	176	57	63	120	4	2	6	102	104	206	74	62	136	5	5	10
Non-Hispanic/Latino**																		
Black	105	72	177	62	56	118	5	2	7	109	81	190	68	63	131	1	4	5
Native American/AK	3	1	4	2	1	3	0	0	0	3	5	8	2	4	6	0	0	0
Native Hawaiian/OPI	3	2	5	2	2	4	0	0	0	3	4	7	3	3	6	0	1	1
White	800	1,179	1,979	655	883	1,538	52	71	123	741	1,106	1,847	579	798	1,377	50	54	104
Asian	226	297	523	158	209	367	2	5	7	211	281	492	145	176	321	11	7	18
Other Race	0	3	3	0	2	2	0	0	0	0	3	3	0	3	3	0	0	0
Multiple Race*	27	34	61	22	27	49	2	2	4	31	35	66	22	20	42	2	1	3
Unknown	5	13	18	5	11	16	1	0	1	24	49	73	24	42	66	2	5	7
Subtotal	1,169	1,601	2,770	906	1,191	2,097	62	80	142	1,122	1,564	2,686	843	1,109	1,952	66	72	138
Foreign	4	6	10	3	6	9	0	0	0	2	0	2	2	0	2	0	0	0
Total	1,255	1,701	2,956	966	1,260	2,226	66	82	148	1,226	1,668	2,894	919	1,171	2,090	71	77	148

*Since 2002, students can select more than one race and / or ethnicity. **Those who did not choose 'Hispanic/Latino' or 'Non-Hispanic/Latino' are listed under 'Non-Hispanic/Latino'. Data Source: AAMC Data Warehouse: Applicant-Matriculant File, as of 1/16/2009.

Academic Support Programs

The Office of Student Affairs and Curriculum provides individual and/or group counseling for all medical students. Services provided include career development, academic planning, personal advising, financial need and planning, and debt management counseling. Students are encouraged to utilize these services throughout their matriculation in the College of Medicine.

Free tutorial assistance is available for all first- and second-year courses, starting in the first two weeks of class. With their tutors (upper-class students, medical fellows and/or residents), students discuss their needs and determine a schedule of meetings. Sessions are conducted on a one-to-one basis or in small groups.

Students who have personal or academic difficulty can ask to have their academic schedule modified. Any required or necessary deviation from the curriculum schedule is determined by the dean and reviewed on an individual basis.

United States Medical Licensing Examination (USMLE) Study Groups
These groups are available for students registered to take the USMLE Step 1. Groups, consisting of six or seven students, meet weekly and are led by M3 or M4 students who scored high on the exam. There is no charge to participants.

Enrichment Programs

Summer Programs
All students accepted to the University of Iowa College of Medicine are invited to participate in this program during the summer preceding their entry into the college. The program introduces new students to the medical curriculum, provides personal and career development information, and conducts seminars emphasizing study skills, time management, and test-taking strategies. Orientation activities and assistance in adjusting to the local community are included. Tuition is free, and a grant from the university is provided to cover books and living expenses.

Early Mentoring Program
A program has been established with upper-class students and with clinical faculty. Each summer program student is matched with a second-year student and a clinical faculty mentor. Effective mentoring programs, combined with a supportive campus environment, assist new students in adjusting more readily to unfamiliar surroundings. This, in turn, helps in learning.

Student Financial Assistance

The university will waive the admission application fee, upon request, for economically disadvantaged students who received a fee waiver from AMCAS. All students desiring consideration for financial aid must complete the Free Application for Federal Student Aid (FAFSA). The information provided on this application will be used to do a need assessment and to determine the level of financial assistance that can be awarded to each student. To assist students in meeting additional demonstrated need, other federal or national foundation grants are also utilized, as are loans from federal, collegiate, or private programs. Financial aid and debt management advising are available in the Office of Medical Student Affairs. College of Medicine staff strive to assist students in meeting 100 percent of demonstrated financial need so that every admitted student will be able to finance a medical education at the University of Iowa.

Other Pertinent Information

The College of Medicine's curriculum was redesigned beginning with the fall 1995 entering class. Major changes in emphasis include earlier patient exposure, increased integration and clinical relevance in the basic science courses and community-based primary care in the clinical years. Running concurrently with the basic science courses found in the first two years will be a new course, Foundations of Clinical Practice, which will provide students with their first exposure to patients, to disciplines such as preventive medicine, and to critical appraisal skills. Major goals for this course include development of the interpersonal skills critical for patient interactions and the facilitation of students' transition to an adult style of learning. Another unique feature of the revised curriculum is the greater emphasis placed on the skills and body of knowledge required by the generalist, which will coincide with the minimum core of material that the college envisions having all students master prior to graduation. One of the ways in which the new curriculum seeks to meet this goal is through the Generalist Core of Clerkships, including community-based primary care, family practice and internal medicine ambulatory care, general internal medicine, obstetrics and gynecology, and pediatrics. The inclusion of a Community-Based Primary Care six-week rotation will serve to further acquaint students with the settings in which generalist physicians practice medicine.

University of Kansas School of Medicine

Gwendolyn Swoop, Executive Director Office of Cultural Enhancement and Diversity
University of Kansas School of Medicine
Mail Stop 3022
3901 Rainbow Boulevard
Kansas City, KS 66160
913-588-1547; 913-588-8890 fax
gswoop@kumc.edu
www2.kumc.edu/oced

Introduction

Diversity is one of our core values at the University of Kansas School of Medicine, and we are deeply committed to creating the very best and stimulating educational environment for our students and delivering the best health care to our patients through diversity.

Recruitment

The Office of Cultural Enhancement and Diversity (OCED) was established in 1998 to address the cultural and diversity needs of the school. Objectives included in the office's mission are 1) to assist in recruiting a diverse student body; 2) to support an educational environment that fosters the vigorous exchange of ideas without fear of prejudice or persecution; 3) to train culturally and clinically skilled physicians and thereby improve access to high quality health care and biomedical research for underserved and special patient populations; and 4) to prepare students for leadership roles in the state of Kansas. In addition to recruitment, OCED accomplishes activities around diversity, such as retention, academic support services, cultural diversity and competency programming and education, and student career counseling and mentoring through several federally funded programs.

Admissions

Each August, the School of Medicine enrolls 175 students in the M.D. program. Prior to matriculation into the medical school, applicants must complete a course of studies leading to a baccalaureate degree as well as the following: (one year) general biology with lab; (one year) inorganic chemistry with lab; (one year) organic chemistry with lab; (one year) physics with lab; (one year) English composition or writing-intensive course; and (one semester) mathematics, college-level algebra, or above.

In addition, applicants must take the Medical College Admission Test (MCAT). We believe that a diverse student body provides for the most optimal learning experience to prepare graduates for the success in their careers, and we consider a number of Diversity Characteristics during our review of applications and deliberations.

Diversity Characteristics Desired of School of Medicine Matriculants:

• Significant life experiences in rural, inner city urban, or diverse cultural communities
• Significant life experiences in "non-western" countries or third-world countries
• Bilingual or multilingual abilities
• Previous careers before pursuing medicine
• Success in overcoming financial, social, family, physical, or educational hardships
• Success in overcoming adversity due to societal biases
• Successful experience in scientific or social research as measured by first-author publications
• Significant life experiences with individuals from cultural backgrounds other than their own

University of Kansas School of Medicine
Applicants, First-Time Applicants, Matriculants by Gender, Race and Ethnicity, 2007-2008

| | 2007 | | | | | | | | | 2008 | | | | | | | | |
| | APP | | | F-time APP | | | MAT | | | APP | | | F-time APP | | | MAT | | |
	Women	Men	Total	Women	Men	Total	Women	Men	Total	Women	Men	Total	Women	Men	Total	Women	Men	Total
Hispanic/Latino																		
Cuban	1	2	3	1	2	3	0	0	0	3	10	13	1	9	10	0	0	0
Mexican American	25	36	61	16	22	38	2	7	9	20	30	50	15	19	34	1	6	7
Puerto Rican	0	1	1	0	0	0	0	0	0	3	3	6	3	3	6	0	0	0
Other Hispanic	12	28	40	8	17	25	0	2	2	20	19	39	12	10	22	0	1	1
Multiple Hispanic/Latino*	2	1	3	2	1	3	0	0	0	7	1	8	6	0	6	0	0	0
Subtotal	40	68	108	27	42	69	2	9	11	53	63	116	37	41	78	1	7	8
Non-Hispanic/Latino**																		
Black	70	40	110	38	25	63	8	6	14	65	47	112	38	35	73	6	4	10
Native American/AK	12	8	20	10	7	17	1	0	1	4	8	12	2	7	9	1	0	1
Native Hawaiian/OPI	4	3	7	4	3	7	0	0	0	8	1	9	4	0	4	0	0	0
White	552	690	1,242	442	497	939	69	64	133	520	752	1,272	390	520	910	61	67	128
Asian	155	201	356	109	133	242	9	4	13	186	243	429	131	164	295	12	7	19
Other Race	0	1	1	0	1	1	0	0	0	0	1	1	0	1	1	0	0	0
Multiple Race*	20	27	47	16	22	38	4	0	4	15	29	44	12	15	27	1	3	4
Unknown	5	8	13	4	7	11	0	0	0	14	20	34	14	18	32	3	2	5
Subtotal	818	978	1,796	623	695	1,318	91	74	165	812	1,101	1,913	591	760	1,351	84	83	167
Foreign	6	8	14	4	6	10	0	0	0	8	10	18	6	8	14	0	0	0
Total	864	1,054	1,918	654	743	1,397	93	83	176	873	1,174	2,047	634	809	1,443	85	90	175

*Since 2002, students can select more than one race and / or ethnicity. **Those who did not choose 'Hispanic/Latino' or 'Non-Hispanic/Latino' are listed under 'Non-Hispanic/Latino'. Data Source: AAMC Data Warehouse: Applicant-Matriculant File, as of 1/16/2009.

Academic Support Programs

The Center of Excellence for Minority Medical Education (COE) is one of the federally funded programs administered by OCED. COE funds support the COE Learning Resource Center, which is located in close proximity to student classrooms. It contains a wealth of resources for students, serves as a gathering place used to discuss problems and exchange ideas, provides academic enrichment information, and provides an opportunity for students and OCED staff to interact on a regular basis. The Center employs a learning-skills specialist, offers United States Medical Licensing Examination (USMLE) board preparation workshops, supports a minority faculty—student mentoring program, and supplemental instruction. The Center and staff support student-led research on minority health care issues in the Minority Students and Faculty Summer Research Training Program. In addition to these programs, which are specifically designed for students in our federally funded diversity programs, more services are available through the campus-wide Student Center (*http://www.kumc.edu/studentcenter/scess*).

Enrichment Program

The School of Medicine support and grows a continuous and vigorous K-20 Educational Pipeline Program. Developed in 1986, the University of Kansas Medical Center (KUMC) Health Careers Pathways Program (HCPP) has served 5,268 students via three Satellite Centers, Saturday Academy, and through the summer enrichment programs.

Educational Partnerships

The Greater Kansas City—Health Professions Pipeway Initiative (HPPI) is a visionary and innovative bi-state alliance between the KUMC (Schools of Nursing, Allied Health, and Medicine), the University of Missouri-Kansas City, United School District (USD) 500, KCMO School

District and key churches
This Pipeway provides educational and

support programs to students and their teachers and families from kindergarten all the way through board examination, licensure, and employment, by linking with our other enrichment programs and community resources. The program's focus is on increasing the number of academically well-prepared underrepresented minority applicants in health care and other science-intensive careers. We have three church-based HPPI Cyber Learning Centers for partner families and their children (*http://www.gkc-hppi.org/ cyber.htm*).

Student Financial Assistance

Several guaranteed federal student loan programs are available to medical students at the KUMC, including Stafford Loans, Perkins Loans, and Primary Care Loans. In addition, the University of Kansas Endowment Association provides scholarship and loan assistance to medical students. One of the ways the School of Medicine strives to ensure diversity in the student body is through the scholarship-awarding process. KUMC is the recipient of a NIH Endowment grant for increasing research and training capacity, through the National Center on Minority Health and Health Disparities, a program that assists in enabling us to do this. KUMC also awards the federal Scholarship for Disadvantaged Students annually. This scholarship is available to students from either economically or educationally disadvantaged backgrounds, as defined by program guidelines. KUMC also offers the Kansas Medical Student Loan program. This program, created by the Kansas legislature, provides full tuition scholarships plus stipends in return for practice in rural and underserved parts of the state.

Other Pertinent Information

Multiple programs are available to support and educate students, faculty, and staff and impart cultural competence in this diverse learning environment.

There are close to 60 student organizations and interest groups that students have to choose from, and we encourage and support student participation in

these important organizations. Among them are the Student National Medical Association, the Latino Midwest Medical Student Association, the Asian American Medical Students Association, the Muslim Student Organization, and Students Educating and Advocating for Diversity (SEAD). Medical students are also actively involved in providing health care to the uninsured residents of Wyandotte County at the student-run JayDoc Clinic and participate in Medical Mission trips several times a year through the International Outreach Program. Members of these organizations not only provide personal support to one another, but they also educate and enrich the campus and local communities through their outreach and service projects.

The Office of Cultural Enhancement and Diversity and the school support cultural immersion experiences within the state and abroad. The Nicodemus Project is one such program that takes place in rural Kansas in a unique setting—the only remaining all-African American settlement founded by Exudusters in the post-civil-war era. Each summer descendants of the original settlers come together for a Homecoming Celebration, and our students participate by providing health screenings and prevention and health education as they learn about the culture of Nicodemus.

The Multicultural Health Care Information Resource Center (MIRC) houses, books, journals, posters, CDs, videos, and online access to its resource cache, as well as an electronic resource via the Dykes Library Voyager online catalog and the MIRC Web site located at (*http://www2. kumc.edu/oced/mirc.htm*). The MIRC Library has become a regional resource and clearinghouse, with its focus on health disparities and medical education opportunities for cultural minorities and underserved populations.

The Program on Diversity and Disparities in Health (PDDH), established within the Center of Excellence in Minority Medical Education in September 2001, was designed to enhance minority health research activities throughout KUMC. The program also sponsors a Distinguished Visiting Lectureship Series, which brings in speakers nationally and internationally renowned in health disparities research.

KUMC has a Diversity Initiative that includes a Diversity Advisory Council. This campus-wide initiative supported by a structure which is used to promote diversity *(http://www2.kumc.edu/hr/ diversity/ DefFiles/DivInt.htm)*.

University of Kentucky College of Medicine

Dr. Carol Elam, Associate Dean for Admissions and Institutional Advancement
University of Kentucky College of Medicine
138 Leader Avenue
Lexington, KY 40506-9983
859-323-6161; 859-257-3633 fax-
Clelam1@email.uky.edu
http://www.mc.uky.edu/medicine

Recruitment

The University of Kentucky has a commitment to provide health career information and counseling to high school and college students from minority and low-income groups in an effort to ensure such students have the opportunity to be admitted to, and succeed in, medical school. Special outreach programs designed to stimulate the interest of students from medically underserved populations in all health professions, especially medicine, have been developed for students attending Kentucky schools.

A full-time health science college recruiter is located in the Medical Center Multicultural Affairs Office.

Additionally, the Center for Academic Resources and Enrichment Services (CARES) sponsors a yearly session for students on our undergraduate campus to meet with student affairs officers who can address their specific issues and concerns regarding their anticipated health profession. Medical center students also sponsor an annual Hispanic Health Fair.

Admissions

Academic considerations are the primary determinant of who receives an interview at our institution. Non-academic considerations include leadership, caliber of recommendations, exposure to medicine, interest in primary care research involvement, and willingness to establish practice in Kentucky. Non-cognitive factors play a role in the selection of all candidates.

The Committee on Admissions of the College of Medicine is composed of basic science and clinical faculty members, junior and senior medical students, and community practitioners.

Academic Support Programs

The Center for Academic Resources and Enrichment Services (CARES) administers a short pre-entry program for all entering health profession students in late July. The program emphasizes activities and mentor relationships with faculty and continuing students.

The Office of Medical Education provides all students of the College of Medicine with assistance in achieving their educational goals and in adjusting to the special demands of medical education. The following programs are available to students: individual and group counseling, educational resources, preparation for national licensure examinations, tutorial service, and specialized support services as required.

Student Financial Assistance

The College of Medicine works closely with students to establish a reasonable financial budget and to provide financial assistance within the resources available.

The College of Medicine participates in the following federal assistance programs for disadvantaged students:

University of Kentucky College of Medicine
Applicants, First-Time Applicants, Matriculants by Gender, Race and Ethnicity, 2007-2008

	2007									2008								
	APP			F-time APP			MAT			APP			F-time APP			MAT		
	Women	Men	Total	Women	Men	Total	Women	Men	Total	Women	Men	Total	Women	Men	Total	Women	Men	Total
Hispanic/Latino																		
Cuban	1	10	11	0	8	8	0	0	0	4	6	10	2	6	8	0	0	0
Mexican American	10	16	26	9	12	21	0	0	0	14	14	28	10	10	20	0	0	0
Puerto Rican	1	4	5	1	3	4	0	0	0	2	2	4	2	0	2	0	0	0
Other Hispanic	11	20	31	8	17	25	0	0	0	11	23	34	7	16	23	1	1	2
Multiple Hispanic/Latino*	1	0	1	0	0	0	0	0	0	2	4	6	2	3	5	0	0	0
Subtotal	24	50	74	18	40	58	0	0	0	33	49	82	23	35	58	1	1	2
Non-Hispanic/Latino**																		
Black	66	38	104	46	26	72	3	0	3	61	29	90	45	16	61	3	1	4
Native American/AK	0	2	2	0	2	2	0	0	0	3	1	4	3	1	4	0	0	0
Native Hawaiian/OPI	3	2	5	3	2	5	0	0	0	4	0	4	2	0	2	0	0	0
White	554	829	1,383	441	622	1,063	33	50	83	588	869	1,457	458	616	1,074	39	55	94
Asian	154	198	352	107	141	248	6	5	11	138	207	345	96	138	234	1	6	7
Other Race	2	1	3	2	1	3	0	0	0	0	1	1	0	1	1	0	0	0
Multiple Race*	15	25	40	13	15	28	0	2	2	22	27	49	15	13	28	0	0	0
Unknown	5	7	12	5	6	11	0	0	0	10	27	37	9	25	34	1	0	1
Subtotal	799	1,102	1,901	617	815	1,432	42	57	99	826	1,161	1,987	628	810	1,438	44	62	106
Foreign	48	59	107	40	42	82	1	3	4	62	88	150	42	68	110	1	4	5
Total	871	1,211	2,082	675	897	1,572	43	60	103	921	1,298	2,219	693	913	1,606	46	67	113

*Since 2002, students can select more than one race and / or ethnicity. **Those who did not choose 'Hispanic/Latino' or 'Non-Hispanic/Latino' are listed under 'Non-Hispanic/Latino'. Data Source: AAMC Data Warehouse: Applicant-Matriculant File, as of 1/16/2009.

- Scholarships for Disadvantaged Students (SDS)
- National Health Service Corps (NHSC) Scholarship (Service Commitment)
- Primary Care Loan

The following institutional programs provide limited assistance to disadvantaged/minority students enrolled in the College of Medicine:

- College of Medicine Diversity Scholarship
- Jonas Scholarship Enhancement
- Provost Enhancement Scholarship

The College of Medicine also has institutional subsidized student loan programs to assist students in addition to federal financial aid.

University of Louisville School of Medicine

Mary S. Joshua, Associate Director, Minority and Rural Affairs, Special Programs Office
University of Louisville School of Medicine
Health Sciences Center
Abell Administration Center - 323 E. Chestnut Street, Room 502
Louisville, KY 40202
502-852-7159; 502-852-8866 fax
msjosh01@gwise.louisville.edu
www.louisville.edu/medschool/ahec/special.programs

Recruitment

To insure a quality education for our matriculants, an aggressive effort to identify and recruit a diverse student population is in place. Health career information and counseling are provided to high school and college students. A concerted effort is made to follow up with students from racial/ethnic groups underrepresented in medicine, counties underserved in health professions, and those with disadvantaged backgrounds. Also, information exchange occurs frequently with students and many pre-medical advisors throughout the United States.

The School of Medicine/Special Programs Office staff identifies high school and college students, encouraging them to participate in special summer preparatory programs to strengthen their academic skills and broaden their health career and research awareness. Throughout the year, mentorship activities, workshops and shadowing or visits with medical students, physicians, and basic science faculty are scheduled.

The Student National Medical Association and the Black Biomedical Graduate Student Organization assist with recruitment and retention of a diverse group of students.

Admissions

Applicants to the School of Medicine are considered individually and are selected based on merit. There is no separate admissions committee for screening applicants from underrepresented groups. However, there are individuals from underrepresented racial/ethnic groups who serve as members of the regular admissions committee.

The Admissions Committee evaluates an applicant's acceptability based on the entire academic record (undergraduate and graduate), Medical College Admission Test (MCAT) scores, and letters of recommendation. The applicant's personality and motivation are evaluated by interviews with members of the committee. Extracurricular activities and medical exposure are also important elements of the applicant evaluation.

The Medical Education Development (MED) Program provides a supplemental year for promising applicants who do not gain acceptance through the regular process. MED Program students are selected from the pool of regular applicants and are invited to take selected courses from the first-year medical school curriculum and graduate-level courses. Upon passing these courses and completing other program requirements, MED Program participants are considered for admission to the medical school to take the remainder of the first-year courses. Preference is granted to denied applicants from the targeted recruitment groups.

University of Louisville School of Medicine
Applicants, First-Time Applicants, Matriculants by Gender, Race and Ethnicity, 2007-2008

| | | 2007 | | | | | | | | | 2008 | | | | | | | | |
| | | APP | | | F-time APP | | | MAT | | | APP | | | F-time APP | | | MAT | | |
		Wo-men	Men	Total	Wo-men	Men	Total	Wo-men	Men	Total	Wo-men	Men	Total	Wo-men	Men	Total	Wo-men	Men	Total
Hispanic/Latino																			
Cuban		2	12	14	1	8	9	0	0	0	7	8	15	6	7	13	1	0	1
Mexican American		16	13	29	10	8	18	0	0	0	11	15	26	8	12	20	2	0	2
Puerto Rican		4	3	7	3	2	5	0	0	0	2	5	7	1	3	4	0	0	0
Other Hispanic		13	19	32	12	15	27	1	0	1	22	25	47	16	16	32	0	1	1
Multiple Hispanic/Latino*		1	1	2	1	1	2	0	0	0	4	1	5	3	0	3	0	0	0
	Subtotal	36	48	84	27	34	61	1	0	1	46	54	100	34	38	72	3	1	4
Non-Hispanic/Latino**																			
Black		106	44	150	71	30	101	7	3	10	102	46	148	62	35	97	9	4	13
Native American/AK		3	3	6	3	2	5	0	0	0	3	1	4	3	1	4	1	0	1
Native Hawaiian/OPI		2	1	3	2	1	3	0	0	0	2	2	4	0	0	0	0	0	0
White		596	857	1,453	462	645	1,107	48	71	119	572	969	1,541	414	680	1,094	42	70	112
Asian		182	235	417	127	164	291	9	6	15	168	262	430	122	167	289	7	10	17
Other Race		2	1	3	2	1	3	0	0	0	0	2	2	0	1	1	0	0	0
Multiple Race*		18	31	49	14	20	34	2	1	3	22	26	48	17	17	34	3	0	3
Unknown		4	5	9	4	5	9	0	0	0	16	32	48	15	27	42	1	2	3
	Subtotal	913	1,177	2,090	685	868	1,553	66	81	147	885	1,340	2,225	633	928	1,561	63	86	149
Foreign		10	10	20	6	9	15	0	0	0	7	16	23	5	13	18	2	0	2
	Total	959	1,235	2,194	718	911	1,629	67	81	148	938	1,410	2,348	672	979	1,651	68	87	155

*Since 2002, students can select more than one race and / or ethnicity. **Those who did not choose 'Hispanic/Latino' or 'Non-Hispanic/Latino' are listed under 'Non-Hispanic/Latino'. Data Source: AAMC Data Warehouse: Applicant-Matriculant File, as of 1/16/2009.

Academic Support Programs

Services are available to assist students in achieving their educational and career goals. These activities and services include: a four-week pre-matriculation program prior to entry into medical school; relocation, housing, and financial aid information; individual counseling and faculty-student-resident interaction; faculty advisors and a director of academic support; a tutorial program; assistance in preparation for the United States Medical Licensing Examination; educational resource material; and other workshops and individualized support as needed.

Enrichment Programs

Go to:
(www.louisville.edu/medschool/ahec/ special.programs).

Health Careers Adventure Program

This is an intensive effort of the North-West Area Health Education Center, which includes a four-week summer enrichment component for sixth-through tenth-grade students to encourage interest in a health career. Each summer, students participate and enhance academic skills in biology, math, chemistry, reading, and writing. They learn about health care and health careers through presentations and field trips to health care facilities with health professionals and professional students. Programs during the academic year, after school, and Saturdays include tutoring, volunteer opportunities, and presentations.

The Pre-freshman Professional Education Preparation Program

This program is a four-week residential academic program for graduating high school seniors interested in medicine or dentistry. Priority is given to graduating seniors from medically underserved counties in Kentucky and students from underrepresented groups. Students receive academic enrichment in math and science, study skills, and test-taking strategies. Participants gain career and clinical exposure to medicine and dentistry while adjusting to college life.

Summer Medical and Dental Education Program (SMDEP)

This innovative six-week residential academic program is for pre-medical and pre-dental students upon completion of one or two years of college. Funded by The Robert Wood Johnson Foundation, the program introduces students to the academic realities of medical and dental education. The hallmark activity is a course for credit entitled "Introduction to Fundamentals of Biomedical Sciences." Participants focus on integrating and applying the basic sciences utilizing team-based medial/dental applications for college credit, tuition-free. In addition to science enrichment, students receive intensive instruction and workshops centered on financial planning, career planning, health disparities, written and oral communication, learning-skills development, and cultural competency training. Students are divided into clusters with medical and dental students serving as Student Development Assistants and Cluster Leaders. The academic component is taught by Health Sciences Center faculty.

MCAT/DAT Training Conference

After completion of two years of college, pre-medical and pre-dental students may apply to a five-week summer residential program to assist them in preparation for the MCAT or the Dental Admission Test (DAT). Students review biology, general chemistry, organic chemistry, physics, verbal reasoning, and quantitative reasoning. Pre-dental students review an additional course in perceptual ability. In addition to review, students participate in professional and personal development workshops, clinical activities, and hospital tours. Supervised practice test sessions on the MCAT and DAT are conducted. Application, personal statement, and interview assistance are also provided.

Pre-matriculation Program

Upon their admission to the University of Louisville School of Medicine, students from disadvantaged backgrounds, underrepresented groups, or medically underserved counties are invited to participate in the four-week summer Pre-matriculation Program. This program is conducted during the weeks immediately preceding the beginning of the school year. The areas of emphasis include human physiology, medical biochemistry, and anatomical science. Time is also devoted to overall orientation to medical school, study and test-taking skills, stress management, computing, financial management, practice opportunities, research options, and clinical activity. In addition to academic preparation, this program provides for the development of peer groups, establishment of support systems, familiarity with the city and school, dialogue with faculty and upper-level students, and an early establishment of day-to-day routine.

Student Financial Assistance

The University of Louisville School of Medicine waives the secondary application fee for disadvantaged students. Financial assistance for interview trips cannot be provided. The university offers scholarships for students with strong academic credentials. Based on available resources, the School of Medicine makes a concerted effort to assist students in meeting their financial needs. During the Pre-matriculation Program and academic year, workshops on debt management and financial planning are provided.

Educational Partnerships

University of Kentucky, State Council on Higher Education, Pikeville Osteopathic Medical School, Kentucky State University, Western Kentucky University

Louisiana State University Health Science Center School of Medicine in New Orleans

Dr. Edward G. Helm, Associate Dean and Professor of Surgery
Louisiana State University School of Medicine in New Orleans
Office of Community & Minority Health Education
1901 Perdido Street
Suite 310, Box P3-2
New Orleans, LA 70112-1393
504-568-8501; 504-568-6319 fax
http://www.medschool.lsuhsc.edu/cmhe/

Recruitment

The Louisiana State University (LSU) School of Medicine in New Orleans actively recruits minority and disadvantaged students. The Office of Community & Minority Health Education (CMHE) directs its retention activities at the K-12 and college level. Recruitment workshops are held annually at the health sciences center. Invitations are extended to all Louisiana college pre-medical advisors and students. A workshop consists of an overview of the medical school curriculum and presentations by the faculty and administrators. High school recruitment activities include working with high school science clubs, Career Awareness and Competition Days held at the health sciences center, and visits to high schools. Recruitment activities are carried out by the CMHE staff, medical students, and faculty. The school's recruitment efforts encompass an integrated program of visits, lectures, films, tours, and actual assistance in completing applications.

Admissions

The LSU School of Medicine in New Orleans is dedicated to providing the opportunity for an excellent medical education to all Louisiana applicants who are prepared to benefit from its curriculum and instruction. To this end, the Admissions Committee of the School of Medicine will strive to recruit and admit Louisiana residents from every geographic, economic, social, and cultural dimension of the state of Louisiana.

The primary goal of the School of Medicine in New Orleans is to produce competent, humanistic physicians. In order to achieve this goal, the School of Medicine finds that having a diverse student body is essential. Diversity in all its forms benefits students by creating a dynamic, productive, and positive learning environment that promotes better cross-cultural and cross-racial understanding. Ultimately the benefit of classroom diversity will help the School of Medicine produce individuals who are able to be effective clinicians within a multi-cultural environment.

Our present policy precludes us from accepting applications from individual who are not residents of Louisiana unless the applicant is the son/daughter of an alumnus of LSU School of Medicine in New Orleans who no longer resides in the state or an applicant who is applying to the M.D./Ph.D. program.* There is no discrimination because of race, religion, sex, age, disability, national origin, or financial status. Minority and disadvantaged students are strongly encouraged to apply. The Office of Community & Minority Health Education may be reached by calling

Louisiana State University School of Medicine in New Orleans
Applicants, First-Time Applicants, Matriculants by Gender, Race and Ethnicity, 2007-2008

	2007 APP Women	Men	Total	F-time APP Women	Men	Total	MAT Women	Men	Total	2008 APP Women	Men	Total	F-time APP Women	Men	Total	MAT Women	Men	Total
Hispanic/Latino																		
Cuban	2	10	12	1	8	9	0	0	0	3	6	9	3	3	6	0	1	1
Mexican American	14	18	32	9	13	22	1	2	3	4	4	8	2	3	5	1	0	1
Puerto Rican	3	4	7	2	3	5	0	0	0	0	3	3	0	0	0	0	0	0
Other Hispanic	17	20	37	11	13	24	1	2	3	18	11	29	13	6	19	3	4	7
Multiple Hispanic/Latino*	1	2	3	1	2	3	0	0	0	4	2	6	3	1	4	0	1	1
Subtotal	37	54	91	24	39	63	2	4	6	29	26	55	21	13	34	4	6	10
Non-Hispanic/Latino**																		
Black	99	38	137	72	27	99	8	3	11	86	36	122	54	31	85	8	2	10
Native American/AK	1	1	2	1	1	2	0	0	0	1	0	1	0	0	0	0	0	0
Native Hawaiian/OPI	3	2	5	3	2	5	0	1	1	0	4	4	0	2	2	0	1	1
White	345	492	837	253	323	576	59	82	141	262	361	623	189	240	429	57	80	137
Asian	105	144	249	77	99	176	10	4	14	64	62	126	50	41	91	9	8	17
Other Race	1	1	2	1	0	1	0	0	0	0	0	0	0	0	0	0	0	0
Multiple Race*	8	28	36	5	20	25	2	4	6	10	15	25	7	7	14	0	1	1
Unknown	3	3	6	2	3	5	0	0	0	4	6	10	4	6	10	1	2	3
Subtotal	565	709	1,274	414	475	889	79	94	173	427	484	911	304	327	631	75	94	169
Foreign	16	33	49	12	22	34	0	0	0	10	14	24	10	12	22	0	0	0
Total	618	796	1,414	450	536	986	81	98	179	466	524	990	335	352	687	79	100	179

*Since 2002, students can select more than one race and / or ethnicity. **Those who did not choose 'Hispanic/Latino' or 'Non-Hispanic/Latino' are listed under 'Non-Hispanic/Latino'. Data Source: AAMC Data Warehouse: Applicant-Matriculant File, as of 1/16/2009.

504-568-8501. Dr. Edward G. Helm is the associate dean for this office.

If you are not sure of your residency status as it pertains to Louisiana or you would like information on the residency requirements, you should make an inquiry to W. Bryant Faust, Acting Registrar; LSU Health Sciences Center, 433 Bolivar Street, New Orleans, LA 70112; 504-568-4829.

Rural Scholars' Track
LSU School of Medicine in New Orleans has implemented a Rural Scholars' Track. The goal of this pathway is to identify and train physicians who will most likely practice medicine in rural settings, particularly in the state of Louisiana. This rural track is in response to the growing shortage of physicians in certain areas of Louisiana. The Rural Scholars' Track will improve the delivery and quality of the rural health care system through a combination of education, service, collaboration, and research specific to these underserved areas of the state.

The students admitted to this program will have to meet the same admissions criteria as all other students applying to the school. The students who are chosen to enter this track will be selected from applicants who have already been accepted into the entering class. Admission to this program will be limited to students coming from rural parishes defined as primary care shortage areas by the Louisiana State Board of Medical Examiners. In addition, students from parishes designated as rural by the Office of Rural Health Policy will be given further consideration.

Academic Support Programs
The School of Medicine has tutorial programs in the basic sciences, as well as in the clinical areas. In addition, the CMHE staff provides basic science course review sessions and study-skills workshops during the academic year for all minority/disadvantaged students. A structured four-week United States Medical Licensing Examination Step 1 review is available to all second-year LSU students.

Enrichment Programs
Science Enrichment Program (SEP)
The SEP is an after-school program for 30 seventh graders conducted at a New Orleans public middle school. SEP is for students who have expressed an interest in health careers and enjoy math and science. The classes, held two days per week for one-hour sessions, will not only sharpen science and mathematics skills but also improve test-taking skills for the eighth grade LEAP exam. High School Science Club members and LSU School of Medicine minority and disadvantaged medical students serve as SEP tutors.

Junior Summer Science Program (JrSSP)
The JrSSP is a four-week summer hands-on research experience at LSU Health Sciences Center for ten SEP students to apply learned science and mathematics principles in a biomedical hands-on laboratory setting. Minority and disadvantaged medial students assist the instructor for the program.

Summer Science Program (SSP)
This eight-week enrichment program is for rising and graduating disadvantaged high school seniors who have demonstrated an interest in the health professions. The students must be Louisiana residents. The purpose of the program is to provide academically talented students an opportunity to interact with scientists, clinicians, and faculty of the Louisiana State University Health Sciences Center. This program provides classroom, as well as hands-on, laboratory experiences. Students are assigned sites in the university-affiliated hospitals, research laboratories of faculty, and clinical settings. Minority and disadvantaged medical students serve as program coordinators.

Medical College Admission Test (MCAT) Review
A comprehensive preparatory to review the MCAT is offered to potential applicants. This course includes a preliminary diagnostic examination, lectures in each area of the MCAT, a review of test-taking techniques, home-study materials, and access to the online data-based computer library. Upon completion of the course, a mock MCAT is given.

Pre-matriculation Program
The goal of the program is to provide entering disadvantaged medical students with experiences that will facilitate academic, environmental, and emotional adjustment to medical school. It is intended that participation in this program will enable the student to begin medical school with greater ease and competency. The program consists of lectures and lab experiences in histology, biochemistry, physiology, and gross anatomy. In addition, sessions in personal development, study skills, note taking, test-taking skills, memorization, and time management are also offered. Students will be given Career Exploration and Cultural Competency Workshops, a one-week rotation in a Community Health Clinic, and a two-week Primary Care Shadowing experience.

Student Financial Assistance
Incoming freshman students who are of the opinion that they are disadvantaged from an educational, economic, or social point of view are encouraged to apply for a scholarship. Members of the Medical School Scholarship Committee interview the applicants and the committee decides on who is most deserving for the award. A base award of $1,500-$3,000 per year is available for four years. The program is available for approximately 15 disadvantaged students/year.

Educational Partnerships
An educational network exists with the New Orleans Public School System (NOPS). Through this LSU–NOPS linkage, students receive information, support, and encouragement to explore health care fields as professions. School-based science clubs serve as the forum. Club sponsors—high school science teachers and counselors with LSU faculty—direct activities and field trips. Programmatic components of the net-

work are Awareness Day, Competition Day, the High School Summer Science Program, and the seventh Grade SEP and Junior Summer Science Program. In addition, CMHE has a Young Healers Mentorship Program with the Louisiana Medical Association. This program offers a variety of opportunities for African-American medical students to work with practicing minority physicians.

In addition, partnerships with Louisiana's Historically Black Colleges and Universities exist for the recruitment and facilitation of entry into the School of Medicine.

Louisiana State University School of Medicine in Shreveport

Shirley Roberson, Director Multicultural Affairs
LSUHSC School of Medicine in Shreveport
1501 Kings Highway
Shreveport, LA 71130-3932
(318) 675-5049; (318) 675-4332 fax
srober1@lsuhsc.edu

Recruitment

The Director of Multicultural Affairs, along with the Assistant Dean of Admissions, visits college campuses in Louisiana each year with special attention given to the Historically Black Colleges and Universities in the state. Students are presented information pertaining to admissions procedures, scholarships, support services, student activities, curriculum, and other programs provided by the Louisiana State University Health Sciences Center School of Medicine. In an effort to inform pre-college students about the health care professions, visits to local high schools are made as requested and students are encouraged to participate in K-12 pipeline programs which introduce them to healthcare careers. Minority medical students and faculty participate in both the interview and recruiting processes.

Admissions

The Louisiana State University Health Sciences Center School of Medicine in Shreveport is an American Medical College Application Service (AMCAS) affiliated school, and all applicants must apply through that agency. All Louisiana applicants completing the AMCAS process are sent a secondary application. Applicants who are granted a fee waiver from AMCAS can request a waiver of the $50 fee that normally accompanies the secondary application filed directly with the Louisiana State University Health Sciences Center School of Medicine in Shreveport. Applicants are admitted to the Louisiana State University Health Sciences Center School of Medicine without regard to race, sex, marital status, disability, age, or creed. Students are evaluated on their scholastic records, Medical College Admission Test (MCAT) scores, interview evaluations, and letters of recommendation. Non-cognitive variables are also considered.

The Admissions Committee is composed of basic and clinical science faculty as well as physicians from the community and medical students. Minorities are represented on this committee.

Academic Support Programs

The Louisiana State University Health Sciences Center (LSUHSC) School of Medicine in Shreveport has a peer tutoring program for students experiencing academic difficulty. Academic progress of all students is monitored closely throughout the year by the Student Promotions Committee who are a part of the Medical Curriculum Counsel, which works closely with the Director of Multicultural Affairs. Academic and personal counseling is coordinated through the Offices of Student Affairs and Multicultural Affairs.

Student Financial Assistance

LSUHSC School of Medicine in Shreveport has re-established a scholarship program directed at medical students who come from disadvantaged backgrounds educationally, economically, and/or socially. This program is designed to help reduce the educational debt incurred during medical school for those medical students who have lacked the traditional benefits available to most students in the areas of primary

Louisiana State University School of Medicine in Shreveport
Applicants, First-Time Applicants, Matriculants by Gender, Race and Ethnicity, 2007-2008

| | 2007 | | | | | | | | | 2008 | | | | | | | | |
| | APP | | | F-time APP | | | MAT | | | APP | | | F-time APP | | | MAT | | |
	Women	Men	Total	Women	Men	Total	Women	Men	Total	Women	Men	Total	Women	Men	Total	Women	Men	Total
Hispanic/Latino																		
Cuban	3	4	7	1	3	4	0	0	0	1	5	6	1	2	3	0	1	1
Mexican American	11	8	19	7	5	12	1	0	1	3	4	7	2	3	5	0	1	1
Puerto Rican	2	3	5	2	2	4	0	1	1	0	4	4	0	1	1	0	0	0
Other Hispanic	9	16	25	7	7	14	0	0	0	14	9	23	10	3	13	0	0	0
Multiple Hispanic/Latino*	0	2	2	0	1	1	0	1	1	3	1	4	3	0	3	0	0	0
Subtotal	25	33	58	17	18	35	1	2	3	21	23	44	16	9	25	0	2	2
Non-Hispanic/Latino**																		
Black	76	35	111	58	30	88	4	3	7	61	22	83	40	17	57	3	0	3
Native American/AK	2	0	2	1	0	1	0	0	0	0	0	0	0	0	0	0	0	0
Native Hawaiian/OPI	2	2	4	2	2	4	0	0	0	0	3	3	0	1	1	0	0	0
White	255	380	635	179	255	434	40	60	100	196	276	472	143	179	322	47	53	100
Asian	69	91	160	49	63	112	1	3	4	32	48	80	22	30	52	3	5	8
Multiple Race*	3	16	19	1	12	13	0	3	3	4	10	14	3	4	7	1	1	2
Unknown	3	1	4	3	1	4	0	0	0	3	3	6	3	3	6	1	0	1
Subtotal	410	525	935	293	363	656	45	69	114	296	362	658	211	234	445	55	59	114
Foreign	4	7	11	3	6	9	0	0	0	0	1	1	0	1	1	0	0	0
Total	439	565	1,004	313	387	700	46	71	117	317	386	703	227	244	471	55	61	116

*Since 2002, students can select more than one race and / or ethnicity. **Those who did not choose 'Hispanic/Latino' or 'Non-Hispanic/Latino' are listed under 'Non-Hispanic/Latino'. Data Source: AAMC Data Warehouse: Applicant-Matriculant File, as of 1/16/2009.

and secondary education, family income and assets, social and cultural experiences. Students are also encouraged to compete for national merit and need-based awards and grants. There is an emergency loan program funded by faculty donations to assist students who have an urgent need. All applicants are advised to be aggressive in making their financial needs known to medical school officials.

Other Pertinent Information

In addition to numerous intramural activities, there is a chapter of the Student National Medical Association (SNMA), a non-profit organization that is composed of minority and non-minority medical, graduate and allied health students.

Tulane University School of Medicine

Dr. Ernest Sneed, Assistant Dean
of Students
Office of Admissions and Student
Affairs
Tulane University School of Medicine
1430 Tulane Avenue, SL 67
New Orleans, LA 70112
esneed@tulane.edu

Recruitment

The diversity of our student body is an important factor in ensuring that our students have an enriched learning environment and that they become culturally competent physicians. Members of our Office of Admissions and Student Affairs, along with student and faculty representatives, make visits to both local and national undergraduate institutions with significant minority populations to encourage interest in medicine in general and in our institution in particular. Through the Student National Medical Association and the Office of Diversity, undergraduate and high school minority students from various colleges and local high schools visit our institution throughout the year. They interact with students, residents, and faculty while here and are encouraged to contact members of our medical community with any questions or concerns after they leave our campus. Tulane is a host site for the National Youth Leadership Forum on Medicine each summer, and we are able to encourage these exceptional high school students to return to Tulane for medical school. Tulane is also linked with the Center for Math and Science High School here in New Orleans, which also provides an opportunity to directly engage the interest of local, talented minority students.

Admissions

Tulane does not have a separate admissions process for minority students. Rather, all applications are considered individually, with race/ethnicity being only one of a number of factors that make up an individual's unique profile. We seek to admit a diversity of well-rounded, committed, involved students who will make positive contributions to our medical school and to the community in which they serve, and who will make competent, compassionate, and able physicians. The Admissions Committee always has at least three minority representatives (one student and two faculty) out of 25 total members. When minority students come for interviews, we routinely have our minority students and faculty available to interact with them, to answer any questions, and just to talk. We encourage the applicants to keep in touch after the interview process, and to feel free to contact anyone they have met here, or the Assistant Dean of Student Affairs, for specific questions. We have several Early Acceptance Programs with colleges in the area, which help to ensure that qualified minority students from those institutions choose our medical school to attend. We also have the Tulane Rural Medical Education (TRuMEd) program, which helps guide interested students to eventually practice in a rural and underserved setting.

Academic Support Programs

All students accepted to Tulane University School of Medicine are capable of excelling academically, and we monitor their progress via the Academic Performance Committee, whose purpose is

Tulane University School of Medicine
Applicants, First-Time Applicants, Matriculants by Gender, Race and Ethnicity, 2007-2008

	2007									2008								
	APP			F-time APP			MAT			APP			F-time APP			MAT		
	Women	Men	Total	Women	Men	Total	Women	Men	Total	Women	Men	Total	Women	Men	Total	Women	Men	Total
Hispanic/Latino																		
Cuban	26	41	67	18	30	48	0	0	0	36	43	79	30	35	65	1	0	1
Mexican American	59	62	121	50	41	91	0	0	0	61	68	129	48	44	92	0	0	0
Puerto Rican	20	20	40	15	16	31	0	0	0	11	24	35	9	17	26	0	0	0
Other Hispanic	80	90	170	56	62	118	1	1	2	118	117	235	88	74	162	2	0	2
Multiple Hispanic/Latino*	8	9	17	7	6	13	0	0	0	20	14	34	17	6	23	0	0	0
Subtotal	193	222	415	146	155	301	1	1	2	246	266	512	192	176	368	3	0	3
Non-Hispanic/Latino**																		
Black	223	112	335	172	82	254	4	0	4	322	126	448	219	96	315	0	2	2
Native American/AK	4	6	10	3	6	9	0	0	0	9	9	18	7	7	14	0	0	0
Native Hawaiian/OPI	12	11	23	10	7	17	0	1	1	14	14	28	8	9	17	0	0	0
White	1,692	2,070	3,762	1,291	1,437	2,728	55	71	126	1,930	2,557	4,487	1,427	1,709	3,136	61	74	135
Asian	807	971	1,778	559	658	1,217	17	16	33	997	1,122	2,119	690	687	1,377	14	17	31
Other Race	1	6	7	1	1	2	0	0	0	4	8	12	3	7	10	0	0	0
Multiple Race*	78	92	170	61	59	120	2	3	5	109	101	210	83	62	145	1	2	3
Unknown	33	37	70	31	30	61	0	2	2	73	93	166	66	77	143	1	2	3
Subtotal	2,850	3,305	6,155	2,128	2,280	4,408	78	93	171	3,458	4,030	7,488	2,503	2,654	5,157	77	97	174
Foreign	119	111	230	94	83	177	2	0	2	135	171	306	103	131	234	1	0	1
Total	3,162	3,638	6,800	2,368	2,518	4,886	81	94	175	3,839	4,467	8,306	2,798	2,961	5,759	81	97	178

Note: In 2008, one applicant, who declined to report gender, was not included here.
*Since 2002, students can select more than one race and / or ethnicity. **Those who did not choose 'Hispanic/Latino' or 'Non-Hispanic/Latino' are listed under 'Non-Hispanic/Latino'. Data Source: AAMC Data Warehouse: Applicant-Matriculant File, as of 1/16/2009.

to identify students with problems early on so that they can get the help they need to succeed. The course directors are proactive in assisting students with difficulties via individual or group tutoring by members of the department. Our Office of Education in the medical school, and the Educational

Resource Center on the nearby undergraduate campus, are both available to assist with study skills and time management issues, as well as with testing for learning disabilities. A Peer Tutoring Program is in place that trains and funds upper-level students to work with first- or second-year students that are having course difficulties, and it has been very successful. There is also a system in place to assist any student with psychological or personal issues in a confidential and compassionate manner. We stress to all of our students that we will help in whatever way necessary to ensure their success in these often challenging medical school years.

Student Financial Assistance
Some application fee waivers are granted but no financial assistance is available for interview trips. Tulane offers financial assistance to qualified students through scholarships or loans, federal, private, or institutional. While most available financial aid is need-based, Tulane offers a limited number of scholarships that are awarded on the basis of academic achievement.

Inquiries concerning financial aid should be directed to the Financial Aid Office, Tulane School of Medicine, New Orleans, LA 70112.

Johns Hopkins University School of Medicine

Dr. Daniel Hiroyaki Teraguchi,
Assistant Dean, Student Affairs
Director,
Office for Student Diversity
Johns Hopkins University School of
Medicine
Broadway Research Building,
Suite 137
733 North Broadway
Baltimore, MD 21205
410-614-8759; 410-955-0544 fax
dteraguchi@jhu.edu
http://www.hopkinsmedicine.org/
som/students/diversity

Recruitment

The Johns Hopkins University School of Medicine is committed to enrolling and educating individuals from disadvantaged groups. Minority faculty and students participate in all admissions and recruitment activities. Representatives of the Admissions Committee, faculty, student body, and the Assistant Dean for Student Affairs visit colleges throughout the country to provide pre-medical advisors and minority students with information about educational opportunities available at the Johns Hopkins medical institutions. This is followed by direct mailings to the students to encourage them to apply. Informal counseling is also available for pre-medical students. Tours of the medical school and hospital facilities are conducted for all applicants selected for interview, and similar tours can be conducted, upon request, to minority student groups interested in medical careers.

Admissions

There are no state residency requirements, and the Committee on Admission welcomes applications from minority students throughout the country. The B.A. degree, or equivalent, must be received prior to matriculation. All students are encouraged to complete degrees in the liberal arts or sciences consistent with their undergraduate major. Admitted applicants may request a deferral of their admission for a period of up to three years. The Medical College Admission Test (MCAT) is required.

Minority students are considered on an equal basis with other candidates. Selection factors include: proven academic competence in college courses, strong personal qualities, demonstrated leadership, creative abilities, commitment to humanistic concerns, and supporting recommendations provided by premedical advisors or faculty members. Applications to the Johns Hopkins University School of Medicine are made through the American Medical College Application Service (AMCAS).

Academic Support Programs

The curriculum schedule emphasizes adequate time for self-study and exploration. In the first year, formal classroom activities end at 1:00 p.m. Students have the afternoon hours for further study or for extracurricular activities. Tutorial programs are provided in each of the courses and are subscribed to on a voluntary basis. Small-group sessions emphasize mentoring by individual faculty as well as open faculty office hours in the afternoon. The Student Assistance Program offers workshops on study skills, time management, and test taking. These programs are offered to all students on a voluntary basis. Programs emphasize individual students and are not targeted toward any subgroup in the student body.

Johns Hopkins University School of Medicine
Applicants, First-Time Applicants, Matriculants by Gender, Race and Ethnicity, 2007-2008

	2007									2008								
	APP			F-time APP			MAT			APP			F-time APP			MAT		
	Wo-men	Men	Total	Wo-men	Men	Total	Wo-men	Men	Total	Wo-men	Men	Total	Wo-men	Men	Total	Wo-men	Men	Total
Hispanic/Latino																		
Cuban	10	20	30	10	17	27	0	0	0	18	15	33	15	14	29	0	0	0
Mexican American	58	68	126	49	56	105	0	0	0	49	62	111	40	48	88	0	0	0
Puerto Rican	30	26	56	27	22	49	0	0	0	14	21	35	11	16	27	0	1	1
Other Hispanic	77	86	163	64	72	136	3	0	3	65	78	143	52	65	117	1	2	3
Multiple Hispanic/Latino*	9	7	16	9	7	16	0	0	0	12	15	27	10	13	23	1	0	1
Subtotal	184	207	391	159	174	333	3	0	3	158	191	349	128	156	284	2	3	5
Non-Hispanic/Latino**																		
Black	293	177	470	234	153	387	7	5	12	303	155	458	242	128	370	4	3	7
Native American/AK	8	3	11	6	3	9	0	0	0	4	6	10	4	6	10	0	0	0
Native Hawaiian/OPI	10	3	13	8	2	10	0	0	0	12	3	15	9	1	10	0	1	1
White	1,297	1,775	3,072	1,152	1,519	2,671	27	26	53	1,224	1,877	3,101	1,077	1,624	2,701	31	34	65
Asian	728	842	1,570	645	706	1,351	17	20	37	641	831	1,472	545	658	1,203	13	15	28
Other Race	1	2	3	1	2	3	0	0	0	0	2	2	0	1	1	0	0	0
Multiple Race*	95	87	182	83	76	159	2	5	7	81	86	167	70	75	145	2	0	2
Unknown	37	49	86	36	44	80	0	1	1	68	104	172	66	96	162	3	0	3
Subtotal	2,469	2,938	5,407	2,165	2,505	4,670	53	57	110	2,333	3,064	5,397	2,013	2,589	4,602	53	53	106
Foreign	169	181	350	134	151	285	3	2	5	154	189	343	138	145	283	4	3	7
Total	2,822	3,326	6,148	2,458	2,830	5,288	59	59	118	2,645	3,444	6,089	2,279	2,890	5,169	59	59	118

*Since 2002, students can select more than one race and / or ethnicity. **Those who did not choose 'Hispanic/Latino' or 'Non-Hispanic/Latino' are listed under 'Non-Hispanic/Latino'. Data Source: AAMC Data Warehouse: Applicant-Matriculant File, as of 1/16/2009.

Student Financial Assistance

All financial aid is need-based. Qualified aid applicants receive a package of scholarship and loan funds. Every aid recipient is first given a standard unit loan to meet their need. The amount of the unit loan varies annually and is the same for every student. Remaining financial need above the unit loan is awarded in scholarship monies. The application fee can be waived if the applicant has received an AMCAS fee waiver or if a letter is sent from their financial aid officer or pre-medical advisor to certify their inability to pay the fee.

For several years, the average debt of our graduating seniors has been less than that for graduating seniors from state supported schools.

The financial aid office is actively searching for scholarships and grant awards for which our students are eligible and make application when such sources are identified. All funds received in this manner reduce the amount the student has to borrow or reduces their parents' contribution.

Enrichment Programs

Minority Summer Internship Program {Undergraduates}
This is a ten-week program for undergraduates interested in graduate biomedical research. Students accepted to the program are placed in the laboratories of faculty members and work on projects designed for them by faculty. While at Hopkins the students learn about the M.D./Ph.D admissions processes, interact with graduate students, and participate in a number of enrichment activities including journal clubs with faculty members and research seminars. The students receive full support in this program including stipend, housing, and travel.

Contact Person: Dr. Peter Maloney, Director; Phone: 410-614-3385; FAX: 410-614-3386

High School Summer Research Placements
Each year five to ten students from local high schools are placed in research laboratories here at Johns Hopkins. The students are paired with advanced Ph.D. students who serve as their mentors for six to eight weeks. The high school students carry out research projects designed for them by the Ph.D. student or faculty member and also participate in activities of the Minority Summer Internship Program for undergraduate students. These include journal clubs, seminar presentations, and field trips to the National Institutes of Health.

Summer Research Project
During the summer following their first year of medical school, the students may participate in summer research fellowships with faculty from the School of Medicine.

Educational Partnerships

The Dunbar-Hopkins Health Partnership is Baltimore City's and Maryland's most strategically positioned school, university, and business-community partnership for the health professions. Dunbar Senior High School is a citywide school that is envisioned as becoming a magnet health science school in the near future. This multifaceted collaboration involves Dunbar Senior High School; Johns Hopkins Schools of Medicine, Nursing, and Public Health; the Johns Hopkins Hospital; and the Johns Hopkins Center for the Social Organization of Schools. Under the direction of Dunbar's principal, the initiative prepares students for admission to college and to a variety of careers in the health professions. This goal is realized, in part, through a variety of programs and interventions, including: curricular view and consultation, faculty development, field work and internships, grant writing, information technology donations and planning, longitudinal program evaluation, mentoring, public relations assistance, special seminars, and visiting scholars and faculty.

A critical element of the students program at Dunbar High School is research. The initial research course, Scientific Research in Health Care Delivery Systems: Theory and Application, will be offered in the second year of high school. This course will provide the foundation for students who will learn to read, understand, and apply research to their pathway of study. Throughout the third and fourth year of high school, the students will continue to conduct more sophisticated research that will culminate in a senior project. This Senior Project for the Health Professions Majors will be a research project using all types of research resources, Internet, journals, and current unpublished research. The senior project will include an exhibition with a presentation to a panel of health care professionals, educators, and peers.

The Student National Medical Association of the Johns Hopkins University School of Medicine sponsors a tutorial program at the Dunbar Senior High School. Students are tutored from 3:30 p.m. to 4:30 p.m. once or twice weekly as their schedule permits. Students are tutored in mathematics, chemistry, physics, biology, history, English, and foreign languages. Special programs are also provided to prepare these students for college and to acquaint them with health career opportunities. This group of medical students also participates in a Teen Sex Education Program at the Dunbar Middle School.

In doing these things for the Dunbar Middle and High Schools, the minority medical students serve as role models to encourage disadvantaged youth to pursue careers in medicine.

Uniformed Services University of the Health Sciences
F. Edward Hébert School of Medicine

Dr. Margaret Calloway, CDR, MC, USN, Associate Dean for Recruitment and Admissions, Uniformed Services University of the Health Sciences Office of Recruitment and Admissions
Room A1041
4301 Jones Bridge Road
Bethesda, MD 20814-4799
301- 295-3383; 301-295-3545 fax
mcalloway@usuhs.mil
http://www.usuhs.mil

Introduction

The Uniformed Services University of the Health Sciences (USU) was established by Congress in 1972 to provide a comprehensive education in medicine to select young men and women who demonstrate potential for and commitment to careers as medical corps officers in the uniformed services. USU serves the uniformed services and the nation as an outstanding academic health sciences center with a worldwide perspective for education, research, service, and consultation. It is unique in relating these activities to military medical readiness, public health, disaster medicine, and humanitarian medical assistance worldwide. The university provides the nation with health professionals committed to careers in public service and scientists dedicated to inquiry, research, and technological advances that serve the common good.

USU is a tuition-free medical school. Students are commissioned as active duty reserve officers in one of the four branches of the uniformed services – Army, Navy, Air Force, or Public Health Service—and afforded all of the pay and allowances, privileges and responsibilities of an active duty officer. In 2009, the annual average salary of a USU medical student was approximately $54,000, plus medical and dental benefits (prior Service Officers and enlisted personnel are at a slightly higher rate).

The Office of Recruitment and Admissions is instrumental in the recruitment and retention of a student body that mirrors the diversity of this nation through a multi-faceted approach to enhancing the cultural, ethnic, and experiential diversity within the university.

Recruitment

Seaman to Admiral Medical Corps Option (STA-21)
This unique program was designed specifically with our nation's service members in mind. Its goal is to draw highly motivated, academically sound students from the current active duty community who are interested in pursuing military medical careers. The STA-21 Medical Corps Option, still in its infancy, will facilitate the completion of a baccalaureate degree, acceptance to medical school, and the completion of a Doctor of Medicine or Doctor of Osteopathy degree, by providing an opportunity for enlisted personnel to complete their education without a break in service, and finally to obtain a commission in the U.S. Navy. Current USU medical students would serve as mentors and tutors for this talented group of service members.

Student Ambassador Program
Representatives from USU attend various career fairs and national confer-

Uniformed Services University of the Health Sciences F. Edward Hebert School of Medicine
Applicants, First-Time Applicants, Matriculants by Gender, Race and Ethnicity, 2007-2008

	2007									2008								
	APP			F-time APP			MAT			APP			F-time APP			MAT		
	Women	Men	Total	Women	Men	Total	Women	Men	Total	Women	Men	Total	Women	Men	Total	Women	Men	Total
Hispanic/Latino																		
Cuban	2	6	8	1	5	6	0	0	0	4	8	12	3	7	10	1	1	2
Mexican American	18	32	50	13	23	36	1	3	4	16	36	52	14	24	38	1	1	2
Puerto Rican	9	5	14	7	4	11	1	1	2	12	11	23	9	9	18	3	0	3
Other Hispanic	23	36	59	19	21	40	1	3	4	26	42	68	18	29	47	2	4	6
	4	2	6	3	1	4	0	0	0	1	4	5	1	2	3	0	0	0
Subtotal	56	81	137	43	54	97	3	7	10	59	101	160	45	71	116	7	6	13
Non-Hispanic/Latino**																		
Black	65	47	112	47	37	84	0	0	0	69	35	104	45	28	73	0	2	2
Native American/AK	1	7	8	1	6	7	1	0	1	1	7	8	1	4	5	0	1	1
Native Hawaiian/OPI	6	0	6	4	0	4	0	0	0	5	2	7	2	2	4	0	0	0
White	346	724	1,070	264	504	768	45	80	125	334	802	1,136	221	556	777	36	95	131
Asian	166	303	469	113	187	300	8	19	27	153	258	411	102	136	238	3	13	16
Other Race	1	1	2	1	0	1	0	0	0	1	1	2	1	1	2	0	0	0
Multiple Race*	28	44	72	17	26	43	1	8	9	30	37	67	19	26	45	3	2	5
Unknown	7	12	19	7	11	18	1	0	1	12	35	47	12	30	42	1	2	3
Subtotal	620	1,138	1,758	454	771	1,225	56	107	163	605	1,177	1,782	403	783	1,186	43	115	158
Foreign	7	6	13	5	5	10	0	0	0	4	4	8	3	3	6	0	0	0
Total	683	1,225	1,908	502	830	1,332	59	114	173	668	1,282	1,950	451	857	1,308	50	121	171

*Since 2002, students can select more than one race and / or ethnicity. **Those who did not choose 'Hispanic/Latino' or 'Non-Hispanic/Latino' are listed under 'Non-Hispanic/Latino'. Data Source: AAMC Data Warehouse: Applicant-Matriculant File, as of 1/16/2009.

ences, both as participants and exhibitors. First- and second-year students are invited to serve on medical student panels, admissions workshops, and other activities at many of these venues. USU students are encouraged to seek leadership positions in regional and national organizations and to attend the corresponding national meetings. Descriptive materials are mailed to prospective applicants and to undergraduate health professions advisors and career counselors nationwide. In conjunction with the Office of Recruitment and Admissions, current medical students often participate in workshops, seminars, and medical student panels throughout the United States.

Open House Tours
USU welcomes pre-medical and pre-health societies, undergraduate groups, health professions advisors, and high school classes or interest groups for tours of the campus and medical school. In cooperation with many different departments at the university and the National Naval Medical Center, the Office of Recruitment and Admissions coordinates a tour of the facilities, a meeting with the admissions counselors, and at least one hands-on activity for groups of three or more visiting prospective students, faculty, or advisors. Students from groups underrepresented in medicine and science are highly encouraged to take advantage of this opportunity.

Once matriculated, a student's academic progress is closely monitored. Academic issues in any course are immediately identified by faculty members and students are strongly encouraged to seek counsel in the Office of Student Affairs where a strategic plan of action is enacted.

Retention
Students accepted to the school of medicine are assigned current first- or second-year medical students as peer mentors in order to ease their transition into the military medical school environment. Later in the spring, official sponsors are assigned. In the immediate pre-matriculation time frame, incom-

ing students are invited to attend impromptu sessions on time management, study skills, and other topics designed by volunteer faculty educators to prepare students for the academic rigors of the first year's course load.

The Office of Student Affairs (OSA) closely monitors the progress of all students. Individual counseling is provided as soon as problem areas are identified. Peer tutoring, faculty mentoring, study groups, and small tutorial sessions are available and tailored to the learning style and needs of the individual student. Higher performing classmates volunteer to lead study groups to clarify lecture or lab material. In addition, faculty volunteers assist students with preparation for exams, [including the United States Medical Licensing Exam (USMLE) Steps 1 and 2], complete with clinical diagnostic testing.

Admissions
Minority applicants follow the standard American Medical College Application Service (AMCAS) procedures. The Admissions Committee considers cognitive and non-cognitive factors in the evaluation and admissions process. Other than standard AMCAS fees, there are no additional charges for USU applications.

Academic Support Programs
Faculty Mentor Program
Early in each academic year, all students receive a form to request a faculty mentor. The overall goal of the mentor program is to allow the development of a personal and a professional relationship between the mentor and student such that the mentor is aware of all issues that may impact the student's professional and personal success.

Post-Baccalaureate Program
This unique program selects students from among the pool of candidates to the school of medicine who are not offered acceptance to the first-year class of the medical school by the full Admissions Committee because of some slight weakness in their dossier. Three students whose applications demonstrate

significant potential are given the opportunity to attend USU as a civilian graduate student, taking a portion of the first-year courses, in an effort to better prepare them for the rigors of the school's full curriculum. Successful participants, maintaining a 3.00 or better in all classes, are offered commissioning and matriculation into the next entering class. (Students must meet commissioning physical standards prior to acceptance into the post-baccalaureate program.)

Enrichment Programs
Center for Health Disparities
In 2004, the School of Medicine received a substantial grant to conduct research in health disparities. The Center for Health Disparities offers a ten-week paid summer research internship for qualified college students through the graduate school. Participants also receive the benefit of faculty mentors who are pioneers in medical research. Applications are available online.

Educational Partnerships
USU has a close affiliation with many of the other federal institutions in the Washington Metropolitan Area, and several faculty members have dual appointments with the National Naval Medical Center, Malcolm Grow U.S. Air Force Medical Center, Walter Reed Army Medical Center, the Armed Forces Radiobiology Research Institute, the National Institutes of Health, the U.S. Army Institute of Research, the Naval Medical Research Command, and others. Medical students are welcome to participate in ongoing research programs through prior arrangement with faculty in any of these closely affiliated institutions.

Medical Student Professional Development
USU actively supports student-run organizations. The university provides administrative support as well as a modest amount of financial assistance for student officers to attend national or regional meetings of their respective organizations. It should be noted that all medical, graduate, and graduate

nursing students and spouses are welcome to participate in any of the organizations supported by the medical school. This enhances the ethnic, cultural, and experiential diversity of the medical school.

Among the student groups at USU are:

Student National Medical Association (SNMA)
This is the largest and most influential national organization for minority medical students. The USU chapter is active in recruitment of students for both the medical school as well as for science-related careers. SNMA members are involved in mentoring programs for high school students, and two members served as peer mentors for the 2004 S2M2 inaugural program. These students annually participate in the Pre-Medical Forum at the SNMA national meeting. Additionally, SNMA members serve as role models for elementary, middle, and high school students in the Washington Metropolitan Area.

Asian Pacific American Medical Student Association (APAMSA)
Student leaders select activities and learning sessions that increase cultural awareness to both the USU community and the local medical community. As an active APAMSA chapter, USU students co-hosted the tenth annual conference at the Marvin Center on the George Washington University campus in 2003. These students also served as translators for a community-wide career awareness program at a local high school.

American Medical Student Association (AMSA)
This chapter made AMSA history by presenting a resolution to establish a military medicine interest group at the AMSA national meeting. In addition to informing the membership of the many contributions of military medicine, the USU chapter leadership now serves as the point of contact for all military sponsored medical students nationwide.

Women in Medicine and Science (WIMS)
Under student leadership with clinical faculty support, students are exposed to lectures and local events highlighting the accomplishments of women in medicine and science. Together with APAMSA and SNMA, WIMS co-sponsors monthly student activities at faculty members' homes including information sessions, professional development seminars, and team building exercises.

Other student-led organizations include the American Medical Association Medical Student Section (AMA-MSS), specialty interest groups (Surgery, Pediatrics, OB/ GYN, Psychiatry, Internal Medicine and subspecialties, Aerospace Medicine, Wilderness Medicine, Dive Medicine, etc.), and the Alpha Omega Alpha Medical Honor Society. There are a host of additional intramural and county recreational league athletic teams composed of USU students and faculty members.

University of Maryland School of Medicine

Dawn Roberts, Associate Director
University of Maryland School of Medicine
655 West Baltimore Street
Room M-004
Baltimore, MD 21201
410-706-7689; 410-706-1407 fax
droberts@som.umaryland.edu
www.umaryland.edu

Recruitment

The University of Maryland School of Medicine sponsors a number of undergraduate and high school programs that are designed to encourage, prepare, and facilitate the entry of minority students into the field of medicine. These include visits to undergraduate colleges and universities, seminars, workshops, and summer programs. An important focus of the school's recruitment effort is to provide information on admissions requirements, the admissions process, undergraduate preparation for medicine, the M.D./Ph.D. program, and other educational opportunities.

Applicants and prospective applicants are encouraged to contact the medical school admissions personnel. Visit our Web site at (www.umaryland.edu). On the day of the interview, applicants have the opportunity to meet with medical students and faculty and tour the medical school.

Admissions

The University of Maryland School of Medicine participates in the American Medical College Application Service (AMCAS). Minority students from all states are encouraged to apply. The admissions procedure for minority students is the same as that for all applicants. Among the selection factors emphasized by the Admissions Committee are: undergraduate or graduate grade-point average, Medical College Admission Test scores, application essay, and personal characteristics of the applicant including work or research experience. The interview, letters of recommendation, and the applicant's life experiences help the committee to evaluate the subjective qualities. The University of Maryland does not grant extensions for the initial application.

Academic Support Programs

Retention services are available for all students through the Office of Medical Education and the Office of Student Affairs. Services provided include tutorials; academic monitoring; personal, academic, career, and financial counseling; interaction with faculty through the advisory system; and skills development workshops. Because of the school's commitment to recruiting and graduating in-creased numbers of students, a number of retention activities, such as the Pre-matriculation Summer Program, are available. The school's emphasis is on providing personalized services relative to the needs of each student.

Enrichment Programs

Pre-matriculation Summer Program (PSP)
This program is offered to students who are scheduled to matriculate at the University of Maryland School of Medicine. The PSP provides an orientation to the medical school curriculum, gives a review of learning skills, and simulates the first semester schedule.

Short-Term Research Training Program
This program, which provides supervised full-time research experience, is offered

University of Maryland School of Medicine
Applicants, First-Time Applicants, Matriculants by Gender, Race and Ethnicity, 2007-2008

	2007									2008								
	APP			F-time APP			MAT			APP			F-time APP			MAT		
	Women	Men	Total	Women	Men	Total	Women	Men	Total	Women	Men	Total	Women	Men	Total	Women	Men	Total
Hispanic/Latino																		
Cuban	9	12	21	8	10	18	0	0	0	13	14	27	12	12	24	0	0	0
Mexican American	31	26	57	23	19	42	0	0	0	29	29	58	23	19	42	0	0	0
Puerto Rican	14	19	33	9	16	25	0	0	0	17	14	31	15	10	25	1	0	1
Other Hispanic	58	34	92	46	25	71	2	0	2	60	58	118	43	44	87	2	0	2
Multiple Hispanic/Latino*	10	1	11	10	1	11	0	0	0	8	4	12	6	2	8	0	1	1
Subtotal	122	92	214	96	71	167	2	0	2	127	119	246	99	87	186	3	1	4
Non-Hispanic/Latino**																		
Black	336	152	488	254	130	384	12	5	17	329	125	454	243	101	344	7	9	16
Native American/AK	3	2	5	2	2	4	0	0	0	4	4	8	4	3	7	0	0	0
Native Hawaiian/OPI	9	3	12	8	3	11	0	0	0	7	3	10	5	2	7	0	0	0
White	1,084	1,231	2,315	892	948	1,840	51	41	92	1,103	1,249	2,352	906	940	1,846	55	44	99
Asian	560	554	1,114	438	420	858	20	19	39	542	560	1,102	394	392	786	19	15	34
Other Race	1	2	3	1	1	2	0	0	0	1	5	6	1	4	5	0	0	0
Multiple Race*	66	52	118	55	40	95	6	2	8	62	41	103	52	33	85	1	0	1
Unknown	30	26	56	29	22	51	1	0	1	58	58	116	54	51	105	5	1	6
Subtotal	2,089	2,022	4,111	1,679	1,566	3,245	90	67	157	2,106	2,045	4,151	1,659	1,526	3,185	87	69	156
Foreign	89	89	178	73	67	140	1	0	1	82	105	187	61	76	137	0	0	0
Total	2,300	2,203	4,503	1,848	1,704	3,552	93	67	160	2,315	2,269	4,584	1,819	1,689	3,508	90	70	160

*Since 2002, students can select more than one race and / or ethnicity. **Those who did not choose 'Hispanic/Latino' or 'Non-Hispanic/Latino' are listed under 'Non-Hispanic/Latino'. Data Source: AAMC Data Warehouse: Applicant-Matriculant File, as of 1/16/2009.

to pre-matriculants. Students can participate in this program at any stage during the four-year curriculum. Both programs provide participants with a stipend, supervision, and support from both the faculty and administration.

Student Financial Assistance

A variety of university, state, and federally funded programs provide financial aid to students in need. Students are encouraged to apply for financial aid as soon as applications become available—usually during the latter part of December to mid-January. Priority processing of financial aid applications is provided for those received prior to February 15th. Detailed information on programs and application procedures can be obtained by contacting the Student Financial Aid Office, 111 S. Greene Street, Suite 104, Baltimore, MD 21201, 410-706-7347.

Educational Partnerships

The University of Maryland School of Medicine is committed to increasing the number of underrepresented minority students (African American, American Indian/Alaskan Native, Mexican American/ Chicano, and mainland Puerto Rican) at the medical school. The school has developed programs to increase the pipeline that supplies the minority applicant pool by developing partnerships with area high schools, colleges, and universities, and community programs, which will enhance the development/academic preparation of students through a variety of educational/professional experiences.

The High School Mini Medical School is an entertaining, educational program designed to provide high school students with interactive classroom instruction on a variety of medical subjects. Mini Medical School courses are taught by the University of Maryland School of Medicine Medical Students. Student participants, will learn directly from our medical students about many health subjects that impact them and specifically their communities. They also will get a chance to find out how they can break cycles

of health care disparities and create positive changes in their families and communities. They will also learn how to take an active role in maintaining their own health.

Boston University School of Medicine

Dr. Jonathan Woodson, Associate
Dean for Student, Diversity and
Multicultural Affairs
Director, Early Medical Selection
Program
Boston University School of Medicine
715 Albany Street, Suite A206
Boston, MA 02118
617-638-4163; 617-638-4433 fax
jwoodson@bu.edu

Recruitment

The Boston University School of Medicine (BUSM) is committed to the recruitment, admission, and retention of minority students. The Office of Diversity and Multicultural Affairs (ODMA) recruits nationwide for applicants to BUSM. The recruitment program involves visiting undergraduate schools to speak to individuals and groups. Staff also visit summer pre-medical programs to interview prospective applicants.

Admissions

BUSM has no special admissions committee for minority students. The ODMA actively participates in the processing and screening of applications

from minority students. The associate dean and director are active members of the Admissions Committee, participating in the medical school interviews and the selection process. Candidates for admission to BUSM must apply through the American Medical College Application Service, 2450 N Street, NW, Washington, DC 20037.

Academic Support Programs

All students receive group or individual tutorial assistance as the need arises. Academic counseling is offered by the associate dean, director, and other student affairs staff. In addition, each first-year student is assigned a faculty advisor. Various seminars are conducted by the OMA to assist students in:

- developing their clinical acumen and interpersonal relationships;
- meeting faculty who can serve as mentors and role models; and
- selecting appropriate house officer training programs.

Students have available to them the alternative curriculum that permits them to take the first year over two years, or the second year over two years. Our policies state that a student must not

take longer than three years to complete the first two years of the curriculum. We offer the students a variety of support services from the Office of Student Affairs, Office of Student Support Services, and the Office of Minority Affairs, including tutoring, counseling, testing, psychiatric evaluation and support, etc. Our objective is to help the student reach his/her full potential. Each student has a faculty advisor with whom they meet at least twice per year, and more if needed. In addition, the Associate Dean for Students and Minority Affairs is a member of all of the promotions committees and receives all students exam results throughout the year. This permits early intervention if needed.

Student Financial Assistance

Application fees are waived upon request when proof of need is submitted. The Office of Student Financial Management actively works with students in identifying sources of direct grants, loans, and service commitment programs.

Educational Partnerships

Early Medical School Selection Program (EMSSP)
EMSSP was developed 25 years ago with a consortium of eight Historically

Boston University School of Medicine
Applicants, First-Time Applicants, Matriculants by Gender, Race and Ethnicity, 2007-2008

| | | 2007 | | | | | | | | | 2008 | | | | | | | | |
| | APP | | | F-time APP | | | MAT | | | APP | | | F-time APP | | | MAT | | |
	Wo-men	Men	Total	Wo-men	Men	Total	Wo-men	Men	Total	Wo-men	Men	Total	Wo-men	Men	Total	Wo-men	Men	Total
Hispanic/Latino																		
Cuban	32	32	64	24	26	50	1	0	1	40	39	79	33	33	66	1	1	2
Mexican American	107	99	206	84	81	165	3	5	8	88	100	188	76	81	157	1	6	7
Puerto Rican	47	36	83	38	32	70	0	0	0	31	33	64	26	27	53	0	0	0
Other Hispanic	140	121	261	114	97	211	6	5	11	137	116	253	110	85	195	4	4	8
Multiple Hispanic/Latino*	21	13	34	15	9	24	0	0	0	24	20	44	22	14	36	1	0	1
Subtotal	347	301	648	275	245	520	10	10	20	320	308	628	267	240	507	7	11	18
Non-Hispanic/Latino**																		
Black	243	144	387	187	124	311	13	3	16	264	148	412	205	125	330	11	5	16
Native American/AK	8	8	16	6	7	13	0	0	0	9	7	16	6	5	11	0	0	0
Native Hawaiian/OPI	24	12	36	19	8	27	0	0	0	20	8	28	15	5	20	0	0	0
White	2,943	2,983	5,926	2,454	2,351	4,805	35	32	67	2,594	2,943	5,537	2,090	2,279	4,369	38	40	78
Asian	1,565	1,506	3,071	1,269	1,149	2,418	19	22	41	1,393	1,459	2,852	1,082	1,056	2,138	27	22	49
Other Race	2	5	7	2	4	6	0	0	0	4	9	13	3	8	11	0	0	0
Multiple Race*	148	150	298	129	110	239	4	3	7	160	136	296	129	97	226	1	4	5
Unknown	59	78	137	55	72	127	2	3	5	144	153	297	137	134	271	1	2	3
Subtotal	4,992	4,886	9,878	4,121	3,825	7,946	73	63	136	4,588	4,863	9,451	3,667	3,709	7,376	78	73	151
Foreign	294	317	611	230	242	472	6	6	12	338	321	659	276	254	530	6	3	9
Total	5,633	5,504	11,137	4,626	4,312	8,938	89	79	168	5,246	5,492	10,738	4,210	4,203	8,413	91	87	178

*Since 2002, students can select more than one race and / or ethnicity. **Those who did not choose 'Hispanic/Latino' or 'Non-Hispanic/Latino' are listed under 'Non-Hispanic/Latino'. Data Source: AAMC Data Warehouse: Applicant-Matriculant File, as of 1/16/2009.

Black Colleges and Universities. In order to further diversify the program, it was expanded to include students from colleges with large Hispanic populations and the Indian Health Service. The program provides an early and more gradual transition into the medical school curriculum, through provisional acceptance into BUSM at the completion of the first two years of undergraduate study.

Students accepted into the program remain at their undergraduate colleges through their junior year and complete the maximum number of science courses required by their respective schools for graduation. Following their sophomore and junior years, the students take summer science courses at Boston University. The students complete their senior year at Boston University, taking first-year medical school courses at BUSM, while retaining bachelor degree candidacy at their home institutions. Applications may be requested from Boston University School of Medicine Office of Minority Affairs, 715 Albany Street Boston, MA 02118.

CityLab

This is a National Institutes of Health–Science Education Partnership Award and Howard Hughes Medical Institute-funded biotechnology learning laboratory designed to give high school students and their science teachers hands-on learning experiences. The laboratory is located within the Boston University Medical Center complex. A full-time high school teacher and laboratory manager coordinate laboratory experiences, including DNA finger-printing, protein quantitation, and restriction analysis.

Boston University School of Medicine has a commitment to providing research training to underrepresented minorities through mentorship in Program Center Grants.

Boston University School of Medicine has as its flagship hospital the Boston Medical Center which serves a large diverse population in the City of Boston.

Twenty six languages may be spoken on any given day. The staff and residents reflect the institutions commitment to diversity.

The Center for Community Health Education, Research, and Service (CCHERS)
CCHERS represents a consortium of 15 partners: 12 Boston neighborhood health centers, Boston University School of Medicine, Northeastern University College of Nursing, and Boston's Department of Health and Hospitals. CCHERS is an innovative model of community health care systems. It is an educational experience that not only satisfies the traditional medical school course objectives, but also achieves new goals that are fundamental to the health care provider in the 21st century—increasing the supply of generalist physicians and exposing students to community-based primary care.

Boston Area Health Education Center (BAHEC)
The center is located at Boston City Hospital and affiliated with the Boston Department of Health and Hospitals, Boston University School of Medicine, and a network of neighborhood health centers. With a mission of alleviating health manpower shortages in medically underserved areas of Boston, BAHEC offers programs in three areas designed to make opportunities in health care available to minority populations and to improve the quality of health care in Boston's inner-city neighborhoods.

Harvard Medical School

Dr. Alvin F. Poussaint, Faculty
Associate Dean for Student Affairs
Rosa Soler DaSilva, Program Director
Jennifer S. Brown, Program
Coordinator
Office of Recruitment and
Multicultural Affairs
Harvard Medical School
260 Longwood Suite 244
Boston, MA 02115
617-432-2159; 617-432-0997 fax
rosa-dasilva@hms.harvard.edu
http://www.hms.harvard.edu/orma/

Recruitment

Harvard Medical School (HMS) seeks diverse student populations. Our commitment to diversity is not only reflected in the variety of institutions from which students are accepted, but also in the ethnic and economic backgrounds of the student body. The Office of Recruitment and Multicultural Affairs was established in 1969. This office is responsible for recruiting and providing supportive services to individuals from groups underrepresented in medicine. HMS has been very successful in admitting and graduating students from these groups. In the past 39 years,

Harvard has graduated over 1,000 minority physicians and the current student body is composed of 22% underrepresented minority students.

The Office of Recruitment and Multicultural Affairs works closely with the underrepresented miinority student's health organizations (The Multicultural Student Alliance composed of the Black Health Organization, Medical Students of Las Americas, and the Native American Health Organization), to recruit underrepresented students in medicine.

Students registered on the Minority Applicant Registry list, published by the AAMC, receive admission information from the Office of Recruitment and Multicultural Affairs. The office coordinates campus visits for student organizations at other colleges and universities to meet HMS faculty, students, and staff. It also mails brochures and general information to undergraduate minority affairs and pre-medical advisors throughout the country.

Admissions

A student's entire record is evaluated when deciding on admission. The factors emphasized in the selection of ap-

plicants are academic strength, involvement in extracurricular activities, commitment to the community, and leadership potential. Research and comments contained in letters of recommendations are also considered.

Harvard Medical School does not have cutoff scores for grade-point averages and Medical College Admission Test (MCAT) scores. The grade-point averages of admitted students are within a broad range in keeping with the national average.

HMS students come from a variety of undergraduate institutions and academic backgrounds. The 2008 entering class came from several different colleges and universities. Forty nine percent were women and 21 percent were minorities. Although the majority of students admitted were science majors, non-science majors are given equal consideration.

Academic Support Programs

Medical education at Harvard Medical School includes the following curricular elements: the biological and social sciences important to medicine, pathophysiology and mechanisms of disease,

Harvard Medical School
Applicants, First-Time Applicants, Matriculants by Gender, Race and Ethnicity, 2007-2008

	2007 APP Women	2007 APP Men	2007 APP Total	2007 F-time APP Women	2007 F-time APP Men	2007 F-time APP Total	2007 MAT Women	2007 MAT Men	2007 MAT Total	2008 APP Women	2008 APP Men	2008 APP Total	2008 F-time APP Women	2008 F-time APP Men	2008 F-time APP Total	2008 MAT Women	2008 MAT Men	2008 MAT Total
Hispanic/Latino																		
Cuban	15	22	37	14	17	31	1	1	2	21	16	37	18	15	33	0	1	1
Mexican American	74	105	179	65	88	153	3	1	4	67	86	153	58	68	126	3	2	5
Puerto Rican	28	35	63	27	29	56	0	0	0	17	25	42	13	21	34	0	2	2
Other Hispanic	94	113	207	84	90	174	2	5	7	81	111	192	70	87	157	3	3	6
Multiple Hispanic/Latino*	14	15	29	13	10	23	0	1	1	11	19	30	9	15	24	0	0	0
Subtotal	225	290	515	203	234	437	6	8	14	197	257	454	168	206	374	6	8	14
Non-Hispanic/Latino**																		
Black	217	170	387	179	146	325	6	10	16	219	149	368	178	120	298	8	6	14
Native American/AK	8	11	19	6	10	16	1	1	2	9	11	20	7	11	18	0	1	1
Native Hawaiian/OPI	12	5	17	11	5	16	0	0	0	8	6	14	7	4	11	0	0	0
White	1,364	1,840	3,204	1,256	1,623	2,879	29	34	63	1,241	1,876	3,117	1,099	1,636	2,735	33	35	68
Asian	791	971	1,762	714	817	1,531	23	23	46	717	900	1,617	611	742	1,353	23	25	48
Other Race	1	4	5	1	4	5	0	0	0	2	5	7	1	3	4	0	0	0
Multiple Race*	105	107	212	98	92	190	4	4	8	98	102	200	85	80	165	3	4	7
Unknown	40	48	88	38	45	83	1	1	2	89	123	212	88	110	198	3	2	5
Subtotal	2,538	3,156	5,694	2,303	2,742	5,045	64	73	137	2,383	3,172	5,555	2,076	2,706	4,782	70	73	143
Foreign	188	245	433	156	204	360	7	7	14	216	237	453	190	194	384	4	4	8
Total	2,951	3,691	6,642	2,662	3,180	5,842	77	88	165	2,796	3,666	6,462	2,434	3,106	5,540	80	85	165

*Since 2002, students can select more than one race and / or ethnicity. **Those who did not choose 'Hispanic/Latino' or 'Non-Hispanic/Latino' are listed under 'Non-Hispanic/Latino'. Data Source: AAMC Data Warehouse: Applicant-Matriculant File, as of 1/16/2009.

the patient-doctor relationship, clinical experiences in patient care, and electives. The first three elements form the common core of general medical education, which is taken by all students; the elective program encourages individual variation and emphasis.

The Academic Societies were established in 1987 to serve as the organizational framework for each student's experience in general medical education. Students in the Division of Health Science and Technology (HST) are members of its own society. All other students are assigned randomly to one of four societies: Cannon Society, Castle Society, Peabody Society, or Holmes Society. Each society is composed of faculty members including a Master, Associate Masters, Educators, Senior Fellows, Tutors, Preceptors, and Advisors, plus students from all four classes and administrative staff.

Members of a society share a society cluster area and classrooms in the Tosteson Medical Education Center (TMEC). Society-based academic activities support a problem-based learning approach and include the organization of tutorial groups, small-course evaluation and feedback sessions, and a mechanism for vertical integration of faculty and student curricular planning. Each society organizes a program of student advising, whose core is a four-year relationship between student and advisor to foster goals of self-assessment and professional development. The societies also plan para-curricular and social functions that bring faculty and students together.

Throughout its history, HMS has influenced the design of medical school education. From Harvard University President Charles Eliot's 19th century reform—developing the concept of a medical school as we know it today—to the ground breaking New Pathway curriculum of the 1980s, HMS has been in a continual process of growth and change. HMS recently redesigned its curriculum to meet the needs of 21st century medicine by integrating clinical and basic science across the curriculum,

developing new models for clinical education, and engaging students in an in-depth scholarly experience.

The curriculum began mid-August 2006 with a new course, Introduction to the Profession, designed to introduce students to the profession, the practice of medicine, and the experiences that lie before them as they embark on the process of becoming physicians. Courses focused on the scientific basis of medical practice (basic, population, and behavioral sciences) and the patient-doctor relationship (professionalism, communication, physical diagnosis) span the first three and one-half semesters of the curriculum. In April of Year II, students begin making the transition from classroom to the clinical realm. Individual clerkships in the major disciplines of medicine (medicine, surgery, pediatrics, obstetrics and gynecology, psychiatry, neurology, radiology) are unified in a "Principal Clinical Experience," which will provide opportunities for longitudinal experiences with patients and faculty mentors as well as an interdisciplinary curriculum that integrates the scientific and clinical aspects of important diseases. Throughout the four years of medical school, students will have many opportunities to work one-on-one with faculty mentors. In this vein, a capstone experience for our students will be a several year, faculty-mentored, in-depth scholarly experience culminating in a written work product. This exploration of a topic in-depth will allow students to participate with faculty in the excitement of discovery and scholarship. The new HMS curriculum will prepare graduates to function in an increasingly multicultural landscape undergoing radical scientific, social, economic, and technological transformation. HMS seeks to ready students for this new world by providing them with the ideal educational environment and carefully integrated global experience to foster their growth as clinicians, scholars, discoverer, and leaders.

Students with a declared interest in a

career in biomedical research or a strong interest and background in quantitative or molecular science may want to consider applying to Health Sciences and Technology (HST).

The following academic support services are provided for all students: tutorials for basic science courses, academic and personal counseling, and review materials and sessions for the United States Licensing Medical Examination.

The Faculty Associate Dean for Student Affairs is available to students for personal and academic counseling. There are no special academic programs or tracks for underrepresented students since the attrition rate for underrepresented minority students at HMS is negligible. All Harvard students go through the regular program.

Enrichment Programs

Pre-matriculation Summer Enrichment and Minority Faculty Development Program (PMSP)
The Office of Recruitment and Multicultural Affairs sponsor this eight- to ten-week program for admitted HMS/HSDM underrepresented minority students. PMSP is directed to developing faculty from entering minority dental and medical students by fostering student interest in academic medicine and providing a mechanism for minority students and faculty to exchange ideas and interests. Through laboratory investigation seminars, site visits, and interaction with scientists and physicians, students gain a better understanding of career options in academic medicine. Participants receive a stipend for housing in the medical area dormitory, and payment for transportation to Boston.

Student Financial Assistance

Approximately 70 percent of all enrolled medical students receive some form of financial aid (grants and/or loans). All applications for admission are considered without regard to the financial resources of the applicant. Harvard awards financial aid according to need. There are several need-based scholarships and low-interest loans administered by the HMS Financial Aid Office. Parent information is an important component in determining eligibility for these programs.

Educational Partnerships

At present there are no formal educational partnerships that exist between Harvard Medical School and other institutions. However, there are several informal relationships between the medical school and city colleges, state colleges, and local high schools that have been established over the past years. Minority medical students volunteer as education counselors in local high schools and tutor high school students who attend after school programs.

Tufts University School of Medicine

Dr. Joyce A. Sackey, FACP
Dean for Multicultural Affairs and
Global Health
Tufts University School of Medicine
145 Harrison Avenue
Boston, MA 02111
617-636-6576; 617-636-0375 fax

Colleen Romain, Director for Student
Programs and Minority Affairs
Tufts University School of Medicine
145 Harrison Avenue
Boston, MA 02111
617-636-6576; 617-636-0375 fax

Recruitment

Tufts University School of Medicine (TUSM) attracts students from all across the country. Approximately 51 percent of each class of 168 has been from the northeastern U.S. The rest of the class is principally from the west and southwest. Most recruitment occurs at the undergraduate schools. Contacts are made by faculty, staff, students, and alumni through pre-medical organizations on individual campuses, as well as through national or regional student meetings, career day programs, and by being in communication with summer and post-baccalaureate program staff.

Admissions

Minority student applications are evaluated by members of the Admissions Committee, which includes minority faculty. The committee is careful to evaluate the total person, including socioeconomic background, academic, and extracurricular accomplishments, and experience, as well as initiative, personal goals, and interests.

Academic Support Programs

Throughout the academic years, tutorial aid in the form of individualized or group instruction by faculty, graduate students, and upperclassmen has been provided to students who request it. In addition, workshops on study skills and stress management are offered. Students organize their own board reviews with support of faculty and staff and arrange for a simulated or Practice Board exam during the month of March and April. Students are assigned both peer and faculty advisors. Workshops on specialty selection are made available to assist students in choosing a professional path. Carefully selected clinical faculty in each discipline work with third-year students to choose appropriate fourth-year courses and help plan the residency application process.

The Curriculum

Because rapid demographic, biomedical, technical, and scientific changes require that physicians confront new issues, practices, and information, Tufts initiated a new, integrated, cell to organism, interdisciplinary curricular model in 1985. The curriculum includes non-biological sciences relevant to health and health care delivery. A problem-based case study approach is closely coordinated with the material presented in each segment of the curriculum. Opportunities to participate in population health, primary care, and subspecialty clinical as well as research settings have also been accommodated in the regular curriculum.

M.D.-M.P.H.

At Tufts it is possible to complete an M.D. and a Masters in Public Health within four years. The faculty have designed a challenging program for a very select group of students interested in examining the changes in population

Tufts University School of Medicine
Applicants, First-Time Applicants, Matriculants by Gender, Race and Ethnicity, 2007-2008

	2007									2008								
	APP			F-time APP			MAT			APP			F-time APP			MAT		
	Wo-men	Men	Total	Wo-men	Men	Total	Wo-men	Men	Total	Wo-men	Men	Total	Wo-men	Men	Total	Wo-men	Men	Total
Hispanic/Latino																		
Cuban	31	26	57	22	18	40	1	1	2	36	32	68	32	29	61	0	2	2
Mexican American	75	65	140	61	50	111	1	0	1	75	59	134	63	46	109	3	2	5
Puerto Rican	30	18	48	25	15	40	1	1	2	28	23	51	23	19	42	0	0	0
Other Hispanic	115	96	211	93	72	165	0	5	5	115	98	213	94	71	165	3	1	4
Multiple Hispanic/Latino*	15	7	22	10	6	16	0	1	1	16	14	30	14	9	23	0	0	0
Subtotal	266	212	478	211	161	372	3	8	11	270	226	496	226	174	400	6	5	11
Non-Hispanic/Latino**																		
Black	160	96	256	124	79	203	2	1	3	179	101	280	145	79	224	5	4	9
Native American/AK	8	4	12	6	4	10	0	0	0	10	3	13	8	2	10	0	0	0
Native Hawaiian/OPI	17	15	32	15	10	25	0	0	0	20	8	28	15	5	20	0	0	0
White	2,414	2,345	4,759	1,984	1,826	3,810	51	53	104	2,277	2,529	4,806	1,821	1,910	3,731	49	63	112
Asian	1,338	1,291	2,629	1,050	969	2,019	20	22	42	1,274	1,296	2,570	930	893	1,823	13	23	36
Other Race	3	3	6	2	2	4	0	0	0	3	9	12	2	8	10	0	0	0
Multiple Race*	122	106	228	104	78	182	3	1	4	133	104	237	113	71	184	6	0	6
Unknown	49	66	115	44	60	104	4	2	6	117	143	260	114	124	238	1	2	3
Subtotal	4,111	3,926	8,037	3,329	3,028	6,357	80	79	159	4,013	4,193	8,206	3,148	3,092	6,240	74	92	166
Foreign	171	197	368	138	154	292	0	3	3	209	192	401	168	148	316	1	0	1
Total	4,548	4,335	8,883	3,678	3,343	7,021	83	90	173	4,492	4,611	9,103	3,542	3,414	6,956	81	97	178

*Since 2002, students can select more than one race and / or ethnicity. **Those who did not choose 'Hispanic/Latino' or 'Non-Hispanic/Latino' are listed under 'Non-Hispanic/Latino'. Data Source: AAMC Data Warehouse: Applicant-Matriculant File, as of 1/16/2009.

composition; the structure of health care delivery; or environmental, economic, and social factors that shape health services delivery.

M.D.-Ph.D.

The Sackler School of Graduate Biomedical Sciences, in conjunction with the School of Medicine, offers an M.D.-Ph.D. degree program in biochemistry; pharmacology; cell, molecular, and developmental biology; cellular and molecular physiology; immunology, molecular biology, and microbiology; and neuroscience. Degree requirements are designed to be completed in approximately seven years.

The first two years include a modified first- and second-year medical school curriculum in which advanced graduate-level courses, research experience, and seminars supplement the standard curriculum. The following three to four years are devoted to graduate courses and individual research. The dissertation and the final two years are devoted to the clinical portion of the M.D. curriculum.

M.D.-M.B.A. in Health Management

TUSM, in collaboration with the Florence Heller Graduate School for Advanced Studies in Social Welfare at Brandeis University and the Northeastern University Graduate School of Business Administration, now offers a combined M.D.-M.B.A. in Health Management degree. This program is believed to be the first in the nation to enable medical students to earn a Master of Business Administration (M.B.A.) in Health Management in the same four calendar years in which they earn the Doctor of Medicine (M.D.) degree. The program capitalizes on the strengths of three outstanding educational institutions—TUSM in medicine, Brandeis in health policy and social services, and Northeastern in business administration—to produce a new breed of physician capable of effectively participating in the planning and management of the changing health care environment.

Enrichment Programs

Pre-matriculation Summer Program

This program is a comprehensive introduction to courses that are encountered in the first year of medical school. The areas of study include:

- Anatomy
- Molecular Biology
- Neuropsychology
- Biochemistry
- Physical Diagnosis
- Genetics
- Histology
- Neuroscience
- Immunology
- Problem-Based Learning

Courses are taught by faculty members who are closely involved with the teaching of these general medical school courses, by graduate students in each of the disciplines, and by medical students who have recently completed the courses. Workshops run by upper-class students on such issues as surviving in medical school and preparing for classes, are also a part of the curriculum. The program runs for six weeks prior to the beginning of the first year.

An introduction to the new problem-based school curriculum, all explanation of Promotions and Evaluation Committee policies and procedures, as well as opportunities to meet with key staff (i.e., Deans, Financial Aid Counselors, the Registrar) are also incorporated into the program. Second-year students work with the new incoming students to familiarize them with the school and affiliated hospitals.

Students are given the opportunity to become involved in clinical exposure. These elective periods are over a three-week period and are under the supervision of mentor physicians. This can prove invaluable in providing an introduction to an environment in which exposure during medical school will help them in making informed career choices for graduate training.

Teachers and High School Students Program (TAHSS)

Along with the traditional recruitment programs by faculty, alumni, and staff at the undergraduate level, Tufts focuses on the high school student. In 1988, TUSM started the Minority High School Program. The TAHSS is an integral part of the medical school's community outreach. The program's objectives are to motivate, guide, and advise high school students from disadvantaged backgrounds in the health and science professions. The program consists of presentations during the academic year and a seven-week summer research experience. These experiences are in bench research and clinical settings to further increase their knowledge of the health sciences. Faculty, students, and staff present career and financial planning information for college along with workshops on the health fields, courses in gross anatomy and, nutrition, and a special workshop for parents.

High school students in the Massachusetts area applying and receiving an acceptance to college may apply to the Colleen Romain Scholarship Fund. The fund was created by the Dr. Larnie Booker a 1998 graduate for Mrs. Romain's extensive outreach with high school students.

Student Financial Assistance

The application fee may be waived upon receipt of documentation from the American Medical College Application Service certifying that payment of the fee would constitute a financial burden. In certain cases, regional interviews may be scheduled.

Although scholarship resources are scarce, the dean provides a limited number of one-half scholarships for four years. In addition, the Financial Aid Office provides assistance to students in identifying sources of grants, low interest loans, and other programs.

University of Massachusetts Medical School

55 Lake Avenue North
Worcester, MA 01655
http://www.ummassmed.edu

Dr. Danna B. Peterson,
Assistant Dean
Student Affairs/
Diversity and Minority Affairs
508-856-3866; 508-856-5911 fax
danna.peterson@umassmed.edu

Dr. Deborah Harmon Hines
Vice Provost for School Services
508-856-2444; 508-856-4888 fax
Toll Free 877-395-3149 #1
Deborah-Harmon.Hines@
umassmed.edu

Outreach Programs
508-856-2707; 508-856-6540 fax
Toll Free 877-395-3149 #2
Outreach.programs@umassmed.edu

Introduction

Activities related to minority students are pre-matriculation activities and matriculation activities. All pre-matriculation activities reside in the Office of School Services under the direction of the Vice Provost. They include the High School Health Careers Program, Summer Enrichment Program for Undergraduates, National Institutes of Health Funded Summer Research Fellowship Program for Minority Undergraduate Students, The Worcester Pipeline Collaborative, and all recruitment for University of Massachusetts Medical School (UMMS) programs. Matriculation activities are under the Assistant Dean for Students Affairs/ Diversity and Minority Affairs. They include career counseling, social activities, advising the UMMS Student National Medical Association (SNMA) Chapter, advising, and mentoring the academic progress of all minority students. Other matriculation support/activities are under the supervision of the Vice Provost for School Services, Student Financial Aid, and Student Americans with Disabilities Act Services.

Recruitment

Recruitment to the University of Massachusetts Medical School is handled by the Office of School Services through recruitment visits to college fairs, recruitment events, high schools, colleges, and universities throughout the Commonwealth of Massachusetts. Recruitment is not conducted outside the Commonwealth because of very stringent residency requirements. Students who have graduated from Massachusetts high schools meet the residency requirements. Students attending colleges and universities may satisfy the residency requirement. Students can call 508-856-2323 for clarification.

Admissions

All applicants must complete an American Medical College Application Service (AMCAS) application. Upon receipt of the verified AMCAS application, the UMMS Admissions Office will send a UMMS Secondary Application and a proof of Massachusetts Residency form to all applicants. UMMS automatically waives application fees for students who have received fee waivers from AMCAS. All letters of recommendation should be sent directly to the Associate Dean for Admissions. A letter of recommendation from the Pre-medical Committee is preferred. If those are not available, two letters of recommendation should come from instructors in the pre-requisite courses. Applicants must have taken the Medical College Admission Test (MCAT) within the three years prior to application.

Selected applicants are invited for interviews. They are given the option of hav-

University of Massachusetts Medical School
Applicants, First-Time Applicants, Matriculants by Gender, Race and Ethnicity, 2007-2008

	2007 APP Women	2007 APP Men	2007 APP Total	2007 F-time APP Women	2007 F-time APP Men	2007 F-time APP Total	2007 MAT Women	2007 MAT Men	2007 MAT Total	2008 APP Women	2008 APP Men	2008 APP Total	2008 F-time APP Women	2008 F-time APP Men	2008 F-time APP Total	2008 MAT Women	2008 MAT Men	2008 MAT Total
Hispanic/Latino																		
Cuban	0	0	0	0	0	0	0	0	0	2	1	3	2	1	3	1	0	1
Mexican American	3	0	3	3	0	3	0	0	0	2	0	2	2	0	2	1	0	1
Puerto Rican	5	1	6	3	0	3	0	1	1	4	2	6	3	2	5	1	0	1
Other Hispanic	17	7	24	14	6	20	2	0	2	4	10	14	3	7	10	0	1	1
Multiple Hispanic/Latino*	2	0	2	2	0	2	0	0	0	1	1	2	0	1	1	1	0	1
Subtotal	27	8	35	22	6	28	2	1	3	13	14	27	10	11	21	4	1	5
Non-Hispanic/Latino **																		
Black	21	9	30	19	7	26	4	4	8	24	20	44	16	18	34	2	3	5
Native American/AK	0	0	0	0	0	0	0	0	0	1	0	1	0	0	0	0	0	0
White	306	280	586	231	213	444	45	34	79	272	280	552	209	211	420	50	45	95
Asian	72	75	147	54	60	114	6	5	11	63	83	146	50	53	103	2	6	8
Other Race	0	0	0	0	0	0	0	0	0	1	1	2	1	1	2	0	0	0
Multiple Race*	9	8	17	9	6	15	0	2	2	9	10	19	6	5	11	1	0	1
Unknown	7	4	11	7	3	10	0	0	0	6	14	20	6	12	18	0	0	0
Subtotal	415	376	791	320	289	609	55	45	100	376	408	784	288	300	588	55	54	109
Foreign	1	3	4	1	1	2	0	0	0	3	0	3	3	0	3	0	0	0
Total	443	387	830	343	296	639	57	46	103	392	422	814	301	311	612	59	55	114

*Since 2002, students can select more than one race and / or ethnicity. **Those who did not choose 'Hispanic/Latino' or 'Non-Hispanic/Latino' are listed under 'Non-Hispanic/Latino'. Data Source: AAMC Data Warehouse: Applicant-Matriculant File, as of 1/16/2009.

ing one of two interviews at an off-campus site. A tour of the campus by students is also a part of the Interview Day. On the interview day, meetings are arranged for minority applicants and minority medical students, the Associate Vice Chancellor for School Services, and the Assistant Dean of Student Affairs/Diversity and Minority Affairs.

In the admission process service, volunteer activities and work with underserved populations are noted in all candidates as well as their academic achievement. The ability to work with diverse patients, professionalism, team work, communication, and leadership skills are key attributes for today's physicians. The interview process is geared towards assessing these and other non-cognitive factors. Both the Assistant Dean of Student Affairs/Diversity and Minority Affairs and the Vice Provost for School Services are voting members of the Admissions Committee. Additionally, minority faculty and staff participate in the interviewing process.

Academic Support Programs
Tutorial services are available through the Office of Academic Achievement at no additional cost to the student. This includes content and skills tutoring. Students may elect to be in an extended program for a number of reasons. Such requests must be made in writing to the Associate Dean for Student Affairs. Participation in the Extended Program is aided by the fact that all students pay tuition for only four years. Each medical student is assigned to a faculty advisor and to a Second-Year Student Buddy by the Assistant Dean for Student Advising.

The faculty advisor monitors the student's academic progress. The Assistant Dean of Student Affairs/Diversity and Minority Affairs is closely involved with the minority students' academic progress. Both the Assistant Dean of Student Affairs/Diversity and Minority Affairs and the Vice Provost for School Services are on the Academic Evaluation Boards. The Assistant Dean follows up on all aca-

demic issues related to matriculated students underrepresented in medicine. The Assistant Dean provides an additional advisory role for these students. *(http://www.umassmed.edu/studentaffairs/minority/index.aspx)*

Enrichment Programs
For information on the following please contact *(outreach.programs@umassmed.edu):*

• High School Health Careers Program (Massachusetts residents only)-five weeks in the summer
• Summer Enrichment Programfor Disadvantaged Undergraduate Students (Massachusetts residents only)-four weeks in May/June
• Post-Baccalaureate Program for Disadvantaged Students (Massachusetts residents only)-one year

For information on the following please contact *(summer.research@umassmed.edu):*
• NIH and Summer Undergraduate Research Experience (SURE) Program

Educational Partnerships
• Worcester Pipeline Collaborative: K-12 (www.umassmed.edu/wpc)
• Clark University's Worcester Education Partnership: *(http://www.clarku.edu/departments/hiattcenter/wep/about/index.shtml)*
• Central Massachusetts STEM Pipeline Network K-12: *(http://www.umassmed.edu/rsrc/CentralMAStem/index.aspx)*
• Colleges of Worcester Consortium (www.cowc.org)

Student Financial Assistance
UMMS financial aid is need based. There is limited gift aid available. All students must file a Free Application Federal Student Aid (FAFSA) form. Also available to UMMS students is the Learning Contract. The Learning Contract, provided by the Massachusetts State Legislature, defers tuition and fees annually for a service payback commitment of four years in the Commonwealth of Massachusetts. Service payback may be in the areas of 1) primary care, or 2) public service, or 3)

community service, or 4) an underserved area. The Learning Contract is administered by the Office of School Services/Financial Aid.

Other Information
Career in Medicine
Each medical student is appointed an advisor through the office of the Assistant Dean of Student Affairs/Advising. The Assistant Dean/Advising provides faculty development in the Careers in Medicine program for the advisors. The Office of Student Affairs schedules several programs a year in career advising:

• The "Big Picture" for first-year students
• "Introduction to Clerkships" for second-year students
• "Career Day," "Soup to Nuts" (application to residency) for third-year students
• After each session for the whole class the Assistant Dean/Diversity and Minority Affairs reviews these Careers in Medicine programs with the first-, second- and third-year minority medical students respectively both in groups and individually. Throughout the year, the Assistant Dean is available for career counseling.

Cultural Diversity
• International Pathways Program: (www.umassmed.edu/intmeded/) Twenty students are selected each year to participate in this four-year longitudinal program. The program emphasizes language immersion and health education and supports travel abroad for the aforementioned activities.
• Special Electives: *(www.umassmed.edu/ome/electives/opt.electives.aspx)*
  Rural Medicine Electives
  Medical Interviewing in Spanish
  Pathways Program/Serving Underserved and Multicultural Populations
  American Sign Language
• The SNMA (Student National Medical Association) Chapter has been active in promoting awareness of dis-

parities in medical access and treatment for minority populations. The Chapter has organized panels on the cultural diversity of different African countries. Each year the focus of the culture varies. The panels are open to the whole student body and faculty. The Chapter has become very involved in providing education assistance to African immigrant populations.

- The Asian students started a community outreach program to the Asian population in Worcester. All students are invited to participate in the program. The goal is to provide health care education and other assistance to the Asian community.
- In order to serve the increasingly changing diverse population of the Commonwealth, many UMMS students elect to participate in our growing International Program. Many of the people of Massachusetts are immigrants. UMMS students do electives in the countries of origins to learn language and social skills to assist them in serving our patient population.

Cultural Competency
Multicultural Interclerkship: *http://www.umassmed.edu/ome/interclerkships/* This interclerkship is mandatory for third-year students. The focus is on immigrant populations, how to obtain a history over cross-cultural barriers.

Cultural competency is taught longitudinally in the first- and second-year course "Physician, Patient and Society" and during the third-year clerkships and fourth-year electives.

Mentoring Programs
The Advising program includes a mentoring program for students in their clinical years. A student may elect to choose a field specific mentor in the specialty chosen for residency. The mentor may help with applications, choosing residency programs and advising on clinical aspects of the specialty.

In a team approach the Diversity and Equal Opportunity Office and the As-sistant Dean have initiated an informal mentoring process with medical students, residents and faculty which stared in 2006.

Other Events
The Diversity and the Equal Opportunity Office sponsors annual celebrations for the Rev. Dr. Martin Luther King, Jr., Day and Black History Month (February).

UMMS is home to the statewide Area Health Education Office (AHEC).

Michigan State University College of Human Medicine

Letitia V. Fowler, Admissions Senior Counselor
Michigan State University College of Human Medicine
A-239 Life Sciences
East Lansing, MI 48824-1317
517-353-9620; 517-432-0021 fax
Letitia.Fowler@Chm.msu.edu
http://www.mdadmissions.msu.edu

Recruitment

The Michigan State University (MSU) College of Human Medicine seeks a broadly diverse student body using a mission-based admission process that carefully evaluates applicants' non-academic attributes. Consistent with our motto, "Serving the People," we actively seek, consider, and maintain minority and disadvantaged students as well as students from underserved areas and populations in our applicant pool. As part of the recruitment and outreach efforts, the Office of Admissions works with our Student National Medical Association (SNMA) and Latino Medical Student Association groups to welcome accepted applicants through follow-up contacts by e-mail and phone while applicants are making their final decisions.

In the development of the applicant pool and support of students from broadly diverse backgrounds, the Dean for Admissions and the Admissions Senior Counselor work with MSU undergraduates individually and in groups through the Charles Drew Enrichment Program and LANE Scholars Society — both programs for select MSU undergraduates from disadvantaged backgrounds. The Office of Admissions regularly seeks opportunities for recruitment and engagement with students at other colleges and universities who are interested in medicine to best capture an incoming class reflective of our ever-changing and broadly diverse society.

The College of Human Medicine has demonstrated a strong commitment to the recruitment and retention of applicants from a variety of backgrounds including socioeconomically disadvantaged and educationally disadvantaged. Reaching beyond our campus, we routinely make college visits around the State and beyond; place advertisements in relevant publications that are student-focused and advisor-focused (such as the National Association of Advisors for the Health Professions annual directory featuring special programs); and participate in national recruitment events sponsored by the Association of American Medical Colleges (AAMC).

MSUCHM supports student attendance at regional national meetings; these include meetings for the SNMA Region V and American Medical Student Association.

Admission

The Michigan State University College of Human Medicine seeks a broadly diverse class. The preliminary screening process identifies students with academic potential and experience to support their decision to pursue a medical career. Students from disadvantaged backgrounds are given close attention to discern potential and assess opportunity as well as accomplishment to evaluate the many non-cognitive variables addressed in our mission-based admission process. This attention to potential and the experience of the individual continues throughout the admission process as applicants are evaluated by four independent evaluators. Non-cog-

MI, Michigan State University College of Human Medicine
Applicants, First-Time Applicants, Matriculants by Gender, Race and Ethnicity, 2007-2008

	2007 APP Women	2007 APP Men	2007 APP Total	2007 F-time APP Women	2007 F-time APP Men	2007 F-time APP Total	2007 MAT Women	2007 MAT Men	2007 MAT Total	2008 APP Women	2008 APP Men	2008 APP Total	2008 F-time APP Women	2008 F-time APP Men	2008 F-time APP Total	2008 MAT Women	2008 MAT Men	2008 MAT Total
Hispanic/Latino																		
Cuban	7	11	18	7	9	16	0	0	0	12	21	33	9	18	27	0	0	0
Mexican American	65	65	130	49	47	96	3	2	5	51	53	104	42	42	84	2	0	2
Puerto Rican	13	5	18	10	3	13	0	0	0	13	14	27	11	11	22	0	1	1
Other Hispanic	51	49	100	33	31	64	0	1	1	52	57	109	37	39	76	5	0	5
Multiple Hispanic/Latino*	8	5	13	4	4	8	1	0	1	11	5	16	10	1	11	0	0	0
Subtotal	144	135	279	103	94	197	4	3	7	139	150	289	109	111	220	7	1	8
Non-Hispanic/Latino**																		
Black	178	118	296	113	91	204	6	2	8	199	86	285	140	67	207	2	5	7
Native American/AK	6	3	9	4	3	7	0	0	0	7	6	13	4	4	8	0	0	0
Native Hawaiian/OPI	10	6	16	8	6	14	0	0	0	13	8	21	9	7	16	0	0	0
White	1,167	1,424	2,591	954	1,078	2,032	51	49	100	1,070	1,409	2,479	812	1,004	1,816	51	56	107
Asian	607	719	1,326	448	513	961	15	14	29	578	665	1,243	416	415	831	11	12	23
Other Race	0	3	3	0	1	1	0	0	0	0	5	5	0	5	5	0	0	0
Multiple Race*	58	73	131	39	51	90	2	1	3	45	64	109	31	39	70	1	1	2
Unknown	16	29	45	15	28	43	2	4	6	44	67	111	42	56	98	3	2	5
Subtotal	2,042	2,375	4,417	1,581	1,771	3,352	76	70	146	1,956	2,310	4,266	1,454	1,597	3,051	68	76	144
Foreign	151	154	305	128	118	246	3	0	3	129	174	303	94	130	224	2	2	4
Total	2,337	2,664	5,001	1,812	1,983	3,795	83	73	156	2,224	2,634	4,858	1,657	1,838	3,495	77	79	156

*Since 2002, students can select more than one race and / or ethnicity. **Those who did not choose 'Hispanic/Latino' or 'Non-Hispanic/Latino' are listed under 'Non-Hispanic/Latino'. Data Source: AAMC Data Warehouse: Applicant-Matriculant File, as of 1/16/2009.

nitive variables include commitment and motivation for medicine, depth, and breadth of clinical experience, compassion, communication skills, judgment and problem solving, service and leadership, and potential to contribute to the profession.

In keeping with the above, the Committee on Admissions seeks to admit a class that is not only academically competent but also representative of a wide spectrum of personalities, backgrounds, talents, and motivations. The College does not have a separate review system for minority applicants but strongly encourages applications from students who have the desire and the aptitude to become physicians but have experienced unequal educational opportunities for social, cultural, geographical or other reasons. Over the years, the College has shown an increased, steady enrollment of students from one or more of the aforementioned backgrounds.

The requirements for admission are the Medical College Admission Test and the specific course requirements, which are outlined in the AAMC's *Medical School Admission Requirements (MSAR)*. Academic major is not a critical factor for admission; a solid background in the arts, humanities, or social sciences is of value to the future doctor along with strong preparation in the biosciences. Completion of B.S., B.A., or equivalent is required.

For information on admissions, please contact Dr. Christine Shafer, Assistant Dean for Admissions, Office of Admissions, Michigan State University, College of Human Medicine, A-239 Life Sciences Building, East Lansing, MI 48824-1317 or visit: *(http://www.mdadmissions.msu.edu)*.

Academic Support Programs

Academic support at MSUCHM is provided through the Academic Support Unit. The Director of Academic Support manages the implementation of an academic skills program and highly structured learning activities. Beginning in year 1, all students have the option of individual tutoring, small-group tutor-

ing, and/or discipline-based small group supplemental instruction. In the pre-clinical phase, students are given the opportunity to extend their programs. Students are guided by faculty to develop a schedule that extends over a two-year period rather than the customary one-year program.

The faculty and professional staff of the Office of Academic Programs and the Office of Student Affairs and Services are available to assist in the retention of medical students through personal assistance and counseling.

Enrichment Programs

Post-Baccalaureate Program
The Advanced Baccalaureate Learning Experience (ABLE) ABLE is an academic year post-baccalaureate program that is designed to improve the qualifications of students from disadvantaged backgrounds in order to facilitate their entry into medical school. The program is designed to accommodate a maximum of 15 students. ABLE participants enroll as second baccalaureate degree students in the College of Natural Science, which makes them eligible for campus housing, student privileges, and financial aid, provided they meet the required guidelines.

Admission to the ABLE Program is offered by the College of Human Medicine Committee on Admissions to students from disadvantaged backgrounds who apply to the College in the usual manner (i.e., through the American Medical College Application Service), work their way through the admissions process to the committee level, and are referred to the ABLE Review Committee for consideration. A follow-up application is sent to each ABLE candidate. The ABLE Review Committee then selects the final ABLE Program participants.

Students enroll in selected medical school basic science courses (maximum of two per academic year), which are offered by the College of Human Medicine. Passing medical school courses during this post-baccalaureate year will allow ABLE students, ultimately admitted to the College

of Human Medicine, an opportunity to waive a portion of their medical school courses once they begin medical school. They also enroll in upper division and graduate science courses offered by the College of Natural Science.

The ABLE program guarantees admission to the College of Human Medicine for those students who successfully complete the program. Criteria for successful completion are established and defined at the time of acceptance into the program.

For information on the ABLE Program, please contact: Dr. Christine Shafer, College of Human Medicine, A-239 Life Sciences Building, Michigan State University, East Lansing, MI 48824, 517-353-9620.

Student Financial Assistance

The Michigan State University Office of Financial Aid has a staff of health professions advisors to counsel medical students and assist them in financial planning. There are some scholarships and grants available to entering students through the Office of Admissions. Most scholarships and grants awarded at Michigan State University are made on the basis of demonstrated financial need. Workshops are conducted during the week of pre-matriculation to encourage students to begin financial planning for their medical school education early. If financial problems are anticipated, students are urged to speak with a health professions counselor at the Office of Financial Aid or with the Assistant Dean for Student Affairs and Services.

Financial aid is not available for student interview trips. Students who receive the American Medical College Application Service (AMCAS) fee waiver pay no additional application fees. Other students may request this accommodation with documentation of need.

Educational Partnerships

The College of Human Medicine has developed alliances with many organizations for mutual benefit. Collaboration has produced workshops on health careers, college admissions, and financial aid. Presentations are made to community constituents and tutorial sessions in math, science, and language arts are available.

Service learning opportunities are also arranged for high school, college, and medical student volunteers.

MSUCHM is engaging with colleges and universities in Michigan to establish Early Assurance Programs for students who are interested in practicing in an underserved area of medicine. Such programs will provide an enhanced opportunity for admission to medical school to those who otherwise might not have access to or be familiar with the intricacies of premedical preparation and medical school application by virtue of being a first generation college student, graduating from a low income high school as defined by the United States Department of Education or in an underserved (health professional shortage) urban or rural area, or experiencing disadvantages due to their socio-economic level.

University of Michigan Medical School

Dr. David Gordon, Associate Dean for Diversity and Career Development
University of Michigan
Medical School
1135 Catherine Street
2919C Taubman Medical Library
Ann Arbor, MI 48109-0603
734-764-8185 x0; 734-615-4248 fax
dgordon@umich.edu
www.med.umich.edu/medschool/diversity

Introduction

The University of Michigan Medical School has a number of programs and opportunities, described below, that may be of particular interest to students from U.S. populations that are underrepresented in medicine. These programs and opportunities are open to all students, regardless of race/ethnicity or gender, and we clearly value the ways in which students of all backgrounds contribute to forming an academically excellent, exciting, and broadly diverse educational environment.

Recruitment

The Medical School has maintained its longstanding commitment to recruit, retain, and graduate members of those underrepresented and disadvantaged groups that have been historically (and continue to be) underrepresented in medicine. This has been accomplished with a number of programs that are co-ordinated through the Diversity & Career Development Office (DCDO) and the Office of Student Programs' Admissions Office.

Diversity & Career Development Web site: *(http://www.med.umich.edu/medschool/diversity/).*

Office of Student Programs Web site: *(http://www.med.umich.edulmedschool/osp/).*

Admissions Web site: *(http://www.med.umich.edu/medschool/admissions/).*

These efforts begin at the high school level (see Enrichment Programs and Educational Partnerships) and continue beyond graduation through assistance in placement of graduating medical students.

The school also has a dual science M.D./ Ph.D. program, either through the Medical Scientist Training Program or individually arranged. Dual degrees are also available in business administration, public health, and law.

Minority and other disadvantaged students in the College of Literature, Science, and the Arts at the University of Michigan and other regional schools are encouraged to develop early linkages with our offices and medical student groups, particularly our Black Medical Association and Latino American Native American Medical Association, for pre-application support. Additionally, DCDO staff, minority and majority faculty members, medical students, and alumni visit selected health professions summer programs, regional and national meetings, college career days, etc., to recruit. In addition, medical students who are members of the Black Medical Association, and the Latin American Native American Medical Association, acting on behalf of those student associations, also greet interviewees, conduct school tours, and respond to requests for information from applicants. Our aim is to help any student in need of career advice.

University of Michigan Medical School
Applicants, First-Time Applicants, Matriculants by Gender, Race and Ethnicity, 2007-2008

	2007 APP Women	2007 APP Men	2007 APP Total	2007 F-time APP Women	2007 F-time APP Men	2007 F-time APP Total	2007 MAT Women	2007 MAT Men	2007 MAT Total	2008 APP Women	2008 APP Men	2008 APP Total	2008 F-time APP Women	2008 F-time APP Men	2008 F-time APP Total	2008 MAT Women	2008 MAT Men	2008 MAT Total
Hispanic/Latino																		
Cuban	6	15	21	5	10	15	1	0	1	9	14	23	7	11	18	0	1	1
Mexican American	51	74	125	38	58	96	2	0	2	64	67	131	49	53	102	0	1	1
Puerto Rican	16	13	29	13	10	23	0	1	1	11	14	25	10	11	21	1	0	1
Other Hispanic	49	50	99	37	42	79	3	0	3	52	73	125	45	62	107	3	3	6
Multiple Hispanic/Latino*	7	8	15	6	6	12	0	0	0	9	10	19	8	7	15	0	0	0
Subtotal	129	160	289	99	126	225	6	1	7	145	178	323	119	144	263	4	5	9
Non-Hispanic/Latino**																		
Black	181	130	311	137	111	248	4	6	10	226	117	343	177	95	272	2	2	4
Native American/AK	7	3	10	5	3	8	0	0	0	10	12	22	5	10	15	0	1	1
Native Hawaiian/OPI	11	4	15	9	4	13	0	0	0	8	8	16	7	6	13	0	0	0
White	1,360	1,739	3,099	1,167	1,447	2,614	59	45	104	1,309	1,795	3,104	1,113	1,465	2,578	57	44	101
Asian	721	890	1,611	615	712	1,327	18	20	38	683	896	1,579	544	701	1,245	19	22	41
Other Race	1	4	5	1	3	4	0	0	0	1	6	7	1	4	5	0	1	1
Multiple Race*	83	98	181	73	78	151	6	2	8	66	91	157	54	69	123	2	3	5
Unknown	14	49	63	13	45	58	0	2	2	66	106	172	64	92	156	4	2	6
Subtotal	2,378	2,917	5,295	2,020	2,403	4,423	87	75	162	2,369	3,031	5,400	1,965	2,442	4,407	84	75	159
Foreign	41	44	85	36	41	77	0	1	1	34	49	83	30	40	70	1	0	1
Total	2,548	3,121	5,669	2,155	2,570	4,725	93	77	170	2,548	3,258	5,806	2,114	2,626	4,740	89	80	169

*Since 2002, students can select more than one race and / or ethnicity. **Those who did not choose 'Hispanic/Latino' or 'Non-Hispanic/Latino' are listed under 'Non-Hispanic/Latino'. Data Source: AAMC Data Warehouse: Applicant-Matriculant File. as of 1/16/2009.

Admissions

All students are considered on the basis of individual qualifications. Cognitive and non-cognitive variables are given careful consideration. Attributes evaluated include motivation, competence, character, and personal fitness for the study of medicine. The academic record and the Medical College Admission Test (MCAT) are used to assess the student's level of academic preparedness. We are also particularly interested in students, minority or majority, who have overcome major life hurdles in order to achieve what they have, as well as students with a demonstrated commitment to improve the health of underserved and disadvantaged populations. The Admissions Committee is a diverse group that includes medical students and members of the basic science and clinical faculties. Women and members of minority groups are represented on the committee. As a state-assisted institution, the University of Michigan Medical School has a primary responsibility to train future physicians of this state. However, approximately half of the class consists of non-residents.

All applicants must be U.S. citizens or have a U.S. permanent resident visa in order to be considered for admission. A permanent resident must have completed at least one year of pre-medical education at an accredited college in North America.

Our Medical School generally does not accept transfers from other medical schools. If an exception is to be considered, the student must have been previously enrolled in a medical school program leading to the M.D., and he/she must be in good standing and eligible for re-entry to that school.

The school participates in the American Medical College Application Service (AMCAS). The deadline for receipt of the application by AMCAS is November 15th.

Academic Support Programs

Study skills, academic counseling, and tutorial assistance are available in each of the courses for all matriculated students. Assistance is available on an individual and/or group basis. From time to time, students who are having academic difficulty in the medical school are permitted to proceed on a reduced schedule of courses. Plans are generated on an individual as-needed basis and have to be approved by our Academic Review Boards.

The medical school has a very effective counseling program that is available to all students. These various programs account for a high rate of student retention and graduate medical placement.

Pre-matriculation Program

Entering students are recommended by the Admissions Committee for participation in the three-week pre-matriculation summer program. This program is designed to facilitate the academic transition to medical school, and is particularly offered to any students who may have been away from a curriculum-intensive environment for some time, or who feel they need supplemental academic enrichment. This program provides a background in study and reading skills to enhance performance in medical school, provides personal development workshops and individual counseling, and orients the students to the faculty, staff, and advanced students, as well as the Medical School and university campus. Students focus on courses in anatomy and molecular and cell biology, study-skills training, and personal development workshops.

Enrichment Programs

Summer Science Academy

This is a two-week summer program for tenth- and 11th-grade students in the State of Michigan who desire educational experiences which showcase careers in medicine and the biomedical sciences. Although open to any student, we especially target disadvantaged students (including from underserved backgrounds) who might not otherwise have access to such an enrichment opportunity. Many of our faculty and trainees participate by giving career talks and providing hands-on activities for the students. We also follow up with students to advise them on the college application process. Over the years of running this program, several such students have gained entry into medical schools, including our own.

Medical School Summer Opportunities for Apprenticeships in Research (Med-SOAR)

The Medical School also administers the Medical School Summer Opportunities for Apprenticeships in Research Program, which is for Michigan undergraduate residents and those who have participated in DCDO outreach programs. The Medical School provides funding to permit hosting a number of local disadvantaged students (including from underserved backgrounds) to attend this ten-week program, for which they receive a stipend. Students work with a member of the faculty involved in an ongoing research investigation. Academic counseling support services are also offered. At the end of the program, students give a poster presentation to their respective laboratories/programs, families, and invited guests.

Summer Research Opportunity Program (SROP)

Research opportunities are available for disadvantaged undergraduate students (including from underserved backgrounds) from institutions outside the State of Michigan to participate in research projects at the University of Michigan. Several of these research opportunities are within the Medical School, where students work with established investigators in both the basic and clinical sciences. The research work, the SROP seminars, and workshops give participants a realistic groundwork for advanced study, helping them prepare for graduate/professional degrees. Medicine-oriented students who participate in this program are encouraged to apply to the Medical School. This program is administered by our Rackham School of Graduate Studies (http://www.rackham.umich.edu/ Recruitment/SROP/index.php).

Student Financial Assistance

Financial aid at the University of Michigan Medical School is provided on the basis of financial need. The Medical School offers financial assistance in the form of scholarships, loans, and grants. Eligibility is based on current federal, state, and institutional regulations and recruiting goals. The Medical School also administers a Financial Program, funded by the regents of the university, which provides a limited number of tuition scholarships and supplemental grants to economically disadvantaged minority students who encounter unexpected expenses.

Educational Partnerships

The Medical School partners with several of the other health sciences schools at the University of Michigan (i.e., dental, pharmacy, public health, and others) and with the Ypsilanti School District and schools in Detroit, Michigan to provide science education and mentoring to local high school students. The Medical School is committed to creating a strong pipeline to improve the numbers of underrepresented minorities in medicine as well as all sciences. Specific programs run by the Medical School include the following:

Profiles for Success Program
(Formerly a Health Careers Opportunity Program funded by the federal Health Resources Services Administration). This is a six-week summer program run by the University of Michigan School of Dentistry and the Medical School for economically or educationally disadvantaged individuals, as well as for those who have shown a commitment to working with underserved or disadvantaged populations. This program provides enrichment and skill-building activities for specific pre-medical courses (e.g., chemistry, biology), as well as preparation for the MCAT examination and the medical school admission process. We also provide students opportunities to meet with various medicine specialists and research investigators to talk about their careers *(http://www.dent.umich.edu/ mac/pfs.html)*.

Wayne State University School of Medicine

Dr. Kertia L. Black, Assistant Dean
Office of Student Affairs
Wayne State University
School of Medicine
540 East Canfield Avenue
Rm. 1369 Scott Hall
Detroit, MI 48201
313-577-1463; 313-577-0361 fax
kblack@med.wayne.edu

Recruitment

The Office of Diversity at Wayne State University School of Medicine plans, directs, and implements the medical school's recruitment activities for disadvantaged students. The primary purpose of the Recruitment Outreach Program is to provide an access system for students to the medical school and to aid prospective disadvantaged students in their efforts to become stronger candidates for admission to medical school. The intent of the outreach program is to increase the pool of disadvantaged applicants by strengthening the students' academic and personal background. It is the policy of the Office of Diversity to establish communication and involvement with prospective disadvantaged applicants early in the admissions process.

The School of Medicine Office of Diversity has a Pre-medical Career counseling staff that provides academic and developmental counseling to students. The staff counselors work in the field serving target populations, such as the Detroit Public Schools, two- and four year colleges other than Wayne State University, and Wayne State University's undergraduate pre-medical program.

Admissions

All students are admitted through the school's Admissions Committee. Membership on the Admissions Committee includes minority and female faculty members as well as students. Factors such as a broad educational background, competitive performance in the basic sciences and on the Medical College Admission Test, related experiences in the biomedical field, and personal characteristics are considered by the Admissions Committee.

Academic Support Programs

Tutoring, academic, and personal counseling are available on an individual or group basis to all medical students through the Office of Student Affairs. Faculty and advanced level students serve as tutors.

Enrichment Programs

Pre-Matriculation Program
Entering students are invited to participate in a summer program designed to facilitate the transition to medical school. The students are familiarized with the school and are introduced to the organ systems curriculum. Concepts in biochemistry, anatomy, histology, physiology, and embryology are presented. The students' regular course work begins in the fall. Students are given an opportunity to work on those study skills pertinent to medical school. Counseling and directional work are provided to reinforce confidence. In addition, students are given the opportunity to meet faculty and advanced students.

Post-Baccalaureate Program
This program assists students whose prior academic performances have been compromised by economic and educational disadvantages. The program is restricted to legal Michigan residents. The program offers a year of structured and intensive preparation for medical

Wayne State University School of Medicine
Applicants, First-Time Applicants, Matriculants by Gender, Race and Ethnicity, 2007-2008

	2007									2008								
	APP			F-time APP			MAT			APP			F-time APP			MAT		
	Women	Men	Total	Women	Men	Total	Women	Men	Total	Women	Men	Total	Women	Men	Total	Women	Men	Total
Hispanic/Latino																		
Cuban	7	9	16	7	7	14	0	1	1	8	7	15	4	7	11	0	1	1
Mexican American	39	20	59	30	16	46	2	2	4	23	30	53	19	20	39	0	1	1
Puerto Rican	11	6	17	9	6	15	0	1	1	5	7	12	5	5	10	0	0	0
Other Hispanic	27	25	52	16	19	35	1	1	2	37	40	77	26	21	47	1	0	1
Multiple Hispanic/Latino*	2	5	7	1	2	3	0	0	0	6	6	12	6	2	8	0	0	0
Subtotal	86	65	151	63	50	113	3	5	8	79	90	169	60	55	115	1	2	3
Non-Hispanic/Latino**																		
Black	272	158	430	164	117	281	13	9	22	272	121	393	182	76	258	9	4	13
Native American/AK	3	6	9	2	6	8	0	1	1	5	5	10	1	4	5	2	2	4
Native Hawaiian/OPI	5	4	9	4	3	7	0	0	0	8	7	15	6	7	13	0	0	0
White	814	1,018	1,832	660	741	1,401	77	118	195	816	1,089	1,905	603	757	1,360	84	96	180
Asian	449	557	1,006	327	378	705	22	40	62	508	609	1,117	357	379	736	26	36	62
Other Race	3	7	10	2	2	4	0	0	0	0	5	5	0	4	4	0	0	0
Multiple Race*	36	43	79	26	28	54	4	4	8	44	54	98	29	39	68	1	2	3
Unknown	15	24	39	14	21	35	0	2	2	39	55	94	32	45	77	5	3	8
Subtotal	1,597	1,817	3,414	1,199	1,296	2,495	116	174	290	1,692	1,945	3,637	1,210	1,311	2,521	127	143	270
Foreign	209	194	403	168	154	322	2	2	4	207	245	452	155	189	344	6	11	17
Total	1,892	2,076	3,968	1,430	1,500	2,930	121	181	302	1,978	2,280	4,258	1,425	1,555	2,980	134	156	290

Note: In 2008, one applicant, who declined to report gender, was not included here.
*Since 2002. students can select more than one race and / or ethnicity. **Those who did not choose 'Hispanic/Latino' or 'Non-Hispanic/Latino' are

school. The submission of an application for admission to Wayne State University School of Medicine is one of the prerequisites to candidacy for the school's Post-Baccalaureate Program. Fourteen to 16 students participate in the Post-Baccalaureate Program each year. Successful completion of the program assures admission to Wayne State University School of Medicine. The program strengthens the student's academic and non-academic preparation for medical school. The program is divided into three semesters and a summer program. During the fall and winter semesters the students take specific science courses in the university's College of Liberal Arts. Course selection is based on individual needs. Specially designed study skills and reading programs are provided. Students also receive personal counseling. The spring term classes are held at the medical school. Medical school faculty present anatomy, histology, biochemistry, and physiology course material. The intent of this term's work is to facilitate the development of discipline and the necessary mechanisms to handle the volume of work in medical school. During the summer the students participate in the Entering Freshman Summer Program described above.

Student Financial Assistance

All students admitted to Wayne State University School of Medicine who apply for financial aid are awarded assistance based on need and the availability of funds.

Mayo Medical School

Dr. Eddie Greene, Director, Office for
Diversity
Barbara Porter, Assistant Dean for
Student Affairs
Mayo Medical School
200 First Street, S.W.
Rochester, MN 55905
507-293-0028; 507-538-4897;
507-284-2634 fax
eddie.eddie@mayo.edu
porter.barbara@mayo.edu

Recruitment

Mayo Medical School actively works to encourage and assist underrepresented minority students to pursue careers in medicine and biomedical research. These activities are coordinated by the Office of Minority Student Affairs, which serves the Mayo Medical School, Mayo Graduate School, Mayo School of Health Sciences (allied health), and Mayo School of Graduate Medical Education (residency training programs). Faculty, students, and administrators attend national recruitment meetings, as well as visit selected universities and colleges. Upon request, colleges and universities may arrange to bring groups of students to Mayo for tours and visits. Students who are considering applying to Mayo Medical School may, depending upon availability, tour the school and sit in on classes.

Admissions

Entering class size at Mayo Medical School is 42 students, including six M.D./Ph.D. students, and two Oral and Maxiofacial Surgery (O.M.S.) students. More than 3,400 applications are received each year. The Admissions Committee of Mayo Medical School reviews applications of minority students looking at factors such as grade-point average, Medical College Admission Test scores, as well as non-cogitative attributes of leadership, service, research experiences, health care exploration activities, and commitment to medicine. The Admissions Committee is composed of physician and basic science faculty, two student members, one public member, and one administrator. Mayo Medical School actively recruits students from diverse groups underrepresented in medicine. Since 1992, entering classes have averaged about 20 percent underrepresented minority students.

Academic Support Programs

Mayo Medical School does not have a formal program for pre-admission academic reinforcement. Upon entering, each student is paired with a mentor who works to guide them throughout their time at Mayo. For all students, close personal relationships with faculty and administration are maintained, and any student in academic difficulty is offered help as soon as the need is evident. Mayo is prepared to offer whatever academic support is needed including tutoring and repeating a particular course or an entire academic year. It is uncommon for any of Mayo's students to take more than four years to complete the curriculum.

Enrichment Programs

An extensive series of programs and activities are offered to assist minority students in their professional development (http://www.mayo.edu/msgme/diversity.html.) These include:

- summer research for undergraduates (SURF) *(www.mayo.edu/mgs/surf.html)*
- a post-baccalaureate research program for recent college graduates *(http://www.mayo.edu/mgs/post-bacprogram .html)*

MN, Mayo Medical School
Applicants, First-Time Applicants, Matriculants by Gender, Race and Ethnicity, 2007-2008

	2007									2008								
	APP			F-time APP			MAT			APP			F-time APP			MAT		
	Wo-men	Men	Total	Wo-men	Men	Total	Wo-men	Men	Total	Wo-men	Men	Total	Wo-men	Men	Total	Wo-men	Men	Total
Hispanic/Latino																		
Cuban	8	11	19	8	8	16	0	0	0	10	6	16	7	6	13	0	0	0
Mexican American	28	36	64	25	31	56	1	0	1	25	38	63	21	30	51	1	1	2
Puerto Rican	9	7	16	7	7	14	1	1	2	15	7	22	12	7	19	0	0	0
Other Hispanic	28	25	53	23	21	44	0	0	0	19	53	72	12	40	52	0	0	0
Multiple Hispanic/Latino*	3	2	5	3	2	5	0	0	0	6	3	9	6	3	9	0	0	0
Subtotal	76	81	157	66	69	135	2	1	3	75	107	182	58	86	144	1	1	2
Non-Hispanic/Latino**																		
Black	76	52	128	58	45	103	1	3	4	83	48	131	68	35	103	0	1	1
Native American/AK	7	5	12	5	5	10	0	0	0	3	5	8	3	5	8	1	0	1
Native Hawaiian/OPI	5	3	8	5	3	8	1	0	1	7	6	13	6	4	10	1	1	2
White	894	1,267	2,161	782	1,049	1,831	12	16	28	868	1,378	2,246	731	1,142	1,873	15	13	28
Asian	290	418	708	255	341	596	3	1	4	319	457	776	259	353	612	4	7	11
Other Race	2	4	6	2	3	5	0	0	0	1	4	5	1	3	4	0	0	0
Multiple Race*	45	53	98	38	40	78	0	1	1	46	52	98	38	43	81	2	0	2
Unknown	12	27	39	12	24	36	0	0	0	38	67	105	37	59	96	1	0	1
Subtotal	1,331	1,829	3,160	1,157	1,510	2,667	17	21	38	1,365	2,017	3,382	1,143	1,644	2,787	24	22	46
Foreign	53	59	112	45	48	93	0	1	1	74	101	175	66	82	148	1	1	2
Total	1,460	1,969	3,429	1,268	1,627	2,895	19	23	42	1,514	2,225	3,739	1,267	1,812	3,079	26	24	50

*Since 2002, students can select more than one race and / or ethnicity. **Those who did not choose 'Hispanic/Latino' or 'Non-Hispanic/Latino' are listed under 'Non-Hispanic/Latino'. Data Source: AAMC Data Warehouse: Applicant-Matriculant File, as of 1/16/2009.

- summer research (SRF) for medical students *(http://www. mayo.edu.msgme/diversity-srf.html)*,
- career development for medical students *(http://www.mayo.edu/ msgme/diversitysep.html)*
- career development program (CDP) *(http://www.mayo.edu/ msgme/diversity cdc.html)*
- both a one-year Certificate and two-year Masters in Clinical Research. The Clinical Research Training Program (CRTP) allows minority medical students to acquire clinical research skills while taking an appropriate leave of absence from their home school *(http://www.mayo.edu/ msgme/crtp.html)*.

All of these programs are coordinated through the Office of Minority Student Affairs, and most are supported by the Mayo Clinic's initiative for minority student development, "Training in Trans-lational Research: Bench to Bedsides." This initiative, founded by the National Institutes of Health (NIH), is focused on increasing the number of minority basic science and clinical investigators and addressing the shortage of minority academic physicians.

Student Financial Assistance

Students are admitted to Mayo Medical School without regard to their financial circumstances. If the applicant's American Medical College Application Service (AMCAS) fee is waived, Mayo also waives their application fee. Merit scholarships are available equal to the full cost of tuition. Students may also qualify for other need-based financial aid. Financial aid counseling is available to applicants and is required for accepted students. Mayo also has loan funds available to supplemental federally-sponsored loan and grant programs. These funds, combined with Mayo's generous scholarship program, enable students to avoid excessive debt. Mayo's average debt upon graduation is routinely half the national average for medical student loan debt. Summer and other programs may provide one or more of the following: scholarships, stipends/salaries travel, meals, and housing.

Educational Partnerships

Mayo has ongoing relationships with minority serving high schools, colleges, and universities. Institutional resources are committed to providing minority college students from around the United States with opportunities to learn more about Mayo Medical School and the medical field. Extensive effort is made to bring Mayo programs to the attention of students and to provide high-quality experiences.

Other Pertinent Information

There is an active branch of the Student National Medical Association on campus. Mayo Medical School sponsors delegate travel to meetings held elsewhere and occasionally hosts regional meetings.

University of Minnesota Medical School

University of Minnesota Medical School - Duluth Campus
Mary Tate, Director, Office of Minority Affairs and Diversity
University of Minnesota Medical School-Twin Cities
B-608 Mayo Memorial Building
MMC 293, 420 Delaware Street, SE
Minneapolis, MN 55455-0374
612-626-2173,612-625-1494;
612-626-9340 fax
minaff@umn.edu

Dr. Joycelyn Dorscher
Director, CAIMH Duluth
218-726-7235; 612-624-0465;
218-726-8948 fax
caimh@d.umn.edu
http://www.meded.umn.edu/
minority/index.cfm

Recruitment

The University of Minnesota Medical School strongly believes in the importance of having a culturally diverse student body. Therefore, the university actively seeks the recruitment of competitive and talented students of color interested in pursuing their medical

education. Representatives in the Office of Minority Affairs and Diversity (OMA&D) and the Center of American Indian and Minority Health (CAIMH) visit high schools, colleges, and universities and attend local or national pre-health professions student recruitment fairs.

At the University of Minnesota Medical School, faculty, staff, and students assist by spending time with pre-medical students providing clarification regarding the application materials, the application process, and answering general questions or concerns. The Medical School is strongly committed to the recruitment and education of students from groups underrepresented in medicine and encourages and welcomes interested prospective students to contact the OMA&D and CAIMH at the address, telephone, and fax numbers, or e-mail address listed above. Prospective students are also encouraged and invited to explore the medical school's Web site at *(www.med.umn.edu)*.

Admissions

Once the Office of Admissions has received a verified application from the American Medical College Application

Service, the application is screened by members of the Admissions Committee to determine the applicant's overall qualifications. Qualified applicants are then mailed the University of Minnesota-Twin Cities Medical School supplemental application materials, including a supplemental information form and instructions on how to complete the online portion of the supplemental application. Once all application materials are received and reviewed by the Admissions Committee, competitive applicants are invited for interviews. Limited travel assistance for interviews may be available through the Office of Minority Affairs and Diversity. Applicants are notified of acceptance through a rolling admissions process.

Significant qualifications considered by the Admissions Committee are that an applicant

- is academically qualified to complete the Medical School curriculum;
- demonstrates past experience and commitment of service to others through volunteer or community service activity;

demonstrates a strong motivation for a career in medicine, excellent interper-

University of Minnesota Medical School
Applicants, First-Time Applicants, Matriculants by Gender, Race and Ethnicity, 2007-2008

		2007									2008								
		APP			F-time APP			MAT			APP			F-time APP			MAT		
		Wo-men	Men	Total	Wo-men	Men	Total	Wo-men	Men	Total	Wo-men	Men	Total	Wo-men	Men	Total	Wo-men	Men	Total
Hispanic/Latino																			
Cuban		2	6	8	2	6	8	0	0	0	5	5	10	2	4	6	0	0	0
Mexican American		22	30	52	20	24	44	2	2	4	22	25	47	18	18	36	1	2	3
Puerto Rican		6	2	8	5	1	6	0	1	1	11	7	18	9	6	15	2	1	3
Other Hispanic		20	21	41	18	17	35	3	1	4	19	28	47	10	21	31	0	0	0
Multiple Hispanic/Latino*		1	2	3	0	1	1	0	0	0	4	6	10	3	4	7	0	1	1
Subtotal		51	61	112	45	49	94	5	4	9	61	71	132	42	53	95	3	4	7
Non-Hispanic/Latino**																			
Black		48	43	91	39	36	75	3	2	5	66	46	112	48	36	84	0	6	6
Native American/AK		10	12	22	8	10	18	2	0	2	9	12	21	6	10	16	0	0	0
Native Hawaiian/OPI		1	3	4	1	3	4	0	0	0	5	2	7	4	1	5	0	0	0
White		874	1,086	1,960	722	810	1,532	70	68	138	884	1,104	1,988	704	810	1,514	58	63	121
Asian		227	287	514	175	215	390	10	11	21	246	267	513	182	187	369	9	11	20
Other Race		0	2	2	0	2	2	0	0	0	0	0	0	0	0	0	0	0	0
Multiple Race*		33	35	68	28	29	57	1	2	3	43	48	91	36	31	67	4	3	7
Unknown		11	19	30	11	17	28	0	3	3	40	39	79	38	37	75	2	4	6
Subtotal		1,204	1,487	2,691	984	1,122	2,106	86	86	172	1,293	1,518	2,811	1,018	1,112	2,130	73	87	160
Foreign		101	124	225	78	86	164	1	1	2	99	119	218	76	93	169	2	1	3
Total		1,356	1,672	3,028	1,107	1,257	2,364	92	91	183	1,453	1,708	3,161	1,136	1,258	2,394	78	92	170

Note: In 2008, one applicant, who declined to report gender, was not included here.
*Since 2002, students can select more than one race and / or ethnicity. **Those who did not choose 'Hispanic/Latino' or 'Non-Hispanic/Latino' are listed under 'Non-Hispanic/Latino'. Data Source: AAMC Data Warehouse: Applicant-Matriculant File, as of 1/16/2009.

sonal and communication skills, maturity, and compassion;

- demonstrates the skills and talents necessary to develop mastery of the foundations of a medical education; and
- contributes to the diversity of the medical student body and/or demonstrates a commitment to serving the health needs of a diverse society.

The Admissions Committee is composed of clinical and basic science faculty, physician representatives of medical societies, and student representatives.

Academic Support Programs

The academic success of students is promoted by a number of academic support and student service programs. Highlighted below are some of the programs offered by the school.

Learner Development
Individual assistance and special workshops/presentations are provided to assist students in adapting their study techniques, time management, and learning strategies to the unique challenges of medical education, and in developing skills for lifelong learning in medicine. Examples of service include counseling for improving study techniques and test-taking skills, assistance with specific learning for performance problems and (e.g., difficulties in concentration/attention, procrastination, test anxiety, etc.), and assistance with preparation for the United States Medical Licensing Examination (USMLE) Step 1 and Step 2. The office also arranges for tutoring assistance and provides referrals as needed.

Knowledge Co-op: A Student Peer Teaching Program
The year-two students are organized to provide academic peer support for year-one students in the basic sciences. Students have created a Medical Wiki for all Yr1 and Yr2 courses. Yr2 Knowledge Co-op coordinators take responsibility for coordinating the ongoing updating of content for all courses. The benefits of the wiki format include hav-

ing the material instantly available, collaborative editing, and the option of expansion. Topics can be kept brief and to the point for Knowledge Co-op, but easily expanded on by linking to different topic pages.

Knowledge Co-op also supports Yr 1 students by arranging practice practicals preceding actual exams in lab courses.

Careers in Medicine
Programming and advisor services are provided to assist students in understanding medical career options and in selecting and applying to residency programs.

Physician Mentor and Advisor Programs
University faculty and community physicians provide guidance for academic progress and for students' professional development as future physicians.

Confidential Assistance and Referral Program (C.A.R.E.)
Counselors are available to meet with students to assist in resolving difficulties that affect academic work and overall well-being (i.e., financial problems, stress, personal and family issues, etc.). C.A.R.E. services may also be utilized by students' families.

Center of American Indian and Minority Health
The University of Minnesota Center of American Indian and Minority Health is one of four Centers of Excellence in Indian Health. The center creates a culturally supportive environment and provides counseling, and academic and research resources to American Indian medical students on both the Duluth and Twin Cities campuses. Interested students may visit the Web site at *(www.caimh.org)* or call 218-726-7235.

Medical School Office of Minority Affairs and Diversity (OMA&D)
OMA&D's mission is to create a welcoming and supportive environment for minority medical students and to enhance the student's educational experience at the University of Minnesota Medical School. Students can contact

OMA&D for more information about other services available.

Student Financial Assistance
The Medical School's Financial Aid Office is available to assist students in all aspects of the financial aid process including general information, financial counseling, debt management, and loan processing. Questions, comments, or concerns regarding the financial aid process should be directed to this office.

The University of Minnesota Medical School, Office of Minority Affairs and Diversity, or the Financial Aid Office should be contacted for information regarding the University of Minnesota scholarship for the non-resident portion of tuition.

Other Pertinent Information
We in the University of Minnesota Medical School want your educational experience to be a positive and rewarding one. The Medical School faculty and staff are here to serve and assist you in achieving your goal of becoming a Doctor of Medicine.

University of Mississippi School of Medicine

Dr. Jasmine P. Taylor, Associate Vice Chancellor for Multicultural Affairs
University of Mississippi School of Medicine
University of Mississippi Medical Center
2500 North State Street
Jackson, MS 39216-4505
601-984-1340; 601-984-1335 fax
jptaylor@som.umsmed.edu
http://mca.umc.edu

Recruitment

A comprehensive program is designed to accomplish the goals of increased enrollment and retention to assure the academic progression and timely graduation of an increased number of disadvantaged individuals in the fields of medicine, dentistry, and health-related professions. The Health Professional Alliance Partnership (HPAP) consists of formal partnerships with: 1) The University of Mississippi Medical Center and two undergraduate institutions, Alcorn State University and Tougaloo College; 2) Community organizations and the University of Mississippi Medical Center Area Health Education Center (AHEC) Program; and 3) Secondary school systems in the following regions: Southern region

(Claiborne and Jefferson County Public School Systems), Central region (Jackson County Public School, Rural Hinds, and Madison Public School Systems), and Philadelphia (Choctaw Indian Reservation).

The University of Mississippi Medical Center (UMMC) and its partner schools, universities, and community organizations has developed a very comprehensive plan to increase the number of disadvantaged students in the state of Mississippi who enter UMMC or other professional schools. This plan will be accomplished by developing an elementary school through post-secondary health science education pipeline. Through the linkages with each partner institution, substantial changes are planned that will improve educational opportunities for and achievement levels of disadvantaged students who are interested in health careers.

The goal of HPAP is to provide students from disadvantaged backgrounds an opportunity to develop skills needed to successfully enter and complete health profession schools. UMMC and its partner schools, universities, and community organizations have developed a comprehensive plan to increase the admission and retention of disadvantaged students in the state of Mississippi in health professions schools.

Admissions

Selection of applicants is made by the Admissions Committee on a competitive basis, without regard to race, age, sex, color, religion, marital status, national origin, veteran status, or handicap. Preference is given to applicants who are legal residents of Mississippi.

The first evaluation of applicants is made on the basis of scholastic record and scores on the Medical College Admission Test (MCAT). Those applicants possessing the scholastic competency necessary to successfully pursue the course of study required of students in the School of Medicine are further evaluated on the basis of character, motivation, and promise of fitness for the practice of medicine. Selection is made on the basis of all these evaluations. The Admissions Committee is composed of members of the faculty of the School of Medicine who are appointed by the Dean. There is minority representation on the committee.

Academic Support Programs

Throughout the academic year, tutorial assistance is available to underrepresented and disadvantaged students on an individual and/or group basis. Academic progress is closely monitored by the Division of Multicultural Affairs for early identification and intervention.

University of Mississippi School of Medicine
Applicants, First-Time Applicants, Matriculants by Gender, Race and Ethnicity, 2007-2008

		2007									2008								
		APP			F-time APP			MAT			APP			F-time APP			MAT		
		Women	Men	Total	Women	Men	Total	Women	Men	Total	Women	Men	Total	Women	Men	Total	Women	Men	Total
Hispanic/Latino																			
Cuban		0	0	0	0	0	0	0	0	0	1	0	1	1	0	1	1	0	1
Other Hispanic		1	3	4	1	0	1	0	0	0	3	1	4	3	0	3	0	0	0
	Subtotal	1	3	4	1	0	1	0	0	0	4	1	5	4	0	4	1	0	1
Non-Hispanic/Latino**																			
Black		35	12	47	24	10	34	8	3	11	26	10	36	20	9	29	8	2	10
Native American/AK		0	1	1	0	1	1	0	0	0	0	0	0	0	0	0	0	0	0
White		81	118	199	63	86	149	34	54	88	82	115	197	54	79	133	37	52	89
Asian		6	9	15	3	5	8	3	6	9	14	5	19	9	5	14	8	1	9
Multiple Race*		1	2	3	0	1	1	1	1	2	4	1	5	2	0	2	1	0	1
Unknown		0	1	1	0	1	1	0	0	0	1	2	3	1	1	2	0	0	0
	Subtotal	123	143	266	90	104	194	46	64	110	127	133	260	86	94	180	54	55	109
Foreign		1	0	1	1	0	1	0	0	0	0	1	1	0	0	0	0	0	0
	Total	125	146	271	92	104	196	46	64	110	131	135	266	90	94	184	55	55	110

*Since 2002, students can select more than one race and / or ethnicity. **Those who did not choose 'Hispanic/Latino' or 'Non-Hispanic/Latino' are listed under 'Non-Hispanic/Latino'. Data Source: AAMC Data Warehouse: Applicant-Matriculant File, as of 1/16/2009.

The academic year Tutorial Program provides tutorial assistance in gross anatomy, histology, neuroanatomy, biochemistry, pharmacology, pathology and microbiology. Assistance with learning skills, test-taking techniques, and academic counseling are also available through the Division of Multicultural Affairs.

You are not alone. When you arrive on this campus, you will have a family watching over you. We offer a formal mentoring program where students are paired with a School of Medicine faculty member whose primary focus will be guiding you through your health professions school experience. Students who are informed and feel connected tend to perform better and are generally happier. Also, each incoming student meets with the Associate Vice Chancellor for Multicultural Affairs for a one-on-one lunch meeting in the fall of the year. The Associate Vice Chancellor will serve as one of your main advocates during your training at the School of Medicine. The URL for these programs is *(http://mca.umc.edu)*.

Enrichment Programs
Summer Enrichment Programs
These programs are offered by the UMMC, through the Division of Multicultural Affairs, to assist disadvantaged students with medical school admission, retention, regular academic progress, and graduation and are conducted under HPAP.

Science Training Enrichment Program (STEP)
STEP is a Saturday Science Institute for students in grades six to eight that consists of ten months of activities that will encourage students to pursue science and math and ultimately choose a career in the health professions or health sciences. The program offers specialized courses and hands-on-experience in science, mathematics, writing, computer skills, cultural awareness and health careers in collaboration with The University of Mississippi Medical Center, Jackson Public Schools, Madison County Schools, Canton

Schools, and Hinds County Schools.

EXCEL Program
The Project EXCEL is conducted at Jackson State University and Alcorn State University. Students are from high schools in the undergraduate linkage school geographic area. High school students (grades nine-12) spend the six-week summer program preparing for college matriculation. College representatives, health care professionals, and students are invited to share information about their college, the admissions process, health care careers, and being a health care professional. Parents are also invited to participate in special activities. The following is the breakdown of participants:

MEDCORP I & II
The MEDCORP I & II program is a six-week summer program designed to provide individuals from disadvantaged backgrounds with mathematics and science education that will enhance their preparation for health profession school. The MEDCORP is conducted at Alcorn and Jackson State Universities. The students at this level of the program are pre-freshman and pre-sophomores.

MEDCORP III & IV
The Facilitating Entry (MEDCORP III & IV) level includes an intense seven-week summer academic enrichment, reinforcement, and motivational program conducted at UMMC. The program provides a concise and thorough review of the knowledge and various skills tested on the MCAT or Dental Admissions Test (DAT).

Clinical correlation and hospital rotations are offered from 1-5 pm (or later, depending on rotations) three days per week. Emergency room rotations are on Friday evenings and weekends, including Sundays.

Pre-matriculation Summer Enrichment Program (PRE-MAT)
PRE-MAT is a seven-week program for entering disadvantaged medical and dental students is conducted by the Division of Multicultural Affairs beginning in June. The program affords

students a preview of gross anatomy and biochemistry. The program structure is designed to significantly increase the competitive basis upon which the participants would approach more advanced professional studies and provide an early and controlled measures of their predicted performance in basic science areas.

The Professional Portal Track Program is a program that seeks to improve the health care and biomedical education of the underserved citizens of Mississippi. It is a comprehensive two-year, mentor based program that offers a non-thesis-requiring Master of Biomedical Science degree. This terminal degree is suitable for preparation for teaching at the community/junior college level, as advanced training for governmental and industrial positions, and as an indication of competitiveness for admission to the University of Mississippi Schools of Medicine (M.D. program), Dentistry (D.M.D. program), and Graduate Studies in the Health Sciences (Ph.D. program). Criteria for admission to the Professional Portal Track include: 1) formal application and denial of admission to either the School of Medicine, School of Dentistry, or School of Graduate Studies in Health Sciences at the University of Mississippi Medical Center; 2) MCAT or DAT scores not more than four years old; 3) belonging to racial or ethnic groups underrepresented in medicine or coming from an environmentally or economically disadvantaged background; 4) recommendation by the medical, dental, or graduate school's admission officer; 5) invitation to apply by the Professional Portal Track Program Director; and 6) submission of acceptable Graduate Record Examination (GRE) scores. Residency requirements and time limitations for the Professional Portal Track are the same as those listed in the University of Mississippi Medical Center Bulletin for the Master of Science program. The degree requires the completion of 45 quarter hours of graduate level credit and the maintenance of a B average. The Professional Portal Track Program will begin with the onset of the 2004-2005 academic year; a maximum of 15 students will be enrolled in each class.

Student Financial Assistance

The School of Medicine's financial aid program is designed to meet the needs of any Mississippi resident admitted to the school whose financial need can be documented.

Educational Partnerships

A comprehensive program is designed to accomplish the goals of increased enrollment and retention to assure the academic progression and timely graduation of an increased number of disadvantaged individuals in the fields of medicine, dentistry, and health-related professions. The Health Professional Alliance Partnership consists of formal partnerships with: 1) The University of Mississippi Medical Center (UMMC) and two undergraduate institutions, Alcorn State University and Tougaloo College; 2) Community organizations and the University of Mississippi Medical Center AHEC Program; and 3) Secondary school systems in the following regions: Southern Region (Claiborne and Jefferson County Public School Systems), Central Region (Jackson Public Schools, Hinds County Public Schools, and Madison County Public School Systems) and the Mississippi Band of Choctaw Indians.

Saint Louis University School of Medicine

Office of Multicultural Affairs
Saint Louis University School
of Medicine
1402 South Grand Boulevard, C120
St. Louis, MO 63104-1085
314-977-8730; 314-977-8779 fax
http://medschool.slu.edu/oma

Mission Statement

The Office of Multicultural Affairs (OMA) at Saint Louis University (SLU) is dedicated to ensuring that disadvantaged and underrepresented physicians are reflective of their numbers in the overall population. The office endeavors to assist students from diverse backgrounds to be successful as they progress along the educational pathway in pursuit of a career as a physician. The focus of the OMA initiatives is prevention rather than crisis intervention.

The OMA is a student-centered, student-friendly office and a resource center for underrepresented and other students who are seeking a diverse and caring environment in which to reach their greatest potential. The charge of the OMA is to support and enhance the academic, educational, social, and cultural interests of the diverse student constituency at Saint Louis University School of Medicine and to maximize the students' abilities in pursuit of a medical career.

The OMA is a first line point of contact for the underrepresented undergraduate student and the secondary student who is in search of information related to a health career in medicine. To this end, the office seeks to entice, encourage, enable, and empower students who have medicine as their career goal.

The OMA initiatives are intended to increase the number of disadvantaged and underrepresented students matriculating into the School of Medicine. More specifically, the initiatives are intended to better prepare entering students for the rigors of a medical school curriculum and are designed to improve the probability of underrepresented students successfully completing the course curriculum as expeditiously as possible.

Academic Support Programs

The Skills Enhancement Component is designed to increase the academic opportunities available to currently enrolled underrepresented medical students through individual and group sessions related to time management, auxiliary management (note taking, study skills, memory techniques, etc.), and academic/ personal management, (i.e., how to cope in a medical school environment).

The Supplemental Instruction (SI) Initiative
The initiative is a proactive, participatory, collaborative, approach to learning that utilizes small-group discussion and emphasizes long-term retention of material.

For Males Only and Woman-to-Woman
These sessions are separate informal sessions for underrepresented male and female medical students, respectively. The sessions, facilitated by School of Medicine male and female physicians of color, focus on such pertinent topics as successfully negotiating medical school, being a student of

Saint Louis University School of Medicine
Applicants, First-Time Applicants, Matriculants by Gender, Race and Ethnicity, 2007-2008

	2007									2008								
	APP			F-time APP			MAT			APP			F-time APP			MAT		
	Women	Men	Total	Women	Men	Total	Women	Men	Total	Women	Men	Total	Women	Men	Total	Women	Men	Total
Hispanic/Latino																		
Cuban	11	14	25	8	10	18	0	0	0	11	19	30	8	13	21	1	0	1
Mexican American	59	71	130	43	54	97	0	1	1	44	57	101	34	42	76	0	1	1
Puerto Rican	11	13	24	10	11	21	0	0	0	13	15	28	12	11	23	0	1	1
Other Hispanic	52	68	120	38	47	85	0	0	0	54	73	127	44	41	85	0	2	2
Multiple Hispanic/Latino*	7	5	12	4	2	6	0	0	0	11	9	20	8	4	12	0	0	0
Subtotal	140	171	311	103	124	227	0	1	1	133	173	306	106	111	217	1	4	5
Non-Hispanic/Latino**																		
Black	190	92	282	126	66	192	3	2	5	158	84	242	112	58	170	5	0	5
Native American/AK	8	5	13	6	5	11	0	0	0	4	7	11	3	3	6	0	0	0
Native Hawaiian/OPI	10	6	16	9	4	13	0	0	0	15	9	24	6	8	14	0	0	0
White	1,529	2,103	3,632	1,167	1,525	2,692	52	73	125	1,467	2,148	3,615	1,058	1,467	2,525	45	57	102
Asian	731	895	1,626	506	613	1,119	15	30	45	747	879	1,626	505	539	1,044	18	29	47
Other Race	2	5	7	2	1	3	0	0	0	3	4	7	3	4	7	0	0	0
Multiple Race*	76	87	163	50	62	112	2	0	2	63	80	143	50	50	100	3	4	7
Unknown	23	32	55	22	27	49	1	0	1	51	74	125	46	60	106	3	2	5
Subtotal	2,569	3,225	5,794	1,888	2,303	4,191	73	105	178	2,508	3,285	5,793	1,783	2,189	3,972	74	92	166
Foreign	110	144	254	80	99	179	0	0	0	115	142	257	85	100	185	3	2	5
Total	2,819	3,540	6,359	2,071	2,526	4,597	73	106	179	2,756	3,600	6,356	1,974	2,400	4,374	78	98	176

Note: In 2008, one applicant, who declined to report gender, was not included here.
*Since 2002, students can select more than one race and / or ethnicity. **Those who did not choose 'Hispanic/Latino' or 'Non-Hispanic/Latino' are listed under 'Non-Hispanic/Latino'. Data Source: AAMC Data Warehouse: Applicant-Matriculant File, as of 1/16/2009.

color in a predominantly white medical school, staying focused, and maintaining balance in one's life.

United States Medical Licensing Examination (USMLE)
Step 1 Board Review utilizes the SI model, described above and focuses upon the specific subject areas covered in the Step 1 examination.

The Clinical Survival Skills Booklet
This booklet is designed as a guide for students while they acclimate themselves to clinical medicine and build their knowledge base.

The Smart Track Support Group
This group is designed to provide a diverse student constituency of high school, undergraduate, and graduate students with the necessary tools to be successful as they progress along the educational pathway in pursuit of a career in medicine.

Enrichment Programs
The Summer Enrichment Program
This program is a three-week experience for 20 St. Louis metropolitan area high school disadvantaged juniors and seniors designed to stimulate and sustain their interest in a career in medicine.

The Summer Research Apprenticeship Program
This program is an eight-week activity that places underrepresented students in a research setting with the intent of stimulating their interest in pursuing a career in academic medicine by giving them an opportunity to participate in a "hands-on" research experience.

Other Pertinent Information
Saint Louis University's School of Medicine is committed to enrolling and graduating disadvantaged individuals and those underrepresented in medicine. To this end, the OMA initiatives delineated above are designed to ensure the matriculation, even progression, and graduation of underrepresented students from the medical school in an expeditious manner.

For information please contact the Office of Multicultural Affairs Saint Louis University School of Medicine1402 South Grand Blvd., St. Louis, MO 63104Phone: 314-977-8730; Fax: 314-977-8779 (oma@wpogate.slu.edu)

University of Missouri—Columbia School of Medicine

Dr. Rachel M.A. Brown, Associate Dean for Student Programs
MA215 Medical Sciences Building
University of Missouri—Columbia School of Medicine
Columbia, MO 65212
573-882-2923; 573-884-2988 fax
brownrac@health.missouri.edu
www.muhealth.org/~medicine

Traci Wilson-Kleekamp
Diversity Coordinator
573-882-2472 (office)
kleekampt@health.missouri.edu

Recruitment

The University of Missouri—Columbia School of Medicine is committed to the recruitment and retention of students from underrepresented groups and underserved areas. Recruitment activities occur at the high-school and undergraduate levels and include participation in campus diversity programming, recruitment fairs, and on-site campus visits. Our dedicated Diversity Coordinator focuses on increased minority student enrollment through extensive communication by mail, email, and telephone and by attending local, regional, and national events. We have expanded our recruitment efforts to include colleges/institutions with large enrollments of underrepresented student groups.

The School of Medicine holds an annual Pre-Med Day to invite interested students to visit the campus for a day of scheduled events to learn more about the admissions process, our internationally recognized problem-based learning (PBL) curriculum, and financial aid; tour the campus and new simulation center; as well as meet enrolled minority students. An increased effort has been made to recruit from our undergraduate class of Minority Association of Pre-Health Students (MAPS) and high-achieving science majors. Medical students, staff, and faculty participate in all of the above activities.

Admissions

The Admissions Committee is composed of faculty, students, and alumni. Assessment of all applicants is based upon academic record, pattern of academic performance, personal characteristics, motivation, extracurricular and community activities, interpersonal skills, work experiences, and emotional stability. The Admissions Committee has two goals. The first is to select the most qualified applicants, particularly those who will excel as patient-centered physicians. The second is to focus on selecting students from diverse backgrounds who are likely to serve the needs of the state of Missouri, with a special emphasis on the underserved and rural communities. Minority students invited to interview for medical school will have an additional opportunity to meet one-on-one with enrolled minority students and/or the Diversity Coordinator for additional inquiry. The diversity coordinator participates in the application review and the interviews with all minority applicants.

Academic Support Programs

Academic support activities are designed to meet the needs of the student and may include flexible curriculum scheduling, tutoring, skill development, and counseling. Study-skills instruction is provided in note taking, test taking,

University of Missouri-Columbia School of Medicine
Applicants, First-Time Applicants, Matriculants by Gender, Race and Ethnicity, 2007-2008

| | 2007 | | | | | | | | | 2008 | | | | | | | | |
| | APP | | | F-time APP | | | MAT | | | APP | | | F-time APP | | | MAT | | |
	Women	Men	Total	Women	Men	Total	Women	Men	Total	Women	Men	Total	Women	Men	Total	Women	Men	Total
Hispanic/Latino																		
Cuban	1	4	5	1	2	3	0	0	0	3	4	7	0	4	4	0	0	0
Mexican American	7	10	17	6	9	15	1	2	3	9	14	23	8	8	16	0	0	0
Puerto Rican	2	1	3	2	1	3	0	0	0	3	1	4	1	0	1	0	0	0
Other Hispanic	4	14	18	4	11	15	0	0	0	7	18	25	5	9	14	0	1	1
Multiple Hispanic/Latino*	0	3	3	0	1	1	0	0	0	1	3	4	1	2	3	0	0	0
Subtotal	14	32	46	13	24	37	1	2	3	23	40	63	15	23	38	0	1	1
Non-Hispanic/Latino**																		
Black	24	25	49	17	19	36	0	0	0	45	31	76	37	23	60	3	3	6
Native American/AK	3	4	7	3	4	7	0	0	0	1	2	3	1	2	3	0	2	2
Native Hawaiian/OPI	3	2	5	3	2	5	0	0	0	3	1	4	2	1	3	0	0	0
White	373	479	852	310	354	664	40	50	90	345	534	879	260	370	630	34	37	71
Asian	114	130	244	86	97	183	3	0	3	109	128	237	86	87	173	4	6	10
Other Race	0	1	1	0	0	0	0	0	0	0	2	2	0	1	1	0	0	0
Multiple Race*	16	18	34	11	18	29	0	0	0	20	14	34	12	9	21	3	1	4
Unknown	2	9	11	2	8	10	0	0	0	12	19	31	12	18	30	1	0	1
Subtotal	535	668	1,203	432	502	934	43	50	93	535	731	1,266	410	511	921	45	49	94
Foreign	5	10	15	4	7	11	0	0	0	3	12	15	3	7	10	0	0	0
Total	554	710	1,264	449	533	982	44	52	96	561	783	1,344	428	541	969	45	50	95

Note: In 2008, one applicant, who declined to report gender, was not included here.

*Since 2002, students can select more than one race and / or ethnicity. **Those who did not choose 'Hispanic/Latino' or 'Non-Hispanic/Latino' are listed under 'Non-Hispanic/Latino'. Data Source: AAMC Data Warehouse: Applicant-Matriculant File, as of 1/16/2009.

time management, and textbook reading. Individual-sized academic programs are available to students as needed. Students are assigned a faculty advisor to assist with curricular and career planning.

Student Financial Assistance

The School of Medicine's Financial Aid Office provides access to the institutional and federal programs aimed at increasing the attendance of underrepresented and disadvantaged students. Besides traditional need-based scholarships and loans, the University of Missouri-Columbia offers the Professional Degree Assistance Program, which provides significant scholarship assistance to first-year underrepresented medical students. The School of Medicine also participates in the Scholarships for Disadvantaged Students program funded by the federal Department of Health and Human Services. Once students are accepted by the school, they are mailed the necessary forms for applying for financial aid.

Enrichment Programs

High School Mini-Medical School Program
Each summer the School of Medicine conducts a one-week High School Mini-Medical School Program, which is designed to motivate high school students to enter careers in medicine and to give them a sample of the medical student curriculum. Preference is given to students from underrepresented groups and students from underserved areas of Missouri.

Excellence in Learning
The School of Medicine supports this two-day program, designed to give disadvantaged and underrepresented high school students from St. Louis the opportunity to experience the university environment and to explore health-related careers. Students shadow physicians and work through a problem-based learning case in small groups.
(http://excelearn.missouri.edu/)

Other Pertinent Information

The School of Medicine is strongly committed to the recruitment, enrollment, and graduation of a diverse student body. The Office of Medical Education staff works with all units of the School of Medicine and the university to maintain a high retention rate. There is an active branch of the Student National Medical Association (SNMA) on campus. The SNMA works cooperatively with the Office of Medical Education in their recruitment activities.

University of Missouri—Kansas City School of Medicine

Dr. Susan B. Wilson, Associate Dean,
Office of Cultural Enhancement
and Diversity
University of Missouri—Kansas City
School of Medicine
2411 Holmes Street
Kansas City, MO 64108
816-235-1780; 816-235-5277 fax
Wilsonsb2@umkc.edu
http://www.umkc.edu/medicine

Recruitment

The program at the University of Missouri-Kansas City (UMKC) is a six-year program leading to baccalaureate and M.D. degrees and is designed primarily for high school seniors entering college for the first time. Students who are freshman and have not accumulated more than 24 credit hours are also eligible to apply. In either case, students are required to complete both degrees. A limited number of students already having a baccalaureate degree are admitted at the year-three level to fill any existing vacancies. These students are referred to as, M.D. only.

The Office of Cultural Enhancement and Diversity (OCED) serves as the medical school's central division for diversity initiatives, including community engagement, recruitment, facilitation of admission, and retention.

An Associate Dean directs this office, which provides support in academic, administrative, financial, and personal matters for underrepresented minorities. OCED staff include a medical recruiter, who is responsible for recruiting activities that focus on attracting a diverse applicant pool, and a program assistant who coordinates community bases service learning projects. The OCED also draws attention to minority health through an endowed lectureship that addresses health disparities.

A minority Recruitment Committee works with the Council on Selection at the School of Medicine to identify students interested in health sciences early in secondary schooling. A Summer Scholars Program provides a four-week educational/preparatory realistic exposure to the health professions to selected high school students. Saturday Academy, a core program of the Health Professional Partner-ship Initiative, provides Saturday didactic sessions on science subjects and topic for students in grades six through 12. Additionally, a Medical Explorer Post provides continuing exposure to the health field.

Admissions

All admissions are the responsibility of the Council on Selection, which is a diverse group of about 18 people. The council consists of ten physicians, two student physicians, three basic scientists, and three arts and sciences faculty representatives. The chairman of the council is a physician appointed by the dean. Students seeking admission directly from high school should complete four units of English; three units of social studies; one unit of fine arts; four units of mathematics; three units of science including one unit biology and one unit of chemistry; and two units of a single foreign language. One unit of physics and one-half unit of computer science are highly recommended. Applicants must also submit their scores from the ACT or SAT Test. An initial academic screen to identify applicants for interview is based on class rank and the ACT or SAT composite scores. All applicants not meeting this initial screen are reviewed by a subcommittee of the council. All application information, both cognitive and non-cognitive, is examined for evidence of academic potential.

Academic Support Programs

The university's Center for Academic Development offers a wide range of free services to students. These include tutorial assistance, a writing lab, a math lab, and learning and study skills services in note taking, test taking, reading comprehension, memory, anxiety reduction, and supplemental instruction. The medical school has a strong Academic

University of Missouri-Kansas City School of Medicine
Applicants, First-Time Applicants, Matriculants by Gender, Race and Ethnicity, 2007-2008

| | 2007 | | | | | | | | | 2008 | | | | | | | | |
| | APP | | | F-time APP | | | MAT | | | APP | | | F-time APP | | | MAT | | |
	Women	Men	Total	Women	Men	Total	Women	Men	Total	Women	Men	Total	Women	Men	Total	Women	Men	Total
Hispanic/Latino																		
Other Hispanic	2	2	4	2	2	4	2	2	4	2	0	2	2	0	2	2	0	2
Subtotal	2	2	4	2	2	4	2	2	4	2	0	2	2	0	2	2	0	2
Non-Hispanic/Latino**																		
Black	5	2	7	5	2	7	5	2	7	2	0	2	1	0	1	2	0	2
Native American/AK	1	0	1	1	0	1	1	0	1	0	0	0	0	0	0	0	0	0
White	24	14	38	24	14	38	24	14	38	20	18	38	18	16	34	20	18	38
Asian	22	20	42	22	20	42	22	20	42	20	20	40	19	18	37	20	20	40
Multiple Race*	0	0	0	0	0	0	0	0	0	0	1	1	0	0	0	0	1	1
Unknown	2	0	2	2	0	2	2	0	2	2	1	3	2	1	3	2	1	3
Subtotal	54	36	90	54	36	90	54	36	90	44	40	84	40	35	75	44	40	84
Total	56	38	94	56	38	94	56	38	94	46	40	86	42	35	77	46	40	86

*Since 2002, students can select more than one race and / or ethnicity. **Those who did not choose 'Hispanic/Latino' or 'Non-Hispanic/Latino' are listed under 'Non-Hispanic/Latino'. Data Source: AAMC Data Warehouse: Applicant-Matriculant File, as of 1/16/2009.

and Advisory Support Program:

- Education Assistants: Help tailor a curriculum that fulfills individual needs.
- Clinical Medical Librarian: Locates information pertinent to patient care.
- Clinical Pharmacologist: Teaches patient-oriented pharmacology at the bedside.
- Supplemental Instruction (SI): Meets weekly in small groups to discuss course content for enhanced learning, application, and retention of basic science disciplines.

Enrichment Programs

Summer Scholars
The medical school sponsors a four-week educational/preparatory program for high school juniors and seniors who are interested in a career in health care. This program is designed to identify and motivate promising minority students toward careers in medicine and other health careers by providing educational experiences to enhance academic performance and supplying realistic information and clinical experiences to clarify their perceptions of health care roles.

Saturday Academy
This is a core program developed for the Health Professionals Partnership Initiative (HPPI). The program is strictly didactic with an emphasis on math and sciences. The curriculum is designed to prepare students to excel in their academic coursework, expand their quest for knowledge, and motivate them to enroll in higher level science and mathematics courses. The program runs concurrently with the school year.

Student Financial Assistance

There are four types of student financial aid. They are scholarships and grants, which are gifts and do not require repayment; long-term loans repayable after termination of schooling at reduced interest rates; short-term loans repayable within the same academic period; and employment in the College Work-Study Program. In general, aid is based on financial need. Gift assistance for minority students is available in

years three and four of the six-year curriculum from the National Medical Fellowships, Inc. The out-of-state tuition fee is waived for minorities.

Educational Partnerships

The UMKC had a partnership established through The Robert Wood Johnson Foundation HPPI Program. Although the granting period ended in 2003, the school has retained many of those partnerships, particularly with area high schools.

Other Pertinent Information

The medical program at the University of Missouri—Kansas City limits approximately 75 percent of the entering class to residents of Missouri.

Washington University in St. Louis, School of Medicine

Dr. Will Ross, Associate Dean for Diversity, Associate Professor of Medicine
Lisa Stevenson, MBA, Director of Diversity Programs
Office of Diversity Programs
660 South Euclid, Box 8023
Washington University School of Medicine
St. Louis, MO 63110
314-362-6854; 314-747-3974 fax
diversity@msnotes.wustl.edu
medschooldiversity.wustl.edu

Recruitment

The mission of the Office of Diversity Programs is to promote cultural diversity no only within the student body but also within the entire academic workforce as a means of enhancing the educational environment at Washington University School of Medicine.

The recruitment and retention of students from underrepresented and economically disadvantaged groups is our main activity and is accomplished through visits to undergraduate colleges and universities as well as a select science- and medical-exposure programs across the country.

Additionally, admissions information is mailed twice yearly to registrants of the Medical Minority Applicant Registry. The associate dean and the director work closely with the Student National Medical Association (SNMA) in welcoming applicants from underrepresented groups to campus during their admission interviews.

In April each year, we sponsor a Revisit Program designed to encourage accepted students who are underrepresented in medicine to enroll at the School of Medicine by taking an in-depth look at the school through a series of activities on campus and in the St. Louis area. The program provides the visiting students with ample opportunity to get to know each other as well as currently enrolled students, faculty, and administrators.

Providing a supportive community for students is an ongoing objective as well. By sponsoring social gatherings throughout the year, the office provides networking opportunities for medical students, residents, and fellows from underrepresented groups. Students are invited to monthly dinners with faculty as well as physicians from the community through the Mound City Medical Forum, a local component of the National Medical Association.

Admissions

The Committee on Admissions consists of faculty and administrators including the Associate Director and the Director of Diversity Programs. Individual attention is given to all applicants of the School of Medicine. All underrepresented minority applicants who apply, or who are considering applying, are encouraged to contact the office. Medical students are selected on the basis of academic performance, aptitude and motivation for the study of medicine, and the personal characteristics required for the effective and compassionate practice of medicine. Selected applicants are invited for a personal interview and tour of the medical center campus. Generally, the Associate Dean for Diversity and the director along with other members meet with minority candidates during their visit to the School of Medicine. The admissions

Washington University in St. Louis School of Medicine
Applicants, First-Time Applicants, Matriculants by Gender, Race and Ethnicity, 2007-2008

	2007									2008								
	APP			F-time APP			MAT			APP			F-time APP			MAT		
	Women	Men	Total	Women	Men	Total	Women	Men	Total	Women	Men	Total	Women	Men	Total	Women	Men	Total
Hispanic/Latino																		
Cuban	9	13	22	8	12	20	0	0	0	10	8	18	8	7	15	0	0	0
Mexican American	30	44	74	26	36	62	1	1	2	31	44	75	27	34	61	2	3	5
Puerto Rican	13	16	29	13	13	26	0	1	1	3	16	19	3	13	16	0	0	0
Other Hispanic	43	38	81	38	31	69	0	1	1	32	51	83	30	43	73	0	1	1
Multiple Hispanic/Latino*	6	6	12	6	5	11	0	0	0	8	7	15	7	7	14	1	0	1
Subtotal	101	117	218	91	97	188	1	3	4	84	126	210	75	104	179	3	4	7
Non-Hispanic/Latino**																		
Black	213	139	352	168	115	283	3	4	7	183	92	275	146	70	216	4	3	7
Native American/AK	5	6	11	3	5	8	0	0	0	3	5	8	2	4	6	0	0	0
Native Hawaiian/OPI	3	2	5	3	2	5	0	0	0	6	3	9	5	2	7	0	0	0
White	798	1,215	2,013	706	1,027	1,733	36	33	69	764	1,280	2,044	679	1,094	1,773	28	37	65
Asian	450	612	1,062	406	504	910	16	19	35	402	586	988	343	461	804	17	13	30
Other Race	2	2	4	2	2	4	0	0	0	1	1	2	1	1	2	0	0	0
Multiple Race*	67	73	140	61	62	123	2	1	3	53	59	112	43	46	89	1	2	3
Unknown	12	30	42	10	28	38	0	0	0	46	66	112	44	58	102	2	1	3
Subtotal	1,550	2,079	3,629	1,359	1,745	3,104	57	57	114	1,458	2,092	3,550	1,263	1,736	2,999	52	56	108
Foreign	123	142	265	100	121	221	2	2	4	116	146	262	107	106	213	4	3	7
Total	1,774	2,338	4,112	1,550	1,963	3,513	60	62	122	1,658	2,364	4,022	1,445	1,946	3,391	59	63	122

*Since 2002, students can select more than one race and / or ethnicity. **Those who did not choose 'Hispanic/Latino' or 'Non-Hispanic/Latino' are listed under 'Non-Hispanic/Latino'. Data Source: AAMC Data Warehouse: Applicant-Matriculant File, as of 1/16/2009.

committee consists of several faculty who are from underrepresented groups. Members of the SNMA are also available to meet for breakfast with applicants the day of their interview.

Academic Support Programs
The educational program of Washington University School of Medicine is designed to meet the needs of all students in an individualized and personalized way. The school can provide tutorial aid, on a one-to-one basis, to students at no cost. Academic and personal counseling are provided to anyone experiencing academic difficulty. Individualized academic programs can be devised to help students adjust to the medical school curriculum. Individualized programs permit students two years to complete the first year's coursework. Thereafter, it is anticipated that the student would continue his/her regular course work in an uninterrupted fashion, receiving the M.D. degree in five years rather than four.

Enrichment Programs
The Division of Biology and Biomedical Sciences offers BiomedRap, a ten-week summer biomedical research program for undergraduates. Applications can be obtained at biomedrap.wustl.edu. Through the Health Care Advocacy Program (HCAP) the Office of Diversity Programs provides Washington University freshman and sophomores with the opportunity to explore the health care setting as part of an eight-week patient care unit assignment at Barnes-Jewish Hospital. For more information, visit (*medschooldiversity.wustl.edu*).

Research
Summer opportunities in basic science and clinical research are available to undergraduates. Please contact Dr. Koong-Nah Chung, Assistant Dean for Admissions and Student Affairs at Washington University School of Medicine at 314-362-6844 or (chungkmsnotes.wustl.edu). The Division of Biology and Bio-medical Sciences offers BiomedRap, a ten-week biomedical research program for undergraduates. Ap-

plications can be obtained online at (www.biomedrap.wustl.edu).

Educational Partnerships
We sponsor a number of outreach programs throughout the educational pipeline to enhance the exposure and preparation of underrepresented students and other students from disadvantaged groups who are interested in careers in medicine:

The Health Professions Fair
The Fair provides a forum for St. Louis City and County high school students to explore various health-related career opportunities. The program is sponsored by the Office of Diversity Programs and the St. Louis Public Schools. Each year approximately 160 students from area schools are selected to participate in the fair.

The Saturday Scholars Program
The program is sponsored by the School of Medicine in collaboration with the St. Louis Public Schools. Students from area high schools are selected by their science teachers to attend this four-week human anatomy and physiology course taught by Dr. Ross with first- and second-year medical students.

The Young Scientist Program
The program is sponsored by the Washington University Division of Biomedical Sciences and the Office of Diversity Programs. This summer program provides high school students with an eight-week laboratory research experience that introduces them to careers in science.

Cultural Diversity
We promote an atmosphere of multiculturalism on the campus through a variety of activities. Examples include Diversity Week, a lunch-time series that further explores multiculturalism and effective health care delivery. Featured lecturers include faculty from the medical school as well as experts from the St. Louis community. The Fall orientation retreat begins with an evening diversity workshop that allows students to explore ways to communicate and relate to others in cross-cultural situations through small-group case-based discussions.

Student Financial Assistance
The applicant's ability to finance medical education at Washington University School of Medicine does not influence the selection process. All students accepted have proven scholastic ability. Financial aid, based solely on demonstrated need, is available to all students in the School of Medicine. Within its financial capabilities, the school is prepared to assist each student with financial aid in the form of loans and grants. Beginning with the 2006-2007 academic year, need-based loans are capped at $20,000 annually. In addition, the secondary application fee of $50 may be waived upon written request documenting financial hardship. Merit-based scholarships are also available and are awarded to candidates presenting exceptional academic and personal credentials.

Other Pertinent Information
Washington University School of Medicine and its faculty believe that the school enters into a partnership with its students in the pursuit of excellence in the medical and scientific educational experience. The Office of Diversity Programs was established to help meet the needs of underrepresented minority students.

The Washington University School of Medicine is committed to recruit, admit, enroll, educate, and graduate an increased number of students from diverse underrepresented racial and cultural groups. Underrepresented minority students in colleges and universities throughout the country are strongly encouraged to file application for admission to the school. Candidates should feel free to contact us at our Web site located at (*http://medicine.wustl.edu/diversity*).

The school participates in the America Medical College Application Service (AMCAS) of the Association of American Medical Colleges. All applicants must apply through AMCAS by December 1st of the year prior to actually attending the school. The school's AMCAS number is 184.

Creighton University School of Medicine

Dr. Sade Kosoko-Lasaki,
Associate Vice President
for Health Sciences—Multicultural
and Community Affairs
Creighton University School of
Medicine
2500 California Plaza
Omaha, NE 68178
Toll Free: 1-877-857-2854;
402-280-2981; 402-280-4030 fax
skosoko@creighton.edu

Recruitment

The Office of Health Sciences - Multicultural and Community Affairs, (HS-MACA), under the direction of an Associate Vice President, has a mission to help Creighton University in the training and development of future leaders for an increasingly multicultural society. HS-MACA provides support and retention services to students by providing diversity awareness to the entire campus community. HS-MACA promotes minority affairs through recruiting and retaining disadvantaged students in the Creighton University Health Sciences Schools. HS-MACA also promotes local involvement in multicultural communities, civic functions, and community service organizations. HS-MACA coordinates multicultural activities with other areas of the University and works to enhance cultural awareness of Health Sciences faculty, students, and staff.

HS-MACA's recruiting activities include annual visits to conference meetings, colleges, universities, and organizations with a high concentration of underrepresented students. Pre-college recruitment includes frequent visits to area high schools to educate underrepresented individuals and motivate them to pursue a health profession career. Recruiting materials consist of diversity brochures, fliers, and health sciences program information. The Recruitment & Retention Manager in HS-MACA distributes recruiting materials and tracks responses from potential applicants to the Health Sciences Schools. Recruitment is through mass mailings, health professional career fairs, national association conferences, college/university campus visits, and invitations to Creighton University campus.

Admission

HS-MACA and Creighton University School of Medicine (CUSOM) work closely to maximize diversity in the medical school. In addition, recruitment by both offices on college campuses and at recruitment fairs actively encourages applications from students listed in the Association of American Medical Colleges (AAMC) Medical Minority Applicant Registry (MedMAR). Applications through the American Medical College Application Service (AMCAS) are regularly reviewed by the Assistant Dean for Admissions, and qualified applicants are encouraged to complete their applications by sending references and completing the Secondary Application. Interviews are then offered to qualified applicants.

During the interview, the applicant is invited to stay in the home of a medical student participating in the "Host Program." The applicant may request to stay in the home of an underrepresented medical student. The interviews are conducted on Fridays and require presence on campus for the full day. Applicants interview with Admissions Committee Members – both student and faculty (or alumni). Both inter-

Creighton University School of Medicine
Applicants, First-Time Applicants, Matriculants by Gender, Race and Ethnicity, 2007-2008

	2007									2008								
	APP			**F-time APP**			**MAT**			**APP**			**F-time APP**			**MAT**		
	Women	Men	Total	Women	Men	Total	Women	Men	Total	Women	Men	Total	Women	Men	Total	Women	Men	Total
Hispanic/Latino																		
Cuban	6	12	18	3	10	13	0	1	1	8	14	22	7	10	17	1	1	2
Mexican American	62	62	124	46	44	90	1	0	1	33	74	107	26	49	75	0	3	3
Puerto Rican	7	16	23	4	14	18	0	0	0	8	7	15	7	5	12	0	0	0
Other Hispanic	54	45	99	37	29	66	0	2	2	51	53	104	33	34	67	0	0	0
Multiple Hispanic/Latino*	9	7	16	5	4	9	0	0	0	7	6	13	6	3	9	0	0	0
Subtotal	138	142	280	95	101	196	1	3	4	107	154	261	79	101	180	1	4	5
Non-Hispanic/Latino**																		
Black	91	77	168	56	51	107	1	3	4	70	71	141	39	49	88	2	1	3
Native American/AK	8	10	18	5	8	13	0	0	0	7	8	15	6	6	12	0	1	1
Native Hawaiian/OPI	13	7	20	9	5	14	1	0	1	14	9	23	7	7	14	1	0	1
White	1,436	1,938	3,374	1,062	1,320	2,382	43	50	93	1,416	2,165	3,581	979	1,427	2,406	49	50	99
Asian	538	683	1,221	356	432	788	8	9	17	570	644	1,214	362	383	745	8	6	14
Other Race	1	4	5	0	2	2	0	0	0	4	6	10	3	5	8	0	0	0
Multiple Race*	72	70	142	49	44	93	2	2	4	59	81	140	40	52	92	0	0	0
Unknown	15	27	42	13	22	35	1	1	2	43	74	117	41	57	98	2	0	2
Subtotal	2,174	2,816	4,990	1,550	1,884	3,434	56	65	121	2,183	3,058	5,241	1,477	1,986	3,463	62	58	120
Foreign	71	92	163	53	61	114	0	1	1	63	90	153	46	66	112	0	1	1
Total	2,383	3,050	5,433	1,698	2,046	3,744	57	69	126	2,353	3,302	5,655	1,602	2,153	3,755	63	63	126

*Since 2002, students can select more than one race and / or ethnicity. **Those who did not choose 'Hispanic/Latino' or 'Non-Hispanic/Latino' are listed under 'Non-Hispanic/Latino'. Data Source: AAMC Data Warehouse: Applicant-Matriculant File, as of 1/16/2009.

views are rated equally and concentrate on motivation for medicine and the applicant's demonstrated activities in service to others. During the campus tour, the applicants have an opportunity to visit the HS-MACA. A presentation "View HS-MACA" introducing the student to the diversity program at Creighton University is given.

Completed applications are reviewed by the School of Medicine Committee on Admissions for scoring. The committee score is based on academics, MCAT scores and evaluation of the applicant's non-cognitive skills including service to others, involvement in community projects, health care experience as well as academic achievement. Acceptance decisions take into account the committee rating and the interview scores.

Scholarship application is encouraged and required for consideration by the School of Medicine Scholarship Committee. Admitted applicants are automatically reviewed for scholarship awards by the committee. The applicant whose record demonstrates strong commitment to serving others in addition to academic achievement is valued.

Academic Support Programs

The Office of Academic Advancement within the School of Medicine provides formal tutoring for all basic science courses. Assistance with clinical clerkship and elective material is provided on request. This office also coordinates training sessions on study skills, test-taking skills, time management, stress management, and general wellness topics. Each first-year student is assigned a "buddy" from the second-year class who assists in the transition to medical school. A mentoring system is also in place in which all first-year students meet informally with a designated faculty member throughout the year in order to discuss concerns and to build camaraderie. All students are assigned a formal faculty advisor according to his/her curricular, research, and clinical interests.

Enrichment Programs

Cultural Proficiency for Medical Residents, Students, Faculty, and Staff
A seminar setting, consisting of didactic presentations on the definition of cultural competency, its benefits and barriers, is correlated with the changing demographics in the United States. This presentation also includes discussions on the importance of diversity and cultural sensitivity in health care. A diverse group of physicians and community members are invited to discuss their various cultures in small break out sessions and in a panel discussion. Case studies are presented and discussed in small groups followed by group interactions. The students are also trained on the effective use of an interpreter in the clinical setting. The seminar concludes with a "reflection" assignment to the students who are also instructed to submit their own cultural awareness story.

Community Oriented Primary Care (COPC)
The program is designed to help reduce health disparities affecting our nation's communities. The mission of the Creighton University Medical Center (CUMC) COPC Public Health Research Endowment program is to increase the number of health professionals who are committed to addressing health disparities through their research and service in medically underserved communities. This mission supports the core values of Creighton University; "service to others, the importance of family life, the inalienable worth of each individual, and appreciation of ethnic and cultural diversity." It also supports the goals of Healthy People of 2010 to eliminate health disparities.

Starting with financially and/or educationally disadvantaged students in the seventh grade, and proceeding through the high school and college years, Creighton's Health Careers Opportunity Program (HCOP): Pipeline to Success at Creighton University provides educational activities so that students will be prepared to handle medical school and other health professions programs. HCOP shepherds young stu-

dents in the seventh and eighth grades as they participate in a Health Careers Exploration Club. High school students attend monthly meetings, a Saturday Academy program, and a six-week summer program. College students attend a monthly meeting and a six-week summer program that focuses on math, science, reading, and writing. Creighton's College of Arts and Sciences and community partners such as the Omaha Public Schools and Boys and Girls Clubs collaborate with HS-MACA on this initiative.

HS-MACA Mentoring Program
This program provides students in the health science schools formal and informal opportunities for counseling, mentoring, and group support. Short-term results include: improvement in academic performance of mentee, enhancement of interpersonal relationships, mutual feelings of honesty and respect, and rewarding and enriching experiences for all involved.

HS-MACA Tutoring
This program is designed to provide tutorial assistance in most academic subject areas like math, science, reading, and Spanish for the students from public and private schools. This will enable underrepresented high school students to excel in their academic work, expand their quest for knowledge, and motivate them to strengthen their study skills.

Student Financial Assistance

The School of Medicine's application fee is waived for any student who receives the same waiver from AMCAS. Financial aid counseling and debt management counseling are provided to all students. Two full tuition Medical Dean's Diversity Scholarships are available to underrepresented minority students each year. In addition, students from economically disadvantaged backgrounds qualify for Disadvantaged Scholarships.

Educational Partnership

Creighton University has a pre-medical Post-Baccalaureate Program. The goal of this program is to increase the number of qualified minority students enrolled in and successfully completing medical school. The target population for this program is disadvantaged students who have applied for but failed to qualify for admission to a medical school. The curriculum is designed to correct educational deficiencies and to provide a rigorous academic program that improves the ability of the student to deal with all fundamental concepts necessary for successful completion of a medical school curriculum. This intensive academic program has been highly successful. Since its inception in 1975, 298 minority students have completed the course and 270 have been admitted to a health professions program.

University of Nebraska College of Medicine

Dr. Jeffrey W. Hill, Associate Dean for Admissions and Student Affairs
University of Nebraska College of Medicine
985527 Nebraska Medical Center
Omaha, NE 68198-5527
402-559-2259; 402-559-6840 fax
jwhill@unmc.edu

Recruitment

Recruitment and career awareness activities at the University of Nebraska Medical Center (UNMC) campus are conducted at the elementary, junior high, high school, and college levels. These activities include, but are not limited to, contact through science clubs, health clubs, minority student organizations, career and/or health fairs, school visits, and by participation in community activities.

Recruitment visits are made annually to colleges in Nebraska that have the largest percentages of minority students enrolled. Contacts with non-resident minorities are made by attending national conferences including the Society for the Advancement of Chicanos and Native Americans in Science, and Minority Access to Research Careers/Minority Biomedical Research Support. In addition, contact is made with students on lists such as the Talent Roster of Outstanding Minority Community College Graduates, and through correspondence with members of the National Association of Medical Minority Educators. Voluntary recruiters—University of Nebraska faculty members—assist the multicultural affairs office staff with recruitment visits to out-of-state colleges.

Affiliation agreements exist with several colleges and universities that have a predominant enrollment of students that are underrepresented minorities. These agreements exist to increase awareness of the many academic opportunities available to potential students at the University of Nebraska Medical Center. Summer research opportunities that are fully funded exist for students from these affiliated institutions.

Admissions

Applications should be filed through the American Medical College Application Service (AMCAS), ten to 14 months prior to the proposed matriculation date. Students are selected on the basis of scholarship, appraisals of character, personal interviews, scores on Medical College Admission Test (MCAT), and general motivation and promise. Although a specific minority admissions program does not exist in the medical school, minority applications are encouraged.

Academic Support Programs

All basic science departments at the University of Nebraska College of Medicine offer tutorial support to all students. Additionally, student services sponsors an Academic Support Program for minority students. Activities in this program include workshops on study skills, test-taking skills, stress management, and an introduction to campus resources. Individual and small-group tutorials are provided free of charge in the basic science areas.

Other services of the office include personal development seminars; scholarship, fellowship, and externship reference library; as well as academic and personal advisement and referrals.

A minority faculty preceptorship pro-

University of Nebraska College of Medicine
Applicants, First-Time Applicants, Matriculants by Gender, Race and Ethnicity, 2007-2008

	2007									2008								
	APP			F-time APP			MAT			APP			F-time APP			MAT		
	Women	Men	Total	Women	Men	Total	Women	Men	Total	Women	Men	Total	Women	Men	Total	Women	Men	Total
Hispanic/Latino																		
Cuban	0	3	3	0	2	2	0	0	0	1	4	5	0	4	4	0	0	0
Mexican American	18	23	41	14	16	30	1	2	3	13	17	30	10	9	19	1	2	3
Puerto Rican	1	2	3	1	2	3	0	0	0	1	1	2	1	0	1	0	0	0
Other Hispanic	7	12	19	6	7	13	0	1	1	11	20	31	6	13	19	0	0	0
Multiple Hispanic/Latino*	0	3	3	0	2	2	0	0	0	3	2	5	3	2	5	0	0	0
Subtotal	26	43	69	21	29	50	1	3	4	29	44	73	20	28	48	1	2	3
Non-Hispanic/Latino**																		
Black	20	28	48	13	22	35	0	2	2	27	32	59	16	21	37	1	3	4
Native American/AK	5	3	8	4	3	7	0	1	1	4	1	5	2	1	3	0	0	0
Native Hawaiian/OPI	3	1	4	3	1	4	0	0	0	3	0	3	3	0	3	0	0	0
White	415	515	930	329	364	693	43	62	105	390	574	964	302	400	702	43	66	109
Asian	105	147	252	66	97	163	2	2	4	100	149	249	67	102	169	4	1	5
Other Race	0	1	1	0	1	1	0	0	0	0	0	0	0	0	0	0	0	0
Multiple Race*	12	19	31	8	13	21	0	1	1	12	13	25	5	8	13	1	1	2
Unknown	1	5	6	1	4	5	0	0	0	9	11	20	9	9	18	1	0	1
Subtotal	561	719	1,280	424	505	929	45	68	113	545	780	1,325	404	541	945	50	71	121
Foreign	10	11	21	9	10	19	0	2	2	4	9	13	4	5	9	0	0	0
Total	597	773	1,370	454	544	998	46	73	119	578	833	1,411	428	574	1,002	51	73	124

Note: In 2008, one applicant, who declined to report gender, was not included here.

*Since 2002, students can select more than one race and / or ethnicity. **Those who did not choose 'Hispanic/Latino' or 'Non-Hispanic/Latino' are listed under 'Non-Hispanic/Latino'. Data Source: AAMC Data Warehouse: Applicant-Matriculant File, as of 1/16/2009.

gram is offered to first-year medical students to develop clinical skills and to provide a mentor for freshman and sophomore students.

Enrichment Programs

Summer programs at the University of Nebraska Medical Center are generally contingent upon available grant funds. Currently a Summer Research Enrichment Program is being sponsored for juniors and seniors in college. The program is designed to provide academic enrichment in the following areas: communications with an emphasis on technical writing, medical terminology, research skills, clinical and laboratory work experiences, and seminars to explore the health status of minorities. Preference is given to Nebraska residents, but all students are encouraged to apply. The University of Nebraska is also a program site for the Summer Medical Dental Education Program (SMDEP).

Student Financial Assistance

The University of Nebraska Medical Center is committed to the goal that no student should be forced to withdraw from school because of financial constraints. Financial assistance is offered in the form of scholarships, grants, and loans administered by an experienced financial aid office staff.

The University of Nebraska College of Medicine requires an application fee. Disadvantaged students may apply for an application fee waiver directly through AMCAS. Financial assistance for interview trips is not available.

University of Nevada School of Medicine

Ann E. Diggins, Director of Recruitment and Student Services
University of Nevada School of Medicine
2040 W. Charleston, Ste. 503
Las Vegas, NV 89102
702-671-6457; 702-671-6414 fax
adiggins@medicine.nevada.edu
www.medicine.nevada.edu

Recruitment

The University of Nevada School of Medicine (UNSOM) has a successful history of providing physicians to the state's communities. In continuation of that mission, the school strongly believes in recruiting, retaining, and graduating minority physicians to provide quality medical care for Nevada's increasingly diverse minority communities.

The school is committed to:

- Maintaining diversity among its students by accepting students from a variety of backgrounds, ethnic cultures, and experiences, and
- Advancing the participation of underrepresented minorities in medicine and science.

Outreach focuses on students in grades seven through 12 and college. Programs for Nevada residents include:

- Physician Shadowing – Students are paired with UNSOM physicians for clinical observational experiences. Efforts are targeted to match underrepresented students with potential role model/mentor physicians.
- Pre-Medical Student Conference – The medical school hosts two all-day pre-medical student conferences. Diverse students and faculty are featured throughout each event.
- Science Partners – Undergraduate pre-medical science majors are paired with elementary teachers to increase inquiry based science for students in grades K-six.
- Nevadans Into Medicine – This is an admissions preparation program for college juniors and seniors. (www.unr.edu/undergrad-nevadans.htm)

Admissions

The School of Medicine's Admissions Selection Committee has adopted a policy that enables applicants from all socioeconomic, sex, racial, religious, and educational backgrounds to be equally considered. All students must meet residency and admissions criteria. Applications from underrepresented minority students are encouraged. (www.unr.edu/med/admissions)

Academic Support Programs

The medical school offers an intentionally small, personalized atmosphere for students. Services include:

- Tuition scholarships
- Mentoring and colleague programs
- Academic support
- Community service opportunities
- Minority student organizations
- Physician seminars

At the school, students receive personalized instruction and attention from faculty, staff, and colleagues. A class size of only 62 students gives them the opportunity to learn medicine in an environment of caring. The school prides itself on graduating physicians who understand the value of caring for their patients, the importance of receiving a top-notch medical education, and the opportunity to give back to the community.

Mentoring and Colleague Program
First-year medical students are matched with a community physician for an ongoing clinical education and mentoring relationship. Volunteer primary care

NV, University of Nevada School of Medicine
Applicants, First-Time Applicants, Matriculants by Gender, Race and Ethnicity, 2007-2008

	2007									2008								
	APP			F-time APP			MAT			APP			F-time APP			MAT		
	men	Men	Total	men	Men	Total	men	Men	Total	men	Men	Total	men	Men	Total	men	Men	Total
Hispanic/Latino																		
Cuban	1	4	5	0	3	3	0	0	0	5	4	9	3	3	6	0	1	1
Mexican American	18	18	36	13	12	25	1	1	2	19	21	40	17	12	29	0	0	0
Puerto Rican	2	4	6	2	3	5	0	0	0	2	0	2	2	0	2	0	0	0
Other Hispanic	21	7	28	15	4	19	1	1	2	16	17	33	12	14	26	0	0	0
Multiple Hispanic/Latino*	2	2	4	2	1	3	0	0	0	2	3	5	2	3	5	0	0	0
Subtotal	44	35	79	32	23	55	2	2	4	44	45	89	36	32	68	0	1	1
Non-Hispanic/Latino**																		
Black	20	21	41	15	17	32	0	0	0	29	14	43	22	13	35	0	1	1
Native American/AK	0	5	5	0	5	5	0	1	1	3	4	7	3	4	7	0	0	0
Native Hawaiian/OPI	8	2	10	7	2	9	0	0	0	8	4	12	6	4	10	0	0	0
White	278	374	652	208	281	489	19	25	44	271	420	691	206	308	514	23	20	43
Asian	130	126	256	106	88	194	4	6	10	149	139	288	114	95	209	10	5	15
Other Race	0	0	0	0	0	0	0	0	0	0	1	1	0	1	1	0	0	0
Multiple Race*	19	18	37	16	13	29	3	0	3	22	16	38	15	13	28	0	0	0
Unknown	7	7	14	7	7	14	0	0	0	13	24	37	13	22	35	0	2	2
Subtotal	462	553	1,015	359	413	772	26	32	58	495	622	1,117	379	460	839	33	28	61
Foreign	8	7	15	6	4	10	0	0	0	3	12	15	2	10	12	0	0	0
Total	514	595	1,109	397	440	837	28	34	62	542	679	1,221	417	502	919	33	29	62

*Since 2002, students can select more than one race and / or ethnicity. **Those who did not choose 'Hispanic/Latino' or 'Non-Hispanic/Latino' are listed under 'Non-Hispanic/Latino'. Data Source: AAMC Data Warehouse: Applicant-Matriculant File, as of 1/16/2009.

physicians donate their time and host medical students in clinical settings four days each month. This program gives students hands-on experience in clinical care beginning the second week of school.

The Colleague Program
This program matches an incoming student with a veteran second-year student for help in study skills, managing the work of medical school, and balancing his/her personal life with school responsibilities. This program gives students a ready-made "big brother or sister" to help ease the transition into medical school.

Academic Support
The medical school Wellness Program provides an ongoing series of seminars dealing with such issues as study skills, test-taking strategies, and time management. In addition, students are encouraged to seek assistance from faculty. Nevada maintains a very high faculty to student ratio for the purpose of enhancing instruction and support for students.

Community Service Opportunities
The School of Medicine believes in the importance of giving back to the community. Students are involved in caring for patients in clinics for AIDS patients, the medically indigent and homeless, and other populations throughout the state. These activities combine medical education for the students and the need in the community for high-quality health care for those who do not have the ability to pay. Students are also asked to volunteer for mentor programs with high schools and assist in programs designed to provide science enrichment activities for middle and high school minority students.

Physician Seminars
Every six weeks the medical school hosts a luncheon for minority students with minority physicians. During these seminars, the doctors share their experiences and expertise with students. The meetings also give students the chance to discuss practice options and engage in career planning, as well as gather tips for success in medical school.

Student Financial Assistance
The School of Medicine has an increasing endowment for minority student scholarships. In addition, tuition and recruitment scholarships are awarded each year. The school is committed to easing the financial demands of medical school for all students.

Educational Partnerships
The School of Medicine has a partnership with Hug High School in Reno. This program includes a high school mentoring program that pairs first-year medical students with underrepresented minority students in the ninth and tenth grades.

BS/MD Accelerated Pathway
This program offers a seven-year accelerated pathway to medical school for a small number of motivated, mature high school seniors who are serious and focused on a career in medicine. Students accepted into this program will complete the first three years of the required undergraduate curriculum at the University of Nevada, Reno (URN) or University of Nevada, Las Vegas (UNLV), then enter the University of Nevada School of Medicine. Applicants are limited to those students who are residents of Nevada and a graduate of a Nevada high school.

Dartmouth Medical School

Dr. Lori Arviso Alvord, Associate Dean of Student and Multicultural Affairs
Shawn O'Leary
Dartmouth Medical School
301 Remsen Building
Hanover, NH 03755-3833
603-650-1582; 603-650-1169 fax

Introduction

Dartmouth Medical School (DMS) is dedicated to advancing health through the dissemination and discovery of knowledge. Our chief responsibility is to select students of exceptional character and accomplishment and prepare them to become superb and caring physicians, scientists, and teachers.

DMS has a strong commitment to diversity. Our Office of Multicultural Affairs takes a leading role in creating a community that honors the diverse backgrounds of our students, faculty, and administrators. We initiate programs that teach our students to be culturally versatile and practice medicine appropriately in the world as it exists today.

Recruitment

A multifaceted approach to minority recruitment is taken at DMS. Faculty, students, and administrators visit a number of summer and health profession career programs, as well as many undergraduate colleges. Information about DMS is sent to select candidates identified through the Medical Minority Applicant Registry (Med-MAR) of the AAMC. A student hosting program allows candidates who have been invited to interview to stay overnight in the homes of current students during the interview visit. The Admissions Office is also pleased to respond on an individual basis to inquiries from applicants. Please feel free to contact the Admissions Office at 603-650-1505. The Director of Multicultural Affairs at the Medical School can be reached at 603-650-1553.

Admissions

DMS, the nation's fourth oldest medical school, is committed to making its opportunities available to students from a wide range of backgrounds and experiences. We seek a diverse student body. The admissions process at DMS involves a holistic review of all applications. Though the process is very selective, it does not employ rigid cutoffs in making decisions. All applications are considered carefully, with attention given to the unique qualities, background, and characteristics of each individual. Applications from those underrepresented in medicine are particularly encouraged. The DMS student body is national in scope, with residents from approximately 25 states and 60 undergraduate institutions represented in a typical entering class.

Academic Support Programs

The relatively small class size at DMS permits close and meaningful interaction with faculty and a supportive relationship with classmates on an ongoing basis. Formal academic support programs include a Senior Advising Dean who meets individually with students on an as-needed basis, and a Big Sibling Program, through which each student is matched with a volunteer second-year medical student mentor. In addition, the faculty preceptor, with whom each first- and second-year student works as part of DMS's On-Doctoring course, is

Dartmouth Medical School
Applicants, First-Time Applicants, Matriculants by Gender, Race and Ethnicity, 2007-2008

	2007									2008								
	APP			F-time APP			MAT			APP			F-time APP			MAT		
	Women	Men	Total	Women	Men	Total	Women	Men	Total	Women	Men	Total	Women	Men	Total	Women	Men	Total
Hispanic/Latino																		
Cuban	12	10	22	9	7	16	1	0	1	13	17	30	9	14	23	0	0	0
Mexican American	41	46	87	35	36	71	1	2	3	33	29	62	30	22	52	1	0	1
Puerto Rican	10	14	24	10	10	20	0	0	0	7	13	20	7	11	18	0	0	0
Other Hispanic	47	45	92	43	36	79	0	1	1	51	66	117	45	51	96	2	2	4
Multiple Hispanic/Latino*	6	4	10	4	4	8	0	0	0	11	8	19	9	6	15	0	0	0
Subtotal	116	119	235	101	93	194	2	3	5	115	133	248	100	104	204	3	2	5
Non-Hispanic/Latino**																		
Black	67	50	117	54	43	97	0	0	0	81	60	141	57	48	105	0	1	1
Native American/AK	13	8	21	9	6	15	0	0	0	8	10	18	5	8	13	0	0	0
Native Hawaiian/OPI	10	6	16	8	3	11	0	0	0	11	6	17	7	3	10	0	0	0
White	1,385	1,591	2,976	1,179	1,300	2,479	19	16	35	1,322	1,711	3,033	1,103	1,351	2,454	20	23	43
Asian	623	661	1,284	511	507	1,018	10	6	16	569	725	1,294	452	532	984	4	6	10
Other Race	0	3	3	0	2	2	0	0	0	0	4	4	0	3	3	0	0	0
Multiple Race*	70	79	149	60	61	121	1	0	1	76	74	150	64	54	118	0	1	1
Unknown	30	36	66	29	30	59	3	1	4	64	95	159	62	81	143	1	5	6
Subtotal	2,198	2,434	4,632	1,850	1,952	3,802	33	23	56	2,131	2,685	4,816	1,750	2,080	3,830	25	36	61
Foreign	207	236	443	170	180	350	6	6	12	238	284	522	204	219	423	6	6	12
Total	2,521	2,789	5,310	2,121	2,225	4,346	41	32	73	2,484	3,102	5,586	2,054	2,403	4,457	34	44	78

*Since 2002, students can select more than one race and / or ethnicity. **Those who did not choose 'Hispanic/Latino' or 'Non-Hispanic/Latino' are listed under 'Non-Hispanic/Latino'. Data Source: AAMC Data Warehouse: Applicant-Matriculant File, as of 1/16/2009.

an important source of advice and counsel. Students also participate in an active chapter of the Student National Medical Association, which addresses the concerns of minority medical students at the campus and national levels.

The Office for Learning and Disability Services (OLADS) at Dartmouth Medical School is committed to helping students live up to their highest potential. In addition to coordinating services for students with disabilities, OLADS assists all DMS students in understanding their learning styles, their strengths and weaknesses, and their individual paths to excellence. The coordinator of that office is both a learning and disabilities specialist and a professional counselor. In addition to working one-on-one with students, a series of Success Seminars are offered in the first year and small-group tutoring is available to students who need assistance in a particular course.

Enrichment Programs

The Advanced Readiness Course (ARC) takes place during the week preceding first-year orientation. ARC is a voluntary course open to any incoming student who feels that he/she could benefit from additional preparation in order to begin medical school with the utmost confidence. Students in ARC are exposed to representative lectures from all the first-term courses and are guided through the advanced skills that insure learning and prepare them to handle the increased workload of medical school. There are also activities during that week designed to help students make the transition to Dartmouth Medical School and to the Upper Valley area.

Student Financial Assistance

DMS is committed to providing an excellent medical education to any accepted student. Students are admitted on a need-blind basis. Once a student accepts the offer of admission, the institution and the student work together to develop a sound approach to financing medical school. We provide institutional need-based financial aid in the form of loans and scholarships to meet

the cost of a medical education for those students with documented financial need.

Financial need is defined as the difference between educational costs and the resources that are available from the student and his or her spouse and family. DMS encourages financial aid applicants to complete the Free Application for Federal Student Aid (FAFSA), the Need Access Application, and the free DMS application to be considered for institutional need- based aid. These forms are accessible at *(www.dms.dartmouth.edu/ admin/fin_aid/)*.

Other Pertinent Information

In addition to the clinical facilities at Dartmouth, students also participate in Dartmouth-affiliated clerkships in settings as diverse as the Tuba City Indian Health Service Hospital in Arizona; Children's Hospital Orange County, California; Key West, Florida; Connecticut's Hartford Hospital; Kuskokwim Delta Regional Hospital in Bethel, Alaska; Hawkes Bay Regional Hospital in Hastings, New Zealand; and other sites as well. Although many students complete their clerkships in Dartmouth's environs, these off-campus programs ensure that DMS students will have access to a broad variety of patient populations that represent the full spectrum of health care delivery.

University of Medicine and Dentistry of New Jersey— New Jersey Medical School

Dr. Maria L. Soto-Greene, Professor and Vice Dean
UMDNJ—New Jersey Medical School
185 South Orange Avenue C671
Newark, NJ 07103
973-972-9151; 973-972-7104 fax
sotogrml@umdnj.edu
http://njms.umdnj.edu

Introduction

The New Jersey Medical School (NJMS) is the oldest of eight schools that form the University of Medicine and Dentistry of New Jersey (UMDNJ), the nation's largest freestanding health sciences university. The mission of the NJMS is to educate students, physicians, and scientists to meet society's current and future health care needs through patient-centered education; pioneering research; innovative clinical, rehabilitative and preventive care; and collaborative community outreach.

The NJMS takes pride in the diversity of its faculty, alumni, staff and students, as well as the strengths of its community programs. NJMS is proud of its commitment to recruiting and retaining minority students. The school's commitment to diversity is far reaching with programs beginning at the third-grade level through faculty levels. We are united by our commitment to scholarship, professionalism, and dedication to science, but above all excellence.

Recruitment

The NJMS has faculty, staff, administrators, and students who participate in recruitment initiatives by visiting colleges, high schools, health career programs as well as graduate and professional recruitment fairs looking for prospective applicants and disseminating information about the curriculum and life at NJMS.

Admissions

NJMS continues to have a diverse student body and strong, dedicated commitment to the recruitment, retention, and graduation of underrepresented minorities. The Board of Trustees of the UMDNJ has committed itself, the university, and its component units to a policy of equal opportunity without regard to race, color, creed or religion, sex, national origin, age, military status, marital status, handicap if otherwise qualified, or other factors prohibited by law. This is the governing principle in student admissions and other student services and employment.

Annually, the NJMS accepts 170 entering students. All applicants must take the Medical College Admission Test (MCAT), either in the spring or fall, the year before their planned matriculation date. It is the responsibility of the applicant to have the results of the test forwarded to the Committee on Admissions. The committee will consider no application for final action until the test results have been received.

NJMS also has a five-year program. This curriculum offers students an opportunity to extend the first two years of coursework over a period of three years, thus completing the requirements for the M.D. degree in five years rather than four. This option is open to accepted students who request it because of family, financial, or education considerations. It is also available to matriculated students who experience academic difficulty during the first year. Further information may be obtained from the Office of Admissions at the time of application.

University of Medicine and Dentistry of New Jersey-New Jersey Medical School
Applicants, First-Time Applicants, Matriculants by Gender, Race and Ethnicity, 2007-2008

| | 2007 | | | | | | | | | 2008 | | | | | | | | |
| | APP | | | F-time APP | | | MAT | | | APP | | | F-time APP | | | MAT | | |
	Women	Men	Total	Women	Men	Total	Women	Men	Total	Women	Men	Total	Women	Men	Total	Women	Men	Total
Hispanic/Latino																		
Cuban	29	27	56	24	22	46	5	3	8	21	31	52	16	24	40	1	2	3
Mexican American	44	39	83	35	23	58	0	0	0	22	16	38	16	12	28	0	0	0
Puerto Rican	38	20	58	27	20	47	1	3	4	25	15	40	22	10	32	2	3	5
Other Hispanic	89	87	176	70	62	132	2	7	9	91	80	171	71	62	133	5	7	12
Multiple Hispanic/Latino*	13	10	23	9	9	18	1	0	1	12	9	21	10	3	13	0	0	0
Subtotal	213	183	396	165	136	301	9	13	22	171	151	322	135	111	246	8	12	20
Non-Hispanic/Latino**																		
Black	372	153	525	266	115	381	12	3	15	316	136	452	233	96	329	12	4	16
Native American/AK	2	2	4	2	2	4	0	0	0	1	1	2	1	1	2	0	0	0
Native Hawaiian/OPI	18	10	28	16	7	23	0	1	1	9	6	15	6	2	8	0	0	0
White	913	1,022	1,935	737	746	1,483	26	33	59	806	943	1,749	627	669	1,296	25	55	80
Asian	826	779	1,605	623	572	1,195	33	41	74	762	686	1,448	561	445	1,006	25	45	70
Other Race	2	5	7	2	1	3	0	0	0	1	2	3	0	2	2	0	0	0
Multiple Race*	57	64	121	45	42	87	1	2	3	54	44	98	40	33	73	2	1	3
Unknown	26	33	59	24	29	53	2	2	4	49	53	102	46	45	91	1	4	5
Subtotal	2,216	2,068	4,284	1,715	1,514	3,229	74	82	156	1,998	1,871	3,869	1,514	1,293	2,807	65	109	174
Foreign	7	8	15	4	7	11	0	0	0	22	30	52	21	21	42	0	0	0
Total	2,436	2,259	4,695	1,884	1,657	3,541	83	95	178	2,191	2,052	4,243	1,670	1,425	3,095	73	121	194

*Since 2002, students can select more than one race and / or ethnicity. **Those who did not choose 'Hispanic/Latino' or 'Non-Hispanic/Latino' are listed under 'Non-Hispanic/Latino'. Data Source: AAMC Data Warehouse: Applicant-Matriculant File, as of 1/16/2009.

Academic Support Programs

The NJMS Office of Student Affairs provides programs and individual consultations for all medical students. Students can acquire advanced skills needed to achieve optimally in professional-level courses and licensing examinations. All incoming medical students are given direction in how to adapt their study techniques, time management, and learning strategies to the unique challenges of medical education. This guidance begins with an optional pre-matriculation program, continues through orientation in the first year of medical school, and is available throughout the four years of medical education whenever the student requests it.

During the first year, small-group tutorials guided by upper class students provide a rich learning environment outside the traditional curriculum. In addition, a teaching elective is provided for medical students who wish to improve their own educational/teaching skills.

NJMS also has a five-year program. The curriculum offers students an opportunity to extend the first two years of coursework over a period of three years, thus completing the requirements for the M.D. degree in five years rather than four. However, this option is only available to matriculated students under extenuating circumstances, such as family or financial hardships, or for those who experience academic difficulty during the first year.

A lending library, stocked by donations from upper class students, is also available to assist students in deciding which resource materials are best for their individual study. Upper class tutors, supervised by the Office of Academic Success and Enrichment (CASE), are assigned to help students who require their services.

Customized programs are available for medical board preparation. These include practice examinations, which are given to the second-year medical school class as they prepare for the first step of the United States Medical Licensing Examination.

Enrichment Opportunities

At the NJMS, the Office of Special Programs (OSP) develops, implements, and supports, the pre-professional/professional health education and community service programs. The OSP has established educational pipeline programs to address the entire educational spectrum. The educational pipeline programs target pre-college students through the professional level, including their entry at NJMS.

The Hispanic Center of Excellence (HCOE)

This center was established in 1991 with the primary goal of improving the health status of the Latino population by increasing the number of Latinos in the health professions and medicine in particular. Over the past 18 years, there has been a continuous refinement of institutional policies and programs that have permitted the HCOE to implement initiatives aimed at enhancing academic performance, improving the recruitment and retention of faculty, and developing the capacity of the school's graduates to provide culturally competent health care services. HCOE seeks to reduce disparities in health care by supporting individuals committed to advancing the goals of diversity in the medical profession and improved health care to underserved populations.

The Student Health Advocates for Resources and Education (S.H.A.R.E.) Center

Founded in 1996, is a student-run organization that promotes community service at NJMS. The S.H.A.R.E. Center supports a diverse group of programs whereby NJMS students may pursue direct patient care, community education, youth mentoring, and more.

Robert Wood Johnson Foundation's Summer Medical and Dental Education Program (SMDEP)

SMDEP is a six-week residential summer program designed to provide rising freshmen and sophomore college students interested in medicine and dentistry a problem-based learning model of science education. The curriculum has been carefully designed to enhance the students' academic and personal skills required to succeed in medical and dental school. This is accomplished by providing opportunities for the development and practice of critical-thinking skills, problem-based learning skills, and self-assessment.

Northeast Regional Alliance MedPrep Scholars Program (NERA)

NERA is a partnership between New Jersey Medical School, Mount Sinai School of Medicine Center for Multicultural and Community Affairs, Columbia University College of Physicians and Surgeons and the Manhattan Staten Island Area Health Education Center. The summer program uniquely builds on the collective expertise of four outstanding institutions to expand health careers preparation for minority and disadvantaged students from junior high school through medical school with the goal of increasing competitiveness for medical school. Ultimately, we expect that our scholars will have the humanism, professionalism and interpersonal skills required of a future physician caring for a diverse population.

The Pre-Medical Honors Program

This program is designed to attract promising high school students to medicine and the health sciences and is offered during the fall.

Mini-Med School

Mini-Med School is a similar program offered to adults; each program includes 195 minutes of lectures and seminars. The programs address recent findings in medical research and health care, raise consciousness about the routes to medical care, and enhance one of the principle missions of NJMS—to train socially conscious and humane physicians.

The Richard Pozen & Ann Silver Pozen Community Scholars Endowment

Established in 2008 to support and encourage medical student participation in community service projects, students in this program will gain a community service understanding under the tutelage of faculty and/or sponsors. The aim of this program is to stimulate a student's ongoing interest and develop their community skills in service to others, with the ultimate goal of motivating them to pursue careers in medicine in which service to the community is an integral part.

Freshman Introduction to Resources and Skills Training (F.I.R.S.T)
Funded by AmeriChoice F.I.R.S.T. provides an early exposure to the rigors of medical school and acclimates incoming NJMS/NJDS students to different teaching techniques and study strategies including a rigorous, skills-oriented foundation for successful performance in the basic science curriculum of medical school.

The SMART Initiative (Science, Medicine and Related Topics Pipeline)
This initiative is a set of pre-college health-related educational enrichment programs for students entering grades six through 12. Its mission is to assist participants in acquiring a strong background in the sciences and to cultivate interest in health careers. Programs are offered during the winter and summer.

The Healthcare Foundation Center for Humanism and Medicine
The Center focuses the ideals of humanism not just in educational programs but in research endeavors, clinical practice and community outreach activities as well. They are the proud sponsors of Student Doctor Day, which works with children from grades five through 12, mostly from underrepresented backgrounds.

Mentoring Programs

The mentoring/career advising services at New Jersey Medical School (NJMS) serve three main functions: physician faculty-student mentoring meetings, web-based advising, and "career fair" events. With regard to the faculty-student mentoring meetings, first- and second-year students have regularly scheduled advisory group meetings, usually during the lunch hour, with free

food being served to all participants. Students are required to attend all sessions. Individual mentoring meetings between third- and fourth-year NJMS students and the specialty-specific faculty advisors of their choice continue to be arranged. All clinical department chairs have committed to actively supporting this effort.

All NJMS students receive access codes to the AAMC's Careers in Medicine Web site, along with specific instructions and clear guidance on how to gain the most benefit from its use. To date, the Web site has generated a response rate over 98.5% among first-year students, with 191 out of 194 students actively using the site. Also, 498 out of the total student body of 737 are currently using the Web site (67.5 % total response rate), significantly exceeding the national average. All participating physician faculty advisors also receive access codes to the faculty version of the same site, resulting in a response rate of 80%, with 28 out of 35 advisors having logged on to the site.

Finally, two "Careers Night" events are organized by the NJMS Alumni Association each year. Students feedback for these sessions has historically been very strong, and with the increase in participating specialties, we expect this to continue to hold true.

Student Financial Assistance

The UMDNJ Student Financial Aid Office awards financial aid. The amount and type of aid is based on need, specific eligibility requirements, and UMDNJ's financial aid packaging policy, which is a formula developed to determine the amount of aid to be given to the student from university administered aid programs. The total amount of need-based aid awarded to the student cannot exceed his or her financial need.

The primary source of financial assistance at UMDNJ and most other graduate and professional schools is student loans. However, there is also an unlimited number of Dean's Academic Schol-

arships and other alumni scholarships available to students who meet the criteria. Students who come from backgrounds underrepresented in medicine may also qualify for assistance from the Disadvantaged Student Fund (DSF).

UMDNJ—Robert Wood Johnson Medical School

Dr. Cheryl A. Dickson, Assistant Dean, Student Affairs Multicultural Affairs
UMDNJ—Robert Wood Johnson Medical School
675 Hoes Lane
Piscataway, NJ 08854-5635
732-235-2143/2144;
732-235-3972 fax
dicksoca@umdnj.edu
http://rwjms.umdnj.edu/osap

Introduction

Robert Wood Johnson Medical School (RWJMS) established the Office of Multicultural Affairs in 1996 to address cultural sensitivity and diversity at RWJMS. The office develops, sponsors, and supports programs and activities that foster cultural awareness and an understanding of diversity. Activities include a multicultural appreciation week, cultural competence workshops, and a presentation on diversity during first-year orientation. Activities are also done in celebration of Asian, Black, and Latin Heritage Months. RWJMS offers several courses addressing multiculturalism that in-clude a complimentary/alternative medicine elective, a medical Spanish elective, a cultural diversity module as part of Introduction to the Patient, and panel presentation on culture, religion and sexuality. The Office of Multicultural Affairs works collaboratively with other departments, offices, and centers within the school that promote the understanding of diversity and delivery of culturally competent health care. Additional resources include a Center for Healthy Families and Cultural Diversity, a Cultural Diversity Committee, and a Student Committee for Multicultural Affairs. For more information contact: Cynthia Ferrer 732-235-3467.

Recruitment

RWJMS actively seeks to increase the number of underrepresented minority and disadvantaged students who are interested in pursuing careers in medicine. To achieve this goal, RWJMS sponsors enrichment programs for students at the high school and undergraduate levels and has developed articulated admissions programs with Rutgers University and Seton Hall University.

RWJMS welcomes the opportunity to speak with prospective pre-medical students. The Recruiter/Counselors are available to visit high schools, colleges, and universities and to speak with students about the medical school application process and about the diverse programs and opportunities at RWJMS. The school is also delighted to host visits to the RWJMS campus by student groups as this affords an excellent opportunity to meet with students, faculty, and administrators. The Recruiter/Counselors will help to plan such a visit and will arrange for speakers who can address topics of particular interest to the visiting group.

The Recruiter/Counselors also welcome the opportunity to meet individually with prospective applicants. They are very experienced with all aspects of the medical school admissions process, and can discuss with each student his/her individual situation, whether it involves long-range planning and preparation for medical school or the immediate details of the application process.

University of Medicine and Dentistry of New Jersey-Robert Wood Johnson Medical School
Applicants, First-Time Applicants, Matriculants by Gender, Race and Ethnicity, 2007-2008

| | 2007 | | | | | | | | | 2008 | | | | | | | | |
| | APP | | | F-time APP | | | MAT | | | APP | | | F-time APP | | | MAT | | |
	Women	Men	Total	Women	Men	Total	Women	Men	Total	Women	Men	Total	Women	Men	Total	Women	Men	Total
Hispanic/Latino																		
Cuban	17	12	29	12	10	22	0	0	0	11	15	26	7	12	19	0	2	2
Mexican American	35	15	50	31	10	41	0	0	0	19	13	32	12	11	23	2	0	2
Puerto Rican	32	23	55	25	22	47	1	0	1	22	14	36	19	10	29	1	0	1
Other Hispanic	64	59	123	49	44	93	5	3	8	63	64	127	50	51	101	1	3	4
Multiple Hispanic/Latino*	13	10	23	10	8	18	2	0	2	6	8	14	5	3	8	0	1	1
Subtotal	161	119	280	127	94	221	8	3	11	121	114	235	93	87	180	4	6	10
Non-Hispanic/Latino**																		
Black	256	124	380	184	95	279	7	5	12	244	119	363	182	79	261	11	4	15
Native American/AK	2	3	5	2	3	5	0	0	0	2	1	3	2	1	3	0	0	0
Native Hawaiian/OPI	13	11	24	12	7	19	0	0	0	4	4	8	4	1	5	0	0	0
White	700	814	1,514	580	609	1,189	45	26	71	661	817	1,478	537	595	1,132	47	40	87
Asian	585	572	1,157	449	430	879	33	28	61	541	553	1,094	409	374	783	24	18	42
Other Race	3	4	7	1	1	2	0	0	0	0	1	1	0	1	1	0	0	0
Multiple Race*	39	48	87	33	35	68	2	2	4	37	36	73	27	25	52	1	2	3
Unknown	22	32	54	21	28	49	3	4	7	48	43	91	46	38	84	5	4	9
Subtotal	1,620	1,608	3,228	1,282	1,208	2,490	90	65	155	1,537	1,574	3,111	1,207	1,114	2,321	88	68	156
Foreign	21	22	43	15	19	34	0	0	0	17	15	32	16	12	28	0	0	0
Total	1,802	1,749	3,551	1,424	1,321	2,745	98	68	166	1,675	1,703	3,378	1,316	1,213	2,529	92	74	166

*Since 2002, students can select more than one race and / or ethnicity. **Those who did not choose 'Hispanic/Latino' or 'Non-Hispanic/Latino' are listed under 'Non-Hispanic/Latino'. Data Source: AAMC Data Warehouse: Applicant-Matriculant File, as of 1/16/2009.

Admissions

The RWJMS Admissions Committee plays a pivotal role in the school's efforts to increase the number of physicians from disadvantaged and underrepresented minority groups. Every minority/disadvantaged applicant is assured an individualized review of his/her completed application. Admissions Committee members are sensitive to the diverse factors that are important in evaluating medical school applicants. Life experiences, economic background, leadership experiences, and other factors are carefully considered along with the traditional numeric criteria such as GPA and Medical College Admission Test scores. The interview provides the applicant an opportunity to discuss in detail his/her qualifications and to learn about the academic program, environment, and special services offered at RWJMS. Committee membership includes faculty and students (who are full voting members). The Recruiter/Counselors work in the Office of Multicultural affairs and works with the admissions office to help to facilitate the admissions process for minority/ disadvantaged applicants.

Academic Support Programs

RWJMS is committed to the success of all its students and has developed a variety of programs to help every student achieve his/her goal of becoming a physician. The atmosphere at RWJMS is cooperative and supportive and faculty are accessible and receptive to answering questions and discussing course work. Many first-year courses incorporate faculty-led review periods into the class schedule and some designate a particular faculty member as an academic resource person.

Cognitive Skills Program (CSP)

This program provides individual consultation in a variety of learning-related areas, including study strategies, test-taking skills, and time management. The CSP also offers preparation programs for the United States Medical Licensing Examination and academic year tutorials.

RWJMS offers a flexible curriculum option that provides the opportunity for a limited number of students to personalize the sequence of courses. This option accommodates students with special circumstances, including those enrolled in combined degree programs (M.D./M.P.H., M.D./Ph.D.), those who wish to pursue other academic or research interests, and those with particular employment or family needs. Flexible curriculum students pay eight semesters of tuition during their matriculation. Tuition payments are prorated over the duration of their educational program.

As part of its commitment to increasing minority representation in medicine, for nearly 30 years, RWJMS has offered comprehensive academic support programs, a pre-matriculation summer program (discussed in more detail below, Enrichment Programs) and academic year tutorials, as well as individualized assistance with study and test-taking skills are offered. The Office of Special Academic Programs, which administers enrichment programs, also serves as a liaison to effectively present minority students' concerns to the senior administration of RWJMS.

Enrichment Programs

Pre-matriculation Summer Program (PSP)

Disadvantaged students, who have been accepted to the first-year class at RWJMS, are invited to attend the four week Pre-matriculation Summer Program. The goal of the program is to introduce students to course content they will encounter during their first year of medical school, as well as to give participants the opportunity to familiarize themselves with the RWJMS faculty and staff and the school environment. Cognitive skills seminars and individual cognitive skills assessments are incorporated into the summer program to assist students in identifying efficient and effective methods of studying medical information.

Second-year medical students serve as teaching fellows and also help the new

students with such things as locating apartments for the fall. Campus housing is available for students attending the program and scholarships are available to cover tuition, on-campus housing, and living expenses. Contact: Dr. Cheryl Dickson, 732-235-2144, or Cindy Ford 732-235-2808.

Biomedical Careers Program (BCP)

For the past 30 years, RWJMS has co-sponsored a summer enrichment program for disadvantaged students with Rutgers, The State University of New Jersey. BCP is designed for undergraduate students interested in pursuing a career in medicine and other health-related professions. This six-week summer program offers three levels and seven different curricula to meet the academic needs of all participants. Each level offers a set of academic coursework and activities complemented by career-related counseling and life-skills seminars. In order to be eligible, students must have completed one year of college, one semester of biology, and one semester of math. Students enrolled in BCP are eligible for three college credits through Rutgers University, and housing is available. Full and partial need-based scholarships are available to cover tuition, housing, and living expenses. Contact: Cindy Ford, 732-235-2808 *(http://rwjms.umdnj.edu/ osap)*

Summer Science Scholars Program (S3A)

The academy is a four-week science enrichment program designed for highly motivated and academically committed high school students achieving excellence in the sciences. The curriculum focuses on exploring the human body through a series of lectures, organ laboratories, and clinical experiences. The academy provides a bridge between high school and undergraduate studies in the sciences and ultimately a career in medicine. Students participate in college preparatory workshops, health profession seminars, cognitive skills sessions, and community service opportunities. Additionally, students complete a research project to present at the Summer Science Scholars Academy symposium. S3A classes are small to foster individualized learning and enhance the student's personal experience. Financial assistance is available to cover tuition and housing expenses. Contact: Cynthia Ferrer, 732-235-2143. *(http://rwjms.umdnj.edu/osap)*

Summer Enrichment Program (SEP)

A four week program for high school students in the Abbott District School districts, (districts which in general are lower socioeconomic and lower funding for educational programs) to help prepare them in basic science skills and math and introduce students to possible careers in health related fields. Students have the opportunity to work with medical students in panel presentations and special sessions. Students work with cognitive skills throughout the summer and have help with preparation for the SAT examination. Students are given encouragement and skills to utilize to help them get to the next step of college education. Students have the opportunity to stay on campus or commute from home. Contact: Cindy Ford, 732-235-2808. *(http://rwjms.umdnj.edu/osap)*

Research in Science and Engineering (RISE)

This eight-week summer enrichment program is for minority and disadvantaged students interested in pursuing careers in research. Students are paired with research mentors from Rutgers or UMDNJ-RWJMS. Four days per week are spent in the lab with one day spent in classroom preparation for the Graduate Record Exam (GRE) and scientific seminars. The program concludes with a scientific symposium where students present the results of their summer research. There is no tuition charge, housing is provided, and a stipend is provided to cover living expenses. Contact: *rise@umdnj.edu (http://rwjms.umdnj.edu/education/gsbs/prospective/rise_2.html)*.

Student Financial Assistance

The RWJMS application fee will be waived for any student who receives an American Medical College Application Service fee waiver. Overnight accommodations with our medical students can be arranged for applicants coming to interview. To ensure that every student who matriculates at RWJMS has adequate financial support, a financial needs assessment (based on the Free Application for Federal Student Aid form) is made for each student and an individualized financial aid package is developed. The types of financial aid include scholarships and grants (including a special institutional fund for disadvantaged minority students), loans, and college work-study programs. Financial aid counselors are available to assist students in planning effective personal budgets.

Educational Partnerships

RWJMS has articulated admissions programs with Rutgers University (B.A./M.D. program). Eligibility for these programs is not restricted to particular racial/ethnic categories. In addition, RWJMS, in conjunction with Rutgers University and Seton Hall University, offers a special articulated admissions program, Access-Med, for disadvantaged students participating in that program their respective undergraduate institutions. Contact: Dr. Cheryl Dickson, 732-235-2144.

Other Pertinent Information

RWJMS was founded in 1966 as a professional school within Rutgers University. Since 1971, RWJMS has been associated with the University of Medicine and Dentistry of New Jersey (UMDNJ), New Jersey's health sciences university. RWJMS continues to enjoy the benefits of its close proximity to, and relationship with, Rutgers University. RWJMS has facilities at several locations in the central and southern parts of New Jersey. The basic science building, where all students receive two years of pre-clinical instruction, is located in Piscataway, adjacent to the main science campus of Rutgers University. The medical science complex also includes a UMDNJ—Community Mental Health Center and several facilities operated jointly with Rutgers University, including the Library of Science and Medicine, the Center for Advanced Biotechnology and Medicine, and the Environmental and Occupational Health Sciences Institute.

RWJMS offers clinical education at training sites both in central New Jersey (the Piscataway program) and in southern New Jersey (the Camden program). Major teaching affiliations with Robert Wood Johnson University Hospital in New Brunswick and Cooper Hospital/University Medical Center in Camden, plus affiliations with numerous community hospitals in central New Jersey, provide students with a diverse range of clinical training facilities.

Joint Degree Programs

M.D./Ph.D. Students may pursue a Ph.D. degree in the discipline of their choice through one of the graduate programs sponsored by the UMDNJ-Graduate School of Biomedical Sciences (GSBS) or one of the graduate programs sponsored jointly by GSBS and Rutgers University. Tuition remission and stipend support are available. Typically, students take about three years to complete the degree between the second and third year of medical school.

M.D./M.P.H. Students may pursue an M.P.H. through the New Jersey Graduate Program in Public Health sponsored jointly by UMDNJ-RWJMS and Rutgers University. Students may study in any one of several "tracks" including: Health Care Organization, Family Health, Epidemiology, and Toxicology. Medical-school funded positions for this M.P.H. are available. In addition, a few stipends for living expenses are available to students who take a year off for full-time study in the M.P.H. program. Typically students can complete this degree by taking some courses concurrent with their medical school courses (some courses replace medical school courses) plus an additional year of study.

M.D./J.D. Students may pursue a J.D. degree through either Rutgers Law

School (Camden) or Seton Hall Law School (Newark). Typically, two and one-half years of additional study are required. This degree may be taken between years two and three or between years three and four of medical school.

M.D./M.S.J. Students may pursue a Masters of Science in Jurisprudence at Seton Hall Law School. One additional year of full-time study is required. Students would typically complete this degree between years two and three of medical school.

M.D./M.B.A.. Students may pursue an M.B.A. through a joint program sponsored by Rutgers University and RWJMS. Medical-school funded positions are available.

M.D./M.S. in Medical Informatics. Students may pursue the M.S. in Medical Informatics through this joint program with New Jersey Institute of Technology and UMDNJ-School of Health Related Professions. Some scholarships support is available.

Robert Wood Johnson Medical School has a long-standing commitment to increasing access to education for under-represented minority and disadvantaged students. This commitment is evident in institutional policies and procedures, in the programs and services which RWJMS offers, and in the major fiscal commitments that the institution has made to these programs.

University of New Mexico School of Medicine

Dr. Valerie Romero-Leggott, Vice President for Diversity
University of New Mexico School of Medicine
MSC 08 4680
1 University of New Mexico
Albuquerque, NM 87131-0001
505-272-2728; 505-272-6857 fax
http://hsc.unm.edu/som/diversity

Introduction

The mission of the University of New Mexico School of Medicine Office of Diversity is to promote racial, ethnic, socioeconomic, and geographic diversity in the University of New Mexico Health Sciences Center (UNMHSC) and to develop a variety of opportunities addressing key issues in diversity.

Strategies to achieve this mission include creating college awareness and identifying, recruiting, and supporting students, residents, and faculty from diverse backgrounds. The Office of Diversity addresses the challenges of students from minority groups that are underrepresented in the context of collaborative partnerships and programs. A critical component to the success of our students and programs has been our partnerships with communities, other colleges and entities within the HSC, other educational institutions, community health centers, health professionals and educators.

Recruitment

Recruitment takes place all year round throughout New Mexico at the community level through career fairs, high school and institutions of higher education site visits, and special events. Presentations are given about the School of Medicine's admissions process, UN-MHSC colleges and programs, combined B.A./M.D. degree program, and the Health Career Pathways Programs. The programs range from special speakers talking to students about careers to shadowing opportunities and educational events in collaboration with area physicians, local community leaders, medical students, high school teachers, and counselors.

The Office of Diversity also organizes several tours of the UNMHSC for students and educators from all areas of New Mexico. These tours include presentations from faculty and students from a variety of health professions, centers, and institutes, information on student opportunities, and interactive simulated sessions.

The Office of Diversity collaborates in recruitment efforts with other UN-MHSC colleges and programs including, the Hispanic and Native American Center of Excellence, the Center for Native American Health, and School Based Health Centers, in addition to UNM main campus recruitment and student support services such as, El Centro de la Raza, American Indian Student Services, African American Student Services, and Minority Science Programs. Misty Salaz, BAIMD Recruiter, or Liliana Sosa, Program Coordinator, 505-272-2728; 505-272-6857 Fax; (http://hsc.unm.edu/ som/diversity/)

The School of Medicine's Office of Admissions hosts an Annual Pre-Med/Health Day in collaboration with the other UNMHSC programs in an effort to provide pre-med/health students throughout the state an opportunity to visit our campus and learn about all of the opportunities offered by UNM. Pre-med/health students and advisors from two-year community colleges and four-

University of New Mexico School of Medicine
Applicants, First-Time Applicants, Matriculants by Gender, Race and Ethnicity, 2007-2008

	2007									2008								
	APP			F-time APP			MAT			APP			F-time APP			MAT		
	Wo-men	Men	Total	Wo-men	Men	Total	Wo-men	Men	Total	Wo-men	Men	Total	Wo-men	Men	Total	Wo-men	Men	Total
Hispanic/Latino																		
Cuban	2	2	4	1	2	3	0	0	0	0	1	1	0	1	1	0	1	1
Mexican American	43	51	94	25	34	59	5	7	12	28	30	58	20	20	40	8	7	15
Puerto Rican	2	0	2	2	0	2	0	0	0	0	2	2	0	2	2	0	0	0
Other Hispanic	30	16	46	22	9	31	5	3	8	15	20	35	9	15	24	6	1	7
Multiple Hispanic/Latino*	6	6	12	6	3	9	0	0	0	6	4	10	3	3	6	2	0	2
Subtotal	83	75	158	56	48	104	10	10	20	49	57	106	32	41	73	16	9	25
Non-Hispanic/Latino**																		
Black	23	16	39	15	14	29	0	1	1	8	8	16	4	5	9	1	0	1
Native American/AK	16	6	22	9	4	13	3	0	3	7	10	17	4	7	11	1	1	2
Native Hawaiian/OPI	2	4	6	2	3	5	0	1	1	0	1	1	0	1	1	0	0	0
White	259	298	557	199	227	426	23	19	42	162	152	314	129	110	239	21	18	39
Asian	94	104	198	79	71	150	2	3	5	39	39	78	24	30	54	3	1	4
Other Race	2	1	3	1	0	1	0	0	0	0	0	0	0	0	0	0	0	0
Multiple Race*	9	19	28	8	12	20	2	1	3	6	15	21	5	6	11	0	3	3
Unknown	10	7	17	10	7	17	0	0	0	8	10	18	7	9	16	0	1	1
Subtotal	415	455	870	323	338	661	30	25	55	230	235	465	173	168	341	26	24	50
Foreign	5	8	13	4	8	12	0	0	0	4	1	5	3	0	3	0	0	0
Total	503	538	1,041	383	394	777	40	35	75	283	293	576	208	209	417	42	33	75

*Since 2002, students can select more than one race and / or ethnicity. **Those who did not choose 'Hispanic/Latino' or 'Non-Hispanic/Latino' are listed under 'Non-Hispanic/Latino'. Data Source: AAMC Data Warehouse: Applicant-Matriculant File, as of 1/16/2009.

year institutions are invited from all over New Mexico to participate in this event. The program consists of an introduction to all of the UNMHSC programs, information regarding the School of Medicine's curriculum, a presentation on financing medical education, a panel of students from various programs providing a question/answer session, lunch, afternoon tours of the Health Science Center, and mock interviews. Contact: Marlene Ballejos, Admissions Director; 505-272-4766; 505-925-6031 Fax; *(http://hsc.unm.edu/som/admissions/)*

The Center for Native American Health (CNAH), in collaboration with the UNM Health Sciences Center programs, students, and recruiters,

- Conducts orientations of the campus for high school students, school counselors, school administrators, and parents from Native American (NA) schools and communities.
- Conducts outreach to rural NA schools with NA HSC students and NA faculty, traveling long distances to meet with high school students and their parents within their local communities. This allows potential HSC students to gain insight into the determination and commitment that's necessary for their journey to becoming a healthcare provider.
- Acts as a bridge between the UNMHSC campus and the UNM main campus for the NA undergraduates, and other tribal colleges, hosting a NA Health Science Interest Forum to encourage and foster interest in health careers.
- Invites undergraduates interested in medicine to meet other NA medical students at the monthly meetings and to visit the HSC campus.
- Provides the NA medical students support to recruit and mentor other native students interested in medical school. Interested students are also connected with NA faculty for additional encouragement and guidance. Contact: Dr. Gayle Dine'Chacon, Director; 505-272-4100; 505-272-6019 Fax; *(http://hsc.unm.edu/*

som/fcm/CNAH/SDevelopment.shtml)

Admissions

Because the School of Medicine is publicly supported, it has an implied obligation to train students who are likely to serve the state's expanding medical needs. For this reason, residents of New Mexico are given primary consideration for admission. In addition to a 3.0 grade-point average (GPA) and a composite Medical College Admission Test (MCAT) score of 22, the School of Medicine seeks a diverse student body and considers a wide range of factors when evaluating applicants for admission, including but not limited to, demonstrated intellectual capacity, academic achievement, work experiences, life experiences, academic and personal motivation, commitment to public service, the extent to which the applicant has overcome educational and/or economic obstacles, and other indicators that the applicant can succeed in medical studies and make a significant contribution to the School of Medicine community and the state of New Mexico. Furthermore, the UNM School of Medicine seeks the inclusion of students from groups that are underrepresented in medicine in New Mexico. An active minority recruitment program encourages applications from Hispanic, Native-American, and African-American residents of New Mexico. All applicants meeting the residency, GPA, and MCAT requirements receive individualized consideration and are reviewed competitively in one pool. Applicants who are not residents of New Mexico, but who have a demonstrated tie to the state or who live in a state with a Western Interstate Commission on Higher Education (WICHE) agreement, must apply through the Early Decision Program (EDP).

The Office of Admissions offers post-admissions workshops to applicants who were not successful in gaining admission into medical school. Students are provided an assessment form to complete regarding various aspects of their application. The Assistant Dean for Admissions meets with applicants individually to help applicants improve

their applications and become more competitive in the application process. Contact: Marlene Ballejos, Admissions Director; 505-272-4766; 505-925-6031 Fax; *(http://hsc.unm.edu/som/admissions/)*

Academic Support Programs

Through the Academic Success Center (ASC), the UNM School of Medicine provides assistance to students to enhance their learning skills. Consultation is available regarding study habits, learning skills, test-taking strategies, test anxiety, time management, problem-solving conceptualization, Myers-Briggs Type Indicator administration and interpretation, and other related areas of concern. After initial consultation, students may be directed toward available UNM or community resources, begin working on skills through ASC, or be referred to special courses (Board Review) or diagnostics as needed.

The Peer Tutorial Program is a partnership between the ASC and the Office of Diversity funded by the Office of Diversity. This program provides tutoring in basic science courses for medical students in their first and second years. Tutors are third- or fourth-year students who have generally excelled in the disciplines in which they tutor. Contact: Pamela DeVoe, Program Manager; 505-272-8972; 505-272-5084 Fax; *(http://hsc.unm.edu/som/excellence)*

As part of the counseling program that has emphasis on eventual career choice, the Office of Student Services has established a Medical Student Mentors program to supplement the formal career advisement. This program pairs up four to five Phase I medical students with a practicing clinician at the UNM Hospital or affiliated VA hospital systems. The student meets with the advisor in group settings as well as one on one, as needed, to assist in developing balance between studies, career, and personal life. Contact: Office of Student Services; 505-272-3414; 505-272-8239 Fax; *(http://hsc.unm.edu/som/oss/)*

The CNAH provides mentoring and role modeling opportunities for Native-

American HSC students, as well as high school and undergraduate students interested in health careers and health research. On campus, CNAH shares all announcements of internships, scholarships, etc. with the Native-American students by e-mail. Contact: Dr. Gayle Dine'Chacon, Director; 505-272-4100; 505-272-6019 Fax; *(http://hsc.unm.edu/som/fcm/CNAH/SDevelopment.shtml)*

Enrichment Programs

The UNM School of Medicine's Office of Diversity offers five distinct, yet interrelated, pipeline programs to increase the disadvantaged applicant pool into health professions in New Mexico. The Office of Diversity was awarded a $1.6 million federal grant from the Health Resources and Services Administration in 2005 "to assist individuals from disadvantaged backgrounds to enter and graduate from a health or allied health professions program." Although the grant was not renewed, as of 2007 due to Title VII funding cuts, the School of Medicine has committed to continuing the education pipeline programs because of their importance to the people of New Mexico. The other colleges and partners involved in these programs have also committed to their continued participation and support of the following *Health Careers Pathway Programs:*

Dream Makers
The Dream Makers program is designed to establish and facilitate health career clubs at middle schools in the Albuquerque area, including the Native American Charter Academy, and rural areas including Las Vegas, Chaparral, and the Native-American community in Ramah, NM. The program's primary goals are to introduce young people to health professions, stimulate interest in science and math, and increase imagination in the areas of medicine and health. Current medical and other UNM Health Sciences Center students regularly assist with Dream Makers workshops in order to give middle school students a realistic sense of opportunities and potential for success in the health sciences fields. The program

is offered during the regular school year.

Health Careers Academy (HCA)
The Health Careers Academy is a six-week, nonresidential, summer program for rising high school freshmen, sophomores, and juniors. The HCA is designed to help strengthen ACT scores and provide academic enrichment in math, science, English and study skills. The program is also designed to provide exposure to various professions in the health care field. Participants attend presentations by UNM Health Sciences Center professionals, engage in hands-on activities, and learn about various health careers.

Undergraduate Health Sciences Enrichment Program (UHSEP)
The Undergraduate Health Science Enrichment Program is a six-week residential summer program that assists disadvantaged undergraduate students who attend or plan to attend an institution of higher learning in New Mexico. The program is designed to enhance academic preparation and facilitate entry into medical or allied health professions schools. The UHSEP program is separated into two separate residential summer sessions. UHSEP I takes place the summer before a student's freshman year. USHEP II takes place the summer before a student's junior year. UHSEP students attend classes in math, science, English, study skills, and humanities in medicine. They attend health professions seminars and educational and cultural field trips and participate in clinical volunteer job shadowing through community health clinics where preceptors will serve as mentors.

New Mexico Clinical Education Program
The New Mexico Clinical Education Program provides a six-week experience in a rural clinic setting by placing students in primary care facilities and community health centers throughout New Mexico. Students shadow physicians and participate in all areas of the clinic and the community. This program is offered to students who are seriously pursuing a medical or physical therapy career. Prior to placement in a

rural clinic, students receive training in CPR/First Aid, intake procedures, and cultural competency and ethics. During the program, students volunteer for a 40-hour work week and are exposed to a variety of different opportunities such as community outreach and patient education; patient intake procedures; physical exams; diagnosis and treatments; emergency medical services and treatments; laboratory, pharmacy, and x-ray; and business management and administration.

Pathways to Pharmacy Program (PPP)
Participants in the Pathways to Pharmacy Program (PPP) are selected from the pool of pharmacy school applicants by the UNM College of Pharmacy (COP) Admissions Committee. PPP is a 12-month program where students will participate in a two-semester academic program and a final summer enrichment experience that will help prepare students for the rigors of the curriculum at the UNM College of Pharmacy. Upon successful completion of the program, students will matriculate into the following fall pharmacy school class. The PPP participants receive counseling, mentoring, and advising throughout the PPP from UNM COP faculty and admissions committee members. Contact: Peter Couse, Program Manager, or Liliana Sosa, Program Coordinator, 505-272-2728; 505-272-6857 Fax; *(http://hsc.unm.edu/som/diversity/)*

The Hispanic Center of Excellence (COE)
provides enrichment and professional development opportunities for Hispanic medical students and special programs for the general Health Sciences Center student population. The COE sponsors and coordinates the student lending library, the Academic Success Center, and the medical school's USMLE (United States Medical Licensing Exam), Step 1 support program. The COE sponsors Hispanic medical students with off-campus board review programs, as well as professional development experiences through conference travel. In addition, COE sponsors a Junior Faculty Development program which supports selected junior faculty

members with research and professional development training and opportunities. Contact: Pamela DeVoe, Program Manager; 505-272-8972; 505-272-5084 Fax; *(http://hsc.unm.edu/som/excellence)*

The student development initiative at the Center for Native American Health is establishing health career clubs in coordination with school counselors within NA communities. The students from these rural, isolated communities are:

- Provided financial support to attend national conferences where they are exposed to the possibilities in medicine,
- Given guidance from Native-American health professionals, and
- Able to participate in a one-day session to shadow a clinician in their local health centers so they can gain a better understanding of a career in medicine.

CNAH conducts a one-day event for high school students, teachers, and parents. "C.O.L.O.R.S." is a university-based project designed to:

- Familiarize students, teachers and the community with health career programs and university facilities;
- Offer information on application processes;
- Introduce the numerous university support programs available to NA students;
- Introduce NA role models to attendees; and
- Demonstrate the university's commitment to listening to, and addressing community specific needs.

CNAH conducts a one-day event for high school students, teachers, and parents. "On the Road" Program is geared towards familiarizing students and family members within tribal communities about health careers and the need for more Native-American health professionals. Native-American faculty and students who are role models and potential mentors are the primary representatives from the university to visit the communities. The activities may in-

clude: students "shadowing" at a local clinic, hospital, dental office etc.; a session on how to prepare for a health career; and a hands-on workshop with UNM faculty presentations. Contact: Dr. Gayle Dine'Chacon, Director; 505-272-4100; 505-272-6019 Fax; *(http://hsc.unm.edu/som/fcm/CNAH/SDevelopment.shtml)*

Student Financial Assistance

UNM offers a full range of federal, state and institutional scholarship, loan, and grant programs to eligible School of Medicine students. Of particular interest to M.D. students who plan to practice in an underserved area of New Mexico is the Loan-for-Service program. This program provides up to $25,000 in funding per academic year to contracted individuals and is a state-funded program for New Mexico residents only. The School of Medicine has also been the beneficiary over the years of generous funding from the Federal Scholarships for Disadvantaged Students program (approximately $106,166 for the 2008-2009 academic year). Students who meet the federal definition of a student from a disadvantaged background, either economic or environmental, are awarded through this grant program.

In addition, the School of Medicine offers significant scholarship aid to students from its own endowed funds donated by affiliated agencies and groups. This includes a few full tuition scholarships as well as many smaller awards. The school also provides comprehensive loan exit counseling sessions to each graduating class. One of our loan partners, New Mexico Student Loans, offers zero percent interest repayment on Stafford Loans for graduates who practice in New Mexico. Applicants to the University of New Mexico School of Medicine normally must remit a $50.00 application fee. Fee waivers will be considered when the applicant indicates he or she is disadvantaged on the American Medical College Application Service (AMCAS) application and writes a brief letter to the Assistant Dean for Admissions describing

the reason for the waiver request. Contact: Janell Valdez, Financial Aid Supervisor, Office of Financial Aid; 505-272-8008; 505-272-8063 Fax; *(http://hsc.unm.edu/som/finaid/)*

Educational Partnerships

The School of Medicine's Office of Diversity facilitates access to medical school for students from minority groups that are underrepresented in medicine in a collaborative effort with various educational partners.

Since August 2006, the Office of Diversity has led in the outreach, recruitment, and admissions for the combined B.A./M.D. Degree Program in partnership with the School of Medicine and College of Arts and Sciences. This program allows New Mexico high school seniors the opportunity to complete their Bachelor of Arts degree and, upon meeting program requirements, students will transfer into the School of Medicine to pursue their Doctor of Medicine (M.D.) degree. The program is an innovative approach to contributing to the diversity of the student body and to growing native New Mexican physicians who are committed to staying in the state and practicing medicine in the areas with the greatest need.

The Office of Diversity has established partnerships regarding educational pipeline and cultural competency issues. Some of our partners within UNM and the Health Science Center include the Colleges of Pharmacy and Nursing, the School of Law, the Southwest Hispanic Research Institute, the Student Services Ethnic Centers and Career Enrichment Programs, Recruitment Services, the Center for Native American Health, the Center of Excellence, and the Institute of Ethics. The Office of Diversity has also partnered with other departments within UNM and the Health Science Center as well as other New Mexico educational institutions and the Area Health Education Centers.

The Office of Diversity has established several community partnerships to encourage New Mexico's children to consider all the various opportunities available in the health professions fields. The Office of Diversity is collaborating with Engaging Latino Communities for Education (ENLACE), School Based Health Centers, the New Mexico Math, Engineering, and Science Achievement Program (NMMESA), and the Albuquerque Public Schools to name a few. The Office of Diversity also serves on the Health Careers Workforce Education Alliance, an Albuquerque area high schools and partners with the Health Occupations Students of America organization. In addition, partnerships with First Choice Community Health Centers and many rural health clinics offer clinical volunteer job shadowing through community health clinics where preceptors will serve as mentors for students.

Albany Medical College

Dr. Ingrid Allard, Associate Dean
Community Outreach and Medical Education
Albany Medical College
47 New Scotland Avenue, MC1
Albany, NY 12208
518-262-5634; 518-262-5138 fax
Allardi@mail.amc.edu

Recruitment

The Office of Community Outreach and Medical Education works together with the Albany Medical College (AMC) Office of Admissions to recruit diverse students from underrepresented backgrounds. The process includes visits to pre-medical summer programs, career days, and participation in many conferences with a pre-medical minority focus. Underrepresented diverse applicants receive follow-up from the Office of Community Outreach and Medical Education regarding the status of their application and are encouraged to visit the Medical College. Campus visits and accommodations with students of color and other students from diverse backgrounds can be arranged

Admissions

All applicants apply through the Albany Medical College Admissions Office. The Associate Dean for Community Outreach and Medical Education works closely with the Admissions Office to assist them in identifying quality applicants from underrepresented diverse backgrounds. Once students are invited for an interview, the Associate Dean can meet with the students on an informal basis to answer questions or address any concerns the students may have.

In identifying students for interview and for acceptance, Albany Medical College actively looks for other qualities in addition to a good grade-point average and scores on the Medical College Admissions Test (MCAT). We look for qualities such as motivation, persistence, and compassion, and in some cases what the student has had to overcome to get to this point.

All applicants are invited to an informal session hosted by currently enrolled students. In addition, all applicants are invited to attend a luncheon and tour of the school on the day of the interview. Albany Medical College students are present and can at the time give applicants further insight into the school and the admission process.

Academic Support Programs

Science and Technology Entry Program (STEP)
This program is designed to provide support for screening, testing, counseling, tutoring, and teaching of New York state residents who are enrolled in secondary school; who exhibit the potential for college-level study, if provided with special services; and are either minority, historically underrepresented in the scientific, technical, health-related, and licensed professions, or economically disadvantaged. Albany Medical College has been involved with the Science and Technology Entry Program for at least 15 years.

Student Financial Assistance

Scholarship monies are available specifically for underrepresented students of color. This scholarship is made available by a member of the Albany City Community. All other financial assistance is based on demonstrable need. Applicants may apply for a waiver of the application fee if they consider themselves financially disadvantaged.

Albany Medical College
Applicants, First-Time Applicants, Matriculants by Gender, Race and Ethnicity, 2007-2008

	2007									2008								
	APP			F-time APP			MAT			APP			F-time APP			MAT		
	Wo-men	Men	Total	Wo-men	Men	Total	Wo-men	Men	Total	Wo-men	Men	Total	Wo-men	Men	Total	Wo-men	Men	Total
Hispanic/Latino																		
Cuban	26	23	49	20	17	37	0	0	0	27	30	57	21	25	46	0	0	0
Mexican American	76	64	140	59	42	101	1	0	1	65	72	137	54	55	109	0	2	2
Puerto Rican	28	14	42	20	13	33	1	0	1	25	23	48	23	20	43	0	0	0
Other Hispanic	98	99	197	70	65	135	0	1	1	123	118	241	91	80	171	1	0	1
Multiple Hispanic/Latino*	15	8	23	9	6	15	1	0	1	17	14	31	14	8	22	1	0	1
Subtotal	243	208	451	178	143	321	3	1	4	257	257	514	203	188	391	2	2	4
Non-Hispanic/Latino**																		
Black	210	121	331	140	98	238	3	2	5	191	95	286	128	79	207	0	0	0
Native American/AK	6	4	10	5	4	9	1	0	1	6	5	11	6	3	9	0	0	0
Native Hawaiian/OPI	22	11	33	16	8	24	0	0	0	16	14	30	10	7	17	0	0	0
White	2,067	2,231	4,298	1,576	1,577	3,153	34	44	78	1,866	2,413	4,279	1,349	1,649	2,998	40	40	80
Asian	1,396	1,447	2,843	1,012	999	2,011	22	18	40	1,350	1,399	2,749	944	896	1,840	22	25	47
Other Race	3	5	8	1	2	3	0	1	1	3	7	10	3	5	8	0	0	0
Multiple Race*	100	120	220	74	81	155	1	1	2	106	89	195	70	60	130	1	3	4
Unknown	50	47	97	47	43	90	7	3	10	84	115	199	77	99	176	1	4	5
Subtotal	3,854	3,986	7,840	2,871	2,812	5,683	68	69	137	3,622	4,137	7,759	2,587	2,798	5,385	64	72	136
Foreign	300	306	606	238	234	472	2	1	3	284	326	610	214	244	458	2	1	3
Total	4,397	4,500	8,897	3,287	3,189	6,476	73	71	144	4,163	4,720	8,883	3,004	3,230	6,234	68	75	143

Note: In 2008, one applicant, who declined to report gender, was not included here.

*Since 2002, students can select more than one race and / or ethnicity. **Those who did not choose 'Hispanic/Latino' or 'Non-Hispanic/Latino' are listed under 'Non-Hispanic/Latino'. Data Source: AAMC Data Warehouse: Applicant-Matriculant File, as of 1/16/2009.

Educational Partnerships

Students who participate in STEP are from the local high schools and elementary schools. Albany Medical College does offer an automatic complimentary interview to former AMC STEP participants if they apply to AMC. There are no formal partnerships. Albany Medical College has a partnership with several local colleges in the area. The Medical College has accelerated B.S./M.D. programs where students will do three or four years at the undergraduate institution and then matriculate into Albany Medical College.

Albert Einstein College of Medicine of Yeshiva University

Dr. Yvette Calderon, Assistant Dean,
Nilda I. Soto, Assistant Dean,
Dr. Milton Gumbs, Associate Dean
Office of Diversity Enhancement
Albert Einstein College of Medicine
of Yeshiva University
1300 Morris Park Avenue, Belfer 205
Bronx, NY 10461
718-430-3091; 718-430-8825 fax
soto@aecom.yu.edu

Recruitment

Minority student recruitment is conducted through the Office of Diversity Enhancement. Faculty members and enrolled medical students also take an active part in these efforts. The College of Medicine participates annually in the National Association of Medical Minority Educators, Inc.'s Student Recruitment Workshop and the Health Careers Conferences sponsored by the various ASPIRA organizations. In addition, visits are made to colleges, both local and out-of-state, in order to speak to student groups interested in medicine as a career. The Office of Diversity Enhancement works closely with pre-

medical advisors at various undergraduate institutions.

The Office of Diversity Enhancement and enrolled minority students sponsor an annual recruitment luncheon for prospective applicants.

Admissions

In selecting students for interview and for acceptance, attention is paid not only to the traditional indicators of success, such as grade-point average and Medical College Admission Test scores, but also to those qualities that a student must possess in order to become a good physician. Among these are good character, strong motivation, perseverance, and compassion.

All students are invited to attend a luncheon and tour of the school on the day of the interview. Einstein medical students are present and can, at that time, give applicants further insight into the school and the admissions process.

Academic Support Programs

The Office of Diversity Enhancement, in conjunction with the Associate Dean for Students Affairs and the Office of

Academic Support and Counseling, closely follows the academic progress of students. Should difficulties arise; students are counseled and may be advised to avail themselves of tutorial assistance or the services of the Office of Academic Support and Counseling. These services are provided to all students free of charge upon their request. Extensive syllabi, which cover the lecture material, are provided for most subjects in the basic sciences.

Since many academic problems arise because of personal difficulties rather than intellectual unpreparedness, a large part of the retention effort involves non-academic supports.

There are chapters of the Student National Medical Association and the Latino Medical Student Association at Einstein. Both are quite active in undergraduate advisement, recruitment efforts, and important issues of society and health. The Office of Diversity Enhancement assigns each incoming student a Big Brother/Sister from the second-year class. The support that the students provide to each other, both directly and through their various activities is invaluable and can, literally,

Albert Einstein College of Medicine of Yeshiva University
Applicants, First-Time Applicants, Matriculants by Gender, Race and Ethnicity, 2007-2008

	2007 APP Women	Men	Total	2007 F-time APP Women	Men	Total	2007 MAT Women	Men	Total	2008 APP Women	Men	Total	2008 F-time APP Women	Men	Total	2008 MAT Women	Men	Total
Hispanic/Latino																		
Cuban	23	20	43	18	15	33	0	1	1	20	25	45	16	20	36	0	0	0
Mexican American	57	65	122	45	48	93	1	1	2	50	56	106	41	38	79	0	2	2
Puerto Rican	32	22	54	26	19	45	0	1	1	28	28	56	25	23	48	0	3	3
Other Hispanic	114	102	216	90	77	167	0	1	1	105	99	204	88	78	166	4	4	8
Multiple Hispanic/Latino*	15	9	24	10	6	16	0	0	0	14	11	25	11	6	17	1	0	1
Subtotal	241	218	459	189	165	354	1	4	5	217	219	436	181	165	346	5	9	14
Non-Hispanic/Latino**																		
Black	210	107	317	154	87	241	7	5	12	203	116	319	159	87	246	2	7	9
Native American/AK	2	2	4	2	2	4	0	0	0	3	4	7	3	4	7	0	0	0
Native Hawaiian/OPI	17	9	26	14	8	22	1	0	1	17	9	26	12	5	17	0	0	0
White	1,603	1,807	3,410	1,323	1,411	2,734	49	63	112	1,554	1,849	3,403	1,214	1,401	2,615	56	44	100
Asian	1,151	1,231	2,382	917	937	1,854	21	18	39	1,068	1,195	2,263	797	835	1,632	22	17	39
Other Race	1	3	4	0	1	1	0	0	0	2	6	8	1	5	6	0	0	0
Multiple Race*	96	103	199	77	74	151	1	2	3	83	81	164	70	54	124	4	2	6
Unknown	52	50	102	49	43	92	5	0	5	106	110	216	100	94	194	6	4	10
Subtotal	3,132	3,312	6,444	2,536	2,563	5,099	84	88	172	3,036	3,370	6,406	2,356	2,485	4,841	90	74	164
Foreign	240	273	513	193	205	398	3	4	7	259	282	541	209	221	430	2	2	4
Total	3,613	3,803	7,416	2,918	2,933	5,851	88	96	184	3,512	3,871	7,383	2,746	2,871	5,617	97	85	182

*Since 2002, students can select more than one race and / or ethnicity. **Those who did not choose 'Hispanic/Latino' or 'Non-Hispanic/Latino' are listed under 'Non-Hispanic/Latino'. Data Source: AAMC Data Warehouse: Applicant-Matriculant File, as of 1/16/2009.

mean the difference between success and failure.

Faculty members interested in providing support and assistance to minority medical students make themselves available to students. They provide mentorship, advise and guidance through the medical school process and with career and specialty selection.

Enrichment Programs

The Department of Biochemistry offers a preparatory course in medical genetics, immunology, and biochemistry during the two-week period preceding the start of classes. Aside from serving to introduce the students to courses in the first-year curriculum, the course helps to introduce the students to each other, to some faculty members, and to the school environment. Participation is voluntary and is recommended to students whose basic science background is weak or limited in content or scope. In addition, incoming minority students are invited to a special Retreat Weekend prior to the start of classes.

Minority Student Summer Research Opportunity Program
Designed for undergraduates who have completed their sophomore or junior year, this program provides eight and one-half weeks of experience in biomedical research. Students receive a stipend and free housing for students not able to commute.

Hispanic Center of Excellence
The Institute for Community and Collaborative Health of the Albert Einstein College of Medicine was awarded a grant from the Department of Health and Human Services to initiate a Hispanic Center of Excellence. Einstein has provided support to continue the funding and activities of the Hispanic Center of Excellence. It is the first Center of Excellence in New York State, and it serves to reinforce the participation and presence of the college in all areas of the Bronx community and the Hispanic populations of New York. The Center highlights the college's longstanding institutional commitment to underrepresented minorities in the Bronx and

throughout the city and state and provides leadership in research and education on Hispanic health issues and disparities in health care. The Center develops innovative methods to strengthen and enhance the academic performance by minority students, improves educational diversity and cultural competency for all students and faculty, and fosters minority faculty development and promotion.

The center assists with mentoring programs for minority students at Albert Einstein in order to enhance the academic success of the minority students by offering a faculty-mentoring program, which includes office-based experiences with community-based Hispanic physicians. It also provides an annual career-planning workshop for pre-clinical and clinical minority students. The center is active in the development of culturally competent problem-based learning (PBL) seminars in the four-week clerkship in family medicine required of all third-year medical schools. The center provides assistance with the cross-cultural interviewing session that is included in the introduction to clinical medicine course in the first year.

Student Financial Assistance

Application fees are waived for financially-needy students. Financial aid is available to minority students on the basis of financial need and consists of scholarships and awards, in addition to the well-known loan programs. No students should be discouraged from applying due to lack of funds.

Educational Partnerships

The Einstein Enrichment Program (EEP) is an after school program for high school students from the Bronx who are either economically disadvantaged or minorities historically underrepresented in scientific, medical, and health related professions. EEP is funded through the New York State Education Department's Science and Technology Entry Program (STEP). EEP renders a holistic approach and provides support, at all levels, in order

to enhance the academic abilities and address the special needs of secondary school students. Academic support is provided in the form of regents review, SAT preparation, cognitive instruction in writing, study skills, and critical thinking. Career advisement and college admission and information workshops, on career paths and options, are presented. Individual and group counseling is offered. The program runs for 30 weeks during the academic year and six weeks in the summer. During the summer, all students are put in placements. The placements allow students to acquire actual hands-on experiences that provide them with the knowledge and skills necessary for careers in medicine, science, and technology.

Columbia University College of Physicians and Surgeons

Dr. Hilda Y. Hutcherson,
Associate Dean
Richele Jordan-Davis, Assistant Dean
Office of Diversity
Columbia University College of
Physicians and Surgeons
630 West 168th Street
Third Floor, Suite 401
New York, NY 10032
212-305-4157; 212-305-1049 fax
www.oda-ps.cumc.columbia.edu

Recruitment

The Office of Diversity assists with the recruitment and nurturing of underrepresented and/or disadvantaged students. Activities include Web and e-mail outreach, participation at recruitment seminars and conferences, and visits to colleges by faculty, administrators and students. Organized visits by prospective applicants are scheduled whenever possible. Such visits feature counseling sessions, opportunities to see the campus, and discussions with medical students. The Office of Diversity regularly provides pre-medical career counseling and advice to individual high school and college students.

The Office of Diversity presents an annual Recruitment Day Conference that provides detailed information to potential underrepresented in medicine students. General topics are covered as well as specific information about the College of Physicians and Surgeons (P&S). P&S has a very active, cohesive, and effective Black and Latino Students Organization (BALSO), which is supported by the Office of Diversity. BALSO is active internally and externally with all Office of Diversity recruitment efforts. BALSO students sponsor pre-enrollment orientation activities for new students, as well as a variety of academic support and social programs.

The Office of Diversity works closely with community outreach programs sponsored by Columbia University Medical Center.

Admissions

Columbia University College of Physicians and Surgeons participates in the American Medical College Application Service (AMCAS) application process. Admission information can be located on the admissions Web site. The Office of Diversity works closely with the Admissions Office. Applicants are encour-

aged to visit the Office of Diversity at the time of their interviews. Arrangements such as breakfast meetings are made for provision of additional information, tours and meetings with other underrepresented students. Minority faculty serve as active members of the Admissions Committee.

Academic Support Programs

Academic support programs are available to all P&S students, including a student-skills assessment and building program for entering first-year students. During the first year, the program includes the formation of intense, course-oriented study groups, which are popular among students. The Student Success Network (SSN) offers services to help make first-year students' adjustment to medical school a smooth one. SSN promotes a sense of teamwork through regular small-group review sessions, facilitated by second-year students. Tutors are also available free of charge.

Advisory Deans serve as mentors who enhance each P&S student's education by providing support in curriculum, academic progress, professional development, residency choices and all things

Columbia University College of Physicians and Surgeons
Applicants, First-Time Applicants, Matriculants by Gender, Race and Ethnicity, 2007-2008

	2007									2008								
	APP			F-time APP			MAT			APP			F-time APP			MAT		
	Women	Men	Total	Women	Men	Total	Women	Men	Total	Women	Men	Total	Women	Men	Total	Women	Men	Total
Hispanic/Latino																		
Cuban	20	28	48	19	23	42	0	2	2	20	18	38	16	16	32	0	0	0
Mexican American	64	78	142	54	62	116	3	1	4	51	53	104	44	45	89	1	1	2
Puerto Rican	34	38	72	30	34	64	1	1	2	22	30	52	20	24	44	0	1	1
Other Hispanic	100	89	189	92	69	161	6	2	8	100	98	198	91	82	173	2	1	3
Multiple Hispanic/Latino*	14	10	24	12	8	20	0	0	0	17	15	32	15	13	28	1	0	1
Subtotal	232	243	475	207	196	403	10	6	16	210	214	424	186	180	366	4	3	7
Non-Hispanic/Latino**																		
Black	223	143	366	188	121	309	7	4	11	235	145	380	191	115	306	16	7	23
Native American/AK	5	5	10	4	5	9	0	0	0	5	4	9	5	4	9	0	0	0
Native Hawaiian/OPI	17	5	22	15	5	20	0	0	0	12	4	16	8	4	12	0	0	0
White	1,474	1,718	3,192	1,301	1,470	2,771	42	52	94	1,402	1,851	3,253	1,212	1,566	2,778	36	45	81
Asian	988	1,038	2,026	874	885	1,759	11	10	21	894	1,057	1,951	750	856	1,606	12	12	24
Other Race	2	3	5	2	3	5	0	0	0	4	6	10	3	4	7	0	0	0
Multiple Race*	113	110	223	104	94	198	1	2	3	113	83	196	93	67	160	2	0	2
Unknown	38	56	94	37	53	90	0	0	0	112	122	234	109	108	217	1	7	8
Subtotal	2,860	3,078	5,938	2,525	2,636	5,161	61	68	129	2,777	3,272	6,049	2,371	2,724	5,095	67	71	138
Foreign	206	220	426	167	177	344	6	3	9	237	216	453	205	177	382	5	3	8
Total	3,298	3,541	6,839	2,899	3,009	5,908	77	77	154	3,224	3,702	6,926	2,762	3,081	5,843	76	77	153

*Since 2002, students can select more than one race and / or ethnicity. **Those who did not choose 'Hispanic/Latino' or 'Non-Hispanic/Latino' are listed under 'Non-Hispanic/Latino'. Data Source: AAMC Data Warehouse: Applicant-Matriculant File, as of 1/16/2009.

necessary to make P&S students even more successful in their careers and personal achievements. In addition, each new student is assigned an advisor from among members of the second-year class.

BALSO students provide extensive counseling with strong ties established between members of the second- and first-year classes. Brother/Sister arrangements provide valuable guidance from more senior students. Also, BALSO features several special group tutorials.

Retention rates for underrepresented minority students at P&S are very high. Students are recognized annually as recipients of nationally competitive awards for academic scholarships and are frequently selected for graduation prizes and awards. Students are highly sought after for residency programs.

Enrichment Programs

Summer Medical and Dental Education Program (SMDEP)
Columbia is a SMDEP site hosting approximately 80 (60 pre-medical/20 pre-dental) college students for a six-week in-residence program for academic and study skills enrichment, clinical experiences and counseling. Web site: (www.smdep.org)

The New York State Science and Technology Entry Program
This program supports S-PREP, an innovative, year-long program for underrepresented students who are seriously interested in pursuing a career in medicine or in other health professions. The program, organized and run by the Office of Diversity for over 20 years, features medical science courses taught on Saturdays at P&S with P&S students functioning as teachers and preceptors. Academically talented high school students in grades nine-12 are encouraged to participate in the program. Web site: *(www.oda-ps.cumc.columbia.edu/prep.html)*

Health Careers Opportunity Program (HCOP)
Columbia is a member of the Northeast Regional HCOP Alliance that includes Mount Sinai School of Medicine and UMDNJ New Jersey Medical School. HCOP is a year-long program with an intensive six-week summer component. Eighty college students from New York and New Jersey participate in academic enrichment, study skills development, MCAT prep, clinical experiences and career counseling at two of the three campuses over the course of three years.

Student Financial Assistance

Application fees are waived for financially-needy students. Financial aid is available to students on the basis of financial need and consists of scholarships and awards, in addition to the well-known loan programs. No student should be discouraged from applying due to lack of funds. The Student Financial Planning office works closely with the Office of Diversity during the recruiting and post-admissions process. All P&S students are assigned a counselor upon entry for their class. This will determine need, financial aid packages, and work closely with that class throughout medical school. Financial Aid Officers have posted walk-in hours each week to handle questions that can be quickly resolved. Intense financial planning and debt management seminars are held regularly for students. All students complete an exit interview upon graduation. Web site: (http://cpmcnet.columbia.edu/student/finaid/aboutus.html)

Educational Partnerships

P&S is actively involved with community groups, state and national organizations, and partnerships with many local school systems to ensure the achievement of students underrepresented in medicine. Web sites: *(www.amsny.org)*, *(www.msiahec.org)*, *(www.heaf.org)*.

Weill Cornell Medical College of Cornell University

Dr. Carlyle H. Miller, Associate Dean for Student Affairs and Equal Opportunity Programs
Weill Cornell Medical College of Cornell University
445 East 69th Street, Room 110
New York, NY 10021
212-746-1058; 212-746-8211 fax
chm2031@med.cornell.edu
http://www.med.cornell.edu

Recruitment

The faculty at Weill Cornell University's Weill Medical College (WCMC) has long recognized that society's needs will be better met by increasing the numbers of men and women in the health science fields from minority groups underrepresented in medicine. Accordingly, a studious effort is made to attract talented minority students to WCMC. WCMC actively recruits on a nationwide basis to assure that each entering medical school class will be a diverse group of capable, prospective physicians. At WMC, diversity means the inclusion of students representative of populations that are most affected by physician shortages.

Since New York City is one of the great urban academic centers in the United States, Weill Cornell welcomes visits to its facilities from prospective medical school students who live in the area or who may be visiting. Faculty and students are also eager to participate in pre-medical conferences sponsored by various minority organizations.

Admissions

Weill Cornell Medical College does not have a separate admissions committee or subcommittee for applicants from minority groups underrepresented in medicine. Students from minority backgrounds apply to WCMC in the same way as other applicants. The Admissions Committee consists of approximately 30 people and, at present, eight members are from underrepresented minority groups.

Academic Support Programs

There is no specific academic support program for students prior to or during their stay at WCMC as medical students. When any student encounters academic difficulties, the problem is handled by assistance from faculty.

Enrichment Programs

Travelers Summer Research Fellowship Program for Pre-medical Students
The primary purpose of this program is not to entice students to WCMC for their medical education, but to provide pre-medical students from diverse backgrounds with an experience in medical research. It also gives them deeper insights into the field of medicine, including issues that greatly affect the health of traditionally underserved groups. Participants in the program come from a wide range of undergraduate institutions and, to be eligible, must have completed their junior year in a pre-medical curriculum. Through the experiences of laboratory research, classroom lectures, and seminars on public health issues, the fellows gain a clear picture of the demands and opportunities they will encounter in choosing medicine as a career. A popular feature of this seven-week program is the assignment of each participant to a fourth-year medical student, who serves as a clinical tutor and takes the summer student on weekly rounds at New York Presbyterian Hospital Weill Cornell campus to observe the care of patients. A number of the participants

Weill Cornell Medical College
Applicants, First-Time Applicants, Matriculants by Gender, Race and Ethnicity, 2007-2008

		2007								2008							
		APP			F-time APP			MAT			APP			F-time APP			MAT		
		Women	Men	Total	Women	Men	Total	Women	Men	Total	Women	Men	Total	Women	Men	Total	Women	Men	Total
Hispanic/Latino																			
Cuban		17	24	41	17	21	38	0	0	0	17	16	33	16	16	32	0	0	0
Mexican American		48	63	111	39	57	96	0	2	2	39	47	86	34	37	71	2	1	3
Puerto Rican		35	36	71	30	33	63	1	0	1	16	26	42	15	19	34	0	0	0
Other Hispanic		94	90	184	83	70	153	6	0	6	72	94	166	66	80	146	3	5	8
Multiple Hispanic/Latino*		10	12	22	9	9	18	0	0	0	11	11	22	10	10	20	0	1	1
Subtotal		204	225	429	178	190	368	7	2	9	155	194	349	141	162	303	5	7	12
Non-Hispanic/Latino**																			
Black		165	114	279	135	95	230	6	9	15	162	104	266	136	87	223	2	3	5
Native American/AK		3	5	8	2	4	6	0	1	1	1	5	6	1	5	6	0	1	1
Native Hawaiian/OPI		17	3	20	15	2	17	0	0	0	7	3	10	6	3	9	0	0	0
White		1,281	1,487	2,768	1,157	1,292	2,449	27	28	55	1,211	1,586	2,797	1,072	1,361	2,433	29	35	64
Asian		843	911	1,754	748	779	1,527	10	6	16	778	900	1,678	652	741	1,393	7	5	12
Other Race		2	4	6	2	4	6	0	0	0	2	5	7	1	4	5	0	0	0
Multiple Race*		98	84	182	92	76	168	1	1	2	110	76	186	93	60	153	2	2	4
Unknown		33	52	85	31	47	78	0	1	1	85	104	189	83	94	177	1	1	2
Subtotal		2,442	2,660	5,102	2,182	2,299	4,481	44	46	90	2,356	2,783	5,139	2,044	2,355	4,399	41	47	88
Foreign		153	169	322	122	135	257	2	0	2	167	172	339	149	136	285	1	0	1
Total		2,799	3,054	5,853	2,482	2,624	5,106	53	48	101	2,678	3,149	5,827	2,334	2,653	4,987	47	54	101

*Since 2002, students can select more than one race and / or ethnicity. **Those who did not choose 'Hispanic/Latino' or 'Non-Hispanic/Latino' are listed under 'Non-Hispanic/Latino'. Data Source: AAMC Data Warehouse: Applicant-Matriculant File, as of 1/16/2009.

in this program subsequently apply to WCMC. The Travelers Foundation funds this summer program.

Tri-Institutional M.D.-Ph.D. Program
This program sponsors a summer program in biomedical research for college students who have completed their freshman or sophomore years with distinction. This is an opportunity for students to test and develop their interest in pursuing a combined degree program, while providing the student hands-on research experience that is considered highly among the criteria for admission to M.D.–Ph.D. programs. Students should contact Dr. Olaf Anderson, Program Director, 212-746-6023, for further information.

Student Financial Assistance
The application fee will be waived for students with the American Medical College Application Service (AMCAS) fee waiver. Others who would find it extremely difficult financially to pay the application fee should contact the Office of Admissions. There are no special funds set aside specifically for minority group students, but financial aid in the form of grants and loans is made available to all students according to financial need, within the limits of available funds for a given year. Although tuition is high, there is subsidized student housing available for all medical students.

Mount Sinai School of Medicine of New York University

Dr. Gary Butts, Associate Dean for Multicultural Affairs and Director, Center for Multicultural & Community Affairs
Mount Sinai School of Medicine
One Gustave Levy Place—Box 1035
5th Floor Annenberg Building, Room 5-16
New York, NY 10029
212-241-8276; 212-241-3594 fax
gary.butts@mssm.edu;
cmca@mssm.edu
www.mssm.edu/cmca

Center for Multicultural & Community Affairs

The Center for Multicultural and Community Affairs (CMCA), formerly the Office of Multicultural and Community Affairs, was established by the Mount Sinai School of Medicine (MSSM) in 1998 to increase underrepresented minority groups (URMs) in medicine, adding to the diversity of the school and the hospital and to Mount Sinai's effectiveness in serving the ethnically and racially diverse communities of East Harlem, Harlem, the Bronx, Queens, and New York City. CMCA is the interface for educational pipeline programs, minority affairs, institution-wide diversity initiatives, academic supports for medical students, and culture and medicine programs within the School of Medicine. The center's mission is to support improving community health outcomes and reducing race/ethnic health outcome disparities through increasing health care work force diversity and scientific inquiry, which impacts health policy.

Recruitment

The School of Medicine's recruitment program includes visits by the Center for Multicultural & Community Affairs, faculty, admissions, and students to colleges in the New York metropolitan area, the northeastern states, and selected undergraduate institutions in other areas of the country (i.e., Historically Black Colleges and Universities and Hispanic-Serving Institutions). Information on the MSSM is provided to selected students on the Medical Minority Applicant Registry and from individual requests.

The Center for Multicultural & Community Affairs conducts an annual Open House event for minority student applicants in the fall. The Center for Multicultural & Community Affairs and the Office of Admissions may arrange on-site visits for students in pre-medical clubs and societies. The MSSM conducts a summer internship program and a winter Medical College Admission Test (MCAT) preparation and review program for undergraduate students. On-campus year-round high school science enrichment and internship programs are conducted under the Secondary Education Through Health (SETH) program, the Life Sciences Secondary School, and the Mount Sinai Scholars Program at the Manhattan Center for Science and Mathematics. In a multicultural environment, these programs serve educationally and economically disadvantaged students who have strong interest in careers in medicine and biomedical sciences.

Admissions

All applicants to MSSM are evaluated on the basis of academic performance, MCAT scores, pre-medical committee letters of recommendation, extracurric-

Mount Sinai School of Medicine of New York University
Applicants, First-Time Applicants, Matriculants by Gender, Race and Ethnicity, 2007-2008

	2007 APP Women	Men	Total	F-time APP Women	Men	Total	MAT Women	Men	Total	2008 APP Women	Men	Total	F-time APP Women	Men	Total	MAT Women	Men	Total
Hispanic/Latino																		
Cuban	24	22	46	21	19	40	1	3	4	26	24	50	23	22	45	2	3	5
Mexican American	60	56	116	51	38	89	3	0	3	55	44	99	45	33	78	1	1	2
Puerto Rican	33	31	64	28	29	57	2	4	6	27	24	51	25	18	43	0	2	2
Other Hispanic	116	97	213	94	78	172	2	4	6	106	104	210	96	81	177	2	5	7
Multiple Hispanic/Latino*	15	11	26	9	8	17	0	0	0	14	10	24	12	9	21	0	0	0
Subtotal	248	217	465	203	172	375	8	11	19	228	206	434	201	163	364	5	11	16
Non-Hispanic/Latino**																		
Black	224	113	337	176	94	270	5	1	6	219	109	328	179	89	268	5	2	7
Native American/AK	3	3	6	2	3	5	0	0	0	4	3	7	4	3	7	0	0	0
Native Hawaiian/OPI	15	10	25	14	8	22	0	0	0	15	7	22	12	4	16	0	0	0
White	1,579	1,560	3,139	1,347	1,263	2,610	37	33	70	1,494	1,641	3,135	1,243	1,345	2,588	36	29	65
Asian	1,036	962	1,998	849	755	1,604	15	14	29	974	982	1,956	767	720	1,487	11	21	32
Other Race	2	3	5	2	2	4	0	0	0	2	6	8	1	5	6	0	0	0
Multiple Race*	105	93	198	94	69	163	1	3	4	108	70	178	86	55	141	2	2	4
Unknown	52	58	110	49	50	99	4	2	6	104	113	217	99	98	197	7	5	12
Subtotal	3,016	2,802	5,818	2,533	2,244	4,777	62	53	115	2,920	2,931	5,851	2,391	2,319	4,710	61	59	120
Foreign	192	183	375	150	144	294	4	3	7	234	211	445	195	156	351	2	2	4
Total	3,456	3,202	6,658	2,886	2,560	5,446	74	67	141	3,382	3,348	6,730	2,787	2,638	5,425	68	72	140

*Since 2002, students can select more than one race and / or ethnicity. **Those who did not choose 'Hispanic/Latino' or 'Non-Hispanic/Latino' are listed under 'Non-Hispanic/Latino'. Data Source: AAMC Data Warehouse: Applicant-Matriculant File, as of 1/16/2009.

ular activities, and the degree of interest and motivation apparent in the application or evidenced upon interview. The Admissions Committee thoroughly reviews the applications of students from underrepresented minority and educationally disadvantaged backgrounds. Actions are then taken based on these recommendations. Minority faculty and minority student representation are present on the Admissions Committee. Application fees may be waived upon appropriate request.

Enrichment Programs

Medical Education and Research
Recognizing the importance of treating patients as community, CMCA works to infuse a public health orientation to the scope of thinking, training, research, and future practice of medical students.

Health Career Educational Pipeline Programs
CMCA oversees several educational pipeline programs with secondary schools and colleges in New York City. Since the inception of the School of Medicine in 1968, the school has offered programs for youth from disadvantaged backgrounds to obtain early exposure and advance towards careers in health and science. With HRSA and HCOP support, Mount Sinai's Center for Excellence in Youth Education (CEYE) was created (1988) to oversee high school and collegiate programs.

Addressing Cultural Competence in Medicine
The Culture and Health Work Group is charged by the Dean and directed by CMCA to develop programs, activities and projects to expand culturally focused themes and assessments throughout the medical school and residency curriculum. The committee is comprised of faculty, deans and medical students and works to address education, research and community relevant topics related to culture and health.

Medical Students and the Community
Mount Sinai medical students have traditionally been involved in volunteer and service-learning activities in East Harlem and in our surrounding communities. CMCA serves as an advisor to various medical student groups and provide support in coordinating clinical and educational activities and opportunities with surrounding community-based health and social service organizations.

Student Financial Assistance
It is the policy of the school to provide as much financial assistance as possible to all students who require such assistance in order to maintain attendance. Students who are accepted for admissions are provided financial assistance applications on which they may document their requests for financial aid. Applications are treated confidentially and awards are made by a faculty committee on financial aid. Each application is considered on an individual basis so that the greatest support for the most needy students may be distributed.

Educational Partnerships
Through the Center of Excellence in Youth Education (CEYE), overseen by the Center for Multicultural & Community Affairs, the majority of educational pipeline programs are administered and directed for high schools and colleges, representing a 30-year institutional commitment. It has a remarkable science enrichment and career exploration infrastructure for educating students from diverse backgrounds. CEYE's year-round programs include: Science Technology Entry Program (STEP), Scholars and Mentoring Program, the Bio-Science Studies Institute, a Collegiate Careers in Medicine and Research Program, and SAT and MCAT Prep Programs.

New York Medical College

Joan June, Assistant Dean
New York Medical College
Office of Minority Affairs
Administration Building
Valhalla, New York 10595
914-594-3016; 914-594-4514 fax
joan_june@nymc.edu

Recruitment

The New York Medical College recruitment strategy includes recruitment visits to undergraduate colleges, participation in career day programs, attendance at professional organization recruitment conferences, and individual counseling of students interested in pursuing a medical career. Also information on the Medical College is provided through individual requests. The Assistant Dean, medical students, alumni, faculty, and administrators participate in the recruitment efforts.

The College conducts a college preparatory program for minority and disadvantaged high school students, which exposes the students to the academic excellence necessary to pursue career in medicine.

Admissions

The Admissions Committee has no preference as to a major field of undergraduate study; however, any college work submitted must include specified credits in chemistry, physics, biology, and English. Science courses must include substantial laboratory work. The Admissions Committee members consist of faculty from the basic sciences departments, clinical departments and administrators. The Assistant Dean for Minority Affairs is a member of the Admission Committee.

Academic Support Programs

The following services are available to all students throughout the year: the decelerated program, individualized tutorial assistance arranged at no cost to the student, personal guidance, career advisement, and the Student Counseling Services.

Student Financial Assistance

Financial aid is awarded on the basis of need; scholarships, based on academic merit and need, are available to entering students. The College provides debt management and loan counseling services.

New York Medical College
Applicants, First-Time Applicants, Matriculants by Gender, Race and Ethnicity, 2007-2008

	2007 APP Women	APP Men	APP Total	F-time APP Women	F-time APP Men	F-time APP Total	MAT Women	MAT Men	MAT Total	2008 APP Women	APP Men	APP Total	F-time APP Women	F-time APP Men	F-time APP Total	MAT Women	MAT Men	MAT Total
Hispanic/Latino																		
Cuban	40	30	70	28	22	50	0	0	0	36	32	68	32	29	61	1	2	3
Mexican American	91	83	174	70	62	132	0	0	0	83	90	173	66	64	130	0	1	1
Puerto Rican	36	27	63	25	22	47	0	0	0	34	27	61	30	19	49	3	0	3
Other Hispanic	131	131	262	102	85	187	0	2	2	149	154	303	117	110	227	1	0	1
Multiple Hispanic/Latino*	23	13	36	15	9	24	0	0	0	20	13	33	17	7	24	1	0	1
Subtotal	321	284	605	240	200	440	0	2	2	322	316	638	262	229	491	6	3	9
Non-Hispanic/Latino**																		
Black	299	158	457	219	129	348	2	0	2	292	151	443	217	121	338	7	2	9
Native American/AK	3	8	11	2	8	10	0	0	0	6	6	12	6	3	9	0	0	0
Native Hawaiian/OPI	27	14	41	22	10	32	1	0	1	26	17	43	15	10	25	1	0	1
White	2,442	2,627	5,069	1,889	1,857	3,746	61	46	107	2,429	2,930	5,359	1,808	2,031	3,839	49	52	101
Asian	1,701	1,762	3,463	1,254	1,253	2,507	39	30	69	1,710	1,796	3,506	1,228	1,184	2,412	25	29	54
Other Race	2	8	10	1	3	4	0	0	0	4	5	9	4	4	8	0	0	0
Multiple Race*	152	151	303	115	95	210	4	2	6	131	130	261	99	80	179	2	2	4
Unknown	54	60	114	48	51	99	1	3	4	135	139	274	124	117	241	3	4	7
Subtotal	4,680	4,788	9,468	3,550	3,406	6,956	108	81	189	4,733	5,174	9,907	3,501	3,550	7,051	87	89	176
Foreign	294	285	579	235	213	448	2	2	4	262	287	549	209	212	421	2	0	2
Total	5,295	5,357	10,652	4,025	3,819	7,844	110	85	195	5,317	5,777	11,094	3,972	3,991	7,963	95	92	187

Note: In 2008, one applicant, who declined to report gender, was not included here.
*Since 2002, students can select more than one race and / or ethnicity. **Those who did not choose 'Hispanic/Latino' or 'Non-Hispanic/Latino' are listed under 'Non-Hispanic/Latino'. Data Source: AAMC Data Warehouse: Applicant-Matriculant File, as of 1/16/2009.

New York University School of Medicine

Mekbib Gemeda
Assistant Dean for Diversity Affairs and Community Health
New York University School of Medicine
550 First Avenue, SLH
New York, NY 10016
212-263 8948; 212-263 6526 fax
mekbib.gemeda@nyumc.org
http://www.med.nyu.edu/diversity_affairs/

Recruitment

New York University School of Medicine conducts a robust recruitment, retention, and pipeline cultivation program. Faculty, students, deans, and administrators are actively involved in the programs which include the following:

Outreach to universities and colleges across the United States and Puerto Rico
Visits are coordinated by the Office of Diversity Affairs, the Sackler Institute for Graduate Biomedical Sciences, and the M.D./Ph.D. program, and the presentations are given by the Director of the Institute, Joel Oppenheim, the Co-Director of the M.D./Ph.D. program, Eva Hernando-Monge, and the Director of the Office of Diversity Affairs, Mekbib Gemeda. Contact person: Mekbib Gemeda, *(mekbib.gemeda@nyumc.org)*.

Visits for student groups from universities and colleges
Tours and visits of the school and hospitals and meeting with current minority students, faculty and administrators at the medical school are organized for student groups interested in exploring training and life at NYU School of Medicine. We organize these visits through minority student clubs, biology and premed clubs and pre-medical offices at institutions in the area. Contact person: Allison Avery *(Allison.Avery@nyumc.org)*. We also organize a revisit for students admitted into the medical school.

Exhibits at national meetings for underrepresented students interested in science and medicine
These meetings include the Annual Biomedical Research Conference for Minority Students (ABRCMS), the Annual Conference of the Society for the Advancement of Chicanos and Native Americans in Science (SACNAS), The Student National Medical Association Meeting (SNMA), the Latino Medical Student Association (LMSA), as well as the AAMC, NAMEE, AMSA, NMA, and AMA conferences.

An *annual career day* for students in the tri-state area interested in pursuing biomedical careers is also hosted by the school. Contact Person: Allison Avery *(Allison.Avery@nyumc.org)*

A ten-week Summer Undergraduate Research Program for students from institutions across the U.S. and Puerto Rico who are interested in pursuing graduate biomedical and medical training
The program is part of the Leadership Alliance program, a consortium of 33 leading research and teaching institutions. At the end of the program, the students attend a three-day Leadership Alliance Symposium where they present their research findings to deans, faculty, and administrators from Alliance Institutions. *(http://www.med.nyu.edu/sackler/programs/summer.html)*

Network for minorities in science
The Assistant Dean for Diversity Affairs and Community Health was one of the developers of the largest online network for minorities in science,

New York University School of Medicine
Applicants, First-Time Applicants, Matriculants by Gender, Race and Ethnicity, 2007-2008

| | 2007 | | | | | | | | | 2008 | | | | | | | | |
| | APP | | | F-time APP | | | MAT | | | APP | | | F-time APP | | | MAT | | |
	Women	Men	Total	Women	Men	Total	Women	Men	Total	Women	Men	Total	Women	Men	Total	Women	Men	Total
Hispanic/Latino																		
Cuban	29	29	58	26	24	50	0	1	1	23	23	46	20	22	42	1	1	2
Mexican American	53	66	119	47	55	102	2	0	2	44	54	98	39	44	83	0	1	1
Puerto Rican	40	38	78	36	35	71	2	0	2	25	32	57	23	25	48	1	1	2
Other Hispanic	122	102	224	100	82	182	5	5	10	97	104	201	85	83	168	0	2	2
Multiple Hispanic/Latino*	12	10	22	9	9	18	1	1	2	18	16	34	14	11	25	0	1	1
Subtotal	256	245	501	218	205	423	10	7	17	207	229	436	181	185	366	2	6	8
Non-Hispanic/Latino**																		
Black	251	138	389	198	121	319	2	3	5	215	119	334	174	100	274	4	1	5
Native American/AK	5	4	9	3	4	7	0	0	0	5	5	10	5	4	9	0	0	0
Native Hawaiian/OPI	21	8	29	20	6	26	1	0	1	15	11	26	12	7	19	0	0	0
White	1,769	1,914	3,683	1,539	1,557	3,096	43	48	91	1,594	1,970	3,564	1,331	1,597	2,928	40	51	91
Asian	1,196	1,226	2,422	1,014	995	2,009	22	16	38	1,069	1,194	2,263	857	903	1,760	24	25	49
Other Race	2	3	5	2	2	4	0	0	0	3	7	10	2	6	8	0	0	0
Multiple Race*	110	111	221	102	90	192	1	4	5	127	72	199	103	58	161	2	1	3
Unknown	49	67	116	47	57	104	0	2	2	111	122	233	109	109	218	5	3	8
Subtotal	3,403	3,471	6,874	2,925	2,832	5,757	69	73	142	3,139	3,500	6,639	2,593	2,784	5,377	75	81	156
Foreign	94	104	198	73	83	156	1	0	1	118	127	245	101	98	199	1	0	1
Total	3,753	3,820	7,573	3,216	3,120	6,336	80	80	160	3,464	3,856	7,320	2,875	3,067	5,942	78	87	165

*Since 2002, students can select more than one race and / or ethnicity. **Those who did not choose 'Hispanic/Latino' or 'Non-Hispanic/Latino' are listed under 'Non-Hispanic/Latino'. Data Source: AAMC Data Warehouse: Applicant-Matriculant File, as of 1/16/2009.

(JustGarciaHill.org). The site has a growing membership of over 6,000 underrepresented minorities at all levels in the pipeline, from undergraduates to senior scientists.

Admissions

New York University School of Medicine participates in the American Medical College Application Service (AMCAS). The Admissions Committee evaluates applications and selected candidates are invited for an interview. The candidate's academic, professional, and personal experience is evaluated to determine eligibility for admission. This allows candidates to present their best qualities to the admissions committee.

Academic Support Programs

A robust mentoring and advisement program is made available to all students. Friendly, accessible faculty make it easy for students to seek assistance when they need it. The Office of Diversity Affairs has an open door policy that encourages all students to come with any concerns. The office also reaches out to student groups and hosts seminars and workshops focused on cultivating mentoring opportunities and career development. In addition, underrepresented minority students are linked to resident and faculty role-models.

Institute of Community Health and Research
Students have opportunities to participate in community outreach, education and research through a robust institute consisting of centers or Latino Health, Asian Health and the Health of the African Diaspora.
(www.med.nyu.edu/ichr)

Enrichment Programs

A ten-week Summer Undergraduate Research Program is offered for students from institutions across the United States and Puerto Rico who are interested in pursuing graduate biomedical and medical training. The program is part of the Leadership Alliance program a consortium of 33 leading research and teaching institutions. At the end of the program, the students attend a three-day Leadership Alliance Symposium where they present their research findings to deans, faculty and administrators from Alliance institutions.
http://www.med.nyu.edu/sackler/programs/summer.html
Contact Person: Mekbib Gemeda *(mekbib.gemeda@nyumc.org)*.

Bridging the Gap is a mentoring program for minority undergraduate students at New York University who are interested in medicine. The program involves minority medical students and faculty at New York University School of Medicine and is coordinated by the Pre-Professional Office and the Black and Latino Student Association at the School of Medicine.

High School Fellows Program
This program is a science enrichment and direct clinical and/or research experience at NYU Medical Center for motivated high school junior and senior students in the New York City school system. The program includes an intensive summer semester and a fall/spring session. Contact Person: Carlos Restrepo,
(Carlos.Restrepo@nyumc.org)

MiniMed Program
This program is supported by the office of Diversity Affairs and run by first-year and second-year medical students to expose middle school and high school ninth and tenth graders from underserved communities to medicine and medical careers. The program is structured around hands-on workshops and projects scaling down the first-year medical curriculum to expose the students to basic human body structure and function and pathophysiology as well as health disparities.

Student Financial Assistance

Financial need-based scholarships and fee waivers are available for students. Students are encouraged to demonstrate financial need in their AMCAS applications. Debt management and financial planning programs and workshops are also offered.

Educational Partnerships

Salk School of Science
Established in 1995 as a joint program of the NYU School of Medicine and New York City's School District 2, the Salk School of Science is an innovative attempt to improve science teaching in a middle school by involving members of the medical/scientific community. The school emphasizes hands-on, in-depth exploration of the physical/chemical, life, and earth sciences. NYU faculty and students work directly with Salk pupils in a variety of activities that create a connection between biomedical science and the sciences in the Salk curriculum.

State University of New York Downstate Medical Center College of Medicine

Dr. Constance H. Hill, Associate Dean for Minority Affairs
State University of New York Downstate Medical Center, College of Medicine
450 Clarkson Avenue, Box 1186
Brooklyn, NY 11201
718-270-3033; 718-270-1929 fax
chill@downstate.edu
http://sls.downstate.edu/minority_affairs

Recruitment

The State University of New York (SUNY) Downstate's Office of Minority Affairs in the College of Medicine participates in recruitment activities sponsored by the Association of American Medical Colleges, Historically Black Colleges and Universities (HBCUs), the National Association of Medical Minority Educators (NAMME), and local colleges and universities.

The College of Medicine offers students a broad professional education that provides exceptional opportunities for those committed to promoting healthcare in urban communities and addressing the complex challenges of research and preventive care that confront clinicians, researchers and educators. This unique aspect of Downstate's mission is reflected in the students we attract and select. Many of our students are members of minority and cultural groups underrepresented in the health professions and/or come from families of first generation immigrants or from economically disadvantaged backgrounds.

The differences in background and outlook that students bring can enhance the quality of the educational experience of all students at SUNY Downstate. The belief that diversity adds an essential ingredient to the educational process is one of the tenets of SUNY Downstate. Many factors, such as race, ethnic or cultural background, academic achievement, geographic location, diversity of experiences, leadership roles, and socioeconomic background, are taken into consideration in the admissions process. A diverse health care work force will be better equipped to provide culturally competent care to an increasingly diverse population.

Admissions

The Committee on Admissions considers the total qualifications of each applicant without regard to sex, race, color, creed, national origin, religion, age, sexual orientation, marital status, or disability. Decisions regarding admission are based on multiple factors including academic performance, completion of the courses required for admission, the potential for academic success including performance on standardized tests such as the Medical College Admission Test (MCAT), communication skills, character, personal skills, health related experiences, and motivation for a career in medicine. New York State residents are given admissions preference, although well-qualified out-of-state applicants are also accepted. We welcome and encourage applications from women and members of groups underrepresented in medicine.

State University of New York Downstate Medical Center College of Medicine
Applicants, First-Time Applicants, Matriculants by Gender, Race and Ethnicity, 2007-2008

	2007									2008								
	APP			F-time APP			MAT			APP			F-time APP			MAT		
	Women	Men	Total	Women	Men	Total	Women	Men	Total	Women	Men	Total	Women	Men	Total	Women	Men	Total
Hispanic/Latino																		
Cuban	15	14	29	12	10	22	1	0	1	15	13	28	13	9	22	0	0	0
Mexican American	27	32	59	22	22	44	1	1	2	26	23	49	21	15	36	0	0	0
Puerto Rican	35	23	58	30	22	52	0	1	1	16	16	32	14	13	27	0	0	0
Other Hispanic	78	70	148	60	48	108	3	5	8	100	84	184	80	65	145	5	2	7
Multiple Hispanic/Latino*	12	11	23	9	7	16	1	0	1	6	8	14	5	5	10	0	1	1
Subtotal	167	150	317	133	109	242	6	7	13	163	144	307	133	107	240	5	3	8
Non-Hispanic/Latino**																		
Black	258	111	369	185	90	275	12	2	14	282	126	408	204	94	298	11	3	14
Native American/AK	1	5	6	1	5	6	0	1	1	2	1	3	2	1	3	0	0	0
Native Hawaiian/OPI	10	5	15	8	4	12	1	0	1	11	9	20	9	7	16	0	0	0
White	1,053	1,141	2,194	850	861	1,711	35	47	82	1,165	1,354	2,519	915	993	1,908	38	53	91
Asian	692	651	1,343	531	480	1,011	28	20	48	810	835	1,645	588	565	1,153	29	32	61
Other Race	1	3	4	1	1	2	0	0	0	2	6	8	1	4	5	0	0	0
Multiple Race*	72	63	135	58	47	105	2	4	6	59	53	112	44	38	82	1	1	2
Unknown	34	36	70	32	33	65	1	3	4	81	73	154	77	63	140	1	6	7
Subtotal	2,121	2,015	4,136	1,666	1,521	3,187	79	77	156	2,412	2,457	4,869	1,840	1,765	3,605	80	95	175
Foreign	64	48	112	60	41	101	0	0	0	41	60	101	34	49	83	0	0	0
Total	2,352	2,213	4,565	1,859	1,671	3,530	85	84	169	2,616	2,661	5,277	2,007	1,921	3,928	85	98	183

Note: In 2008, one applicant, who declined to report gender, was not included here.
*Since 2002, students can select more than one race and / or ethnicity. **Those who did not choose 'Hispanic/Latino' or 'Non-Hispanic/Latino' are listed under 'Non-Hispanic/Latino'. Data Source: AAMC Data Warehouse: Applicant-Matriculant File, as of 1/16/2009.

Academic Support Programs

The Office of Academic Development was established to help ensure that medical students, at every stage of their education, will achieve their full academic potential. Comprehensive and individualized programs of academic assistance are available to all students. A full range of academic services helps students develop optimal study strategies such as time management, study organization, note taking, problem solving, reading, and test-taking skills.

The office also offers programs to help students effectively prepare for the United States Medical Licensing Examination (USMLE) Steps 1 and 2. During the second academic year, a series of general lectures on licensure exam preparation is provided. Students are also able to receive individual counseling on a wide range of academic issues. A three-week preparatory course is sponsored by the medical school at the completion of the second year.

Enrichment Programs

Operation Success
This program is restricted to those students admitted to the next entering class and provides an introduction to basic medical sciences. Operation Success is a six-week residential program directed by medical school faculty with the assistance of rising second-year students. No applications are necessary and information is sent once admission has been granted.

Summer Research
This is an eight-week program designed for undergraduate students who have historically been underrepresented in the biomedical and health related professions. The program is open to all qualified applicants, but it is preferred that students will have completed the sophomore year of college.

Science and Technology Entry Program
The Science and Technology Entry Program at SUNY Downstate Medical Center, funded by the Associated Medical Schools of New York, is designed to encourage minority and economically disadvantaged junior/high school students to pursue scientific, technological, and health related careers. This program provides mathematics and science enrichment through the use of New York State Board of Education certified teachers, as well as medical students and medical school faculty.

Student Financial Assistance

All students admitted to the SUNY Downstate Medical Center College of Medicine who apply for financial consideration are given financial assistance based on need and available funds. Total financial counseling for the student and his/her parents will be provided during the summer programs and throughout the year.

Educational Partnerships

There is a combined program with the Sophie Davis School of Biomedical Education-City University of New York. The goals of this combined degree program are to train primary care physicians who will work in medically underserved areas and to increase the number of minority physicians.

Students are selected for this program in the senior year of high school. Only residents of New York are eligible to apply. This seven-year program leads to a baccalaureate degree granted by the City College of New York and to the M.D. degree awarded by one of seven participating New York medical schools.

The Office of Minority Affairs is dedicated to providing students with an opportunity to further their education in the health care field.

Other Pertinent Information

SUNY Downstate Medical Center College of Medicine is a teaching institution educating health care professionals; a research facility seeking answers to the medical problems that beset humankind; a teaching hospital caring for people with special problems; an outpatient facility serving the health needs of the community; a public service institution; and a unit of the State University of New York.

SUNY Downstate Medical Center is an institution that exists to educate, conduct research, and patient care. As a large urban medical center, which is part of a large public university system, SUNY Downstate Medical Center College of Medicine is keenly aware of its special obligation for public service and is a vital contributor to the health care needs of the underserved and underprivileged citizens of Brooklyn, the state, and the nation.

State University of New York Upstate Medical University College of Medicine

Dr. Greg Threatte, Interim Assistant Dean of Multicultural Resources
State University of New York Upstate Medical University College of Medicine
716 Irving Avenue
215 Weiskotten Hall
Syracuse, NY 13210
315-464-5433; 315-464-5431 fax
admiss@upstate.edu

Recruitment

The Office of Multicultural Resources provides access for historically underserved students to the College of Medicine. The curriculum adapts to the skills and background of the individual student. This is reflective of the College of Medicine at the State University of New York (SUNY) Upstate Medical University commitment towards increasing the enrollment, retention, and graduation of historically underserved students interested in medicine.

Recruiting activities are geared toward high school and college students. Recruitment visits are made to regional health career meetings and to individual undergraduate schools. Liaison relationships have been established with some undergraduate schools to enable SUNY Upstate Medical University to assist students on a continuing basis to better prepare for medical school.

Admissions

SUNY Upstate Medical University has one Admissions Committee for all applicants to the College of Medicine, including historically underserved applicants. There are historically underserved faculty and staff on the Admissions Committee. Applications from the historically underserved are carefully and thoroughly reviewed by this committee. Every applicant is evaluated on the merits of her/his total application rather than any one specific parameter. Both the academic and clinical faculty have historically underserved individuals.

Academic Support Programs

All students in the College of Medicine, including historically underserved students, participate in a comprehensive program of academic support. The basic components include a summer human anatomy class and faculty- and student-run tutorials in each of the major basic science courses.

There is advisement and counseling to help orient, direct, and guide students throughout their medical education. Each medical student is assigned to an advisory team that includes 12 students, an advisory dean, a clinician, and a senior medical student. First- and second-year students are required to meet once per month in small-group sessions to discuss academic commonalities. Students are also encouraged to meet privately with their advisory deans as needed. This process assures that each student has an advisor who will track the student's progress and serve as a mentor through the four years in medical school.

Enrichment Programs

Summer Programs
Human anatomy is offered for those enrolled as first-year students. The course is eight weeks long. Students successfully completing this summer course are exempt from taking human anatomy during the first year. Students have the opportunity to develop basic

State University of New York Upstate Medical University
Applicants, First-Time Applicants, Matriculants by Gender, Race and Ethnicity, 2007-2008

	2007 APP Women	Men	Total	2007 F-time APP Women	Men	Total	2007 MAT Women	Men	Total	2008 APP Women	Men	Total	2008 F-time APP Women	Men	Total	2008 MAT Women	Men	Total
Hispanic/Latino																		
Cuban	14	8	22	10	6	16	0	0	0	11	9	20	8	6	14	0	0	0
Mexican American	30	30	60	25	21	46	0	0	0	19	22	41	13	14	27	0	1	1
Puerto Rican	17	16	33	14	15	29	0	0	0	17	14	31	14	13	27	1	0	1
Other Hispanic	57	50	107	43	38	81	0	0	0	61	74	135	47	52	99	0	1	1
Multiple Hispanic/Latino*	10	4	14	7	4	11	0	0	0	8	5	13	6	2	8	0	0	0
Subtotal	128	108	236	99	84	183	0	0	0	116	124	240	88	87	175	1	2	3
Non-Hispanic/Latino**																		
Black	153	82	235	101	63	164	15	2	17	164	73	237	105	56	161	15	2	17
Native American/AK	4	6	10	3	5	8	0	0	0	3	2	5	3	2	5	0	0	0
Native Hawaiian/OPI	9	9	18	8	7	15	0	0	0	12	6	18	6	4	10	0	0	0
White	1,001	1,153	2,154	789	866	1,655	39	48	87	1,044	1,378	2,422	799	974	1,773	43	55	98
Asian	635	631	1,266	473	431	904	15	19	34	733	772	1,505	513	482	995	9	10	19
Other Race	1	4	5	1	2	3	0	0	0	2	4	6	2	3	5	0	0	0
Multiple Race*	54	38	92	41	30	71	1	0	1	49	52	101	32	35	67	3	4	7
Unknown	27	28	55	24	25	49	3	1	4	55	78	133	53	69	122	3	5	8
Subtotal	1,884	1,951	3,835	1,440	1,429	2,869	73	70	143	2,062	2,365	4,427	1,513	1,625	3,138	73	76	149
Foreign	200	210	410	155	157	312	8	9	17	229	283	512	175	212	387	3	5	8
Total	2,212	2,269	4,481	1,694	1,670	3,364	81	79	160	2,407	2,772	5,179	1,776	1,924	3,700	77	83	160

*Since 2002, students can select more than one race and / or ethnicity. **Those who did not choose 'Hispanic/Latino' or 'Non-Hispanic/Latino' are listed under 'Non-Hispanic/Latino'. Data Source: AAMC Data Warehouse: Applicant-Matriculant File, as of 1/16/2009.

learning skills in the context of one of their major academic courses.

USMLE Step 1 and Step 2
United States Medical Licensing Examination Step 1 and Step 2 preparation is available to students. The preparation includes a three-hour diagnostic test and a questionnaire. The data are computer-analyzed, and each student receives a customized study strategy, test-taking hints, diagnostic exam with computer-assisted feedback, individual study plan, and practice questions with explanations.

Student Financial Assistance

Costs. For 2006-07, the cost of tuition is $18,800 for New York residents and $33,500 for non-residents. Fees for first-year students are $1,090, and books and supplies (including diagnostic kit) cost approximately $2,000 for the year. Students should plan on $1,300 per month for living expenses (rent, food, personal, and travel). Health insurance is required. The total budget for a first-year student is $37,461 for a New York resident, or $52,161 for a non-resident.

Scholarships and grants
Over $1.9 million in scholarship and grant aid was provided to students in the College of Medicine in 2006-07. Many scholarships and grants are need-based, with eligibility based on family circumstances. In general, need-based funds are targeted to those students whose total family incomes are under $70,000 per year. Students are encouraged to provide parents' information on the Free Application for Federal Student Aid. This does not affect the overall eligibility for aid and allows students to be considered for all need- based programs. On average, about 10 percent of the financial aid at SUNY Upstate is in the form of scholarship and grant assistance.

Loans. Borrowing money to pay for medical school is a fact of life for most students. While average debt levels seem high (Upstate's class of 2006 borrowed an average of $124,429 for their pre-medical and medical school educa-

tion), the amounts are manageable when compared to average incomes of physicians. The Financial Aid Office staff work closely with students to ensure that each has the information and tools needed to effectively manage their student loan repayments. Students can control the amount of loans that they must borrow by planning and budgeting their finances carefully. The Financial Aid Office staff provides assistance with this also.

Application Process. SUNY Upstate Medical University uses the Free Application for Federal Student Aid (FAFSA). Students are encouraged to file on line at (www.fafsa.ed.gov) as soon as possible after January 1. The priority filing date for Upstate is March 1. Admission to Upstate is not required for filing. While completion of income tax returns before filing is helpful, applicants can estimate their income and then provide corrections, if necessary, after tax filing. Applicants are encouraged to provide parental income on the FAFSA so that consideration can be given for need-based scholarships and grants.

Students who have had recent changes in their financial circumstances or their family's circumstances are encouraged to send a letter to the Financial Aid Office outlining the changes. Upstate also makes available an optional financial aid application form that applicants can use to report these changes.

Educational Partnerships

Early Decision Program
This program is offered to applicants who are interested in applying only to Upstate. Requirements for the Early Decision Program are the same as for regular admissions, except that the American Medical College Application Service (AMCAS) Early Decision application deadline is August 1, and the deadline to have a complete application on file is August 15. Acceptance decisions are made prior to October 1. Candidates not accepted early decision may apply to other schools and will automatically be considered under the regular admissions process after October 1.

The Early Assurance Program (EAP)
EAP offers early acceptance to undergraduate students in their second year of college. Applicants must have sophomore standing and be enrolled at any accredited undergraduate institution. The EAP program is designed to free students from the pressures associated with medical school application and MCAT preparation so they may pursue unique academic interests. It is not intended to accelerate the length of time of the undergraduate education. Accepted students are required to complete their remaining two years of college, maintain a 3.50 science and overall GPA, continue relevant volunteer experiences, and do not have to take the MCAT exam. Applicants to the Early Assurance Program must have a minimum GPA of 3.50, a minimum combined SAT score of 1,300 (or ACT composite score of 29) and three of the four science sequences* (see below) completed prior to application:

- General biology or zoology - six-eight semester hours
- General chemistry - six-eight semester hours
- Organic chemistry - six-eight semester hours
- General physics - six-eight semester hours

*All sciences must have the corresponding lab.

The admissions office must have a complete application on file by July 1. Applications are reviewed over the summer, and interviews are scheduled for the end of August into the beginning of September of the junior year.

A completed application consists of:

- EAP Application
- SAT/ACT Score Report
- Official High School Transcript
- Health Professions Committee Letter of Recommendation
- Personal Statement
- Official College Transcript(s)·
- $100 Application Fee

Cobleskill Medical School Early Assurance Program
This is a guaranteed acceptance program for first-year students at SUNY Cobleskill who are interested in primary care careers and who meet the following academic requirements:

- 90 percent high school GPA
- 1,200 combined SAT scores or 27 ACT composite
- Three years of high school math & science courses
- 3.50 Cobleskill OPA

Students enrolled in this program will spend two years at SUNY Cobleskill, two years at either Siena College or Cornell University's College of Agriculture and Life Sciences, and then enter the medical program at SUNY Upstate. For more information on applying to this programs, please contact Anita Wright, Director of Transfer Services at SUNY Cobleskill.

Guthrie Pre-Medical Scholars Program
This is a guaranteed acceptance program involving Wilkes University, SUNY Upstate, the Binghamton Clinical Campus, and the Guthrie Health Care System. This program assures high school seniors of admission to the College of Medicine before they enter Wilkes University for undergraduate course work. To be considered, you must:

- Have a 1,200 combined SAT Scores or 27 ACT
- Obtain a competitive high school GPA rank in the top 10 percent of your high school class
- Reside in a rural county in the southern tier of New York State

Students in this program study the rural health care delivery system by completing clinical coursework and performing basic science research at Guthrie's Robert Packer Medical Center in Sayre, Pennsylvania. Eligibility information is available from Elleen Sharp, Pre-Health Advisor, Wilkes University.

Blackwell Medical Scholarship Program
This program is for high school students who are from rural areas, from underrepresented minority groups, or are among the first generation in their families to attend college. To be considered, you must:

- Have 1,250 combined SAT Scores (or 27 ACT)
- Have a minimum 90 percent high school GPA
- Demonstrate commitment to a career in medicine

Students accepted into this program will complete their undergraduate degree at Hobart and William Smith Colleges and are guaranteed admission to Upstate's College of Medicine, pending all program standards are met. More information is available from the Admissions Office or Laura Vanniel, Pre-Health Counselor at Hobart and William Smith Colleges.

Elmira College Program
This is a guaranteed acceptance program for first-year students at Elmira College who are interested in pursuing a career in medicine and meet academic and other eligibility requirements. Students accepted into this program will complete their undergraduate degree at Elmira College and then enter the College of Medicine at Upstate. More information is available from Dr. Larry Stevens, Pre-Health Advisor, Elmira College.

The Post-baccalaureate Program
This program is a 19-month program providing students with a Master's Degree in Medical Technology and the opportunity to improve their credentials and skills for entrance into medical school. Students who have been interviewed and denied admission into medical school at Upstate medical university school will be considered for admissions.

The Post-baccalaureate Program provides 45 credit hours of graduate coursework in the basic sciences (i.e., biochemistry, cell and molecular biology, genetics, immunology) and advanced coursework in the clinical laboratory sciences. A thesis proposal and thesis work are also part of the curriculum. Further, the curriculum contains internships in clinical laboratories providing the students with practical experience as well as developing the communication and professional skills needed to deal with patients and other health care professionals. The combination of coursework and clinical experience will be an excellent preparation for students entering medical school.

Stony Brook University Medical Center School of Medicine

Dr. Aldustus E. Jordan,
Associate Dean for Student and Minority Affairs
Stony Brook University School of Medicine
Health Sciences Center
Level 4, Room 147
Stony Brook, NY 11794-8436
631-444-2341; 631-444-8921 fax
aldustus.jordan@stonybrook.edu
www.stonybrookmedicalcenter.org/som

Recruitment

Recruitment visits are made upon request by undergraduate schools, student groups, and community organizations, or through contacts made by staff and students from Stony Brook University. Staff from the School of Medicine visit undergraduate institutions and summer programs, and also work closely with other campus groups in hosting visits from high school students from the Long Island and New York City area. Faculty, staff, and the Black and Latin Students Association are active participants in these activities.

Admissions

The admissions procedures for minority students are the same as those for all applicants to the School of Medicine. A subcommittee of the Admissions Committee reviews applications and provides an initial evaluation. Final admissions decisions are made by the full Admissions Committee. The subcommittee includes minority members from the Admissions Committee, students, and others.

Academic Support Programs

Academic assistance programs are available for all students. These include faculty advisement, student and faculty tutorials, and small-group seminars, all of which are available upon request by the student or by advisement to the student. Individual arrangements may be made for students who would benefit from different curricular arrangements.

Enrichment Programs

A one-week early academic pre-orientation is provided for entering students who need or desire an orientation to the curriculum. Students work with faculty and upperclass students and focus on anatomy and biochemistry.

Student Financial Assistance

All students admitted, who apply for financial consideration, are given financial assistance based on need and on available funds. Total financial counseling for student and or his/her parents is provided.

Educational Partnerships

The School of Medicine receives funding from the National Institutes of Health for the Minority High School Student Research Apprenticeship Program to provide research opportunities for high school students. Students are assigned to a scientific investigator for a six-week period. The Towards Early Admission to Medicine Program is a six-week program designed to increase student awareness of medical school and support activities such as academic coursework, research, career advising, and counseling, for minority students in grades 11 and 12. The Science and Technology Entry Program is designed for students in grades seven to 12 from local school districts with high enrollments of African American, Latino, and Native American students. The program has a six-week summer component as well as an academic year component.

The School of Medicine at Stony Brook University Medical Center
Applicants, First-Time Applicants, Matriculants by Gender, Race and Ethnicity, 2007-2008

	2007									2008								
	APP			F-time APP			MAT			APP			F-time APP			MAT		
	Women	Men	Total	Women	Men	Total	Women	Men	Total	Women	Men	Total	Women	Men	Total	Women	Men	Total
Hispanic/Latino																		
Cuban	13	10	23	10	9	19	0	1	1	11	9	20	10	7	17	3	2	5
Mexican American	18	14	32	16	9	25	1	1	2	21	13	34	17	8	25	0	0	0
Puerto Rican	21	22	43	17	21	38	1	1	2	17	15	32	14	13	27	0	1	1
Other Hispanic	59	54	113	52	42	94	2	0	2	58	65	123	49	51	100	1	0	1
Multiple Hispanic/Latino*	7	3	10	5	3	8	0	0	0	7	4	11	7	3	10	1	0	1
Subtotal	118	103	221	100	84	184	4	3	7	114	106	220	97	82	179	5	3	8
Non-Hispanic/Latino**																		
Black	182	104	286	137	89	226	1	2	3	154	90	244	116	63	179	6	6	12
Native American/AK	3	2	5	3	2	5	0	0	0	3	1	4	2	1	3	0	0	0
Native Hawaiian/OPI	10	8	18	9	6	15	0	0	0	8	4	12	5	2	7	0	0	0
White	798	881	1,679	657	683	1,340	28	27	55	793	972	1,765	637	741	1,378	28	36	64
Asian	499	474	973	393	370	763	22	24	46	536	532	1,068	418	355	773	16	20	36
Other Race	2	4	6	1	1	2	0	0	0	0	2	2	0	1	1	0	0	0
Multiple Race*	44	36	80	37	28	65	1	0	1	30	31	61	23	26	49	0	1	1
Unknown	28	29	57	26	25	51	0	2	2	52	63	115	49	57	106	1	1	2
Subtotal	1,566	1,538	3,104	1,263	1,204	2,467	52	55	107	1,576	1,695	3,271	1,250	1,246	2,496	51	64	115
Foreign	108	98	206	86	75	161	1	1	2	100	108	208	80	85	165	1	0	1
Total	1,792	1,739	3,531	1,449	1,363	2,812	57	59	116	1,790	1,909	3,699	1,427	1,413	2,840	57	67	124

*Since 2002, students can select more than one race and / or ethnicity. **Those who did not choose 'Hispanic/Latino' or 'Non-Hispanic/Latino' are listed under 'Non-Hispanic/Latino'. Data Source: AAMC Data Warehouse: Applicant-Matriculant File, as of 1/16/2009.

Students may receive college credit for successful course completion in selected areas. All of these programs are partnerships between the medical school, undergraduate campus, local school districts, and community-based agencies.

University at Buffalo School of Medicine and Biomedical Sciences, State University of New York

Dr. David A. Milling, Associate Dean for Multicultural Affairs
University at Buffalo School of Medicine and Biomedical Sciences, State University of New York
Office of Multicultural Affairs
3435 Main Street, Room 40 BEB
Buffalo, NY 14214-3013
716-829-2802; 716-829-2798 fax
sbudzillo@buffalo.edu

Recruitment

Recruitment of students underrepresented in medicine is coordinated through the Office of Multicultural Affairs. Our efforts focus on undergraduate institutions in New York State and the northeast region. Visits to undergraduate institutions and summer programs are conducted by the Assistant Dean for Multicultural Affairs and minority medical students. Multi-cultural Affairs staff and University of Buffalo Student National Medical Association members host visitations for local and regional high school and college groups.

Admissions

The SUNY/Buffalo School of Medicine participates in the American Medical College Application Service. All completed applications are evaluated by the Admissions Committee and a determination is made with regard to a personal interview. The interview is a prerequisite to admission and is the final stage of the admissions process. Multiple criteria are used to determine candidate eligibility for admissions. This allows minority students, as well as others, an opportunity to present their very best qualities to the Admissions Committee.

Academic Support Programs

Faculty advisement, tutoring, counseling, and study skills are offered to all students. Close communication regarding academic progress is maintained between the students, faculty, and Office of Medical Education. Additional academic assistance is always available for students experiencing difficulty.

Student Financial Aid

All accepted students are encouraged to apply for a scholarship and/or other financial assistance. Information regarding our scholarship program and other available financial opportunities is mailed to the student at the time of acceptance. Scholarships are awarded based on financial need and academic performance.

Educational Partnership

The Post-Baccalaureate Program is sponsored by the Associated Medical Schools of New York, a consortium of public and private medical schools in New York State. This program is housed at the State University of New York at Buffalo. The program is designed to bridge the gap between undergraduate education and matriculation into medical school. The year-long program addresses weaknesses in the student's preparation for medical school including instruction in study skills. The goal of the program is to increase the enrollment and retention of educationally qualified or economically disadvantaged students in New York State medical schools.

The Science and Technology Entry Program is a New York State initiative sponsored by the Associated Medical Schools of New York. The program is designed to acquaint and academically

University at Buffalo State University of New York School of Medicine & Biomedical Sciences
Applicants, First-Time Applicants, Matriculants by Gender, Race and Ethnicity, 2007-2008

	2007									2008								
	APP			F-time APP			MAT			APP			F-time APP			MAT		
	Women	Men	Total	Women	Men	Total	Women	Men	Total	Women	Men	Total	Women	Men	Total	Women	Men	Total
Hispanic/Latino																		
Cuban	13	10	23	11	8	19	1	0	1	8	9	17	5	7	12	0	0	0
Mexican American	25	21	46	19	15	34	0	0	0	18	16	34	15	11	26	1	0	1
Puerto Rican	20	12	32	17	11	28	0	0	0	12	11	23	10	11	21	0	0	0
Other Hispanic	46	50	96	31	34	65	0	1	1	47	60	107	37	40	77	0	0	0
Multiple Hispanic/Latino*	8	6	14	6	5	11	0	0	0	7	4	11	6	2	8	0	0	0
Subtotal	112	99	211	84	73	157	1	1	2	92	100	192	73	71	144	1	0	1
Non-Hispanic/Latino**																		
Black	125	81	206	93	63	156	0	2	2	122	65	187	85	50	135	3	1	4
Native American/AK	2	2	4	2	2	4	0	0	0	1	0	1	1	0	1	0	0	0
Native Hawaiian/OPI	9	7	16	9	6	15	0	0	0	9	5	14	6	3	9	0	0	0
White	871	1,001	1,872	685	742	1,427	43	47	90	818	1,078	1,896	614	766	1,380	51	43	94
Asian	613	647	1,260	463	454	917	30	11	41	606	652	1,258	430	413	843	19	13	32
Other Race	1	4	5	1	2	3	0	0	0	0	4	4	0	3	3	0	0	0
Multiple Race*	48	49	97	34	35	69	1	2	3	44	43	87	29	27	56	2	1	3
Unknown	20	32	52	18	26	44	0	1	1	47	55	102	44	47	91	1	1	2
Subtotal	1,689	1,823	3,512	1,305	1,330	2,635	74	63	137	1,647	1,902	3,549	1,209	1,309	2,518	76	59	135
Foreign	48	55	103	40	45	85	0	0	0	46	52	98	40	38	78	0	0	0
Total	1,849	1,977	3,826	1,429	1,448	2,877	75	64	139	1,785	2,054	3,839	1,322	1,418	2,740	77	59	136

*Since 2002, students can select more than one race and / or ethnicity. **Those who did not choose 'Hispanic/Latino' or 'Non-Hispanic/Latino' are listed under 'Non-Hispanic/Latino'. Data Source: AAMC Data Warehouse: Applicant-Matriculant File, as of 1/16/2009.

prepare high school students for subsequent admission into the health related and licensed professions. Students historically underrepresented in the health related and licensed professions in grades nine through 12 from Buffalo area high schools are targeted for participation in the program.

University of Rochester School of Medicine and Dentistry

Adrienne Morgan, Senior Director
The Center for Advocacy, Community Health, Education, and Diversity (CACHED)
University of Rochester Medical Center School of Medicine and Dentistry
Office of Medical Education
601 Elmwood Avenue, Box 601
Rochester, NY 14642
585-275-7203; 585-275-4172;
585-273-1016 fax
adrienne_morgan@urmc.
rochester.edu

Recruitment

The Center for Advocacy, Community Health, Education and Diversity (CACHED) and the University of Rochester Medical Center (URMC) mission is to meet the urgent need for underrepresented physicians in all aspects of the medical profession through an active recruitment program that seeks applicants for the M.D., Ph.D., and M.D./Ph.D., M.D./M.P.H., and M.D./M.B.A. programs. In closely coordinated efforts with the Office of Admissions and CACHED, campus visits and recruitment trips are made to career and summer programs and to meet pre-medical advisors and students. Undergraduate students are invited to tour the school and meet with faculty and/or students.

Admissions

URMC is interested in the composite profile of each applicant including his/her academic preparation, performance on the Medical College Admission Test (MCAT), personal background, experiences, commitment, and motivation. Applications are individually reviewed by the Admissions Committee consisting of faculty, administrators and students. Applicants invited to the school for interviews typically meet with faculty and students.

Early application is encouraged and the MCAT is required for admission. Applicants who receive fee waiver assistance from AAMC are eligible for the URMC fee waiver.

Academic Support Programs

The URMC Advisory Dean (AD) Program
The AD Program is designed to enhance the personal and professional development of medical students throughout the course of their undergraduate medical education. This program helps facilitate the many transitions that students face during their medical school tenure, including from college student to medical student, classroom to clinic office, and medical school to residency. The interaction of each Advisory Dean with a small cohort of students (25) in each class helps to foster trusting relationships, enhance students' personal development, and ultimately assists in each student's professional growth and development in medicine. The Advisory Dean system is a model advising program for undergraduate medical education.

Peer Tutoring
As part of the institutional effort to nurture and assist students, tutoring and study skills enhancement are provided free of charge. The peer tutorial service has been established to assist students with basic science strand courses. In addition to providing student tutors who have developed successful approaches to mastering the material, peer tutor sessions present material in a manner that is consistent with individual students' learning styles.

University of Rochester School of Medicine and Dentistry
Applicants, First-Time Applicants, Matriculants by Gender, Race and Ethnicity, 2007-2008

| | | 2007 | | | | | | | | | 2008 | | | | | | | |
| | APP | | | F-time APP | | | MAT | | | APP | | | F-time APP | | | MAT | | |
	Wo-men	Men	Total	Wo-men	Men	Total	Wo-men	Men	Total	Wo-men	Men	Total	Wo-men	Men	Total	Wo-men	Men	Total
Hispanic/Latino																		
Cuban	17	8	25	14	7	21	0	0	0	10	10	20	9	9	18	0	0	0
Mexican American	31	30	61	26	20	46	1	1	2	22	28	50	18	22	40	1	1	2
Puerto Rican	12	12	24	10	11	21	0	1	1	12	12	24	12	12	24	1	1	2
Other Hispanic	45	48	93	37	33	70	1	0	1	49	62	111	45	44	89	3	3	6
Multiple Hispanic/Latino*	8	1	9	7	1	8	0	0	0	10	4	14	9	3	12	0	0	0
Subtotal	113	99	212	94	72	166	2	2	4	103	116	219	93	90	183	5	5	10
Non-Hispanic/Latino**																		
Black	100	71	171	67	54	121	4	6	10	120	76	196	85	57	142	8	2	10
Native American/AK	1	2	3	1	2	3	0	0	0	3	2	5	3	2	5	0	0	0
Native Hawaiian/OPI	12	7	19	11	7	18	0	0	0	7	4	11	5	4	9	0	0	0
White	1,125	1,214	2,339	926	937	1,863	30	31	61	1,134	1,433	2,567	904	1,079	1,983	30	35	65
Asian	720	707	1,427	570	526	1,096	8	13	21	705	782	1,487	537	544	1,081	8	7	15
Other Race	1	4	5	1	2	3	0	0	0	2	4	6	2	4	6	0	0	0
Multiple Race*	55	54	109	45	38	83	1	1	2	65	53	118	45	38	83	1	1	2
Unknown	28	31	59	27	27	54	3	0	3	55	89	144	53	76	129	2	0	2
Subtotal	2,042	2,090	4,132	1,648	1,593	3,241	46	51	97	2,091	2,443	4,534	1,634	1,804	3,438	49	45	94
Foreign	6	3	9	3	3	6	0	0	0	7	8	15	5	6	11	0	0	0
Total	2,161	2,192	4,353	1,745	1,668	3,413	48	53	101	2,201	2,567	4,768	1,732	1,900	3,632	54	50	104

*Since 2002, students can select more than one race and / or ethnicity. **Those who did not choose 'Hispanic/Latino' or 'Non-Hispanic/Latino' are listed under 'Non-Hispanic/Latino'. Data Source: AAMC Data Warehouse: Applicant-Matriculant File, as of 1/16/2009.

The Learning Assistance Center is also available to assist students in assessing and enhancing the effectiveness of their study skills and techniques. In particular, assistance is available to help students with organizing information for review, note taking, problem-solving skills.

Enrichment Programs

The CACHED coordinates the Community Outreach, International Medicine, and Student Research Programs. These programs broaden the scope of medical education to include health, social, and academic experiences beyond the classroom.

The University of Rochester Medical Center also sponsors pipeline programs that are designed to enhance the preparation of students from underrepresented groups and disadvantaged backgrounds for careers in the biomedical sciences and in the health professions.

Summer Research Fellowship Program (SURF)

SURF is an eight-week program designed to enhance the competitiveness of undergraduate students interested in careers in the biomedical sciences and the health professions and who belong to groups historically underrepresented within these areas. Students are individually matched with preceptors (clinicians and scientists) and conduct biomedical and clinically focused research in medical center laboratories. Participants also attend evening presentations, departmental seminars, conferences, and lectures; MCAT prep classes; problem-based learning (PBL) sessions; gross anatomy lectures and labs; and perform weekly rotations in the Emergency Medicine Department. Applicants must have an introduction to their scientific field of interest and must have completed at least two years of college.

Science and Technology Entry Program (STEP)

The Science and Technology Entry Program (STEP) is an academic and career development program designed to stimulate and maintain participants' interest in career opportunities in the sciences, medicine, and the health professions. This program targets students in grades eight through 12. STEP participants are exposed to a variety of academic and professional development opportunities to enhance their problem-solving, critical-thinking, and test-taking skills. STEP students have the opportunity to work directly with physicians, technical staff, certified teachers, and medical and graduate students.

Student Financial Assistance

The URMC offers financial aid on the basis of need and works closely with all granting agencies. The Office of Financial Aid's primary goal is to distribute scholarships and loans so that no student will be deprived of a medical education at Rochester because of unmet financial need. About 80 percent of Rochester students finance their medical education through the use of low-cost student loans. For this reason, a variety of debt management services are provided, designed to support decision making from the beginning to the end of training and throughout the entire repayment process.

Educational Partnerships

Rochester sponsors several limited-access special admissions programs. One program, Rochester Early Medical Scholars Program (REMS), with the undergraduate campus of the university, provides provisional early acceptance to a very select and highly qualified group of high school students who are accepted by the University for Undergraduate Study. Other affiliations include early assurance post-baccalaureate programs with the Associated Medical Schools of New York, Bryn Mawr and Johns Hopkins.

The Brody School of Medicine at East Carolina University

Dr. Virginia D. Hardy, Senior Associate Dean, Academic Affairs
The Brody School of Medicine at East Carolina University
AD47 Brody Medical Sciences Building
600 Moye Boulevard
Greenville, NC 27893
252-744-3078; 252-744-3073 fax
hardyv@ecu.edu
www.ecu.edu/med

Recruitment

The Academic Support and Enrichment Center (ASEC) of The Brody School of Medicine plays an integral role in increasing the number of underrepresented minorities in medicine. A counselor coordinates activities that include providing information about opportunities at The Brody School of Medicine, inviting interested individuals and groups to visit the medical school, visiting undergraduate institutions in North Carolina and Virginia with an emphasis on the Historically Black Colleges and Universities, and assisting prospective minority medical

students in completing the application materials for admission to medical school. Medical students, the Dean of Admissions, faculty from the Academic Support and Enrichment Center, and other faculty participate in the various activities on and off campus.

Annual workshops for pre-medical advisors are conducted on the campus of The Brody School of Medicine. Undergraduate students have access to academic assessment, interventions and psychoeducational workshops. Secondary school students are provided with life and career planning opportunities that include skill enhancement workshops and health career education. For additional information, contact the Academic Support and Enrichment Center, Brody School of Medicine, *(www.ecu.edu/ascc)*, 252-744-2500.

Admissions

The Admissions Committee of The Brody School of Medicine includes members who represent a variety of backgrounds and medical school responsibilities. The committee gives serious consideration to applicants who are members of minority groups and/or have disadvantaged backgrounds. Addi-

tional contact is available for minority students. The Admissions Committee seeks to admit a class that is educationally competent and represents diverse backgrounds. To achieve this diverse class, different factors, such as intellectual, clinical, personal, and social, are used in the selection process.

As a state-supported medical school, The Brody School of Medicine at East Carolina University has an obligation to educate students who have an interest in serving the medical needs of North Carolina. Therefore, preference is given to qualified residents of North Carolina. The School of Medicine strives to include students from a variety of geographical, economic, and ethnic groups. The application procedure includes the submission of a completed application to the American Medical College Application Service (AMCAS). The application forms may be obtained from the Internet at *(www.aamc.org/students)*. The Brody School of Medicine may request the applicant to submit a supplementary application. The supplemental application includes an application form, a statement of residence form, at least three academic letters of recommendation or one preprofessional com-

Brody School of Medicine at East Carolina University
Applicants, First-Time Applicants, Matriculants by Gender, Race and Ethnicity, 2007-2008

		2007 APP			2007 F-time APP			2007 MAT			2008 APP			2008 F-time APP			2008 MAT		
		Women	Men	Total	Women	Men	Total	Women	Men	Total	Women	Men	Total	Women	Men	Total	Women	Men	Total
Hispanic/Latino																			
Cuban		0	1	1	0	1	1	0	0	0	0	2	2	0	2	2	0	0	0
Mexican American		0	2	2	0	1	1	0	0	0	1	0	1	1	0	1	0	0	0
Puerto Rican		2	1	3	2	1	3	0	0	0	1	2	3	0	0	0	0	0	0
Other Hispanic		5	7	12	3	5	8	2	2	4	8	7	15	5	3	8	0	1	1
Multiple Hispanic/Latino*		2	0	2	1	0	1	0	0	0	0	1	1	0	1	1	0	0	0
Subtotal		9	11	20	6	8	14	2	2	4	10	12	22	6	6	12	0	1	1
Non-Hispanic/Latino																			
Black		54	22	76	38	14	52	4	4	8	78	25	103	50	19	69	8	3	11
Native American/AK		3	3	6	3	2	5	0	1	1	4	6	10	3	5	8	1	1	2
Native Hawaiian/OPI		2	0	2	1	0	1	0	0	0	0	1	1	0	0	0	0	0	0
White		264	305	569	189	211	400	24	24	48	265	331	596	186	215	401	23	25	48
Asian		53	68	121	36	45	81	5	5	10	67	50	117	49	29	78	3	6	9
Multiple Race*		7	10	17	6	7	13	2	0	2	9	6	15	7	3	10	1	0	1
Unknown		4	0	4	4	0	4	0	0	0	8	5	13	8	5	13	2	2	4
Subtotal		387	408	795	277	279	556	35	34	69	431	424	855	303	276	579	38	37	75
Foreign		0	0	0	0	0	0	0	0	0	1	0	1	1	0	1	0	0	0
Total		396	419	815	283	287	570	37	36	73	442	436	878	310	282	592	38	38	76

*Since 2002, students can select more than one race and / or ethnicity. **Those who did not choose 'Hispanic/Latino' or 'Non-Hispanic/Latino' are listed under 'Non-Hispanic/Latino'. Data Source: AAMC Data Warehouse: Applicant-Matriculant File, as of 1/16/2009.

mittee evaluation, a recent photograph, and an application fee of $60.00. In addition, a handwritten narrative is requested detailing the following information: the applicant's reason for desiring a career in medicine, a vocational area of interest, reaction to contemporary life, and future professional aspirations.

Applicants are required to take the Medical College Admission Test (MCAT). It should be taken in the spring and no later than the fall semester of the year prior to the desired matriculation date in medical school. Most successful applicants have earned an undergraduate degree. Prior to matriculation, the applicant must have the equivalent of at least three years of acceptable study at an accredited college or university. Regardless of major field of study, applicants must have completed one year of general biology or zoology (including laboratory), general chemistry (including laboratory), organic chemistry (including laboratories), physics (including laboratory), and English. Even though they are not required, additional courses in genetics, biostatistics, social sciences, humanities, and English are recommended.

Academic Support Programs

Academic support services are available at the Academic Support and Enrichment Center (ASEC). Services include counseling, academic enrichment sessions, reading skills assistance, and learning skills instruction.

Counseling is available in response to the individual needs of the student. Areas of counseling include personal, social, career, financial, and academic concerns. Personal development services and multicultural awareness seminars are offered to all students. The Student National Medical Association collaborates with the Academic Support and Enrichment Center to provide various activities and information. Academic services include assessment, interventions and counseling related to academic performance anxiety, time management, reading and study skills,

licensure preparation, and learning and cognitive development. Academic facilitators or tutors are assigned to students based on academic and attitudinal factors. Reading and learning assistance strengthens reading speed and comprehension, study techniques, note-taking techniques, and test-taking skills.

The Academic Support and Enrichment Center has licensed doctoral-level counselors, an administrative assistant, and one secretary. During the summer, School of Medicine faculty members teach in the ASEC Summer Program for Future Doctors. Faculty contributions to the summer program complement, enhance, and expand the work of the ASEC staff.

Enrichment Programs
Summer Program for Future Doctors
The ASEC Summer Program for Future Doctors (SPFD) at The Brody School of Medicine at East Carolina University has an impressive record in preparing students for admission to medical school. The SPFD includes basic sciences as well as cognitive skill development that are necessary for medical school success. The program provides students with a glimpse into the pedagogical style and demands of the medical school curriculum. The Summer Program for Future Doctors introduces participants to the quality and quantity of work that medical schools expect from students. The program helps participants overcome obstacles caused by either educational disadvantage or cultural deprivation, and it improves the students' learning and behavioral skills for success in medical school. Eligible participants for the Summer Program for Future Doctors are students from the sophomore through the graduate level of college. Minority, disadvantaged, and non-traditional students given preference.

The content of the eight-week, tuition-free summer program concentrates on problem-solving experiences that help the student to identify, analyze, and synthesize concepts relevant to understanding complex subject matter. In-

structional modules include basic science courses, medical ethics, MCAT review, along with the opportunity to have practical clinical experience.

The other component of the SPFD is designed for incoming first-year students. The program provides medical students an exposure to the medical school curriculum and the chance to enhance their learning, studying, and test-taking skills.

Student Financial Assistance
Financially disadvantaged students should submit an application for financial assistance as soon as applications become available.

Financial needs of economically disadvantaged students can be met through loans and scholarships. The available loans include, but are not limited to, the Federal Perkins Loan; the Federal Stafford Loan; Primary Care Loan; the Scholarship for Disadvantaged Students; National Health Service Corps; North Carolina Student Loan Program for Health, Science and Mathematics; the North Carolina Academy of Family Physicians Foundation Scholarship Loan; and the Armed Forces Health Professions Scholarship Programs. Other financial aid opportunities are the Board of Governors Medical Scholarship, the Brody Scholarship Program, the Fullerton Scholarship, and the Southern Medical Association of Scholarship.

For additional information about financial aid, contact Kelly Lancaster, Director of Financial Aid and Student Services, Brody School of Medicine at East Carolina University, 252-744-2278; *(lancasterk@ecu.edu)*.

Educational Partnerships
The Brody School of Medicine collaborates with various entities to accomplish its mission. The Brody School of Medicine works closely with the 16 Historically Black Colleges and Universities to provide opportunities and seminars for professional and educational development of pre-medical students. The Brody School of Medicine partners with

local school systems to expose both students and educators to the requirements of medical school and other health careers. The Eastern Area Health Education Center plays a significant role in helping to provide educational, clinical, and professional opportunities to prospective and current students.

Duke University School of Medicine

Dr. Delbert R. Wigfall, Associate
Dean of Medical Education
Associate Clinical, Professor
of Pediatrics
Director, Multicultural
Resource Center
Division of Pediatric Nephrology
Duke University School of Medicine
Box 3005, Rm 0109, DS Purple Zone
Durham, NC 27710
919-668-1670; 919-684-2593 fax
wigfa001@mc.duke.edu
www.medschool.duke.edu

Recruitment

Duke University School of Medicine is committed to strong minority representation in the student body. Faculty and students visit summer enrichment programs and undergraduate colleges where minority candidates are present in significant numbers. This university offers a summer program for talented high school students and a program for undergraduates interested in health science careers (the Summer Medical and Dental Education Program). All qualified minority candidates for medical school are invited to the campus for an interview and formal and informal interaction with minority students and minority faculty. The Dean's Office, the Office of Admissions, and many regional representatives are all involved in helping minority candidates consider Duke University School of Medicine as a place where their academic education will be excellent and their personal needs will be met.

Admissions

All applications are screened by two members of the Committee on Admissions. Attention is paid to evidence of leadership skills, commitment to a medical career, and the candidate's faculty recommendations, in addition to academic record and Medical College Admission Test scores. Students with significant educational disadvantage in their K-12 education are given especially careful consideration as their early academic performance in college may have been negatively affected. Evidence of greater success in later college work is favorably reviewed.

Academic Support Program

All medical school matriculants are assigned to an Associate Dean who works with the student during all four years of medical school. Students also obtain academic advice from study track directors and research preceptors during their third year. Individual and group tutors are available to students requesting help at no cost. There are no special programs for retention of minority students. The attrition rate is less than 1 percent.

Enrichment Programs

See Recruitment for more information.

Student Financial Assistance

In addition to being eligible for a number of merit awards at Duke University School of Medicine, the following two scholarships are specifically for minority students: The Family Dollar Merit Award is available to a North Carolina minority student enrolled at Duke University School of Medicine and seven Dean's Tuition Merit Awards are available each year to minority students based on prior academic achievement. The scholarships are in the amount of full tuition, and they are annually renewable based on satisfactory academic progress.

Duke University School of Medicine
Applicants, First-Time Applicants, Matriculants by Gender, Race and Ethnicity, 2007-2008

	2007									2008								
	APP			F-time APP			MAT			APP			F-time APP			MAT		
	Wo-men	Men	Total	Wo-men	Men	Total	Wo-men	Men	Total	Wo-men	Men	Total	Wo-men	Men	Total	Wo-men	Men	Total
Hispanic/Latino																		
Cuban	14	23	37	13	18	31	0	2	2	17	21	38	12	18	30	0	2	2
Mexican American	44	49	93	37	44	81	0	0	0	39	51	90	32	45	77	0	0	0
Puerto Rican	21	25	46	19	21	40	0	0	0	16	15	31	12	12	24	0	0	0
Other Hispanic	57	61	118	50	51	101	0	0	0	51	68	119	47	59	106	0	0	0
Multiple Hispanic/Latino*	11	9	20	10	5	15	0	0	0	12	9	21	12	7	19	1	0	1
Subtotal	147	167	314	129	139	268	0	2	2	135	164	299	115	141	256	1	2	3
Non-Hispanic/Latino**																		
Black	261	142	403	214	120	334	14	7	21	264	146	410	212	117	329	16	2	18
Native American/AK	7	7	14	6	6	12	0	0	0	6	8	14	5	7	12	0	0	0
Native Hawaiian/OPI	9	5	14	7	4	11	0	0	0	9	2	11	7	1	8	0	0	0
White	1,064	1,708	2,772	936	1,466	2,402	18	30	48	1,047	1,645	2,692	917	1,403	2,320	9	36	45
Asian	566	706	1,272	504	595	1,099	13	11	24	478	686	1,164	405	552	957	14	10	24
Other Race	2	3	5	2	3	5	0	0	0	3	1	4	1	0	1	1	0	1
Multiple Race*	67	79	146	61	63	124	1	0	1	73	71	144	63	53	116	0	1	1
Unknown	27	42	69	27	39	66	0	0	0	59	90	149	57	82	139	1	1	2
Subtotal	2,003	2,692	4,695	1,757	2,296	4,053	46	48	94	1,939	2,649	4,588	1,667	2,215	3,882	41	50	91
Foreign	134	166	300	109	137	246	3	1	4	149	165	314	130	130	260	6	0	6
Total	2,284	3,025	5,309	1,995	2,572	4,567	49	51	100	2,223	2,978	5,201	1,912	2,486	4,398	48	52	100

*Since 2002, students can select more than one race and / or ethnicity. **Those who did not choose 'Hispanic/Latino' or 'Non-Hispanic/Latino' are listed under 'Non-Hispanic/Latino'. Data Source: AAMC Data Warehouse: Applicant-Matriculant File, as of 1/16/2009.

Twenty North Carolina Board of Governors Medical Scholarships are awarded each year to financially disadvantaged state residents who enroll in one of the four medical schools in the state. Recipients are selected from qualified nominations submitted by one of the four medical schools in the state. The award pays full tuition, fees, and a $5,000 stipend each year based on satisfactory academic progress.

The Student Loan Program for Health, Science, and Math provides a $7,500 per year loan to financially needy North Carolinians who enroll in medical school. After completion of residency, the recipient's loan is forgiven on a year-of-service for a year-of-funding basis to those who serve in an eligible practice location within the state. Duke University School of Medicine participates in the federally-funded First Year Scholarship for Students of Exceptional Need and Financial Aid for Disadvantaged Health Professions Students programs. The school's financial aid package for qualified North Carolinians, who document financial need, is based on a tuition grant up to $11,750. Financial need in excess of $11,750 must come next from a $5,000 Stafford Student Loan. Need in excess of $16,750 comes from one-half school grant and one-half loan. The package for students outside North Carolina is based on a $5,000 Stafford Student Loan. Financial need in excess of $5,000 comes from one-half school grant and one-half from loan up to $25,000. Need in excess of $25,000 is funded with three-fourths grant and one-fourth loan.

Educational Partnerships
Duke University has begun specific partnerships with the Durham County School System through its junior and senior high magnet programs. In addition, specific programs are being initiated with Hillside High School and North Carolina Central University to encourage and mentor minority medical students who desire pursuing careers in medical science.

University of North Carolina at Chapel Hill School of Medicine

Larry Keith, Assistant Dean of Admissions and Director of Special Programs
University of North Carolina at Chapel Hill School of Medicine
322 MacNider Building, CB #7530
Chapel Hill, NC 27599-7530
919-966-7673; 919-966-7734 fax
med-info@listserv.med.unc.edu
www.med.unc.edu/medprogram

Recruitment

The University of North Carolina School of Medicine actively recruits minority students in the state, region, and nation. Primarily, the recruitment of minority students is directed at undergraduate institutions with large numbers of economically disadvantaged North Carolina residents. Information seminars are conducted for many pre-college programs. The Assistant Dean of Admissions and Director of Special Programs, Larry Keith, and Recruitment Specialist, Dr. Nerissa Price accompanied by volunteer medical students, regularly visit these institutions to conduct group and individual advisory sessions with students enrolled in science and pre-medical programs. Prospective students are encouraged to visit the campus and explore their interests with members of the dean's staff, faculty, and members of the Student National Medical Association.

Workshops for pre-medical advisors from colleges and universities throughout the region are periodically held on campus. Admissions Committee members regularly participate in events sponsored by pre-medical student organizations.

Admissions

The University of North Carolina (UNC) at Chapel Hill School of Medicine is committed to the principle of equal opportunity. It is the policy of the university not to discriminate on the basis of race, sex, color, national origin, religion, or handicap with regard to its students, employees, or applicants for admission or employment. Admission preference is given to North Carolina residents.

It is the duty of the Admissions Committee, acting for the dean and the faculty, to select the students who, in their judgment, will best provide excellence and beneficial diversity in the student body. In making its selections, the committee considers evidence of each candidate's motivation, maturity, industry, and integrity, as well as the scholastic record. To provide a diverse student body, the committee considers a variety of individual qualifications including non-academic accomplishments and special talents; work and service experience; research experience; resourcefulness and a history of overcoming a disadvantaged background; demonstrated compassion and concern for the welfare of others; the ability to establish rapport and communicate with others; and racial, ethnic, and economic background. No single factor is given overriding emphasis.

Members of the Admissions Committee are appointed from the basic science faculty, the clinical faculty, and physicians in private practice. Minority and female representation on the committee is maintained. There is medical student representation on the committee and in the admissions process.

University of North Carolina at Chapel Hill School of Medicine
Applicants, First-Time Applicants, Matriculants by Gender, Race and Ethnicity, 2007-2008

	2007									2008								
	APP			F-time APP			MAT			APP			F-time APP			MAT		
	Wo-men	Men	Total	Wo-men	Men	Total	Wo-men	Men	Total	Wo-men	Men	Total	Wo-men	Men	Total	Wo-men	Men	Total
Hispanic/Latino																		
Cuban	5	11	16	4	10	14	0	0	0	23	16	39	18	13	31	0	0	0
Mexican American	20	20	40	16	13	29	1	0	1	21	31	52	17	27	44	1	0	1
Puerto Rican	14	19	33	11	17	28	1	0	1	10	12	22	8	9	17	0	0	0
Other Hispanic	51	42	93	38	34	72	1	0	1	45	39	84	37	29	66	2	0	2
Multiple Hispanic/Latino*	6	3	9	5	2	7	0	0	0	7	4	11	7	3	10	0	0	0
Subtotal	96	95	191	74	76	150	3	0	3	106	102	208	87	81	168	3	0	3
Non-Hispanic/Latino**																		
Black	274	117	391	213	96	309	11	6	17	267	118	385	209	97	306	16	5	21
Native American/AK	9	5	14	7	5	12	0	0	0	7	10	17	5	9	14	0	0	0
Native Hawaiian/OPI	4	0	4	3	0	3	0	0	0	3	4	7	3	2	5	0	0	0
White	1,103	1,331	2,434	943	1,069	2,012	51	62	113	1,037	1,353	2,390	869	1,068	1,937	54	65	119
Asian	305	359	664	247	275	522	13	9	22	310	344	654	253	266	519	11	4	15
Other Race	1	4	5	1	3	4	0	0	0	1	3	4	1	2	3	0	0	0
Multiple Race*	57	48	105	51	37	88	3	2	5	52	51	103	43	35	78	2	0	2
Unknown	15	12	27	15	12	27	1	0	1	35	55	90	34	51	85	0	0	0
Subtotal	1,768	1,876	3,644	1,480	1,497	2,977	79	79	158	1,712	1,938	3,650	1,417	1,530	2,947	83	74	157
Foreign	55	75	130	42	60	102	0	0	0	79	85	164	60	64	124	0	0	0
Total	1,919	2,046	3,965	1,596	1,633	3,229	82	79	161	1,897	2,125	4,022	1,564	1,675	3,239	86	74	160

*Since 2002, students can select more than one race and / or ethnicity. **Those who did not choose 'Hispanic/Latino' or 'Non-Hispanic/Latino' are listed under 'Non-Hispanic/Latino'. Data Source: AAMC Data Warehouse: Applicant-Matriculant File, as of 1/16/2009.

Academic Support Programs

Academic Assistance Program
The Associate Dean for Student Affairs is director of this program, which provides tutorial assistance to students. Advanced graduate students and medical students, or postdoctoral fellows and house staff officers, who are certified by the course directors, provide tutoring. Tutors are paid by the Office of Student Affairs. The Associate Dean monitors all students' academic progress, counsels them, and directs them to resources within the medical school and university for academic assistance.

Summer Review Program
This program, directed by the associate dean, is designed for students who have failed a limited number of courses in the first or second year of medical school. Faculty is available during the summer to assist the student in reviewing the courses that were failed. The student is retested in the course at the end of the summer and promoted after successful completion of the program.

The Associate Dean for Student Affairs works directly with class advisors to advise students on academic matters. Students are assigned to Faculty Advisors upon matriculation (ratio of one per four students). Faculty Advisors serve as student advocates and assist students with their academic and non-academic adjustment to medical school. The Associate Dean for Student Affairs reports to class advisors on the academic progress of their assigned students.

A Learning Skills and Assessment Laboratory is available to any student seeking to improve study and other academic skills.

The Associate Dean for Student Affairs identifies and directs students to academic enrichment programs such as research and foreign travel experiences.

Enrichment Programs

Medical Education Development (MED) Program
In operation since 1974, with a cumulative total of nearly 2,288 participants as of 2008, this nine-week program is committed to expanding opportunities for students from non-traditional backgrounds. It provides a chance to enhance academic credentials, while preparing for admission, and increases personal and academic skills for coping with professional training. Approximately 90 percent of former participants have successfully entered health professional schools. Among those who were North Carolina residents, former participants have represented 72 percent of minority matriculants to the UNC Schools of Medicine and Dentistry.

Each summer, the program enrolls 75 to 80 students who show educational and professional promise and a strong commitment to a health career, but who have had limited opportunities in the past that may place them at a disadvantage in competing for admission and in adjusting to medical or dental school. Priority is given to North Carolina residents, typically leaving 12 to 15 spaces for out-of-state applicants. Generally, 10 to 15 percent of participants are new matriculants to the UNC Schools of Medicine and Dentistry. The remainder are rising college seniors or postgraduates preparing to apply to medical or dental school the following fall. A minimum grade-point average of 2.7 is recommended for realistic consideration, and it is highly desirable, although not required, for applicants to take the Medical College Admission Test or DAT in the spring session unless already available for counseling purposes. Financial aid is available on the basis of demonstrated need. A copy of the Financial Aid Form of the College Scholarship Service is required.

The program simulates the experience of beginning medical or dental studies including over 217 hours of basic medical sciences. Courses in gross anatomy, histology, microbiology/immunology, MCAT/DAT Prep, and clinical biochemistry, taught by regular medical faculty and KAPLAN, introduce students to the intense pace and volume of a medical or dental curriculum. These courses are integrated with individualized work or learning, study, reading, and test-taking skills requisite to success in professional education. Other activities include seminars on clinical or health care issues; pre-professional workshops and counseling; exposure to health facilities; and regular contact with enrolled professional students, faculty, and other members of the professional community.

Support for the program comes from school and state resources. For information contact Georgia Njagu, Business Services Coordinator, CB# 7530/322 MacNider Building, University of North Carolina School of Medicine, Chapel Hill, NC 27599-7530, *med-info@listserv.med.unc.edu*, 919-966-7673. Application deadline is February 15.

Student Financial Assistance

The Medical School Student Aid Committee, with the approval of the dean, is responsible for recommending the recipients of school scholarships and loans. The University of North Carolina at Chapel Hill School of Medicine has long upheld a tradition of helping individuals of modest financial means to reach their full potential. In accord with this tradition, financial assistance is available in a variety of forms to supplement funds provided by family, savings, summer work, and other sources. The medical school has a well-established scholarship program to supplement state and federal loans. Also, the admissions office may waive the supplementary application fee for disadvantaged students.

To provide increased medical education opportunities for minorities and disadvantaged students, the medical school participates in the Minority Presence Program and the North Carolina Board of Governors' Medical Scholarship Program. Minority presence is need-based for residents of North Carolina and is primarily used as an incentive for recruitment purposes. The Board of Governors was established in the spring of 1974 by the North Carolina General Assembly. It is a four-year scholarship that provides full tuition, fees, and an annual stipend for selected students.

Educational Partnerships

The Office of Educational Development at UNC School of Medicine, through a collaborative partnership with UNC School of Dentistry, six undergraduate campuses of the UNC System, an inter-institutional health careers program at the UNC System, a medical student organization, three public school systems, and nine regional Area Health Education Centers (AHECs), will conduct activities to increase the number of disadvantaged students entering the health professions with the ultimate aim of improving access to and quality of health care for disadvantaged North Carolinians.

Wake Forest University Health Services School of Medicine

Dr. Brenda Latham-Sadler, Assistant Dean for Student Services
Director, Office of Diversity & Development Initiatives
Wake Forest University Health Services School of Medicine
Medical Center Boulevard
Winston-Salem, NC 27157-1037
336-716-4271; 336-716-5807 fax
http://www1.wfubmc.edu/
MDProgram
http://www1.wfubmc.edu/
MDProgram/Student+Services/
diversity

Recruitment

The director and staff of the Office of Diversity and Development Initiatives, as well as students, participate in special career day programs and panel discussions at high schools, colleges, and universities. Historically Black Colleges and Universities (HBCUs) are also visited. Wake Forest University School of Medicine annually hosts a Medical and Allied Health Professions Seminar for minority students from colleges throughout North

Carolina. An extensive recruitment program is maintained at the community, middle and high school, and undergraduate levels through the Office of Diversity and Development Initiatives in conjunction with Northwest AHEC Wake Forest University School of Medicine, Office of Student Services, Office of Medical Student Admissions, and Diversity and Development Initiatives. These efforts strive to provide the best service to prospective medical students by recruiting and selecting from medical school applicants a diverse population representative of our society who best reflect the core mission of Wake Forest University School of Medicine and who desire to learn according to the goals defined by the curriculum.

Admissions

Wake Forest University School of Medicine participates in the American Medical College Application Service (AMCAS) of the Association of American Medical Colleges. Formal application to the first-year class must be submitted through AMCAS. Applications are received from AMCAS from July 1 through the November 1 deadline. Upon receipt, the applications are considered by the Committee on Admissions (COA), composed of 17

voting members and four advisory members selected by the dean from a variety of disciplines and clinical areas. All faculty members hold either a Ph.D. or M.D. degree. Diversity is also sought for composition of this committee.

All applicants are screened using a formula that considers GPA, MCAT scores, and the undergraduate institution attended. Competitive applicants are sent a secondary application and non-competitive applicants are rejected. The secondary application asks for more detailed information, demographics, pre-college test scores, a processing fee, and evaluations from either a pre-medical committee or two professors–one science and one non-science. Completed applications are then reviewed and placed in interview pools according to the competitiveness of the completed application. Applicants are then selected from the top interview pool for interview. After the interview, the interviewers make recommendations and vote. These votes and recommendations are taken to the Admissions Committee that then considers each interviewed applicant and votes. Final decisions are then made from the committee's cumulative vote report and offers made.

Wake Forest University School of Medicine
Applicants, First-Time Applicants, Matriculants by Gender, Race and Ethnicity, 2007-2008

	2007 APP Women	2007 APP Men	2007 APP Total	2007 F-time APP Women	2007 F-time APP Men	2007 F-time APP Total	2007 MAT Women	2007 MAT Men	2007 MAT Total	2008 APP Women	2008 APP Men	2008 APP Total	2008 F-time APP Women	2008 F-time APP Men	2008 F-time APP Total	2008 MAT Women	2008 MAT Men	2008 MAT Total
Hispanic/Latino																		
Cuban	19	28	47	12	23	35	0	0	0	14	32	46	10	27	37	0	0	0
Mexican American	44	39	83	34	30	64	2	1	3	35	53	88	28	40	68	0	1	1
Puerto Rican	15	13	28	10	11	21	1	0	1	17	25	42	15	20	35	0	1	1
Other Hispanic	59	73	132	44	59	103	0	1	1	85	77	162	64	57	121	0	0	0
Multiple Hispanic/Latino*	15	6	21	12	4	16	0	0	0	13	7	20	11	2	13	0	0	0
Subtotal	152	159	311	112	127	239	3	2	5	164	194	358	128	146	274	0	2	2
Non-Hispanic/Latino**																		
Black	323	153	476	238	122	360	7	2	9	277	140	417	201	107	308	4	3	7
Native American/AK	8	6	14	7	6	13	0	0	0	6	12	18	5	9	14	0	1	1
Native Hawaiian/OPI	4	6	10	4	6	10	0	0	0	10	4	14	5	3	8	0	0	0
White	2,040	2,460	4,500	1,675	1,876	3,551	43	43	86	1,827	2,606	4,433	1,442	1,960	3,402	29	54	83
Asian	735	807	1,542	536	588	1,124	5	11	16	733	803	1,536	516	536	1,052	5	6	11
Other Race	3	3	6	0	1	1	0	0	0	1	5	6	1	3	4	0	0	0
Multiple Race*	78	83	161	60	60	120	0	1	1	74	94	168	62	64	126	4	4	8
Unknown	25	35	60	25	31	56	0	0	0	64	99	163	61	85	146	2	3	5
Subtotal	3,216	3,553	6,769	2,545	2,690	5,235	55	57	112	2,992	3,763	6,755	2,293	2,767	5,060	44	71	115
Foreign	203	202	405	161	153	314	1	2	3	182	207	389	128	153	281	3	0	3
Total	3,571	3,914	7,485	2,818	2,970	5,788	59	61	120	3,338	4,164	7,502	2,549	3,066	5,615	47	73	120

*Since 2002, students can select more than one race and / or ethnicity. **Those who did not choose 'Hispanic/Latino' or 'Non-Hispanic/Latino' are listed under 'Non-Hispanic/Latino'. Data Source: AAMC Data Warehouse: Applicant-Matriculant File, as of 1/16/2009.

An applicant, who is accepted, is asked to respond in writing within two weeks. Upon acceptance of an offer, a holding place fee must be submitted. This fee, which is credited towards tuition, is refundable until May 15th.

Factors considered for admissions include academic achievement, personal qualifications, evaluation by the pre-medical evaluators, state of residence, and with appropriate attention to diversity with regard to race, creed, age, and sex.

Academic Support Programs

Comprehensive academic counseling, personal counseling, and tutoring are offered at no cost to the student. In addition, the Office of Student Services provides test-taking, study skills, and time-management counseling. Second-year students attend seminars to prepare for the United States Medical Licensing Examination Step 1.

Enrichment Programs

Post-Baccalaureate Pre-medical Program
Wake Forest University Campus
The purpose of the program is to identify, encourage, and support minority/disadvantaged students in order to facilitate their entry into medical school. The curriculum includes microbiology, gross anatomy, and Phys/Pharm graduate-level science courses. Workshops in study skills and problem solving are among the support services offered.

- Cost: The program is tuition free however, there is a small program fee and participants are responsible for their own living expenses, books, etc.
- Eligibility: Underrepresented minority/disadvantaged college graduates; cumulative GPA of 2.7; a minimum score of seven on each section of the MCAT; "N" or better on MCAT writing sample.
- Duration: ten months.
- Enrollment: Ten students.
- Application deadline: December 15th through AMCAS.

CERTL Summer Research Program.
The purpose of this program is to increase interest in science and mathematics research among high school

students. The program provides hands-on research experience with distinguished faculty from Winston-Salem State University and Wake Forest University School of Medicine.

- Cost: None. Program participants receive a stipend.
- Eligibility: High school students from Winston-Salem/Forsyth County Schools. Duration: Six weeks.
- Enrollment: 15 students.
- Application deadline: February 18th.

CERTL Science and Mathematics Summer Camp
A hands-on, interactive, fun look at science and mathematics. The purpose of the program is to enhance students' interest in science and mathematics. The students attend problem-based learning sessions daily. In these sessions, students work in teams and use resource materials to discover potential solutions to problems presented in their cases.

- Cost: None.
- Eligibility: Kindergarten through eighth graders from Winston-Salem/Forsyth County Schools.
- Duration: Two weeks.
- Enrollment: 90 students per session.
- Application deadline: February 18th.

Camp Med Summer Program
The program is designed to recruit, educate, and prepare high school students for careers in the health professions. Activities include 20-25 contact hours of presentation, tours/observations and clinical experiences.

- Cost: None.
- Eligibility: High school students from Winston-Salem/Forsyth County Schools.
- Duration: One week.
- Enrollment: 15 students.
- Application deadline: May 7th.

Student Financial Assistance

Wake Forest University School of Medicine attempts to assure that every student's needs for financial aid are met. Federal, state, and institutional resources are available through both scholarship and loan sources. Tuition scholarships are awarded to minority students on the

basis of financial need and academic standing. On the day of the interview, applicants meet with the Financial Aid Officer and are provided general information about financial aid and appropriate application materials.

The Office of Financial Aid provides individual debt management counseling to all students annually. Students are provided estimated repayment plans based on their current level of educational debt and projections of repayment plans estimating their repayment amounts at graduation. Financial planning workshops are conducted annually.

Application fees are waived for students validating financial hardship. A letter of support from the undergraduate financial aid office is adequate.

Educational Partnerships

Winston-Salem/Forsyth County Schools and Winston-Salem State University
This educational partnership was developed among the Winston-Salem/Forsyth County Schools, Winston-Salem State University, and Wake Forest University School of Medicine to develop the Winston-Salem Center of Excellence for Research, Teaching, and Learning (CERTL). The goals of the partnership are to improve students' problem-based learning (PBL) skills and increase the number of kindergarten through 12th-grade students who sustain their interest in science and mathematics.

Other Pertinent Information

Wake Forest University School of Medicine offers all the advantages of a small school and is affiliated with an excellent progressive medical center that maintains state-of-the-art technology. In addition, Wake Forest University School of Medicine has a strong commitment to providing equal access to medical education for minority students. This commitment is expressed in the distribution of resources to minority students.

These resources include not only financial aid but also the availability of advisors and special programs to provide support so that, once enrolled, students are retained through graduation.

University of North Dakota School of Medicine and Health Sciences

Eugene DeLorme, Director
Indians Into Medicine Program
(INMED)
University of North Dakota School
of Medicine and Health Sciences
501 North Columbia Road
Grand Forks, ND 58203
701-777-3037; 701-777-3277 Fax
gdelorme@medicine.nodak.edu

Recruitment

The Indians Into Medicine (INMED) Program recruits American-Indian students for health careers and assists these students in completing health professions degrees. The University of North Dakota (UND) School of Medicine and Health Sciences adds slots in its entering class each year for fully qualified INMED students.

Program participants come from throughout the United States, but INMED's most intensive recruitment efforts focus on the 24 reservations in North and South Dakota, Montana, Nebraska, and Wyoming. This primary service area was designated, at the time of INMED's inception in 1973, because

of severe and continuing staffing problems at Indian health facilities within this 24-reservation, five-state area. The program maintains an all-Indian Tribal Advisory Board with representatives from these tribes.

INMED serves students from junior high school through medical school. Staff members make recruitment visits to high schools and community colleges with large Indian populations, provide health career workshops, and set up recruitment booths at Indian health and minority education conferences.

INMED contacts Indian students who are listed each year in the Medical Minority Applicant Registry. The program also receives referrals from educators and from tribal organizations. INMED distributes a newsletter and recruitment and motivational publications. The INMED Web site provides valuable information regarding programs to rural reservation communities.

Admissions

The UND School of Medicine and Health Sciences adds up to seven positions in its entering class each year for Indian students who are enrolled members of federally recognized tribes. INMED applicants are expected to meet

the same admissions criteria as non-Indian applicants to the School of Medicine. The deadline for application to the UND School of Medicine and Health Sciences is November 1st each year.

Applicants must complete a standardized form that requests basic personal and academic information and submit a personal statement, letters of recommendation, academic transcripts, and Medical College Admission Test (MCAT) scores.

Candidates who meet basic admissions requirements are granted interviews with the school's 11-member admissions committee. The committee members are both appointed by the Dean of the School of Medicine and elected by the faculty or the student body. The committee includes basic science and clinical faculty members, medical students, and a consumer. The Dean of Student Affairs and Admissions and the INMED Director are available to the committee throughout the interview process.

Most INMED medical students at UND earn their medical degrees in the state. Due to the limited number of clinical placement sites, however, some INMED students transfer to the University of

University of North Dakota School of Medicine and Health Sciences
Applicants, First-Time Applicants, Matriculants by Gender, Race and Ethnicity, 2007-2008

| | 2007 | | | | | | | | | 2008 | | | | | | | | |
| | APP | | | F-time APP | | | MAT | | | APP | | | F-time APP | | | MAT | | |
	Wo-men	Men	Total	Wo-men	Men	Total	Wo-men	Men	Total	Wo-men	Men	Total	Wo-men	Men	Total	Wo-men	Men	Total
Hispanic/Latino																		
Mexican American	1	2	3	1	1	2	0	0	0	0	2	2	0	1	1	0	1	1
Puerto Rican	0	0	0	0	0	0	0	0	0	1	0	1	1	0	1	0	0	0
Other Hispanic	0	0	0	0	0	0	0	0	0	2	0	2	2	0	2	0	0	0
Subtotal	1	2	3	1	1	2	0	0	0	3	2	5	3	1	4	0	1	1
Non-Hispanic/Latino**																		
Black	1	2	3	1	2	3	0	0	0	1	0	1	1	0	1	0	0	0
Native American/AK	11	10	21	9	5	14	4	3	7	14	6	20	8	5	13	7	1	8
White	129	129	258	95	88	183	20	35	55	127	116	243	91	75	166	27	22	49
Asian	2	5	7	1	2	3	0	0	0	8	11	19	5	6	11	0	2	2
Multiple Race*	5	6	11	4	2	6	0	0	0	4	3	7	3	2	5	0	0	0
Unknown	0	1	1	0	1	1	0	0	0	7	2	9	7	2	9	0	0	0
Subtotal	148	153	301	110	100	210	24	38	62	161	138	299	115	90	205	34	25	59
Foreign	0	0	0	0	0	0	0	0	0	1	0	1	1	0	1	1	0	1
Unknown Citizenship	0	0	0	0	0	0	0	0	0	1	0	1	0	0	0	1	0	1
Subtotal	0	0	0	0	0	0	0	0	0	2	0	2	1	0	1	2	0	2
Total	149	155	304	111	101	212	24	38	62	166	140	306	119	91	210	36	26	62

*Since 2002, students can select more than one race and / or ethnicity. **Those who did not choose 'Hispanic/Latino' or 'Non-Hispanic/Latino' are listed under 'Non-Hispanic/Latino'. Data Source: AAMC Data Warehouse: Applicant-Matriculant File, as of 1/16/2009.

South Dakota School of Medicine for third- and fourth-year clinical training. INMED maintains a South Dakota Satellite Office at the School of Medicine in Sioux Falls, and South Dakota transfer students are designated at the time of matriculation.

Academic Support Programs

The UND School of Medicine and Health Sciences and INMED provide academic support and retention services for medical students at the University of North Dakota. These services can include faculty advisement, computer-assisted instruction, and study-skills courses. UND has recently instituted a patient-centered learning curriculum. All biomedical sciences are incorporated and integrated in this approach.

INMED's additional support services for Indian undergraduate and medical students include a Learning Resource Center library, study centers, and a student computer room. The program also provides counseling and academic tutoring.

Enrichment Programs

Med Prep

INMED offers Med Prep, an annual summer academic enrichment program with two separate tiers. One tier is for up to ten college juniors and seniors who participate in a six-week Med Prep course designed to assist students who are planning to take or retake the MCAT. These students are offered sessions focusing on the basic sciences and on verbal reasoning and writing to establish a solid academic foundation in the medical sciences in preparation for medical school. The course is taught by medical school faculty and Indian medical students and may include course work in the areas of biochemistry, histology, neurology, embryology, microbiology, and study skills.

The second tier is for up to ten Med Prep participants who are entering medical school in the fall. The program is designed to enhance study skills, introduce patient-centered learning, and provide clinical experiences and inde-

pendent, life-long learning skills.

Pathway

INMED also offers Pathway, a six-week summer enrichment program for up to ten tribal community college students transferring to the university in health care or pre-health care fields. University instructors teach Pathway courses in the areas of anatomy, physiology, biology, and physics.

A learning skills component promotes successful study habits and learning styles.

The Summer Institute

In addition, INMED offers this six-week academic enrichment program for 90 junior high and high school students. The program can also assist college and medical students in applying for summer Indian Health Service (HIS) externships at health facilities.

Student Financial Assistance.

The University of North Dakota School of Medicine and Health Sciences does not assess an application fee to Indian students who apply for admission through INMED. Once accepted into medical school, the Office of Student Financial Aid and INMED can assist students in applying for financial aid through a variety of sources. Most of INMED's medical students utilize IHS scholarships. These scholarships fund tuition and fees, travel, and textbook expenses, and include a monthly stipend for living expenses. IHS scholarship students, enrolled in professional degree programs, are obligated to year-for-year service paybacks in the Indian Health Service.

INMED also maintains a student emergency loan fund for two-month, interest-free loans to students.

Educational Partnerships

The UND School of Medicine and Health Sciences and INMED entered into a Satellite Office Agreement with the University of South Dakota School of Medicine in 1990. The agreement enabled an increase in the number of Indian students who are admitted each

year through the INMED program with some medical students designated at the time of enrollment for transfer to USD for third- and fourth-year clinical training.

The UND School of Medicine and Health Sciences also maintains placement linkages with several IHS clinical facilities. Most Indian students at the UND School of Medicine and Health Sciences complete Phase III and Phase V clinical clerkships at IHS facilities as part of their medical curricula.

INMED staff members maintain contact with health and Indian education organizations throughout the country. Since the program's inception in 1973, INMED has received recruitment assistance, support, and guidance from an all-Indian Tribal Advisory Board, which includes representatives from 24 tribal governments.

Case Western Reserve University School of Medicine

Dr. Robert C. Haynes, Associate Dean for Student Affairs
Joseph Williams, Director, Multicultural Programs
Case Western Reserve University School of Medicine
2109 Delbert Road, Room E 421
Cleveland, OH 44106-4920
216-368-2212; 216-368-8597 Fax
joseph.williams@case.edu

Recruitment

The recruitment of minority students to the Case Western Reserve University (CWRU) School of Medicine is under the direction of the Office of Multicultural Programs. Visits are made on a regular basis to colleges throughout the United States and to graduate school Career Day Fairs. High schools in greater Cleveland and health professions fairs are also visited regularly.

The office also works with the Office of Graduate Education to recruit minority students into graduate programs in the medical school.

Admissions

The Admissions Committee is composed of a diverse group of faculty and students. Any minority student can request a meeting with the Director of the Office of Minority Programs.

Academic Support Programs

The Director of the Office of Multicultural Programs, the Society Deans, and other staff organize programs, monitor progress of the students, counsel, and maintain the main support system for minority students. All students have access to a school-wide tutorial program. Tutors are available to all students at any time the student or faculty feels one is needed. This service is provided at no cost to the recipient. Many upper-class minority students serve as tutors.

Physician Mentors
All entering minority students are matched with a minority alumnus or faculty person. The mentor serves as a role model and is available to counsel and advise the student. This one-on-one interaction enhances the student's adjustment to medical school life.

Student National Medical Association
There is a very active chapter of the Student National Medical Association. Its members mentor undergraduate minority pre-medical students and students in the public schools. Study aids have also been developed for its members.

Enrichment Programs
Short Term Research
With funding from the National Institutes of Health, we are able to provide summer biomedical research opportunities for students interested in research or academic medicine. A stipend and other support are provided. We strongly encourage all students to undertake summer research.

Over the past 18 years, the Case Western Reserve University School of Medicine (CWRU) has conducted a six-week summer enrollment program designed to assist highly motivated and capable minority students in preparing for a career in medicine and in dentistry. Our Summer Medical and Dental and Education Program (SMDEP) is designed to enrich students who are completing their freshman or sophomore year of

Case Western Reserve University School of Medicine
Applicants, First-Time Applicants, Matriculants by Gender, Race and Ethnicity, 2007-2008

	2007 APP Women	Men	Total	2007 F-time APP Women	Men	Total	2007 MAT Women	Men	Total	2008 APP Women	Men	Total	2008 F-time APP Women	Men	Total	2008 MAT Women	Men	Total
Hispanic/Latino																		
Cuban	9	11	20	8	8	16	1	0	1	5	13	18	5	12	17	0	1	1
Mexican American	45	40	85	30	32	62	1	1	2	34	39	73	22	31	53	1	1	2
Puerto Rican	10	18	28	7	16	23	1	1	2	3	14	17	3	11	14	0	0	0
Other Hispanic	49	40	89	37	28	65	3	2	5	43	63	106	36	47	83	2	2	4
Multiple Hispanic/Latino*	7	3	10	2	2	4	0	0	0	3	4	7	3	3	6	0	0	0
Subtotal	120	112	232	84	86	170	6	4	10	88	133	221	69	104	173	3	4	7
Non-Hispanic/Latino**																		
Black	197	142	339	151	112	263	6	9	15	224	109	333	158	78	236	6	3	9
Native American/AK	4	4	8	3	3	6	0	0	0	3	3	6	3	1	4	0	0	0
Native Hawaiian/OPI	8	6	14	7	4	11	0	0	0	7	7	14	3	6	9	0	0	0
White	1,376	1,803	3,179	1,118	1,396	2,514	39	52	91	1,190	1,717	2,907	972	1,297	2,269	43	52	95
Asian	776	911	1,687	613	673	1,286	24	22	46	726	878	1,604	567	615	1,182	33	26	59
Other Race	2	3	5	1	1	2	0	0	0	0	2	2	0	1	1	0	0	0
Multiple Race*	77	104	181	62	76	138	4	5	9	71	73	144	56	55	111	3	1	4
Unknown	16	36	52	15	31	46	0	5	5	64	97	161	63	79	142	1	7	8
Subtotal	2,456	3,009	5,465	1,970	2,296	4,266	73	93	166	2,285	2,886	5,171	1,822	2,132	3,954	86	89	175
Foreign	161	170	331	127	128	255	5	4	9	183	210	393	145	157	302	6	6	12
Total	2,737	3,291	6,028	2,181	2,510	4,691	84	101	185	2,556	3,229	5,785	2,036	2,393	4,429	95	99	194

*Since 2002, students can select more than one race and / or ethnicity. **Those who did not choose 'Hispanic/Latino' or 'Non-Hispanic/Latino' are listed under 'Non-Hispanic/Latino'. Data Source: AAMC Data Warehouse: Applicant-Matriculant File, as of 1/16/2009.

college and are considering professional careers in medicine and dentistry. SMDEP targets those from communities that are historically underrepresented in medicine and dentistry: African-Americans, Latinos, Native-Americans, and those who are economically disadvantaged. All are welcome to apply. SMDEP is a FREE summer program. We provide campus housing and meals at no cost to students. We will also assist with travel expenses.

Student Financial Assistance

The School of Medicine may waive the application fee. No student is denied admission because of financial incapability. Over 85 percent of all students at the School of Medicine receive some form of financial assistance.

Northeastern Ohio Universities College of Medicine

Dr. Tenille N. Kaus, Assistant Director, Diversity and Student Affairs
Northeastern Ohio Universities College of Medicine
4209 State Route 44
P.O. Box 95
Rootstown, OH 44272-0095
330-325-6758; 330-325-5927 Fax
tkaus@neoucom.edu
http://www.neoucom.edu

Recruitment

One of the goals of Northeastern Ohio Universities College of Medicine (NEOUCOM) is to recruit and support qualified medical school applicants from underrepresented minority groups. In addition to the traditional recruitment activities such as mailings, high school visits, college fairs, and receptions, NEOUCOM has several outreach programs that have been developed to increase the enrollment of medical minority students. These programs include telephone calls to medical minority candidates, scholarship mailings, program development luncheons with current medical minority students, and receptions with prospective medical minority students and their families. Contact Person(s): Dawn Jenkins, Ph.D.

Admissions

The definition of diversity embraces a holistic approach that considers life experiences, talents, backgrounds, and personal characteristics, including but not limited to race, ethnicity, gender, religion, age, socioeconomic background, geographic origin, sexual orientation, disability, and current geographic location. NEOUCOM engages in a holistic process that evaluates each qualified candidate as an individual, using a number of criteria to identify those who can best contribute to, and benefit from, membership in the academic community and its various programs. Achieving and promoting diversity remains flexible and the manner in which race, ethnicity, and gender are considered will adhere to federal and Ohio law.

NEOUCOM accepts applications for admissions to the medical school through three separate programs: *The Combined B.S./M.D. Degree Program*, which offers high school seniors a reserved seat in medical school; the traditional *M.D. Degree Program Direct Entry*; and the *Advanced Standing Program* for transfer applicants into their third year of medical school. The Combined B.S./M.D. Degree Program is limited to students who have not taken college course work following high school graduation. Requirements for consideration to this program include high school transcripts and the results of the ACT (American College Test) or SAT (Scholastic Aptitude Test). Applications may be requested after August 1st. The Early Action (non-binding) application deadline is October 1st, and the application deadline is December 15th.

Admission requirements for consideration to the M.D. Degree Program Direct Entry include completion of at least three years of undergraduate study; one year of both university-level organic chemistry, physics, and one semester of biology; and the results of the MCAT (Medical College Admission Test). Applicants to the M.D. Degree Program Direct Entry should request the AMCAS (American Medical College Application Service) application in April of the year preceding anticipated enrollment. The deadline for the

Northeastern Ohio Universities Colleges of Medicine and Pharmacy
Applicants, First-Time Applicants, Matriculants by Gender, Race and Ethnicity, 2007-2008

	2007 APP Women	Men	Total	F-time APP Women	Men	Total	MAT Women	Men	Total	2008 APP Women	Men	Total	F-time APP Women	Men	Total	MAT Women	Men	Total
Hispanic/Latino																		
Cuban	2	8	10	2	6	8	1	0	1	8	6	14	5	5	10	0	0	0
Mexican American	14	21	35	13	18	31	1	0	1	8	12	20	8	10	18	0	1	1
Puerto Rican	4	2	6	4	2	6	0	0	0	4	7	11	4	5	9	0	0	0
Other Hispanic	11	15	26	7	10	17	1	2	3	22	20	42	15	9	24	2	1	3
Multiple Hispanic/Latino*	2	4	6	1	4	5	0	0	0	3	3	6	2	1	3	0	0	0
Subtotal	33	50	83	27	40	67	3	2	5	45	48	93	34	30	64	2	2	4
Non-Hispanic/Latino**																		
Black	58	44	102	40	28	68	2	1	3	74	41	115	54	24	78	2	1	3
Native American/AK	1	4	5	1	3	4	0	0	0	0	3	3	0	2	2	0	0	0
Native Hawaiian/OPI	7	3	10	6	2	8	1	0	1	7	5	12	5	3	8	0	0	0
White	528	615	1,143	425	430	855	29	40	69	499	663	1,162	379	495	874	34	39	73
Asian	253	277	530	187	197	384	22	13	35	265	268	533	202	179	381	19	12	31
Other Race	0	2	2	0	1	1	0	0	0	1	2	3	0	1	1	0	0	0
Multiple Race*	19	27	46	10	17	27	3	5	8	16	23	39	9	13	22	0	0	0
Unknown	7	6	13	6	6	12	0	0	0	25	32	57	24	28	52	1	2	3
Subtotal	873	978	1,851	675	684	1,359	57	59	116	887	1,037	1,924	673	745	1,418	56	54	110
Foreign	13	18	31	9	16	25	0	0	0	10	23	33	8	20	28	0	0	0
Total	919	1,046	1,965	711	740	1,451	60	61	121	942	1,108	2,050	715	795	1,510	58	56	114

*Since 2002, students can select more than one race and / or ethnicity. **Those who did not choose 'Hispanic/Latino' or 'Non-Hispanic/Latino' are listed under 'Non-Hispanic/Latino'. Data Source: AAMC Data Warehouse: Applicant-Matriculant File, as of 1/16/2009.

AMCAS application is November 1st, and the NEOUCOM Supplemental Application should be submitted by December 1st. Early decision is also available.

The Advanced Standing Program is for applicants in good standing at another LCME (Liaison Committee on Medical Education) accredited schools or are graduates of osteopathic medical schools. Applicants are eligible to apply for transfer to NEOUCOM while in the third year of medical school Applicants must have at least two years of medical coursework and pass the USMLE (United States Medical Licensing Examination) Step 1. NEOUCOM's Admission Office can be reached via the internet at *(www.neoucom.edu)*. Contact Person(s): Luke Gloeckhes and Dawn Jenkins, Ph.D.

Academic Support Programs

The Office of Career Development and Advising coordinates the advising efforts during the four years of medical school. Personnel in this office provide services that encourage and enhance students' professional, career, academic, and personal development.

Coordinated by the Director of Career Development and Advising, career development is an integral part of the longitudinal Doctoring course through the Professional Identity Development module. Individual assistance is also offered related to resume/CV preparation, personal statements, identification of fellowships and externships and individual consultation related to specialty choice, residency program selection, and the match process. The office also fosters and promotes development of leadership skills through participation in student government, professional organizations and student interest groups. Students also have the opportunity to hone their leadership skills through the NEOUCOM Leadership Certificate Program.

Academic success and lifelong learning skills are also integrated in the Doctoring curriculum and supported by the Office of Career Development and Ad-

vising. The Learning Specialist offers a learning skills program to help students study more efficiently and effectively. Learning skills assistance is offered in large-group meetings and in small-group and individual sessions. Materials such as Users Guides, newsletters, and Web-based materials are also supplied.

Professional Development Advising Teams (PDAT)

The work of the Office of Career Development and Advising is supplemented by the Professional Development Advising Team (PDAT) program. The PDAT program began in 1995 and has assisted students with continuity in advising from the first year of medical school until graduation. Becoming a physician involves integrating both the science and art of the medicine with health care practice. Students have many questions about the curriculum, about clinical practice, and about the current environment in which medicine is practiced. The PDAT program offers students and faculty an opportunity to work closely together, learning to integrate the complexities of both basic sciences and clinical practice. The goal of the program is to support professional development of all students as they progress through the medical school curriculum.

PDAT consists of a team of advisors that ensures continuity of advising during the basic science and clinical years of medical school. Students interact with their advisors as a team and on an individual basis beginning the first year of medical school.

Clinical Advisors

Clinical Advisors are practicing physicians who provide leadership and direction to student advisees with primary responsibilities in areas of career development and professional socialization of students. Students meet with their Clinical Advisors to discuss issues such as summer plans (research fellowships, shadowing, internships/externships), activities related to career development, self-assessment, and specialty exploration, involvement in extra-curricular activities such as community service,

student organizations and leadership development, and goals for life-long learning and professional development. In the third and fourth years of medical school, interaction with Clinical Advisors includes topics such as the transition from basic science to clinical clerkships, expectations and evaluation of clinical skills, specialty/career choice, and residency program selection and interviewing.

Academic Advisors

Academic Advisors are members of the Academic Affairs professional staff and serve as a resource to address a wide variety of inquiries and concerns related to academic progress and campus resources, including those about student health issues and requirements, student counseling and advising, harassment or student abuse.

Peer Advisors

Peer Advisors assist students in adjusting to the many pressures and stresses of medical education within a small group context. Peer Advisors provide a formal forum for first-year students to interact with a second year student who can be relied upon as a resource person who provides an opportunity for guidance and support, assist students in finding appropriate campus resources and models professional behavior. Peer Advisors assist students in subsequent years with adjustments to clinical experiences and clerkships. Peer Advisors also plan extra-curricular and social functions that bring faculty and students together.

Enrichment Programs

NEOUCOM offers several recruitment programs aimed to encourage young people interested in the sciences from the sixth grade through high school graduation.

These programs include MEDCAMP and HealthSuccess.

- *MEDCAMP* is a program is a three-day intensive experience designed to stimulate students' interests in the basic sciences and medicine and to expose them to opportunities for careers in the science and medicine fields. The program is fashioned after the SPACE-CAMP Program, and includes biomedical science workshops involving research, problem solving, computers, and an introduction to the field of clinical medicine. MEDCAMP is held in the summer and is designed for students who will enter the ninth grade when they begin school in the fall. Preference is given to minorities, females, rural students, and other underrepresented groups in medicine, who have demonstrated achievement in science and an interest in medicine as a possible career. Contact Person: Patricia Thornborough.

- *HealthSuccess* is an enrichment program for ninth- through 11th-grade students from underrepresented groups in medicine. HealthSuccess was developed to better prepare minority students for careers in medicine early in their education. Students gain college readiness skills and medical school preparation through their participation in various activities and workshops. Students have an opportunity to explore careers in medicine, interact with medical students and physicians, tour associated hospitals, and attend college planning and test-taking workshops. The HealthSuccess program is held from January to May of each year, and students participate in activities once a month. Students can remain in the program through their junior year in high school. Contact Person: Jonathan Jackson.

Student Financial Assistance

NEOUCOM provides a debt management curriculum that identifies financial competencies for students to understand and master during each academic year. The curriculum consists of workshops, downloadable handouts, books, interactive calculators, and online videos designed to assist students in making confident financial decisions now and in the future. Not only does NEOUCOM provide this in addition to the formal curriculum, but debt management is placed in the formal fourth-year medical curriculum. Fourth-year

students learn about personal budgeting and investing, filing personal income taxes and managing life, disability, property, and casualty insurance policies.

The following are scholarship funds that exist in support of minority medical students at Northeastern Ohio Universities College of Medicine who demonstrate financial need. Contact Person: Michael Kempe.

- *The Eleanor Smith Bozeman, M.D., Minority Endowment Fund* was personally established by Dr. Bozeman, an internist from Akron, for the purpose of assisting a financially deserving female minority medical student.
- *The Kenneth L. Calhoun Trust Scholarship* was created through a bequest by Mr. Calhoun. The fund distributes annual restricted scholarship funds of $5,000 to a minority medical student attending NEOUCOM who demonstrates financial need.
- *The Dr. Melvin and Mrs. Leona Farris Minority Scholarship* was established for Dr. Melvin Farris, a family physician, who served as a member of the Board of Trustees for both the Northeastern Ohio Universities College of Medicine and The University of Akron. These scholarship funds are designated for underrepresented medical minority students admitted through the traditional four-year Direct Entry Admissions Program at NEOUCOM. The underrepresented medical minority students must demonstrate financial need and meet eligibility criteria. This scholarship is renewable for the four years of the student's enrollment and renewal mounts will remain consistent with the original award, but new award amounts may vary annually.
- *The John D. Finnegan Foundation Minority Medical Student Scholarship Fund* was provided by the Finnegan Foundation as a $10,000 gift for scholarship support over two years, to a financially underrepresented minority medical student from Youngstown State University. Contingent upon good academic stand-

ing, the student will receive the second award for the following academic year.

- *The Clarence E. Josephson Minority Medical Student Scholarship Endowment* was established by Dr. Josephson for minority medical students attending NEOUCOM. A former president of Heidelberg College, Dr. Josephson was concerned about the future of the American health care system and equality among all races.
- *The Minority Scholarship Fund* was established to attract a more diverse student body to the College of Medicine. This scholarship is available to underrepresented minority medical students demonstrating financial need. Students entering through the Direct Entry Admissions Program will be given top priority, followed by students entering through the B.S./M.D. program.
- *The NEOUCOM Minority Scholarship Matching Fund* was created in 1999 to support minority medical students attending NEOUCOM. All non-endowment gifts to the NEOUCOM Foundation in support of minority medical scholarships will be matched by the college for this award.
- *The NEOUCOM Foundation Minority Student Aid Fund* is used for scholarship support for minority students, as well as a minority student recruitment and retention program.
- *The Luther H. Robinson Memorial Endowment Fund* was established by staff physicians at Children's Hospital Medical Center of Akron in memory of Dr. Luther Robinson, who was a pediatrician at Children's Hospital and one of the original members of the NEOUCOM Admissions Committee. Dr. Robinson passed away in 1989. The Luther H. Robinson Memorial Scholarship provides scholarship aid to financially deserving minority medical students entering their junior year of medical school who rank in the top quartile of their class academically.
- *The Links Scholarship Fund* was established by the Kent, Ohio, chapter

of The Links, Inc. The scholarship benefits a minority medical student attending NEOUCOM.

- *The Shirali Family Scholarship Endowment.* Drs. Sudheer and Charulata Shirali, pediatricians in Canton, Ohio, and parents of Swati Shirali M.D. ('90), established the Shirali Family Scholarship Fund to benefit NEOUCOM medical students. The scholarship provides aid to a financially deserving underrepresented minority student from Stark County.

Ohio State University College of Medicine

Dr. Leon McDougle, Assistant Dean, Diversity & Cultural Affairs
Muntagima Furgan,
Associate Director
Office for Diversity and
Cultural Affairs
Ohio State University
College of Medicine
066 Meiling Hall
370 West Ninth Avenue
Columbus, OH 43210-1238
614-688-8489; 614-292-2556 fax

Recruitment

Active recruitment of underrepresented minority and disadvantaged students at the community, junior high school, high school, and undergraduate levels is conducted by members of the Ohio State college administration, faculty, students, and alumni. Recruitment is coordinated through the Admissions Office, the Office for Diversity and Cultural Affairs, and the other health professional schools at the Ohio State University (OSU): 1) (http://medicine.osu.edu/odca) and 2) (http://medicine.osu.edu).

Graduate and Professional Schools Visitation Days
The OSU Office of Minority Affairs, the Graduate School, and Professional Colleges invite five to eight high-ranking seniors and an administrative or faculty representative from a college or university to visit the Ohio State University's campus to explore graduate and professional study opportunities. Hotel accommodations and mileage reimbursement are provided for all guest institutions. A small honorarium is also provided to institutions traveling from outside of Ohio. Certain qualifications and requirements are necessary: (http://oma.osu.edu/future-students/ graduate-student-resources/ visitation-days/index.php).

Admissions

All applicants for admission are evaluated by the Admissions Committee of the College of Medicine and Public Health. Every effort is made to include students who represent all segments of society with a variety of backgrounds, medical career goals, and aspirations. Applications from underrepresented minority students are encouraged and every effort is made, by the Admissions Committee to assist students in becoming successful

applicants. The committee is made up of faculty members of the College of Medicine: (http://medicine.osu.edu/futurestudents/admissions/).

Academic Support Programs

A strong academic support program is available to all students enrolled in the OSU College of Medicine. The MED-PATH Office staff can assist students experiencing academic difficulty with assistance in learning strategies and test-taking development and provides academic advising. The Medical Student Advisory Center offers students test preparation guidance, academic advising, and general counseling services. The Academic Program Committees, for first through fourth year, also offer a variety of academic support options for students as they progress through each of the four years of the curriculum: (http://medicine.osu.edu/odca).

Visiting Student Program
The VSP is designed to provide a unique opportunity for fourth year medical students from other medical schools to rotate on an inpatient service of the specialty that they are strongly considering for a career choice. This diversity program aims to enhance the

Ohio State University College of Medicine
Applicants, First-Time Applicants, Matriculants by Gender, Race and Ethnicity, 2007-2008

	2007									2008								
	APP			F-time APP			MAT			APP			F-time APP			MAT		
	Wo-men	Men	Total	Wo-men	Men	Total	Wo-men	Men	Total	Wo-men	Men	Total	Wo-men	Men	Total	Wo-men	Men	Total
Hispanic/Latino																		
Cuban	4	9	13	4	7	11	0	0	0	5	13	18	4	12	16	1	3	4
Mexican American	45	62	107	31	49	80	0	1	1	31	49	80	23	31	54	2	4	6
Puerto Rican	14	14	28	13	10	23	0	6	6	4	9	13	3	7	10	0	1	1
Other Hispanic	34	47	81	26	34	60	0	1	1	38	47	85	29	33	62	1	0	1
Multiple Hispanic/Latino*	5	6	11	3	3	6	0	0	0	4	6	10	3	5	8	0	0	0
Subtotal	102	138	240	77	103	180	0	8	8	82	124	206	62	88	150	4	8	12
Non-Hispanic/Latino**																		
Black	232	135	367	157	106	263	8	2	10	177	107	284	121	73	194	5	4	9
Native American/AK	5	4	9	5	3	8	0	0	0	5	3	8	4	1	5	0	0	0
Native Hawaiian/OPI	6	3	9	6	3	9	0	0	0	11	4	15	5	3	8	0	0	0
White	1,127	1,669	2,796	927	1,312	2,239	59	86	145	988	1,670	2,658	782	1,273	2,055	50	76	126
Asian	461	588	1,049	361	415	776	22	20	42	426	592	1,018	321	431	752	26	24	50
Other Race	2	0	2	2	0	2	0	0	0	0	3	3	0	3	3	0	0	0
Multiple Race*	55	64	119	48	49	97	3	1	4	45	58	103	34	39	73	2	5	7
Unknown	9	26	35	8	24	32	0	1	1	43	68	111	41	58	99	4	3	7
Subtotal	1,897	2,489	4,386	1,514	1,912	3,426	92	110	202	1,695	2,505	4,200	1,308	1,881	3,189	87	112	199
Foreign	5	6	11	4	4	8	0	0	0	18	22	40	14	19	33	0	0	0
Total	2,004	2,633	4,637	1,595	2,019	3,614	92	118	210	1,795	2,651	4,446	1,384	1,988	3,372	91	120	211

*Since 2002, students can select more than one race and / or ethnicity. **Those who did not choose 'Hispanic/Latino' or 'Non-Hispanic/Latino' are listed under 'Non-Hispanic/Latino'. Data Source: AAMC Data Warehouse: Applicant-Matriculant File, as of 1/16/2009.

growing diversity of our highly ranked OSU College of Medicine residency training programs. A stipend and travel funds are provided for this selective program: *(http://medicine.osu.edu/odca/7280.cfm)*

Enrichment Programs

Summer Pre-Entry Program for medical students matriculating to OSU
The College of Medicine offers a six-week summer enrichment program for entering medical students in order to strengthen their academic background and skills prior to starting the first year. The program is designed for students who are non-science majors, students who may need special preparation prior to beginning medical school or students who have been out of school for a period of time. Instruction in human gross anatomy, neuroanatomy, and immunology are offered. In addition, learning strategies and test-taking seminars are included in the curriculum. Invitations to attend this pre-entry program are sent out to all OSU matriculating first-year medical students.

The program allows students to meet and become acquainted with their faculty and classmates. It also gives students time to acclimate to the medical school environment and the surrounding community. A limited number of stipends for the program will be allotted to underrepresented minority and disadvantaged students in financial need.

MEDPATH Postbaccalaureate Program
A legacy of care for underserved communities has been established by graduates of this innovative diversity program: *(http://medicine.osu.edu/odca/7277.cfm)*.

The Medical Pathways (MEDPATH) Post-baccalaureate program has enhanced the diversity of the College of Medicine since 1991. Annually, up to15 underrepresented in medicine and disadvantaged students have matriculated to the medical school class of 210. In addition, in 2004 a Continuous Quality Improvement plan was implemented to improve the first-attempt success rate

for passing the United States Medical Licensing Examination (USMLE) Step 1 for MEDPATH graduates in medical school. Data collection is ongoing and student performance is improving.

Undergraduate Diversity Seminar
Dr. McDougle serves as the principal investigator for the outcomes study entitled Introduction to Diversity, Communication, and Ethics in Clinical Medicine: The Use of Student-run Introductory Undergraduate Seminar to Increase the Number of Qualified Underrepresented Minority Medical School Applicants. The goals of this annual six-week seminar course created by OSU medical students include: (1) helping students to develop effective communication skills, (2) exposing students to issues regarding today's diverse patient populations, 3) providing students with valuable clinical skills, 4) providing underrepresented in medicine students with medical student mentors, 5) increasing the recruitment and retention of qualified minority physicians, and 6) facilitating teaching opportunities for medical school students. This is a longitudinal study with a participant group and control group comprised of 20 underrepresented in medicine students each. The first course was successfully completed November 29, 2005.

High School MD Camp
Established in the summer of 2004, MD Camp continues to grow in scope and impact to provide academic enrichment activities and mentoring for gifted underrepresented in medicine and disadvantaged high school juniors and seniors. In 2004, MD Camp was two weeks long and involved 12 high school students from Columbus Public High Schools. In 2005, The Office for Diversity & Cultural Affairs worked with five medical students to extend the camp to three weeks and to make it possible for 20 students from Columbus Public Schools and Franklin County suburbs to participate. In addition to medical students who serve primarily as counselors and mentors, College of Medicine faculty provide age-appropriate lectures

of medical school subjects such as anatomy and physiology, and demonstrations of clinical procedures in the College of Medicine's Clinical Skills Center. Minority physicians in the College of Medicine also volunteer to talk to students about their lives as physicians and their clinical practices. A longitudinal outcomes protocol was approved by the IRB in March 2009: *(http://medicine.osu.edu/odca/7278.cfm)*

High School Research Apprentice Program (RAP)
The RAP provides an excellent opportunity for tenth graders to explore a career in research and to build their college resumes. To be eligible students must be a student underrepresented in medicine (African-American, Mexican-American, Puerto Rican or Native-American) or disadvantaged. Eligible students will enter the 11th grade in September. Also, must have good grades (As and Bs), maturity and enthusiasm for working in a laboratory: *(http://medicine.osu.edu/odca/7279.cfm)*

Student Financial Assistance

The OSU Office of Financial Aid has a friendly staff to counsel medical students and assist them in financial planning. There are need-based and merit-based university scholarships and grants available to underrepresented minority students. The National Medical Fellowships Inc. provides assistance to some first- and second-year students. Financial aid, in the form of loans, is also available (e.g., Stafford Student Loan, the Perkins Loan, and the Primary Care Loan). Students are encouraged to begin financial planning for their medical school education early. If financial problems are anticipated, students are urged to contact the Office of Medical Student Affairs: *(http://medicine.osu.edu/futurestudents/financialaid/)*

University of Cincinnati College of Medicine

Dr. Charles W. Collins, Associate Dean, Diversity and Community Affairs
Associate Professor, Child & Adolescent Psychiatry
University of Cincinnati College of Medicine
231 Albert Sabin Way, Suite E251
P.O. Box 670552
Cincinnati, Ohio 45267-0052
513-558-4898; 513-558-1100 fax
charles.collins@uc.edu
www.med.uc.edu

Recruitment

The University of Cincinnati College of Medicine (UCCOM) actively recruits minority, disadvantaged, and non-traditional students. The college encourages individuals from diverse backgrounds to consider the many exceptional educational programs that are offered. Commitment to recruiting, admitting, and graduating students begins with several enrichment programs for middle school, high school, and college students, and extends through medical school graduation.

Under the umbrella of Pathways to Health Careers, the Office of Student Affairs sponsors programs for high school and college students/graduates, one program for high school teachers, and one year-round program for middle school students. All programs introduce students to the sciences, facilitate the development of their critical thinking skills, and expose them to health careers through research and clinical experiences. Note: Middle and high school programs are for students in the Cincinnati area.

Pathways Programs

Saturday Science Academy
Seventh- and eighth-grade students and their parents meet once a month to explore health careers via a hands-on, interactive approach to the sciences.

Health Careers Exploration (HCARE)
Eleventh- and 12th-grade students focus on critical thinking skills and problem-solving skills while learning biology and chemistry and exploring health related careers.

Excellence in Science Education and Learning (ExSEL)
This is a summer program for 11th-

and-12th grade students. This program is for gifted and academically talented students who are interested in the sciences.

Teachers' Initiative Program in Biomedical Research
Middle and high school teachers' complete research with UC faculty members, present their research, and share ideas for teaching science courses and promoting careers in the sciences, particularly the medical sciences in their schools.

Summer Premedical Enrichment Program
This program exposes rising college juniors and seniors and recent college graduates from all over the country to clinical experiences, medical school curriculum, and to the medical school admissions process.

For further information or applications to the above programs, please contact: Pathways to Health Careers, University of Cincinnati College of Medicine, P.O. Box 670552, Cincinnati, OH 45267-0552, (P) 513-558-7212, (F) 513-558-6259. *(http//:medonestop.uc.edu/ pathways).*

University of Cincinnati College of Medicine
Applicants, First-Time Applicants, Matriculants by Gender, Race and Ethnicity, 2007-2008

	2007 APP Women	Men	Total	2007 F-time APP Women	Men	Total	2007 MAT Women	Men	Total	2008 APP Women	Men	Total	2008 F-time APP Women	Men	Total	2008 MAT Women	Men	Total
Hispanic/Latino																		
Cuban	4	7	11	1	4	5	0	0	0	4	6	10	3	5	8	0	0	0
Mexican American	25	28	53	19	18	37	0	0	0	19	33	52	13	25	38	1	2	3
Puerto Rican	7	9	16	6	7	13	0	0	0	3	8	11	2	6	8	0	1	1
Other Hispanic	26	27	53	14	20	34	0	0	0	31	40	71	24	26	50	0	1	1
Multiple Hispanic/Latino*	2	1	3	2	1	3	0	0	0	1	1	2	1	1	2	0	0	0
Subtotal	64	72	136	42	50	92	0	0	0	58	88	146	43	63	106	1	4	5
Non-Hispanic/Latino**																		
Black	152	92	244	93	71	164	2	9	11	133	78	211	93	49	142	7	4	11
Native American/AK	8	3	11	7	2	9	0	0	0	1	4	5	1	3	4	0	0	0
Native Hawaiian/OPI	4	2	6	4	2	6	0	0	0	8	2	10	4	2	6	0	0	0
White	1,095	1,449	2,544	885	1,063	1,948	53	63	116	1,020	1,340	2,360	799	947	1,746	33	67	100
Asian	443	592	1,035	339	396	735	10	20	30	426	536	962	305	353	658	10	23	33
Other Race	1	0	1	1	0	1	0	0	0	0	1	1	0	1	1	0	0	0
Multiple Race*	53	50	103	46	36	82	1	2	3	32	40	72	21	21	42	1	1	2
Unknown	11	23	34	10	20	30	0	0	0	42	64	106	39	53	92	0	8	8
Subtotal	1,767	2,211	3,978	1,385	1,590	2,975	66	94	160	1,662	2,065	3,727	1,262	1,429	2,691	51	103	154
Foreign	21	20	41	20	14	34	0	1	1	6	19	25	3	17	20	0	0	0
Total	1,852	2,303	4,155	1,447	1,654	3,101	66	95	161	1,726	2,172	3,898	1,308	1,509	2,817	52	107	159

*Since 2002, students can select more than one race and / or ethnicity. **Those who did not choose 'Hispanic/Latino' or 'Non-Hispanic/Latino' are listed under 'Non-Hispanic/Latino'. Data Source: AAMC Data Warehouse: Applicant-Matriculant File, as of 1/16/2009.

Admissions

All applicants are invited to complete the University of Cincinnati College of Medicine On-Line Secondary Application. The Application fee is $25 except for those students applying through the AMCAS Fee Assistance Program seeking a fee waiver. Other students who have extenuating circumstances may also submit a request that will be handled on a case by case bases. UC has a holistic evaluation system and applicants are selected for an interview based on the strength and breadth of their credentials. The application essay, undergraduate grade-point average, postbaccalaureate/graduate work, letters of recommendation, community involvement, health-related experiences, nonacademic activities, and Medical College Admission Test (MCAT) scores are all considered in this evaluation for an interview. Disadvantaged students will be evaluated within the context of their larger peer group. Competitive applicants are expected to have medically-related experiences and community service involvement. Research is valued but only required for those applying to the M.D./Ph.D. program.

Applicants invited for an interview will normally participate in a 2.5 hour program introducing them to the college, including a session with the Director of Financial Aid, lunch, and a tour.

Final decisions are based on a combination of academic achievement and personal attributes. The academic assessment may include but is not limited to a competitive science and cumulative GPA, honors course work, independent study, research, and performance on the MCAT. Personal qualities may include, but are not limited to, interpersonal skills, leadership abilities, evidence of commitment to helping others, clinical experiences, the ability to establish priorities, coping skills, motivation, and maturity.

Early Decision Admissions Program (EDP)
The University of Cincinnati encourages students to consider this process if the College of Medicine is their first choice for medical school. There are no special requirements such as higher MCAT scores or grade point averages. A competitive applicant for regular admissions will be competitive for EDP.

For further information, please contact: Admissions Office, University of Cincinnati College of Medicine, P.O. Box 670552, Cincinnati, OH 45267-0552, (P) 513-558-7314, (F) 513-558-1165. *(www.med.uc.edu/).*

Academic Support Programs

Extensive support programs are available for all students. Tutorial services, learning-skills development (including test taking, note taking, study, and reading strategies), and counseling are available. Preparation for the United States Medical Licensing Examination Step 1 is available through the Office of Student Affairs working closely with the faculty. The pass rate for the college has been very high; over the past five years, an average of 98 percent of students pass Step 1 on their first attempt.

The Minority Mentoring Program
This program enhances the medical school experience for minority students. It includes personal, academic, and career counseling. Support groups introduce students to each phase of the medical education experience, prepare them for residency, and discuss gender issues (women's support group). The program also provides students with a supportive link to and interaction with minority physicians in the community. For more information on recruitment and retention services, please contact: Office of Diversity and Community Affairs, University of Cincinnati College of Medicine, P.O. Box 670552, Cincinnati, OH 45267-0552, (P) 513-558-4898, (F) 513-558-1100.

Special Programs

Physician Scientist Training Program (PSTP)
The Physician Scientist Training Program integrates graduate and clinical education to develop physician-scientists who are interested in combining clinical and research careers. Students are awarded an M.D./Ph.D. degree upon completion of the seven- to eight-year program. The program matriculates up to six students each year. To learn more about this exciting career, please contact: Physician Scientist Training Program, University of Cincinnati College of Medicine, P.O. Box 670548, Cincinnati, OH 45267-0548, (P) 513-558-2380, *(www.med.uc.edu/pstp).*

M.D. /M.B.A. Program
A five-year Medical Degree and Masters in Business Administration is available. This combined experience provides unique preparation for a career in medicine and business in the 21st century. Students apply to the M.B.A. program after their first year in medical school.

High School Dual Admissions Program
Outstanding high school students who are interested in a career in medicine are invited to explore this exciting program. The University of Cincinnati College of Medicine has formed a partnership with five universities in the state of Ohio to accept academically talented high school seniors into medical school when they are accepted to their undergraduate college. The universities who currently participate in the program are John Carroll University, University of Dayton, Miami University, Xavier University, and University of Cincinnati. The University of Cincinnati has two programmatic tracts to medical school, one for students in engineering and one for any undergraduate student regardless of their major. For additional information, please contact Dual Admissions Program, University of Cincinnati College of Medicine, P.O. Box 670552, Cincinnati, OH 45267, (P) 513-558-5581, *(www.med.uc.edu/hs2md/).*

Enrichment Programs

See Recruitment and Academic Support Programs.

Student Financial Assistance

The secondary application fee charged by the Admissions Office can be waived if the applicant makes a written request and supplies documentation of financial need. Financial aid is not available for interview trips.

The Assistant Dean for Student Financial Planning is proactive in working with students to finance their medical education. Financial Aid at the University of Cincinnati College of Medicine is awarded on the basis of need. During the interview day program, the Assistant Dean presents financial aid information and is available to meet with applicants individually if appointments are made in advance. The debt management and financial planning programs offered by the College of Medicine are designed for all students. These programs extend throughout student matriculation.

In addition to a group Entrance Interview, first-year students are invited to take part in one-on-one counseling sessions, which include personal financial planning advisement. Seminars on budgeting, financial planning, and debt management are presented during each academic year. Students receive a quarterly financial aid newsletter.

A series of financial planning programs are presented to graduating seniors in the weeks following Match Day. Senior students also receive one-on-one debt management counseling as a part of their financial aid Exit Interview. Graduates are encouraged to contact the financial aid office for debt management assistance whenever necessary.

Educational Partnerships

See High School Dual Admissions Programs.

Other Pertinent Information

University of Cincinnati College of Medicine offers an exciting medical education program. Beginning early in year I and continuing through year II, students work with patients to develop a proficiency in interviewing, history taking, and physical diagnosis. This early clinical experience is designed to facilitate the transition to the third year. In addition, there are several enrichment opportunities available the first

two years of medical school (e.g., Maternal Healthcare—an opportunity to work with a pregnant patient and follow her progress through delivery; Homeless Healthcare—an opportunity to work with the homeless in an inner city clinic; and the Family Medicine Scholars Program—for students who wish to explore career opportunities in Family Medicine). Other unique experiences include participation in the Urban Health Project and the Leadership in Medicine selective.

The University of Cincinnati College of Medicine has a national reputation for providing excellent clinical training. The Clinical Biennium (third and fourth year) includes core clerkships in internal medicine, surgery, pediatrics, psychiatry and obstetrics/gynecology. Other required clerkships include primary care, radiology, and specialty clerkships. Students gain valuable learning experiences by working with faculty in several clinical settings (e.g., The University Hospital, Veterans' Administration Hospital, the nationally known Cincinnati Children's Hospital Medical Center, urban and rural health clinics, geriatrics facilities, private physician offices and other community hospitals).

In the fourth year, students complete an eight-week Acting Internship. This experience is designed to allow students to assume greater responsibility in patient care management, further preparing them for the demands of residency. If a student's interest is highly specialized, students may select to rotate in outstanding subspecialty electives at The University Hospital. Students spend 12 weeks of electives at the College of Medicine. The remaining electives may be taken anywhere in the United States or in a variety of international health care settings.

The University of Toledo, College of Medicine

Dr. Imran I. Ali, Associate Dean for Medical Education, Professionalism & Diversity and Professor, Department of Neurology
The University of Toledo, College of Medicine
Health Science Campus
3000 Arlington Avenue, MS 1195
Toledo, OH 43614-5805
419-383-3544; 419-383-3093 fax
imran.ali@utoledo.edu
http://www.utoledo.edu/med/diversity/index.html

Recruitment

The Office of Institutional Diversity and The Office of Faculty and Student Diversity supports the Office of Admissions by visiting high schools, community organizations, and colleges. High school and college students are invited to visit the medical school either individually or in groups. The Associate Dean of Admissions, The Assistant Dean of Diversity and The Director of Diversity makes a number of recruiting trips on a national basis. The recruitment program is administered by the Office of Admissions with participatory

support from medical students and faculty. The Student National Medical Association (SNMA) is an integral part of this effort.

Admissions

The University of Toledo, College of Medicine is committed to the goal of student body diversity. The College of Medicine believes that obtaining the benefits that flow from a diverse student body is a compelling interest for building an environment of educational excellence. Minority and disadvantaged applicants are evaluated by the admissions committee holistically, looking at all the ways in which an applicant might contribute to a diverse educational experience. The committee reviews the academic background of applicants, as well as the non-academic responsibilities, stated interest in medicine, manifestation of that interest, and potential contribution to the field. Minority faculty and students are represented on the admissions committee and its related activities.

Academic Support Programs

The Academic Enrichment Center is available to assist students in optimiz-

ing performance. This program offers comprehensive support through activities related to study and test-taking skills, a tutorial program, and coordinating of academic advising.

Student Financial Assistance

The application fee is waived if requested and documented through American Medical College Application Service or the undergraduate institution. The institution has established The Medical University of Ohio Scholarship Program. The scholarships are renewable for a four-year period. Individuals from diversified backgrounds, who demonstrate the potential for academic excellence, will be considered.

Educational Partnerships

The SNMA has established an outstanding mentoring program with community schools, whose student bodies are predominantly minority. In addition to social activities, the medical students assist in the academic development of their mentees through career counseling and tutorial support. For the past several years the Office of Institutional Diversity has participated in the University of Toledo Excel Program's

University of Toledo College of Medicine
Applicants, First-Time Applicants, Matriculants by Gender, Race and Ethnicity, 2007-2008

| | 2007 | | | | | | | | | 2008 | | | | | | | | |
| | APP | | | F-time APP | | | MAT | | | APP | | | F-time APP | | | MAT | | |
	Women	Men	Total	Women	Men	Total	Women	Men	Total	Women	Men	Total	Women	Men	Total	Women	Men	Total
Hispanic/Latino																		
Cuban	1	6	7	1	5	6	0	0	0	9	8	17	5	7	12	2	0	2
Mexican American	18	25	43	13	17	30	0	2	2	16	22	38	12	15	27	0	0	0
Puerto Rican	3	5	8	2	4	6	0	0	0	1	3	4	1	2	3	0	0	0
Other Hispanic	13	23	36	6	17	23	0	0	0	24	26	50	19	14	33	1	1	2
Multiple Hispanic/Latino*	1	5	6	1	3	4	0	0	0	1	0	1	1	0	1	0	0	0
Subtotal	36	64	100	23	46	69	0	2	2	51	59	110	38	38	76	3	1	4
Non-Hispanic/Latino**																		
Black	93	58	151	59	42	101	3	4	7	87	56	143	62	35	97	4	3	7
Native American/AK	2	3	5	1	2	3	0	0	0	4	3	7	3	1	4	0	1	1
Native Hawaiian/OPI	4	6	10	3	4	7	0	0	0	8	7	15	4	5	9	0	0	0
White	913	1,140	2,053	716	806	1,522	42	69	111	833	1,204	2,037	603	819	1,422	52	67	119
Asian	401	509	910	270	336	606	19	19	38	420	524	944	289	313	602	13	20	33
Other Race	1	1	2	1	1	2	0	0	0	2	1	3	2	1	3	0	0	0
Multiple Race*	39	50	89	30	29	59	3	1	4	33	36	69	23	19	42	3	3	6
Unknown	11	14	25	9	13	22	1	1	2	34	47	81	30	39	69	2	3	5
Subtotal	1,464	1,781	3,245	1,089	1,233	2,322	68	94	162	1,421	1,878	3,299	1,016	1,232	2,248	74	97	171
Foreign	10	14	24	8	12	20	0	1	1	6	16	22	4	13	17	1	0	1
Total	1,510	1,859	3,369	1,120	1,291	2,411	68	97	165	1,478	1,953	3,431	1,058	1,283	2,341	78	98	176

*Since 2002, students can select more than one race and / or ethnicity. **Those who did not choose 'Hispanic/Latino' or 'Non-Hispanic/Latino' are listed under 'Non-Hispanic/Latino'. Data Source: AAMC Data Warehouse: Applicant-Matriculant File, as of 1/16/2009.

Summer Institute, assisting this program with lectures and tours of the campus to minority high school students in the Toledo community.

Other Pertinent Information

The University of Toledo, College of Medicine Department of Family Medicine has been awarded a federal grant, "Multicultural Predoctoral Training in Family Medicine," to facilitate the development of cultural competence in medical students. First- and second-year students are presented with the clinical significance of cultural factors. Additionally students have the opportunity to gain clinical experience in community health centers serving underserved populations.

Wright State University Boonshoft School of Medicine

Dr. Kevin J. Watt, Assistant Dean, Office of Diversity and Inclusion
Wright State University Boonshoft School of Medicine
3640 Colonel Glenn Highway – 190 White Hall
Dayton, OH 45435-0001
937-775-2934; 937-775-3322 fax
kevin.watt@wright.edu
http://www.med.wright.edu

Recruitment

The academic medical community at Wright State is intensely interested in the maintenance of a diverse student body. Wright State University Boonshoft School of Medicine is a strong supporter of equality in educational opportunities. Every effort is made to recruit qualified minority students who wish to pursue a medical career. The school's philosophy is to seek students with diverse social, ethnic, and cultural heritages. This includes not only minority students, but also the older and non-traditional student.

The School of Medicine offers a number of programs intended to increase the number of minority students entering the medical profession. To reach minority students as early as possible, one summer program is aimed at high school juniors and seniors. Horizons in Medicine provides exposure to the medical sciences as well as work experiences in area health care settings. In association with the Student National Medical Association chapter, the Office of Student Affairs and Admissions has supported the establishment of an undergraduate Minority Association of Pre-Health Students (MAPS) chapter at Wright State University that is made up of minority students interested in health careers and assists them in developing seminars and workshops throughout the year on topics concerning the medical profession and the process of applying to medical school.

Admissions

Admission to the Boonshoft School of Medicine is guided by a philosophy dedicated to increasing the number of students from racial, ethnic, and socioeconomic backgrounds underrepresented in medicine. The Admissions Committee considers not only the academic record, but also the biographical and personal comments of all applicants. The School of Medicine does not set quotas or numerical goals. We select students who have the qualities that will make excellent, dedicated physicians no matter what specialty they choose. The membership of the Admissions Committee includes not only full-time faculty, but also medical students, practicing physicians, and undergraduate instructors as representatives of the local community. There is significant minority representation on the committee.

Academic Support Programs

Strong academic support is provided jointly by the Office of Academic Affairs and the Office of Student Affairs and Admissions. First-year students are offered group and individualized programs that help improve skills such as time management, note taking, organization, and test taking. Support in mastering subject material of the freshman year is provided by a peer tutorial system that is available to all students. For the individual who experiences difficulty with a particular subject, an opportunity to remediate exists in courses during the basic science biennium.

Wright State University Boonshoft School of Medicine
Applicants, First-Time Applicants, Matriculants by Gender, Race and Ethnicity, 2007-2008

	2007									2008								
	APP			F-time APP			MAT			APP			F-time APP			MAT		
	Wo-men	Men	Total	Wo-men	Men	Total	Wo-men	Men	Total	Wo-men	Men	Total	Wo-men	Men	Total	Wo-men	Men	Total
Hispanic/Latino																		
Cuban	5	11	16	3	7	10	0	0	0	4	8	12	2	6	8	0	0	0
Mexican American	27	25	52	19	19	38	0	1	1	16	20	36	13	15	28	2	0	2
Puerto Rican	7	4	11	5	3	8	0	0	0	8	8	16	7	5	12	0	0	0
Other Hispanic	26	29	55	16	15	31	0	1	1	32	36	68	22	20	42	0	0	0
Multiple Hispanic/Latino*	2	4	6	1	2	3	0	0	0	3	5	8	2	1	3	0	0	0
Subtotal	67	73	140	44	46	90	0	2	2	63	77	140	46	47	93	2	0	2
Non-Hispanic/Latino**																		
Black	174	107	281	103	75	178	3	0	3	158	72	230	96	39	135	3	3	6
Native American/AK	3	3	6	1	2	3	0	0	0	5	2	7	4	1	5	0	1	1
Native Hawaiian/OPI	7	3	10	6	2	8	0	0	0	9	4	13	5	3	8	0	0	0
White	826	982	1,808	657	691	1,348	35	43	78	778	977	1,755	570	675	1,245	29	42	71
Asian	347	416	763	248	270	518	7	6	13	346	379	725	254	241	495	11	7	18
Other Race	1	3	4	1	2	3	0	0	0	1	3	4	1	3	4	0	0	0
Multiple Race*	40	41	81	28	28	56	3	0	3	29	27	56	18	15	33	2	0	2
Unknown	13	11	24	12	10	22	1	0	1	28	38	66	25	32	57	0	0	0
Subtotal	1,411	1,566	2,977	1,056	1,080	2,136	49	49	98	1,354	1,502	2,856	973	1,009	1,982	45	53	98
Foreign	14	22	36	13	19	32	0	0	0	14	21	35	10	19	29	0	0	0
Total	1,492	1,661	3,153	1,113	1,145	2,258	49	51	100	1,431	1,600	3,031	1,029	1,075	2,104	47	53	100

*Since 2002, students can select more than one race and / or ethnicity. **Those who did not choose 'Hispanic/Latino' or 'Non-Hispanic/Latino' are listed under 'Non-Hispanic/Latino'. Data Source: AAMC Data Warehouse: Applicant-Matriculant File, as of 1/16/2009.

Enrichment Programs

In addition to Horizons in Medicine, which is available to high school students, a short-term research training program is held each summer for minority undergraduate, graduate, and health professional students. The Short-term Training Program to Increase Diversity in Health-Related Research (STREAMS) is an eight-week program that matches underrepresented minority undergraduate students from around the country with basic science faculty to provide the opportunity to participate in laboratory research focused on the cardiovascular system. This allows students to develop a sound research base as well as hone scientific writing and presentation skills with the faculty of an academic medical center that ranks near the top nationally in the amount of research funding received by community-based medical schools.

A four-week summer program is available to students who have been accepted and will enroll in the next freshman class at the School of Medicine. This pre-matriculation program emphasizes preparation for gross anatomy, a major topic covered in the first year curriculum. This program, which is available to all matriculating students, also helps develop strong study skills and smooth transition to medical school.

Student Financial Assistance

Applicants whose American Medical College Application Service fee has been waived may request a waiver of the Wright State application fee at the time they submit their supplemental applications. The Office of Student Affairs and Admissions of the School of Medicine in cooperation with the Office of Financial Aid of the university administer financial aid. Information concerning available loans and scholarships can be obtained from the Office of Student Affairs and Admissions. Each year, the local minority medical professional society awards several scholarships specifically to minority students.

University of Oklahoma College of Medicine

James F. Albertson, Director of Student Services
University of Oklahoma College of Medicine
P.O. Box 26901
Oklahoma City, OK 73126
405-271-2316; 405-271-3032 fax
james-albertson@ouhsc.edu

Recruitment

University of Oklahoma Health Sciences Center (HSC) Student Affairs helps develop a Sooner community of health care professionals through recruitment, retention, and recreational programs and services. HSC Student Affairs staff is responsible for student recruitment and student services; provides oversight for all campus student organizations and student government; coordinates student development and community-based programs for health professions awareness; oversees the campus' Union facilities; and provides counseling services for Health Sciences Center students through HSC Counseling Services.

HSC Student Affairs' outreach and recruitment programs strive to reach all populations throughout the state of Oklahoma by introducing them to the excitement and rewards awaiting a health care professional. Through transfer-advising services, recruiters visit higher education institutions across the state assisting students through the matriculation and admissions process. HSC Student Affairs welcomes all prospective students for an inside look of campus life during SEE HSC Day hosted each fall semester. Please call HSC Student Affairs for campus tours and program information at (405) 271-2416 or visit *(http://student-affairs.ouhsc.edu/).*

Admissions

The Admissions Committee is designed to include representatives from underrepresented groups in medicine and to select students that will contribute to a diverse educational environment. The academic potential of the successful applicant is complimented by self-awareness, self-discipline, empathy, personal competence, and social competence.

Academic Support Programs

The college retains the services of an academic counselor and a counselor with special expertise in study skills, time management, and test taking. Students may self-refer or be referred if difficulties are recognized. Five sessions may be conducted at no cost to the student. Access to services is coordinated through the Office of Student Affairs. Faculty and Course Directors are available to students for advice, counseling, and assistance with course work.

With support from the college, African-American and Hispanic student groups sponsor health fairs in communities as well as pre-medical advising programs/workshops.

Student Financial Assistance

All College of Medicine students, including minority students, are invited each spring to apply for college scholarships to be applied the following academic year. Disadvantaged students are also invited to apply for the Scholarships for Disadvantaged Students (SDS) each spring through the Office of Financial Aid.

There are various state and federal monies available, both as stipends and loans. Information regarding financial assistance may be obtained from: Office of Financial Aid, University of Oklahoma Health Sciences Center, P.O. Box 26901, Oklahoma City, OK 73126, 405-271-2118. The College of Medicine does not provide financial help to any students for expenses associated with interviews.

University of Oklahoma College of Medicine
Applicants, First-Time Applicants, Matriculants by Gender, Race and Ethnicity, 2007-2008

	2007 APP			2007 F-time APP			2007 MAT			2008 APP			2008 F-time APP			2008 MAT		
	Women	Men	Total	Women	Men	Total	Women	Men	Total	Women	Men	Total	Women	Men	Total	Women	Men	Total
Hispanic/Latino																		
Cuban	0	3	3	0	3	3	0	0	0	2	6	8	1	3	4	0	0	0
Mexican American	16	25	41	10	16	26	0	1	1	16	23	39	13	13	26	0	2	2
Puerto Rican	2	1	3	2	1	3	0	0	0	6	3	9	5	2	7	0	0	0
Other Hispanic	11	16	27	9	9	18	1	2	3	16	15	31	11	10	21	2	0	2
Multiple Hispanic/Latino*	0	3	3	0	3	3	0	0	0	6	4	10	5	1	6	1	0	1
Subtotal	29	48	77	21	32	53	1	3	4	46	51	97	35	29	64	3	2	5
Non-Hispanic/Latino**																		
Black	44	15	59	29	9	38	2	1	3	47	32	79	28	20	48	1	0	1
Native American/AK	24	29	53	19	25	44	5	10	15	18	14	32	13	10	23	2	4	6
Native Hawaiian/OPI	1	1	2	1	1	2	0	0	0	5	1	6	4	1	5	0	0	0
White	315	439	754	242	336	578	41	66	107	358	505	863	279	360	639	49	79	128
Asian	135	138	273	93	85	178	13	16	29	154	177	331	107	109	216	5	12	17
Other Race	1	2	3	1	0	1	0	1	1	3	1	4	2	1	3	1	0	1
Multiple Race*	24	26	50	17	19	36	4	1	5	21	29	50	14	20	34	3	4	7
Unknown	4	1	5	4	0	4	0	0	0	6	12	18	6	10	16	0	1	1
Subtotal	548	651	1,199	406	475	881	65	95	160	612	771	1,383	453	531	984	61	100	161
Foreign	6	6	12	4	5	9	0	0	0	4	3	7	3	2	5	0	0	0
Total	583	705	1,288	431	512	943	66	98	164	662	825	1,487	491	562	1,053	64	102	166

*Since 2002, students can select more than one race and / or ethnicity. **Those who did not choose 'Hispanic/Latino' or 'Non-Hispanic/Latino' are listed under 'Non-Hispanic/Latino'. Data Source: AAMC Data Warehouse: Applicant-Matriculant File, as of 1/16/2009.

Oregon Health & Science University School of Medicine

Leslie Garcia, Director of Center for Diversity & Multicultural Affairs, L601
Oregon Health & Science University School of Medicine
3181 SW Sam Jackson Park Rd
Portland, OR 97239
503-494-5657; 503-494-4916 fax
garcial@ohsu.edu
www.ohsu.edu/academic/diversity
http://www.ohsu.edu/diversity/
http://www.ohsu.edu/ohsuedu/academic/som/diversity/

Recruitment

Oregon Health & Science University (OHSU) has a long history of dedication to providing community services while improving access to health care for underserved and disadvantaged communities. In addition, OHSU has offered outreach programs for at least 23 years to increase the number of underrepresented and disadvantaged individuals entering medicine, dentistry, nursing and biomedical research. The university-wide Center for Diversity and Multicultural Affairs (CeDMA)

works in collaboration with the schools of medicine, nursing, and dentistry to enhance collaboration to increase OHSU's visibility and recruitment efforts of diverse students at the local and national levels. CeDMA and other recruiters within the schools participate in career fairs, offer campus visitations, advising sessions, and maintain ties statewide with counselors in secondary schools, community colleges, and universities. These activities help reach out to prospective students from disadvantaged areas and underserved populations. Specific programs include the CURE project, provides participants their first exposure to a laboratory; the well known AHEC MedStars program provides 40 disadvantaged high school students from urban and rural settings a chance to experience medicine at OHSU for three days in the summer. In partnership with OHSU's academic schools, the Annual Health and Science Careers Conference serves as a catalyst for academic programs to identify prospective underrepresented and/or disadvantaged high school and college students by introducing the students to health and science tracks offered by OHSU. This conference attracts more

than 180 students annually. Formal academic advising and support programs are made available to all participants of the conference and other prospective students year-round. CeDMA also collaborates with OHSU's Healthcare Volunteer Services to highlight volunteer student opportunities at our hospitals to increase experience and candidacy of the applicants. (*http://www.ohsu.edu/volserv/areas.htmlt*)

For information on CeDMA services and programs and the Multicultural Resource Guide, visit *http://www.ohsu.edu/academic/diversity/*).

Admissions

The Admissions Committee seeks students who have demonstrated academic excellence and who will contribute to the diversity and enhance the medical education of all students. Applicants are selected on the basis of demonstrated motivation for medicine, humanistic qualities, and a realistic understanding of the role of the physician in providing health care to all communities in need. The School of Medicine Admissions Committee fully recognizes the importance of diversity in its student body

Oregon Health & Science University School of Medicine
Applicants, First-Time Applicants, Matriculants by Gender, Race and Ethnicity, 2007-2008

	2007									2008								
	APP			F-time APP			MAT			APP			F-time APP			MAT		
	Wo-men	Men	Total	Wo-men	Men	Total	Wo-men	Men	Total	Wo-men	Men	Total	Wo-men	Men	Total	Wo-men	Men	Total
Hispanic/Latino																		
Cuban	8	4	12	5	3	8	0	0	0	6	5	11	6	4	10	0	0	0
Mexican American	69	53	122	57	41	98	1	1	2	51	61	112	42	41	83	1	2	3
Puerto Rican	7	9	16	3	5	8	0	0	0	1	3	4	1	3	4	0	0	0
Other Hispanic	39	36	75	29	24	53	2	0	2	44	43	87	36	33	69	1	0	1
Multiple Hispanic/Latino*	5	3	8	3	3	6	0	0	0	6	5	11	3	3	6	0	0	0
Subtotal	128	105	233	97	76	173	3	1	4	108	117	225	88	84	172	2	2	4
Non-Hispanic/Latino**																		
Black	36	25	61	24	16	40	1	0	1	37	32	69	27	25	52	1	0	1
Native American/AK	7	5	12	6	5	11	0	1	1	5	5	10	5	4	9	0	0	0
Native Hawaiian/OPI	8	4	12	6	3	9	0	0	0	10	8	18	7	6	13	0	0	0
White	1,310	1,511	2,821	1,034	1,139	2,173	49	41	90	1,228	1,576	2,804	929	1,156	2,085	41	35	76
Asian	490	512	1,002	371	356	727	9	9	18	479	454	933	332	292	624	11	11	22
Other Race	0	4	4	0	1	1	0	1	1	1	2	3	1	1	2	1	1	2
Multiple Race*	71	77	148	64	61	125	0	2	2	87	81	168	66	62	128	6	1	7
Unknown	20	31	51	18	29	47	0	1	1	59	68	127	57	57	114	1	2	3
Subtotal	1,942	2,169	4,111	1,523	1,610	3,133	59	55	114	1,906	2,226	4,132	1,424	1,603	3,027	61	50	111
Foreign	14	13	27	14	10	24	0	0	0	12	16	28	11	14	25	0	0	0
Total	2,084	2,287	4,371	1,634	1,696	3,330	62	56	118	2,026	2,359	4,385	1,523	1,701	3,224	63	52	115

*Since 2002, students can select more than one race and / or ethnicity. **Those who did not choose 'Hispanic/Latino' or 'Non-Hispanic/Latino' are listed under 'Non-Hispanic/Latino'. Data Source: AAMC Data Warehouse: Applicant-Matriculant File, as of 1/16/2009.

and in the physician workforce in providing effective delivery of health care to all. The Admissions Committee strongly encourages applications from people from all socioeconomic, racial, ethnic, religious, and educational backgrounds, particularly those groups that are underrepresented in medicine. The directors of CeDMA participate in the admissions process by meeting with prospective students and providing resources pertaining to diversity and multiculturalism at OHSU.

Academic Support Programs

The OHSU School of Medicine (SOM) believes in enabling all of its students to discover their individual career paths in medicine. The Career Advising Program is designed specifically to assist students in developing the knowledge, skills, and attitudes to make satisfying career decisions by offering developmental activities and seminars in all four years of medical school. First year students are assigned a Faculty or Community Physician Advisor based on the student's initial specialty interests. The advisor provides a source of support and information about his or her life as a physician, and specifically about his or her specialty area. The Big and Little Sib Program matches first and second year students on the basis of common interests. Summer opportunities are also provided for first year students to learn about educational opportunities available during the summer between first and second year of medical school. Additionally, "Specialty Talks" provides 13 one-hour sessions for first and second year students to learn more about medical specialty areas. Finally, MedNet is a program that integrates students from all four year's medical school classes into groups consisting of 12-16 students, with three to four students from each class. The purpose is to discuss issues related to the professional development of a physician, explore issues pertinent to each class, and have students share their experiences.

Academic counseling and tutoring is provided through informal and formal mechanism, including consulting with

course and clerkship directors and with the the Associate Dean for Student Affairs regarding academic difficulty and using tutoring services when a student is not making satisfactory progress in a course. Additionally, resources for academic support and learning strategies are available through the Center for Diversity and Multicultural Affairs (CeDMA). Individual meetings and academic success workshops are offered to students to support increased academic skill development. The Associate Dean for Student Affairs also works closely with the Center for Diversity and Multicultural Affairs by referring students for academic and social support and meets with the directors to address needs of underrepresented minority students. CeDMA also maintains a library of resources for the MCAT, USLME, GRE, DAT, SAT ACT and other resources accessible to medical and other students.

Enrichment Programs

OHSU offers over 40 enrichment programs and formal opportunities for both secondary and post-secondary students interested in research, medicine, and other related fields. Programs can be viewed at the below links: *(http://www.ohsu.edu/ohsuedu/ academic/som/dean/som-internships.cfm)* *(http://www.ohsu.edu/xd/outreach/ find-k12.cfm)*

CeDMA staff work with the program coordinators to recruit underrepresented and economically disadvantaged students to the various programs offered at OHSU. CeDMA and other programs within the School of Medicine offer various enrichment programs. Each of these programs is designed to provide support to students interested in medicine, research, or other related health careers. CeDMA also provides specific programs for educationally and economically disadvantaged students to specifically achieve degrees as physician assistants, physicians, researchers, and other related health and science fields. Some of the programs include:

Continuing the Umbrella Research Experience
CURE Program is a research mentorship supported by the Knight Cancer Institute and Center for Diversity & Multicultural Affairs. The program provides research experience, mentorship, academic support year round, workshops, and a stipend to students from socially and economically disadvantaged populations. The long-term goals of this program are increase interest and representation of disadvantaged students in biomedical research and other health-related programs. CURE is a two-summer commitment and students must be in their junior year of high school when they apply. Students in the CURE program and are supported for seven years. *(www.ohsu.edu/academic/diversity)*

Discover OHSU!
Provides educational visits to the OHSU campus for high school and college-age students enrolled in science, health science or health career programs throughout Oregon and Southwest Washington. Students learn of current research, technology, and health disparities, and participate in a cadaver presentation led by a medical student. Health career students may visit the angiography lab, the CAT scan facility, or an MRI lab. Medical students from the SNMLA, LMSA and other OHSU student interest groups are recruited to support disadvantaged and underrepresented student visiting OHSU campus *(http://seo.ohsu.edu/index.php?mw_nam e=discoverohsu.php)*

OHSU Health and Science Conference
An annual conference to assist underrepresented minority and disadvantaged high school and college students by providing them information regarding career preparation, insight, application information and opportunities to meet OHSU's medical students, faculty members and admission recruiters. All participating students are encouraged to seek academic support from OHSU's various health professions, including medicine, nursing, dentistry, allied health, engineering, and biomedical re-

search. (http://www.ohsu.edu/
academic/diversity/hsecconf.html)

MedStars
Designed to help rural Oregon high
school and college students learn about
and experience career options in health
care, including medicine. Emphasis is
placed on recruiting underrepresented
minorities and disadvantaged students
from rural areas throughout Oregon interested in medicine and other health
professions. The Area Health and Education Centers (AHEC) offers various
programs and services statewide and
administrative office is located at
OHSU. The AHEC Director oversees all
five regional areas and maintains a close
relationship with CeDMA.
*(http://www.ohsu.edu/ahec/events/
med_stars.html)*

Equity Summer Research
This is an 8-10 week summer research internship through the OHSU School of
Medicine Graduate Studies Program.
Students receive a stipend to work on a
research project alongside, a faculty principal investigator. They also meet with
basic science faculty, attend lectures, and
learn about the M.D./Ph.D. program
from medical and graduate students.
*(http://www.ohsu.edu/ohsuedu/academic/
som/diversity/equity.cfm)*

Educational Partnerships
The Center for Diversity and Multicultural Affairs partners with numerous
local civic community organizations,
professional organizations, schools, colleges and universities. These partnerships include but are not limited to
Portland public schools, Portland Community College System, Oregon University System and others. The large
majority of the partnerships have formal agreements to promote student
success and diversification. The CeDMA
team conducts quarterly visits to colleges and universities and provide formal
student advising. The Center for Diversity
& Multicultural Affairs also has a formal,
longstanding partnership with Oregon
Area Health Education Centers as well.

The CeDMA collaborates with OHSU's
student interest groups and assist to de-

velop community and educational partnerships

Minority medical student organizations:

*Student National Medical Association
(SNMA)*
SNMA is committed to supporting current and future underrepresented minority medical students, addressing the
needs of underserved communities, and
providing culturally competent and socially conscious physicians.

LMSA
The Latino Medical Student Association (LMSA) meeting is a network of
students, alumni, and health professionals whose mission is to promote the
development of Latino students
through educational, volunteer, professional and networking opportunities to
foster diversity, higher education and
the improvement of the Latino community.

*Asian Pacific American Medical Students
Association (APAMSA)*
The mission of APAMSA at OHSU is
o promote the dissemination of information relative to Asian Pacific American issues in the field of medical
education and to explore and possibly
resolve the unique challenges, obstacles, and responsibilities specific to
Asian Pacific American medical students and physicians .

*Queers and Allies in Health Care
(QAHC)*
The mission of Queers and Allies in
Health Care (is to educate and raise
awareness about queer issues, particularly related to health care, and to provide a welcoming, safe, and supportive
environment for fellow queer and allied
students.

Student Financial Assistance
The Financial Aid Office also offers eligible students funding from several federal and institutional aid programs.
Eligible students can apply for funding
in the Federal Scholarship for Disadvantaged Students program, Federal Perkins
Loan program, Federal Stafford and Unsubsidized Stafford Loan programs,

Federal Graduate PLUS Loan program
and the Federal College Work Study
program. In addition to the federal financial aid programs available to eligible students, OHSU also offers several
institutional scholarships. Institutional
scholarships are based on need and/or
merit and help to alleviate the heavy
loan burden that many medical students
face. Institutional loan programs are
also available to help students pay for
the cost of their medical education. Underrepresented minority and disadvantaged students are considered for four
Diversity Achievement Scholarships offered by the School of Medicine. These
awards are available to Oregon residents
as well as non-residents. Other scholarships that provide assistance for disadvantaged students come from endowed
scholarship programs. The Center for
Diversity & Multicultural Affairs has
also compiled a listing of scholarships
available to high school, undergraduate,
graduate and doctorate students found
at *(http://www.ohsu.edu/academic/
diversity/scholarships.html)*

Educational Partnerships
The Center for Diversity and Multicultural Affairs has partnerships with multiple Oregon institutions and civic
organizations. These partnerships include Benson, Jefferson, Roosevelt, Century, and Woodburn high schools,
Oregon State University, Willamette University, and Portland State University.
The large majority of these schools have
formal agreements to promote student
success and diversification. We also actively support local organizations such as
Self Enhancement Inc. http://www.self-
enhancement.org/home.asp . Additionally, we offer internships to SEI high
school and college students interested in
medicine and other health related areas.
Other formal and longstanding partnerships are with the Oregon Area Health
Education Centers
*(http://www.ohsu.edu/ahec/home/
k-12programs.html)*

The Commonwealth Medical College

Ida L. Castro, MA, JD, Vice President
Social Justice & Diversity
The Commonwealth Medical College
150 N. Washington Avenue
Scranton, PA 18503
570-504-9647; 570-504-7289 fax
icastro@tcmedc.org
www.thecommonwealthmedical.com

Recruitment

The Commonwealth Medical College (TCMC) M.D. program is distinctive for its personal education style and its community service component that grounds students in medical education, research issues, and the health care needs of the community. The College functions with a distributive model of medical education, developing initially three regional campuses (Scranton, Wilkes-Barre, and Williamsport) to provide students with experiences in diverse clinical settings. This distributive model calls for immediate involvement in clinical settings, greatly enhancing the educational experience. The strong research component of the M.D. Program builds a solid foundation for collaborative relationships with allied health professionals and greater real world experience. TCMC's VP for Social Justice and Diversity, Admissions Director, faculty, and students coordinate visits to a number of programs in which minority pre-medical students are enrolled throughout the country in addition to career-day programs in the State of Pennsylvania and the tri-state area abutting the state's northeastern region. In addition, specific outreach to a number of minority students on the Medical Minority Applicant Registry list will be conducted yearly. TCMC's Center for Learning Excellence, the Office of Admissions, and the TCMC Center for Social Justice and Diversity cosponsor a summer internship program for disadvantaged and minority students and are developing our first Summer Enrichment Program for 2010.

Admissions

The Commonwealth Medical College is the newest premier medical college in the United States committed to educating aspiring physicians and scientists to serve society using a community-based, patient-centered, inter-professional, and evidence-based model of education that promotes discovery and utilizes innovative techniques. Applicants admitted into our first classes will define what it means to be a 21st century doctor by creating a legacy of physicians and health care professionals that are knowledgeable, compassionate, innovative, creative, community-oriented, and dedicated to improving the quality and delivery of healthcare for all. At TCMC, we seek to attract students who share the passion for fulfilling the health care needs in the region beyond a strict academic experience, furthering the college's commitment to scholarship, teaching, and service.

Our goal is to educate a generation of diverse physicians dedicated to continuously enhancing their skills throughout their careers; physicians who use new knowledge and technology to adopt best practices and care for a growing spectrum of health issues within an increasingly diverse community setting; physicians who are communicators as well as healers. We are committed to ensuring that each and every one of our students fully explores his/her potential as a scholar and as a student, contributing to community health improvement projects throughout their medical school experience. Our curriculum is competency based with an integrated basic and clinical science approach providing clinical education throughout our curriculum utilizing our state of the art Clinical Skills and Simulation Center. Candidates accepted into this program will be assigned a family in one of our regions and begin their clinical experience during the first year. Clinical experiences provide students with training in an inter-professional setting fully preparing our students for their required clerkships and medical profession. Clinical and didactic experiences are enriched by 21st century labs and a strong research program focused on the health care issues of the northeastern Pennsylvania region. Our students will participate in a public health project during the first two years and will be encouraged to work with research faculty further developing hands-on experiences with the methods by which new scholarly information is generated.

TCMC is more than a medical school; we are an integral part of the community in northeast Pennsylvania dedicated to improving the quality of healthcare for everyone in this region and beyond. Our curriculum is academically challenging, technologically driven, as well as patient-centered. The College welcomes applicants with diverse experiences and backgrounds to enrich academic performance and service. We are firmly committed to the creation and maintenance of a non-discriminatory environment for its faculty, staff, and students and extend every effort to embrace the diverse experiences to strengthen and expand the overall academic life at TCMC.

The TCMC Admissions Office supports the institutional mission statement by admitting academically successful, passionate, diverse, innovative; and community-minded students with an aptitude for biomedical sciences and a sincere commitment to improving the quality of health care overall. Applicants' evaluation criteria will include academic accomplishments; research and health care experiences; community service; MCAT scores (admission of applicants with scores below national averages are highly unlikely); interview; recommendation letters; secondary application essay; personal statements; and personal traits such as character, work ethic, motivation to make positive contributions to society, and the profession. Courses are graded honors, pass/fail.

TCMC does not discriminate on the basis of race, sex, national origin, religion age, marital status, sexual orientation, or disability.

*No data available; new medical school.

For more details, please see Medical School Admission Requirements, published by the AAMC or visit our Web site: *(www.thecommonwealthmedical.com)*.

Academic Support Programs

The TCMC Center for Learning Excellence provides a host of personal, academic, and referral services to enhance the interpersonal and educational experiences of students at the Commonwealth Medical College. Academic services include academic support and advising, tutoring, computer-based modules, disability services, and mentoring. The focus of academic support is to provide assistance with specific course content through peer and professional tutoring as well as to assist students in developing specific learning strategies that will support life-long, self-directed learning.

Personal support services include short-term counseling assistance with transient or time-limited challenges as well as assistance in enhancing interpersonal communications and professional behaviors. Therapeutic counseling services are available to students off site through a group of community psychologists that are not associated with The Commonwealth Medical College. Students may access these services directly, 24 hours per day.

Individual academic support and on-line and group workshops are provided to students who wish to enhance their learning experiences. The staff of the Center for Learning Excellence is prepared to assist students with issues related to time management, stress management, memory techniques, higher level study skills, organization, presentation skills, and reading efficiency. In addition, services are offered to assist students in enhancing self-directed, life-long learning strategies to support their professional development. Tutorial services are available for all students through faculty office hours, a peer-tutoring program and on-line tutorials. All peer tutors are recommended by faculty and are trained in effective learning and referral techniques. Tutorial services are offered at no cost to students through small group and individual formats. Faculty is available to assist students with course content and research activities through office hours and on-line chats.

Enrichment Programs

The Commonwealth Medical College is the newest medical college in the United States committed to educating aspiring physicians and scientists to serve society using a community-based, patient-centered, inter-professional, and evidence-based model of education. The Center for Social Justice and Diversity is currently working with Academic Affairs, Student Affairs, its charter class, and the TCMC Community Advisory Board members to develop enrichment programs to motivate and support children, high school students, community college, and four-year College students who have an interest and aptitude for the sciences to pursue higher education and careers in the medical profession.

Student Financial Assistance

The charter class (2013) received scholarships equivalent to one half of their tuition if out of state residents and higher if they were Pennsylvania residents. TCMC will seek to provide similar scholarships to subsequent classes when possible. To support promising students from disadvantaged backgrounds, TCMC may award aid to students on the basis of demonstrated need.

Drexel University College of Medicine

Dr. Anthony R. Rodriguez, Associate Dean, Student Affairs & Diversity
Drexel University College of Medicine
2900 Queen Lane
Philadelphia, PA 19129-1096
215-991-8265; 215-843-1766 fax
Anthony.Rodriguez@DrexelMed.edu

Recruitment

Two institutions with a rich history of excellence and diversity in medical education, the Medical College of Pennsylvania and Hahnemann University, joined their strengths to create a single school with a common goal—providing expanded educational opportunities for minorities in the field of medicine. Drexel University College of Medicine (formerly MCP/ Hahnemann School of Medicine) is committed to providing each of its graduates with superior clinical skills, combined with an in-depth understanding of, and dedication to, community needs.

The school draws on traditions of diversity that extend back almost 150 years. Hahnemann University was founded in 1848 and the Medical College of Pennsylvania was founded in 1850. Over their histories, the schools educated hundreds of minority physicians, including the second African-American woman in the United States to become a physician, in 1867. Through the Office of Diversity, the medical school continues its historical mission by devoting major energies in the identification, admission, retention, and graduation of students who are members of racial/ethnic groups traditionally underrepresented in the medical profession (i.e., African-American/ Black Non-Hispanic, Puerto Rican American-Mainland, American Indian or Alaskan Native, Mexican-American, and Native-American, Native Hawaiian, Cuban-American, Other Hispanic, Disadvantaged, as well as rural birth county, rural legal county, and first generation higher education students). Recruitment activities include visitation to colleges and graduate and professional career awareness conferences. In addition, orientation visits to the medical school are encouraged and provided to pre-medical advisors and student groups. In cooperation with the campus chapters of the Student National Medical Association and the Latin Medical Student Association, a Minority Applicant Host Program has been established. Preceding, during, and after the interview day, members of the program serve as an important student link between the applicant and the medical school. Individuals are encouraged to contact the Office of Diversity regarding pre-application information or to request a campus visit.

Program for Integrated Learning Curriculum

All students entering the medical school have the opportunity to complete their first two years of medical school in a curriculum that is an alternative to the traditional lecture-based, large-group, faculty-directed curriculum. Under this alternate curriculum, students meet in small groups to pursue self-directed, problem-based learning. Guided by a faculty facilitator, they learn the basic science principles of medical ethics and community and preventive medicine, as well as elements of patient communication, physical diagnosis, and history-taking in this integrated interactive format.

Drexel University College of Medicine
Applicants, First-Time Applicants, Matriculants by Gender, Race and Ethnicity, 2007-2008

	2007									2008								
	APP			F-time APP			MAT			APP			F-time APP			MAT		
	Wo-men	Men	Total	Wo-men	Men	Total	Wo-men	Men	Total	Wo-men	Men	Total	Wo-men	Men	Total	Wo-men	Men	Total
Hispanic/Latino																		
Cuban	39	33	72	28	25	53	0	0	0	35	42	77	27	36	63	0	2	2
Mexican American	109	95	204	81	73	154	1	1	2	93	102	195	69	72	141	2	2	4
Puerto Rican	37	29	66	25	24	49	1	0	1	28	27	55	21	20	41	0	0	0
Other Hispanic	148	135	283	107	90	197	3	2	5	149	158	307	105	117	222	8	2	10
Multiple Hispanic/Latino*	18	12	30	11	8	19	0	0	0	20	14	34	16	9	25	0	0	0
Subtotal	351	304	655	252	220	472	5	3	8	325	343	668	238	254	492	10	6	16
Non-Hispanic/Latino**																		
Black	548	251	799	372	187	559	5	4	9	484	214	698	330	157	487	10	5	15
Native American/AK	7	8	15	5	7	12	1	0	1	4	7	11	4	6	10	1	0	1
Native Hawaiian/OPI	23	17	40	18	11	29	0	1	1	24	20	44	13	11	24	0	0	0
White	3,085	3,351	6,436	2,413	2,394	4,807	70	90	160	2,811	3,423	6,234	2,079	2,357	4,436	40	69	109
Asian	1,783	1,918	3,701	1,320	1,363	2,683	47	49	96	1,772	1,897	3,669	1,259	1,248	2,507	60	42	102
Other Race	5	6	11	3	3	6	0	0	0	6	10	16	5	6	11	0	1	1
Multiple Race*	160	162	322	126	102	228	1	1	2	152	148	300	109	98	207	4	4	8
Unknown	60	68	128	54	58	112	3	1	4	136	162	298	126	142	268	1	3	4
Subtotal	5,671	5,781	11,452	4,311	4,125	8,436	127	146	273	5,389	5,881	11,270	3,925	4,025	7,950	116	124	240
Foreign	35	32	67	29	28	57	0	0	0	25	41	66	20	29	49	0	0	0
Total	6,057	6,117	12,174	4,592	4,373	8,965	132	149	281	5,739	6,265	12,004	4,183	4,308	8,491	126	130	256

Note: In 2008, one applicant, who declined to report gender, was not included here.

*Since 2002, students can select more than one race and / or ethnicity. **Those who did not choose 'Hispanic/Latino' or 'Non-Hispanic/Latino' are listed under 'Non-Hispanic/Latino'. Data Source: AAMC Data Warehouse: Applicant-Matriculant File, as of 1/16/2009.

Admissions

All applicants must apply through the American Medical College Application Service (AMCAS) and request their application, letters of recommendation, and Medical College Admission Test (MCAT) results be forwarded to the Office of Admissions, Drexel University College of Medicine. All applications are reviewed by a member or members of the Admissions Committee.

All applicants must complete the application process prior to consideration for an admission interview. The successful applicant will show evidence of a caring personality, leadership skills, service-oriented activities, and a true commitment to a medical career, in conjunction with strong academic credentials.

Academic Support Services

At Drexel University College of Medicine there is a university-wide commitment to the retention and graduation of underrepresented minority (URM) students. The administration, Office of Diversity personnel, faculty, and the Director of Enrichment and Assessment are all an integral part of a comprehensive retention effort. Students have the option of participating in several enrichment and support programs each which has been implemented to assist in the academic success of each student.

These programs include individual and group tutorial assistance, academic and personal counseling, structured study groups, workshops on stress management, standardized test management, effective study techniques, and diagnostic testing to identify learning styles and academic strengths and weaknesses. Departments in the basic sciences provide regularly scheduled review sessions, and pre-clinical faculty are assigned as advisors to members of the first-year class. First-year students are encouraged to attend the weekly Medical Scholars Review Program. This program is designed to assist the student in the review of course content and information presented the previous week.

Enrichment Programs

Drexel Pathway to Medical School Program (DPMS)
The DPMS program is designed for students from a lower socioeconomic/disadvantaged backgrounds. Students are required to have at least the minimum courses required of medical school acceptance; one year each of biology, chemistry, organic chemistry, and physics, (each with laboratory); and one year of English literature and behavioral science courses. In addition, a 2.90 undergraduate math/science GPA and a minimum MCAT score of 20, with no section below a 6, is necessary.

If an applicant meets these requirements, they may be granted an interview with Drexel University College of Medicine. If, after the interview, they are granted provisional acceptance into the School of Medicine, the applicant will be accepted into this Early Assurance Program.

Student Financial Assistance

The Office of Student Financial Planning administers a comprehensive financial assistance program. Financial assistance eligibility is determined on the basis of need as assessed by Free Application for Federal Student Aid (FAFSA). The Director of Financial Planning provides counseling to each student and develops a financial assistance package commensurate with the needs of the individual student. The office assists students in obtaining funds from private sources and counsels students on locating additional resources. Waiver of the application fee is granted to students who have been approved for American Medical College Application Service (AMCAS) fee waivers. The university provides Academic Merit Scholarships. In order to be considered for the Academic Merit Scholarship, an applicant must meet the criteria established by the Admissions Committee.

Woman One
The Institute for Women's Health and Leadership is the home of the Woman One Award and Scholarship Fund. Woman One has the dual purpose of raising medical scholarships for talented under-represented minority women who intend to serve disadvantaged communities and honoring annually a woman of outstanding leadership. Woman One honorees have included Robert Wood Johnson Foundation President and CEO Risa Lavizzo-Mourey and Olympic Gold Medalist Dawn Staley. In its seventh year, Woman One continues to connect Drexel University College of Medicine to the greater Philadelphia community by engaging businesses and foundations in supporting Drexel's diversity initiatives. The Scholarship Fund provides $80,000 to each Woman One scholar over the course of four years of medical school. There are currently 11 scholars spanning all four classes at Drexel University College of Medicine, one of whom is an M.D./Ph.D. candidate; two scholars have graduated and are working in underserved communities in North Philadelphia and Houston.

Jefferson Medical College of Thomas Jefferson University

Dr. Edward B. Christian,
Associate Dean
Luz Ortiz, Assistant Dean
Office of Diversity and Minority
Affairs
Jefferson Medical College of
Thomas Jefferson University
1020 Locust Street, Suite 163
Philadelphia, PA 19107-6799
215-503-4795; 215-503-4096 fax
Edward.christian@jefferson.edu
Luz.Ortiz@jefferson.edu

Recruitment

The Office of Diversity and Minority Affairs (ODAMA) invites you to visit Jefferson Medical College (JMC) of Thomas Jefferson University, one of the oldest and largest academic health centers in the country. At Jefferson Medical College, we are committed to the active recruitment and retention of a diverse student population. The staff of ODAMA provides information on opportunities at Jefferson as well as assistance with the application process for students who are underrepresented in the field of medicine. Throughout the year, recruiting opportunities are provided through attendance at regional and national conferences and visits to college campuses nationwide. The ODAMA staff attends recruitment fairs and conferences to meet, seek, and recruit potential students. In addition, any group that desires to visit Jefferson Medical College or wishes to have an ODAMA representative visit your home campus should contact our office for arrangements.

Admissions

Jefferson Medical College participates in the American Medical College Application Service (AMCAS). Minority students from all states are encouraged to apply for admissions and are urged to identify themselves on the AMCAS application form. All underrepresented applications are reviewed and qualified students receive an invitation for an interview. Individuals of diverse social, racial, and economical backgrounds are encouraged to apply. Jefferson Medical College has a strong commitment to matriculating a diverse student body to take care of a diverse patient population.

Only completed applications, both the AMCAS and Jefferson secondary application, are processed and considered by the Admissions Committee. The criteria for selection are those that will produce competent and compassionate physicians. Selection factors include, but are not limited to, academic record, Medical College Admission Test (MCAT) scores, recommendations, breadth of medical and community exposure and knowledge-base, personal characteristics, and communication skills. The Admissions Committee takes actions on all applicants.

Academic Support Programs

Jefferson Medical College encourages its students to utilize the numerous resources and faculty that are available to them. The Offices of Undergraduate Medical Education and Student Affairs and Career Counseling are two of the major support service areas for all students. There are a wide variety of skilled personnel, faculty, and materials to assist students throughout their four years.

Computerized and traditional tutorial programs are available for those who need academic reinforcement. Mentoring programs are provided in conjunction with the Office of Student Affairs

Jefferson Medical College of Thomas Jefferson University
Applicants, First-Time Applicants, Matriculants by Gender, Race and Ethnicity, 2007-2008

	2007									2008								
	APP			F-time APP			MAT			APP			F-time APP			MAT		
	Women	Men	Total	Women	Men	Total	Women	Men	Total	Women	Men	Total	Women	Men	Total	Women	Men	Total
Hispanic/Latino																		
Cuban	24	22	46	19	17	36	0	0	0	20	28	48	16	25	41	2	3	5
Mexican American	55	46	101	45	37	82	0	1	1	56	57	113	48	43	91	2	1	3
Puerto Rican	26	17	43	18	16	34	0	0	0	20	18	38	18	13	31	1	1	2
Other Hispanic	99	76	175	81	56	137	0	3	3	117	109	226	87	81	168	4	1	5
Multiple Hispanic/Latino*	18	7	25	13	5	18	0	0	0	12	9	21	9	4	13	1	0	1
Subtotal	222	168	390	176	131	307	0	4	4	225	221	446	178	166	344	10	6	16
Non-Hispanic/Latino**																		
Black	235	120	355	165	94	259	2	3	5	210	118	328	158	90	248	2	1	3
Native American/AK	2	8	10	2	8	10	0	1	1	3	4	7	3	4	7	0	0	0
Native Hawaiian/OPI	20	12	32	15	10	25	0	0	0	16	8	24	10	6	16	0	0	0
White	2,331	2,500	4,831	1,891	1,886	3,777	71	85	156	2,165	2,685	4,850	1,665	1,945	3,610	74	85	159
Asian	1,265	1,274	2,539	963	921	1,884	35	37	72	1,307	1,390	2,697	976	924	1,900	24	30	54
Other Race	1	4	5	1	1	2	0	0	0	5	7	12	3	5	8	0	0	0
Multiple Race*	125	117	242	99	80	179	3	5	8	119	100	219	94	67	161	1	1	2
Unknown	41	58	99	35	52	87	0	1	1	97	131	228	93	114	207	5	2	7
Subtotal	4,020	4,093	8,113	3,171	3,052	6,223	111	132	243	3,922	4,443	8,365	3,002	3,155	6,157	106	119	225
Foreign	253	241	494	200	185	385	8	4	12	256	256	512	201	185	386	7	7	14
Total	4,495	4,502	8,997	3,547	3,368	6,915	119	140	259	4,403	4,920	9,323	3,381	3,506	6,887	123	132	255

*Since 2002, students can select more than one race and / or ethnicity. **Those who did not choose 'Hispanic/Latino' or 'Non-Hispanic/Latino' are listed under 'Non-Hispanic/Latino'. Data Source: AAMC Data Warehouse: Applicant-Matriculant File, as of 1/16/2009.

221

and Career Counseling.

Additional support is provided to underrepresented students through organizations such as the JMC Diversity Council, Student National Medical Association (SNMA), Jefferson African American Student Society (JAASS), and Jefferson Boricua Latino Health Organization (JBLHO).

Student Financial Assistance

JMC students who demonstrate financial need are considered for financial assistance from the school's institutional financial aid programs. Minority and disadvantaged students have additional funding options available to them through the Algernon B. Jackson Scholarship Program.

If AMCAS has previously granted a fee waiver, Jefferson's admissions application fee is waived as well.

Other Pertinent Information

Whether your interest is clinical medicine, academic medicine, or research, Jefferson can meet your academic and social needs. Three dual degree programs are offered in academic medicine: M.D./Ph.D., M.D./ M.B.A., and M.D./M.P.H. Participation in research and community opportunities are plentiful. Students are eligible to apply for research programs and gain experience in research in the summer between the first and second years. We provide hands on clinical experience in the first and second years in addition to a wide range of hospital sites in the third and fourth years. Opportunities to participate in research, community outreach, and global health programs are plentiful.

Jefferson Medical College maintains its focus on the recruitment, retention, and graduation of underrepresented students, while simultaneously advancing the diversity initiatives.

Pennsylvania State University College of Medicine

Dr. Alphonse E. Leure-duPree, Associate Dean for Academic Achievement
Pennsylvania State University College of Medicine
P.O. Box 850, 500 University Drive
Hershey, PA 17033
717-531-6411; 717-531-4045 Fax
tkurzinger@hmc.psu.edu

Recruitment

The Pennsylvania State University College of Medicine is actively involved and strongly committed to the recruitment of minority groups who are underrepresented in medicine.

The recruitment program includes:

• Visitations by faculty and students to high schools and universities in Pennsylvania and neighboring states.
• Orientation visits to medical schools. Students, faculty, and administrators host groups of interested minority students who visit the campus.
• National minority conferences and workshops. Faculty and students are registrants and participants in na-

tional conferences and workshops.
• Career days. School representation is apparent at selected career day programs.

Admissions

Although there is neither a separate Admissions Committee nor a separate policy employed in the selection of minority students, the Committee recognizes and gives consideration to special features of an applicant's background and experience. There is minority representation on the Medical Selection Committee, and both minority faculty and currently enrolled students are participants in the candidate's interview schedule. No student is admitted who cannot, in the judgment of the Committee, complete the graduation requirements and fulfill the school's academic standards.

Academic Support Programs

The Associate Dean of Academic Achievement, the Director of Special Programs, and the course directors work together to identify students who may be experiencing academic difficulty. Students can obtain individual tutorial assistance or group tutorial help. Computerized assistance is also

available in selected courses. In addition, each student has a faculty advisor who is an important part of the educational system. The faculty advisor is a source of general support for students in the areas of academic, personal, and social counseling. Study skills, time management, and stress management programs are also available. A restructuring of the student's curriculum may also be employed to assist in mastery of course material.

Enrichment Programs

The Pennsylvania State University College of Medicine does not offer a summer academic reinforcement program. Individual employment opportunities may be available.

Student Financial Assistance

In addition to need-based financial aid, the school provides four-year Dean's Scholarships to competitive minority applicants who have been accepted to the College of Medicine.

Pennsylvania State University College of Medicine
Applicants, First-Time Applicants, Matriculants by Gender, Race and Ethnicity, 2007-2008

	2007									2008								
	APP			F-time APP			MAT			APP			F-time APP			MAT		
	Women	Men	Total	Women	Men	Total	Women	Men	Total	Women	Men	Total	Women	Men	Total	Women	Men	Total
Hispanic/Latino																		
Cuban	13	15	28	10	12	22	0	1	1	20	21	41	18	17	35	0	1	1
Mexican American	46	41	87	39	30	69	1	1	2	38	44	82	33	37	70	0	2	2
Puerto Rican	19	14	33	15	14	29	0	0	0	20	15	35	17	11	28	0	1	1
Other Hispanic	65	73	138	49	47	96	0	0	0	80	81	161	61	63	124	2	1	3
Multiple Hispanic/Latino*	10	2	12	8	1	9	1	0	1	10	4	14	7	2	9	0	0	0
Subtotal	153	145	298	121	104	225	2	2	4	168	165	333	136	130	266	2	5	7
Non-Hispanic/Latino**																		
Black	184	99	283	135	77	212	5	3	8	181	92	273	134	71	205	2	5	7
Native American/AK	2	4	6	1	4	5	0	0	0	2	6	8	2	5	7	0	0	0
Native Hawaiian/OPI	10	9	19	8	6	14	1	0	1	15	8	23	8	5	13	0	0	0
White	1,687	1,954	3,641	1,330	1,459	2,789	51	51	102	1,569	2,144	3,713	1,208	1,528	2,736	47	47	94
Asian	884	896	1,780	649	637	1,286	7	11	18	882	957	1,839	610	591	1,201	14	12	26
Other Race	2	2	4	2	1	3	0	0	0	4	5	9	2	3	5	0	0	0
Multiple Race*	67	75	142	48	52	100	3	2	5	67	72	139	51	43	94	0	1	1
Unknown	27	33	60	25	30	55	1	0	1	73	82	155	67	69	136	1	1	2
Subtotal	2,863	3,072	5,935	2,198	2,266	4,464	68	67	135	2,793	3,366	6,159	2,082	2,315	4,397	64	66	130
Foreign	227	231	458	188	177	365	7	8	15	263	258	521	199	187	386	2	4	6
Total	3,243	3,448	6,691	2,507	2,547	5,054	77	77	154	3,224	3,789	7,013	2,417	2,632	5,049	68	75	143

*Since 2002, students can select more than one race and / or ethnicity. **Those who did not choose 'Hispanic/Latino' or 'Non-Hispanic/Latino' are listed under 'Non-Hispanic/Latino'. Data Source: AAMC Data Warehouse: Applicant-Matriculant File, as of 1/16/2009.

223

Temple University School of Medicine

Dr. Raul A. DeLa Cadena, Assistant Dean & Director Recruitment, Admissions and Retention Program
Temple University School of Medicine
3400 North Broad Street
Philadelphia, PA 19140
215-707-3595; 215-707-3597 fax
cadena@temple.edu
www.temple.edu/medicine/departments_centers/research/center_minority_health_recruiment_retention.htm

Admissions

Candidates interested in Temple University School of Medicine apply through the American Medical College Application Service (AMCAS). Applications must be completed online at AMCAS.

The deadline for submitting an application to AMCAS is December 15th. After an application is verified by AMCAS, it will be forwarded to Temple University School of Medicine. Once a verified application is received, all applicants are sent a link to complete the supplemental application online and submit a nonrefundable $70 application fee.

Applicants also are asked to have recommendations forwarded from their undergraduate pre-medical committee, a school compilation service, or two (2) individual science faculty. If you are submitting a compilation packet or individual letters, two (2) letters must be from Biology, Chemistry, or Physics professors with whom you completed course work. Students are welcome to submit additional letters to support their application. Applicants who have enrolled in masters or doctoral programs should have additional references submitted by faculty from such programs.

Temple University School of Medicine is participating in the AMCAS Letters of Evaluation/Recommendation Pilot for the current application cycle. As outlined on the AMCAS Letters FAQ page:

Your letter writer can forward your letter to AMCAS in one of the following ways:

• VirtualEvals (VE): VE is available to members of the National Association of Advisors for the Health Professions (NAAHP). If your advisor is a VE user, provide your AAMC ID and AMCAS Letter ID to your advisor, as these IDs must accompany your letter in order for your letter to be matched with your application.

• AMCAS Letter Writer Application: This application enables letter writers to upload documents securely to AMCAS rather than send letters via the mail (anticipated to be available in late fall 2009).

• Interfolio: AMCAS can receive letters sent to Interfolio if you are an Interfolio user or your institution/organization uses Interfolio to deliver letters of evaluation/recommendation. Make certain to add your AAMC ID and AMCAS Letter ID in your Interfolio account, as these IDs must accompany your letter in order for your letter to be matched with your application.

• Mail: Make sure your letter writer has a copy of the AMCAS Letter Request form, which includes your AAMC ID and AMCAS Letter ID. Your letter writer should include this form when sending your letter in order to guarantee that your letter is correctly matched to your application.

The deadline for submitting supplementary materials is January 15th. Applicants who are reapplying to Temple

Temple University School of Medicine
Applicants, First-Time Applicants, Matriculants by Gender, Race and Ethnicity, 2007-2008

	2007									2008								
	APP			F-time APP			MAT			APP			F-time APP			MAT		
	Women	Men	Total	Women	Men	Total	Women	Men	Total	Women	Men	Total	Women	Men	Total	Women	Men	Total
Hispanic/Latino																		
Cuban	33	36	69	24	29	53	3	3	6	38	39	77	29	31	60	0	2	2
Mexican American	78	71	149	59	46	105	0	3	3	63	70	133	47	47	94	0	1	1
Puerto Rican	38	29	67	26	27	53	4	1	5	23	20	43	17	14	31	1	1	2
Other Hispanic	112	107	219	88	79	167	2	3	5	134	130	264	100	97	197	2	5	7
Multiple Hispanic/Latino*	17	9	26	10	7	17	1	0	1	19	11	30	16	7	23	2	1	3
Subtotal	278	252	530	207	188	395	10	10	20	277	270	547	209	196	405	5	10	15
Non-Hispanic/Latino**																		
Black	533	238	771	388	185	573	10	3	13	518	200	718	372	151	523	7	2	9
Native American/AK	5	7	12	4	7	11	0	1	1	4	7	11	2	6	8	0	1	1
Native Hawaiian/OPI	16	18	34	11	13	24	0	0	0	18	13	31	12	8	20	1	0	1
White	2,353	2,685	5,038	1,873	1,953	3,826	42	68	110	2,155	2,742	4,897	1,626	1,924	3,550	49	60	109
Asian	1,385	1,491	2,876	1,031	1,055	2,086	18	8	26	1,417	1,459	2,876	1,003	946	1,949	21	15	36
Other Race	3	4	7	2	1	3	0	0	0	3	7	10	2	5	7	0	0	0
Multiple Race*	138	129	267	107	86	193	2	3	5	112	102	214	81	70	151	2	3	5
Unknown	47	53	100	42	44	86	1	2	3	111	137	248	104	116	220	1	5	6
Subtotal	4,480	4,625	9,105	3,458	3,344	6,802	73	85	158	4,338	4,667	9,005	3,202	3,226	6,428	81	86	167
Foreign	36	44	80	33	37	70	0	0	0	37	50	87	33	39	72	0	0	0
Total	4,794	4,921	9,715	3,698	3,569	7,267	83	95	178	4,652	4,987	9,639	3,444	3,461	6,905	86	96	182

*Since 2002, students can select more than one race and / or ethnicity. **Those who did not choose 'Hispanic/Latino' or 'Non-Hispanic/Latino' are listed under 'Non-Hispanic/Latino'. Data Source: AAMC Data Warehouse: Applicant-Matriculant File, as of 1/16/2009.

University must resubmit all application materials including letters of reference. Once your application has been verified by AMCAS, applicants can check which materials have been processed by the Office of Admissions.

Temple is a private, state-related medical school and welcomes applications from non-residents of Pennsylvania. Tuition is higher for nonresidents, but it is comparable to the tuition at many private medical schools.

For tuition information, please go to (*http://www.temple.edu/cashops/about/ tuitionrates.htm*).

Admission Requirements. Completion of a minimum of 90 semester hours from an accredited college or university is required for admission. Students who have not completed a baccalaureate degree but who have demonstrated exceptional academic capability and evidence of unusual maturity may apply. It is recommended that all required courses be completed prior to applying. Applicants must be U.S. citizens or have permanent residency status at the time of application.

The pre-medical requirements for Temple University School of Medicine include the courses listed below. Generally, the required courses will be eight credit hours and directed to the needs of premedical students. Courses designed for non-science majors, allied health students, etc., are not acceptable.

Course	Semester Hours
Biology (with laboratory)	8
General Chemistry (with laboratory)	8
Organic Chemistry (with laboratory)	8
General Physics (with laboratory)	8
Humanities	6

Although the Admissions Committee forms no preference for science majors, all applicants, whether science majors or not, must demonstrate their capacity for excellent achievement in the sciences. In addition, students should have a broad education in the humanities and should have developed facility in writing. College courses in history, philosophy, literature, foreign languages, religion, the arts, etc., are desirable.

Every applicant must take the Medical College Admissions Test (MCAT) of the Association of American Medical Colleges. Preferably, this test will be taken in the spring of the year before application; however, it must be taken no later than September of the year in which the candidate applies. For the entering class of 2009, Temple will consider applicants who took the MCAT between April 2006 and September 2008. For the entering 2009 application cycle, the latest MCAT scores we will consider are from the September 2008 exam. The January 2009 MCAT scores will not be considered for the entering 2009 application.

Academic Support Programs

The Recruitment, Admissions and Retention Program (RAR)
RAR at Temple University School of Medicine (TUSM) provides support and opportunities for the medical education of educational and/or financially disadvantaged students. The primary purpose of the program is to help TUSM identify, enroll, and graduate physicians from disadvantaged backgrounds and retain them in the profession of medicine. These backgrounds include but are not limited to the traditionally medically underrepresented groups of African Americans, mainland Puerto Ricans, Mexican Americans, and Native Americans. The RAR Program has a legacy of over 30 years of ongoing support services to hundreds of minority applicants and medical students of these and other groups that are underrepresented in the profession of medicine (URM).

Temple is concerned with more than the façade of equal opportunity. It is devoted to its substance – the effort to help disadvantaged students overcome the academic and economic obstacles that are the reasons for their underrep-

resentation among our nation's physicians.

Since 1971, nearly 700 underrepresented African-American and Latino physicians alone completed their medical training at TUSM. Of the 126 medical schools in the United States, TUSM has for many years has been among the top ten medical schools in enrolling and graduating very large numbers of minority physicians. Over 120 minority medical students attend TUSM each year, representing 17% of its total student enrollment. TUSM is committed to this leadership role in securing diversity in our student body, as well as maintaining excellence in our academic programs.

The RAR Program has a staff of full-time counselors responsible for:

• Increasing the number of RAR Program applicants to TUSM;
• Maintaining a high level of RAR Program enrollment; and
• Helping to promote students' academic successes and ensuring retention and on-time graduation.

Enrichment Programs
We provide a wide range of year-round student support services for enrolled underrepresented medical students and conduct a voluntary two-week Summer Program during July for qualified students who will enroll in the first-year class. In keeping with Temple's goal to academically retain all students it enrolls, our RAR Program Counselor and the faculty of the medical school have long agreed that entering first-year students who participate in our Summer Program, called SERA (Summer Educational Reinforcement Activity), better their chances for an academically successful first year.

The SERA is a no-penalty simulation of what it is like to experience the first year of medical education. In the first week, students are introduced to the faculty, staff, upper-class students, and the facilities of the medical school. During the remainder of the week, medical school faculty present lectures, conferences, and laboratory experiences from segments of the first-year courses in gross anatomy, biochemistry, and physiology. Students attend seminars designed to sharpen their learning skills; participate in Learning Teams with their new classmates; experience a variety of early patient care activities; and have Clinical Conferences about medical topics presented by physicians, many of whom are graduates of Temple.

Throughout the two-week SERA, the RAR Program Counselor assists students with planning for their enrollment in the fall, with particular attention directed to their initial adjustment to the first-year curriculum, financial planning, and housing. Year-round student support services provided by our RAR Program help with students' concerns in many areas including adjustment to the rigors of the first-year medical school curriculum and, in subsequent years, timely preparation for taking the licensure examinations as well as residency selection in the fourth year.

The RAR Program Counselor also works very closely with the Office of Admissions to assist in the timely processing of applications from students underrepresented in the health profession of medicine. We provide follow-up communications with applicants when necessary and are advocates for applicants at all stages of their admissions process, including the medical school's Admissions Committee.

Applicants meet with members of the RAR Program staff at the time of their Personal Interview and talk with currently enrolled medical students in order to obtain a realistic picture of what is like to be a medical student at Temple University.

Enrichment Programs
Student National Medical Association (SNMA).
The SNMA is the oldest and largest medical student organization dedicated to people of color and underserved communities. Community service is the heart and soul of the SNMA and eliminating disparities in health care

delivery, disease morbidity, and disease mortality are among our highest priorities. SNMA community service programs are implemented by local chapters based at allopathic and osteopathic medical schools throughout the nation. Our programs are designed to promote healthy living and stress the preventative nature of health care delivery. Committed to increasing the number of culturally capable and sensitive physicians, the SNMA is also dedicated to the academic and clinical success of medical students and pre-medical students. Through our signature MAPS, HPREP, and YSEP programs, SNMA members work with youth from elementary school to college, introducing them to science and serving as mentors. In this way, the SNMA strengthens the educational pipeline that leads from elementary school to medical school.

Boricua Latino Health Organization (BLHO)
Boricua Latino Health Organization (BLHO) is a student organization committed to developing a network of support for minority medical students, particularly those of Latino background. ALL students interested in learning about the Latino culture are welcome and encouraged to participate.

Associated Activities and Events:
- Charlas: Student-run medical terminology and conversational Spanish course (Elective)
- VOICES: Volunteer Spanish interpreter program
- Blood pressure and health screening
- Latino Heritage Month
- Dar Vida: Bone Marrow Drive
- Speakers, fundraisers, and other social activities
- Mentoring, networking and support for medical students

Student Financial Assistance
Provide as much information as possible concerning financial aid for students. Please indicate if the application fee is waived and if financial aid is available for interview trips. Emphasis should be placed on opportunities available only at your institution (that is, non-need-based awards, fellowships,

grants, local loan possibilities, state scholarships or loan programs, and so on). Provide as much information as possible concerning institutional debt management and financial planning programs that are offered for all students.

Educational Partnerships
Temple University School of Medicine maintains the following educational partnerships:

(http://www.aspiringdocs.org/site/c.luIU L9MUJtE/b.2011035/k.C6A4/ WELCOME/apps/lk/content3.aspx) (http://ncmhd.nih.gov/our_programs/ strategic/volumes.asp) (http://www.nhlbi.nih.gov/training/ index.htm) (http://www.temple.edu/medicine/ departments_centers/research/ minority_health.htm)

University of Pennsylvania School of Medicine

Dr. Karen E. Hamilton, Assistant Dean for Diversity and Community Outreach in Undergraduate Medical Education
University of Pennsylvania School of Medicine
3450 Hamilton Walk, Suite 100
Stemmler Hall
Philadelphia, PA 19104
215-898-4409; 215-898-0833 fax
odco@mail.med.upenn
http://www.med.upenn.edu/diversityume

Recruitment

The University of Pennsylvania School of Medicine is committed to sustaining a diverse student body in keeping with the view that interaction among students from different backgrounds enriches the educational experiences of all students, faculty, and the Penn community at large.

In 1968, it established the Office of Minority Affairs, now known as the Office of Diversity and Community Outreach in Undergraduate Medical Education. Among its many responsibilities are efforts to recruit and retain students from groups that are underrepresented in medicine. Currently, 119 students from underrepresented groups compose approximately 16.5 percent of the student body. The recruitment and subsequent graduation of 571 students from these groups since 1968 reflects the School of Medicine's contribution to diversity within the university and within the medical profession.

The office hosts student groups from various undergraduate colleges and community-based organizations in order to provide general information about medical school preparation and details of the School of Medicine's admissions process, curriculum, student life, research opportunities, and financial aid. Similarly, students and office staff participate in outreach activities at local high schools, undergraduate colleges, summer enrichment programs, as well as at the annual career fairs of the Association of American Medical Colleges and the National Association of Medical Minority Educators (NAMME).

The most significant recruitment effort on the part of the office has been coordinating the publication of Getting into Medical School: A Planning Guide for Minority Students. This book was conceived of and written by Penn Medical minority students. To date, it is the only commercially published book of its kind written by and for minority students.

During the admissions season, the office and the Penn Medical chapters of the Student National Medical Association and the Boricua Latino Health Organization sponsor informational sessions about their programs and activities. Applicants from underrepresented groups and those interested in minority health issues and health care delivery for underserved communities are encouraged to attend these sessions.

Admissions

The Committee on Admissions is composed of a diverse group of faculty and students, some of whom are from groups underrepresented in medicine. In its mission to enroll a student body reflective of cultural diversity, consideration is given to an applicant's special features of background and experiences that may contribute to a candidate's potential for a career in medicine. The committee evaluates applicants whom it

University of Pennsylvania School of Medicine
Applicants, First-Time Applicants, Matriculants by Gender, Race and Ethnicity, 2007-2008

	2007									2008								
	APP			F-time APP			MAT			APP			F-time APP			MAT		
	Women	Men	Total	Women	Men	Total	Women	Men	Total	Women	Men	Total	Women	Men	Total	Women	Men	Total
Hispanic/Latino																		
Cuban	18	21	39	17	16	33	1	0	1	19	16	35	15	15	30	0	1	1
Mexican American	39	41	80	33	34	67	0	0	0	40	41	81	35	33	68	1	1	2
Puerto Rican	18	26	44	14	22	36	2	1	3	16	18	34	14	15	29	1	0	1
Other Hispanic	73	67	140	65	55	120	1	2	3	68	77	145	64	67	131	5	7	12
Multiple Hispanic/Latino*	5	5	10	5	5	10	0	0	0	9	10	19	8	9	17	1	0	1
Subtotal	153	160	313	134	132	266	4	3	7	152	162	314	136	139	275	8	9	17
Non-Hispanic/Latino**																		
Black	208	132	340	173	115	288	8	5	13	217	110	327	181	92	273	8	2	10
Native American/AK	0	6	6	0	5	5	0	0	0	2	4	6	2	4	6	0	0	0
Native Hawaiian/OPI	9	5	14	6	4	10	0	0	0	7	5	12	5	3	8	0	0	0
White	1,553	1,760	3,313	1,390	1,515	2,905	49	46	95	1,473	1,897	3,370	1,283	1,594	2,877	38	48	86
Asian	861	929	1,790	762	784	1,546	8	15	23	807	982	1,789	675	787	1,462	11	13	24
Other Race	1	3	4	1	3	4	0	0	0	2	2	4	1	1	2	0	0	0
Multiple Race*	106	92	198	96	77	173	3	3	6	91	87	178	72	69	141	6	3	9
Unknown	34	40	74	32	38	70	3	1	4	96	130	226	94	116	210	1	4	5
Subtotal	2,772	2,967	5,739	2,460	2,541	5,001	71	70	141	2,695	3,217	5,912	2,313	2,666	4,979	64	70	134
Foreign	147	145	292	120	114	234	4	1	5	153	167	320	136	129	265	1	2	3
Total	3,072	3,272	6,344	2,714	2,787	5,501	79	74	153	3,000	3,546	6,546	2,585	2,934	5,519	73	81	154

*Since 2002, students can select more than one race and / or ethnicity. **Those who did not choose 'Hispanic/Latino' or 'Non-Hispanic/Latino' are listed under 'Non-Hispanic/Latino'. Data Source: AAMC Data Warehouse: Applicant-Matriculant File, as of 1/16/2009.

admits on the basis of their academic potential, service, and leadership.

Applications for admission must be submitted through the American Medical Application Service (AMCAS) between June 1 and October 15. The Committee on Admissions will begin processing the application when all supplemental materials have been received, including the application supplemental, application fee or AMCAS fee waiver, Medical College Admission Test (MCAT) scores, and letters of recommendation. In addition to the M.D. program, students may pursue the M.D./Ph.D. degree or the M.D. and Master's degree. The Master's programs most commonly combined with the M.D. degree are the M.B.A., the Master's in Bioethics, and the Master's in Clinical Epidemiology.

Academic Support Programs

Curriculum flexibility is maintained to assure meeting students' individual needs in preparing for a future career. All students will have at least one and one-half years of elective time available to develop a personalized educational program. While most students will enter clinical clerkships at the midpoint of the second year, some are permitted to arrange an alternative schedule.

Counseling is an integral part of the School of Medicine's retention efforts. It is offered in all areas: personal, financial, residential, and academic. The summer prior to matriculation, each entering first-year student is assigned to an upper-class student peer advisor. Moreover, the Student Affairs administrators, the Associate Dean, Assistant Dean, and Associate Director for Diversity and Community Outreach in Undergraduate Medical Education Programs also serve as advisors.

With guidance from the Office for Diversity and Community Outreach in Undergraduate Medical Education, the Student National Medical Association (SNMA) and the Boricua Latino Health Organization (BLHO) have developed academic enrichment activities that include review sessions for the basic sci-

ences, tutoring, cultural competency lectures, and health education projects for underserved communities. These two student organizations also produce an ethnic guide to Philadelphia as part of the larger Guide to the First Year, an on-line publication sponsored by the Penn Med Student Government with the Office for Diversity and Community Outreach in Undergraduate Medical Education. The SNMA and BLHO also organize the Case Presentation Seminar Series in which minority faculty and residents give advice about successful academic performance for each required clerkship. These sessions, open to all, are continuous and facilitate interaction among students, minority faculty, and residents.

Enrichment Programs

Summer Internships in the Biological Sciences
This internship program offers hands-on research experience in a laboratory setting for undergraduate students interested in the biological sciences. Each undergraduate intern is matched with a faculty member and participates for ten weeks in the on-going research of the investigator's laboratory or performs a specific and supervised research project related to the goals of the laboratory. A weekly seminar provides an overview of the breadth of contemporary biomedical science. Formal courses are not offered.

Applicants may specify their research interest: biochemistry and molecular biophysics, cell and molecular biology, developmental biology, genetics, genomics and computational biology, immunology, microbiology, parasitology, and virology neuroscience and pharmacological sciences. Previous research experience is not necessary.

The program is open to students of all racial and ethnic backgrounds. Approximately 30 college sophomores and juniors participate each year. The stipend is $250/ week, round-trip transportation to Philadelphia, and on-campus housing. February 1st is the application deadline.

For an application or further information, contact *(http:// www.med.upenn.edu/bgs/ suip.shtml)* Summer Internship Coordinator, Biomedical Graduate Studies, 160 BRB 2/3, Currie Blvd., University of Pennsylvania, Philadelphia, PA 19104-6064.

Undergraduate Student Scholars Program
The Undergraduate Student Scholars Program in the NIH Center for Molecular Studies in Digestive and Liver Disease at the University of Pennsylvania is an organized program of summer lectures and presentations combined with basic research experience in the laboratory of an expert investigator. This program is open to students from the University of Pennsylvania as well as outside of the university. The curriculum is designed specifically for undergraduate students with an interest in biomedical research, with the eventual goal of M.D., Ph.D., or M.D.-Ph.D. degrees. Applications from women and members of underrepresented minorities are strongly encouraged.

During the program, students attend weekly seminars on introductory topics in biomedical research. At the end of the course, all participants present their research to members of the Center for Molecular Studies in Digestive and Liver Disease in a focused seminar and receive a certificate recognizing their completion of the program. For the research experience, students are paired with individual mentors. The research program is thus individualized to each student and each laboratory. Research interests of program faculty are available at *(http://www.med.upenn.edu/ molecular/)*

The stipend this year is expected to be $3,500 for the ten-week program. Applications, may be obtained at: *(http://www.med.upenn. edu/molecular/)* or by contacting Ms. Rose Garrity at the address below:

Rose Garrity
Administrative Assistant
415 Curie Boulevard
600 Clinical Research Building
Philadelphia, PA 19104-6160
Email: *djolly@mail.med.upenn.edu*

Student Financial Assistance

The School of Medicine is committed to assisting students to fund their medical educational, minimizing debt, and providing financial counseling. The school awards both need based and merit scholarships. Need is documented after a financial analysis of the student's financial situation, including the parents' and spouse's financial situation. This data is requested on the financial aid application.

A successful applicant must be a United States citizen or hold a permanent residence visa, or an immigrant visa to be eligible for financial aid. The types of aid available include the following:

- School of Medicine scholarships
- School of Medicine loans
- MSTP funding (for M.D./Ph.D. program candidates)
- Federal loan programs
- Federal programs emphasizing primary care careers
- Alternative loan programs

Educational Partnerships

In partnership with the School of Medicine, the School of Dental Medicine, School of Veterinary Medicine, and the School of Nursing, along with the Office of Career Services Review have developed the Pre-health Professions Mentor Program. The goal of the program is to increase the number of undergraduates admitted to highly competitive health professional schools. Although the program is a structured network of support for undergraduates who are from groups underrepresented in the health professions, its workshops and other programmatic activities are open to all Penn undergraduates. These include:

- Academic monitoring, counseling, and advising
- Medical College Admissions Test (MCAT) preparation
- Dental School Admissions Test (DAT) preparation
- Graduate Record Exam (GRE) preparation
- Mentoring by faculty; medical, dental, veterinary, and nursing students; and peers
- Interaction with faculty and professionals in the field
- Research experience
- Educational programs and workshops
- Tutoring

University of Pittsburgh School of Medicine

Dr. Chenits Pettigrew, Jr., Assistant Dean of Student Affairs/Director of Diversity Programs
University of Pittsburgh School of Medicine
M-247 Scaife Hall
Pittsburgh, PA 15261
412-648-8987; 412-624-2516 fax
diversityaffairs@medschool.pitt.edu
http://www.medschool.pitt.edu

Recruitment

The Office of Student Affairs/Diversity Programs was instituted in 1979 to enhance and support the increasingly diverse student body of the school and to assist the Office of Admissions in recruiting underrepresented, underprivileged, and non-traditional students. Office staff and members of the Student National Medical Association (SNMA) participate in recruitment visits to various campuses nationwide during the school year and at summer programs.

Recruitment visits are made to majority as well as Historically Black Colleges and Universities and Hispanic-serving campuses. Staff actively utilize the Medical Minority Applicant Registry (Med-MAR) to identify and contact prospective applicants. High school students are contacted via guidance counselors and during recruitment for the university's summer and enrichment programs (see Enrichment Programs). The staff has a great deal of interaction with the University of Pittsburgh undergraduate students through active involvement with the Pre-health Organization for Minority Students, which is a Student National Medical Association MAPS chapter.

Admissions

The school's student body is composed of over 40 states, various undergraduate majors, and many students for whom medicine was not a first career choice. All of these perspectives blend to create a diverse and enriching community. All candidates are considered via the common American Medcial College Application Service (AMCAS) admissions process. An applicant's application is evaluated holistically during a thorough admission process. Community service and other demonstrations of caring for others are extremely important.

Academic Support Programs

The curriculum is a blend of basic sciences, organ system study, small-group learning, lectures, field experience, and self-directed learning. Significant emphasis is placed upon the physician/patient relationship; students begin interacting with patients in the first week of the first year. Course syllabi and study guides are distributed prior to the beginning of each course. The curriculum is quite effective, as evidenced by a 100 percent pass rate on United States Medical Licensing Examination (USMLE) Steps 1 and 2 in most recent years. The school offers an Advisory Deans Program, which is a four-year advising partnership that addresses academic, career, professional, and personal development.

First-year students are assigned to FAST (Faculty and Students Working Together) groups led by faculty advisors and peer mentors who are available for advice and guidance during the first year transition to medical school. In addition, the Student Academic Resource Consortium, a team of second-year students also helps

University of Pittsburgh School of Medicine
Applicants, First-Time Applicants, Matriculants by Gender, Race and Ethnicity, 2007-2008

	2007 APP Women	Men	Total	2007 F-time APP Women	Men	Total	2007 MAT Women	Men	Total	2008 APP Women	Men	Total	2008 F-time APP Women	Men	Total	2008 MAT Women	Men	Total
Hispanic/Latino																		
Cuban	11	14	25	7	11	18	1	0	1	7	14	21	5	11	16	0	0	0
Mexican American	31	37	68	22	29	51	0	0	0	37	37	74	34	29	63	1	2	3
Puerto Rican	15	19	34	10	15	25	2	0	2	15	14	29	12	12	24	0	0	0
Other Hispanic	66	51	117	52	35	87	6	0	6	52	66	118	41	53	94	2	3	5
Multiple Hispanic/Latino*	6	4	10	5	3	8	0	0	0	8	5	13	7	3	10	0	1	1
Subtotal	129	125	254	96	93	189	9	0	9	119	136	255	99	108	207	3	6	9
Non-Hispanic/Latino**																		
Black	206	127	333	152	101	253	8	5	13	186	101	287	145	77	222	8	8	16
Native American/AK	4	2	6	3	2	5	0	0	0	5	4	9	4	4	8	0	0	0
Native Hawaiian/OPI	8	6	14	5	6	11	1	0	1	11	4	15	7	2	9	0	0	0
White	1,363	1,697	3,060	1,141	1,352	2,493	41	42	83	1,248	1,694	2,942	1,025	1,311	2,336	27	51	78
Asian	774	868	1,642	634	683	1,317	14	20	34	698	864	1,562	544	627	1,171	17	17	34
Other Race	1	5	6	1	2	3	0	0	0	1	4	5	1	2	3	0	0	0
Multiple Race*	80	78	158	70	57	127	3	3	6	70	74	144	49	54	103	1	0	1
Unknown	21	51	72	20	46	66	0	0	0	64	92	156	62	79	141	3	6	9
Subtotal	2,457	2,834	5,291	2,026	2,249	4,275	67	70	137	2,283	2,837	5,120	1,837	2,156	3,993	56	82	138
Foreign	33	38	71	29	31	60	0	0	0	15	23	38	14	18	32	0	0	0
Total	2,619	2,997	5,616	2,151	2,373	4,524	76	70	146	2,417	2,996	5,413	1,950	2,282	4,232	59	88	147

*Since 2002, students can select more than one race and / or ethnicity. **Those who did not choose 'Hispanic/Latino' or 'Non-Hispanic/Latino' are listed under 'Non-Hispanic/Latino'. Data Source: AAMC Data Warehouse: Applicant-Matriculant File, as of 1/16/2009.

first-year students adjust to the rigors of medical school.

In support of academic success, the University of Pittsburgh School of Medicine provides a proactive program of academic support. The Office of Academic Development provides assistance in learning strategies, time management, test taking, and coordinates a peer tutorial service. Faculty are always available for assistance on a group review and individual basis. The Office of Academic Development also works with students on pretest assessment and study plans for the USMLE Step 1 in the Spring of the second year. A staff psychologist who has intimate knowledge of the medical School curriculum and medical student life is available to assist students with personal issues that might arise.

Physician Partners Mentoring Program
The Physician Partners Mentoring Program links underrepresented (URM), first-generation, and non-traditional medical students with faculty and community physicians in supportive relationships.

Enrichment Programs

For further information on any of the following programs, contact Dr. Chenits Pettigrew, Assistant Dean of Student Affairs/ Director of Diversity Programs at 412-648-8987, or visit (http://www.medschool.pitt.edu)

Medical Explorers
Hosted in cooperation with the Boy Scouts of Southwestern Pennsylvania, this program provides high school students with exposure to the field of medicine through presentations given by physicians and medical students clinical pathology conferences, field trips, and laboratory experiences. The program operates through the academic year. Students meet twice per week in the Fall semester and once per week in the Spring semester. Planning for the programs is completed by the program participants at the end of each Spring. While designed for high school students, middle school students are also encouraged to attend.

Summer Pre-medical Academic Enrichment Program (SPAEP) Level I
A seven-week program offered to underrepresented and first-generation rising college freshmen and sophomores. Its purpose is to 1) expose students to the pre-medical basic sciences through studying diseases that affect underserved communities (e.g., AIDS, sickle-cell anemia, hypertension); 2) motivate students to pursue careers in medicine; and 3) familiarize students with the medical school environment, the required academic preparation for and with the medical school application process. Students participate in lectures, presentations, research and a course in scientific communication. They shadow physicians. Study-skills diagnostics and tutorials are included. Physicians speak about their fields of practice at a weekly "Brown Bag Lunch" series. At the end-of-program forum each student gives an oral presentation of research on a selected disease. Preference in admission is given to Pennsylvania students, particularly those from Pittsburgh. However, students from across the nation can (and do) participate. Room, board, and travel are included. The application deadline is March 1st.

SPAEP Level II
A seven-week summer research program where participants spend four days per week engaged in mentored laboratory research. Fridays are dedicated to study skills, medical school admissions workshops, and physician shadowing. Room, board, travel, and MCAT preparation are included.

Pre-matriculation Program
This program is offered only to students who have been accepted into the first-year class of the University of Pittsburgh School of Medicine. In addition to providing a look at the curriculum, the program seeks to help students adapt to the medical school, the city, and the university. Participants begin to form support networks during the program. Lectures are given by School of Medicine faculty. Study skills diagnostics are administered, and survival skills workshops are held bi-weekly. Students

meet weekly with the school's administrative deans and participate in problem-based learning small-group sessions.

Medical Crossroads
A day-long medical school preparation program co-sponsored by the University of Pittsburgh School of Medicine chapter of the SNMA. Medical students provide all the lectures and focus on pre-medical academic preparation: the MCAT, the American Medical College Application Service (AMCAS) application, and interview skills. Students participate in a problem-based learning group and sample physical diagnosis sessions facilitated by medical students. All pre-medical students in the state of Pennsylvania are invited to attend.

Student Financial Assistance

The University of Pittsburgh works diligently to help students to overcome any financial barriers. Secondary application fees are waived for those who have received AMCAS fee waivers. Other requests for waivers are considered on an individual basis. For students who have been invited to interview, overnight housing is available through student hosts (this request must be made in advance of the interview day).

Financial aid is awarded based on financial need, as determined from information supplied on the Free Application for Federal Student Aid (FAFSA), and other school-specific documents. Locally-funded aid for underrepresented or first-generation students includes grants and emergency loans through the Negro Educational Emergency Drive (NEED), which are available to residents of Southwestern Pennsylvania. Contact NEED at 412-566-2760.

Students are counseled throughout their matriculation on debt management. To facilitate financial planning and awareness, a debt-counseling session is offered for students in the second semester of the first year. Fourth-year students participate in "Your Financial Rx," a debt-counseling seminar co-sponsored by the Association of American Medical Colleges, the Pennsylvania Medical Society, and the School of Medicine. Sessions include information on negotiating residency contracts, managing student loan repayment, budgeting, investing, and handling stress during residency. Students may participate in "Your Financial Rx" or have an individual debt-counseling exit interview.

Other School of Medicine resources include Dean's Scholarships (available to all students); the alumni-funded Charles M. Hefflin Medical Student Scholarship; The Gateway Medical Society Award; and the Chi Delta Mu Award. The Medical Alumni Scholarship is awarded on a competitive basis to three freshmen from Pennsylvania who have demonstrated exceptional academic achievement.

Educational Partnerships

The Office of Student Affairs/Diversity Programs maintains an active relationship with the City of Pittsburgh Public School System and the Urban League Charter School. These relationships allow the School of Medicine to involve students with its Medical Explorers Post and Summer Pre-medical Academic Enrichment Program. The school of medicine also partners with the Boy Scouts of Southwestern Pennsylvania. The PITTMED Medical Explorers Post is the largest and longest existing Exploring post in the nation.

The Office of Admissions of the University of Pittsburgh identifies potential candidates for its Guarantee Program whereby a limited number of undergraduate students accepted to the university may be considered for guaranteed admission to medical school if they maintain the required grade-point average.

Ponce School of Medicine

Dr. Arvin Báez
Assistant Dean for Student Affairs
Ponce School of Medicine
PO Box 7004
Ponce, PR 00732-7004
787-840-2575; 787-259-1931 fax

Recruitment

Ponce School of Medicine actively recruits highly qualified students who have completed the pre-medical requirements. The medical student body's composition is diversified, consisting primarily of Puerto Ricans and students from the mainland who are bilingual.

Recruitment efforts and academic programs are designed to ensure equal opportunity. Specific information about requirements for admission at Ponce School of Medicine is provided to all public and private colleges and universities, particularly those with pre-medical programs. The same information is provided to any applicant within Puerto Rico or the continental United States.

Admissions

The following criteria are considered by the Admission Committee to evaluate all applicants:

Bachelor degree or its equivalent in a college level institution accredited by the Council of Higher Education of Puerto Rico or by a U.S. accrediting organization,

1. Grade-point average,
2. Medical College Admission Test (MCAT) scores,
3. Ability to communicate in English and Spanish,
4. Interview reports by Admissions Committee members,
5. Certificate of No Penal Record, and
6. Letters of recommendation.

Minority status and economic factors are not used as criteria for admission. Puerto Rican students account for about 85 percent of the student population.

Academic Support Programs

Students identified to have special educational needs during the first semester of the first year are offered the choice to change to a five-year program. This schedule allows students to take three

years for the completion of the basic science curriculum, therefore, allowing five years to complete the degree. The different student associations are active in student support. Male and female students could be members of the organizations.

The Office of Student Affairs coordinates a program of student tutorships in conjunction with the basic sciences departments. Also, students receive counseling in study strategies and test-taking skills at the Office of Student Affairs. Activities directed toward career counseling are scheduled along the academic year. Counseling Program is available to students. The program offers professional counseling, psychological, or psychiatric services.

Enrichment Programs

Medical Student Summer Research Program (MSSRP)
This program is intended to increase the number of medical students participating in biomedical research activities. This allows students to integrate and develop skills necessary for research in the basic sciences through active research participation.

Ponce School of Medicine
Applicants, First-Time Applicants, Matriculants by Gender, Race and Ethnicity, 2007-2008

	2007									2008								
	APP			F-time APP			MAT			APP			F-time APP			MAT		
	Wo-men	Men	Total	Wo-men	Men	Total	Wo-men	Men	Total	Wo-men	Men	Total	Wo-men	Men	Total	Wo-men	Men	Total
Hispanic/Latino																		
Cuban	21	39	60	15	31	46	2	3	5	39	24	63	32	18	50	0	2	2
Mexican American	21	25	46	13	13	26	0	0	0	16	12	28	8	3	11	1	0	1
Puerto Rican	208	159	367	176	129	305	24	20	44	261	156	417	227	134	361	30	24	54
Other Hispanic	54	36	90	44	24	68	3	2	5	61	57	118	42	38	80	1	1	2
Multiple Hispanic/Latino*	15	8	23	11	7	18	3	0	3	15	11	26	12	9	21	0	1	1
Subtotal	319	267	586	259	204	463	32	25	57	392	260	652	321	202	523	32	28	60
Non-Hispanic/Latino**																		
Black	36	29	65	28	21	49	0	0	0	36	21	57	14	13	27	0	0	0
Native American/AK	0	0	0	0	0	0	0	0	0	2	1	3	2	1	3	0	0	0
Native Hawaiian/OPI	3	2	5	3	2	5	0	0	0	3	4	7	3	3	6	0	0	0
White	148	187	335	109	133	242	2	3	5	132	186	318	98	130	228	0	4	4
Asian	109	116	225	84	85	169	0	0	0	102	96	198	76	65	141	1	0	1
Other Race	3	1	4	2	1	3	0	0	0	2	2	4	1	2	3	0	0	0
Multiple Race*	10	7	17	7	5	12	1	0	1	7	12	19	3	6	9	0	0	0
Unknown	5	3	8	5	2	7	0	0	0	6	6	12	6	5	11	0	0	0
Subtotal	314	345	659	238	249	487	3	3	6	290	328	618	203	225	428	1	4	5
Foreign	16	19	35	14	16	30	0	0	0	24	26	50	18	21	39	0	0	0
Total	649	631	1,280	511	469	980	35	28	63	706	614	1,320	542	448	990	33	32	65

*Since 2002, students can select more than one race and / or ethnicity. **Those who did not choose 'Hispanic/Latino' or 'Non-Hispanic/Latino' are listed under 'Non-Hispanic/Latino'. Data Source: AAMC Data Warehouse: Applicant-Matriculant File, as of 1/16/2009.

Student Financial Assistance

To be eligible for assistance, students must be U.S. citizens, be registered on a full-time basis, be in good standing, and have demonstrated financial need.

The following loans are currently available: Federal Stafford, Alternative Loans, and Unsubsidized Stafford Loan. The Student Financial Aid Office assists all qualified students with their applications to available state and federal financial aid programs. Scholarships for the U.S. Army, U.S. Navy, and National Health Service Corps are available. Students receive all information about financial aid upon being admitted to the school.

Educational Partnerships

Ponce School of Medicine has a program with the Pontifical Catholic University of Puerto Rico and Interamerican University-Ponce Campus called the Binary Program. This program allows for academically exceptional students to complete their pre-medical requirements in two years, finishing their college and medical education in six years. The students receive a Bachelor in Science degree from their respective university after completing the second year (basic sciences) of medical studies.

Other Pertinent Information

The Ponce Medical School Foundation is a non-profit organization responsible for the operation of the Ponce School of Medicine. The Foundation took over the operation of the school July 1, 1980, under the government of a Board of Trustees.

The Ponce School of Medicine is located in Ponce, Puerto Rico, the second largest city of the island. Applications for admission are considered based on the qualifications of the applicants without regard to race, age, creed, sex, national origin, or physical handicaps. Students, faculty, and staff are assured of participation in programs and the use of facilities without discrimination.

San Juan Bautista School of Medicine

Dr. Myraida Rivera, Admission's Director and Minority Affairs Officer
San Juan Bautista School of Medicine
P.O. Box 4968
Caguas, PR 00725-4968
787-743-3038; 787-746-3093 fax
mrivera@sanjuanbautista.edu

Recruitment

Since 1978, the SJBSM has been focused to teach and train students in a bilingual environment to serve the communities in health needs in Puerto Rico and in the mainland. Recruitment activities vary from educational and health fairs, to visiting the Science departments at the local undergraduates colleges, and open house activities. The Admission's Committee with the support from the Associate Deanship for Students Affairs, is in charge of programming and coordination of the recruitment activities. Volunteer students are part of this recruitment team.

Admissions

SJBSM look for all candidates that have the intellectual, emotional and physical abilities, with reasonable accommodations as needed for those with disabilities, to acquire the knowledge, behavior, and clinical skills that they will need to successfully complete the core curriculum (technical standards) and comply with the School requirements, established by the Admission's Committee: MCAT Score, GPA, pre-medical credits or Baccalaureate degree in Sciences, background check, technical standards and the ability to communicate in both English and Spanish. The SJBSM does not discriminate by race, sex, gender orientation, religion, physical disability, economic status, national origin or political ideology.

Academic support programs

The School offers a decelerated program in which the biomedical courses are completed in three years instead of the usual two. At the beginning of the first academic year, students have an orientation program that includes formal school presentation of the faculty and staff, academic program description, assessment methodology, and a learning style diagnosis.

There is a tutorial program compulsory for all students who have a non-satisfactory performance during the first course exam. There is also a mentoring program, where a faculty member is assigned a group of students (first and second years) to guide them in all academic and non-academic concerns.

The assessment and promotions committee identify academic risk and the aggravating factors and advise the curriculum committee and the student himself to make the arrangements to avoid an academic failure.

Enrichment Programs

Improvement of Language Skills
Because SJBSM has a non-biased admissions policy, all incoming students are oriented to reinforce their language skills in Spanish and English. Students who are identified through the application process as non-native speakers of Spanish are encouraged to take a Spanish language course. The School has an agreement with the Universidad del Turabo regarding immersion courses in Spanish and/or English for those students who desire enrollment in either.

San Juan Bautista School of Medicine
Applicants, First-Time Applicants, Matriculants by Gender, Race and Ethnicity, 2007-2008

	2008								
	APP			F-time APP			MAT		
	Women	Men	Total	Women	Men	Total	Women	Men	Total
Hispanic/Latino									
Cuban	6	3	9	6	2	8	1	1	2
Mexican American	4	7	11	3	4	7	0	0	0
Puerto Rican	199	108	307	170	95	265	24	16	40
Other Hispanic	12	19	31	9	16	25	2	3	5
Multiple Hispanic/Latino*	2	6	8	2	5	7	1	1	2
Subtotal	223	143	366	190	122	312	28	21	49
Non-Hispanic/Latino**									
Black	14	14	28	8	9	17	0	2	2
Native American/AK	1	0	1	1	0	1	0	0	0
Native Hawaiian/OPI	1	0	1	1	0	1	0	0	0
White	16	40	56	11	31	42	2	2	4
Asian	19	22	41	13	20	33	3	2	5
Unknown	1	1	2	1	1	2	0	0	0
Subtotal	52	77	129	35	61	96	5	6	11
Foreign	3	6	9	3	4	7	0	0	0
Total	278	226	504	228	187	415	33	27	60

*Since 2002, students can select more than one race and / or ethnicity. **Those who did not choose 'Hispanic/Latino' or 'Non-Hispanic/Latino' are listed under 'Non-Hispanic/Latino'. Data Source: AAMC Data Warehouse: Applicant-Matriculant File, as of 1/16/2009.

Basic Science Medical Student Summer Research (BSMSSR) clerkship

This BSMSSR was designed in order to provide a fundamental understanding of the subject under investigation. In this type of research, students will be able to develop critical thinking and to expand their knowledge on the basic science subject chosen. The students will be under direct supervision of a proctor expert on the chosen field. Students will meet individually with the research proctor of their preference, to discuss the subject to be addressed and the standards to be followed. They will schedule appointments throughout the program, as needed, and should meet on a weekly basis with their proctor. Upon completion of the summer research program, students will be encouraged to continue on their investigation.

Notification Process: The proctor should send a formal letter of acceptance of the student and a description of the project to be conducted and the research protocol will be revised and approved by the Associate Dean for Research.

Objectives: a) the student should be able to integrate biomedical sciences and research skills, in order to demonstrate a broad comprehension on the chosen topic, b) the student will be able to associate the biomedical sciences with clinical correlations according to his or her level.

- Proctor: Chosen by the student, and approved by the Associate Dean of Research.
- Duration: Six (6) weeks.
- Credit Hours: Three (3) credits.
- Contact Hours: 40 hours weekly (240 hours).
- Days Offered: As established by proctor
- Enrollment: One (1) student by proctor
- Pre-Requisites: First year medical school basic science courses.
- Meeting time and place: As established by proctor
- Evaluation: It will be submitted at the conclusion of the clerkship by the

proctor, based on the assessment of student's performance on the research study as well as other parameters established by the proctor.

Clinical Science Medical Student Summer Research (CSMSSR)

CSMSSR was designed to develop a broad experience with clinically oriented research activities. In this type of research, students will be able to explore thoroughly specific topics of current clinical interest and correlate with the biomedical sciences knowledge. They may work directly with patients, who either have a specific clinical condition, or have undergone a specific treatment related with the topic of interest. The students will be under direct supervision of a proctor expert on the chosen subject. Students will meet individually with the research proctor of their preference, to discuss the subject to be addressed and the standards to be followed. Students will schedule appointments throughout the program as needed and should meet on a weekly basis with their proctor. Upon completion of the summer research program, students will be encouraged to continue their investigation.

Notification Process: Proctor should send a formal letter of acceptance to the student, and a description of the project to be assigned and the research protocol will be revised and approved by the Associate Dean for Research.

Objectives: a) the student should be able to integrate clinical sciences and research skills in order to demonstrate a broad comprehension of treatment and management depending on the specific clinical research study; b) the student will be able to correlate the different clinical conditions with the effectiveness of potential treatments, according to his or her level.

Proctor: Chosen by the student and approved by the Associate Dean for Research.

- Duration: Six (6) weeks.
- Credit Hours: Three (3) credits
- Contact Hours: 40 hours weekly (240 hours)

- Days Offered: As established by proctor
- Enrollment: One (1) student by proctor
- Pre-Requisites: First and second year medical school biomedical science courses; third year medical school clinical science clerkships
- Meeting time and place: As established by proctor
- Evaluation: It will be submitted at the conclusion of the clerkship by the proctor based on the assessment of student's performance on the research study as well as other parameters established by the proctor.

Student Financial Assistance

The Financial Aid Office has the responsibility to guide students through the available economic aids and the procedure to applying for them. Among financial aids available to our students, are:

Stafford Loans: the student who meets the requirements established by the Federal Education Department

Supplemental Educational Assistance Program, the Council of Higher Education of Puerto Rico (CHEPR). This program is intended to give additional financial assistance to economically disadvantaged students, who are enrolled in eligible institutions.

Legislative Scholarships: This program is administered by the Medical Sciences Campus of the University of Puerto Rico. Annually, the Financial Aid Office distributes the forms to be completed by students interested in apply. The assessment and allocation of financial funds are determined by the institution. The amount to be awarded varies, depending on the student's financial need.

Municipal Scholarships: Some municipalities have assistance programs to help students who demonstrate economic need. To apply for such aid, students should visit the mayors of their respective municipalities.

Veterans: Students beneficiaries must apply in the Registrar's Office certifications are required by the Veterans Administration to begin the process.

Vocational Rehabilitation Program: Students beneficiaries must apply in the Registrar's Office certifications are required by the Vocational Rehabilitation Program to initiate the process.

Study/Work program: The institution offers to some students the opportunity to work for a number of hours per week, and receive payment for their services. Some of these opportunities include tutoring, working in the library and working in the research laboratories. They are subject to the need of service.

Career in Medicine
The Career in Medicine Program starts at the entrance to the school, and has a lot of activities until the graduation, and advice students regarding their future aspirations. There is a school officer in charge with this duty, with the support of the counseling staff.

Tutoring programs
Upper rank students in each course could be a tutor for the students, receiving monetary compensation.

Universidad Central del Caribe School of Medicine

Yari M. Marrero-Pagán,
Guidance Counselor
Universidad Central del Caribe
School of Medicine
P O Box 60327
Bayamón, Puerto Rico 00960
Tel. 787-798-3001 ext. 2405;
787-269-7550 fax
yari.marrero@uccaribe.edu
www.uccaribe.edu

Recruitment

The Universidad del Caribe School of Medicine (UCC-SOM) is a private, non-profit institution that has been committed to primary care medical education, serving in local communities and Hispanic populations in the United States. Our mission aims at preparing high-quality physicians to practice in Puerto Rico and the U.S. mainland. As a result, Hispanic, primarily Puerto Ricans, or Spanish-speaking U.S. citizens, constitute the majority of our student body.

The Hispanic population is the fastest growing minority group in the U.S., creating the need for more Hispanic-oriented institutions, particularly in the health-related professions. The significance of Hispanic needs within the health professions is an important factor contributing to the School of Medicine's explicit social contract, which depends to some degree upon enrolling Puerto Ricans and other Hispanics in our educational program.

Recruitment efforts emphasize visits to public and private colleges and universities in Puerto Rico. Tours and orientation sessions on campus, particularly with the medical students' association and counselors of universities and high schools, are coordinated with our faculty members. Also, state educational fairs, community clinics, and open houses are available throughout the year.

Admissions

The admission process is implemented by the Admissions Committee. This is an Advisory Committee composed of faculty members who are responsible to the Office of the Dean of the Medical School. The process is designed to assure that each applicant is evaluated in terms of his/her academic qualifications and potential. Fluency in both English and Spanish is essential.

The admissions process relies on a combination of objective factors such as performance on the Medical College Admission Test, undergraduate record, and the personal qualifications of the applicant as conveyed by letters of recommendations, and a personal interview. There is no discrimination on the basis of sex, color, race, religion, physical disability, economic status, political ideology, or national origin.

Academic Support Programs

New Student Orientation Program
Each summer, the UCC-SOM offers orientation activities for new medical students. This program aims at facilitating the students' transition to the new academic responsibilities and environment. It includes intensive workshops to enhance students' skills in time and stress management, study habits, learning styles, effective communication, spirituality and health, self-care, and problem solving. Emphasis is placed on helping students to identify high-risk situations that might hinder their academic performance and how to obtain adequate assistance to prevent them.

Fellow medical students (peer counselors) assume a significant role during orientation activities in sharing their

Universidad Central del Caribe School of Medicine
Applicants, First-Time Applicants, Matriculants by Gender, Race and Ethnicity, 2007-2008

	2007									2008								
	APP			F-time APP			MAT			APP			F-time APP			MAT		
	Wo-men	Men	Total	Wo-men	Men	Total	Wo-men	Men	Total	Wo-men	Men	Total	Wo-men	Men	Total	Wo-men	Men	Total
Hispanic/Latino																		
Cuban	15	25	40	9	21	30	1	3	4	24	14	38	22	11	33	1	2	3
Mexican American	16	20	36	11	12	23	0	1	1	15	12	27	9	3	12	0	0	0
Puerto Rican	188	136	324	157	108	265	24	25	49	250	137	387	218	117	335	24	24	48
Other Hispanic	38	31	69	31	20	51	3	1	4	41	46	87	28	36	64	1	3	4
Multiple Hispanic/Latino*	6	7	13	3	6	9	2	1	3	9	10	19	9	9	18	1	0	1
Subtotal	263	219	482	211	167	378	30	31	61	339	219	558	286	176	462	27	29	56
Non-Hispanic/Latino**																		
Black	26	17	43	20	8	28	0	0	0	25	13	38	13	8	21	0	0	0
Native American/AK	0	0	0	0	0	0	0	0	0	2	1	3	2	1	3	0	0	0
Native Hawaiian/OPI	0	2	2	0	2	2	0	0	0	3	3	6	3	3	6	0	0	0
White	101	120	221	75	87	162	2	1	3	90	137	227	66	99	165	1	5	6
Asian	65	73	138	52	51	103	0	0	0	73	64	137	56	46	102	0	2	2
Other Race	2	2	4	1	1	2	1	0	1	0	2	2	0	1	1	0	0	0
Multiple Race*	7	7	14	5	4	9	0	0	0	7	11	18	5	5	10	0	0	0
Unknown	7	2	9	6	1	7	0	0	0	6	3	9	6	2	8	0	0	0
Subtotal	208	223	431	159	154	313	3	1	4	206	234	440	151	165	316	1	7	8
Foreign	14	13	27	11	9	20	0	1	1	12	11	23	8	8	16	0	1	1
Total	485	455	940	381	330	711	33	33	66	557	464	1,021	445	349	794	28	37	65

*Since 2002, students can select more than one race and / or ethnicity. **Those who did not choose 'Hispanic/Latino' or 'Non-Hispanic/Latino' are listed under 'Non-Hispanic/Latino'. Data Source: AAMC Data Warehouse: Applicant-Matriculant File, as of 1/16/2009.

stories of success and failure in order to encourage new students to seek help, become motivated and gain self-confidence. This is with the purpose of showing them how to cope with the challenges and opportunities they will face during their medical education. The program also includes activities of integration with faculty, an introduction to the academic program and classes, the methods of evaluation and promotion, and training in computers for the learning- supports system.

Guidance and Counseling Program
All medical students have access to confidential guidance and counseling services with a professional counselor on a self-referred basis. Any student in need of mental health services not available in the UCC-SOM, may be referred to other professionals within the community, with the student's consent and authorization. The guidance and counseling program includes individual and group meetings with the students to discuss issues related to their success in the medical school. This issue includes personal and family problems, academic difficulties, or other daily-life aspects that may interfere in the health and performance of the student. We also provide academic counseling and guidance that include support with the study plans for USMLE, clerkships selection and career counseling.

Academic Monitoring and Tutoring Program
The Coordinators for each medical school year submit an academic monitoring report to the Dean of Students. This report includes the progress of each student and identifies the ones that have academic problems. Those students are referred to the Guidance and Counseling Program to be interviewed and make a work plan to remediate their low performance. This plan may include, but is not limited to, tutoring services, individual counseling, and referrals. The tutoring services are conducted by outstanding fellow medical students who are previously identified by the faculty and Dean of Students as potential tutors. Tutoring

sessions (individual or group) are coordinated by the counselor and this service is free for the students.

P.U.E.D.O. (I CAN) Program
This is a longitudinal program to enhance the performance of the medical students in the United States Medical Licensing Examination (USMLE) Steps 1 and 2. The P.U.E.D.O. program includes individual and group tutoring, reviews, a study plan template, online resources, books, workshops, the USMLE comprehensive exam, and other relevant activities to promote the success of the students in the USMLE.

Enrichment Programs

Prevention and Integral Health Program
This institutional well-being and prevention program includes workshops, health clinics, and lectures throughout the academic year. The program is directed at helping the students develop healthy attitudes and behavior regarding the use of alcohol, tobacco, and other drugs. Also, activities focused on healthy sexual activities, dealing with stress, violence and aggression, and achieving overall well-being among the student body.

Summer Preceptorships Program
Research activities and programs are offered for medical students, both in the UCC-SOM and other universities and health-related agencies.

Co-Curricular Program
Each academic year, the Dean of Students plans and offers co-curricular activities that include social, community, and service activities.

Student Financial Assistance
Federal Pell Grant
This grant is available almost exclusively to undergraduates; all eligible students will receive the Federal Pell Grant amount they qualify for ($400 to $5,350 for 2009-2010).

Federal Supplemental Educational Opportunity Grant (FSEOG)
This grant is for undergraduates with exceptional financial need; priority is given to Federal Pell Grant recipients;

funds depend on availability at school ($100 to $4,000).

Academic Competitiveness Grant (ACG)
This grant is for undergraduates receiving Pell Grant who are U.S. citizens enrolled full-time in their first or second academic year of study. First academic year student: up to $750; Second academic year student: up to $1,300.

Federal Work-Study Program (FWSP)
This grant is for undergraduate and graduate students; jobs can be on campus or off campus; students are paid at least federal minimum wage. No annual minimum or maximum award amounts.

Subsidized FFELP Stafford Loans
These loans must be repaid – 6.8% fix interest. U.S. Department of Education pays interest while borrower is in school and during grace and deferment periods; you must be at least a half-time student and have financial need. The amount students can qualify for is $3,500 to $8,500, depending on grade level.

Unsubsidized FFELP Stafford Loans
These loans must be repaid – 6.8% fix interest. Borrower is responsible for interest during life of the loan; you must be at least a half-time student; financial need is not a requirement. The amount students can qualify for is $6,000 to $32,000 (less any subsidized amounts received for the same period), depending on grade level and dependency status.

Grad Plus Loans
These loans must be repaid – 8.5% fix interest. Plus loans are unsubsidized; borrower is responsible for interest during the life of the loan. Maximum amount is cost of attendance minus any other financial aid the student receives; no minimum award amount.

P.R. Council on Higher Education (CES)
The CES is a state grant for undergraduate and graduate students that does not have to be repaid. Funds depend on availability at school. No annual minimum or maximum award amounts.

Educational Partnership

The UCC-SOM maintains an educational partnership with many health-related agencies and programs in Puerto Rico. For example, an academic partnership is available with two private universities (Sacred Heart University and Pontifical Catholic University) to recruit undergraduate students to our Biomedical Sciences and Substance Abuse Counseling programs. Also, an agreement is taking place with "Hogar Padre Vernard," a non-profit organization that offers primary care services to underrepresented communities.

University of Puerto Rico School of Medicine

Dr. América Facundo, Professor
University of Puerto Rico School of Medicine
Medical Sciences Campus,
Office A-865
P.O. Box 365067
San Juan, Puerto Rico 00936-5067
(787) 758-2525 Ext. 1868;
(787) 765-9182 fax
america.facundo@upr.edu

Admissions

Candidates are admitted to the first-year class on a competitive basis. The admissions process utilizes a formula that takes into consideration academic and non-academic factors. The academic factors include the general and science grade-point averages and the Medical College Admission Test scores. To assess the applicant's skills and attributes, the Admissions Committee requires an evaluation by pre-medical advisors or recommendations from three professors and a personal interview conducted, according to established guidelines, by a School of Medicine faculty member. Fluency in Spanish is required as most of the pa-

tient population is Spanish-speaking.

The Admissions Committee is composed of faculty members, representing both basic and clinical sciences, and student representatives. The admission process is through the American Medical College Application Service. As this is the state-supported medical school, applicants must be residents of Puerto Rico.

Academic Support Programs

Orientation Activities
These activities for new matriculants are typically offered in June, and they include an Orientation Week. They are designed to acquaint the first-year class with the school's academic program, the methods of evaluation, the different services available to students, and with the faculty, administration, and student body.

Introduction to Medical Studies Program
This one-month enrichment program is offered to all admitted students. It includes mini-courses on the basic sciences, as well as workshops on study skills, anxiety management, communication, professionalism, group building, among others.

The Office of Student Affairs provides tutoring services, orientation, and counseling services to all students whose academic or personal problems might interfere with their academic performance. Study-skills services are made available to interested students.

Psychological testing and psychiatric consultation are also available through the Student's Health Service.

The academic performance of each student is followed throughout the year by a Committee on Advancement, appointed by the dean, for each educational level. These committees recommend the student's promotion or advice on other alternatives.

Student Financial Assistance

Financial assistance is available for eligible, qualified students from university, state, and federal government loan funds and other special trust funds. Educational costs covered by financial aid include tuition and fees, books, supplies and equipment, room and board, transportation, and personal expenses. In order to qualify, students must meet the following requirements: U.S. citizen and resident

University of Puerto Rico School of Medicine
Applicants, First-Time Applicants, Matriculants by Gender, Race and Ethnicity, 2007-2008

	2007 APP Women	Men	Total	F-time APP Women	Men	Total	MAT Women	Men	Total	2008 APP Women	Men	Total	F-time APP Women	Men	Total	MAT Women	Men	Total
Hispanic/Latino																		
Cuban	12	19	31	7	15	22	1	0	1	16	5	21	15	4	19	0	0	0
Mexican American	18	20	38	16	13	29	0	0	0	15	9	24	11	3	14	0	0	0
Puerto Rican	182	139	321	157	112	269	47	51	98	212	143	355	193	125	318	65	40	105
Other Hispanic	28	20	48	22	12	34	1	1	2	28	23	51	22	16	38	0	0	0
Multiple Hispanic/Latino*	12	5	17	9	4	13	1	1	2	11	9	20	9	6	15	0	1	1
Subtotal	252	203	455	211	156	367	50	53	103	282	189	471	250	154	404	65	41	106
Non-Hispanic/Latino																		
Black	28	24	52	16	16	32	0	0	0	38	25	63	25	17	42	0	0	0
Native American/AK	0	0	0	0	0	0	0	0	0	1	0	1	1	0	1	0	0	0
Native Hawaiian/OPI	3	3	6	3	3	6	0	0	0	2	3	5	2	2	4	0	0	0
White	88	131	219	62	92	154	1	1	2	96	132	228	74	93	167	0	0	0
Asian	50	61	111	41	44	85	0	0	0	69	67	136	53	49	102	0	0	0
Other Race	2	1	3	1	1	2	0	0	0	1	2	3	0	1	1	0	0	0
Multiple Race*	9	4	13	7	2	9	0	0	0	3	7	10	2	4	6	0	0	0
Unknown	2	1	3	2	1	3	0	0	0	4	5	9	4	4	8	2	0	2
Subtotal	182	225	407	132	159	291	1	1	2	214	241	455	161	170	331	2	0	2
Foreign	6	7	13	4	6	10	0	0	0	5	11	16	4	8	12	0	0	0
Total	440	435	875	347	321	668	51	54	105	501	441	942	415	332	747	67	41	108

*Since 2002, students can select more than one race and / or ethnicity. **Those who did not choose 'Hispanic/Latino' or 'Non-Hispanic/Latino' are listed under 'Non-Hispanic/Latino'. Data Source: AAMC Data Warehouse: Applicant-Matriculant File, as of 1/16/2009.

of Puerto Rico; accepted for enrollment or enrolled in the University of
Puerto Rico School of Medicine; in
need of financial aid; and in good academic standing.

In addition, medical students benefit
from summer research programs,
summer employment opportunities,
and work-study programs.

The Warren Alpert Medical School of Brown University

Dr. Emma Simmons, MPH, Assistant Dean for Minority Medical Affairs
Office of Minority Medical Affairs
Division of Biology and Medicine
Warren Alpert Medical School
97 Waterman Street, Box G-A222C
Providence, RI 02912
401-863-3897; 401-863-3801 fax
Emma_Simmons_MD@Brown.edu
http://med.brown.edu/omma

Recruitment

The Assistant Dean for Minority Medical Affairs and the Associate Dean of Medicine (Minority Recruitment and Retention) are directly involved in the recruitment of minority applicants through multiple routes of admission (see Admissions section). The Assistant Dean for Minority Medical Affairs directly supervises the recruitment process for minority applicants through the Brown–Tougaloo Early Identification Program (EIP). The Associate Dean of Medicine (Minority Recruitment and Retention) directly supervises the recruitment process of applicants to the Program in Liberal Medical Education (PLME).

Each year approximately two to four promising, second-semester sophomore students, enrolled at Tougaloo College, are selected to participate in the Medical School's Early Identification Program. Admission to the Medical School is contingent upon sustained academic achievement at Tougaloo College, satisfactory completion of all pre-medical course requirements, continued recommendation by the pre-medical advisor at Tougaloo College, and documented verification of completed academic record.

The Office of Minority Medical Affairs is a major driving force in the continuous effort to increase the number of underrepresented minority students matriculating to the college and the Medical School. The office not only plays a crucial role at the Medical School level, but also serves as a vital link with undergraduate medical students and participates in several activities to encourage prospective minority students to attend Brown.

Admissions

The Warren Alpert Medical School continues to offer a number of admission routes to the M.D. program. The majority of first-year entrants are from the Program in Liberal Medical Education, or PLME, in which students enter Brown University in their freshman year and commit to an eight-year continuum leading to both the bachelor's degree and the M.D. degree. Brown accepts applications from qualified graduates of any college or university, through the standard route of admission. Students enrolled as undergraduates at Providence College, Rhode Island College, the University of Rhode Island, and Tougaloo College may apply through the EIP, a cooperative venture between the Medical School and these institutions. The remaining places in the class are reserved for students applying through special programs at institutions with which the Medical School has a formal linkage (the pre-medical post-baccalaureate programs). Occasionally, students are admitted to the Medical School with advanced standing.

The Warren Alpert Medical School of Brown University
Applicants, First-Time Applicants, Matriculants by Gender, Race and Ethnicity, 2007-2008

	2007 APP Women	2007 APP Men	2007 APP Total	2007 F-time APP Women	2007 F-time APP Men	2007 F-time APP Total	2007 MAT Women	2007 MAT Men	2007 MAT Total	2008 APP Women	2008 APP Men	2008 APP Total	2008 F-time APP Women	2008 F-time APP Men	2008 F-time APP Total	2008 MAT Women	2008 MAT Men	2008 MAT Total
Hispanic/Latino																		
Cuban	10	12	22	4	10	14	0	1	1	9	15	24	8	14	22	1	0	1
Mexican American	43	44	87	35	36	71	5	0	5	36	34	70	31	24	55	6	0	6
Puerto Rican	18	15	33	15	12	27	1	0	1	10	11	21	9	8	17	0	0	0
Other Hispanic	53	54	107	43	37	80	0	2	2	47	55	102	40	44	84	0	1	1
Multiple Hispanic/Latino*	13	5	18	10	4	14	0	0	0	9	5	14	8	5	13	1	0	1
Subtotal	137	130	267	107	99	206	6	3	9	111	120	231	96	95	191	8	1	9
Non-Hispanic/Latino																		
Black	122	59	181	92	55	147	4	2	6	125	69	194	90	56	146	4	3	7
Native American/AK	8	2	10	7	2	9	0	0	0	7	3	10	6	3	9	1	0	1
Native Hawaiian/OPI	12	6	18	10	5	15	0	0	0	9	3	12	6	2	8	0	0	0
White	1,151	1,220	2,371	1,016	995	2,011	25	19	44	1,042	1,202	2,244	880	959	1,839	21	13	34
Asian	642	665	1,307	543	523	1,066	12	13	25	544	628	1,172	432	466	898	14	19	33
Other Race	1	3	4	1	3	4	0	0	0	0	4	4	0	3	3	0	0	0
Multiple Race*	65	51	116	55	41	96	1	0	1	72	53	125	57	39	96	2	2	4
Unknown	30	30	60	29	26	55	4	4	8	70	78	148	69	68	137	3	3	6
Subtotal	2,031	2,036	4,067	1,753	1,650	3,403	46	38	84	1,869	2,040	3,909	1,540	1,596	3,136	45	40	85
Foreign	200	204	404	170	161	331	1	1	2	205	214	419	177	162	339	0	0	0
Total	2,368	2,370	4,738	2,030	1,910	3,940	53	42	95	2,185	2,374	4,559	1,813	1,853	3,666	53	41	94

*Since 2002, students can select more than one race and / or ethnicity. **Those who did not choose 'Hispanic/Latino' or 'Non-Hispanic/Latino' are listed under 'Non-Hispanic/Latino'. Data Source: AAMC Data Warehouse: Applicant-Matriculant File, as of 1/16/2009.

The Admissions Committee is composed of clinical and basic science faculty, administrators, and medical students, all with equal screening and ranking privileges.

Applicants are selected on the basis of academic achievement, faculty evaluations, and evidence of maturity, motivation, leadership, integrity, and compassion. Applicants to the M.D./Ph.D. program are also evaluated on the basis of their research accomplishments and potential as well.

The Assistant Dean for Minority Medical Affairs is a voting member of the Program in Liberal Medical Education Selection Advisory Council, the M.D. Admissions Committee, and the Early Identification Selection Committee.

Academic Support Programs

The Medical School has a formal tutorial program for all enrolled students. The program provides content tutors for basic science courses required in Years I and II. Students can self-refer or may be referred by an academic advisor, dean, or instructor. Students experiencing academic difficulties related to ineffective learning approaches, test-taking approaches, anxiety, or other cognitive challenges can also be referred to the on-campus Learning Specialist for learning strategy instruction or other therapeutic approaches, including off-campus referrals. These students will be followed by the Director of Academic Enhancement, and may be assisted by learning strategy tutors, trained second, third, and fourth year medical students. A proactive approach, advising, counseling, and supporting students is used.

United States Medical Licensing Examination (USMLE) Step 1 Preparation
Although passage of USMLE Step 1 is not required for promotion into Year III at Brown, individual and group academic coaching is available to all students preparing for their board exams. The Learning Specialist is available to help students develop their board study plans, identify potential weaknesses, hone their test-taking skills, and provide positive reinforcement during the preparation process. In addition, the Medical School offers Step 1 workshops/presentations, one-to-one tutoring by the Learning Specialist and by trained Step 1 tutors from the third and fourth year class, and USMLE study groups.

Student Financial Assistance

Before students may be considered for financial aid from Brown University, they must apply for a federally-insured, guaranteed student loan. Financial aid may then be offered in the form of scholarships, loans, or both. Over 70 percent of the students receive financial aid. Financial aid may be awarded to foreign national students on a limited basis. M.D./Ph.D. students are eligible for a graduate fellowship (tuition and stipend), during the Ph.D. portion of their studies, and a full tuition scholarship for the last two years of medical school following successful completion of the Ph.D. work.

Other Pertinent Information

At Alpert Medical School we want you to succeed, and we stand ready to give you the tools to do so. To serve the interests and aspirations of its students, the Office of Minority Medical Affairs (OMMA) was established in 1981 as a dynamic resource center offering academic, professional, and personal support programs.

In addition to providing highly personalized advising, OMMA is a source of information on fellowships, grants, meetings, and calls for papers. The office also provides guidance regarding fellowship and scholarship awards; advises and assists the Daniel Hale Williams Medical Society, which serves as a venue for advocacy; and provides programming aimed at raising awareness about health care disparities. OMMA also organizes a whole host of events – from lectures to workshops to dinners – that promote cultural competency, awareness, and tolerance throughout the Alpert Medical School community.

OMMA can put you in touch with students and faculty who would be happy to talk to you about the minority experience at Alpert Medical School.

Medical University of South Carolina College of Medicine

Dr. Deborah Deas, M.P.H.,
Senior Associate Dean for Diversity
Associate Dean, College of Medicine Admissions
Medical University of South Carolina
67 President Street, CDAP/4 North
Charleston, South Carolina 29425
843-792-5214; 843-792-7353 fax
deasd@musc.edu

Recruitment

The Medical University of South Carolina (MUSC) is committed to increasing its number of minority students. The Associate Deans for Admissions and the Director of Admissions, along with selected medical students, travel statewide to colleges and universities to recruit students. In addition to regular recruitment visits, the recruiters attend career fairs at all Historically Black Colleges and Universities in South Carolina.

The College of Medicine collaborates with the College of Graduate Studies at MUSC to sponsor the Ernest E. Just annual symposium to present contributions of Just, current science, and topics on diversity. The Ernest E. Just symposium attracts undergraduate students and their advisors from South Carolina, North Carolina, Georgia, and Florida. Students attend information sessions during the afternoon to meet Dr. Reves, Dean of the College of Medicine, Associate Deans, Admissions staff and current medical students to learn about the medical school requirements and resources available to enhance their applications for admission.

Post-baccalaureate Reapplication Education Program (PREP)
The Medical University of South Carolina (MUSC) established the Post-baccalaureate Reapplication Education Program (PREP) in a committed effort to increase the number of qualified South Carolina applicants who are representative of the medically underserved population in the state. The year-long program is jointly administered by the College of Medicine at MUSC and the College of Charleston. It is an integrative, individually tailored course of undergraduate study prescribed for under-prepared, but promising students who seek admission to MUSC's College of Medicine. The PREP program provides enriched academic assistance to students who come from historically medically underserved groups (minority, rural, low income) to prepare them to enter and succeed in medical school.

Students selected for the program must attend the College of Charleston for two semesters and take at least 15 semester hours of science courses each semester. Student must maintain a minimum cumulative grade-point average of 3.0 in science coursework and retake the Medical College Admission Test (MCAT) in April to improve scores. If a student fulfills all requirements, he or she is admitted into College of Medicine's first-year class beginning with the Summer Gross Anatomy course at MUSC. Tuition for PREP is paid by the College of Medicine.

A Gentleman and a Scholar Mentoring Program
Founded in 2007, A Gentleman and A Scholar Mentoring Program is designed to specifically target African-American male high school and college students interested in pursuing a career in medicine. Each student participant is assigned to a College of Medicine male student mentor who advises their re-

Medical University of South Carolina College of Medicine
Applicants, First-Time Applicants, Matriculants by Gender, Race and Ethnicity, 2007-2008

	2007									2008								
	APP			F-time APP			MAT			APP			F-time APP			MAT		
	Women	Men	Total	Women	Men	Total	Women	Men	Total	Women	Men	Total	Women	Men	Total	Women	Men	Total
Hispanic/Latino																		
Cuban	7	11	18	6	10	16	0	0	0	9	14	23	5	14	19	0	0	0
Mexican American	13	15	28	11	12	23	1	1	2	15	12	27	13	11	24	1	0	1
Puerto Rican	9	3	12	7	2	9	0	0	0	9	4	13	8	3	11	0	0	0
Other Hispanic	23	31	54	14	23	37	1	2	3	20	23	43	10	19	29	0	0	0
Multiple Hispanic/Latino*	0	1	1	0	1	1	0	0	0	2	4	6	1	3	4	0	0	0
Subtotal	52	61	113	38	48	86	2	3	5	55	57	112	37	50	87	1	0	1
Non-Hispanic/Latino**																		
Black	124	54	178	84	40	124	9	9	18	109	57	166	78	37	115	11	10	21
Native American/AK	4	4	8	3	3	6	0	1	1	4	6	10	4	6	10	0	0	0
Native Hawaiian/OPI	3	4	7	2	4	6	0	0	0	3	2	5	2	0	2	0	0	0
White	627	717	1,344	505	519	1,024	46	74	120	653	838	1,491	508	604	1,112	49	76	125
Asian	129	168	297	99	128	227	3	6	9	162	159	321	123	113	236	6	5	11
Other Race	0	0	0	0	0	0	0	0	0	0	2	2	0	2	2	0	0	0
Multiple Race*	23	27	50	13	15	28	1	3	4	23	28	51	18	19	37	1	2	3
Unknown	11	9	20	11	8	19	0	0	0	22	25	47	22	23	45	1	2	3
Subtotal	921	983	1,904	717	717	1,434	59	93	152	976	1,117	2,093	755	804	1,559	68	95	163
Foreign	12	14	26	8	13	21	0	1	1	17	23	40	14	19	33	0	1	1
Total	985	1,058	2,043	763	778	1,541	61	97	158	1,048	1,197	2,245	806	873	1,679	69	96	165

*Since 2002, students can select more than one race and / or ethnicity. **Those who did not choose 'Hispanic/Latino' or 'Non-Hispanic/Latino' are listed under 'Non-Hispanic/Latino'. Data Source: AAMC Data Warehouse: Applicant-Matriculant File, as of 1/16/2009.

spective student on scholarly success and leadership. Participants meet monthly at the Medical University of South Carolina as a group and individually with their mentors throughout the academic year. This program provides a competitive advantage through various endeavors such as clinical shadowing experiences, structured inspirational talks, test taking and study skills, exposure to various summer science programs, and academic tutelage where needed. A Gentleman and A Scholar Mentoring Program will equip participants with the necessary tools to go above and beyond in order to increase the numbers of African-American males entering and successfully completing medical school.

Medicine Careers Academy
The Medicine Careers Academy is a College of Medicine program held in collaboration with the South Carolina Area Health Education Consortium (AHEC). The Medicine Careers Academy is a week-long summer program designed to assist underrepresented minority and disadvantaged college students prepare for entry into medical school. It was developed to increase the retention and graduation rates of pre-medicine students by increasing the participant's knowledge in areas of admission requirements of South Carolina medical programs, financial assistance resources, academic success skills, specialties of medicine, and educational/professional opportunities in the field of medicine.

Summer Institute Program
Since 2000, the Office of Student Diversity has sponsored a Summer Institute Program for students interested in health care. In 2005, The College of Medicine assumed sponsorship of this program, which is designed for recent baccalaureate graduates who have applied to the College of Medicine for admission but were not selected. Additionally, a few highly motivated junior and senior college students who have been identified as having the academic potential for medicine are eligible. The eight-week institute includes

intensive courses in organic chemistry, physics, and biochemistry, as well as a MCAT preparation, test-taking skills, verbal reasoning, and mock interviews.

Admissions

The Admissions Committee consists of 25 members – 17 of whom are basic science and clinical faculty members who are appointed by the Dean of the College of Medicine. Members of the committee serve staggered three-year terms, and two student members appointed at the end of their first year serve until graduation. Regular meetings are held from September through March. Special meetings may be called any time during the academic year. All decisions are made by a simple majority of those attending and are presented to the Dean as recommendations. The criteria for admission to the regular M.D. program are the same for all students seeking enrollment in the College of Medicine. Consideration is given to the applicant's grade-point average (GPA), MCAT scores, interviews and accomplishments (i.e., leadership, volunteer efforts and shadowing experiences). Students are also screened for personal qualities and accomplishments that are considered valuable in adding diversity to a class: cultural experiences, research or graduate degrees, significant artistic or athletic achievements, overcoming adversity or some type of disability, a pattern of significant improvement in coursework, or any type of extended post-baccalaureate career experiences. An Added Value subcommittee reviews all applicants considered for these qualities and accomplishments and assigns an adjustment to the applicant's overall ranking index.

Academic Support Programs

The College of Medicine established the Office of Academics and Student Affairs to assist students with academic and personal challenges. Proactive intervention strategies, such as early detection, collaborative consultation, and appropriate referrals to campus resources are utilized to enhance students' academic performance and decrease stress related to personal issues. The Director of Aca-

demics and Student Support provides academic counseling and facilitates the referral process for supplemental instruction. The Center for Academic Excellence is a centrally located university resource, which provides supplemental instruction, test-taking skills, study skills, and time management.

Student Financial Assistance

State and federal loans, specialized scholarships, and fellowships are arranged individually through the University Financial Aid Office. The Graduate Incentive Scholarships coordinated by the Office of Student Diversity and University Financial Aid Office are available to all entering professional and minority medical students. The fellowship is available to all South Carolinians who agree to practice in South Carolina one year for each $5,000 or portion received. Grants and scholarships are also available from an endowment in the Medical University's Health Sciences Foundation and from the Earl B. Higgins Scholarship Fund.

University of South Carolina School of Medicine

Dr. Carol McMahon, Assistant Dean for Minority Affairs and Assistant Professor of Pathology
University of South Carolina
School of Medicine
Building #3, Room 104
Columbia, SC 29208
803-733-3319; 803-733-1513 fax
carol.mcmahon@uscmed.sc.edu

Recruitment

Under–represented minority applicants for admission to the School of Medicine are identified through: site visits to college campuses; college and high school career day programs; collaboration with undergraduate pre-medical advisors, minority physicians and health care agencies, the USC-SOM Role Models for Medicine Program; and correspondence with students referred to the School or identified in relevant regional and national databases. The primary goal of the Office of Minority Affairs is to increase the number of qualified minority applicants, matriculants and graduates through participation in outreach, recruitment and mentoring activities.

The School of Medicine's Student National Medical Association (SNMA) chapter also plays an active role in the recruitment of minority students via collaboration with MAPS chapter activities at South Carolina colleges, and participation in seminars and workshops about medical school, the application and admissions process, the Medical College Admission Test (MCAT) preparation and interviewing skills. SNMA members provide academic assistance and support to enrolled students, and participate health education programs for community groups and students from middle school through college.

Minority students are encouraged and invited to visit the campus of the University of South Carolina School of Medicine to acquaint themselves with its facilities and programs, to participate in the Day in the Life of a Medical Student program, and to meet Admissions personnel, students and the Assistant Dean for Minority Affairs.

Admissions

The School of Medicine seeks qualified applicants from diverse racial, cultural and economic backgrounds to reflect the population of the state of South Carolina. All qualified applicants are admitted through the regular admissions procedure. The selection process involves comparative evaluation and review of all available data: academic record, MCAT scores, medical/extracurricular activities, letters of recommendation and personal interviews with Admissions Committee members. The Admissions Committee is a diverse group composed of faculty members, community physicians, administrators and medical students. Its representative nature assures a thorough and sensitive review of the credentials of every applicant. Potential applicants can readily access significant information about the School under the Future Students tab on the website: http://www.med.sc.edu. The opportunity for admission is greatest for legal residents of South Carolina.

Academic Support Programs

All students accepted into the medical program will find that the nature of the campus and the class size foster close interpersonal relationships between students and faculty members. These relationships facilitate individualized teaching and mentoring and also allow

Medical University of South Carolina College of Medicine
Applicants, First-Time Applicants, Matriculants by Gender, Race and Ethnicity, 2007-2008

| | 2007 | | | | | | | | | 2008 | | | | | | | | |
| | APP | | | F-time APP | | | MAT | | | APP | | | F-time APP | | | MAT | | |
	Wo-men	Men	Total	Wo-men	Men	Total	Wo-men	Men	Total	Wo-men	Men	Total	Wo-men	Men	Total	Wo-men	Men	Total
Hispanic/Latino																		
Cuban	7	11	18	6	10	16	0	0	0	9	14	23	5	14	19	0	0	0
Mexican American	13	15	28	11	12	23	1	1	2	15	12	27	13	11	24	1	0	1
Puerto Rican	9	3	12	7	2	9	0	0	0	9	4	13	8	3	11	0	0	0
Other Hispanic	23	31	54	14	23	37	1	2	3	20	23	43	10	19	29	0	0	0
Multiple Hispanic/Latino*	0	1	1	0	1	1	0	0	0	2	4	6	1	3	4	0	0	0
Subtotal	52	61	113	38	48	86	2	3	5	55	57	112	37	50	87	1	0	1
Non-Hispanic/Latino**																		
Black	124	54	178	84	40	124	9	9	18	109	57	166	78	37	115	11	10	21
Native American/AK	4	4	8	3	3	6	0	1	1	4	6	10	4	6	10	0	0	0
Native Hawaiian/OPI	3	4	7	2	4	6	0	0	0	3	2	5	2	0	2	0	0	0
White	627	717	1,344	505	519	1,024	46	74	120	653	838	1,491	508	604	1,112	49	76	125
Asian	129	168	297	99	128	227	3	6	9	162	159	321	123	113	236	6	5	11
Other Race	0	0	0	0	0	0	0	0	0	0	2	2	0	2	2	0	0	0
Multiple Race*	23	27	50	13	15	28	1	3	4	23	28	51	18	19	37	1	2	3
Unknown	11	9	20	11	8	19	0	0	0	22	25	47	22	23	45	1	2	3
Subtotal	921	983	1,904	717	717	1,434	59	93	152	976	1,117	2,093	755	804	1,559	68	95	163
Foreign	12	14	26	8	13	21	0	1	1	17	23	40	14	19	33	0	1	1
Total	985	1,058	2,043	763	778	1,541	61	97	158	1,048	1,197	2,245	806	873	1,679	69	96	165

*Since 2002, students can select more than one race and / or ethnicity. **Those who did not choose 'Hispanic/Latino' or 'Non-Hispanic/Latino' are listed under 'Non-Hispanic/Latino'. Data Source: AAMC Data Warehouse: Applicant-Matriculant File, as of 1/16/2009.

for early identification of potential or real academic difficulties so that help may be offered as soon as necessary. In addition, an extensive orientation program, prior to the beginning of classes in the first year, and small-group educational activities throughout the curriculum ensure the development of cooperative working relationships among all students. Each incoming student is assigned to an advisory group consisting of first- through fourth-year students and faculty advisors who monitor the student's academic progress and act both as counselors and advisors. Course directors and faculty members are readily available to provide tutorial sessions and individual attention to students who encounter academic difficulty.

Extended Curriculum Program
This program is available to students with compelling personal reasons. It is an appropriately sequenced and individually scheduled track that permits completion of the first two years of medical school in three years.

Student Financial Assistance
The Office of Student and Career Services makes every effort to provide information, assistance and counseling to help students manage and meet their financial obligations. All students are advised of relevant, applicable, available scholarship and loan opportunities. Minority students are also apprised of scholarships offered specifically for under-represented minorities or designed to enhance diversity, e.g. Graduate Incentive Scholarship Loans, Dean's Diversity Scholarships, hospital based scholarships for under-represented students, etc. Such financial assistance is provided on the basis of need and availability of funds.

Educational Partnerships
Because the School is an important component of a comprehensive research university, medical students have many opportunities for interaction with students in other disciplines as well as participation in student organizations, intramural sports, and social events. The University of South Carolina's campus offers access to excellent research facilities. The School also works closely with its seven affiliated hospitals to provide students valuable clinical experience during their four years of medical education.

Other Pertinent Information
The School of Medicine admitted its first class of 24 students in August 1977 and has a current entering class size of 85 new students.

The Office of Minority Affairs was created in 1996 as a result of the School of Medicine's strategic planning efforts and its commitment to diversity. The Assistant Dean for Minority Affairs serves as an advisor to all prospective and enrolled students.

Sanford School of Medicine of the University of South Dakota

Dr. Gerald J. Yutrzenka, Associate Professor, Director of Diversity Affairs
Assistant Director
INMED Satellite Office
Sanford School of Medicine of the University of South Dakota
414 East Clark Street
Vermillion, SD 57069
605-677-5156; 605-677-6381 fax
Gerald.yutrzenka@usd.edu
www.usd.edu/med

Recruitment

In 1990, the Sanford School of Medicine (SSOM) established a satellite office of the Indians into Medicine (INMED) program located at the University of North Dakota School of Medicine. Through this agreement two additional American Indian students are accepted into the University of North Dakota School of Medicine INMED program each year with the intent of transferring into the third year of the medical school curriculum at SSOM. Upon completion of the requirements for graduation these students receive their medical degree from the Sanford School of Medicine of the University of South Dakota. The INMED Satellite Office at SSOM serves the educational and cultural needs of the INMED transfer students, promotes health career opportunities for American Indians in South Dakota and surrounding states, is involved in the recruitment and retention of American Indian students in health career programs at the University of South Dakota, and serves as a valuable resource to the faculty and students of the School of Medicine and the University.

In addition, SSOM faculty are involved in summer enrichment programs designed to enhance recruitment of American Indians into careers in health and/or biomedical research. SSOM faculty work in concert with the Undergraduate Admissions Office, the TRIO Program, and with other departments and disciplines in efforts to enhance the diversity of the medical school and the University.

Admissions

The Sanford School of Medicine gives priority to applicants who are legal residents of South Dakota and to non-residents who have close personal ties to South Dakota. Applications from American Indians who are enrolled members of tribes located in South Dakota and states bordering onto South Dakota are also placed in the priority pool. The INMED Satellite Office and the Office of Medical Student Affairs are available to offer assistance to minority and other disadvantaged applicants.

The Admissions Committee, composed of 15 faculty from the School of Medicine, evaluate all applicants for admission on the basis of intellect, character, and motivation. Information considered in the evaluation of an applicant includes academic achievement, Medical College Admission Test (MCAT) scores, evaluations by former instructors and others who know the individual well, assessment of interpersonal factors and communication skills, and interest in and understanding of medicine and health care, especially as it relates to South Dakota and the mission of SSOM. All applicants being considered for admission are offered two one-on-one personal interviews with members of the Admissions Committee. Any applicant with questions about admission is encouraged to contact the Dean of Student Affairs, SSOM.

Sanford School of Medicine of the University of South Dakota
Applicants, First-Time Applicants, Matriculants by Gender, Race and Ethnicity, 2007-2008

	2007 APP Women	Men	Total	F-time APP Women	Men	Total	MAT Women	Men	Total	2008 APP Women	Men	Total	F-time APP Women	Men	Total	MAT Women	Men	Total
Hispanic/Latino																		
Cuban	2	3	5	1	3	4	0	0	0	0	1	1	0	1	1	0	0	0
Mexican American	5	4	9	5	3	8	0	0	0	0	4	4	0	4	4	0	0	0
Puerto Rican	0	1	1	0	1	1	0	0	0	1	2	3	1	1	2	0	0	0
Other Hispanic	2	2	4	2	1	3	0	0	0	7	5	12	4	5	9	0	0	0
Multiple Hispanic/Latino*	0	1	1	0	0	0	0	0	0	1	2	3	1	1	2	0	0	0
Subtotal	9	11	20	8	8	16	0	0	0	9	14	23	6	12	18	0	0	0
Non-Hispanic/Latino**																		
Black	12	8	20	8	7	15	0	0	0	5	9	14	4	5	9	0	0	0
Native American/AK	4	6	10	3	4	7	0	0	0	5	1	6	3	1	4	0	0	0
Native Hawaiian/OPI	1	0	1	1	0	1	0	0	0	2	2	4	1	2	3	0	0	0
White	241	283	524	198	199	397	29	24	53	180	272	452	135	182	317	23	28	51
Asian	45	61	106	33	48	81	0	1	1	39	48	87	29	37	66	1	1	2
Other Race	1	0	1	0	0	0	0	0	0	0	0	0	0	0	0	0	0	0
Multiple Race*	8	12	20	6	10	16	0	0	0	7	8	15	5	4	9	0	0	0
Unknown	4	5	9	4	5	9	0	0	0	4	10	14	4	10	14	0	1	1
Subtotal	316	375	691	253	273	526	29	25	54	242	350	592	181	241	422	24	30	54
Foreign	11	22	33	7	15	22	0	0	0	9	17	26	6	13	19	0	0	0
Total	336	408	744	268	296	564	29	25	54	260	381	641	193	266	459	24	30	54

*Since 2002, students can select more than one race and / or ethnicity. **Those who did not choose 'Hispanic/Latino' or 'Non-Hispanic/Latino' are listed under 'Non-Hispanic/Latino'. Data Source: AAMC Data Warehouse: Applicant-Matriculant File, as of 1/16/2009.

Academic Support Programs

All students who matriculate at SSOM are assigned a basic science faculty advisor for Year 1 and Year 2 and a clinical faculty advisor for Year 3 and Year 4 who advise the student on academic and career issues. The Longitudinal Follow-up Committee and the Student Progress and Conduct Committee are both involved with assessing the progress of medical students throughout the curriculum and recommending action, when needed, to help the student successfully complete the curriculum. The INMED Satellite Office is available to help address needs of American Indian students. The Office of Student Affairs with its Student Professional Support Services Office is available to all students. The Student Professional Support Services office coordinates training in study skills, referrals for counseling and planning review programs for United States Medical Licensing Examination (USMLE) preparation.

Enrichment Programs

The School of Medicine has established the Research Apprentice Program (RAP) designed to provide opportunities for up to eight disadvantaged high school students from South Dakota to become engaged in seven weeks of hands-on, mentored research activities within the medical school and other departments within the university. RAP participants are selected with the assistance of the University of South Dakota Upward Bound program. The RAP students participate in after hours social and other learning activities along with Upward Bound students. *(www.usd.edu/rap)*

The NIH-funded IDEA Networks of Biomedical Research Excellence (INBRE) project has been established at the University of South Dakota. Part of INBRE's efforts are directed toward working with some of the South Dakota tribal colleges to enhance educational, research, and mentoring opportunities for American Indians and other disadvantaged students attending these tribal colleges. *(www.usd.edu/brin)*

Several School of Medicine faculty members are involved in providing mentoring experiences, with an emphasis on health professions and biomedical research, to high school as well as undergraduate students. *(www.usd.edu/biomed)*.

The INMED (Indians into Medicine) Satellite office is directly involved in providing mentoring and educational opportunities relative to exposing American Indian middle school and high school students to careers in the health professions. The INMED Satellite office provides assistance with enhancing the academic skills and career advising of American Indian students who express interest in pursuing careers in medicine and other health care professions. *(www.usd.edu/med/md/ diversityopp.cfm)* *(www.usd.edu/med/md)* *(www.med.und.nodak.edu/inmed)*

SSOM has established a four-week elective (Asniya) available to fourth-year medical students that is designed to give students the opportunity to interact with the American Indian tribes in South Dakota. Medical students provide career mentoring and health education instruction to middle school and high school students on one of the several reservations in the state. Medical students are required to obtain at least 20 hours of experience in the local health care facility and must submit a paper in which they reflect upon the experience. Asniya provides medical students with the opportunity to become more aware of the health care opportunities and challenges found within the reservations as well as to enhance their own competency in working with American Indian colleagues and in providing health care to American Indian patients. *(www.usd.edu/med/md/diversityopp.cfm)*

School of Medicine faculty members have been actively involved in a variety of enrichment programs at the University of South Dakota including among others: Upward Bound, Math Science Initiative Program, Talent Search, Re-

search Apprentice Program, Lawrence Brothers Summer Science Camp, Health Careers Summer Camp, and the Governors Camp for the Gifted. *(www.usd.edu/events)* *(www.usd.edu/trio)* *(www.usd.edu/lbc)* *(www.usd.edu/rap)* *(www.usd.edu/med/health/camps.cfm)*

Student Financial Assistance

The medical school will waive the $35 application fee upon request and presentation of reasonable evidence of need. A limited number of scholarships, from local sources, are designated especially for American Indian students. The INMED Satellite Office can assist with application for Indian Health Service scholarships.

The Financial Aid officer is responsible for financial aid counseling and debt management counseling for all medical students. (www.usd.edu/med/md)

Educational Partnerships

SSOM has partnered with a number of local, state, and national entities to enhance the opportunities for South Dakota students to gain access to medical school and other health professions programs. These partnerships include the Talent Search, Upward Bound, and Student Support Services components of the USD TRIO programs and the INMED program. SSOM has partnered with the Aberdeen Area Indian Health Service and the Aberdeen Area Tribal Chairman's Health Board (AATCHB) with the purpose of addressing health concerns, health professions mentoring, and educational opportunities in order to positively impact the health care needs of the tribes in South Dakota.

Sanford School of Medicine has taken a leadership role in helping to establish the Pathways into Health (PIH) collaborative. This effort is designed to provide enhanced opportunities for American Indian/Alaskan Native peoples to enter careers in medicine and other health care professions. PIH acts as a mechanism for providing mentoring and role modeling relative to health

care careers, development of education and training utilizing Web-based and distance-education technology, development of "pipeline" programs, and serving as a resource for information on health care professions and health care education opportunities.
(www.med.und.nodak.edu/inmed)
(www.usd.edu/trio)
(www.pathwaysintohealth.org)

East Tennessee State University James H. Quillen College of Medicine

Dr. Thomas E. Kwasigroch,
Associate Dean
East Tennessee State University
James H. Quillen College of Medicine
Office of Student Affairs
Post Office Box 70580
Johnson City, TN 37601
423-439-2019; 423-439-2070 fax
kwasigro@etsu.edu

Recruitment

The James H. Quillen College of Medicine of East Tennessee State University actively seeks applications from minority and disadvantaged groups. Representatives from the Office of Student Affairs conduct visitation and career day programs at many college campuses across the region. This institution is also an active participant in Pre-medical Enrichment Programs at East Tennessee State University and other institutions.

Admissions

The application and admissions process for all prospective students is the same. The Admissions Committee looks at demonstrations of ability to succeed academically, motivation for and knowledge of the profession, and personal skills believed to be desirable in a physician. In addition to grades and test scores, the Admissions Committee considers evidence of an individual's integrity, leadership ability, motivation, maturity, and intellectual curiosity. Applicants are urged to ensure that their American Medical College Application Service (AMCAS) application provides broad preliminary information in these areas.

The Admissions Committee is composed of representatives from a diverse group of people with a variety of backgrounds. Medical school and undergraduate faculty and professional staff, hospital staff, students, and local community representatives make up the committee. Training exercises, such as simulated admissions, are conducted to help committee members improve their skills in analyzing the applications of minority students, utilizing both cognitive and non-cognitive indicators.

Academic Support Programs

The College of Medicine has an effective system of student advisement to help students transition to medical school. Upon matriculation, entering students are assigned a faculty advisor. In addition, all faculty maintain open-door policies and are available to assist students in any way possible. The Offices of Student Affairs and Academic Affairs have staff available to assist students in academic and personal areas. Professional counselors are also available to serve students who may have need of confidential counseling and/or treatment.

Educational Partnerships

The College of Medicine is a partner in the Tennessee Institutes of Pre-professionals (TIP). The Tennessee Institutes for Pre-Professionals (TIP), which is operated by the University of Tennessee Health Sciences Center, is open to members of underrepresented groups who are residents of Tennessee who are interested in a career in medicine, dentistry, pharmacy, or veterinary medicine. The program is designed to promote and to nurture student's interest in the health professions through an array of structured activities. The program's ultimate goal is to increase the representation and active participation of under represented groups in health

East Tennessee State University James H. Quillen College of Medicine
Applicants, First-Time Applicants, Matriculants by Gender, Race and Ethnicity, 2007-2008

| | | 2007 | | | | | | | | | 2008 | | | | | | | |
| | APP | | | F-time APP | | | MAT | | | APP | | | F-time APP | | | MAT | | |
	Women	Men	Total	Women	Men	Total	Women	Men	Total	Women	Men	Total	Women	Men	Total	Women	Men	Total
Hispanic/Latino																		
Cuban	0	4	4	0	4	4	0	0	0	4	10	14	2	8	10	0	0	0
Mexican American	5	7	12	3	5	8	0	0	0	8	8	16	8	8	16	0	1	1
Puerto Rican	2	0	2	1	0	1	1	0	1	6	3	9	3	3	6	0	0	0
Other Hispanic	11	8	19	10	8	18	0	0	0	20	8	28	11	5	16	0	0	0
Multiple Hispanic/Latino*	1	4	5	1	2	3	0	0	0	2	4	6	2	2	4	0	0	0
Subtotal	19	23	42	15	19	34	1	0	1	40	33	73	26	26	52	0	1	1
Non-Hispanic/Latino**																		
Black	85	34	119	60	23	83	2	1	3	70	40	110	47	27	74	1	0	1
Native American/AK	3	2	5	2	1	3	0	0	0	3	4	7	3	3	6	0	0	0
Native Hawaiian/OPI	2	2	4	2	1	3	0	0	0	4	2	6	2	1	3	0	0	0
White	395	556	951	307	395	702	25	24	49	405	618	1,023	305	416	721	17	33	50
Asian	112	138	250	81	105	186	3	1	4	152	147	299	117	102	219	4	2	6
Other Race	0	0	0	0	0	0	0	0	0	0	1	1	0	1	1	0	0	0
Multiple Race*	15	20	35	9	13	22	2	0	2	22	15	37	19	8	27	1	0	1
Unknown	1	8	9	1	7	8	0	1	1	11	13	24	10	13	23	1	0	1
Subtotal	613	760	1,373	462	545	1,007	32	27	59	667	840	1,507	503	571	1,074	24	35	59
Foreign	16	18	34	15	12	27	0	0	0	24	37	61	18	31	49	0	0	0
Total	648	801	1,449	492	576	1,068	33	27	60	731	910	1,641	547	628	1,175	24	36	60

*Since 2002, students can select more than one race and / or ethnicity. **Those who did not choose 'Hispanic/Latino' or 'Non-Hispanic/Latino' are listed under 'Non-Hispanic/Latino'. Data Source: AAMC Data Warehouse: Applicant-Matriculant File, as of 1/16/2009.

professions training and practice. More information on the program can be found at: *(www.utmem.edu/tip)*.

Student Financial Assistance

The James H. Quillen College of Medicine is authorized to provide state and federal financial assistance to minorities under the guidelines set forth by the various programs. The supplemental information fee (application fee) may be waived by action of the Assistant Dean for Admissions upon the written request of the applicant, provided that an AMCAS fee waiver has been granted. In recent years, the Tennessee Higher Education Commission has also provided scholarships to a limited number of African-American students. Other scholarships may be available on a limited basis.

The administration of the College of Medicine is keenly aware of the financial burden that medical students bear. As such, Financial Services strives to aid students in making wise financial decisions to limit students' overall indebtedness by conducting debt management and financial planning workshops throughout the year.

Meharry Medical College School of Medicine

Allen D. Mosley, Director Admissions and Recruitment
Meharry Medical College School of Medicine
1005 Dr. D.B. Todd Jr. Boulevard
Nashville, TN 37208
615-327-6223; 615-327-6228 fax
amosley@mmc.edu

Recruitment

The School of Medicine is the oldest and largest of the three schools at Meharry and admits 105 students per year. Although a historically black medical college, Meharry's student body reflects the diversity of the nation with representation from the Caucasian, Hispanic, Asian, and Native-American communities.

Recruitment is done primarily at the undergraduate college level. Visitations, seminars and interviews are conducted on various college campuses and in communities as requested by the institutions or organizations. Visits are accepted from premed clubs of both undergraduate colleges and high schools. The School

of Medicine directs the recruitment program that is coordinated by the Office of Admissions and Recruitment. Participation in the recruitment program involves faculty, administrators, and students and all three groups conduct visitations.

The majority of Meharry's graduates keep the commitment of the principles upon which the College was founded by overwhelmingly choosing to practice in underserved urban and rural communities. Nearly 50 percent of the medical graduates select primary care specialties each year. Meharry continues to be proud of its leadership role in helping to ensure diversity in the nation's health professions work force. We have an active Afro Caribbean Student Association, an American Latino Medical Association and a South Asia Meharry Student Association.

Admissions

The Office of Admissions and Recruitment coordinates recruitment activities and provides information about the admission process. All applicants must complete the appropriate application for the School of Medicine. Application materials may be obtained online at

Meharry's Web site under the Admissions section at: *(www.mmc.edu)*.

Students are selected for admission to Meharry Medical College by the Admissions committee, which is charged with selecting students who will make suitable candidates for the study and eventual practice of their profession. The number of applicants greatly exceeds the capacity. All applications are considered on a competitive basis from the standpoint of scholarship, intelligence, aptitude, character, and general fitness. In the final selection of applicants comparing most favorably on these factors, the current policy of the institution is to give preferential consideration to applicants who 1) come from areas with inadequate health care as measured by the medical population ratio, 2) have underserved backgrounds, 3) are from Southern Regional Education Board (SREB) states having contracts with Meharry, 4) are from schools that have special contracts with Meharry to admit students who have been in special courses, and 5) have a history of community activities, especially in the health care area. Special consideration is given to minority groups and disadvantaged applicants of all origins.

Meharry Medical College
Applicants, First-Time Applicants, Matriculants by Gender, Race and Ethnicity, 2007-2008

	2007									2008								
	APP			F-time APP			MAT			APP			F-time APP			MAT		
	Wo-men	Men	Total	Wo-men	Men	Total	Wo-men	Men	Total	Wo-men	Men	Total	Wo-men	Men	Total	Wo-men	Men	Total
Hispanic/Latino																		
Cuban	8	23	31	6	18	24	1	1	2	17	12	29	14	9	23	0	0	0
Mexican American	55	33	88	40	21	61	0	0	0	43	30	73	29	19	48	0	2	2
Puerto Rican	18	11	29	14	9	23	0	1	1	16	16	32	11	13	24	0	1	1
Other Hispanic	63	52	115	42	30	72	3	1	4	64	70	134	43	40	83	0	1	1
Multiple Hispanic/Latino*	12	7	19	7	4	11	0	0	0	9	8	17	7	4	11	0	1	1
Subtotal	156	126	282	109	82	191	4	3	7	149	136	285	104	85	189	0	5	5
Non-Hispanic/Latino**																		
Black	1,062	447	1,509	709	314	1,023	53	25	78	1,064	452	1,516	718	307	1,025	46	34	80
Native American/AK	5	8	13	4	5	9	1	0	1	12	5	17	8	4	12	0	1	1
Native Hawaiian/OPI	15	4	19	12	2	14	0	0	0	9	8	17	4	7	11	0	0	0
White	502	608	1,110	375	401	776	1	2	3	516	599	1,115	358	406	764	2	2	4
Asian	552	598	1,150	392	404	796	4	1	5	569	574	1,143	407	382	789	2	5	7
Other Race	2	8	10	1	2	3	0	0	0	0	5	5	0	2	2	0	0	0
Multiple Race*	64	58	122	40	37	77	1	0	1	56	50	106	37	29	66	1	0	1
Unknown	13	13	26	11	9	20	0	0	0	19	32	51	16	27	43	0	0	0
Subtotal	2,215	1,744	3,959	1,544	1,174	2,718	60	28	88	2,245	1,725	3,970	1,548	1,164	2,712	51	42	93
Foreign	170	166	336	134	127	261	1	0	1	132	141	273	97	105	202	0	2	2
Total	2,541	2,036	4,577	1,787	1,383	3,170	65	31	96	2,526	2,002	4,528	1,749	1,354	3,103	51	49	100

Note: In 2008, one applicant, who declined to report gender, was not included here.

*Since 2002, students can select more than one race and / or ethnicity. **Those who did not choose 'Hispanic/Latino' or 'Non-Hispanic/Latino' are

Academic Support Programs

Any student who experiences difficulty at Meharry can expect assistance, as necessary, from the faculty. At the end of the first month, students are evaluated and advised as to whether or not they should accept a reduced load. Also, at the end of each scheduled examination, each department checks to see if any student is having difficulty. If so, the student is assigned to a faculty advisor for tutorial sessions or referred to the Epps Center for Educational Development and Support Services (CEDSS). The CEDSS is devoted to improving the teaching and learning environment. It assists students in developing a variety of skills that can help to improve their learning. Examples of the type of programs offered by the CEDSS include time and stress management; study, test and note-taking skills; analytical reasoning, problem-solving skills, peer tutoring services; small-group instruction; and a comprehensive review program for licensure in medicine.

The Office of the College Chaplain and Counseling Services provides counseling services to students in the following areas:

- Spiritual and theological concerns
- Interpersonal relationships
- Pre-marital concerns
- Family problems/marital counseling
- Grief
- Stress management
- Conflict resolution
- Adjustment problems
- Self-esteem problems
- Time management

These concerns and others, which are of interest to the students, may be discussed in confidence in the Office of the College Chaplain and Counseling Services.

Enrichment Programs

The Health Careers Opportunity Program (HCOP)

HCOP offers minority undergraduates from disadvantaged backgrounds a challenging academic opportunity to realize their dream of becoming a physician, dentist, or public health professional. Rising junior and senior undergraduate students are eligible to apply to the program.

One of the most exciting aspects of HCOP at Meharry is the opportunity to shadow a professional in the discipline that the student might possibly pursue. Students in the dental program will gain exposure to dental specialties through shadowing experiences in the campus clinic. Students in the medical program will shadow physicians, residents, and medical students and spend two evenings in a hospital emergency room. Public health students will spend time with local experts throughout Nashville. Each participant earns a stipend. The program finances travel, room, meals, and tuition.

Student Financial Assistance

Meharry Medical College's Office of Student Financial Aid (OSFA) is committed to providing financial assistance to students from diverse backgrounds that would otherwise be unable to pursue the attainment of their educational and professional goals. Our student-focused employees will provide professional knowledge and personalized service to help students seek and obtain the best use of all financial resources available through various funding avenues.

The OSFA strives to administer funds on the basis of financial need; to contribute to the success of future generations of America by helping to fund their health professions education; to be a leader in innovative financial aid delivery; and to help support institutional enrollment and retention goals.

Meharry Medical College offers grants, scholarships, loans, and federal work study to eligible students. Meharry participates in the student financial aid programs funded by the U.S. Department of Education and the U.S. Department of Health and Human Services, as well as state and regional funding agencies. The College selects student financial aid recipients based on established criteria and demonstrated financial need. Most of the College's institutional scholarships are awarded based on outstanding academic performance.

Degree candidates that are U.S. citizens or eligible non-citizens are eligible to qualify for most federal student aid pro-grams. The Director of Admissions considers application fee waiver request on an individual basis, provided that an AMCAS fee waiver has been granted.

Educational Partnerships

To enhance the educational experience of students and to strengthen our programs, the collaboration between Meharry Medical College (MMC) and Vanderbilt University Medical Center (VUMC) was established in 1998. The Meharry-Vanderbilt Alliance was built on the vision of education and research leading to the best patient care and eliminating disparities in healthcare affecting minorities and the underserved.

The strategic initiative of the Meharry-Vanderbilt Student Alliance (MVSA) is to engage students in a cross-cultural academic environment to enhance their educational experience. Students in the MVSA play a vital role in medical education, communication, and community outreach through several successful endeavors.

To enhance the educational experience of students and to strengthen the programs of Meharry-Vanderbilt Alliance partners, a pediatrics clerkship exchange is celebrating its fifth year of success. Students at Meharry and Vanderbilt are enthusiastic and positive about the exchange program, which is available in their third year of study. VUMC medical students elect to rotate to MMC for additional outpatient exposure on two-week intervals. Similarly, MMC medical students rotate to Vanderbilt for additional inpatient exposure on two-week intervals.

"Confronting AIDS Now" is a forum to foster student interest in dealing with AIDS through basic science, clinical research and community outreach. MVSA's regular sponsorship of events for professional and graduate studies means the formation of new friendships, the enhancement of sensitivities to the diverse needs of patients and the igniting of passions to serve the needs of the community. Simply put, the role of the Alliance in fostering these experiences for our students cannot be overstated.

University of Tennessee, Health Science Center, College of Medicine

Dr. Gerald J. Presbury,
Associate Professor
Department of Pediatrics
University of Tennessee, Health Science Center, College of Medicine
62 South Dunlap,
Memphis, TN 38163
901-572-5394; 901-572-3122 fax

Recruitment

The College of Medicine maintains a long-term, continuing program for the recruitment of underrepresented minority and disadvantaged students. As a means of identifying students, referral information is requested from high school principals, counselors, college pre-med advisors, and other educational referral agencies. Further, admissions and financial aid representatives for each of the six health professions colleges of the University of Tennessee (UT), Memphis make regular high school and college visits throughout Tennessee and adjoining states. Once students are identified, they are tracked throughout their educational experience. Academic progress is monitored;

counsel and reinforcement are provided regarding career decisions; and close association with faculty and students from the College of Medicine is encouraged through numerous on-campus educational enrichment experiences. Students developing interest, motivation, and knowledge about the health profession are stimulated by periodic health profession publications and newsletters; on-campus visitation programs, including tours, seminars, and study-skills workshops; and summer work experience in laboratories and clinics of the College of Medicine. The College of Medicine is committed to increasing the number of underrepresented minority students who will enter the medical profession.

Admissions

To support the work of the Admissions Committee in selecting highly qualified minority students, a select subcommittee, composed of the Assistant Dean for Admissions and Students and other members of the Admissions Committee, carefully review the applications of all minority students prior to their presentation to the full committee.

Academic Support Programs

The Student Academic Support Service at UT, Memphis provides academic support for medical students throughout their training. This program offers individual laboratory assessments of learning difficulties, as well as an integrative program of skill development in reading, time management, problem solving, note taking, test taking, and memorizing. Computer-assisted instruction, based on the curriculum, is available in large-group, small-group, and individual sessions. Tutorial assistance is also available at no charge. In addition, the college sponsors a variety of other support programs that include:

- *The Faculty Advisory System.* This program facilitates interaction among faculty and students. Each entering student becomes a member of a faculty advisor group composed of five first-year students, five second-year students, two faculty advisors, and two student advisors. The faculty share their perspective on medical education and the profession and serve as resource persons for specific questions or problems. The M-2 student advisors coordinate the activities of the group, and the M-4

University of Tennessee Health Science Center College of Medicine
Applicants, First-Time Applicants, Matriculants by Gender, Race and Ethnicity, 2007-2008

| | 2007 | | | | | | | | | 2008 | | | | | | | | |
| | APP | | | F-time APP | | | MAT | | | APP | | | F-time APP | | | MAT | | |
	Wo-men	Men	Total	Wo-men	Men	Total	Wo-men	Men	Total	Wo-men	Men	Total	Wo-men	Men	Total	Wo-men	Men	Total
Hispanic/Latino																		
Cuban	0	6	6	0	6	6	0	0	0	2	2	4	1	1	2	0	0	0
Mexican American	1	7	8	0	6	6	0	0	0	8	5	13	6	4	10	0	1	1
Puerto Rican	0	2	2	0	2	2	0	0	0	4	3	7	4	3	7	0	2	2
Other Hispanic	12	6	18	9	4	13	1	0	1	11	5	16	6	4	10	0	0	0
Multiple Hispanic/Latino*	1	1	2	1	1	2	1	0	1	0	3	3	0	3	3	0	0	0
Subtotal	14	22	36	10	19	29	2	0	2	25	18	43	17	15	32	0	3	3
Non-Hispanic/Latino**																		
Black	142	48	190	101	36	137	12	4	16	120	46	166	74	30	104	7	3	10
Native American/AK	2	2	4	1	2	3	0	0	0	3	4	7	2	3	5	0	0	0
Native Hawaiian/OPI	3	1	4	2	0	2	0	0	0	0	2	2	0	1	1	0	0	0
White	387	590	977	306	411	717	39	71	110	398	571	969	292	384	676	46	64	110
Asian	92	77	169	68	60	128	8	9	17	94	98	192	74	59	133	8	15	23
Multiple Race*	8	17	25	7	12	19	1	2	3	11	18	29	11	13	24	1	1	2
Unknown	3	6	9	3	6	9	0	2	2	8	10	18	8	10	18	2	0	2
Subtotal	637	741	1,378	488	527	1,015	60	88	148	634	749	1,383	461	500	961	64	83	147
Foreign	7	3	10	6	2	8	0	0	0	3	3	6	2	3	5	0	0	0
Total	658	766	1,424	504	548	1,052	62	88	150	662	770	1,432	480	518	998	64	86	150

*Since 2002, students can select more than one race and / or ethnicity. **Those who did not choose 'Hispanic/Latino' or 'Non-Hispanic/Latino' are listed under 'Non-Hispanic/Latino'. Data Source: AAMC Data Warehouse: Applicant-Matriculant File, as of 1/16/2009.

student advisors share perspectives of those further advanced in the curriculum.

- *Big Brother/Big Sister Program.* Each entering student is assigned a Big Sib. The Big Brother or Big Sister offers invaluable insight into the ropes of the first year: which books are best, the first test, best grocery store, where to get a haircut, where to relax and have fun, how to sign up for intramurals, et cetera. Close and lasting relationships often develop through this program.
- *Career Counseling and Residency Placement.* Choosing the specialty most congruent with students' interests, talents, and long-term personal and professional goals is a major life decision. Programs and activities are available to support students as they contemplate this decision and choose their specialties and residencies, beginning in the second year and continuing through the National Residency Match Program (NRMP) Match in the fourth year.
- *Peer Counseling Program.* Peer Counselors are trained, carefully selected volunteers who offer a confidential personal support system to students in all classes. This program teaches physicians-to-be that it is acceptable to need help, to turn to one another for help, and to know how to offer it. This program fosters positive development and a sharing, cooperative approach to education.

Enrichment Programs

The College of Medicine and the UT, Memphis sponsor a host of summer enrichment activities that are designed to promote a greater interest in the health profession, enhance students' competitiveness as applicants, and contribute to their success in the medical curriculum. The following listing is representative of the interest and commitment of the college.

Summer High School Research Apprenticeships. This program offers opportunities for employment in research settings for high school and college students, generally eight weeks in duration.

Tennessee Pre-professional Fellowship Program (PFP)
African-American residents of Tennessee, who have completed two years of undergraduate study with demonstrated interest in medicine, participate in two required eight-week summer enrichment programs following junior and senior years. Students who successfully complete the programs receive an assurance of medical school admission if, by the time of their application, they meet or exceed minimum admission requirements.

Early Admission
The Committee on Admissions invites applications from outstanding minority applicants at the beginning of their junior year. Students may begin their medical study during their senior year or complete their undergraduate training while having a space reserved for them in the next entering class.

All of the above summer programs carry a stipend to replace lost income.

Student Financial Assistance

Financial aid for all students at UT, Memphis is based on need. These needs are met through scholarships, grants, loans, and work-study. The financial aid officers, through a combination of these means, have been successful in supplying enough assistance to complete degree programs. The College of Medicine is very pleased to sponsor scholarship programs for minority students. Scholarships in the amount of $10,000 annually have been available to all minority students accepted for admission.

Vanderbilt University School of Medicine

Dr. George C. Hill, Associate Dean and Levi Watkins, Jr., Professor for Diversity in Medical Education and Professor in the Department of Microbiology and Immunology
Vanderbilt University School of Medicine
301 Light Hall
Nashville, TN 37232-0190
615-322-7498; 615-322-4526 ax

Recruitment

The Vanderbilt University School of Medicine is committed to a diversified student population. To this end, the school administers an active recruitment program that involves visits by students and staff to other campuses and encourages contacts between applicants and matriculating students. Applicants that have been invited to Vanderbilt are encouraged to return for the "second visit" weekend that occurs each April. Currently enrolled minority students and alumni are actively involved in the school's recruitment program.

Vanderbilt University School of Medicine has organized an Office for Diversity in Medical Education under the leadership of an Associate Dean in Medical Education reporting to the Dean of the School of Medicine. This office will focus on increasing the diversity of the medical and graduate students, house staff, and faculty and enhancing an evolving environment that recognizes and embraces diversity.

The regional Student National Medical Association at Vanderbilt University School of Medicine is extremely active in student affairs and received the region award for excellence in 2004. We also have an active Asian Pacific American Medical Student Association (APAMSA) organization, National Network of Latin American Medical Students (NNLAMS), and a Minority Association of Pre-medical Students (MAPS) chapter.

Admissions

The admissions process at Vanderbilt School of Medicine does not use mathematical formulas for choosing applicants. All parts of the American Medical College Application Service (AMCAS) application and secondary application are of value in making selections. There is a stated goal to matriculate a highly diverse class in terms of race, gender, geography, and other elements. The first priority of the process is to ensure that academic credentials suggest that students can graduate from a highly competitive environment. All aspects of the applications are considered to accomplish the goals of diversity, which enhances the educational experience of our students.

Academic Support Programs

The Vanderbilt University School of Medicine provides a supportive, positive environment in which students are treated individually in their pursuit of excellence in careers in medicine. Individual tutoring and counseling, as needed, are provided to all students. There has been minimal attrition.

Enrichment Programs

Students are given special assistance in locating funded summer re-search positions with Vanderbilt faculty.

Vanderbilt Summer Science Academy
The Vanderbilt Summer Science Academy (VSSA) hosts over 70 undergraduates from institutions all over the country who conduct research in one of the basic science research laborato-

Vanderbilt University School of Medicine
Applicants, First-Time Applicants, Matriculants by Gender, Race and Ethnicity, 2007-2008

	2007									2008								
	APP			F-time APP			MAT			APP			F-time APP			MAT		
	Wo-men	Men	Total	Wo-men	Men	Total	Wo-men	Men	Total	Wo-men	Men	Total	Wo-men	Men	Total	Wo-men	Men	Total
Hispanic/Latino																		
Cuban	11	11	22	9	8	17	0	1	1	18	16	34	14	13	27	1	0	1
Mexican American	30	33	63	26	29	55	0	1	1	40	33	73	34	28	62	2	1	3
Puerto Rican	14	10	24	12	9	21	0	0	0	8	10	18	7	9	16	0	0	0
Other Hispanic	47	55	102	43	45	88	2	0	2	38	51	89	35	43	78	1	0	1
Multiple Hispanic/Latino*	6	5	11	6	3	9	0	0	0	11	8	19	11	5	16	1	0	1
Subtotal	108	114	222	96	94	190	2	2	4	115	118	233	101	98	199	5	1	6
Non-Hispanic/Latino**																		
Black	220	105	325	178	84	262	7	0	7	253	111	364	213	89	302	9	3	12
Native American/AK	4	4	8	3	4	7	0	0	0	8	8	16	8	7	15	0	0	0
Native Hawaiian/OPI	7	2	9	4	1	5	0	0	0	5	4	9	4	4	8	0	0	0
White	1,214	1,680	2,894	1,062	1,398	2,460	17	42	59	1,193	1,720	2,913	1,031	1,432	2,463	26	36	62
Asian	424	466	890	355	378	733	16	5	21	386	528	914	308	412	720	6	9	15
Other Race	1	4	5	1	2	3	0	0	0	2	3	5	1	3	4	0	0	0
Multiple Race*	63	61	124	55	49	104	2	1	3	75	75	150	67	55	122	2	1	3
Unknown	15	29	44	13	27	40	1	1	2	50	81	131	48	71	119	0	0	0
Subtotal	1,948	2,351	4,299	1,671	1,943	3,614	43	49	92	1,972	2,530	4,502	1,680	2,073	3,753	43	49	92
Foreign	123	143	266	99	116	215	5	4	9	146	151	297	123	112	235	3	4	7
Total	2,179	2,608	4,787	1,866	2,153	4,019	50	55	105	2,233	2,799	5,032	1,904	2,283	4,187	51	54	105

*Since 2002, students can select more than one race and / or ethnicity. **Those who did not choose 'Hispanic/Latino' or 'Non-Hispanic/Latino' are listed under 'Non-Hispanic/Latino'. Data Source: AAMC Data Warehouse: Applicant-Matriculant File, as of 1/16/2009.

ries at Vanderbilt. Each student has an opportunity to present their research at the Summer Symposium held on the last day of the program. The VSSA also organizes orientation, a research seminar series, a Graduate Record Examination (GRE) preparatory course, enrichment seminars, and social activities. The research seminars cover many of the major areas of investigation in the biomedical sciences and expose students to the newest technology used in these areas of study. In addition, the enrichment seminars provide useful information for working in the laboratory, applying to graduate programs and exposure to the many career options open to individuals with a Ph.D. in the biomedical sciences. This is an excellent opportunity for undergraduates to experience research at a major academic research center and to understand what graduate life would be like were they to decide on a research career. It is also an excellent opportunity for them to network with students at other institutions from across the country.

Our Summer Academy students have the opportunity to work in one of over 200 laboratories in any of the departments or programs affiliated the Office of Biomedical Research Education and Training. These include those affiliated with the Interdisciplinary Graduate Program [biochemistry, biological sciences, cancer biology, cell & developmental biology, human genetics, microbiology & immunology, molecular physiology & biophysics, neurosciences (molecular & cellular, cognitive/integrative), pathology, and pharmacology] and the Chemical and Physical Biology Program (all Interdisciplinary Graduate Program participating departments and programs as well as chemistry, physics, and mathematics). Students are matched with mentors based on research interest as well as with mentors who have an excellent track record of mentoring students during the summer.

More information can be found at: *(https://medschool.mc.vanderbilt.edu/ssa/)*

For questions, please contact: Michelle Grundy, Ph.D. Director Vanderbilt Summer Science *Academymichelle.grundy@vanderbilt.edu*

Initiative for Maximizing Student Diversity
The Office of Biomedical Research Education and Training provides opportunities for individuals holding a bachelors degree to prepare for Ph.D. training through the Initiative for Maximizing Student Diversity (IMSD) training grant funded by the National Institutes of Health. The Vanderbilt Initiative for Maximizing Student Diversity (IMSD) is an NIH-funded program geared toward students who contribute to diversity, who have a real interest in biomedical research, and would like to enter a first-rate graduate program in the biomedical sciences. The Vanderbilt IMSD program is a very highly flexible approach that involves extensive and careful mentoring at all stages. The Vanderbilt IMSD offers a one-year training opportunity (pre-Interdisciplinary Graduate Program) prior to the traditional first or Interdisciplinary Graduate Program year of graduate school. Students will be selected to matriculate into the pre-Interdisciplinary Graduate Program on a holistic basis. Although applicants will be required to submit GPA and GRE scores, future potential for success as evidenced by recommendation letters and a personal interview will be the key basis for selecting applicants. We anticipate that students who complete the two year pre-Interdisciplinary Graduate Program/Interdisciplinary Graduate Program will be fast tracked for success in their later years in research.

More information can be found on the following Web site: *(https://medschool.mc.acksont./imsd)* or contact: Linda Sealy, Ph.D. Associate Director Initiative for Maximizing Student Diversity *linda.sealy@vanderbilt.edu*

Vanderbilt Emphasis Program
The Emphasis Program is a unique mode of self-directed study that takes place during the first two years of medical school. This program aims to harness the student's skills, talents, and passions by allowing them to pursue a project of their choosing.

Perhaps one of the greatest advantages of the Emphasis Program is the opportunity for students to learn more about themselves and what type of physicians they would like to become.

We will match students' areas of interest with those of committed, excellent faculty mentors. Students will cultivate knowledge and skill through these mentorship experiences, as well as hands-on research and study in desired areas of focus.

Program Director
Denis O'Day, MD
denis.m.oday@vanderbilt.edu
615-936-2100

Program Coordinator
Samantha L. Martin
samantha.l.martin@vanderbilt.edu
615-343-2653

More information can be found at: *(https://www.mc.vanderbilt.edu/emphasis).*

Student Financial Assistance
The school grants application fee waivers for students for whom the American Medical College Application Service has granted a fee waiver.

Vanderbilt uses a needs-analysis system for awarding need-based scholarships. There are Dean's Scholarships awarded to students in order to encourage diversity in the medical student population. In addition, there are merit scholarships, based on academic and leadership potential, for which all Vanderbilt students are eligible. Federal loans are also available.

Educational Partnerships
Vanderbilt faculty participate in special programs in community middle and high schools that are designed to enrich the schools' science curricula and to encourage student interest in the sciences and the health professions. Students and teachers are, in turn, accommodated in summer enrichment programs at the medical center.

Baylor College of Medicine

Dr. James L. Phillips, Senior Associate Dean, Office of Diversity & Community Outreach, and Professor of Pediatrics
Baylor College of Medicine
One Baylor Plaza, M108
Houston, TX 77030
713-798-6598; 713-798-8449 fax
phillips@bcm.edu
www.bcm.edu/studentdiversity

Recruitment

Baylor has an active program of visiting colleges and secondary schools to seek out and inform individuals, from groups underrepresented in medicine, about career opportunities. Faculty, medical students, administrators, and alumni participate in these recruitment efforts. The career fairs for underrepresented minority students at the annual meetings of the Association of American Medical Colleges (AAMC), Society for the Advancement of Chicanos and Native Americans in Science (SACNAS), the National Association of Medical Minority Educators (NAMME) are attended by our faculty and students. Individuals and school groups are also encouraged to visit the campus and participate in organized tours conducted by medical students.

Admissions

The Admissions Committee is composed of faculty and students, several of whom are members of groups underrepresented in medicine. Applicants are evaluated on both cognitive and non-cognitive strengths, including review of one's complete academic record. Since 1971, a significant percentage of each year's entering classes has been minority group students underrepresented in medicine. Baylor as an institution is committed to diversity. In addition to having an underrepresented minority enrollment in each class that ranges from 16-22 percent, several enroll in our Medical Scientist Training Program (MSTP), Baylor's M.D./Ph.D. program, and the M.D./M.B.A. program, which is operated in conjunction with Rice University. The faculty and staff at Baylor focus on helping our students maximize their potential, with some being Howard Hughes Scholars and some recipients of other research fellowships.

Applicants should submit their applications as early as possible (June), since admissions are granted on a rolling basis following interviews in the fall semester.

Academic Support Programs

Each basic science department offers tutorial assistance and individual conferences for all students. Tutors and review sessions are available for students, faculty are readily accessible, and videotapes of the lectures may be checked out from the Learning Resource Center. An innovative mentoring program that utilizes clinical and basic science faculty, plus fellows and residents, is also in place.

Enrichment Programs

Michael E. DeBakey Summer Surgery Program.
The Michael E. DeBakey Summer Surgery Program provides students with an opportunity to work with faculty, residents, medical students, and nurses in a surgical hospital environment. During the eight-week program, students become familiar with the hospital environment, the operating room, and the lifestyle of a surgeon through participation in surgical team routines, making daily rounds with an attending

Baylor College of Medicine
Applicants, First-Time Applicants, Matriculants by Gender, Race and Ethnicity, 2007-2008

| | 2007 | | | | | | | | | 2008 | | | | | | | | |
| | APP | | | F-time APP | | | MAT | | | APP | | | F-time APP | | | MAT | | |
	Women	Men	Total	Women	Men	Total	Women	Men	Total	Women	Men	Total	Women	Men	Total	Women	Men	Total
Hispanic/Latino																		
Cuban	12	10	22	11	7	18	0	0	0	12	11	23	12	10	22	1	1	2
Mexican American	103	116	219	85	97	182	8	14	22	88	93	181	74	72	146	3	11	14
Puerto Rican	19	12	31	18	9	27	1	0	1	13	10	23	11	9	20	0	1	1
Other Hispanic	70	66	136	55	49	104	4	2	6	76	85	161	66	67	133	1	4	5
Multiple Hispanic/Latino*	10	10	20	7	6	13	2	0	2	13	7	20	11	6	17	1	0	1
Subtotal	214	214	428	176	168	344	15	16	31	202	206	408	174	164	338	6	17	23
Non-Hispanic/Latino**																		
Black	275	129	404	221	103	324	2	2	4	243	130	373	200	97	297	5	4	9
Native American/AK	6	7	13	6	7	13	0	1	1	5	9	14	5	8	13	1	1	2
Native Hawaiian/OPI	9	6	15	7	4	11	0	0	0	8	6	14	8	3	11	0	0	0
White	1,015	1,358	2,373	857	1,121	1,978	43	37	80	940	1,373	2,313	788	1,097	1,885	35	26	61
Asian	595	689	1,284	510	541	1,051	27	22	49	594	736	1,330	473	555	1,028	35	35	70
Other Race	8	5	13	6	2	8	0	0	0	9	6	15	9	5	14	1	0	1
Multiple Race*	75	57	132	63	42	105	2	1	3	58	53	111	43	42	85	2	6	8
Unknown	14	26	40	14	23	37	0	2	2	37	49	86	35	39	74	1	1	2
Subtotal	1,997	2,277	4,274	1,684	1,843	3,527	74	65	139	1,894	2,362	4,256	1,561	1,846	3,407	80	73	153
Foreign	119	101	220	93	78	171	1	1	2	108	107	215	93	83	176	0	0	0
Total	2,330	2,592	4,922	1,953	2,089	4,042	90	82	172	2,204	2,675	4,879	1,828	2,093	3,921	86	90	176

*Since 2002, students can select more than one race and / or ethnicity. **Those who did not choose 'Hispanic/Latino' or 'Non-Hispanic/Latino' are listed under 'Non-Hispanic/Latino'. Data Source: AAMC Data Warehouse: Applicant-Matriculant File, as of 1/16/2009.

physician, observing surgeries, and attending brown bag lunches and conferences.

Saturday Morning Science Program
This program targets students in grades seven-12 from our underserved communities. Lectures and labs are presented by our faculty, who are assisted by our medical students. Careers in the biosciences for the students constitute the goal of this initiative, which concludes each semester with a career/college fair.

Several High Schools for the Health Professions throughout the state are affiliated with Baylor College of Medicine.

The SMART Program
The ten-week, Summer Medical and Research Training Program is open to undergraduate college students. In addition to a major laboratory experience, there is a daily seminar series and career development workshops and activities. Contact Gayle Slaughter, Ph.D., Program Director, 713-798-5915.

Student Financial Assistance
Significant financial aid is available for students with demonstrated financial need. Applicants may also request waiver of the application fee on the basis of financial need.

Texas A&M Health Science Center College of Medicine

Wanda J. Watson, Director of
Recruitment and Special Programs
Texas A&M Health Science Center
College of Medicine
159 Joe H. Reynolds Medical Building, College Station, TX 77843-1114
979-845-7743; 979-845-5533 fax
Wwatson@medicine.tamhsc.edu
www.medicine.tamhsc.edu

Recruitment

The recruitment program at The Texas
A&M Health Science Center College of
Medicine is an integrated series of activities and efforts primarily focused at Texas
residents. As part of its commitment to
recruit and graduate qualified disadvantaged students, the College of Medicine
through the Office of Admissions and Office of Special Programs administer several summer enrichment programs. The
College of Medicine hosts and sponsors
enrichment programs that identify and
support promising educationally and
economically disadvantaged college students. These programs are designed to
provide guidance, information, and activities that will encourage graduation and
subsequent application to medical school.

In partnership with the Application Center for Medical/Dental/Undergraduate
Research Summer Programs, the College
of Medicine also has a program of annual recruiting visits to undergraduate
institutions throughout the state of
Texas.

The Director of Recruitment and Special
Programs plans, coordinates, and implements the recruitment and outreach activities for the College of Medicine. These
outreach programs target high school
and first-year college students from educationally and economically disadvantaged backgrounds. Additionally, the
college hosts tour groups for high schools
and universities throughout the year.

Admissions

Admission to the College of Medicine is
competitive. The College of Medicine
considers for enrollment only individuals who are U.S. citizens or permanent
residents of the United States, and who
have completed their undergraduate
coursework at a fully accredited college
or university in the United States or its
territories. By state mandate, enrollment of individuals from states other
than Texas may not exceed 10 percent.

Applicants must demonstrate better
than average ability to master a challenging educational experience. Assessment of applicants is based on
academic record, pattern of academic
performance, extracurricular activities,
motivation, and background. The Admissions Committee consists of faculty
from the basic and clinical sciences.
One hundred and seventy students matriculate each year.

Academic Support Programs

Students in academic difficulty receive
assistance from faculty members and
students. Review sessions are periodically scheduled in particular disciplines.
Specific remedial work if necessary is assigned on an individual basis. Workshops on learning strategies and time
management techniques are conducted
during the first year. Assistance in these
areas, upon request or referral, is provided on an individual basis. During the
third and fourth years on the Temple
Clinical Campus, students select a faculty advisor with whom they can meet
and discuss choices of electives, residency training, and career opportunities.

Texas A&M Health Science Center College of Medicine
Applicants, First-Time Applicants, Matriculants by Gender, Race and Ethnicity, 2007-2008

	2007									2008								
	APP			F-time APP			MAT			APP			F-time APP			MAT		
	Wo-men	Men	Total	Wo-men	Men	Total	Wo-men	Men	Total	Wo-men	Men	Total	Wo-men	Men	Total	Wo-men	Men	Total
Hispanic/Latino																		
Cuban	5	4	9	4	3	7	0	0	0	2	5	7	2	5	7	0	0	0
Mexican American	140	162	302	105	121	226	8	0	8	145	132	277	117	95	212	8	4	12
Puerto Rican	5	6	11	5	4	9	0	0	0	10	10	20	7	9	16	1	0	1
Other Hispanic	60	51	111	41	31	72	2	1	3	49	52	101	28	34	62	1	2	3
Multiple Hispanic/Latino*	1	3	4	1	0	1	0	0	0	5	1	6	5	0	5	0	0	0
Subtotal	211	226	437	156	159	315	10	1	11	211	200	411	159	143	302	10	6	16
Non-Hispanic/Latino**																		
Black	138	64	202	98	49	147	3	0	3	125	69	194	89	45	134	6	2	8
Native American/AK	4	5	9	4	4	8	0	0	0	8	5	13	6	3	9	0	0	0
Native Hawaiian/OPI	2	1	3	1	1	2	0	0	0	1	4	5	1	2	3	0	0	0
White	692	850	1,542	529	616	1,145	27	25	52	667	888	1,555	506	600	1,106	24	42	66
Asian	375	384	759	283	264	547	19	15	34	366	384	750	255	252	507	14	25	39
Other Race	34	25	59	23	17	40	0	3	3	38	20	58	29	12	41	1	0	1
Multiple Race*	25	18	43	18	14	32	1	0	1	21	12	33	13	7	20	3	2	5
Unknown	2	1	3	2	1	3	0	0	0	1	5	6	1	4	5	0	0	0
Subtotal	1,272	1,348	2,620	958	966	1,924	50	43	93	1,227	1,387	2,614	900	925	1,825	48	71	119
Foreign	39	37	76	27	23	50	0	1	1	29	34	63	23	27	50	0	4	4
Total	1,522	1,611	3,133	1,141	1,148	2,289	60	45	105	1,467	1,621	3,088	1,082	1,095	2,177	58	81	139

*Since 2002, students can select more than one race and / or ethnicity. **Those who did not choose 'Hispanic/Latino' or 'Non-Hispanic/Latino' are
listed under 'Non-Hispanic/Latino'. Data Source: AAMC Data Warehouse: Applicant-Matriculant File, as of 1/16/2009.

Student Financial Assistance

Scholarship and loan funds are available for disadvantaged students with financial need from local, state, and national sources. Financial need of the applicant is not a consideration in the admission process. After acceptance, every effort is made to assist disadvantaged students in meeting their financial requirements. Approximately 90 percent of the students currently in the program are receiving some form of financial aid.

Educational Partnerships

The Partnership for Primary Care Program

The Texas A&M Health Science Center College of Medicine entered into agreements with member institutions of the Texas A&M University Systems to develop and implement the Partnership for Primary Care Program. This program is designed to recruit and jointly admit a select group of students with a guaranteed admission to the COM. The College of Medicine and A&M system's member institutions work together to develop programs of recruitment, admission, augmentation of undergraduate studies, and targeted opportunities for exposure to medicine during undergraduate years.

A specific Primary Care or Rural Medicine Track provides students with enrichment experiences over the four years of medical school. Also, students will be provided with the opportunity for a significant portion of their clinical training during medical school in the geographic vicinity of either their hometown or the A&M System University of their undergraduate experience. The program is targeted to provide primary care physicians for rural and/or underserved areas and areas of Texas with a disproportionately low number of primary care physicians.

The Joint Admissions Medical Program (JAMP)

The Joint Admissions Medical Program (JAMP) is a program created by Senate Bill 940 of the 77th Texas Legislature to provide services to support and encourage highly qualified, economically disadvantaged students pursuing a medical education. The program awards undergraduate and medical school scholarships and guarantees admission to those students who satisfy both academic and non-academic requirements to one of the eight participating medical schools. The Texas A&M Health Science Center College of Medicine is one of the eight medical schools participating in the program. As part of its commitment to the program, the COM provides JAMP students with stipends, summer enrichment internships; and mentoring and personal assistance to facilitate preparation for medical school while attending college.

The summer enrichment experience is rather intense by design. Part of the experience requires clinical exposure or clinical observational experiences. The bulk of that experience has been worked out with Scott & White Clinic College Station. However, the COM also provides the participants with an all day clinical experience at Scott & White in Temple shadowing physician faculty.

The Texas A&M University System Prairie View A&M University Undergraduate Medical Academy (UMA)

The Texas A&M Health Science Center College of Medicine has entered into an agreement with the Prairie View A&M University to create the Undergraduate Medical Academy. The College of Medicine Office of Special Programs in the Office of Student Affairs and Admissions coordinates the summer enrichment experience for the Academy students. The COM faculty members are highly involved in the program.

As with all of our summer enrichment programs, the Academy students are required to participate in clinical exposure or clinical observational experiences. The bulk of that experience is with Scott & White Clinic in College Station. They participate in all day clinical experience as Scott & White in Temple shadowing physician faculty.

The academy was created through legislation to increase skills needed for students to enter medical school or other health professions schools, to create a cooperative network between the Academy faculty members, students, and the medical community; and to foster and encourage interest in science and mathematics.

The South Texas College

The Texas A&M Health Science Center College of Medicine has entered into an agreement with the South Texas College (STC) in McAllen, Texas. Through the College of Medicine Partnership for Primary Care Program, qualified students are recruited for simultaneous admissions to the STC Valley Scholars Program and to the CCOM, provided students transfer successfully to the Texas A&M University BIMS or Biology programs. Students are expected to complete the associate of science degree at STC, a baccalaureate degree in BIMS or Biology at Texas A&M University, and the M.D. degree at the College of Medicine.

This program is for the purpose of recruiting, enrolling, and graduating significantly greater numbers of physicians to serve the designated health professions shortage areas of south Texas, to correct disproportions in physician distribution, and to meet the health care needs of rural and underserved south Texas.

Texas Tech University Health Sciences Center, Paul L. Foster School of Medicine

Robin Dankovich
Lead Advisor Recruiter
Office of Admissions
Texas Tech University Health
Sciences Center, Paul L.
Foster School of Medicine
5001 El Paso Drive
El Paso, Texas 79905
915-783-1250; 915-783-1265 fax
robin.dankovich@ttuhsc.edu

Recruitment
Texas Tech University Paul L. Foster School of Medicine (PLFSOM) in El Paso is committed to helping meet the needs of an increasingly diverse population by recruiting a diverse medical school class that exhibits qualities of academic success. Students are sought who possess the personal qualities and proven academic abilities to become effective and competent physicians. Admission guidelines call for no discrimination on the basis of race, sex, age, ethnic origin, religion, sexual orientation, or disability. The staff in the Office of Admissions is available to respond to inquiries, and periodically visits undergraduate universities across Texas personally, including our region, to provide information to pre-med students about our school. Information can also be obtained at: (http://www.ttuhsc.edu/fostersom).

Admission
In addition to evidence of high intellectual ability, a strong record of scholastic achievement, medical experiences, motivation to enter medicine, knowledge of issues in medicine, problem-solving ability, and other factors derived from the application package and interview, the PLFSOM Admissions Committee will also consider factors related to financially or educationally disadvantaged background identified in the application. No single factor is used exclusively to admit or eliminate admission of an applicant. With equal qualifications, preference may be given to residents of El Paso and West Texas. Applications to the PLFSOM are channeled through the Texas Medical and Dental School Application System (TMDSAS) at: (http://www.utsystem.edu/tmdsas/).

Academic Support Programs
Guided instruction by discipline experts through lecture, small groups, and laboratory exercises is utilized to teach an integrated curriculum that establishes the relevance of the basic to the clinical sciences. In an effort to support the students along the way, each class is divided into learning communities called colleges, where two College Masters monitor students' performance on a weekly basis. Preparation for the USMLE exams includes cumulative unit exams and periodic use of the Comprehensive Basic Sciences Exam. All students engage in a language course in conversational and medical Spanish. The Office of Student Affairs is well equipped to provide resources when needed for assistance with reading, study and test strategies, time and stress management and other demands related to the challenges of medical school.

Student Financial Assistance
The PLFSOM offers a number of competitive scholarships based on merit. These scholarships are renewable for up to four years contingent on passing all subjects and successful advancement to the next year of studies. Numbers of scholarships and amounts may vary from year to year.

In addition, the TTUHSC Office of Financial Aid serves students desiring financial assistance regarding loans, other type of scholarships, and loan forgiveness programs. A Liaison Financial Aid Officer is part of the staff in the Office of Student Affairs at the PLF SOM. Additional information may be obtained at www.ttuhsc.edu/financialaid or by calling Diana Andrade at 915-783-5130, diana.andrade@ttuhsc.edu .

Educational partnerships
The PLFSOM Office for Promotion of Community Educational Achievement (OPCEA) promotes the excellence in education with several programs for students in junior-high and high school in the El Paso region who are interested in health careers. For students at the pre-med university level, OPCEA also offers a Summer Camp and a Shadowing-A-Physician Program primarily oriented for students from our region. Students from other areas can also be considered for participation on an individual basis. Further information can be obtained from Mrs. Joyce Palmer, 915-545-6555, joyce.palmer@ttuhsc.edu.

The PLFSOM anticipates participating in the Texas Joint Admission Program (JAMP) in the near future. JAMP was created by the Texas Legislature to support and encourage highly qualified, economically disadvantaged Texas resident students pursuing a medical education.

*No data available; new medical school.

Texas Tech University Health Sciences Center School of Medicine

Dr. Bernell K. Dalley, Associate Dean for Admissions and Minority Affairs
Texas Tech University Health Sciences Center School of Medicine
3601 4th St. MS6216
Lubbock, TX 79430
806-743-2297; 806-743-2725 fax
bernell.dalley@ttuhsc.edu

Recruitment

Texas Tech University Health Sciences Center (TTUHSC) School of Medicine is responsive to both the health care needs of the area it serves and to the need for involvement of minority and disadvantaged groups in the health professions. The School of Medicine has a sincere desire to identify, at the earliest stage of high school and undergraduate training, highly motivated and academically qualified students.

The Office of Border Health on the El Paso campus was created to recruit students from the border counties of Texas, with emphasis on the undergraduate programs in those areas, including San Antonio. The effort is supplemented by identifying high school students in the El Paso County area. Due to increased grant support from the Texas Tech University School of Medicine and State of Texas (through the Joint Admission Medical Program, or JAMP) and Office of Rural and Community Health initiatives, the number of applicants as well as matriculants from underrepresented groups has steadily increased. The Offices of Border Health and Rural and Community Health work in coordination with the Office of Admissions and Minority Affairs and the Office of Student Affairs.

Admissions

The Admissions Committee of Texas Tech University Health Sciences Center School of Medicine is composed of basic science faculty, clinical faculty, and medical students. Minorities are represented on the committee. It is the policy of the TTUHSC School of Medicine to select from a pool of applicants those students who have demonstrated strong academic ability and motivation for medicine. The goal of the institution is to recruit a diverse medical class exhibiting the personal experiences and the qualities promising academic success and to meet the needs of an increasingly diverse population. To that end, race/ethnic background, as well as interest in the region will be among the many factors considered in the admissions process. All potentially acceptable minority applicants are invited for interviews and receive full committee consideration. While all applicants are subjected to standard admission procedures and policies, each applicant is reviewed with careful attention to background and extenuating circumstances.

Students enrolled in the School of Medicine, especially through a student group known as the Dean's Ambassadors, act as recruiters and promoters by talking with potential applicants when they visit the school and at pre-medical organization meetings. Applicants, especially those from underrepresented groups, are always encouraged to visit the medical school and talk with faculty and students. Representatives of the Admissions Committee annually attend the Texas Association of Advisors for the Health Professions Meeting. There is also regular participation in recruitment workshops. Visits are scheduled to campuses with significant numbers of minority students.

Texas Tech University Health Sciences Center School of Medicine
Applicants, First-Time Applicants, Matriculants by Gender, Race and Ethnicity, 2007-2008

	2007									2008								
	APP			F-time APP			MAT			APP			F-time APP			MAT		
	Women	Men	Total	Women	Men	Total	Women	Men	Total	Women	Men	Total	Women	Men	Total	Women	Men	Total
Hispanic/Latino																		
Cuban	5	4	9	4	2	6	0	0	0	2	5	7	2	5	7	0	1	1
Mexican American	145	165	310	104	122	226	1	10	11	134	129	263	105	91	196	1	5	6
Puerto Rican	6	6	12	6	4	10	0	0	0	9	10	19	7	9	16	0	0	0
Other Hispanic	57	53	110	39	33	72	3	2	5	47	51	98	28	33	61	1	2	3
Multiple Hispanic/Latino*	3	3	6	3	0	3	1	1	2	6	1	7	5	0	5	0	0	0
Subtotal	216	231	447	156	161	317	5	13	18	198	196	394	147	138	285	2	8	10
Non-Hispanic/Latino**																		
Black	127	61	188	85	46	131	1	1	2	131	67	198	94	42	136	1	1	2
Native American/AK	3	4	7	3	3	6	0	1	1	9	4	13	6	2	8	1	0	1
Native Hawaiian/OPI	2	1	3	1	1	2	0	0	0	2	4	6	2	2	4	0	0	0
White	655	833	1,488	487	589	1,076	29	50	79	612	873	1,485	455	587	1,042	31	53	84
Asian	373	379	752	281	263	544	18	16	34	360	369	729	253	243	496	20	19	39
Other Race	34	26	60	23	17	40	1	1	2	36	19	55	27	11	38	0	1	1
Multiple Race*	25	19	44	20	15	35	1	2	3	21	14	35	11	9	20	0	1	1
Unknown	2	0	2	2	0	2	0	0	0	1	2	3	1	2	3	0	0	0
Subtotal	1,221	1,323	2,544	902	934	1,836	50	71	121	1,172	1,352	2,524	849	898	1,747	53	75	128
Foreign	31	26	57	23	17	40	1	0	1	19	29	48	13	22	35	1	1	2
Total	1,468	1,580	3,048	1,081	1,112	2,193	56	84	140	1,389	1,577	2,966	1,009	1,058	2,067	56	84	140

*Since 2002, students can select more than one race and / or ethnicity. **Those who did not choose 'Hispanic/Latino' or 'Non-Hispanic/Latino' are listed under 'Non-Hispanic/Latino'. Data Source: AAMC Data Warehouse: Applicant-Matriculant File, as of 1/16/2009.

Academic Support Programs

The Admissions Committee accepts students considered to be capable of proceeding through the curriculum. In addition, students have the opportunity for individual instruction, remediation, and extra help from the faculty. A faculty mentoring program in which faculty serve as advisors to a small group of first- and second-year students is designed to assist in the adjustments to the medical school environment. For those students who do experience difficulty, there is also special assistance offered through the Academic and Career Advisor in the Office of Student Affairs. These programs and individuals help to identify student difficulties at an early period, so that academic and other help will be more profitable. Flexible programs, when appropriate, may be designed for students encountering academic difficulties.

Enrichment Programs

Summer enrichment internships are available for disadvantaged and rural high school, undergraduate, and medical students. One of these, the Summer Pre-medical Academy, consists of an all expenses paid six-week intensive course designed for students with 60 or more college credits. It includes shadowing experiences, a short course in gross anatomy, written and oral communication courses, community service activities and a full Medical College Admission Test review course (Stanley Kaplan). Information is available at the following Web site: (www.ttuhsc.edu/som/admissions). Please inquire through the TTUHSC School of Medicine Office of Admissions (806-743-2297).

Student Financial Assistance

TTUHSC School of Medicine personnel believe that no student should be denied a medical education due to lack of funds. A needs-based scholarship fund has been established for assistance during the first year of medical school. No student or prospective student shall be excluded from participation in, or be denied the benefits of any financial aid program on the basis of race, color, national origin, religion, or sex.

All students receive financial assistance in accordance with demonstrated need. Financial capability does not enter into the student selection process, neither is the lack of personal funds permitted to interfere with the completion of medical school education. The needs analysis is determined through the use of the Free Application for Federal Student Aid (FAFSA). Students receive financial aid counseling through the TTUHSC Office of Financial Aid.

Educational Partnerships

The Offices of Admissions and Minority Affairs, Student Affairs, Rural and Community Health, and Border Health coordinate and administer partnership initiatives. The regional campuses at Lubbock, Amarillo, and El Paso have joined the independent school systems of the respective communities via available magnet high schools for the health professions. Undergraduate programs in all three cities are also involved in mentoring programs with the School of Medicine students. In addition, summer employment and community-based elective opportunities for medical students are provided in these areas, especially in the largely Hispanic rural areas of the Lower Valley outside of El Paso.

Other Pertinent Information

TTUHSC School of Medicine particularly maintains a commitment to well-qualified students who are residents of Texas, eastern New Mexico, and southwestern Oklahoma.

University of Texas Health Science Center at San Antonio School of Medicine

Dr. David J. Jones, Associate Dean for Medical School Admissions
University of Texas Health Science Center at San Antonio School of Medicine
7703 Floyd Curl Drive
San Antonio, TX 78229
210-567-6080; 210-567-6962 fax
jonesd@uthscsa.edu

Recruitment

An active recruitment program is currently underway. This effort involves visits by faculty, administrative staff, and students to a variety of undergraduate campuses within the state of Texas. Visits to the School of Medicine campus are encouraged in order that the disadvantaged student may become familiar with available opportunities. These visits are coordinated by the Coordinator of Recruitment and Science Out-reach (210-567-3941). Inquiries from Texas residents attending undergraduate school outside the state are encouraged.

Admissions

The University of Texas Health Science Center at San Antonio School of Medicine (UTHSCSA) seeks to admit a class that reflects the diversity of the population of the state of Texas. Both Texas state resident applicants and out-of-state resident applicants are accepted. Minority applicants and socioeconomically disadvantaged applicants, as with all applicants, are reviewed holistically in an active effort to determine which of these candidates will be able to successfully complete the medical education curriculum. While the grade-point average (GPA) and the Medical College Admission Test (MCAT) score are important ingredients in the assessment process, many other factors enter into the consideration. Early educational experiences, parental influences, socioeconomic factors, clinical/volunteer activities, and life experiences of the applicant are all relevant issues to be reviewed. Evidence of leadership capacities, exceptional motivation, and record of past achievement, whether academic or in other life areas, are also among the factors considered. The records of all applicants are reviewed. Promising candidates are offered interviews. The candidates are interviewed by two members of the Admissions Committee. At the completion of the interview process, the applicants are then discussed in detail. The ultimate selection is by the Selection Sub-Committee of the Admissions Committee.

Academic Support Programs

The Medical Dean's Office has developed an extensive advisor system called Veritas. The Veritas Leader functions as a student advocate and will aid the student in finding help should problems, academic or otherwise, occur. Peer advising is widely incorporated. Additionally, the Health Science Center Counseling Service provides a full range of educational and learning-skills development services. The Office of Student Life also coordinates an extensive peer advisor system for all students.

The primary mission of the Office of Academic Enhancement is to promote the retention and advancement of medical students through their four-year curriculum. This mission is primarily accomplished by using the experiences and resources of the UTHSCSA medical student population. The input helps to develop and implement projects with the consumer in mind—the medical student. Currently the Office of Aca-

University of Texas School of Medicine at San Antonio
Applicants, First-Time Applicants, Matriculants by Gender, Race and Ethnicity, 2007-2008

	2007									2008								
	APP			F-time APP			MAT			APP			F-time APP			MAT		
	Wo-men	Men	Total	Wo-men	Men	Total	Wo-men	Men	Total	Wo-men	Men	Total	Wo-men	Men	Total	Wo-men	Men	Total
Hispanic/Latino																		
Cuban	4	5	9	3	3	6	0	0	0	2	6	8	2	6	8	0	0	0
Mexican American	181	199	380	137	151	288	14	14	28	176	163	339	142	120	262	13	13	26
Puerto Rican	9	9	18	9	6	15	0	1	1	15	14	29	12	13	25	0	0	0
Other Hispanic	68	58	126	48	38	86	5	2	7	58	60	118	38	41	79	4	6	10
Multiple Hispanic/Latino*	5	3	8	4	0	4	0	0	0	7	1	8	6	0	6	2	0	2
Subtotal	267	274	541	201	198	399	19	17	36	258	244	502	200	180	380	19	19	38
Non-Hispanic/Latino**																		
Black	172	79	251	113	61	174	5	6	11	162	87	249	113	57	170	7	4	11
Native American/AK	4	5	9	4	4	8	0	0	0	10	4	14	7	2	9	0	0	0
Native Hawaiian/OPI	2	1	3	1	1	2	0	0	0	3	3	6	3	2	5	0	0	0
White	797	981	1,778	604	711	1,315	59	65	124	744	1,004	1,748	576	686	1,262	61	67	128
Asian	427	422	849	324	292	616	23	19	42	407	429	836	292	286	578	17	20	37
Other Race	36	26	62	24	19	43	1	2	3	40	24	64	30	15	45	5	1	6
Multiple Race*	34	21	55	24	17	41	2	0	2	27	19	46	16	13	29	1	0	1
Unknown	2	1	3	2	1	3	0	1	1	2	5	7	2	3	5	0	0	0
Subtotal	1,474	1,536	3,010	1,096	1,106	2,202	90	93	183	1,395	1,575	2,970	1,039	1,064	2,103	91	92	183
Foreign	35	31	66	25	21	46	0	1	1	24	33	57	18	27	45	0	0	0
Total	1,776	1,841	3,617	1,322	1,325	2,647	109	111	220	1,677	1,852	3,529	1,257	1,271	2,528	110	111	221

*Since 2002, students can select more than one race and / or ethnicity. **Those who did not choose 'Hispanic/Latino' or 'Non-Hispanic/Latino' are listed under 'Non-Hispanic/Latino'. Data Source: AAMC Data Warehouse: Applicant-Matriculant File, as of 1/16/2009.

demic Enhancement offers individual and group tutoring programs for medical students, a pre-matriculation program for incoming medical students, a tutoring elective for those interested in academic medicine, a USMLE preparation course and consultation services for study skills, time management issues, and test-taking assistance.

Student Financial Assistance

Scholarship assistance is available. The Office of Student Financial Assistance works closely with all students in order to identify the most effective aid package for each student. Scholarships are awarded on a yearly basis.

Financial assistance is not routinely available for interviews. Application fee waivers are not granted.

Educational Partnerships

Facilitated Admissions for South Texas Scholars
The University of Texas-Pan American, Texas A&M International University, and St. Mary's University in partnership with the UTHSCSA offer programs to provide for early acceptance to medical school. The objectives of this program are to: 1) select outstanding students from these universities to a program for facilitated acceptance to the School of Medicine; 2) support students who are accepted to the program during their undergraduate studies by providing academic enrichment, MCAT, and medical school preparation courses; 3) provide early acceptance to medical school based on academic/MCAT performance; and finally, 4) offer the opportunity to return to South Texas for clinical training in their third and fourth years of medical school at the Regional Academic Health Center-associated clinical facilities.

University of Texas Medical Branch University of Texas Medical School at Galveston

Dr. Lauree Thomas, Associate Dean for Student Affairs and Admissions
The University of Texas Medical School at Galveston
610 Texas Avenue Building,
Suite 3.416
301 University Boulevard
Galveston, TX 77555-0807
409-772-1442; 409-772-5148 fax
lauthoma@utmb.edu
www.utmb.edu/somstudentaffairs

Recruitment

The Office of Student Affairs and Admissions facilitates the recruitment, admissions, and matriculation of a medical school class that is of the highest quality. The School of Medicine recruits primarily throughout the state as well as on a national level. The Director of Recruitment, faculty, and medical students visit with pre-medical students and advisors at universities in Texas and other states with a significant enrollment of Texas residents from educationally and economically disadvantaged backgrounds. During these visits, presentations on the medical school admission process, academic preparation, curriculum, student life, and financial aid are discussed at length as well as the rigorous and demanding expectations of medical school.

The University of Texas Medical Branch (UTMB) has committed substantial institutional resources towards our core institutional value of diversity. To achieve this goal, UTMB has established partnerships with several Texas colleges and universities, community organizations, and school districts to enhance the recruitment, matriculation, retention, and graduation of educationally and economically disadvantaged premedical and medical students. Every year, the Medical School hosts a number of recruitment programs both on and off campus, which are designed to facilitate acceptance into medical school. These programs include the interview day Night Before Social, the annual Premedical Conference, the Early Medical School Acceptance Program (EMSAP), the Joint Admission Medical Program (JAMP), the Short-Term Research Education Program to Increase Diversity in Health-Related Research, and the Prematriculation Reinforcement and Enrichment Program (PREP). It is praiseworthy to note that UTMB strongly adheres to its core values of diversity in training a cadre of workforce physicians who mirrors the population of the State of Texas.

Admissions

The major goals of the UTMB Medical School include the recruitment, retention, and graduation of students from educationally and economically disadvantaged backgrounds and correcting the physician shortage among medically underserved populations. Therefore, UTMB is well-known for its student body diversity. The Admissions Committee makes sure that all applicants are given adequate consideration when reviewing applications for medical school. All minority and disadvantaged applications are screened by members of the Admissions Committee where special attention is given to the cognitive and non-cognitive attributes of each applicant. Consideration is given to all applicants from disadvantaged backgrounds, rural, and medically underserved areas. Among the factors that are considered are the educational level of parents, occupation of parents, family income and household in which applicant grew up, high school and college attended, percentage of college expenses earned by applicant, hometown, geographic re-

University of Texas Medical Branch School of Medicine
Applicants, First-Time Applicants, Matriculants by Gender, Race and Ethnicity, 2007-2008

	2007									2008								
	APP			F-time APP			MAT			APP			F-time APP			MAT		
	Women	Men	Total	Women	Men	Total	Women	Men	Total	Women	Men	Total	Women	Men	Total	Women	Men	Total
Hispanic/Latino																		
Cuban	5	5	10	4	3	7	0	0	0	2	6	8	2	6	8	0	0	0
Mexican American	174	194	368	129	146	275	11	16	27	171	161	332	137	119	256	11	18	29
Puerto Rican	8	9	17	8	6	14	0	2	2	12	13	25	9	12	21	1	2	3
Other Hispanic	66	64	130	45	42	87	4	4	8	57	59	116	37	41	78	3	3	6
Multiple Hispanic/Latino*	4	3	7	3	0	3	0	0	0	6	1	7	6	0	6	1	0	1
Subtotal	257	275	532	189	197	386	15	22	37	248	240	488	191	178	369	16	23	39
Non-Hispanic/Latino**																		
Black	182	83	265	124	63	187	16	7	23	174	89	263	125	58	183	16	6	22
Native American/AK	5	5	10	5	4	9	0	0	0	10	5	15	7	3	10	1	0	1
Native Hawaiian/OPI	2	1	3	1	1	2	0	0	0	2	4	6	2	2	4	0	0	0
White	791	988	1,779	598	727	1,325	57	68	125	751	1,014	1,765	579	696	1,275	44	77	121
Asian	419	430	849	321	296	617	10	21	31	400	437	837	281	289	570	13	22	35
Other Race	38	26	64	26	18	44	2	0	2	42	27	69	32	17	49	4	3	7
Multiple Race*	30	21	51	22	16	38	0	2	2	27	20	47	18	14	32	1	2	3
Unknown	2	0	2	2	0	2	0	0	0	4	5	9	4	3	7	0	0	0
Subtotal	1,469	1,554	3,023	1,099	1,125	2,224	85	98	183	1,410	1,601	3,011	1,048	1,082	2,130	79	110	189
Foreign	50	42	92	35	28	63	5	2	7	39	42	81	30	33	63	2	0	2
Total	1,776	1,871	3,647	1,323	1,350	2,673	105	122	227	1,697	1,883	3,580	1,269	1,293	2,562	97	133	230

*Since 2002, students can select more than one race and / or ethnicity. **Those who did not choose 'Hispanic/Latino' or 'Non-Hispanic/Latino' are listed under 'Non-Hispanic/Latino'. Data Source: AAMC Data Warehouse: Applicant-Matriculant File, as of 1/16/2009.

gion of state from a medically underserved community, and English as a second language. Each interviewee receives two separate interviews while on campus, and a special effort is made to introduce minority applicants to currently enrolled minority students. As authorized by the Board of Regents, the University of Texas System has granted UTMB permission to use race and ethnicity as one of several factors that are considered for admission into medical school and in awarding scholarships. All applicants are evaluated holistically and individually by members of the Admissions Committee.

Academic Support Programs

The Academic Counseling Program has been developed specifically to aid medical students so that they can achieve academic success. Students are assisted in defining and addressing learning styles and any academic or personal problems that may impact their academic performance. Workshops are conducted for groups of students or they are seen on an individual basis for an assessment of their reading and comprehension ability, learning skills, study skills, time management, and test-taking strategies.

An Early Academic Identification Warning System assesses the student's level of academic performance throughout the basic science curriculum so that proactive interventional strategies can prevent failure. Performance in the problem-based learning small-group discussions, quizzes, and block exams are closely followed. Once a student is identified, they are placed in an automatic academic monitoring tracking system and the student is immediately counseled. An individualized, discipline-specific academic plan is created based upon a thorough assessment of the student's needs. Several workshops are given that cover a variety of topics such as stress management, handling personal relationship issues, relaxation, time management, and dealing with stress and test anxiety.

Tutorial assistance in the basic sciences

courses is offered through the Peer Tutorial Program. Some students receive individual assistance, but most meet in small groups. In the For Students by Students Program, students that have completed an academic year develop a manual for the upcoming class which provides insights into studying for different courses that cover textbooks, labs, web sites, practice tests, and learning tools.

Step Prep is a formal United States Medical Licensing Examination Step 1 intensive board preparation program consisting of several components. A comprehensive manual is distributed to each second-year student in January. In the Spring, a free board review course is taught over a three-week period. Two Comprehensive Basic Science Examinations (CBSEs) are also given to provide feedback to students as to their progress in board preparation. Additionally, a mentoring component allows senior students to advise and/or tutor the sophomores throughout their preparation.

Enrichment Programs

A variety of enrichment programs are offered at UTMB that promote the professional development of perspective candidates so that they become more competitive for medical school entrance:

Short-Term Research Education Program to Increase Diversity in Health-Related Research. This program is supported by the National Heart, Lung and Blood Institute. UTMB supports basic and clinical research directed at the causes, prevention, and treatment of cardiovascular, pulmonary, and hematological diseases. Summer research training opportunities in these areas are available at UTMB School of Medicine for three talented, underrepresented minority undergraduate and six medical students. Each student will work closely with a National Institutes of Health-funded faculty member at UTMB on an exciting research project directed to these specific areas. In order to bolster the already short supply of

minority biomedical researchers, we believe that by providing this opportunity, underrepresented students may become interested in pursuing a career in medical or biomedical research. All trainees will participate in scientific seminars, workshops, or clinical conferences that will be held throughout the summer. At the conclusion of the program, each student will present their research at a scientific symposium held on campus.

Prematriculation Reinforcement Enrichment Program (PREP)
This intensive, academic enrichment program provides a smooth transition from college to the rigorous and demanding expectations of the medical school curriculum. Six-weeks in duration, it gives a realistic preview of selected courses in the first-year curriculum that are taught by UTMB faculty. The demands of the courses, including the pace and examinations are identical to that of courses taught during the academic year. The program provides the opportunity to make the academic, psychological, emotional, and physical adjustments necessary to adapt to the work load of the medical school curriculum.

Early Medical School Acceptance Program (EMSAP)
This program is a formal partnership and contractual agreement for conditional acceptance into medical school between UTMB and six public universities (UT Brownsville, UT El Paso, UT Pan American, Texas A&M, International University at Laredo, Prairie View A&M, and Texas Southern University). A maximum of 30 college students are accepted each year and are offered conditional acceptance to UTMB's Medical School provided they maintain an overall and science GPA of 3.25 and a MCAT score of 24. Five students are selected from each of the partnership universities.

EMSAP enhances the competitiveness of underrepresented and disadvantaged college students for admission into medical school. The students participate in a comprehensive, integrated, six-week intensive summer program at UTMB that provides academic support services, MCAT preparation, clinical exposure, and mentoring. The main objectives of the program are to increase the number of bilingual and bicultural physicians in Texas, to support the drive to cultivate and produce medical professionals with a passion for delivering health care to the underserved, and to offer outstanding college students an opportunity to prepare for the competitiveness of the medical school admissions process.

Student Financial Assistance

UTMB falls in the bottom quartile of all medical schools for tuition and fees; tuition has been raised only twice in a ten-year period. It has made significant strides in awarding scholarships to underrepresented minority students. With the establishment of the Herzog Foundation in 1994, UTMB has more than $8,000,000 in endowments that provide scholarships for students from minority and disadvantaged backgrounds. Several other scholarship programs are available and new ones are added each year. Minority students are encouraged to apply for National Medical Fellowships, the National Hispanic Scholarship Fund, scholarships offered through local medical societies, and any of the other state funded initiatives. Two years ago, UTMB embarked upon a Capital Campaign, which designated scholarships for minority students as a top priority. UTMB's need-based scholarships are primarily awarded to low income minority students.

To assist students with financial planning and debt management, Enrollment Services has specialists who are available for counseling. In addition to this service, students may use the online tools provided on the Enrollment Services Web site to assist them with managing their loan debt and planning a budget. All financial aid students are required to complete online entrance interviews prior to receiving any loan funds.

University of Texas Medical School at Houston

Dr. R. Andrew Harper
Assistant Dean for Educational
Programs
University of Texas Medical School
at Houston
6431 Fannin, JJL 304
Houston, TX 77030
713-500-5140; 713-500-0603 fax
r.andrew.harper@uth.tmc.edu
http://med.uth.tmc.edu/administra-tion/edu_programs/index.htm

Recruitment

The University of Texas Medical School at Houston (UTMS-H) sponsors several substantive recruitment programs. The UTMS-H Office of Admissions sponsors between five and ten Admissions Workshops each year at colleges and universities throughout the state of Texas. Medical students frequently attend career fairs at high schools in the greater Houston metropolitan area to distribute information and promote careers in medicine to high school juniors and seniors.

The UT Medical Summer Research Program is a ten-week hands-on research program for undergraduate and medical students interested in biomedical research. Administered by the Office of Educational Programs, this program offers students opportunities to do basic science research under the direction of UTMS-H faculty and to be introduced to the medical environment. More information about this program can be found at: *(http://med.uth.tmc.edu/administration/edu_programs/ep/summer_research_program/)*.

The University of Texas Medical School at Houston currently has affiliation agreements for assured acceptance programs with several Texas universities. Two agreements of note are with the University of Houston, which has the most culturally diverse student population in the nation, and the University of Texas at El Paso, the only major research university in the nation with a predominately Mexican-American student body. More information about assured acceptance programs can be found at: *(http://med.uth.tmc.edu/administration/admissions/assured-acceptance.html)*.

Admissions

All applicants participate in the same admissions process. Each applicant's file is screened, and those applicants that indicate a potential for success in medicine are invited for an interview. The applicant obtains an interview and subsequent matriculation into medical school based on a number of criteria. Ethnicity is considered in the evaluation of applicants to medical school, but it is considered in conjunction with many additional criteria.

The Admissions Committee is composed of a richly diverse cross section of the school's faculty membership and represents several cultural and ethnic backgrounds. These basic science and clinical faculty evaluate each interviewed applicant. The committee takes into consideration the following criteria in reviewing applicants: Medical College Admission Test (MCAT) scores; non-cognitive variables, such as potential for service, determination, and independence; and commitment of the applicant to practicing in the state of Texas in a needed area or specialty.

The Admissions Committee is frequently apprised of the mission and purpose of the admissions process and the goals for our institution. These goals include attention to underrepresented minorities as well as to candidates from health professions shortage areas, and to those candidates who may be likely to return to these areas of our state.

University of Texas Medical School at Houston
Applicants, First-Time Applicants, Matriculants by Gender, Race and Ethnicity, 2007-2008

	2007									2008								
	APP			F-time APP			MAT			APP			F-time APP			MAT		
	Women	Men	Total	Women	Men	Total	Women	Men	Total	Women	Men	Total	Women	Men	Total	Women	Men	Total
Hispanic/Latino																		
Cuban	5	5	10	4	2	6	1	1	2	2	5	7	2	5	7	0	1	1
Mexican American	182	196	378	138	148	286	10	13	23	172	158	330	140	115	255	11	13	24
Puerto Rican	7	9	16	7	6	13	1	1	2	13	14	27	10	13	23	1	2	3
Other Hispanic	74	62	136	51	42	93	5	2	7	59	66	125	38	46	84	9	8	17
Multiple Hispanic/Latino*	5	4	9	4	1	5	0	0	0	6	1	7	6	0	6	0	0	0
Subtotal	273	276	549	204	199	403	17	17	34	252	244	496	196	179	375	21	24	45
Non-Hispanic/Latino**																		
Black	189	83	272	132	62	194	9	6	15	174	90	264	122	58	180	5	5	10
Native American/AK	5	5	10	5	4	9	0	0	0	9	3	12	7	2	9	0	0	0
Native Hawaiian/OPI	2	1	3	1	1	2	0	0	0	1	4	5	1	2	3	0	0	0
White	814	984	1,798	624	726	1,350	60	81	141	761	1,033	1,794	585	718	1,303	53	90	143
Asian	429	444	873	330	312	642	16	20	36	424	441	865	304	293	597	11	15	26
Other Race	38	28	66	26	20	46	1	0	1	40	26	66	30	17	47	0	3	3
Multiple Race*	30	21	51	22	17	39	0	3	3	29	20	49	18	14	32	2	0	2
Unknown	2	1	3	2	1	3	0	0	0	3	4	7	3	3	6	1	0	1
Subtotal	1,509	1,567	3,076	1,142	1,143	2,285	86	110	196	1,441	1,621	3,062	1,070	1,107	2,177	72	113	185
Foreign	46	38	84	32	25	57	0	0	0	36	42	78	27	31	58	0	0	0
Total	1,828	1,881	3,709	1,378	1,367	2,745	103	127	230	1,729	1,907	3,636	1,293	1,317	2,610	93	137	230

*Since 2002, students can select more than one race and / or ethnicity. **Those who did not choose 'Hispanic/Latino' or 'Non-Hispanic/Latino' are listed under 'Non-Hispanic/Latino'. Data Source: AAMC Data Warehouse: Applicant-Matriculant File, as of 1/16/2009.

Information about admissions requirements and criteria can be found at: *(http://med.uth.tmc.edu/administration/admissions/)*

Academic Support Programs

UTMS-H sponsors several programs that are designed to increase the retention rate of all medical students. A five-week summer Pre-Entry Program is designed to enhance the performance of students in the basic science years. The program is for students who, for a variety of reasons, might benefit from such a program. Services, administered by the Assistant Dean for Education Programs, include the Peer Tutoring Program, which provides tutelage for first- and second-year students by second- and fourth-year student tutors; academic monitoring; and academic and non-academic counseling.

An Alternate Pathway Program (http://med.uth.tmc.edu/students-current/policies.htm#altpath) offers students the option to complete the first-year basic science curriculum in two years. The Master Advisor Program is designed to facilitate interactions between students and members of the medical school faculty and administration. Several organizations whose members are interested in service to historically underserved communities and in recruitment of minority students, such as the Student National Medical Association, have active chapters at UTMS-H.

Enrichment Programs

Elementary School Science Enrichment Program
UTMS-H coordinates an enrichment project designed to spark elementary school students' interest in science. Approximately 700 hours of science enrichment activities are presented to a group of 120 African-American and Hispanic elementary school students during the academic year. This program is organized by first-year medical students with administrative support from the Office of Admissions. Program Contact: UTMS-H Office of Admissions.

Anatomy Enrichment Program
This program is administered through the Office of Admissions. High school students from the greater Houston metropolitan area are invited to participate in a day-long workshop in the Human Anatomy Facility of the UTMS-H. Students are presented with a hands-on lesson in human anatomy and physiology in the morning and tour the medical school facility in the afternoon. Program Contact: Nancy Murphy - *Nancy.D.Murphy@uth.tmc.edu*

Summer Medical and Dental Education Program (SMDEP)
This program is presented in collaboration with The University of Texas Dental Branch (UTDB) and funded by a grant from the Robert Wood Johnson Foundation. The mission of SMDEP is to assist rising sophomore and junior undergraduate students from backgrounds that are historically underrepresented in dentistry and medicine. The program also aims to enhance the students' knowledge, skills, and attitudes to make them more competitive and improve their chances of becoming successful applicants to either a medical or dental school of their choice.

SMDEP serves to advance our institutions' core missions of providing the highest quality education, conducting the highest caliber or research in biomedical and health sciences, and providing exemplary clinical care in a diverse and culturally competent environment.

Students experience academic enrichment in five core areas: microbiology, anatomy and physiology, pre-calculus and calculus, physics, and organic chemistry. In addition, students participate in study and communication skills classes, financial planning and career development workshops, and academic counseling sessions. Students are involved in clinical experiences in emergency medicine, family practice, internal medicine, restorative dentistry, and oral surgery. All SMDEP scholars participate in admission discussions and simulated interviews as preparation for the formal application process. So-

cial interactions with other SMDEP scholars, currently enrolled medical and dental students, and faculty complete the experience. *(http://www.smdep.org/progsites/houston.htm), (http://www.db.uth.tmc.edu/SMDEP/index.htm)*. Program Coordinator: Rebecca Lopez - *Rebecca.lopez@uth.tmc.edu*

Summer Research Program
This program serves to foster a greater understanding of biomedical research among both undergraduate and medical students. Administered by the Office of Educational Programs, this ten-week summer program offers students opportunities to do intensive, hands-on biomedical laboratory research under the direct supervision of a selected UTMS-H faculty sponsor. These preceptorships are in the basic science and clinical departments. The program provides science training workshops, a weekly seminar series featuring top scientists, enrichment series, and special facility/laboratory tours. Participants are awarded $2,500 stipend funded by the Dean of the Medical School. *(http://med.uth.tmc.edu/administration/edu/SRP)*. Program Coordinator: Linda Guardio - *summer.research@uth.tmc.edu*

Summer Pre-Entry Program
This five-week program, administered through the Office of Educational Programs, is offered each year for new matriculants to the UTMS-H. The purpose of the program is to strengthen academic performance of participants by providing a rigorous academic program, tutorial sessions, computer and study-skills workshops, and by establishing support networks with students and faculty. Approximately 30 students who are judged most likely to benefit from enhanced academic preparation and/or an early adjustment to medical school are invited to participate. Scholarships are available for students who require financial assistance.

(http://med.uth.tmc.edu/administration/edu_programs/ep/pre-entry_program.htm)

Program Contact: Wai San Johannson,
wai.san.johannson@uth.tmc.edu

Student Financial Assistance

Financial aid is available primarily in
the form of loans. Students with outstanding credentials are automatically
considered for a Faculty Scholarship
Award.

Other additional scholarships may be
funded by benefactors within the
community.

University of Texas Southwestern Medical Center at Dallas Southwestern Medical School

Dr. Byron Cryer, Associate Dean, Minority Student Affairs
University of Texas Southwestern Medical Center at Dallas
Southwestern Medical School
5323 Harry Hines Boulevard
Dallas, TX 75235-9006
214-648-2168; 214-648-7517 fax
byron.cryer@utsouthwestern.edu
www.utsouthwestern.edu

Recruitment

To recruit undergraduates, members of the faculty make numerous visits to campuses throughout the state of Texas each year. During these visits, meetings with pre-medical student are held to discuss questions and problems of both general and specific natures. These visits may include a meeting with groups of underrepresented minority (URM) pre-medical students. Several of these visits are to historically Black colleges in the state of Texas as well as to south and west Texas where there are large Hispanic populations.

Additionally, every effort is made to arrange opportunities for minorities to visit the UT Southwestern Medical School campus to see the facilities and to talk with faculty and students. Once yearly a minority pre-medical student conference is held on the campus to accomplish this goal.

Other recruiting efforts by the Office of Minority Student Affairs involve sending medical school marketing materials to underrepresented minorities via mail and e-mail, encouraging potential students to set up an appointment for a face to face discussions with the Associate Dean, and providing information on mentoring opportunities such as UT Southwestern Scholar's Program.

Admissions

All admissions decisions are made by a single Admissions Committee. This committee participates in all screening of applications and decides which candidates should be invited for interviews and which ones will be offered places. The admissions policies dictate that a decision be reached for each applicant separately, taking into account the breadth of considerations for each application.

The Admissions Committee carefully considers the complete background of each applicant as well as their specific future medical career aspirations.

Academic Support Programs

Academic or tutorial assistance at Southwestern is an individually tailored program. Students are advised that there are many avenues open to them should they encounter problems of any sort. They are encouraged to use them and, from all indications, they respond. An Office of Medical Education composed of specialists in medical education offers students training in study habits and test-taking skills. Students in academic difficulty are most often identified early and tutorial or special programs are arranged to meet the individual needs of the students. Recently, modifications in the curriculum have been incorporated to assist students having serious difficulty. There is ample flexibility in the curriculum to meet students' needs on an individual basis. Student mental health services provide psychological support to students.

University of Texas Southwestern Medical Center at Dallas Southwestern Medical School
Applicants, First-Time Applicants, Matriculants by Gender, Race and Ethnicity, 2007-2008

| | 2007 | | | | | | | | | 2008 | | | | | | | | |
| | APP | | | F-time APP | | | MAT | | | APP | | | F-time APP | | | MAT | | |
	Women	Men	Total	Women	Men	Total	Women	Men	Total	Women	Men	Total	Women	Men	Total	Women	Men	Total
Hispanic/Latino																		
Cuban	5	3	8	4	1	5	2	0	2	2	4	6	2	4	6	0	0	0
Mexican American	153	166	319	117	127	244	14	12	26	157	143	300	128	109	237	9	10	19
Puerto Rican	8	9	17	8	6	14	2	2	4	9	13	22	6	12	18	1	0	1
Other Hispanic	64	56	120	48	36	84	4	4	8	50	62	112	33	44	77	3	1	4
Multiple Hispanic/Latino*	1	4	5	1	2	3	0	0	0	7	1	8	7	0	7	0	0	0
Subtotal	231	238	469	178	172	350	22	18	40	225	223	448	176	169	345	13	11	24
Non-Hispanic/Latino**																		
Black	164	77	241	116	60	176	13	3	16	165	87	252	122	61	183	5	2	7
Native American/AK	6	6	12	6	5	11	0	0	0	8	4	12	6	3	9	0	0	0
Native Hawaiian/OPI	2	1	3	1	1	2	0	0	0	2	2	4	2	1	3	0	0	0
White	736	963	1,699	580	725	1,305	27	49	76	706	963	1,669	559	683	1,242	49	47	96
Asian	414	435	849	326	315	641	35	39	74	403	437	840	295	297	592	40	43	83
Other Race	34	24	58	23	15	38	1	1	2	39	24	63	30	16	46	1	2	3
Multiple Race*	31	25	56	24	19	43	1	2	3	26	22	48	16	16	32	1	1	2
Unknown	1	0	1	1	0	1	0	0	0	5	10	15	5	8	13	0	0	0
Subtotal	1,388	1,531	2,919	1,077	1,140	2,217	77	94	171	1,354	1,549	2,903	1,035	1,085	2,120	96	95	191
Foreign	53	49	102	41	34	75	5	3	8	45	49	94	34	39	73	2	4	6
Total	1,672	1,818	3,490	1,296	1,346	2,642	104	115	219	1,624	1,821	3,445	1,245	1,293	2,538	111	110	221

*Since 2002, students can select more than one race and / or ethnicity. **Those who did not choose 'Hispanic/Latino' or 'Non-Hispanic/Latino' are listed under 'Non-Hispanic/Latino'. Data Source: AAMC Data Warehouse: Applicant-Matriculant File, as of 1/16/2009.

The Summer Enrichment Program (SEP)

A student pre-matriculation program, provides talented students from academically disadvantaged backgrounds who have received an offer of admission to UT Southwestern Medical School an opportunity to develop the skills needed to successfully enter into and complete the medical school curriculum. The SEP, by invitation, identifies students to participate in the six-week enrichment program in which there is a review of clinical anatomy, embryology, membrane and cardiovascular physiology, and biochemistry.

Enrichment Programs

The Medical School conducts several programs that target minority high school and undergraduate students.

The Health Professions Recruitment and Exposure Program (HPREP)

HPREP is a collaborative effort between UT Southwestern and Dallas Independent School District that enrolls approximately 200, ninth through 12th grade minority students in a program designed to stimulate their interest in health and science careers. The program is held on six consecutive Saturdays beginning in January. Various health care topics are discussed and hands on workshops are conducted.
(http://www8.utsouthwestern.edu/ utsw/home/educ/nondegprog/HPREP/ index.html)

UT Southwestern Summer NIH Sponsored Research Program

This program is for minority undergraduate students interested in biomedical research. The program consists of two successive summers of research (ten weeks each) on the medical school's campus combined with a structured curriculum in research methodology and concepts.
(http://www.utsouthwestern.edu/utsw/ home/educ/nondegprog/SUMR/)

A Pre-medical Conference is conducted each year at UT Southwestern. The conference is designed to increase college students' awareness of the ap-

plication process and of the medical school experience.

The Student National Medical Association (SNMA) Scholars Program

This program offers underrepresented undergraduate students a six week-clinical preceptorship in a physician's office. The program consists of a shadowing experience for the pre-med student working with a physician who provides medical care to underserved patient populations. Eligibility requirements include 30 hours of college coursework with a minimum 3.0 GPA and an interest in health care in underserved communities.*(http://www8.utsouthwestern. edu/home/education/studentsalumni/ index.html)*

The Joint Admission Medical Program (JAMP)

JAMP provides economically disadvantaged students a formalized curriculum that is designed to develop students' knowledge of fundamental scientific concepts. This program provides an MCAT review course, clinical preceptorship, a mock interview workshop, and a laboratory component.
(http://www.utsystem.edu/jamp/)

The Parkland Collegiate Fellows Program

Is a collaborative program between the medical school and the school's primary teaching hospital, Parkland Health & Hospital system. This program provides a six-week paid summer internships for disadvantaged college undergraduate students who may not otherwise have an opportunity to gain hands-on experience in a healthcare setting. Eligibility requirements include at least 36 hours of college work and interest in health care.
(http://www.parklandcareers.com/ content.asp?c=colfelpro)

UT Southwestern has been a collaborating partner in the *Dr. Emmett J. Conrad Leadership Program* that is sponsored by Texas State Senator Royce West. This program selects disadvantaged and minority college students from Texas Senatorial District 23 to participate in paid summer internships in a variety of health care settings.

(http://www.senate.state.tx.us/75r/ Senate/members/dist23/drconrad/ leaderpgm.htm)

Student Financial Assistance

Waiver of the application fee to University of Texas Medical Schools can be solicited from the Texas Medical and Dental Application Center and is granted in extreme cases. UT Southwestern is unable to provide financial assistance for interview trips to any students.

In conjunction with the financial aid application process and prior to entering any financial commitment, all financial aid applicants are provided access to an annual publication of the Office of Student Financial Aid entitled, Meeting College Expenses: A Guide for Seeking Financial Assistance. Much of this publication is designed to provide each student with debt management and budgeting tools for use throughout the student's enrollment. Prior to the disbursement of each student's financial aid, formal counseling is required and made available through the use of established video and Web-based productions.

Financial aid exits interviews are available in individual or group settings, depending on the time of year and volume of students needing to complete the process. During the financial aid exit, each student is provided with detailed information related to each loan received, including the lending agency to whom the student will be processing repayment, a projected payment schedule, and terms and conditions specified in the promissory note. Three full-time financial aid counselors and the director are available throughout the academic year for personal student consult and guidance.

Educational Partnerships

UT Southwestern and Dallas Independent School District collaborate in an educational partnership, HPREP, described previously which provides educational opportunities in healthcare and science to high school students. In 2008, UT Southwestern Office of Minority Student Affairs partnered with Southern Methodist University's Minority Association of Pre-health Students (MAPS) in order to provide mentoring opportunities for college students at Southern Methodist University.

Other Pertinent Information

No other Texas medical school matriculated a greater percentage of minority students in 2007 than UT Southwestern Medical School. [1] In 2007 and 2008, UT Southwestern Medical School was ranked the No.1 medical school in the United States for Hispanics. [2]

1 Association of American Medical Colleges, Data Warehouse: Applicant-Matriculant File.
2 Hispanic Business Magazine

University of Utah School of Medicine

Candelida Ramos, Director Diversity and Community Outreach
University of Utah School of Medicine
30 N. 1900 E. 1C117
Salt Lake City, UT 84132-2101
801-585-2430; 801-585-3300 fax
candi.ramos@hsc.utah.edu
http://medicine.utah.edu/diversity

Recruitment

The University of Utah School of Medicine is committed to recruiting a diverse student body. The School of Medicine believes that students from a broad range of cultural, ethnic, economic, and experiential backgrounds bring different perspectives to the learning environment and enhance the educational experience of the student body. The Office of Diversity and Community Outreach works closely with students from minority groups identified by the state of Utah as underrepresented. These are Africans and African Americans; American Indians; Alaska Natives; Polynesians and Pacific Islanders including Native Hawaiians, Tongans, Samoans, Filipinos, Tahitians, Maoris, Fijians, Niueans, Palauans; and Chicanos/as and Latinos/as including Mainland Puerto Ricans, Mexican Americans, Central Americans, and South Americans. The office provides academic advising and assistance to these students in their preparation for and application to medical school. The Office of Diversity and Community Outreach also offers support for out-of-state interviewees such as student hosting, rides to and from the airport, and mock interviews. Visit our Web site at: *(http://medicine.utah.edu/diversity).*

Recruitment of out-of-state students takes place through targeted mailings and selected on-site visits to pre-medical events within the region. The office will arrange visits for students wanting to check out Utah, with hosting from current medical students. We will also provide application assistance and advice. In-state students are recruited in a similar manner, with visits and seminars to students at various venues and forums around the state. The Association of Minority Medical Students is very active in supporting and assisting in recruitment of students from diverse backgrounds. The group helps with hosting, answering student e-mail inquiries, and anything else applicants need.

Admissions

The University of Utah School of Medicine carefully considers each applicant on the basis of individual merit. The School of Medicine is looking for well-rounded students with a demonstrated commitment to serving people. Some of the characteristics the School of Medicine looks for in students include integrity, composure, maturity, independence, compassion, self-knowledge, interpersonal skills, problem-solving ability, leadership, and intellectual curiosity. The school has eight formal categories for evaluating applicants, which are: Medical College Admission Test (MCAT), GPA, extracurricular activities, leadership, research, medical exposure, physician shadowing, and volunteer service. Applicants are expected to meet minimum performance standards in each category and be average or above average in at least five. We should also mention that we have strict GPA and MCAT minimums—3.0 in both science GPA and cumulative GPA (as calculated by American Medical College Application Service), and 7 in each section of the MCAT (not total

University of Utah School of Medicine
Applicants, First-Time Applicants, Matriculants by Gender, Race and Ethnicity, 2007-2008

| | 2007 | | | | | | | | | 2008 | | | | | | | | |
| | APP | | | F-time APP | | | MAT | | | APP | | | F-time APP | | | MAT | | |
	Wo-men	Men	Total	Wo-men	Men	Total	Wo-men	Men	Total	Wo-men	Men	Total	Wo-men	Men	Total	Wo-men	Men	Total
Hispanic/Latino																		
Cuban	4	10	14	3	9	12	0	0	0	6	5	11	3	2	5	0	0	0
Mexican American	30	40	70	25	30	55	0	0	0	31	44	75	21	31	52	3	0	3
Puerto Rican	4	10	14	4	5	9	0	1	1	3	6	9	2	5	7	0	0	0
Other Hispanic	30	35	65	21	20	41	0	2	2	34	25	59	19	11	30	1	2	3
Multiple Hispanic/Latino*	5	3	8	2	2	4	0	0	0	8	6	14	6	4	10	1	1	2
Subtotal	73	98	171	55	66	121	0	3	3	82	86	168	51	53	104	5	3	8
Non-Hispanic/Latino**																		
Black	34	29	63	21	18	39	0	0	0	68	35	103	28	21	49	0	0	0
Native American/AK	3	4	7	1	3	4	0	0	0	3	6	9	2	4	6	0	0	0
Native Hawaiian/OPI	3	2	5	1	1	2	0	0	0	7	6	13	4	4	8	0	1	1
White	175	638	813	132	481	613	18	60	78	194	650	844	146	460	606	20	54	74
Asian	55	76	131	37	60	97	11	4	15	62	66	128	51	42	93	9	6	15
Other Race	0	0	0	0	0	0	0	0	0	0	1	1	0	1	1	0	0	0
Multiple Race*	11	30	41	10	27	37	1	3	4	22	19	41	14	14	28	1	2	3
Unknown	2	4	6	2	4	6	0	0	0	5	11	16	5	10	15	1	0	1
Subtotal	283	783	1,066	204	594	798	30	67	97	361	794	1,155	250	556	806	31	63	94
Foreign	13	20	33	9	13	22	2	0	2	4	9	13	4	7	11	0	0	0
Total	369	901	1,270	268	673	941	32	70	102	447	889	1,336	305	616	921	36	66	102

*Since 2002, students can select more than one race and / or ethnicity. **Those who did not choose 'Hispanic/Latino' or 'Non-Hispanic/Latino' are listed under 'Non-Hispanic/Latino'. Data Source: AAMC Data Warehouse: Applicant-Matriculant File, as of 1/16/2009.

score). These minimums are balanced out by the total weight of MCAT and GPA being only 20 percent of the final selection score. Interviewers and selection committee members are not given MCAT and GPA information on applicants. The non-cognitive criteria listed above are 80 percent of the applicant's final score. Please see the admissions Web site at *(http://medicine.utah.edu/admissions) or contact the admissions office if you have any questions.*

Academic Support Programs

Tutorial programs are available to all students in both basic and clinical sciences. Peer counseling is available to all freshman and sophomore students, and physician mentors are assigned to all students, upon request, for the duration of their study at Utah. An extensive program of academic and personal counseling is made available to all students. The director of student counseling, a licensed psychologist, sees students and their families by request to resolve personal or academic issues. Students may also access the counseling center on the main campus as an additional resource. The Director of Learning Resources meets with students individually to discuss test-taking strategies, board study and preparation, and learning strategies and tools visit: *(http://medicine.utah.edu/learningresources) for more information.*

The Office of Diversity and Community Outreach informs students of research, fellowship, internship, and externship opportunities offered both locally and nationally and assists them with their applications for these programs. Additionally, the office disseminates information on scholarships locally and nationally to eligible students. Assistance with curriculum vitas and personal statements and residency applications is also provided to students.

Enrichment Programs

The School of Medicine offers over 20 continuous outreach programs over the course of the school year and summer months. Please see our Web site for program descriptions and photos:

(http://medicine.utah.edu/diversity)

We whole-heartedly follow a symbiotic programming and partnership model to ensure continuity and appropriate benefit for all involved. Our school has a strong culture of service, as evidenced by our admissions standards, and we try to provide an outlet for medical students after matriculation. The outreach programs offer medical students a chance to become more acquainted with communities of color in and around Salt Lake City. It is our hope that through programming we can increase the cultural awareness and interaction skills of medical students thereby improving their competence as future practitioners. The students we serve with our programs are gaining exposure to medicine and can begin the planning process of pursuing a career involving higher education in the health sciences.

Some of our programs are community based partnerships that do not fit into grade categories, such as the New Pilgrim Baptist Church Outreach Program, which is a partnership with the African American community through the church. We also have some programming for rural students to reach into Utah's many rural communities and assist medical students with grants received in Glaucoma Screening, Diabetes care, etc.

Programming for elementary aged youth focuses on hands-on exposure to medicine and anatomy, preventive health, and safety. We currently have an outreach program at Edison Elementary School and partner with University Neighborhood Partners, Gear-Up, and Club Ute for summer activities. The office also supports science fairs and community events, by invitation, at schools that align with our outreach goals.

Junior high-aged students are served through on-site outreach at Glendale and Northwest Intermediate schools. Students are taught slightly more advanced anatomyand physiology by volunteer medical students. Glendale's partnership is a Youth Teaching Youth grant model through the Utah Museum of Natural History, where students advance in the program toward teaching responsibilities of younger students. At Northwest our partnership is with the MESA Club, which has been active for over five years. We also have an interdisciplinary program at the School of Medicine called Science Power, which is for junior high-age women interested in science. This program expands hands-on activities through campus partnerships with engineering, math, genetics, etc. Women faculty and students from across campus volunteer to mentor and teach participants throughout the year.

High school student programming is focused on college preparation, more exposure to health sciences careers—particularly medicine—and mentoring. Future Doctors, which began in 1997, is a free after-school program open to all students across the Salt Lake Valley. Each session includes a lecture from a physician in a medical discipline followed by a related hands-on activity. In the past we have covered dermatology/suturing, pathology/gram staining, cardiology/cow heart dissection, and more. The other high school program is specifically for Native American students. Expanded Indian Nations began in 1998 as a program focused on recruiting students to the University of Utah and into higher education in general.

The pre-medical and college outreach programs focus on making students aware of the admissions process and helping students prepare to be successful applicants. Two, day-long seminars are offered each year—one for students of color and one for women students. At each of these seminars, the Associate Dean of Admissions, the Associate Vice President for Diversity in the Health Sciences and the Assistant Dean for Diversity candidly talk with participants about admission policies and procedures. Students openly ask questions and find out about the selection process and ultimately what makes a great applicant. The day also includes a medical student interaction, workshops on personal statements, interviewing, the

AMCAS application, and of course, hands-on lab activities. The Office of Diversity and Community Outreach also advises students throughout the year, offering appointments and monthly workshops to help students tackle issues specific to individual preparation strategies.

The Summer MCAT Preparation and Research/Clinical Training Scholars Program, which began in 2001, selects eight to ten students each year. The program is limited to students who meet Utah's admission standards, and who have an interest in applying to Utah's medical school. Eligibility is based on economic, social, and educational disadvantage. Designed to strengthen each student individually, the program places students in unfilled requisite areas, or areas of the student's application that need to be strengthened. For ten weeks students engage in a MCAT prep course, tutoring sessions, learning and test-taking assessments, and either a research or clinical medicine placement. In addition to these basic tenets, students also receive instruction in application strategies, personal statement writing, the AMCAS application, mock interviewing, financial aid, and more. Weekly seminar lunches are provided for students as a chance to meet current medical students, residents, and faculty at the University of Utah. Although preference is given to Utah residents, the program does accept students from out of state and provides room and board for the summer. All participants receive a stipend for June, July, and August.

Student Financial Assistance

The University of Utah School of Medicine and the Financial Aid and Scholarships Office at the University of Utah assist students in meeting the costs of medical school. The school makes every effort to meet the financial needs of admitted students. Student financial assistance packages may consist of loans, scholarships, and loan repayment programs.

Educational Partnerships

Health Professions Magnet School
The Health Professions Magnet School is a partnership between the Salt Lake City School District and the University of Utah Health Sciences Center. The Health Professions Magnet School began as the Health Professions Academy in 1999. Over the years the program has grown and expanded into a magnet school for students in the Salt Lake City area.

Students are recruited for the program in junior high school and begin the program once in high school. The students' curriculum includes health science courses and opportunities for field trips to the University Hospital and clinics. Additionally, throughout the four years of the Health Professions Magnet School, the students participate in hands-on activities including dissection, first aid, lab experiments, shadowing, and community service projects.

Health Sciences Leap
Begun in 2001, Health Sciences LEAP is a four-year-long pipeline program designed to assist students interested in careers in medicine, nursing, pharmacy, or health who come from populations traditionally underrepresented in the health professions in Utah. This population includes students from minority backgrounds, but also those who meet definitions of educational, social, or economic disadvantage.

In the first year of Health Sciences LEAP, students take two humanities seminars of three credit hours each, thereby fulfilling their general education humanities requirement. In the first semester, they study American autobiography in a course that also fulfills their diversity requirement. In the second semester they read ethical philosophy and apply it to current issues in health care delivery. Students are also eligible for three one-credit-hour add-ons: a library research skills class, a service learning class, and a course on how students of color can better succeed on a predominantly white campus.

The second year of Health Sciences LEAP begins with a two-credit-hour fall semester course in "Health Professions Exploration," called UUHSC 2500. Students shadow professionals in their future fields for two hours per week, and then write about and discuss their experiences in light of readings done and lectures heard on cultural competency in medicine, complementary and alternative medicine, professionalism, collegiality, collaboration, and medical ethics. Wherever possible, arrangements are made for students to shadow providers of color, who add a mentoring aspect to the course. Guest lecturers for the seminar are also drawn from a group of people of color and/or women experts. In their second semester, students take a two-credit-hour course in "Basic Lab Technique" (Biology 2115), taught by a biology professor, which prepares them to work in research laboratories during their third year.

Third year Health Sciences LEAP consists of two semesters that together make up UUHSC 3000 and 3001: "Research Seminar for Advanced LEAP Students." Students are placed with faculty as research assistants for eight months, working ten hours per week in a paid position. Whenever possible, they are placed with Principal Investigators from minority backgrounds and can choose either basic science or social science areas of study. Students reflect on this work in the two seminars, which require them to give oral presentations on their research, first to classmates, then to other Health Sciences LEAP students, and finally to the university as a whole in the context of the Undergraduate Research Symposium. They also visit each other's research labs and learn to write up their research in a form appropriate to a medical or scientific journal.

The final Health Sciences LEAP year asks students to research, design, implement, and evaluate an extended service project in cooperation with the University of Utah's Bennion Center, the Huntsman Cancer Center's Special Populations Office, or the University

Neighborhood Partners. The course sequence, "Service Learning Through Community Partnerships," is two semesters long and carries one credit hour each semester. Students are required to meet regularly as a class and with their service partners. Working alone or in pairs, they contribute at least 100 hours to their community partnerships, 80 of which are in direct service. The course emphasis is on higher education's responsibility to community, and establishing viable partnerships with symbiotic rewards.

Over the course of the program, students are supported by personal advising, peer mentors, library skill and study skills courses, and biannual celebrations of their accomplishments.

University of Vermont College of Medicine

Tiffany J. Delaney,
Director of Admissions and
Minority Affairs Officer
University of Vermont College of
Medicine
E-215 Given Building
89 Beaumont Avenue
Burlington, VT 05405-0068
802-656-2154; 802-656-9663 fax
medadmissions@uvm.edu

Recruitment

The University of Vermont College of Medicine (UVMCOM) prides itself on its goal to select successful individuals from many cultures with unique life experiences to promote diversity among future physicians. Active recruitment of minority students to the College of Medicine is under the leadership of the Director of Admissions with assistance from medical students, faculty, and staff. Information on UVMCOM is sent to targeted candidates identified through the Medical Minority Applicant Registry (Med-MAR) of the AAMC. In addition, minority candidates are encouraged to

visit the campus prior to applying. Please contact the Office of Admissions at 802-656-2154 for information on arranging a visit.

Admissions

Applicants are reviewed for admission on the basis of their personal essays, Medical College Admission Test scores, letters of reference, and grade-point averages. Significant direct human service experience is desirable. The university makes a particular effort to identify applicants who will enhance the overall diversity of the student body. Applicants considered to be promising candidates, based on a review of the application materials, are invited for an interview. The interview takes place at the University of Vermont College of Medicine. It includes an orientation session with the Associate Dean of Admissions, an opportunity to meet informally with medical students, a tour of the College of Medicine, an opportunity to meet with the financial aid counselor, and an interview with a member of the Admissions Committee and a third- or fourth-year medical student when available. The Admissions Committee is composed of 38 faculty

members plus the Associate Dean for Admissions, who chairs the committee. Committee membership varies annually. The committee is seeking applicants who are mature, who are highly motivated for a career in medicine, and who relate well to others.

Academic Support Programs

Initial advisement is provided by the Associate Dean for Student Affairs. The structure of the freshman curriculum allows multiple opportunities for contact with faculty in small-group teaching sessions, thus providing additional opportunity for the development of close relationships with faculty. Tutoring is available for students in academic difficulty, and other academic support services are available. Involvement in clinical medicine from the first week of medical school provides a significant stimulus to academic performance throughout the basic science years. In the third year, students select formal advisors based on their career preferences at that point in their education. The College of Medicine has a tradition of a flexible policy for leaves of absence for students who need to depart from the traditional four-year sequence.

University of Vermont College of Medicine
Applicants, First-Time Applicants, Matriculants by Gender, Race and Ethnicity, 2007-2008

	2007									2008								
	APP			F-time APP			MAT			APP			F-time APP			MAT		
	Wo-men	Men	Total	Wo-men	Men	Total	Wo-men	Men	Total	Wo-men	Men	Total	Wo-men	Men	Total	Wo-men	Men	Total
Hispanic/Latino																		
Cuban	14	15	29	8	10	18	1	0	1	11	9	20	10	8	18	0	0	0
Mexican American	45	39	84	37	29	66	1	0	1	47	37	84	39	28	67	0	0	0
Puerto Rican	10	9	19	6	6	12	1	1	2	11	4	15	10	4	14	1	0	1
Other Hispanic	52	55	107	39	39	78	1	1	2	67	65	132	50	45	95	2	5	7
Multiple Hispanic/Latino*	6	2	8	2	1	3	0	0	0	13	8	21	10	2	12	0	0	0
Subtotal	127	120	247	92	85	177	4	2	6	149	123	272	119	87	206	3	5	8
Non-Hispanic/Latino**																		
Black	63	35	98	39	26	65	2	1	3	69	48	117	47	33	80	2	0	2
Native American/AK	6	3	9	5	3	8	0	0	0	8	1	9	7	0	7	0	0	0
Native Hawaiian/OPI	5	8	13	4	7	11	0	0	0	9	5	14	5	2	7	0	0	0
White	1,768	1,897	3,665	1,342	1,346	2,688	40	39	79	1,537	1,851	3,388	1,102	1,270	2,372	41	42	83
Asian	728	757	1,485	517	505	1,022	9	6	15	631	640	1,271	406	380	786	4	5	9
Other Race	1	3	4	1	1	2	0	0	0	3	5	8	3	3	6	0	0	0
Multiple Race*	76	65	141	62	40	102	1	0	1	79	73	152	53	44	97	3	1	4
Unknown	30	36	66	27	33	60	1	1	2	69	80	149	66	66	132	2	0	2
Subtotal	2,677	2,804	5,481	1,997	1,961	3,958	53	47	100	2,405	2,703	5,108	1,689	1,798	3,487	52	48	100
Foreign	185	188	373	145	138	283	1	5	6	170	222	392	125	167	292	2	1	3
Total	2,989	3,112	6,101	2,234	2,184	4,418	58	54	112	2,724	3,048	5,772	1,933	2,052	3,985	57	54	111

*Since 2002, students can select more than one race and / or ethnicity. **Those who did not choose 'Hispanic/Latino' or 'Non-Hispanic/Latino' are listed under 'Non-Hispanic/Latino'. Data Source: AAMC Data Warehouse: Applicant-Matriculant File, as of 1/16/2009.

Enrichment Programs

During the summer following the freshman year, medical students may participate in Summer Research Fellowships or Preceptorship Placements with practicing physicians. The remaining summer periods of the student's medical education are committed to clinical educational experiences.

Student Financial Assistance

The secondary application fee is waived for those applicants who qualify for a fee waiver from the American Medical College Application Service. The College of Medicine Financial Aid Office provides some low-interest loans to eligible students, as well as grant and scholarship aid to those students from high-need backgrounds. Most students meet the majority of their expenses through these institutional funds (the dollar amount varies from year to year), federal loans, and personal resources.

Educational Partnerships

No such partnerships are in place at this time.

Eastern Virginia Medical School

Gail C. Williams, Assistant Dean for Student Affairs and Director of Minority Affairs
Eastern Virginia Medical School
700 West Olney Road
Norfolk, VA 23507-1980
757-446-5869; 757-446-5817 fax
williagc@evms.edu
www.evms.edu/minority/index.html

Recruitment

Eastern Virginia Medical School (EVMS), Virginia's only privately funded medical school, accepted its first class in October 1973. EVMS offers exciting and challenging opportunities for aspiring physicians through its excellent programs in medical education, research, and clinical care. EVMS has one of the ten largest Clinical Skills Centers in the United States and Canada for teaching and assessment. The Medical School's affiliation with over 33 community based health care facilities across the Hampton Roads area allows students to gain clinical training that is both broad and culturally diverse. Although EVMS provides outstanding training and experience for students entering the full range of medical specialties, the school is committed to help meet the nation's need for producing more primary care physicians.

EVMS is also committed to the recruitment, admission, education, and retention of minority group students who are underrepresented in medicine, as well as students from disadvantaged backgrounds. The recruitment activities are coordinated through collaborative efforts between the Office of Admissions and the Office of Minority Affairs.

EVMS faculty, administrators, and students make visits to area high schools, upon request, and participate fully in career day activities. Counselors, students, and science teachers make periodic visits to the EVMS campus for tours and orientation. Qualified minority high school students attending Norfolk public schools are actively recruited for admission into the EVMS/Norfolk Public Schools Magnet High School for the Sciences and Health Professions.

Primarily in-state undergraduate institutions, as well as select out-of-state institutions, are visited each year by the Associate Dean for Admissions and/or the Director of Minority Affairs. A pre-health coalition of advisors has been established to afford the exchange of information and professional services between EVMS and the undergraduate schools. Special efforts are also made to meet with pre-medical clubs and pre-medical advisors. On-campus visitations are arranged upon request.

The Director of Minority Affairs and the Associate Dean for Admissions are available for individual on-campus meetings, by appointment, with students.

Admissions

EVMS seeks to produce a diverse physician workforce to advance medical education, patient care, and research. The school does not discriminate on the basis of race, color, national origin, gender, age, sexual orientation, citizenship, religion, political affiliation, or handicap.

Early completion of the American Medical College Application Service (AMCAS) application and EVMS supplemental application is strongly encouraged. It is also recommended that the Medical College Admission Test (MCAT) be taken as early as possible. All applications are carefully screened, and an interview is granted to appli-

Eastern Virginia Medical School
Applicants, First-Time Applicants, Matriculants by Gender, Race and Ethnicity, 2007-2008

| | 2007 | | | | | | | | | 2008 | | | | | | | | |
| | APP | | | F-time APP | | | MAT | | | APP | | | F-time APP | | | MAT | | |
	Wo-men	Men	Total	Wo-men	Men	Total	Wo-men	Men	Total	Wo-men	Men	Total	Wo-men	Men	Total	Wo-men	Men	Total
Hispanic/Latino																		
Cuban	12	17	29	8	14	22	0	0	0	12	18	30	9	16	25	0	0	0
Mexican American	33	36	69	27	26	53	0	1	1	28	26	54	24	19	43	0	2	2
Puerto Rican	14	12	26	8	9	17	0	0	0	10	14	24	8	10	18	0	1	1
Other Hispanic	48	42	90	36	32	68	0	0	0	63	59	122	42	38	80	0	1	1
Multiple Hispanic/Latino*	6	1	7	4	1	5	0	0	0	8	4	12	7	2	9	0	0	0
Subtotal	113	108	221	83	82	165	0	1	1	121	121	242	90	85	175	0	4	4
Non-Hispanic/Latino**																		
Black	211	95	306	146	77	223	6	0	6	207	77	284	145	59	204	2	1	3
Native American/AK	5	4	9	5	3	8	0	0	0	4	3	7	4	2	6	1	0	1
Native Hawaiian/OPI	8	8	16	7	6	13	0	0	0	9	6	15	5	4	9	0	0	0
White	1,216	1,374	2,590	934	942	1,876	39	39	78	1,118	1,428	2,546	827	981	1,808	33	41	74
Asian	631	690	1,321	439	467	906	12	10	22	698	671	1,369	489	413	902	9	13	22
Other Race	0	1	1	0	0	0	0	0	0	0	5	5	0	2	2	0	0	0
Multiple Race*	65	59	124	44	37	81	3	0	3	61	67	128	46	47	93	0	0	0
Unknown	26	22	48	23	19	42	0	0	0	52	55	107	47	45	92	2	4	6
Subtotal	2,162	2,253	4,415	1,598	1,551	3,149	60	49	109	2,149	2,312	4,461	1,563	1,553	3,116	47	59	106
Foreign	127	130	257	103	95	198	2	3	5	133	151	284	109	106	215	3	2	5
Total	2,402	2,491	4,893	1,784	1,728	3,512	62	53	115	2,403	2,584	4,987	1,762	1,744	3,506	50	65	115

*Since 2002, students can select more than one race and / or ethnicity. **Those who did not choose 'Hispanic/Latino' or 'Non-Hispanic/Latino' are listed under 'Non-Hispanic/Latino'. Data Source: AAMC Data Warehouse: Applicant-Matriculant File, as of 1/16/2009.

cants being considered for admission to the medical school. On the day of the interview, minority candidates routinely meet with the Director of Minority Affairs in a one-to-one setting.

The Admissions Committee is composed of basic science faculty members, clinical science faculty, and students. Members of minority groups are represented on the committee. All applicants are evaluated on the basis of several factors including science and overall grade-point average (GPA), MCAT scores, medical exposure, community/volunteer work, the personal interview, and letters of recommendation.

Academic Support Programs

The advisor system is coordinated through the Office of Education. Each entering student is assigned a faculty advisor, as well as a second-year student advisor through the Big Brother, Big Sister Partnership Program. During the clinical years, each student selects a faculty advisor for consultation concerning fourth-year electives and choices of medical specialty. An academic support seminar is offered during the fall for all entering students. The foci are on test-taking skills, study and time management, stress management, and processing information and monitoring text comprehension.

Special tutorial sessions are arranged for M1 and M2 students through departmental course directors and through the Office of Education. Flexible curriculum schedules may be devised with approval of the Student Progress Committee.

Ongoing counseling and advising are available through the Offices of Minority, Women, Education, and Academic Affairs, as well as through the Careers in Medicine Program. In addition, the EVMS Chapter of the Student National Medical Association, and the Committee on Minority Group Affairs, actively address minority issues and/or concerns.

Enrichment Programs

On-Campus Visitation Day Program
The on-campus program, for premedical students, "Enhancing Diversity in Medicine," is held in the spring of each year. A few of the day's scheduled activities include a tour of the school's basic educational facilities; a review of the admission selection factors and interview assessment variables; mock admission interviews conducted by members of the EVMS Admissions Committee; and panel presentations by medical students, residents, and physicians. The panel presentations allow students to get a realistic view of each level of the medical education spectrum, including both the rewards and challenges of practicing medicine.

Students learn about the importance of achieving diversity in medicine to improve clinical skills and enhance patient care. This program has received excellent evaluations by attendees.

EVMS Summer Scholars Research Program
EVMS supports the mission of the Virginia-Nebraska Alliance (vanealliance.com) in promoting better health outcomes for minorities by increasing the numbers of health care professionals and researchers from traditionally underrepresented minority groups. EVMS will provide summer research experiences (ten-12 weeks) for students from the Alliance member schools. The program will combine didactic sessions with mentored research projects, including community health, clinical, and bench research.

Participating research programs in the EVMS Medical Center include the Center for Pediatric Research, the Strelitz Diabetes Center, the Clinical Center for Women's Health, and the George L. Wright, Jr. Center for Biomedical Proteomics, to name a few.

For enrichment program dates and registration information, interested students should visit the Web site at: *(www.evms.edu/ minority/index.html).*

Student Financial Assistance

EVMS participates in the Federal Student Loan Program for undergraduate, graduate, and professional studies. There are scholarship opportunities as well, including funds for individuals from socioeconomic and disadvantaged backgrounds who demonstrate financial need. Institutional financial aid is awarded on the basis of demonstrated need without regard to race or ethnicity. Waiver of the admissions application fee will be graded on the basis of an AMCAS application fee waiver.

It is the mission of the Office of Financial at EVMS to provide students the tools and resources to obtain assistance to fund their education. The Office of Financial Aid assists students with debt management and financial planning. This is accomplished through mini sessions offered throughout the year including topics of establishing good credit, information about identity theft, managing student loan debt, and preparing an efficient spending plan. A mandatory Entrance Interview is conducted upon entry into school. This session provides the students pertinent information about their rights and responsibilities. A financial seminar including topics of insurance, investments, and a savings plan, is hosted as the student is entering the last semester at EVMS.

It is the intent of the Office of Financial Aid at EVMS to provide all students the opportunity to gain insight to financial management and planning. We are ready to assist students in areas that are of importance to their particular needs.

Educational Partnerships

EVMS has formal joint B.S./M.D. programs in medicine with ten Virginia undergraduate institutions (including each of the state's Historically Black Colleges and Universities): Christopher Newport University, the College of William and Mary, Hampden-Sydney College, Hampton University, Norfolk State University, Old Dominion University, Saint Paul's College, Virginia Wesleyan University, Virginia

State University, and Virginia Union University.

Students are selected from the sophomore class by the pre-health committee of the undergraduate institutions and the EVMS Admissions Committee based on the merit of their academic performance, including competitive SAT scores, and non-academic factors such as extracurricular and volunteer activities, leadership experience, and health care exposure. Students who meet the continued eligibility requirements will not be required to take the Medical College Admission Test and are given early assurance of positions into medical school. Interested students should contact the premedical advisors at the participating institutions for more program information and an application.

University of Virginia School of Medicine

Dr. Norman Oliver
Associate Dean for Diversity
Associate Professor of Family
Medicine
University of Virginia Health System
Office for Diversity
P.O. Box 800739
Charlottesville, VA 22908-0739
434-924-1867; 434-924-8387 fax
www.healthsystem.virgina.edu/
itemet/diversity

Recruitment

All predominantly African-American schools in the state of Virginia are invited each year to participate in the Day at the Medical Center sponsored by the Medical Alumni Association. Some schools are visited by members of the Admissions Committee for the purpose of recruiting students. Representatives from the School of Medicine also visit summer programs to recruit students. Pre-medical societies may request a visit by the Associate Dean for Diversity throughout the year.

Admissions

Minority students invited for interviews have an opportunity to meet with the Associate Dean for Diversity and a minority faculty member who are able to answer questions informally as well as give advice to prospective students.

Academic Support Programs

Each entering student is assigned a faculty member and a second-year student as advisors. During the clinical years, each student selects a faculty member whom he/she consults about such matters as fourth-year electives program and career choice. The School of Medicine provides academic support services for medical students including structured Peer Tutorial Programs in biochemistry, cell and tissue structure, genetics, gross anatomy, human behavior, introduction to clinical medicine, microbiology, neuroscience, pathology, pharmacology, physiology, and psychopathology. Tutoring is provided by faculty teaching the courses, by fourth-year medical students, and graduate students. Preparatory workshops for Step 1 of the United States Medical Licensing Examination and workshops on time management, stress management,

study skills, and test-taking strategies are offered. Academic and personal counseling and resources for students with special learning needs are also provided. During the clinical experience, individual assistance is available when necessary. The student academic support program is directed by the Associate Dean for Student Academic Support. When necessary, the curriculum can be adjusted to allow additional time for completion by the student with special requirements.

Enrichment Programs
Summer Medical and Dental Education Program (SMDEP)
This six-week program, funded by The Robert Wood Johnson Foundation, is offered each summer to enhance opportunities for minority and other students from disadvantaged backgrounds to enter, remain in, and graduate from medical school. SMDEP is aimed at increasing acceptance rates into medical school for minorities and other students from disadvantaged backgrounds and is designed for students who have completed at least one year of college. SMDEP offers academic enrichment and clinical experience with faculty

University of Virginia School of Medicine
Applicants, First-Time Applicants, Matriculants by Gender, Race and Ethnicity, 2007-2008

	2007									2008								
	APP			F-time APP			MAT			APP			F-time APP			MAT		
	Women	Men	Total	Women	Men	Total	Women	Men	Total	Women	Men	Total	Women	Men	Total	Women	Men	Total
Hispanic/Latino																		
Cuban	7	10	17	6	9	15	2	1	3	18	22	40	16	20	36	2	1	3
Mexican American	21	23	44	15	19	34	2	0	2	13	26	39	12	20	32	0	2	2
Puerto Rican	10	16	26	8	14	22	2	0	2	12	17	29	10	13	23	0	2	2
Other Hispanic	36	45	81	30	35	65	1	4	5	45	48	93	35	35	70	4	5	9
Multiple Hispanic/Latino*	3	0	3	2	0	2	0	0	0	8	4	12	8	3	11	0	0	0
Subtotal	77	94	171	61	77	138	7	5	12	96	117	213	81	91	172	6	10	16
Non-Hispanic/Latino**																		
Black	181	85	266	141	75	216	6	2	8	157	79	236	120	62	182	4	4	8
Native American/AK	5	4	9	5	4	9	0	0	0	3	3	6	3	3	6	0	0	0
Native Hawaiian/OPI	4	3	7	4	2	6	0	0	0	6	0	6	3	0	3	0	0	0
White	1,098	1,381	2,479	921	1,114	2,035	41	50	91	1,055	1,502	2,557	873	1,236	2,109	39	48	87
Asian	399	467	866	326	364	690	11	10	21	440	475	915	336	352	688	12	11	23
Other Race	0	0	0	0	0	0	0	0	0	0	4	4	0	3	3	0	0	0
Multiple Race*	69	54	123	62	41	103	2	5	7	54	48	102	49	36	85	1	3	4
Unknown	23	24	47	21	19	40	1	1	2	45	70	115	44	62	106	1	3	4
Subtotal	1,779	2,018	3,797	1,480	1,619	3,099	61	68	129	1,760	2,181	3,941	1,428	1,754	3,182	57	69	126
Foreign	69	70	139	56	54	110	1	1	2	75	73	148	65	51	116	2	1	3
Total	1,925	2,182	4,107	1,597	1,750	3,347	69	74	143	1,931	2,371	4,302	1,574	1,896	3,470	65	80	145

*Since 2002, students can select more than one race and / or ethnicity. **Those who did not choose 'Hispanic/Latino' or 'Non-Hispanic/Latino' are listed under 'Non-Hispanic/Latino'. Data Source: AAMC Data Warehouse: Applicant-Matriculant File, as of 1/16/2009.

mentors; lectures by eminent scientists in biomedical research; exposure to the real world of medicine through a clinical medicine lecture series; academic and personal counseling; and sessions on admission procedures, financial planning, study skills, time management, and interviewing skills.

Student Financial Assistance

The admission application fee may be waived for financially disadvantaged applicants. The Minority Affairs and Financial Aid offices work closely with minority students to ensure that no applicant is denied access to medical school due to lack of funding.

Virginia Commonwealth University School of Medicine

Donna H. Jackson
Office of Student Outreach Programs
Virginia Commonwealth University
School of Medicine, P.O. Box 980565
Richmond, VA 23298-0565
804-828-9630; 804-828-1246 fax
donna.jackson@vcu.edu

Recruitment

The School of Medicine has undertaken a variety of recruitment efforts for prospective medical school applicants. Admissions representatives, the Director of Diversity Access Programs, along with selected medical students and faculty members annually visit with pre-medical advisors and student groups on the medical campus and at the undergraduate institutions. On-campus recruitment visits include a tour of the medical facilities by medical students. All recruitment sessions conducted include information about the unique and desirable features that the institution offers as well as the medical school curriculum, financial aid, student life-style, and student or-ganizations. Recruitment visits are made to most colleges and universities in the state of Virginia and to most out-state schools that have a large enrollment of Virginia residents. Groups who wish to visit the campus should contact the School of Medicine Admissions Office. Individual tours are not provided; however, interested individuals are welcomed to visit the Admissions Office and pick up a self-guided tour book. Science clubs and other special groups are also invited to tour the facilities.

Recruitment visits are also provided at the middle and high school levels. School of Medicine representatives and selected medical students participate in school career days and college fairs.

The Office of Student Outreach Programs sponsors a "Second Look" Program to accepted students from backgrounds underrepresented in medicine. These students are invited back to the medical campus to meet and speak with medical students, residents, and faculty and learn more about the facilities and opportunities.

Admissions

The School of Medicine has an institutional goal to educate and train students who will meet the health needs of our state and nation. Two important objectives are to increase the population of students from backgrounds underrepresented in medicine and graduate 50 percent of the medical school class who are interested in primary care.

An initial screening is conducted on all applications. The Admissions Committee, who makes the decision to grant interviews, reviews those applicants who are provided with secondary applications. All interviews are conducted on the Medical College of Virginia Campus and are one-on-one interaction. Selection factors include, but are not limited to: Medical College Admission Test (MCAT) scores, GPA, letters of recommendations, essays, and exposure to medicine. No factor is weighted. Acceptances are made to those candidates who clearly demonstrate an ability to be successful students as well as exhibit compassion and other important interpersonal qualities of a physician.

The Admissions Committee is composed of School of Medicine adminis-

Virginia Commonwealth University School of Medicine
Applicants, First-Time Applicants, Matriculants by Gender, Race and Ethnicity, 2007-2008

	2007 APP			2007 F-time APP			2007 MAT			2008 APP			2008 F-time APP			2008 MAT		
	Women	Men	Total	Women	Men	Total	Women	Men	Total	Women	Men	Total	Women	Men	Total	Women	Men	Total
Hispanic/Latino																		
Cuban	12	16	28	8	15	23	0	0	0	13	26	39	11	22	33	0	2	2
Mexican American	39	34	73	32	23	55	0	0	0	37	39	76	30	27	57	0	0	0
Puerto Rican	15	12	27	11	9	20	0	0	0	12	19	31	9	12	21	0	1	1
Other Hispanic	53	61	114	35	40	75	3	0	3	73	68	141	53	41	94	0	0	0
Multiple Hispanic/Latino*	6	4	10	4	2	6	0	0	0	8	6	14	7	3	10	0	0	0
Subtotal	125	127	252	90	89	179	3	0	3	143	158	301	110	105	215	0	3	3
Non-Hispanic/Latino																		
Black	231	94	325	154	74	228	7	2	9	219	113	332	144	86	230	5	3	8
Native American/AK	4	7	11	4	6	10	0	0	0	4	3	7	4	2	6	0	0	0
Native Hawaiian/OPI	14	8	22	9	7	16	0	0	0	10	2	12	4	2	6	2	0	2
White	1,478	1,630	3,108	1,129	1,101	2,230	47	70	117	1,440	1,886	3,326	1,051	1,312	2,363	50	65	115
Asian	822	854	1,676	579	574	1,153	28	21	49	869	886	1,755	612	538	1,150	27	25	52
Other Race	0	4	4	0	1	1	0	0	0	3	5	8	3	3	6	0	0	0
Multiple Race*	77	64	141	57	39	96	1	2	3	84	78	162	61	53	114	2	3	5
Unknown	24	25	49	23	18	41	2	1	3	61	73	134	55	58	113	2	2	4
Subtotal	2,650	2,686	5,336	1,955	1,820	3,775	85	96	181	2,690	3,046	5,736	1,934	2,054	3,988	88	98	186
Foreign	35	40	75	30	26	56	0	0	0	52	65	117	42	47	89	0	3	3
Total	2,810	2,853	5,663	2,075	1,935	4,010	88	96	184	2,885	3,269	6,154	2,086	2,206	4,292	88	104	192

*Since 2002, students can select more than one race and / or ethnicity. **Those who did not choose 'Hispanic/Latino' or 'Non-Hispanic/Latino' are listed under 'Non-Hispanic/Latino'. Data Source: AAMC Data Warehouse: Applicant-Matriculant File, as of 1/16/2009.

trators, physicians, and fourth-year medical students. All are full voting members.

Academic Support Programs

The Associate Dean of Student Affairs, Director of Student Outreach Programs, Director of Curriculum, the Diversity Access Program Director, and professionals in the University Counseling Center are concerned with the progress and maturation of individual medical students. Students who have academic problems are identified early in the academic year, and these individuals are provided with tutorial assistance. A variety of tutorial services are available: individual and group tutoring based upon a personal needs assessment; educational resources such as computer disks, co-op notes, review material, audio tapes of first- and second-year lectures; and study-skills sessions.

The Office of Student Affairs groups students for participation in our Healing with Empathy, Acceptance, Respect and inTegrity Mentoring Groups (HEART Groups). The HEART Group facilitator is also the faculty advisor of record for the group. In addition, the Office of Student Outreach Programs can arrange with Student Affairs to provide students with a minority physician mentor, if desired.

Enrichment Programs

There are a number of enrichment programs available to prospective and matriculating medical students.

Health Careers/Education and Special Services for Students (HC/ESSS)
Virginia Commonwealth University hosts various programs to encourage and educate high school and college-level students about health careers. The programs currently serve students ranging from fourth grade to undergraduate and post-baccalaureate grade levels. In addition, HC/ESSS provides support and resources to enrolled VCU health profession students. For more information, visit (www.vcuhealth.org/vp/sass-dss/programs/).

VCU Acceleration Program
The VCU Acceleration Program provides college students early exposure to the math and science curriculum of pre-health sciences and opportunities for internships and volunteer work in various clinical health service provider settings. The VCU Acceleration Program offers many unique and valuable learning experiences for students. Upon acceptance into the program the students will participate in the four-week Summer Health Sciences program, which exposes them to the math and science curriculum of health sciences. Prior to the start of the sophomore year, a stipend will be given to each student while participating in the summer programs. They also will do internships in various clinical health service provider settings. Other program features include Supplemental Instruction in math and science, and academic and health professions advising.

Project Inquisitive Minds
This one-week program is designed to encourage and educate high school students about the many interdisciplinary programs of health careers. Through activities and educational experiences, high school students in the program will develop and understand the roles and responsibilities of diverse health careers. The program targets underrepresented minority students within the Richmond area who have an interest in pursuing a health career beyond high school graduation.

Diversity Access Programs
This program is designed to provide bachelor and post-bachelor students with the resources, skills, and exposure needed to successfully complete college level work and gain entrance into one of VCU's health professions schools. The programs include a skills development workshop series focusing on topics such as preparing for professional school admissions, improving learning skills, and financial planning and wellness. This program operates through the Office of the Vice President of Health Sciences under the Of-

fice of Students Academic Support Services for Students with Disabilities.

Area Health Education Centers (AHEC)
The Virginia Statewide AHEC Program is located within HC/ESSS and develops health careers recruitment programs for Virginia's students, especially underrepresented and disadvantaged students. The AHEC programs support community-based training of primary care health professions students, residents, and other health professions students in Virginia's underserved communities. AHEC also provides educational and practice support systems for the Commonwealth's primary care providers. The Virginia AHEC regularly collaborates with health, education, and human services organizations to achieve the shared goal of improved health and disease prevention for the citizens of the Commonwealth.

Post-Baccalaureate Program
The School of Medicine offers a one-year pre-medical basic health sciences certificate for individuals seeking to enhance their background in the basic health sciences. This is an opportunity for advanced graduate-level training prior to entry into a professional program. Interested individuals should contact VCU's School of Graduate Studies at 804-828-6916.

Foundations of Clinical Medicine
All first- and second-year medical students must participate in the Foundations of Clinical Medicine course, which is designed to provide the students with patient exposure to help prepare them for their clinical years. Within the course, components address the importance of getting to know the patient individually and gaining an effective history with cultural issues in mind. Cases are provided and students practice with simulated patients.

Project ACEe
The School of Medicine sponsors an educational experience for inner-city minority high school students who have an interest in the medical field. Beginning in January of each year, se-

lected students are provided with educational workshops that will help them to explore the medical profession and provide preparation to become self-sufficient learners in college. This is a major pipeline program.

Cultural Competence

The School of Medicine currently addresses cultural competence at all levels. Students have cultural competencies integrated into their coursework through both lecture and electives during all years. In addition, courses and seminars are given regarding professionalism and ethics. Cultural competency for faculty is addressed through the Office of Faculty and Instructional Development. Diversity Awareness and other training sessions are also provided for all faculty.

Student Financial Assistance

A detailed evaluation of financial aid for each student with a need is conducted after the student has been accepted into the School of Medicine. Available scholarship monies and loans vary in amount and distribution each year. Every effort is made to meet the financial needs of all students. Average expenses for the first year of medical school include tuition and fees, loan fees, room and board, books and supplies, transportation, and personal. These factors are used in the determination of need for financial aid.

In order to serve its student body efficiently and correctly, the School of Medicine maintains its own Office of Financial Aid. Policies for the awarding of institutional financial aid are made by the School of Medicine Scholarship Committee, composed of administrators, faculty, and appointed doctors from various areas of medicine. Financial aid is awarded on the basis of financial need, which is determined through use of the Free Application for Federal Student Aid (FAFSA) financial statement and/or merit.

Applicants seeking consideration for institutional scholarships are requested to report on the FAFSA statement their own income and assets, that of their

parents, and, where applicable, their spouse. In addition, applicants are asked to complete the Needs Access Form, which is an on-line process.

The foundation of all financial aid awards is the presumption of a reasonable level of borrowing, beginning with a federally-subsidized Stafford Student Loan of $8,500. Applicants who have financial need, after factoring in both family resources and loans, may receive institutional scholarship assistance to help meet remaining need. Since aid is based upon financial need, aid recipients are required to notify the Financial Aid Office of changes in their financial resources.

Applicants who anticipate borrowing as a means of financing medical education are advised to assure that their personal credit record has no adverse credit history. The establishment of good credit is not a requirement for obtaining student loans, but the absence of poor credit history is a requirement.

Financial assistance is not available to students who are not U.S. citizens or permanent resident aliens. Financial need is not a factor in decisions regarding admission. Financial aid applications are made available to all students who are invited to the school for admissions interviews.

About 88 percent of Virginia Commonwealth University medical students receive financial aid. Of these students, approximately 38 percent receive some form of school-based aid. School-based aid is composed of revolving loan monies and scholarship funds. Federal funds consist of the subsidized and unsubsidized Stafford student loans, as well as the GRAD Plus loan. In addition, a variety of other outside sources are utilized, such as the Alter-native Loan Program (ALP).

The School of Medicine will waive application fee requirements for all students for whom that fee will be a financial hardship as determined by the American Medical College Application Service.

Educational Partnerships

Guaranteed Admissions Program

The Virginia Commonwealth University's Honors Program offers a Guaranteed Admissions Program to qualified high school seniors. This is an opportunity to gain a guarantee of future admissions to highly selective graduate and professional programs at VCU.

Preferred Admissions Program

Similar to the Guaranteed Admissions Program, Virginia Commonwealth University's Honors Program offers a Preferred Admissions Program to sophomore students currently enrolled at VCU. These students, who have performed well academically for the first two years of undergraduate school, are given the opportunity to gain a guarantee of future admissions to VCU's highly selective graduate and professional programs.

VCU has recently entered into preferred admissions partnerships with Hampton University, Hampden-Sydney College and Virginia Military Institute. Students attending these institutions who are interested in being considered for preferred admissions should talk with the pre-med advisor to discuss program requirements.

Mason Scholar Program

The George Mason University (GMU) chooses 10 Mason Scholars each year. They are high school graduates who have shown superior academic accomplishment, civic involvement, and leadership potential. Each year, a selected number of these scholars are given the opportunity to gain admission to the VCU School of Medicine. In the past, VCU has admitted one to four Mason Scholars to each medical school class. Individuals apply for the GMU Scholars program as they apply for admissions to GMU. The selections are made solely by the GMU Scholars Program administration.

Virginia Tech Carilion School of Medicine*

Dr. Dennis Means, Assistant Dean for Minority Affairs
Virginia Tech Carilion School of Medicine
1 Riverside Circle, Suite 102
Roanoke, VA 24016
549-581-0122; 540-985-3951 fax
demeans@carilion.com

Recruitment

The Virginia Tech Carilion School of Medicine (VTC) has stated its mission "to develop physician thought leaders through inquiry, research, and discovery, using an innovative curriculum based upon adult learning methods in a patient centered context." Diversity within the faculty and student body is critical to this mission and will be sought through the recruitment and admissions processes and managed by the organizational structure. The primary responsibility for overseeing this process is through the Assistant Dean for Minority Affairs, with the management structure provided by the Diversity Committee.

As VTC recruits its first class to matriculate in August 2010, recruitment efforts will be focused on the pre-medical programs at the minority serving institutions of Virginia and the surrounding states and on the region's historically black institutions. VTC will utilize the well developed committees and structures of its partner, Virginia Tech, in recruitment efforts. These efforts will include personal contact and recruitment trips to the pre-medical organizations of the above institutions. In future years, VTC will develop programs for local community colleges, high and middle schools, summer internship programs, and a presence at other organizations and meetings with a high concentration of minority students.

Admission

The VTC Admission Committee is committed to a holistic review of candidates. A consideration of minority status is part of that holistic review. Other considerations include life experience and disadvantaged financial or educational status. These factors are actively sought during the application process and considered throughout the admissions process. The Diversity Committee will have advisory status to the Admissions Committee. Additional details of the admissions process are available at: (http//www.vtc.vt.edu).

Academic Support Programs

The Office of Student Affairs offers formal tutoring for all basic science courses. Assistance with clinical education is available upon request. Students who are struggling with any aspect of the educational program will have individualized assistance programs designed for their particular needs. As our student body grows and matures, a "buddy" program utilizing senior medical students as informal mentors is planned. A full range of academic, career, and personal counseling services will be available.

Enrichment Programs

Plans at VTC include summer enrichment programs for pre-medical students. There are no current plans for summer programs for students accepted for admission to VTC.

Student Financial Assistance

VTC will reduce the fee for our secondary application for students who apply for, and are approved for, the American Medical College Application Service (AMCAS) fee assistance program (FAP). Financial aid and debt management will be available for all students who matriculate to VTC. There will be a full range of scholarship and loan programs on both a merit and need based system. Scholarships directed to minority students are actively being developed.

Educational Partnership

Virginia Tech, one of the founding partners of VTC, has well developed programs in multiculturalism. VTC participates in several of these programs including;

- The Virginia Nebraska Alliance
- The Virginia North Carolina Alliance
- The Multicultural Academic Opportunities Program

VTC is also developing a partnership with Hollins University for the creation of a post baccalaureate program. The intent of this program is to provide students considering medicine as a second career with the academic guidance and clinical experiences necessary for them to be strong candidates for medical school.

*No data available; new medical school.

University of Washington School of Medicine

Dr. David Acosta, Associate Dean for Multicultural Affairs
University of Washington School of Medicine
A-314 Health Sciences Center
Box 346340
Seattle, WA 98195
206-685-2489; 206-543-9063 fax
http://www.uwmedicine.org/
Education/MDProgram/

Recruitment

Founded in 1946, the UW medical school is recognized for its excellence in training primary-care physicians and for advancing medical knowledge through scientific research. It is nationally known for its commitment to community service through the volunteer activities of its students, staff, faculty and alumni. The Office of Multicultural Affairs (OMCA) *(http://myomca.org)* was established in 1980 by the Dean of the School of Medicine as a reaffirmation of the medical school's efforts and intent to matriculate and graduate a diverse group of individuals who are traditionally underrepresented in medicine.

The University of Washington School of Medicine serves as the regional medical school for the five WWAMI states (Washington, Wyoming, Alaska, Montana, and Idaho – for more information, go to *http://www.uwmedicine.org/ Education/WWAMI/).* Students outside of the region who are from disadvantaged backgrounds or who have a demonstrated commitment to work with the underserved populations are encouraged to apply. The OMCA staff coordinates activities that are designed to encourage, assist and support students who have an interest in pursuing a career in medicine.

OMCA works directly with K-12 schools, community colleges, universities, and established community organizations in the Pacific Northwest to identify, encourage, recruit, and train a diverse medical student body. A Diversity Advisory Board consisting of medical students, faculty and community members participate in the development of program activities and strategies to help the OMCA achieve the goals established in our mission statement.

Admissions

The School of Medicine is committed to building and sustaining a diverse academic community of faculty, staff, fellows, residents, and students and to assuring that access to education and training is open to learners from all segments of society, acknowledging a particular responsibility to the diverse populations within the WWAMI region. Given this mission of the school, the Admissions Committee is committed to selecting students with the goal of meeting the needs and demands of our local and regional communities. Using a holistic approach process, applicants are considered not only on the basis of their academic performance and Medical College Admission Test (MCAT) scores, but also on their motivation to pursue medicine, their maturity, demonstrated humanitarian qualities, community service and experiences in serving the underserved. Extenuating circumstances in an applicant's background (such as the barriers that they have overcome) are evaluated as they relate to these selection factors.

All five States in the region offer annual Pre-Admissions Workshops for poten-

University of Washington School of Medicine
Applicants, First-Time Applicants, Matriculants by Gender, Race and Ethnicity, 2007-2008

	2007 APP Women	APP Men	APP Total	F-time APP Women	F-time APP Men	F-time APP Total	MAT Women	MAT Men	MAT Total	2008 APP Women	APP Men	APP Total	F-time APP Women	F-time APP Men	F-time APP Total	MAT Women	MAT Men	MAT Total
Hispanic/Latino																		
Cuban	4	7	11	3	5	8	0	0	0	8	10	18	6	9	15	0	0	0
Mexican American	72	76	148	56	62	118	0	2	2	61	85	146	50	69	119	4	3	7
Puerto Rican	13	10	23	10	9	19	0	1	1	9	7	16	7	5	12	0	1	1
Other Hispanic	55	44	99	48	28	76	3	1	4	48	62	110	37	49	86	2	1	3
Multiple Hispanic/Latino*	7	7	14	7	7	14	1	1	2	9	6	15	6	6	12	1	0	1
Subtotal	151	144	295	124	111	235	4	5	9	135	170	305	106	138	244	7	5	12
Non-Hispanic/Latino**																		
Black	81	54	135	70	46	116	0	2	2	96	50	146	71	43	114	2	1	3
Native American/AK	15	11	26	13	10	23	0	1	1	9	13	22	6	13	19	0	2	2
Native Hawaiian/OPI	14	8	22	10	5	15	0	0	0	22	10	32	15	6	21	0	0	0
White	1,223	1,483	2,706	993	1,192	2,185	87	65	152	1,172	1,526	2,698	935	1,204	2,139	84	73	157
Asian	520	582	1,102	450	457	907	5	13	18	508	532	1,040	416	402	818	16	11	27
Other Race	1	2	3	1	1	2	0	0	0	3	2	5	3	2	5	0	0	0
Multiple Race*	92	83	175	80	71	151	5	2	7	84	85	169	62	68	130	7	4	11
Unknown	23	32	55	22	31	53	1	1	2	68	66	134	66	62	128	2	2	4
Subtotal	1,969	2,255	4,224	1,639	1,813	3,452	98	84	182	1,962	2,284	4,246	1,574	1,800	3,374	111	93	204
Foreign	40	39	79	31	37	68	0	0	0	30	47	77	25	37	62	0	0	0
Total	2,160	2,438	4,598	1,794	1,961	3,755	102	89	191	2,127	2,501	4,628	1,705	1,975	3,680	118	98	216

Note: In 2008, one applicant, who declined to report gender, was not included here.
*Since 2002, students can select more than one race and / or ethnicity. **Those who did not choose 'Hispanic/Latino' or 'Non-Hispanic/Latino' are

tial applicants. The workshops are designed to provide in-depth information on the medical school and the WWAMI model. For more information visit: *(http://www.uwmedicine.org/Education/WWAMI/Medical+School.htm)*, the application process, interview skills, and financial aid.

Academic Support Programs

The School of Medicine offers a variety of services for minority and/or disadvantaged students. A learning specialist is available to assist students with learning skills, study skills and test-taking strategies for their medical school courses and the U.S. Medical Licensing Examination Boards. Individual and small group tutoring services are offered during the academic year for all students. Board preparation programs and diagnostic testing services are offered.

A research advisor is available to provide assistance with the required research project known as the Independent Investigative Inquiry that all medical students are required to complete. Students are encouraged to consider health care disparities research.

Counseling staff provide free, short-term, confidential counseling services to all students and can help the student cope with a variety of personal and/or professional issues surrounding the demands of medical school. An optional expanded curriculum is also available for students requiring more than the traditional four years to complete the curriculum.

Pre-Matriculation Program.

This five-week summer program is offered for new medical school matriculants from minority and/or disadvantaged backgrounds. It provides an introduction to the medical school curriculum (Histology), exposure to local health care systems, and workshops in study skills, test-taking skills, and stress management. *(http://depts.washington.edu/omca/PREMAT/)*. Contact: Mary Walls, *mwalls@u.washington.edu*, 206-616-3047.

Student Organizations. The School of Medicine has a variety of student organizations for minority medical students. These include the Washington Chapter of the Student National Medical Association (Region I: *http://www.snmaregion1.org/;* contact: Margaret Nkechi Onwuka, *mno82@u.washington.edu*), the Washington Chapter of the Latino Medical Student Association *(http://students.washington.edu/lmsa/officers.html;* contact: Lili Peacock-Villada, *lilip05@alum.dartmouth.org;* Christina Arredondo, *arredonc@u.washington.edu);* the Medicine Wheel Society *(http://faculty.washington.edu/dacosta/nacoe/mws.html; contact: Andy Benefield, abd2@u.washington.edu)* and the Asian Pacific American Medical Student Association (Region VII contact: Catherine Delostrinos, *cathetr@u.washington.edu;* Duc Ngo, *ducngo@u.washington.edu).* These student organizations not only provide support, social activities, and cultural events for students, but they also provide students with the opportunities to participate in recruitment, community outreach, and peer mentoring among local K-12 schools, high school and college students. AFERM (Alliance for Equal Representation of Minorities, *aferm@u.washington.edu)* is a new student organization committed to enhancing the diversity of the medical school.

Mentoring Networks

Structured mentoring networks for medical students have been established and are active with local minority community health professionals: African American Mentoring Network *(http://faculty.washington.edu/dacosta/aamn/index.html)*, Chicano/Latino Mentoring Network, and the Medicine Wheel Society. Students participate in support activities with community mentoring networks designed to provide social, moral and academic support. They meet regularly to discuss and address student needs, issues and activities. In addition, the mentors provide career-counseling in medicine.

Enrichment Programs

UDOC

This is a free summer enrichment program for high school students that is offered in Seattle, WA (three-weeks; *http://depts.washington.edu/omca/UDOC/)* and Anchorage, AK (six-weeks; *http://biomed.uaa.alaska.edu/UDOC.htm).* This program encourages high school students from minority and/or disadvantaged backgrounds to pursue a career in the health professions and fosters their development in academics, leadership and community service. Contact: Felicity Abeyta, 206-685-2489, *fabeyta@u.washington.edu.*

Summer Medical and Dental Education Program (SMDEP)

This is a free 6-week summer enrichment program offered to college freshman and sophomores from minority and/or disadvantaged backgrounds that have a demonstrated interest in pursuing a career in medicine or dentistry. The program is located in Seattle, WA *(http://depts.washington.edu/omca/SMDEP/index.html)*, and offers academic preparation in the basic sciences, clinical immersion experiences with an individually assigned physician/dentist mentor, exposure to the local health care system and community, including opportunities for emergency room, surgery observation, and dental procedures and biomedical science research. Participants receive free room and board, travel assistance, and a stipend. Other amenities include textbooks, access to the University's many educational and recreational resources, mentorship and advising. Contact: Pam Racansky, *racansky@u.washington.edu*, 206-616-5866.

Student Financial Assistance

The School of Medicine will waive the application fee for students who qualify under the American Medical College Application Service fee waiver guidelines. Financial aid is available to all students through the Office of Financial Aid and is based on demonstrated financial need. Three full-time officers staff the office to assist students in applying for local and national grants, scholarships, and low-interest loans. Out-of-state students generally can apply for resident status by the second year based on established University guidelines. Once resident status is granted, students pay in-state tuition. OMCA can assist students in meeting the requirements necessary for establishing residency. The school offers a number of scholarships to students who demonstrate academic merit and financial need. Contact: Diane Noecker, *dnoecker@u.washington.edu, 206- 685-9229.*

Educational Partnerships

WWAMI

WWAMI is an enduring partnership between the UW School of Medicine and the states of Wyoming, Alaska, Montana, and Idaho. The UWSOM is the only medical school in the five-state WWAMI region and has established partnerships with the University of Wyoming *(http://uwadmnweb.uwyo.edu/wwami/),* Washington State University *(http://www.wsu.edu/ ~wwami/), University of Alaska-Anchorage (http://biomed.uaa.alaska.edu/), Montana State University (http://www.montana.edu/ wwwwami/),* and University of Idaho *(http://www.webs.uidaho.edu/wwami/).* It collaborates closely with community and regional organizations to implement its programs, community outreach, and mentoring networks to help support students in their pursuit of their medical career. Students from Alaska, Montana, Idaho, and Wyoming take their initial year at state universities in their home states.

Post-Baccalaureate Pre-Medical Certificate Program at Montana State University

This program is offered for those students who have completed their bachelor's level work at a four-year institution who are interested in taking the science courses traditionally required for application to medical and dental schools. These requisite courses include general chemistry, introductory biology, organic chemistry, introductory physics

and biochemistry. Post-baccalaureate students completing 36 of the suggested 45 credits available will receive a Certificate of Completion. Students will be advised in their curricular choices and medical school applications by Jane Cary, Director of Health Professions Advising, at hpa@montana.edu, 406-994-1670.
(http://www.montana.edu/dhs/hpa/ Post-bacc.advising.htm).

National Institute of Diabetes and Digestive and Kidney Diseases-Charles Drew University of Medicine and Sciences National High School Student Summer Research Apprentice Program

In partnership with UCLA, this program is designed to provide high school students with an opportunity to work in a biomedical laboratory in their state. Each student is paired with an established researcher and assigned to a research team to work on a specific biomedical research project. The eight-week program provides students with real experiences working in a laboratory and learning research protocols. In the last week the students travel to Washington, DC to present their research. The purpose of the program is to increase the number of ethnic minorities involved in biomedical research. Contact: Felicity Abeyta, 206-685-2489, *fabeyta@u.washington.edu. (http://www2.niddk.nih.gov/Funding/ FundingOpportunities/Minority_Health _Research_Coordination/ stu-summer.htm).*

Project H.O.P.E. (Health Occupations Preparatory Experience)

In partnership with Western Washington Area Health Education Center (AHEC), this program provides high school students with a 6-week paid internship to learn and be exposed to health careers in local health facilities in their communities. The students spend part of their time at the UWSOM and the OMCA and are exposed to the health sciences.
(http://www.wwahec.org/WWAHEC_ HOPE.htm).

Cultural Diversity

Native American Center of Excellence

(http://uwnacoe.com). The Center provides a unique educational resource and experience for American Indian/Alaskan Native (AI/AN) students and non-Native students who have an interest in learning more about AI/AN culture and health care issues. Program offerings include career advising, pre-matriculation workshops, mentoring, membership in the Medicine Wheel Society, and participation in the Indian Health Pathway (IHP).

The Indian Health Pathway

The IHP provides medical students with the necessary information and experiences to make them better practitioners in urban and rural AI/AN communities. The pathway provides this educational experience through the use of specialized lecture series, small group discussions, immersion clinical experiences in medical practices that serve the AI/AN communities (Indian Health Service and tribal authority contract clinics located in both urban and rural sites). This program is unique in that it utilizes a number of AI/AN faculty to teach these components who have had a vast amount of collective experience in working directly with Native populations. Contact: Vicki Pinkham, *vp@u.washington.edu,* 206-685-2489. *http://faculty. washington.edu/dacosta/nacoe/ihp.html)*

The Hispanic Health Pathway

The HHP was launched in Spring 2008. The goal of the Hispanic Health Pathway is to provide a number of educational opportunities to medical students that better prepares them to care for the Hispanic population. This pathway provides contextual content, problem-based learning experiences, small group discussions, mentoring opportunities with Hispanic faculty or non-Hispanic faculty who have an expertise in providing cultural-responsive care to Hispanics. Elective clerkship rotations in office sites throughout WWAMI that specifically care for a large Hispanic population are available for students to participate in. The pathway provides the students the option to improve Spanish speaking skills through an immersion experience in Central America. Students have the opportunity to obtain certification of completion after meeting all of the set criteria. Contact: Pam Racansky, *racansky@u.washington.edu* , 206-616-5866. *(http://faculty.washington.edu/ dacosta/HHP/index.html).*

Underserved Pathway
The Underserved Pathway is administered by the UW Department of Family Medicine. This pathway provides academic, mentorship and clinical experiential resources to prepare medical students to care for a variety of underserved populations located in both rural and urban communities. Contact: Jennifer Earle, *jearle@u.washington.edu,* 206-543-9425.
(http://courses.washington.edu/ upathway/).

Global Health Pathway
The Global Health Pathway is administered by the UW Department of Global Health. This pathway will provide medical students with the academic resources, research skills, and clinical experiences in international health necessary to practice in international communities both domestically and globally. Contact: Daren Wade, *dwade@u.washington.edu,* 206- 616-1159. *(http://depts. washington.edu/ihg/pathway.htm).*

Center for Cultural Proficiency in Medical Education
CC-PriME is a new Center at the UWSOM, and is administered by the Office of Multicultural Affairs. Supported by grant funding from the National Institute of Health, the Center adds a new dimension and reinforces the mission of the school in its commitment to enhance the diversity in medical training as a unique educational opportunity. The purpose of the Center is to prepare and train our future health professional workforce to provide the best cultural-responsive care. CC-PriME will integrate multicultural health education into the existing medical school curriculum, and develop new innovative programs. In addition, the Center will provide faculty development in cross-

cultural training, and develop faculty trainers in the same area of study. Contact: Amen Tsegai, *amen2@u.washington.edu,* 206-616-3021. CC-PriME's Web site: *(http://cc-prime.com).*

Joan C. Edwards School of Medicine at Marshall University

Dr. Marie C. Veitia, Associate Dean for Student Affairs
Joan C. Edwards School of Medicine at Marshall University
1600 Medical Center Drive, Huntington, WV 25701
304-691-1730; 304-691-1744 fax
veitia@marshall.edu

Recruitment

The Joan C. Edwards School of Medicine does not have a special recruitment program for minority students. An admissions counselor does visit all colleges in West Virginia to discuss medical school opportunities and current medical students are invited to participate. Every effort is made to recruit minority students.

Admissions

The admissions process is the same for all applicants. The Admissions Committee considers the grade-point average for undergraduate studies, particularly in science and related courses; Medical College Admission Test scores; and character qualifications such as motivation, enthusiasm, emotional stability, mature judgment, integrity, leadership, and scope of interests as is evident from letters of recommendation and two interviews with members of the Admissions Committee. Minorities are represented on the Admissions Committee.

Academic Support Programs

All medical school matriculants can receive tutorial assistance and advisement from a particular course professor, an assigned faculty advisor, and/or a student-selected faculty advisor. Academic achievement as well as personal and emotional needs are monitored closely, and the Office of Student Affairs intervenes as is indicated. A Peer-Tutoring Program is available upon request to first-year students at no charge. A U.S. Medical Licensing Exam (USMLE) Step 1 Review Course is offered on campus to all second-year students at no charge. Financial assistance is provided for other review materials. The main campus of Marshall University also provides extensive learning resources through the Higher Education for Learning Problems program.

Enrichment Programs

Several programs are conducted annually with high school and college students designed to stimulate interest in the medical professions. Most notably is the Southwestern West Virginia Area Health Education Center (SWAHEC). This federally funded program aims to recruit disadvantaged students from rural communities and increase retention among those who are educated in the medical professions. The Concord Summer Academy, which partners with Concord University, is an enrichment program aimed at exposing high school students to the health professions. Finally, college students are invited to participate in stipend-supported summer programs. Every effort is made to meet the needs of all students, including especially minority and disadvantaged students.

Student Financial Assistance

Those students receiving a fee waiver from the American Medical College Application Service will also receive a waiver of the application fee for the School of Medicine. Debt management and financial planning are currently offered on a one-on-one basis. Plans are

Joan C. Edwards School of Medicine at Marshall University
Applicants, First-Time Applicants, Matriculants by Gender, Race and Ethnicity, 2007-2008

	2007 APP Women	2007 APP Men	2007 APP Total	2007 F-time APP Women	2007 F-time APP Men	2007 F-time APP Total	2007 MAT Women	2007 MAT Men	2007 MAT Total	2008 APP Women	2008 APP Men	2008 APP Total	2008 F-time APP Women	2008 F-time APP Men	2008 F-time APP Total	2008 MAT Women	2008 MAT Men	2008 MAT Total
Hispanic/Latino																		
Cuban	6	11	17	5	9	14	0	0	0	2	5	7	2	5	7	0	0	0
Mexican American	14	16	30	10	13	23	0	0	0	4	7	11	3	6	9	0	0	0
Puerto Rican	4	4	8	3	4	7	0	0	0	6	4	10	6	2	8	0	1	1
Other Hispanic	22	21	43	18	12	30	1	0	1	10	15	25	6	8	14	0	0	0
Multiple Hispanic/Latino*	2	3	5	1	2	3	0	0	0	2	2	4	2	1	3	0	0	0
Subtotal	48	55	103	37	40	77	1	0	1	24	33	57	19	22	41	0	1	1
Non-Hispanic/Latino**																		
Black	44	41	85	36	30	66	0	0	0	40	26	66	28	19	47	0	1	1
Native American/AK	1	1	2	1	1	2	0	0	0	2	0	2	2	0	2	0	0	0
Native Hawaiian/OPI	5	4	9	4	2	6	0	0	0	2	1	3	0	1	1	0	0	0
White	464	632	1,096	354	462	816	35	27	62	349	468	817	268	355	623	35	26	61
Asian	262	296	558	213	224	437	2	5	7	151	148	299	109	99	208	8	6	14
Other Race	1	2	3	0	1	1	0	0	0	0	1	1	0	1	1	0	0	0
Multiple Race*	15	30	45	10	20	30	0	1	1	12	12	24	9	9	18	0	0	0
Unknown	14	7	21	12	6	18	1	0	1	15	19	34	13	16	29	0	0	0
Subtotal	806	1,013	1,819	630	746	1,376	38	33	71	571	675	1,246	429	500	929	43	33	76
Foreign	7	16	23	4	10	14	0	0	0	4	9	13	4	8	12	0	1	1
Total	861	1,084	1,945	671	796	1,467	39	33	72	599	717	1,316	452	530	982	43	35	78

*Since 2002, students can select more than one race and / or ethnicity. **Those who did not choose 'Hispanic/Latino' or 'Non-Hispanic/Latino' are listed under 'Non-Hispanic/Latino'. Data Source: AAMC Data Warehouse: Applicant-Matriculant File, as of 1/16/2009.

underway to provide more opportunities for students in this area.

Other Pertinent Information

There is no discrimination because of race, gender, religion, age sexual orientation, handicap, or national origin. Qualified members of minority groups are encouraged to apply. The Joan C. Edwards School of Medicine is committed to developing mechanisms by which to enhance diversity. By working with the Office of Multicultural Affairs at Marshall University, the School of Medicine strives to provide fairness and equity in the distribution of opportunity and in the treatment of individuals. Objectives and strategies for doing so are established and/or reviewed annually.

West Virginia University School of Medicine

Dr. Rosemarie Cannarella Lorenzetti , Assistant Dean of Student Services – Eastern Division
West Virginia University School of Medicine
2500 Foundation Way
Martinsburg, WV 25425
304-264-6234; 304-596-6330 fax

Recruitment

The School of Medicine participates in a statewide program called HSTA-Health Science Technology Academy. This program is in most counties in the state, and serves as an initial step in the active recruitment of African-Americans; Hispanic; and poor, underserved/underprivileged white students in our state. It serves to focus interest to secondary school students in health science careers. This program is especially oriented toward minority students, targeting African-American, then Hispanic, and thirdly underprivileged high school students. During this program, the students are exposed to the African – American and Hispanic leaders in the school systems and health care systems, to further serve as role models for aca-demic achievement as active goals for these high school students. There are also 13 programs held at the WVU main campus that are focused on career counseling and discussions, and programs are carried out to help the advisors in their work with students interested in health science careers. Minority advisors are especially welcomed, and every effort is made to indicate our interest in helping needy students. This program is called Mountaineer Visitation Days. Our director of admission attends the AAMC minority fair on a biannual basis.

Admissions

The School of Medicine has no differences in requirements for minority students. Every effort is made to select minority students who are felt to have proper motivation and capabilities for professional school. There is no special screening panel or admissions committee devoted to minority applicants. The criteria used for selection are the same for all students, and these include the grade-point averages, Medical College Admission Test scores, personal interviews, letters of recommendation, and student's motivation and interpersonal skills. The Admissions Committee is made up of both of basic science and clinical faculty. In addition, there are senior students who are full members of the committee. Every effort is made to obtain minority students and faculty for membership on the Admissions Committee.

Academic Support Programs

Every effort is made to make an early identification of students in academic difficulty, regardless of their minority or socioeconomic status. This is done through close supervision, cooperation, and communication among the course instructors, course coordinators, and Office of Student Services. Assistance is routinely given to students with special needs. This assistance may take several forms, such as identification and help with personal problems, improvement in study techniques, and tutorial guidance on a one-to-one basis by faculty members. The Health Sciences Center Campus has a branch Learning Resources Center with learning tutorials, time and stress management help, and overall study-skills enhancement available. Every attempt is made to individualize students' needs, and special

West Virginia University School of Medicine
Applicants, First-Time Applicants, Matriculants by Gender, Race and Ethnicity, 2007-2008

	2007									2008								
	APP			F-time APP			MAT			APP			F-time APP			MAT		
	Women	Men	Total	Women	Men	Total	Women	Men	Total	Women	Men	Total	Women	Men	Total	Women	Men	Total
Hispanic/Latino																		
Cuban	4	12	16	3	10	13	1	0	1	8	14	22	8	11	19	0	0	0
Mexican American	10	16	26	8	13	21	0	0	0	15	17	32	13	15	28	0	0	0
Puerto Rican	1	4	5	1	3	4	0	0	0	5	7	12	4	5	9	0	0	0
Other Hispanic	29	32	61	23	23	46	2	0	2	25	33	58	13	21	34	0	0	0
Multiple Hispanic/Latino*	2	3	5	1	2	3	0	0	0	3	2	5	3	1	4	0	0	0
Subtotal	46	67	113	36	51	87	3	0	3	56	73	129	41	53	94	0	0	0
Non-Hispanic/Latino**																		
Black	49	35	84	27	25	52	3	0	3	66	33	99	45	25	70	0	0	0
Native American/AK	1	5	6	1	5	6	0	0	0	2	4	6	2	3	5	0	0	0
Native Hawaiian/OPI	5	5	10	5	4	9	0	0	0	5	3	8	3	2	5	0	0	0
White	729	981	1,710	580	706	1,286	38	48	86	662	1,054	1,716	502	776	1,278	38	53	91
Asian	341	416	757	273	296	569	7	6	13	358	447	805	257	298	555	5	9	14
Other Race	0	1	1	0	1	1	0	0	0	0	0	0	0	0	0	0	0	0
Multiple Race*	34	42	76	23	31	54	1	1	2	32	31	63	25	18	43	1	1	2
Unknown	14	14	28	14	13	27	1	0	1	29	32	61	26	31	57	0	1	1
Subtotal	1,173	1,499	2,672	923	1,081	2,004	50	55	105	1,154	1,604	2,758	860	1,153	2,013	44	64	108
Foreign	44	52	96	36	36	72	0	0	0	40	52	92	30	40	70	1	0	1
Total	1,263	1,618	2,881	995	1,168	2,163	53	55	108	1,250	1,729	2,979	931	1,246	2,177	45	64	109

*Since 2002, students can select more than one race and / or ethnicity. **Those who did not choose 'Hispanic/Latino' or 'Non-Hispanic/Latino' are listed under 'Non-Hispanic/Latino'. Data Source: AAMC Data Warehouse: Applicant-Matriculant File, as of 1/16/2009.

arrangements for scheduling are, at times, made on an individual basis. All students are encouraged to communicate with the Office of Student Services if they need assistance in the areas of academic achievement, health, or matters of personal concern. Our office can be very proactive in following student progress, as we are a small school, and review all test grades, to keep a pulse on those who may have academic trouble.

Enrichment Programs

Health Careers Opportunity Program (HCOP)
West Virginia University (WVU) recognizes the underrepresentation of health care providers from minority and other underrepresented backgrounds practicing in the state. We have established a program aimed at increasing the number of qualified applicants applying to and graduating from medical, dental, pharmacy, and allied health programs. This program, known as the Central Appalachian Health Careers Opportunity Network (CAHCON), has three components:

- Preliminary Education: supports students as they transition from high school to college
- Facilitating Entry: supports students applying to health and allied health professions schools
- Retention: supports students in health and allied health professions schools

Currently, two HCOP graduates are enrolled in our entering medical school class. One previous HCOP student is serving as a faculty member in Family Medicine as a fellowship-trained OB Family Medicine specialist, after attending medical school and residency at WVU.

Highlights:

- Award of $1.86 million in federal funds
- Over 500 students helped since 1985; all but a handful are WV residents
- Very high retention rate of at risk participants (only seven students have dropped out of college from this program in the past ten years)
- Students from all WV institutions of higher education are eligible for this program and do participate

Health Sciences Seminar (HSS)
HSS has been supported by WVU since 1981 with the purpose of trying to encourage sixth-to-ninth grade disadvantaged youths to examine career possibilities in the health sciences. Nearly 1,100 seventh, eighth, and ninth graders from all over West Virginia along with their parents have participated in this overnight, two-day, cost-free event. The university will provide this seminar free to students and parents/guardians. West Virginia's Division of Student Affairs and HCOP sponsor this program. These students are given hands-on experiences with health care professions illustrating health career opportunities, tours of the extensive health care facilities at WVU, a chance to learn about financial aid opportunities, educational and skill requirements for multiple health professions, and much more. This program has a special emphasis on recruiting financially disadvantaged, first generation, and underrepresented minority participants.

Educational Partnerships

The Health Sciences and Technology Academy (HSTA)
HSTA reaches out to ninth- to 12th-grade underrepresented students and follows them to college and toward professional school to help them prepare for health care careers. The goal is to nurture the ambitions of talented students who, for economic or other reasons, might not ordinarily achieve these career goals. HSTA is a partnership among the numerous units of West Virginia University, West Virginia Rural Health Education Partnership, and many Appalachian communities. The program brings minority and disadvantaged students and their teachers to campus each summer for clinic, laboratory, and classroom training and enrichment activities, and then provides the infrastructure and support for community-based science projects mentored by teachers, health professions

students, and volunteer community leaders during the school year. HSTA aims to share the resources and talent of the partnership, to encourage public school teachers' and community leaders' mentoring of students.

The ultimate goal is to increase the college-going rate among underrepresented students in the Appalachian region, to improve science and math education, to empower communities through leadership development of their youth, and, ultimately, to increase the number of health care providers in West Virginia's currently underserved rural communities.

- Total number of students served by HSTA—2,100
- Total number of students currently served by HSTA—760
- Retention of students who begin the program in high school—64 percent
- Number of graduates to date, academic years 1998-2004—580 (currently 26 counties)
- Percent of graduates to enter college—99 percent
- Average high school GPA of graduates—3.57
- Average college GPA of graduates reporting—3.01

Another program at WVU specially designed to target West Virginia High School students who may be interested in staying in West Virginia for medical school is called the MedSTEP program. This program is a joint venture with Shepherd University in which students accepted in the program are guaranteed a spot in the entering medical school class four years in the future. They receive targeted support throughout college, which has helped students stay focused and be successful in medical school. West Virginia realizes that it is a very homogenous state, and diversity for this school also means getting more of the in-state students from poorer families and families without college graduates, to get into medical school and stay in medical school. This targeted program of support throughout college years is growing and showing effectiveness in this arena.

Student Financial Assistance

Weir Foundation
Scholarship awarded to disadvantaged minority student in the School of Medicine. Students must complete Free Application for Federal Student Aid (FAFSA) by March 1.

Robert D'Alessandri Medical Fund
Scholarship awarded to a medical student with financial need and academic promise. Preference is given to minority/underrepresented students who completed the HSTA, HSS, or HCOP programs. Applicants must be U.S. citizens. To be considered, the FAFSA must be filed by March 1. There is no cost to file the FAFSA. The scholarship is not available for interview trips.

Medical College of Wisconsin

Dr. Dawn St. A. Bragg, Assistant Dean, Student Affairs/Diversity
Assistant Professor, Pediatrics
Medical College of Wisconsin
8701 Watertown Plank Road
Milwaukee, WI 53226
414-456-8734; 414-456-6506 fax
dbragg@mcw.edu
www.mcw.edu/medicalschool/
studentdiversity.htm

Recruitment

The Medical College of Wisconsin (MCW) recognizes the importance of allowing its medical students the opportunity to exchange ideas with others who have talents, backgrounds, viewpoints, experiences, and interests different from their own. To this end, the Medical College is committed to the recruitment, admission, and graduation of talented students from diverse backgrounds. Specifically, students who demonstrate experiences in one or more of the following categories will be deemed to contribute to the diversity of the MCW student body:

- Growing up in poverty or in a disadvantaged socioeconomic status;
- Being the first person from one's family to attend college or graduate school;
- Overcoming educational disadvantage (graduating from a high school with little resources or with a high drop out rate);
- Having a primary language other than English;
- Living in a rural area; or
- Overcoming a significant handicap.

The Office of Student Affairs/Diversity provides support service to enhance students' academic learning. Among the services provided are academic counseling, test-taking strategies, and other services to help students manage all aspects of their student life.

Admissions

The Assistant Dean of Student Affairs/Diversity discusses career options at MCW with all students who are invited for an interview. After the interview process, the Admissions Committee reviews all applications for admissions. Attempts are made to select students who are not only academically talented, but who also demonstrate non-cognitive characteristics believed to predict successful completion of medical school (i.e., motivation, leadership qualities, commitment to helping others, realistic understanding of medicine, and other personal traits). The committee interviewers include basic science and clinical faculty as well as medical students. Application fees may be waived by MCW when requested by the applicant after obtaining an American Medical College Application Service fee waiver. Students are notified of their acceptance to MCW within two weeks after their interview.

Academic Support Programs

The Medical College of Wisconsin provides academic support for all students. In addition to the faculty, there are large- and small-group tutoring sessions as well as study skills workshops. A learning skills specialist assists students in assessing, identifying, and resolving deficiencies to ensure success in medical school. The college offers a decelerated five-year program where students can complete the first two years over a three-year period. Several events are facilitated throughout the year to intro-

Medical College of Wisconsin
Applicants, First-Time Applicants, Matriculants by Gender, Race and Ethnicity, 2007-2008

	2007 APP Women	2007 APP Men	2007 APP Total	2007 F-time APP Women	2007 F-time APP Men	2007 F-time APP Total	2007 MAT Women	2007 MAT Men	2007 MAT Total	2008 APP Women	2008 APP Men	2008 APP Total	2008 F-time APP Women	2008 F-time APP Men	2008 F-time APP Total	2008 MAT Women	2008 MAT Men	2008 MAT Total
Hispanic/Latino																		
Cuban	9	15	24	7	13	20	0	0	0	12	13	25	10	10	20	0	0	0
Mexican American	54	63	117	43	45	88	3	1	4	50	67	117	39	48	87	2	7	9
Puerto Rican	10	11	21	6	11	17	2	1	3	11	11	22	10	8	18	0	1	1
Other Hispanic	58	64	122	36	43	79	0	1	1	58	56	114	43	39	82	0	0	0
Multiple Hispanic/Latino*	5	6	11	2	5	7	0	2	2	10	6	16	6	1	7	0	0	0
Subtotal	136	159	295	94	117	211	5	5	10	141	153	294	108	106	214	2	8	10
Non-Hispanic/Latino**																		
Black	132	82	214	82	60	142	3	4	7	112	70	182	66	47	113	7	1	8
Native American/AK	5	6	11	4	6	10	0	0	0	7	8	15	6	5	11	1	0	1
Native Hawaiian/OPI	13	8	21	10	6	16	0	0	0	13	10	23	8	7	15	0	1	1
White	1,670	2,406	4,076	1,273	1,736	3,009	72	73	145	1,563	2,350	3,913	1,117	1,575	2,692	56	86	142
Asian	690	859	1,549	494	582	1,076	23	13	36	682	793	1,475	452	492	944	25	16	41
Other Race	3	1	4	1	1	2	0	0	0	3	5	8	3	5	8	0	0	0
Multiple Race*	63	77	140	43	49	92	2	1	3	68	81	149	47	46	93	5	1	6
Unknown	21	39	60	20	35	55	2	0	2	52	81	133	49	67	116	0	2	2
Subtotal	2,597	3,478	6,075	1,927	2,475	4,402	102	91	193	2,500	3,398	5,898	1,748	2,244	3,992	94	107	201
Foreign	136	141	277	108	102	210	1	0	1	99	138	237	69	97	166	0	1	1
Total	2,869	3,778	6,647	2,129	2,694	4,823	108	96	204	2,740	3,689	6,429	1,925	2,447	4,372	96	116	212

*Since 2002, students can select more than one race and / or ethnicity. **Those who did not choose 'Hispanic/Latino' or 'Non-Hispanic/Latino' are listed under 'Non-Hispanic/Latino'. Data Source: AAMC Data Warehouse: Applicant-Matriculant File, as of 1/16/2009.

duce the medical students to cultural and professional resources within the greater Milwaukee Metropolitan area.

Enrichment Programs

Academic programs are offered to high-school and college-level students through a series of educational pipeline programs. Sixty percent of students who participate in summer enrichment programs at the Medical College of Wisconsin go on to medical school or graduate studies in biomedical fields. The programs currently offered are the Apprenticeship in Medicine (AIM), the Research Opportunity for Academic Development in Science (ROADS), and the Multicultural Summer Research Training Program (MSRTP).

Apprenticeship In Medicine (AIM)
This program offers local high school students from diverse backgrounds, the opportunity to engage in a variety of clinical hands-on experiences. An intensive six-week program has been designated to increase awareness of common medical problems in underserved communities and career opportunities in fields of medicine. This program offers a stipend upon completion of the program.

Research Opportunity for Academic Development in Science (ROADS)
The ROADS program offers local high school students from diverse backgrounds the opportunity to assist a Medical College of Wisconsin faculty investigator on a current research project. This program is designed to provide participants with a meaningful experience in a health-related field and to stimulate their interest in careers in science, medicine and biomedical research. This program offers a monthly stipend.

Multicultural Summer Research Training Program (MSRTP)
This program offers qualified undergraduate and graduate multicultural students an opportunity to be matched with a full-time faculty investigator(s) to participate in a research project(s) addressing the causes, prevention, and treatment of cardiovascular, pul-

monary and hematological diseases. The program offers a monthly stipend to participants.

Student Support Groups and Community Outreach Programs
Students of diverse backgrounds are encouraged to become active in community outreach programs, which are sponsored by student-led organizations such as the Student National Medical Association (SNMA), LaRaza Medical Student Association (LaRaMA), and the Physicians for Social Responsibility (PSR). Students utilize their creative energies to sponsor health fairs, high school career day visits, and are available to participate in the numerous programs and activities sponsored by the Office of Student Affairs/Diversity.

Student Financial Assistance

Several major competitive scholarships are available to students who contribute to the diversity of the student body and have outstanding academic credentials. For Wisconsin residents, the Dean's Scholarship reflects the college's commitment to ensure that students from diverse backgrounds have an opportunity to pursue their career goals in medicine. Other scholarships available and open to both Wisconsin and out-of-state residents include the Presidential Scholarship and the Advanced Medical Opportunity Scholarship. In addition to these, the Wisconsin Energy Corporation Foundation Endowment and the Hearst Foundation Endowment provide financial support to deserving students.

Scholarships are also funded through several clinical departments for students from diverse backgrounds who possess outstanding academic credentials. Students who would like to be considered for any of these scholarships should contact the Assistant Dean for Student Affairs/ Diversity. Other institutional financial assistance is comprised of need-based scholarships, interest-deferred loans and federal loans (i.e., Stafford loan program). The Office of Student Financial Services provides assistance to students complet-

ing their financial aid application. Application fee waivers for financially disadvantaged applicants are available for those who have received an AMCAS fee waiver. Students are encouraged to contact the Office of Admissions as questions or concerns arise. In addition, students do not have to be accepted to begin the financial aid process; however, a clean credit report is required of all students prior to matriculation.

Educational Partnerships

Realizing the need to stimulate an interest in math and science at an early age, students are encouraged to strive for academic excellence so that they may become more competitive for college. MCW has established a collaborative program with the University of Wisconsin-Milwaukee, called the Center for Science Education, which places strong emphasis on science and math education, starting as early as middle school. Through these initiatives, MCW has strengthened its community ties. Other educational partnerships include the Center for Healthy Communities, Center for the Advancement of Urban Children, and undergraduate higher education institutions throughout the regional area, (i.e., Marquette University, University of Wisconsin Milwaukee, etc.). Thus, underrepresented students in medicine have an ample opportunity to pursue their dream of becoming physicians.

University of Wisconsin School of Medicine and Public Health

Dr. Gloria Hawkins, Assistant Dean for Multicultural Affairs
University of Wisconsin-Madison
750 Highland Ave, Room 2146-HSLC
Madison, WI 53705
608-263-3713; 608-262-4226 fax
gvhawkin@facstaff.wisc.edu
http://www.med.wisc.edu/
education/multicultural/index.php

The mission of the Multicultural Affairs Office in the School of Medicine and Public Health (SMPH) is to provide academic opportunities that will yield an increase in students historically underrepresented in medicine and to work toward the development of learning environments that will foster academic success. To carry out this mission, the Office has outreach programs/activities for pre-college and college students; works collaboratively with undergraduate programs, pre-medical organizations, students, and advisors; and works closely with the school's Office of Admissions. The Multicultural Affairs staff advises and counsels medical students, monitors their academic progress, and makes ap-propriate academic and counseling referrals. Partnerships have been forged with internal and external constituent groups to provide a climate that embraces diversity and supports the professional development of all students, especially students from diverse backgrounds.

Recruitment

The Offices of Admissions and Multicultural Affairs work collaboratively to recruit students from diverse backgrounds, especially those who are from groups historically underrepresented in higher education and medicine. Visits are made during the year to colleges and universities in the state and throughout the country. High school students who are residents of Wisconsin are encouraged to become familiar with the school through the summer Research Apprentice Program. The program provides opportunities for students to participate as research apprentices in the laboratories of university faculty. Working collaboratively with faculty within the school, research opportunities are available to undergraduates who are interested in medicine. Inquiries about undergraduate research opportunities should be made to the Assistant Dean of Multicultural Affairs.

Admissions

The Admissions Committee is composed of faculty and students, some of whom are minority, and considers several factors when reviewing applicants. These factors include: 1) undergraduate and graduate academic performance and the Medical College Admission Test (MCAT) scores; 2) extracurricular activities; 3) the applicant's employment record, volunteer experience, and medical exposure; 4) the personal, educational, and socioeconomic background of the applicant and the response of the applicant to any challenges; 5) the applicant's character with reference to honesty and integrity, empathy, maturity, leadership, self-discipline, and emotional stability; 6) motivation to pursue a career in medicine; and 7) the interest and suitability of the applicant for special programs and/or future specific careers.

Furthermore, in the interests of both enriching the educational environment for all students and better meeting the future medical, educational, and scientific needs of society, the committee makes a special effort to select a class whose members represent a broad range of diverse life experiences, back-

University of Wisconsin School of Medicine and Public Health
Applicants, First-Time Applicants, Matriculants by Gender, Race and Ethnicity, 2007-2008

	2007 APP Women	Men	Total	2007 F-time APP Women	Men	Total	2007 MAT Women	Men	Total	2008 APP Women	Men	Total	2008 F-time APP Women	Men	Total	2008 MAT Women	Men	Total
Hispanic/Latino																		
Cuban	1	3	4	1	3	4	0	0	0	9	7	16	7	7	14	0	0	0
Mexican American	34	29	63	30	24	54	1	1	2	27	39	66	21	31	52	2	3	5
Puerto Rican	10	7	17	9	6	15	0	0	0	8	7	15	7	6	13	1	0	1
Other Hispanic	32	28	60	23	22	45	2	1	3	28	33	61	23	27	50	2	3	5
Multiple Hispanic/Latino*	2	5	7	1	3	4	0	0	0	4	4	8	3	2	5	0	0	0
Subtotal	79	72	151	64	58	122	3	2	5	76	90	166	61	73	134	5	6	11
Non-Hispanic/Latino**																		
Black	94	64	158	70	48	118	3	3	6	82	45	127	55	30	85	6	0	6
Native American/AK	5	8	13	4	8	12	0	0	0	5	4	9	3	2	5	0	0	0
Native Hawaiian/OPI	5	5	10	4	5	9	0	0	0	5	9	14	5	6	11	0	0	0
White	988	1,226	2,214	863	963	1,826	59	47	106	913	1,259	2,172	744	940	1,684	64	51	115
Asian	288	351	639	229	263	492	21	14	35	249	339	588	194	240	434	9	18	27
Other Race	2	1	3	1	1	2	0	0	0	0	2	2	0	2	2	0	0	0
Multiple Race*	29	40	69	25	33	58	0	2	2	39	45	84	32	32	64	3	1	4
Unknown	11	20	31	10	17	27	1	0	1	36	61	97	36	55	91	0	0	0
Subtotal	1,422	1,715	3,137	1,206	1,338	2,544	84	66	150	1,329	1,764	3,093	1,069	1,307	2,376	82	70	152
Foreign	8	4	12	6	4	10	0	0	0	1	4	5	1	3	4	0	0	0
Total	1,509	1,791	3,300	1,276	1,400	2,676	87	68	155	1,406	1,858	3,264	1,131	1,383	2,514	87	76	163

*Since 2002, students can select more than one race and / or ethnicity. **Those who did not choose 'Hispanic/Latino' or 'Non-Hispanic/Latino' are listed under 'Non-Hispanic/Latino'. Data Source: AAMC Data Warehouse: Applicant-Matriculant File, as of 1/16/2009.

grounds, and interests. This diversity may include: 1) ethnic or racial background, 2) socioeconomic background, 3) educational background, 4) regional and geographic background, 5) interests and/or aptitudes for different medical careers, and 6) other cultural experiences. Therefore, non-residents in addition to Wisconsin residents who are from diverse backgrounds are strongly encouraged to apply.

All applicants must take the following courses to be given consideration for admission: 1) one semester of general biology with lab; 2) one semester of advanced biology with lab; 3) two semesters of inorganic/general chemistry with lab; 4) one semester of organic chemistry; 5) one semester of biochemistry; 6) two semesters of physics with lab; and 7) two semesters of mathematics with statistics and calculus recommended to meet this quantitative requirement.

Campus interviews are arranged by the Admissions staff, and the Multicultural Affairs Office plans special outreach activities for minority and disadvantaged applicants on some of the interview days. Applicants who receive acceptance offers from the school are invited to attend the Second Visit Program, sponsored by the Multicultural Affairs Office, for a more in-depth look at the school.

Academic Support Programs

The Multicultural Affairs Office works closely with Student Academic Support Services (SASS) in the school to ensure that students are provided with the academic support required for success. SASS has a highly trained staff to conduct self-assessment tests, study-skills workshops, and exam-preparation sessions. Other services include study materials and tutors for medical school classes and for the United States Medical Licensing Examination Steps 1 and 2. Periodically, consultations are made with other campus and community services in an effort to provide appropriate and effective support for students.

Careers in Medicine and Mentoring
Careers in Medicine is a comprehensive program that connects medical students with clinical faculty through career advising, mentoring, and workshops/seminars. This program is available to first-year medical students and culminates with residency placement. Faculty mentors help students assess their goals and interests, explore their options, choose a specialty, and prepare for residency placement.

Student Support and Community Outreach
Students are encouraged to explore their interests through organizations within the school and community outreach activities. These organizations include Medical Students for Minority Concerns (MSMC), Asian Pacific American Medical Student Association (APAMSA), American Medical Student Association (AMSA), Medical Students for the Arts (MFA), National Network of Latin American Medical Students (NNLAMS), Student National Medical Association (SNMA), and Student Physicians for Social Responsibility (PSR). Community outreach activities include the middle school Mentorship Achievement Program (MAP) and the Health Professions Mentoring Program (HPMP) for high school students. The Native American Health Working Group (NAHWG), a committee within the health sciences, focuses on educational and community issues. All of the organizations and groups have a diverse and active student membership.

Student Financial Assistance

The university makes available financial aid in the form of grants, scholarships, and low-interest loans to all students who demonstrate financial need. These funds are awarded based on the availability of funds and information the student provides on the university financial aid application. The school is committed to helping competitive students from diverse, as well as economically disadvantaged, backgrounds identify resources to finance their education.

Educational Partnerships

The University of Wisconsin SMPH works closely with the University of Wisconsin-Madison and the University of Wisconsin-Milwaukee in preparing students for medical education. In the summer of 2009, SMPH will launch a new partnership with the University of Wisconsin-Platteville and the University of Wisconsin-Milwaukee. This partnership program, Rural and Urban Scholars in Community Health (RUSCH), will give undergraduates who have an interest in and commitment to urban or rural medicine opportunities to:

- learn about health care issues in those communities;
- become knowledgeable of the culture of medicine through interactions and shadowing experiences with physicians, and community-service learning projects; and
- participate in enrichment activities that will enhance student preparation and readiness for application and early admission to medical school.

The Multicultural Affairs Office has pipeline programs and outreach initiatives ranging from middle school through undergraduate studies. These initiatives include a summer research program, hosting campus visits, premedical activities for merit-based and special support program students, and a long-standing partnership with the AHANA Pre-Health Society at the University of Wisconsin-Madison.

Other Pertinent Information

The American Medical College Application Service (AMCAS) application must be filed with AMCAS by November 1. Prospective applicants are strongly encouraged to apply early for consideration for admission to the University of Wisconsin School of Medicine and Public Health.

Enrichment

Programs

Association of
American Medical Colleges

Summer Medical Programs

The Summer Medical and Dental Education Program (SMDEP) is a FREE six week summer academic enrichment program for freshman and sophomore college students who are interested in a career in medicine or dentistry. SMDEP is implemented at 12 sites across the nation, and all programs provide a basic science curriculum, career development activities, clinical exposure and financial planning and health policy workshops.

The program is available at 12 medical and dental schools across the US:

- Case Western Reserve University Schools of Medicine & and Dental Medicine
- Columbia University College of Physicians and Surgeons and College of Dental Medicine
- David Geffen School of Medicine at UCLA and UCLA School of Dentistry
- Duke University School of Medicine
- Howard University Colleges of Arts and Sciences, Dentistry, and Medicine
- University of Louisville Schools of Medicine and Dentistry
- University of Nebraska Medical Center, College of Medicine and Dentistry
- UMDNJ-New Jersey Medical and New Jersey Dental Schools
- University of Texas Dental Branch and Medical School at Houston
- University of Virginia School of Medicine
- University of Washington Schools of Medicine and Dentistry
- Yale University School of Medicine

The program is funded by the Robert Wood Johnson Foundation with direction and technical assistance provided by the Association of American Medical Colleges (AAMC) and the American Dental Education Association (ADEA). SMDEP will launch its 2010 online application on November 1, 2009. The deadline for submitting the online application and all supporting documentation is March 1, 2010. Applications are reviewed on a "first come, first served" basis. Early application is strongly encouraged!

Visit the SMDEP website at www.smdep.org or call our toll free number (866) 58-SMDEP (76337) for more information.

State	School	Pre-K to Kindergarten	Elementary/Junior High School Level	High School Level	Undergraduate College Level	Pre-matriculants to Their Medical School	Combined College/MD Programs for HSS[1]	Post-Baccalaureate	Educational Partnerships	Extended Programs	Other
AL	University of Alabama School of Medicine	✓	✓	✓	✓	✓		✓			
AL	University of South Alabama College of Medicine				✓	✓		✓			
AZ	University of Arizona College of Medicine			✓	✓			✓			INMED[2]
AR	University of Arkansas for Medical Sciences College of Medicine	✓	✓	✓	✓	✓					SDS[5]
CA	Los Angeles (David Geffen) (UCLA)			✓	✓			✓			UCLA PRIME, SMDEP[3]
CA	Keck School of Medicine of the University of Southern California		✓	✓	✓			✓			
CA	Loma Linda University School of Medicine		✓	✓	✓	✓	✓	✓			
CA	Stanford University School of Medicine			✓	✓			✓			COE[4]
CA	UCLA/Drew	✓	✓	✓	✓	✓	✓				
CA	University of California, Davis, School of Medicine			✓	✓	✓		✓		✓	Rural Prime
CA	University of California, Irvine, College of Medicine					✓		✓		✓	Prime - LC
CA	University of California, San Diego, School of Medicine		✓	✓	✓	✓	✓	✓			
CA	University of California, San Francisco, School of Medicine			✓				✓	✓	✓	Prime - LIS
CO	University of Colorado Denver School of Medicine	✓	✓	✓	✓			✓			
CT	University of Connecticut School of Medicine			✓	✓	✓		✓	✓		HCOP[6], MDPP
CT	Yale University School of Medicine			✓	✓			✓			SMDEP[3]
DC	The George Washington University School of Medicine and Health Sciences			✓				✓	✓		ISCOPES
DC	Georgetown University School of Medicine						✓	✓			
DC	Howard University College of Medicine			✓	✓	✓		✓	✓		SMDEP[3]
FL	Florida International University Herbert Wertheim College of Medicine										SDS[5]
FL	Florida State University College of Medicine		✓	✓	✓			✓	✓		
FL	University of Central Florida College of Medicine										SDS[5]
FL	University of Florida College of Medicine			✓	✓			✓			SDS[5]
FL	University of Miami, Miller School of Medicine			✓				✓			
FL	University of South Florida College of Medicine			✓							IMS, SDS[5]
GA	Emory University School of Medicine			✓	✓						
GA	Medical College of Georgia School of Medicine			✓	✓	✓		✓			
GA	Mercer University School of Medicine							✓			
GA	Morehouse School of Medicine		✓	✓	✓	✓		✓	✓		COE[4], SDS[5]
HI	University of Hawai'i at Mānoa John A. Burns School of Medicine			✓				✓	✓		COE[4]
IL	Chicago Medical School at Rosalind Franklin University of Medicine and Science				✓			✓			
IL	Loyola University of Chicago Stritch School of Medicine			✓							
IL	Northwestern University Feinberg School of Medicine			✓	✓	✓	✓				CDM

[1] High School Students
[2] Indians Into Medicine
[3] Summer Medical and Dental Education Program
[4] Centers of Excellence
[5] Scholarships for Disadvantaged Students
[6] Health Careers Opportunity

Additional Note: 1) Many schools offer other types of programs that are not identified on the grid. These are programs such as USMLE preparation, elementary and middle school, and combined degree. 2) We have made every attempt to compile the list of enrichment programs on this chart based on the information reported in the school entries and on the checklist. However, we cannot guarantee the complete accuracy of each entry. Some schools may offer programs listed on the grid but did not identify them. (✓) It is advised that you contact the medical schools for more information. Source: Minority Student Opportunities in United States Medical Schools. L.M.I. Johnson, ed. Washington, DC: Association of American Medical Colleges, 2009.

State	School	Pre-K to Kindergarten	Elementary/Junior High School Level	High School Level	Undergraduate College Level	Pre-matriculants to *Their* Medical School	Combined College/MD Programs for HSS[1]	Post-Baccalaureate	Educational Partnerships	Extended Programs	Other
IL	Rush Medical College of Rush University Medical Center										SDS[5]
IL	Southern Illinois University School of Medicine			✓	✓		✓	✓			
IL	University of Chicago Division of the Biological Sciences Pritzker School of Medicine			✓	✓	✓		✓			
IL	University of Illinois at Chicago College of Medicine			✓	✓	✓	✓	✓			SDS[5]
IN	Indiana University School of Medicine		✓	✓	✓			✓			Bridges to the Docorate Initiative
IA	University of Iowa Roy J. and Lucille A. Carver College of Medicine				✓			✓			SDS[5]
KS	University of Kansas School of Medicine	✓	✓	✓	✓		✓	✓			COE[4] ,SDS[5]
KY	University of Kentucky College of Medicine				✓						
KY	University of Louisville School of Medicine		✓	✓	✓	✓	✓	✓			SMDEP[3]
LA	Louisiana State University Health Sciences Center School of Medicine in New Orleans		✓	✓	✓	✓		✓			Rural Scholar's Track
LA	Louisiana State University School of Medicine in Shreveport		✓	✓	✓	✓		✓			
LA	Tulane University School of Medicine			✓				✓			
MD	Johns Hopkins University School of Medicine		✓	✓	✓		✓				COE[4]
MD	Uniformed Services University of the Health Sciences F. Edward Hébert School of Medicine		✓	✓	✓		✓	✓			
MD	University of Maryland School of Medicine		✓	✓	✓			✓			
MA	Boston University School of Medicine			✓	✓			✓			SDS[5]
MA	Harvard Medical School		✓	✓	✓	✓					Summer Clinical and Translational
MA	Tufts University School of Medicine			✓	✓	✓				✓	MD-MPH, MD-PhD, MD-MBA
MA	University of Massachusetts Medical School	✓	✓	✓	✓			✓	✓		Regional Resource Center, RR Library, SDS[5]
MI	Michigan State University College of Human Medicine			✓	✓			✓	✓		
MI	University of Michigan Medical School			✓	✓	✓		✓			Profile for Success (HCOP[6])
MI	Wayne State University School of Medicine				✓		✓				
MN	Mayo Medical School				✓			✓			
MN	University of Minnesota Medical School		✓	✓	✓	✓					Minnesota Future Doctors, HCOP[6], COE[4]
MS	University of Mississippi School of Medicine		✓	✓	✓	✓		✓			SDS[5]
MO	Saint Louis University School of Medicine			✓	✓		✓				
MO	University of Missouri – Columbia School of Medicine			✓	✓			✓			
MO	University of Missouri – Kansas City School of Medicine		✓	✓	✓			✓	✓		
MO	Washington University in St. Louis School of Medicine			✓	✓			✓			
NE	Creighton University School of Medicine		✓	✓	✓		✓	✓			
NE	University of Nebraska College of Medicine				✓						SMDEP[3]
NV	University of Nevada School of Medicine	✓	✓	✓	✓			✓	✓		

[1] High School Students
[2] Indians Into Medicine
[3] Summer Medical and Dental Education Program
[4] Centers of Excellence
[5] Scholarships for Disadvantaged Students
[6] Health Careers Opportunity

Additional Note: 1) Many schools offer other types of programs that are not identified on the grid. These are programs such as USMLE preparation, elementary and middle school, and combined degree. 2) We have made every attempt to compile the list of enrichment programs on this chart based on the information reported in the school entries and on the checklist. However, we cannot guarantee the complete accuracy of each entry. Some schools may offer programs listed on the grid but did not identify them. (✓) It is advised that you contact the medical schools for more information. Source: Minority Student Opportunities in United States Medical Schools. L.M.I. Johnson, ed. Washington, DC: Association of American Medical Colleges, 2009.

Enrichment Programs

State	School	Pre-K to Kindergarten	Elementary/Junior High School Level	High School Level	Undergraduate College Level	Pre-matriculants to *Their* Medical School	Combined College/MD Programs for HSS[1]	Post-Baccalaureate	Educational Partnerships	Extended Programs	Other
	Dartmouth Medical School				✓						
NJ	UMDNJ – New Jersey Medical School	✓	✓	✓	✓			✓	✓		SMDEP[3], COE[4], SDS[5]
NJ	UMDNJ – Robert Wood Johnson Medical School		✓	✓	✓			✓	✓		Rise, SDS[5]
	University of New Mexico School of Medicine	✓	✓	✓	✓			✓			COE[4], SDS[5]
NY	Albany Medical College			✓				✓	✓		
NY	Albert Einstein College of Medicine of Yeshiva University		✓	✓	✓			✓			COE[4]
NY	Columbia University College of Physicians and Surgeons		✓	✓				✓			SMDEP[3]
NY	Weill Cornell Medical College of Cornell University		✓	✓				✓			SDS[5]
NY	Mount Sinai School of Medicine of New York University		✓	✓				✓			SDS[5]
NY	New York Medical College										
NY	New York University School of Medicine	✓	✓	✓				✓			
NY	State University of New York, Downstate Medical Center College of Medicine	✓	✓	✓	✓		✓	✓		✓	SDS[5]
NY	State University of New York Upstate Medical University College of Medicine		✓	✓	✓		✓	✓			
NY	Stony Brook University Medical Center School of Medicine		✓		✓			✓			
NY	University at Buffalo School of Medicine and Biomedical Sciences		✓				✓	✓			
NY	University of Rochester School of Medicine and Dentistry	✓	✓	✓			✓	✓			
NC	The Brody School of Medicine at East Carolina University			✓	✓			✓			
NC	Duke University School of Medicine	✓	✓	✓				✓			SMDEP[3]
NC	University of North Carolina at Chapel Hill School of Medicine			✓	✓		✓	✓			
NC	Wake Forest University Health Sciences, School of Medicine	✓	✓	✓	✓		✓	✓			COE[4]
	University of North Dakota School of Medicine and Health Sciences		✓	✓	✓	✓		✓			
OH	Case Western Reserve University School of Medicine		✓	✓							SMDEP[3]
OH	Northeastern Ohio Universities College of Medicine	✓	✓	✓			✓	✓	✓		
OH	Ohio State University College of Medicine		✓	✓	✓		✓				Visiting Student Program
OH	University of Cincinnati College of Medicine	✓	✓	✓		✓		✓	✓		
OH	The University of Toledo, College of Medicine		✓					✓			
OH	Wright State University Boonshoft School of Medicine		✓	✓	✓		✓				
OK	University of Oklahoma College of Medicine										
OR	Oregon Health & Sciences University School of Medicine		✓	✓	✓			✓			
PA	Drexel University College of Medicin			✓				✓			
PA	Jefferson Medical College of Thomas Jefferson University									✓	

[1] High School Students
[2] Indians Into Medicine
[3] Summer Medical and Dental Education Program
[4] Centers of Excellence
[5] Scholarships for Disadvantaged Students
[6] Health Careers Opportunity

Additional Note: 1) Many schools offer other types of programs that are not identified on the grid. These are programs such as USMLE preparation, elementary and middle school, and combined degree. 2) We have made every attempt to compile the list of enrichment programs on this chart based on the information reported in the school entries and on the checklist. However, we cannot guarantee the complete accuracy of each entry. Some schools may offer programs listed on the grid but did not identify them. (✓) It is advised that you contact the medical schools for more information. Source: Minority Student Opportunities in United States Medical Schools. L.M.I. Johnson, ed. Washington, DC: Association of American Medical Colleges, 2009.

Enrichment Programs

	Pre-K to Kindergarten	Elementary/Junior High School Level	High School Level	Undergraduate College Level	Pre-matriculants to *Their* Medical School	Combined College/MD Programs for HSS[1]	Post-Baccalaureate	Educational Partnerships	Extended Programs	Other
PA Pennsylvania State University College of Medicine										
Temple University School of Medicine		✓	✓	✓	✓					
The Commonwealth Medical College	✓	✓	✓							COE[4]
University of Pennsylvania School of Medicine				✓			✓			
University of Pittsburgh School of Medicine		✓	✓	✓			✓			
PR Ponce School of Medicine				✓			✓			
San Juan Bautista School of Medicine							✓			
Universidad Central del Caribe School of Medicine				✓			✓			
University of Puerto Rico School of Medicine				✓						SDS[5]
RI The Warren Alpert Medical School of Brown University				✓		✓	✓			
SC Medical University of South Carolina College of Medicine		✓	✓		✓					
University of South Carolina School of Medicine	✓	✓	✓				✓	✓		MAPS
SD Sanford School of Medicine of the University of South Dakota	✓	✓	✓				✓			
TN East Tennessee State University James H. Quillen College of Medicine			✓				✓			
Meharry Medical College School of Medicine			✓				✓			HCOP[6]
University of Tennessee Health Science Center, College of Medicine		✓	✓							SDS[5]
Vanderbilt University School of Medicine			✓	✓		✓	✓			
TX Baylor College of Medicine	✓	✓	✓							
Texas A&M University System Health Science Center College of Medicine			✓			✓	✓		✓	SDS[5]
Texas Tech University Health Sciences Center Paul L. Foster School of Medicine	✓	✓					✓			
Texas Tech University Health Sciences Center School of Medicine		✓	✓			✓	✓			SDS[5]
University of Texas Health Science Center at San Antonio School of Medicine			✓				✓			
University of Texas Medical Branch University of Texas Medical School at Galveston		✓	✓	✓		✓	✓			SDS[5]
University of Texas Medical School at Houston	✓	✓	✓	✓			✓			SMDEP[3]
University of Texas Southwestern Medical Center at Dallas Southwestern Medical School		✓	✓	✓			✓			
UT University of Utah School of Medicine	✓	✓	✓	✓			✓			
VT University of Vermont College of Medicine							✓			
VA Eastern Virginia Medical School		✓	✓			✓	✓		✓	COE[4], SDS[5]
University of Virginia School of Medicine										SMDEP[3]
Virginia Commonwealth University School of Medicine		✓	✓			✓	✓			SDS[5]
Virginia Tech Carillon School of Medicine							✓			
WA University of Washington School of Medicine		✓	✓	✓		✓	✓			SMDEP[3], COE[4]
WV Joan C. Edwards School of Medicine at Marshall University		✓	✓							
West Virginia University School of Medicine		✓	✓							HCOP[6]
WI Medical College of Wisconsin		✓	✓			✓	✓		✓	
University of Wisconsin School of Medicine and Public Health		✓	✓				✓			

[1] High School Students
[2] Indians Into Medicine
[3] Summer Medical and Dental Education Program
[4] Centers of Excellence
[5] Scholarships for Disadvantaged Students
[6] Health Careers Opportunity

Additional Note: 1) Many schools offer other types of programs that are not identified on the grid. These are programs such as USMLE preparation, elementary and middle school, and combined degree. 2) We have made every attempt to compile the list of enrichment programs on this chart based on the information reported in the school entries and on the checklist. However, we cannot guarantee the complete accuracy of each entry. Some schools may offer programs listed on the grid but did not identify them. (✓) It is advised that you contact the medical schools for more information. Source: Minority Student Opportunities in United States Medical Schools. L.M.I. Johnson, ed. Washington, DC: Association of American Medical Colleges, 2009.

You can change the face of medicine.

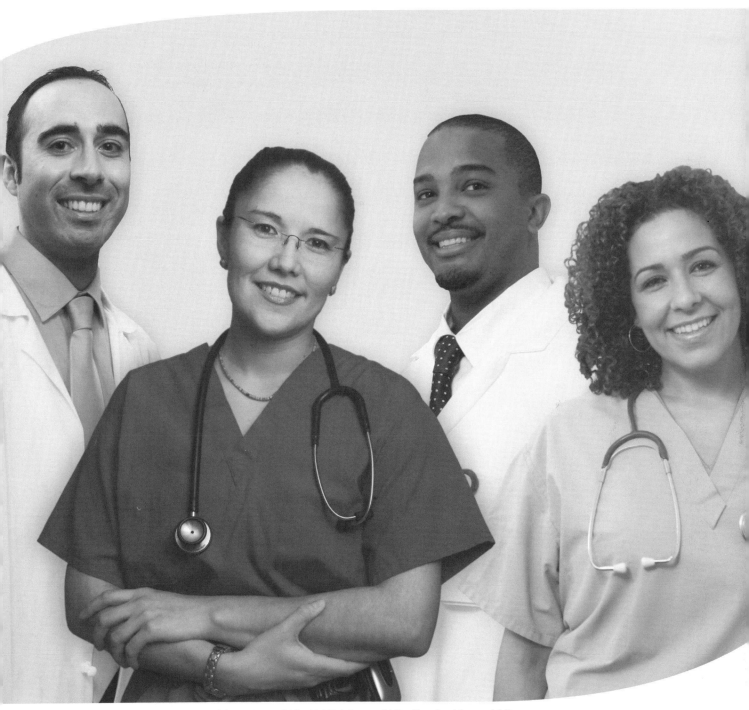

From left: Romeu Azevedo, M.D., Candelaria Martin, M.D., Kahlil Johnson, M.D., Claudine Morcos, M.D.

If you really want to make a difference in people's lives, consider a career in medicine. Too many African Americans, Latinos/as, and Native Americans don't get the care they need. Help us change this reality. Log on to **AspiringDocs.org**®, a new resource from the Association of American Medical Colleges, to learn more.

AAMC

Tomorrow's Doctors, Tomorrow's Cures®

© 2006 AAMC

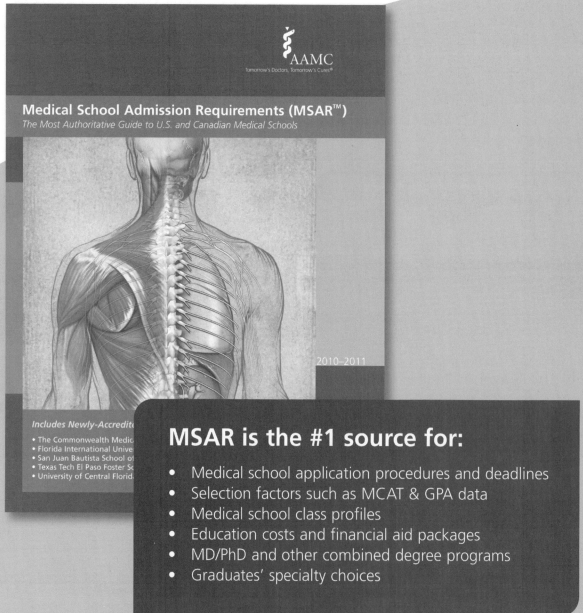

If you are serious about a career in Medicine or Dentistry Let SMDEP give you a competitive advantage

Summer Medical and Dental Education Program

Join the Summer Medical and Dental Education Program (SMDEP) for a FREE six-week summer academic enrichment program at one of 12 sites across the country.

To be eligible for SMDEP, an applicant must:

- be a U.S. citizen or hold a permanent resident visa;
- be currently enrolled as a freshman or sophomore in college; and
- have a minimum overall GPA of 3.0, with 2.75 in the sciences.

Applications available: November 1

Application deadline: March 1

For more information, visit our Web site at www.smdep.org or call the National Program Office at 1.866.58.SMDEP (587-6337)

The Participating SMDEP Institutions include:

Case Western Reserve University
Schools of Medicine and Dental Medicine

Columbia University College of Physicians and
Surgeons and College of Dental Medicine

David Geffen School of Medicine at UCLA
and UCLA School of Dentistry

Duke University School of Medicine

Howard University Colleges of Art &
Sciences, Dentistry, and Medicine

The University of Texas Dental Branch and
Medical School at Houston

UMDNJ New Jersey Medical and
New Jersey Dental Schools

University of Louisville
Schools of Medicine and Dentistry

University of Nebraska Medical Center,
Colleges of Medicine and Dentistry

University of Virginia School of Medicine

University of Washington Schools of
Medicine and Dentistry

Yale University School of Medicine

Robert Wood Johnson Foundation

SMDEP is a national program funded by the Robert Wood Johnson Foundation with direction and technical assistance provided by the Association of American Medical Colleges and the American Dental Education Association.

MCAT
Medical College
Admission Test

AAMC

Taking the MCAT?
Where Do You Start?

Begin with resources from
the test developers....

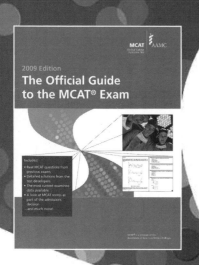

The Official Guide to the MCAT Exam

- Actual exam questions with difficulty ratings
- Detailed explanations and tips for solving problems
- Current data on how scores and GPA factor in admissions
- Info to help you decide about retesting

Online Practice Tests

- A free online practice test available to everyone
- Score and diagnostic reports help improve your study plan
- Additional practice tests available for purchase

Learn more at:
www.aamc.org/mcat

Selected

AAMC Data

Association of
American Medical Colleges

U.S. Medical School Applicants, First-Time Applicants, Acceptees, and Matriculants by Sex and Race/Ethnicity, 2006-2008

	Gender* and Race/Ethnicity**	2006 Applicants	2006 First-Time Applicants	2006 Acceptees	2006 Matriculants	2007 Applicants	2007 First-Time Applicants	2007 Acceptees	2007 Matriculants	2008 Applicants	2008 First-Time Applicants	2008 Acceptees	2008 Matriculants
Women — Hispanic or Latino	Mexican American	492	366	228	218	508	370	223	214	480	369	226	218
	Puerto Rican	294	251	147	145	354	288	155	150	409	349	191	181
	Cuban	106	84	48	46	99	68	49	47	118	96	57	56
	Other Hispanic or Latino	493	376	211	206	524	393	213	199	529	384	216	207
	Multiple Hispanic or Latino	68	49	31	29	68	50	29	26	82	59	39	39
	Subtotal	1,453	1,126	665	644	1,553	1,169	669	636	1,618	1,257	729	701
Non-Hispanic or Latino	Black or African American	2,019	1,425	801	757	2,139	1,466	744	717	2,065	1,386	781	744
	Asian	3,809	2,958	1,718	1,634	4,151	3,178	1,850	1,754	4,078	3,013	1,840	1,745
	American Indian or Alaska Native	75	59	37	35	77	61	31	28	68	46	32	29
	Native Hawaiian or Other Pacific Islander	65	46	18	18	63	48	17	17	62	38	18	17
	White	10,379	8,072	5,114	4,820	11,027	8,652	5,181	4,875	10,570	8,025	5,084	4,768
	Other Race	40	25	11	11	40	28	10	9	47	35	16	15
	No Race Response	200	192	149	141	236	225	156	150	417	396	210	196
	More than One Race	486	375	255	242	528	410	241	228	512	380	265	245
	Subtotal	17,073	13,152	8,103	7,658	18,261	14,068	8,230	7,778	17,819	13,319	8,246	7,759
Non-U.S. or Permanent Resident	Foreign	767	626	175	136	921	757	208	168	922	741	205	153
	Unknown Citizenship	.	.	.	.	.	.	.	.	1	.	1	1
	Subtotal	767	626	175	136	921	757	208	168	923	741	206	154
	Total Women	19,293	14,904	8,943	8,438	20,735	15,994	9,107	8,582	20,360	15,317	9,181	8,614
Men — Hispanic or Latino	Mexican American	464	355	238	230	526	397	241	227	512	367	249	242
	Puerto Rican	266	224	156	149	283	229	154	149	289	229	159	156
	Cuban	100	86	44	42	119	89	53	50	122	91	76	76
	Other Hispanic or Latino	447	326	207	194	474	321	205	196	492	343	229	215
	Multiple Hispanic or Latino	47	39	27	27	44	33	21	19	53	37	27	26
	Subtotal	1,324	1,030	672	642	1,446	1,069	674	641	1,468	1,067	740	715
Non-Hispanic or Latino	Black or African American	910	629	419	399	994	724	444	422	959	675	415	400
	Asian	3,737	2,751	1,706	1,611	4,239	3,118	1,891	1,781	4,201	2,926	1,922	1,833
	American Indian or Alaska Native	72	47	33	33	74	60	35	33	63	47	34	29
	Native Hawaiian or Other Pacific Islander	48	33	16	16	47	31	12	11	50	32	11	11
	White	12,311	9,086	6,077	5,731	13,109	9,638	6,103	5,757	13,243	9,496	6,189	5,864
	Other Race	45	27	13	12	37	21	12	11	37	22	16	14
	No Race Response	219	205	130	125	269	242	152	142	491	429	238	225
	More than One Race	439	318	221	210	476	339	230	221	479	334	203	195
	Subtotal	17,781	13,096	8,615	8,137	19,245	14,173	8,879	8,378	19,523	13,961	9,028	8,571
Non-U.S. or Permanent Resident	Foreign	710	553	188	144	889	710	198	158	879	673	186	136
	Subtotal	710	553	188	144	889	710	198	158	879	673	186	136
	Total Men	19,815	14,679	9,475	8,923	21,580	15,952	9,751	9,177	21,870	15,701	9,954	9,422
Women & Men — Hispanic or Latino	Mexican American	956	721	466	448	1,034	767	464	441	992	736	475	460
	Puerto Rican	560	475	303	294	637	517	309	299	698	578	350	337
	Cuban	206	170	92	88	218	157	102	97	240	187	133	132
	Other Hispanic or Latino	940	702	418	400	998	714	418	395	1,021	727	445	422
	Multiple Hispanic or Latino	115	88	58	56	112	83	50	45	135	96	66	65
	Subtotal	2,777	2,156	1,337	1,286	2,999	2,238	1,343	1,277	3,086	2,324	1,469	1,416
Non-Hispanic or Latino	Black or African American	2,929	2,054	1,220	1,156	3,133	2,190	1,188	1,139	3,024	2,061	1,196	1,144
	Asian	7,546	5,709	3,424	3,245	8,390	6,296	3,741	3,535	8,279	5,939	3,762	3,578
	American Indian or Alaska Native	147	106	70	68	151	121	66	61	131	93	66	58
	Native Hawaiian or Other Pacific Islander	113	79	34	34	110	79	29	28	112	70	29	28
	White	22,690	17,158	11,191	10,551	24,136	18,290	11,284	10,632	23,813	17,521	11,273	10,632
	Other Race	85	52	24	23	77	49	22	20	84	57	32	29
	No Race Response	419	397	279	266	505	467	308	292	909	826	448	421
	More than One Race	925	693	476	452	1,004	749	471	449	991	714	468	440
	Subtotal	34,854	26,248	16,718	15,795	37,506	28,241	17,109	16,156	37,343	27,281	17,274	16,330
Non-U.S. or Permanent Resident	Foreign	1,477	1,179	363	280	1,810	1,467	406	326	1,801	1,414	391	289
	Unknown Citizenship	.	.	.	.	.	.	.	.	1	.	1	1
	Subtotal	1,477	1,179	363	280	1,810	1,467	406	326	1,802	1,414	392	290
	Total Applicants	39,108	29,583	18,418	17,361	42,315	31,946	18,858	17,759	42,231	31,019	19,135	18,036

*In 2008, one applicant, who declined to report gender, is not reflected.

**Since 2002, following U.S. federal guidelines, AMCAS has asked applicants who are U.S. citizens or Permanent Residents to self-identify using two separate questions: the first question ("Ethnicity") asks applicants whether they are "Spanish/Hispanic/Latino(a)" or "Not Spanish/Hispanic/Latino(a)"; the second question ("Race") asks applicants to self-identify using non-Hispanic or Latino race categories, and applicants are asked to "check all that apply." The ethnicity category and several race categories permit further self-identification by sub-categories. Prior to 2002, AMCAS applicants were not able to select more than one race; thus, data prior to 2002 are not directly comparable to later data.

Source: AAMC: Data Warehouse: Applicant Matriculant File as of 10/10/2008.

Applicants to U.S. Medical Schools by Race, Selected Combinations within Hispanic or Latino Ethnicity, and Sex, 2006-2008

	Gender* and Race**	2006 Hispanic or Not*			2007 Hispanic or Not*			2008 Hispanic or Not*		
		No	Yes	Total	No	Yes	Total	No	Yes	Total
Women	American Indian or Alaska Native	75	22	97	77	18	95	68	14	82
	American	17	2	19	16	2	18	12	4	16
	American Indian or Alaska Native, White	60	15	75	66	12	78	69	6	75
	Asian	3,809	49	3,858	4,151	57	4,208	4,078	52	4,130
	Asian, Black or African American	23	2	25	31	3	34	26	4	30
	Asian, White	297	11	308	312	14	326	303	9	312
	Black or African American	2,019	62	2,081	2,139	69	2,208	2,065	81	2,146
	Black or African American, White	35	21	56	47	16	63	41	12	53
	Native Hawaiian or Other Pacific Islander	65	11	76	63	9	72	62	10	72
	White	10,379	852	11,231	11,027	927	11,954	10,570	952	11,522
	White, Other	3	2	5	2	1	3	2	.	2
	Other	40	37	77	40	33	73	47	22	69
	No Race Response	200	350	550	236	381	617	417	440	857
	Non-U.S. Citizen/Permanent Resident	767	.	767	921	.	921	923	.	923
	More than One Race	51	17	68	54	11	65	59	12	71
	Total for Women	17,840	1,453	19,293	19,182	1,553	20,735	18,742	1,618	20,360
Men	American Indian or Alaska Native	72	19	91	74	16	90	63	19	82
	American	4	.	4	9	.	9	4	.	4
	American Indian or Alaska Native, White	79	15	94	82	7	89	100	14	114
	Asian	3,737	35	3,772	4,239	46	4,285	4,201	43	4,244
	Asian, Black or African American	17	1	18	22	1	23	11	1	12
	Asian, White	271	11	282	279	5	284	298	13	311
	Black or African American	910	41	951	994	43	1,037	959	47	1,006
	Black or African American, White	20	7	27	36	12	48	30	17	47
	Native Hawaiian or Other Pacific Islander	48	8	56	47	7	54	50	9	59
	White	12,311	786	13,097	13,109	870	13,979	13,243	845	14,088
	White, Other	1	.	1	1	2	3	.	1	1
	Other	45	40	85	37	33	70	37	25	62
	No Race Response	219	348	567	269	395	664	491	427	918
	Non-U.S. Citizen/Permanent Resident	710	.	710	889	.	889	879	.	879
	More than One Race	47	13	60	47	9	56	36	7	43
	Total for Men	18,491	1,324	19,815	20,134	1,446	21,580	20,402	1,468	21,870
All Applicants	American Indian or Alaska Native	147	41	188	151	34	185	131	33	164
	American	21	2	23	25	2	27	16	4	20
	American Indian or Alaska Native, White	139	30	169	148	19	167	169	20	189
	Asian	7,546	84	7,630	8,390	103	8,493	8,279	95	8,374
	Asian, Black or African American	40	3	43	53	4	57	37	5	42
	Asian, White	568	22	590	591	19	610	601	22	623
	Black or African American	2,929	103	3,032	3,133	112	3,245	3,024	128	3,152
	Black or African American, White	55	28	83	83	28	111	71	29	100
	Native Hawaiian or Other Pacific Islander	113	19	132	110	16	126	112	19	131
	White	22,690	1,638	24,328	24,136	1,797	25,933	23,813	1,797	25,610
	White, Other	4	2	6	3	3	6	2	1	3
	Other	85	77	162	77	66	143	84	47	131
	No Race Response	419	698	1,117	505	776	1,281	909	867	1,776
	Non-U.S. Citizen/Permanent Resident	1,477	.	1,477	1,810	.	1,810	1,802	.	1,802
	More than One Race	98	30	128	101	20	121	95	19	114
	Total	36,331	2,777	39,108	39,316	2,999	42,315	39,145	3,086	42,231

*Since 2002, following U.S. federal guidelines, AMCAS has asked applicants who are U.S. citizens or Permanent Residents to self-identify using two separate questions: the first question ("Ethnicity") asks applicants whether they are "Spanish/Hispanic/Latino/Latina" or "Not Spanish/Hispanic/Latino/Latina"; the second question ("Race") asks applicants to self-identify using non-Hispanic or Latino race categories, and applicants are asked to "check all that apply." The ethnicity category and several race categories permit further self-identification by sub-categories. Prior to 2002, AMCAS applicants were not able to select more than one race; thus, data prior to 2002 are not directly comparable to later data.

Matriculants to U.S. Medical Schools by Race, Selected Combinations within Hispanic or Latino Ethnicity, and Sex, 2006-2008

	Matriculants Race	2006 Hispanic or Not*			2007 Hispanic or Not*			2008 Hispanic or Not*		
		No	Yes	Total	No	Yes	Total	No	Yes	Total
Women	American Indian or Alaska Native	35	7	42	28	4	32	29	4	33
	American Indian or Alaska Native, Black or African American	5	1	6	5	2	7	1	3	4
	American Indian or Alaska Native, White	27	5	32	31	7	38	32	2	34
	Asian	1,634	16	1,650	1,754	13	1,767	1,745	25	1,770
	Asian, Black or African American	6	.	6	9	1	10	11	3	14
	Asian, White	171	7	178	143	7	150	160	4	164
	Black or African American	757	15	772	717	23	740	744	33	777
	Black or African American, White	13	7	20	23	4	27	21	6	27
	Native Hawaiian or Other Pacific Islander	18	5	23	17	2	19	17	3	20
	White	4,820	400	5,220	4,875	405	5,280	4,768	428	5,196
	White, Other	2	.	2	.	.		.	.	
	Other	11	17	28	9	14	23	15	7	22
	No Race Response	141	156	297	150	151	301	196	178	374
	Non-U.S. Citizen/Permanent Resident	136	.	136	168	.	168	154	.	154
	More than One Race	18	8	26	17	3	20	20	5	25
	Total for Women	7,794	644	8,438	7,946	636	8,582	7,913	701	8,614
Men	American Indian or Alaska Native	33	9	42	33	3	36	29	9	38
	American Indian or Alaska Native, Black or African American	2	.	2	2	.	2	2	.	2
	American Indian or Alaska Native, White	34	7	41	29	3	32	46	6	52
	Asian	1,611	14	1,625	1,781	19	1,800	1,833	16	1,849
	Asian, Black or African American	11	.	11	9	1	10	2	1	3
	Asian, White	133	8	141	128	2	130	110	7	117
	Black or African American	399	17	416	422	18	440	400	22	422
	Black or African American, White	8	4	12	28	3	31	20	11	31
	Native Hawaiian or Other Pacific Islander	16	3	19	11	1	12	11	3	14
	White	5,731	376	6,107	5,757	401	6,158	5,864	410	6,274
	White, Other	.	.		.	.		.	1	1
	Other	12	16	28	11	8	19	14	10	24
	No Race Response	125	183	308	142	179	321	225	217	442
	Non-U.S. Citizen/Permanent Resident	144	.	144	158	.	158	136	.	136
	More than One Race	22	5	27	25	3	28	15	2	17
	Total for Men	8,281	642	8,923	8,536	641	9,177	8,707	715	9,422
All Matriculants	American Indian or Alaska Native	68	16	84	61	7	68	58	13	71
	American Indian or Alaska Native, Black or African American	7	1	8	7	2	9	3	3	6
	American Indian or Alaska Native, White	61	12	73	60	10	70	78	8	86
	Asian	3,245	30	3,275	3,535	32	3,567	3,578	41	3,619
	Asian, Black or African American	17	.	17	18	2	20	13	4	17
	Asian, White	304	15	319	271	9	280	270	11	281
	Black or African American	1,156	32	1,188	1,139	41	1,180	1,144	55	1,199
	Black or African American, White	21	11	32	51	7	58	41	17	58
	Native Hawaiian or Other Pacific Islander	34	8	42	28	3	31	28	6	34
	White	10,551	776	11,327	10,632	806	11,438	10,632	838	11,470
	White, Other	2	.	2	.	.		.	1	1
	Other	23	33	56	20	22	42	29	17	46
	No Race Response	266	339	605	292	330	622	421	395	816
	Non-U.S. Citizen/Permanent Resident	280	.	280	326	.	326	290	.	290
	More than One Race	40	13	53	42	6	48	35	7	42
	Total Matriculants	16,075	1,286	17,361	16,482	1,277	17,759	16,620	1,416	18,036

*Since 2002, following U.S. federal guidelines, AMCAS has asked applicants who are U.S. citizens or Permanent Residents to self-identify using two separate questions: the first question ("Ethnicity") asks applicants whether they are "Spanish/Hispanic/Latino/Latina" or "Not Spanish/Hispanic/Latino/Latina"; the second question ("Race") asks applicants to self-identify using non-Hispanic or Latino race categories, and applicants are asked to "check all that apply." The ethnicity category and several race categories permit further self-identification by sub-categories. Prior to 2002, AMCAS applicants were not able to select more than one race; thus, data prior to 2002 are not directly comparable to later data.

Source: AAMC: Data Warehouse: Applicant Matriculant File as of 10/10/2008.

U.S. Medical School Graduates by Sex and Race/Ethnicity, 2006-2008

	Gender and Race/Ethnicity*	2006	2007	2008
Women	Black or African American	733	724	720
	American Indian or Alaska Native	79	66	76
	Asian	1,630	1,657	1,727
	Native Hawaiian or Other Pacific Islander	22	15	16
	White	4,638	4,869	4,867
	Other Race, Non-Hispanic or Latino	124	156	38
	Mexican American	175	179	192
	Puerto Rican	159	151	192
	Cuban**	40	31	41
	Other Hispanic or Latino	164	199	185
	Foreign	99	104	105
	No Rece Response or Unknown Citizen	148	119	105
	Unduplicated Total Women Graduates	7,748	7,926	7,974
Men	Black or African American	389	362	389
	American Indian or Alaska Native	60	57	79
	Asian	1,601	1,643	1,600
	Native Hawaiian or Other Pacific Islander	19	20	17
	White	5,391	5,441	5,492
	Other Race, Non-Hispanic or Latino	176	177	50
	Mexican American	185	193	196
	Puerto Rican	129	131	136
	Cuban**	31	44	52
	Other Hispanic or Latino	174	174	189
	Foreign	86	111	112
	No Rece Response or Unknown Citizen	158	149	140
	Unduplicated Total Men Graduates	8,178	8,217	8,193
All	Black or African American	1,122	1,086	1,109
	American Indian or Alaska Native	139	123	155
	Asian	3,231	3,300	3,327
	Native Hawaiian or Other Pacific Islander	41	35	33
	White	10,029	10,310	10,359
	Other Race, Non-Hispanic or Latino	300	333	88
	Mexican American	360	372	388
	Puerto Rican	288	282	328
	Cuban**	71	75	93
	Other Hispanic or Latino	338	373	374
	Foreign	185	215	217
	No Rece Response or Unknown Citizen	306	268	245
	Total Women and Men Graduates	15,926	16,143	16,167

* Since 2002, following U.S. federal guidelines, AMCAS has asked applicants who are U.S. citizens or Permanent Residents to self-identify using two separate questions: the first question ("Ethnicity") asks applicants whether they are "Spanish/Hispanic/Latino/Latina" or "Not Spanish/Hispanic/Latino/Latina"; the second question ("Race") asks applicants to self-identify using non-Hispanic or Latino race categories, and applicants are asked to "check all that apply." The ethnicity category and several race categories permit further self-identification by sub-categories. Prior to 2002, AMCAS applicants were not able to select more than one race; thus, data prior to 2002 are not directly comparable to later data.

** Before AMCAS year 2002, Cuban was considered to be in the Other Hispanic or Latino category, so counts of Cubans are non-existent or minimal until the graduating class of 2006.

Source: AAMC: Data Warehouse: STUDENT file as of 11/5/2008; Applicant Matriculant File as of 12/3/2008.

U.S. Medical School Faculty by Sex and Race/Hispanic Origin, 2008

Race/Hispanic Origin	Men		Women		Unreported		Total	
	No.	%	No.	%	No.	%	No.	%
Asian	10,439	12.7	5,785	13.5	53	9	16,277	13
Black	1,877	2.3	1,827	4.3	10	1.7	3,714	3
Native American/Alaskan	95	0.1	48	0.1	0	0	143	1
Native Hawaiian/OPI	146	0.2	69	0.2	1	0.2	216	0.2
White	56,889	69.5	26,806	62.7	272	46.4	83,967	67.1
Other	180	0.2	93	0.2	0	0	273	0.2
Unknown	7,122	8.7	5,143	12	227	38.7	12,492	10
Multiple Races	1,868	2.3	1,018	2.4	7	1.2	2,893	2.3
Cuban	38	0	25	0.1	0	0	63	0.1
Mexican American	411	0.5	242	0.6	1	0.2	654	0.5
Puerto Rican	507	0.6	414	1	2	0.3	923	0.7
Other Hispanic	2,213	2.7	1,183	2.8	12	2	3,408	2.7
Multiple Hispanic	110	0.1	81	0.2	1	0.2	192	0.2
Total	81,895	100	42,734	100	586	100	125,215	100

Source: AAMC Faculty Roster System: http://www.aamc.org/data/facultyroster/reports.htm
as of 1/23/2009.